Famous Lines

Famous Lines

A Columbia Dictionary of Familiar Quotations

Robert Andrews

COLUMBIA UNIVERSITY PRESS   NEW YORK

Columbia University Press
Publishers Since 1893
New York   Chichester, West Sussex
Copyright © 1997 Columbia University Press

Library of Congress Cataloging-in-Publication Data

Andrews, Robert, 1957–
Famous lines : a Columbia dictionary of familiar quotations / Robert Andrews.
    p.   cm.
Includes bibliographical references.
ISBN 0-231-10218-6
1. Quotations, English. 2. Quotations. I. Title.
PN6081.A656   1996
082—dc20   96-43879
                          CIP

⊗

Casebound editions of Columbia University Press books are printed
on permanent and durable acid-free paper.
Printed in the United States of America

c 10 9 8 7 6 5 4 3

Contents

Contents · VI

Introduction

When Logan Pearsall Smith was asked what meaning, if any, he had derived from his earthly term, he said there was just one thing which mattered, "to set a chime of words tinkling in the minds of a few fastidious people." For those with an eye to immortality, to be remembered thus eclipses every other form of glory, and even politicians and generals have acknowledged the supremacy of words to carry the most enduring freight. In German, great sayings and quotations are *geflügelte Worte*, or "winged words," because they outdistance everything else. They are the currency of history, evoking personalities in high-contrast cameo, training spotlights on moments of soaring grandeur or intense pathos, high farce and raw grief, retelling tales, distilling the pith of bygone debates and meditations. Endowed with often uncanny resonance, certain remarks and lines have transcended the particular time and circumstances that gave birth to them and sewn themselves into the fabric of our communal experience. Take the words of Jefferson, for example, as used in the *Declaration of Independence*, or the verse of John Keats or Emily Dickinson. Countless other, more contemporary voices have infiltrated our outlook, too—the language of Orwell's *1984*, McLuhan's prophecy of a Global Village, Kerouac's and Ginsberg's jazz talk.

The selection of entries for inclusion in this volume is based on the durability and relevance of the quotations (their capacity for transcendence) and to a large extent, therefore, the quotations selected themselves. These are the most famous lines in the language, embedded in our cultural landscape, each one reflecting a common experience, denoting a shared understanding. They are echoes which we all recognize and respond to, and they are a shorthand, triggering whole chains of association. Where this collection differs from other works is in its absorption of the wealth of new material which has surfaced in the 20th century and which now forms part of our range of expression. Film, in particular, has furnished us with a whole new set of references which are constantly with us, some dating back to the early years of the century. Television has made less impact, barring catch-phrases and running gags, though even here there is a subliminal awareness of lines from TV which have risen above the medium's innate propensity for ephemerality (think of *Monty Python, The Prisoner, Star Trek* or *Twin Peaks*). Fragments of popular song have also made inroads into the common idiom, though here I have tried to distinguish between fine lyrics (i.e. those which it's hard to recall without also evoking the music) and those snatches of song which are quoted, as it were, tunelessly.

The present volume also diverges conspicuously from *The Columbia Dictionary of Quotations*—the collection which preceded this, which was based on altogether different criteria, and which even eschewed the most familiar quotes. Where that book embraced a wide diversity of sources, many of them rescued from "the iniquity of oblivion," this work specializes in those sayings which have survived, and attempts to reintroduce us to what are, in effect, old acquaintances. The arrangement under headings is designed to give priority to the lines themselves, and to the subjects which they originally addressed, a factor too often relegated or lost when old acquaintance becomes over-familiarity. Moreover, as well as presenting these well-honed phrases and remarks in as useful, instructive and entertaining a light as possible, this scheme allows a telling insight into the ways in which different people—powerful individuals, for the most part—have responded to the perennial concerns of the human race. A brief glance at the headings will illustrate what these are: love, death, religion, war, sex, and the arts come top of the list. But the quotations in this book are not just the greatest things ever said or written on these and other topics: more interestingly they are those which are best remembered and retained, which have resounded the most, and found a lodging in our collective consciousness.

The choice of headings was the hardest part of compiling this book. The quotations themselves are extracts from a wider and subtler discourse, and do not take kindly to being compartmentalized, or foreshortened. Sometimes I have applied what might seem an unduly literal interpretation to the lines quoted, on other occasions a more tangential reading. But throughout, the primary consideration has been to place the words where they will be most helpful to the reader in search of *les mots justes* on a particular subject—that eloquent, elusive quip or comment that crystallizes a concept, or encapsulates a philosophy. Copiously cross-referenced and exhaustively cited, the quotations are also larded with context and commentary wherever these may be useful or enlightening, even if it is only to name the speaker in a passage of fiction. As well as providing authenticity and interest, such details are necessary reminders not to associate immortal words too rigidly with their authors' true feelings (and there is enough self-contradiction on these pages to shatter that particular fallacy).

As a rule, quotations have been credited to the people with whom they are most closely connected, on the grounds that the most famous lines from films or songs, say, generally depend for their impact on the persona of those who uttered or sang them rather than those who first penned them. "I could've been a contender." is intrinsically Brando (not Budd Schulberg), just as "I Did It My Way" is pure Sinatra (as opposed to Paul Anka). This is a significant departure from most anthologies which list well-known lines under often obscure lyricists and screenwriters, whose names fail to strike that essential note of recognition which underpins the potency of a quotation. In all cases, background information is supplied to minimize the possibility of misattribution, while the names and keyword indexes should ensure that any particular quote can be traced without difficulty.

The book applies a strict definition to what constitutes a quotation, giving lesser prominence to proverbs, slogans, catchwords, clichés and anthems. A quotation must be linked to a personality, or it is merely lifeless, and few would argue that an advertising formula or political soundbite possesses much soul. By the same rationale, book and song titles by themselves are arid things ("Catch-22" is not enough), as are explanations or summaries of philosophies, frequently included in anthologies because they are historically significant, albeit utterly unquotable. Mathematical principles rarely trip off the tongue, nor do convoluted passages which show the earliest usage of some particular form of words. When we describe someone "at their last gasp," we are not quoting the *Second Book of Maccabees* in the *Apocrypha,* we are simply dipping in the currents of common parlance. On the other hand, three words, "What's up, Doc?" can vividly evoke a complete personality, even if it's only that of a cartoon rabbit. These are quotations to be quoted—which are quoted—when there is knowledge or intention of quoting.

In a similar vein, I have provided sources and context for quotations using modern, accessible works wherever possible, rather than recondite authorities which are frequently as hard to track down as the quote they are said to contain. Quotations do not belong on the dusty shelves of academia, they are part of a living tradition, of the affinities which define us individually and collectively. Yes, we must be exact, but let us not be precious, and let us not forget that a good portion of the things that were supposed to be said were never said at all, or at least not in their enshrined form. The best quotations exist in a myriad variations—no matter: what is important is that they are with us, and, when encountered in the right place, at the right time, in the right mood, they can still move us.

Acknowledgements

Much enthusiasm has gone into the creation of this work, and much has been engendered by it. Happily, this dedicated zeal survived all the painstaking research, detailed commentary and laborious word-processing that were also necessary to bring the book to completion. At Columbia University Press, James Raimes once more demonstrated his encouragement and forbearance in the face of frustrated schedules and missed deadlines ("Ye have heard of the patience of Job"). Ivan Farkas was another source of calm and steadfast support. At my end, Agata Scamporrino endured chaotic routines and added her invaluable assistance as she has done before on many previous occasions; Vikki Fear contributed time and energy in a variety of roles; Kristan Sanderson handled everything with inscrutable competence, and with a flair for creative input at all levels; Tim Munro applied his brain as big as a planet to each technical problem as it arose, concocting miracle cures and blinding me with science; Kate Hughes lent her particular expertise on Latin and Russian authors; Alyson Hallet was helpful in the field of women writers and artists, but even more crucial for her dauntless good humor; Richard Davoll allowed himself to be dragged to techno-hell and back for the sake of art and scrupulous editing—without his incisive contributions, this book would always be unfinished; Philip Krynsky came up trumps (again) and devoted months of his life to what must have seemed at times an endless task. His input is especially appreciated in the fields of cinema and song. Lastly, this book is dedicated to Jo Morgan, my partner, who has seen it all before, and has kept her sanity:

The lyf so short, the craft so longe to lerne,
Th' assay so hard, so sharp the conquerynge,
The dredful joye, alwey that slit so yerne;
Al this mene I be love.

Quotations

Abandonment

1   And about the ninth hour Jesus cried with a loud voice, saying *Eli, Eli, lama sabachthani?* that is to say, My God, my God, why hast thou forsaken me?

   BIBLE: NEW TESTAMENT, *Matthew,* 27:46.

   The words of Jesus were anticipated in *Psalms* 22:1.

Abortion

1   It serves me right for putting all my eggs in one bastard.

   DOROTHY PARKER, (1893–1967) U.S. humorous writer. Quoted in *You Might As Well Live,* pt. 2, ch. 3, John Keats (1970).

   On her abortion.

Absence

1   Absent in body, but present in spirit.

   BIBLE: NEW TESTAMENT
   St. Paul, in *1 Corinthians,* 5:3.

2   I was court-martialled in my absence, and sentenced to death in my absence, so I said they could shoot me in my absence.

   BRENDAN BEHAN, (1923–1964) Irish playwright. Pat, in *The Hostage,* act 1 (1958).

   On his experiences in the I.R.A.

3   The heart may think it knows better: the senses know that absence blots people out. We really have no absent friends. The friend becomes a traitor by breaking, however unwillingly or sadly, out of our own zone: a hard judgment is passed on him, for all the pleas of the heart.

   ELIZABETH BOWEN, (1899–1973) Anglo-Irish novelist. *The Death of the Heart,* pt. 2, ch. 2 (1938).

4   Beneath the rule of men entirely great
   The pen is mightier than the sword.
   Absence is to love what wind is to fire; it extinguishes the small, it enkindles the great.

   ROGER BUSSY–RABUTIN, COMTE DE, (1618–1693) French soldier, writer. "Maximes d'Amour," act 2, sc. 2, *Histoire Amoureuse des Gaules* (1665).

François, Duc de La Rochefoucauld, expressed a similar thought in *Sentences et Maximes Morales*, no. 276 (1678): "Absence lessens the minor passions and increases the great ones, as the wind douses a candle and kindles a fire."

5 If youth but knew; if age but could.
Wives in their husbands' absences
grow subtler,
And daughters sometimes run off
with the butler.

GEORGE GORDON NOEL BYRON, 6TH BARON BYRON, (1788–1824) British poet. *Don Juan*, cto. 3, st. 22 (1819–1824).

6 There was once a man who said, "God
Must think it exceedingly odd
If he finds that this tree
Continues to be
When there's no one about in the Quad."

RONALD KNOX, (1888–1957) British scholar, priest. In *The Complete Limerick Book*, Langford Reed (1924).

Knox's limerick was anonymously answered: "Dear Sir, Your astonishment's odd: *I* am always about in the Quad. And that's why the tree Will continue to be, Since observed by Yours faithfully, God."

7 "Presents," I often say, "endear absents."

CHARLES LAMB, (1775–1834) British essayist, critic. *Essays of Elia*, "A Dissertation Upon Roast Pig" (1820-23).

8 How like a winter hath my absence been
From thee, the pleasure of the fleeting year!
What freezings have I felt, what dark days seen,
What old December's bareness everywhere!

WILLIAM SHAKESPEARE, (1564–1616) British dramatist, poet. "Sonnet 97" (1609).

Abstinence

1 Subdue your appetites, my dears, and you've conquered human natur.'

CHARLES DICKENS, (1812–1870) British novelist. Mr. Squeers, in *Nicholas Nickleby*, ch. 5 (1838–1839).

2 Abstinence is as easy to me, as temperance would be difficult.

SAMUEL JOHNSON, (1709–1784) British author, lexicographer. *Memoirs of the Life and Correspondence of Mrs. Hannah More*, vol. 1, ed. William Roberts (1834).

Absurdity

1 The privilege of absurdity; to which no living creature is subject, but man only.

THOMAS HOBBES, (1588–1679) British philosopher. *Leviathan*, pt. 1, ch. 5 (1651).

2 There is only one step from the sublime to the ridiculous.

NAPOLEON BONAPARTE, (1769–1821) French general, emperor. Quoted in *Histoire de l'Ambassade dans le Grand–duché de Varsovie en 1812*, p. 215, D.G. De Pradt (1815). Remark, Dec. 1812, to Polish Ambassador Abbé De Pradt.

Of Napoleon's return by sledge to Paris after the failure of his Russian campaign; also in Comte de Las Cases' *Mémorial de Sainte–Hélène*. Tom Paine had earlier observed (*The Age of Reason*, pt. 2, 1795): "One step above the sublime, makes the ridiculous; and one step above the ridiculous, makes the sublime again."

3 Oh, life is a glorious cycle of song,
A medley of extemporanea;
And love is a thing that can never go wrong;
And I am Marie of Roumania.

DOROTHY PARKER, (1893–1967) U.S. humorous writer. "Comment," *Enough Rope* (1926).

Abuse

1   It's not a slam at *you* when people are rude—it's a slam at the people they've met before.

    F. Scott Fitzgerald, (1896–1940) U.S. author. Cecilia Brady, in *The Last Tycoon*, ch. 1 (1941).

2   His speech was rather like being savaged by a dead sheep.

    Denis Healey, (b. 1917) British Labour politician. *Hansard*, col. 1027. Speech, June 14, 1978, House of Commons.

    Referring to a criticism of Healey's Budget proposals by Shadow Chancellor, Geoffrey Howe. According to Healey's memoirs, his off–the–cuff remark was inspired by Winston Churchill's comment that an attack by Labour politician Clement Attlee was "like being savaged by a pet lamb." (*The Time of My Life*, pt. 3, ch. 21, 1989). In 1983, after being congratulated by Healey on his appointment as Foreign Secretary, Howe commented that it was "like being nuzzled by an old ram." Healey's rejoinder: "It would be the end of a beautiful friendship if he accused me of necrophilia."

3   A fly, Sir, may sting a stately horse and make him wince; but one is but an insect, and the other is a horse still.

    Samuel Johnson, (1709–1784) British author, lexicographer. Quoted in James Boswell, *Life of Johnson*, vol. 1, note to entry, March 20, 1776, ed. George Birkbeck Hill, rev. L.F. Powell (1934).

Acceptance

1   Ah, when to the heart of man
    Was it ever less than a treason
    To go with the drift of things
    To yield with a grace to reason
    And bow and accept at the end
    Of a love or a season?

    Robert Frost, (1874–1963) U.S. poet. "Reluctance," l. 19-24, *A Boy's Will* (1913).

2   Turning the other cheek is a kind of moral jiu–jitsu.

    Gerald Stanley Lee, (1862–1944) U.S. clergyman, writer. *Crowds*, bk. 4, ch. 9 (1913).

Accounts

1   For which of you, intending to build a tower, sitteth not down first, and counteth the cost, whether he have sufficient to finish it?

    Bible: New Testament, Jesus, in *Luke*, 14:28.

Achievement

1   I have climbed to the top of the greasy pole.

    Benjamin Disraeli, (1804–1881) British statesman, author. Quoted in *The Life of Benjamin Disraeli*, vol. 4, ch. 16, W. Monypenny and G. Buckle (1916).

    Remark to friends on becoming prime minister.

Acquaintance

1   Acquaintance. A person whom we know well enough to borrow from, but not well enough to lend to.

    Ambrose Bierce, (1842–1914) U.S. author. *The Devil's Dictionary* (1881–1906), repr. in *Collected Works of Ambrose Bierce*, vol. 7 (1911).

2   I look upon every day to be lost, in which I do not make a new acquaintance.

    Samuel Johnson, (1709–1784) British author, lexicographer. Quoted in James Boswell, *Life of Dr. Johnson*, entry, Nov. 1784 (1791).

Action

1   Let us honour if we can
    The vertical man,
    Though we value none
    But the horizontal one.

    W.H. (WYSTAN HUGH) AUDEN,
    (1907–1973) Anglo–American poet. *Poems*,
    epigraph (1930). Repr. in *Collected Shorter
    Poems 1927–1957* (1966), "Shorts."

2   He who desires but acts not, breeds
    pestilence.

    WILLIAM BLAKE, (1757–1827) British
    poet, painter, engraver. *The Marriage of
    Heaven and Hell*, plate 7, "Proverbs of Hell,"
    (c. 1793). Repr. in *Complete Writings*, ed.
    Geoffrey Keynes (1957).

3   It is vain to say human beings ought
    to be satisfied with tranquillity: they
    must have action; and they will
    make it if they cannot find it.

    CHARLOTTE BRONTË, (1816–1855)
    British novelist. *Jane Eyre*, ch. 12 (1847).

4   Never confuse movement with
    action.

    ERNEST HEMINGWAY, (1899–1961) U.S.
    author, quoted by Marlene Dietrich in *Papa
    Hemingway*, pt. 1, ch. 1, A.E. Hotchner (1966
    edition).

    "In those five words," Dietrich added, "he
    gave me a whole philosophy."

5   As life is action and passion, it is
    required of a man that he should
    share the passion and action of his
    time, at peril of being judged not to
    have lived.

    OLIVER WENDELL HOLMES, JR.,
    (1841–1935) U.S. jurist. "Memorial Day
    Address," *Speeches of Oliver Wendell
    Holmes* (1934). Speech, May 30, 1884,
    Keene, Hew Hampshire.

6   When the going gets tough, the
    tough get going.

    JOSEPH P. (PATRICK) KENNEDY,
    (1888–1969) U.S. tycoon, diplomat.

Quoted in *Honey Fitz*, p. 291, J.H. Cutler
(1962).

The saying has also been ascribed to football
coach Knute Rockne (1888–1931).

7   Every man feels instinctively that all
    the beautiful sentiments in the
    world weigh less than a single lovely
    action.

    JAMES RUSSELL LOWELL, (1819–1891)
    U.S. poet, editor. "Rousseau and the Senti-
    mentalists," *Among My Books* (1870). Origi-
    nally published in *North American Review*
    (Boston, July 1867).

8   Saying is one thing and doing is
    another.

    MICHEL DE MONTAIGNE, (1533–1592)
    French essayist. *Essays*, bk. 2, ch. 31 (1580).

9   Let's go to work.

    QUENTIN TARANTINO, (b. 1963) U.S.
    filmmaker. Joe Cabot (Lawrence Tierney), in
    Reservoir Dogs (film) (1992).

    The words also appeared as the advertising
    slogan on original posters of the film on
    release.

Activism

1   While there is a lower class, I am in
    it, while there is a criminal element,
    I am of it, and while there is a soul
    in prison, I am not free.

    EUGENE VICTOR DEBS, (1855–1926)
    U.S. trade unionist, Socialist leader. *The Pen-
    guin Book of Twentieth Century Speeches*, ed.
    Brian MacArthur (1992). Speech, Sept. 14,
    1918, from the dock at Cleveland, Ohio.

    Defending himself against charges of violating
    the 1917 Espionage Act. Debs was sentenced
    to jail and was finally released under a pardon
    by the incoming President Harding in 1921.

Actors and Acting

1   For an actress to be a success, she
    must have the face of Venus, the

brains of a Minerva, the grace of Terpsichore, the memory of a Macaulay, the figure of Juno, and the hide of a rhinoceros.

ETHEL BARRYMORE, (1897–1959) U.S. actor. Quoted in *The Theatre in the Fifties*, p. 30, George Jean Nathan (1953).

2 For the theatre one needs long arms; it is better to have them too long than too short. An *artiste* with short arms can never, never make a fine gesture.

SARAH BERNHARDT, (1844–1923) French actor. *Memories of My Life*, ch. 6 (1907).

3 Acting is the expression of a neurotic impulse. It's a bum's life.... The principal benefit acting has afforded me is the money to pay for my psychoanalysis.

MARLON BRANDO, (b. 1924) U.S. screen actor. Quoted in *Marlon Brando: The Only Contender*, ch. 13, Gary Carey (1985).

4 To see him act is like reading Shakespeare by flashes of lightning.

SAMUEL TAYLOR COLERIDGE, (1772–1834) British poet and critic. *Table Talk*, "27 April 1823," *Specimens of the Table Talk of Samuel Taylor Coleridge*, ed. Henry Nelson Coleridge (1835). Repr. in *Collected Works*, vol. 14, ed. Kathleen Coburn (1990).

Referring to the actor Edmund Kean.

5 Don't put your daughter on the stage,
Mrs. Worthington,
Don't put your daughter on the stage.

NOËL COWARD, (1899–1973) British playwright, actor, composer. "Mrs. Worthington" (song), refrain (1935), published in *Cowardy Custard: The World of Noël Coward*, ed. John Hadfield (1973). Noël Coward sang the song in the original recording, with music by Cole Porter.

6 No! I am not Prince Hamlet, nor was meant to be:
Am an attendant lord, one that will do
To swell a progress, start a scene or two,
Advise the prince.

T.S. (THOMAS STEARNS) ELIOT, (1888–1965) Anglo–American poet, critic. "The Love Song of J. Alfred Prufrock," *Prufrock and Other Observations* (1917).

7 An actor is a kind of guy who if you ain't talking about him ain't listening.

GEORGE GLASS, (1910–1984) U.S. film production executive. Quoted in *Brando*, ch. 8, Bob Thomas (1973).

The quote is frequently attributed to Marlon Brando, who may have heard it from Glass; a similar quip is credited to Michael Wilding: "You can pick out actors by the glazed look that comes into their eyes when the conversation wanders away from themselves."

8 Players, Sir! I look on them as no better than creatures set upon tables and joint stools to make faces and produce laughter, like dancing dogs.

SAMUEL JOHNSON, (1709–1784) British author, lexicographer. Quoted in James Boswell, *Life of Dr. Johnson*, entry, October [?] 1775 (1791).

9 Miss Caswell is an actress, a graduate of the Copacabana school of dramatic arts.

JOSEPH L. MANKIEWICZ, (1909–1993) U.S. filmmaker. Addison De Witt (George Sanders), in *All About Eve* (film), introducing his protègé Miss Caswell, played by Marilyn Monroe, to Margo Channing (Bette Davis) (1950). Joseph L. Mankiewicz.

10 She runs the gamut of emotions from A to B.

DOROTHY PARKER, (1893–1967) U.S. humorous writer. Quoted in obituary, *Publishers Weekly* (New York, June 19, 1967).

Referring to Katharine Hepburn, in a theater review of *The Lake.*

11 O, it offends me to the soul to hear a robustious, periwig–pated fellow tear a passion to tatters, to very rags, to split the ears of the groundlings, who for the most part are capable of nothing but inexplicable dumb shows and noise. I would have such a fellow whipped for o'erdoing Termagant. It out–Herods Herod. Pray you avoid it.

WILLIAM SHAKESPEARE, (1564–1616) British dramatist, poet. Hamlet, in *Hamlet,* act 3, sc. 2, l. 8–14 (1604).

Directing the players how to perform the speech he has inserted in the play to be presented before Claudius.

Addiction

1 All sin tends to be addictive, and the terminal point of addiction is what is called damnation.

W.H. (WYSTAN HUGH) AUDEN, (1907–1973) Anglo-American poet. *A Certain World,* "Hell" (1970).

2 Cocaine habit–forming? Of course not. I ought to know. I've been using it for years.

TALLULAH BANKHEAD, (1903–1968) U.S. screen actor. *Tallulah,* ch. 4 (1952).

According to Tallulah, this was the riposte she used to shock people when taking throat–lozenges. Apart from on one occasion, she claimed never to have used cocaine "except medicinally."

3 Every form of addiction is bad, no matter whether the narcotic be alcohol or morphine or idealism.

CARL JUNG, (1875–1961) Swiss psychiatrist. *Memories, Dreams, and Reflections,* ch. 12 (1962).

Admiration

1 Admiration. Our polite recognition of another's resemblance to ourselves.

AMBROSE BIERCE, (1842–1914) U.S. author. *The Devil's Dictionary* (1881–1906), repr. in *Collected Works of Ambrose Bierce,* vol. 7 (1911).

2 However big the fool, there is always a bigger fool to admire him.

NICOLAS BOILEAU–DESPREAUX, (1636–1711) French poet, critic. *L'Art Politique,* cto. 1, l. 232 (1674).

3 Oh! death will find me long before I tire
Of watching you.

RUPERT BROOKE, (1887–1915) British poet. "Sonnet," *Collected Poems* (1966).

Adolescence

1 So much alarmed that she is quite alarming,
All Giggle, Blush, half Pertness, and half Pout.

GEORGE GORDON NOEL BYRON, 6TH BARON BYRON, (1788–1824) British poet. *Beppo,* st. 39 (1818).

2 The imagination of a boy is healthy, and the mature imagination of a man is healthy; but there is a space of life between, in which the soul is in a ferment, the character undecided, the way of life uncertain, the ambition thick–sighted: thence proceeds mawkishness.

JOHN KEATS, (1795–1821) British poet. *Endymion,* preface (1818).

Adultery

1 Can a man take fire in his bosom, and his clothes not be burned? Can

one go upon hot coals, and his feet not be burned? So he that goeth in to his neighbour's wife; whosoever toucheth her shall not be innocent.

BIBLE: HEBREW, *Proverbs*, 6:27–9.

2 Thou shalt not commit adultery.

BIBLE: HEBREW, *Exodus*, 20:14.

The seventh commandment.

3 Whosoever looketh on a woman to lust after her hath committed adultery with her already in his heart.

BIBLE: NEW TESTAMENT, Jesus, in *Matthew*, 5:28.

From the Sermon on the Mount.

4 What men call gallantry, and gods adultery,
Is much more common where the climate's sultry.

GEORGE GORDON NOEL BYRON, 6TH BARON BYRON, (1788–1824) British poet. *Don Juan*, cto. 1, st. 63 (1819–1824).

5 On the breast of her gown, in fine red cloth, surrounded with an elaborate embroidery and fantastic flourishes of gold thread, appeared the letter A.

NATHANIEL HAWTHORNE, (1804–1864) U.S. author. *The Scarlet Letter*, ch. 2 (1850).

Referring to the scarlet letter of Hester Prynne, standing for Adulteress.

6 Adultery? Thou shalt not die. Die for adultery!
No, the wren goes to't, and the small gilded fly
Does lecher in my sight. Let copulation thrive.

WILLIAM SHAKESPEARE, (1564–1616) British dramatist, poet. Lear, in *King Lear*, act 4, sc. 5, l. 110–12 (1623).

Speaking to the blinded Gloucester, whom he believes has come to ask forgiveness.

7 A mistress should be like a little country retreat near the town, not to dwell in constantly, but only for a night and away.

WILLIAM WYCHERLEY, (1640–1716) British dramatist. Dorilant, in *The Country Wife*, act 1 (1675). Repr. in *Plays of William Wycherley*, ed. W.C. Ward (1888).

Adulthood/Adult Development

1 When I was a child, I spake as a child, I understood as a child, I thought as a child: but when I became a man, I put away childish things.

BIBLE: NEW TESTAMENT. St. Paul, in *1 Corinthians*, 13:11.

2 Men are but children of a larger growth,
Our appetites as apt to change as theirs,
And full as craving too, and full as vain.

JOHN DRYDEN, (1631–1700) British poet, dramatist, critic. Dollabella, in *All for Love*, act 4, sc. 1 (1678).

See Chesterfield on women.

3 To be adult is to be alone.

JEAN ROSTAND, (1894–1977) French biologist, writer. *Pensées d'un Biologiste* (1939). Repr. in *The Substance of Man* (1962).

4 A child becomes an adult when he realizes that he has a right not only to be right but also to be wrong.

THOMAS SZASZ, (b. 1920) U.S. psychiatrist. "Childhood," *The Second Sin* (1973).

Adventures and Adventurers

1   An adventure is only an inconvenience rightly considered. An
inconvenience is only an adventure
wrongly considered.

**G.K. (GILBERT KEITH) CHESTER-
TON,** (1874–1936) British author. *All Things
Considered,* "On Running After One's Hat"
(1908).

2   The call of the wild.

JACK LONDON, (1876–1916) U.S. novelist.
The Call of the Wild (1903).

3   Take a walk on the wild side.

LOU REED, (b. 1943) U.S. rock musician.
"Walk on the Wild Side" (song), on the album
Transformer (1972).

4   If we do not find anything very
pleasant, at least we shall find something new.

**VOLTAIRE [FRANÇOIS MARIE
AROUET],** (1694–1778) French philosopher,
author. Cacambo, in *Candide,* ch. 17 (1759).

Said on journeying downriver into unknown
country.

Adversity

1   Against a spike
Kick not, for fear it pain thee if thou
strike.

AESCHYLUS, (525–456 B.C.) Greek dramatist. Aigisthos, in *Agamemnon,* l. 1623–4,
trans. by Gilbert Murray.

Some translations give the more colloquial,
"Do not kick against the pricks." The words
sum up one of the play's major themes, of
helplessness and submission in the face of
life's savage struggle.

2   It is hard for thee to kick against the
pricks.

BIBLE: NEW TESTAMENT, Jesus, in *Acts,*
9:5.

The words of Christ to Saul (St. Paul) on his
way to Damascus. See Aeschylus on adversity.

3   Thou broughtest us into the net;
thou laidst affliction upon our loins.
Thou hast caused men to ride over
our heads; we went through fire and
through water; but thou broughtest
us out into a wealthy place.

BIBLE: HEBREW, *Psalms,* 66:11–2.

4   Adversity is sometimes hard upon a
man; but for one man who can
stand prosperity, there are
a hundred that will stand adversity.

THOMAS CARLYLE, (1795–1881) Scottish
essayist, historian. *On Heroes and Hero–Worship,* "The Hero as Man of Letters" (1841).

5   I needed a drink, I needed a lot of
life insurance, I needed a vacation, I
needed a home in the country.
What I had was a coat, a hat and a
gun.

RAYMOND CHANDLER, (1888–1959)
U.S. author. Philip Marlowe, in *Farewell, My
Lovely,* ch. 34 (1940).

6   For of fortunes sharp adversitee
The worst kynde of infortune is
this,
A man to han ben in prosperitee,
And it remembren, whan it passed
is.

GEOFFREY CHAUCER, (1340–1400)
British poet. Pandarus, in *Troilus and
Criseyde,* bk. 3, l. 1625–8 (c. 1385), repr. in
The Works of Geoffrey Chaucer, ed. Alfred W.
Pollard, et al. (1898).

The same thought appears in bk. 2 of
Boethius's *Consolation of Philosophy,* translated by Chaucer: "For in all adversite of fortune, the most unsely kinde of contrarious fortune is to han been weleful." Similarly in
Dante, *Inferno,* canto 5, see Dante on "regret."

7   I have nothing to offer but blood,
toil, tears and sweat.

WINSTON CHURCHILL, (1874–1965) British statesman, writer. Vol. 6, *Winston S. Churchill: His Complete Speeches, 1897–1963,* ed. Robert Rhodes James (1974). Speech, May 13, 1940,

House of Commons.

Maiden speech as prime minister.

8 Do you not see how necessary a world of pains and troubles is to school an intelligence and make it a soul?

JOHN KEATS, (1795–1821) British poet. *Letters of John Keats,* no. 123, ed. Frederick Page (1954). Letter, Feb. 14–May 3, 1819, to his brother and sister–in–law, George and Georgiana Keats.

9 Christ, you know it ain't easy,
You know how hard it can be,
The way things are going
They're going to crucify me.

JOHN LENNON, (1940–1980) British songwriter, rock musician. "The Ballad of John and Yoko" (song) (1969) on the album *The Beatles Again* (1970).

The song, which was banned for its perceived blasphemy, is also credited to Paul McCartney.

10 I long ago come to the conclusion that all life is six to five against.

DAMON RUNYON, (1884–1946) U.S. author. Sam the Gonoph, in "A Nice Price," *Money from Home* (1935). *Collier's* (New York, Sept. 8, 1934).

11 Sweet are the uses of adversity
Which, like the toad, ugly and
    venomous,
Wears yet a precious jewel in his
    head.

WILLIAM SHAKESPEARE, (1564–1616) British dramatist, poet. Duke Senior, in *As You Like It,* act 2, sc. 1, l. 12–14 (1623).

12 By trying we can easily learn to endure adversity. Another man's, I mean.

MARK TWAIN, (1835–1910) U.S. author. *Following the Equator,* ch. 39, "Pudd'nhead Wilson's New Calendar" (1897).

13 Perhaps one day this too will be pleasant to remember.

VIRGIL [PUBLIUS VERGILIUS MARO], (70–19 B.C.) Roman poet. *Aeneid,* bk. 1, l. 203.

Addressed to his men, referring to the difficulties of the journey to Latium.

Advertising

1 You can tell the ideals of a nation by its advertisements.

NORMAN DOUGLAS, (1868–1952) British author. Don Francesco, in *South Wind,* ch. 7 (1917).

2 Promise, large promise, is the soul of an advertisement.

SAMUEL JOHNSON, (1709–1784) British author, lexicographer. "The Idler," no. 40, *Universal Chronicle* (London, Jan. 20, 1759). Repr. in *Works of Samuel Johnson,* Yale Edition, vol. 2, eds. W.J. Bate, John M. Bullitt and L.F. Powell (1963).

Advice

1 Where no counsel is, the people fall; but in the multitude of counsellors there is safety.

BIBLE: HEBREW, *Proverbs,* 11:14.

Affectation

1 Nothing so much prevents our being natural as the desire to seem so.

FRANÇOIS LA ROCHEFOUCAULD, DUC DE, (1613–1680) French writer, moralist. *Sentences et Maximes Morales,* no. 431 (1678).

Affection

1   Set your affection on things above, not on things on the earth.

    BIBLE: NEW TESTAMENT, St. Paul, in *Colossians*, 3:2.

Africa and Africans

1   Day by day we hear the cry of AFRICA FOR THE AFRICANS. This cry has become a positive, determined one. It is a cry that is raised simultaneously the world over because of the universal oppression that affects the Negro.

    MARCUS GARVEY, (1887–1940) Jamaican civil rights campaigner. Quoted in *The Philosophy and Opinions of Marcus Garvey*, vol. 1, ch. 1, ed. Amy Jacques Garvey (1923).

2   So 'ere's *to* you, Fuzzy–Wuzzy, at your 'ome in the Soudan;
You're a pore benighted 'eathen but a first–class fightin' man;
An' 'ere's *to* you, Fuzzy–Wuzzy, with your 'ayrick 'ead of 'air—
You big black boundin' beggar— for you broke a British square!

    RUDYARD KIPLING, (1865–1936) British writer, poet. "Fuzzy–Wuzzy," *Barrack–Room Ballads* (1892).

3   When old settlers say "One has to understand the country," what they mean is, "You have to get used to our ideas about the native." They are saying, in effect, "Learn our ideas, or otherwise get out; we don't want you."

    DORIS LESSING, (b. 1919) British novelist. *The Grass is Singing*, ch. 1 (1950).

4   There is always something new out of Africa.

    PLINY THE ELDER (GAIUS PLINIUS SECU), (23–79) Roman scholar. *Natural History*, bk. 8, sct. 17.

    Greek proverb quoted by Pliny; *Out of Africa* was the English title for Isak Dinesen's 1937 account of her years in Kenya, filmed in 1985.

African Americans

1   The fact that the adult American Negro female emerges a formidable character is often met with amazement, distaste and even belligerence. It is seldom accepted as an inevitable outcome of the struggle won by survivors, and deserves respect if not enthusiastic acceptance.

    MAYA ANGELOU, (b. 1928) U.S. author. *I Know Why the Caged Bird Sings*, ch. 34 (1969).

2   An American, a Negro ... two souls, two thoughts, two unreconciled strivings; two warring ideals in one dark body, whose dogged strength alone keeps it from being torn asunder.

    W.E.B. (WILLIAM EDWARD BURGHARDT) DU BOIS, (1868–1963) U.S. civil rights leader, author. *The Souls of Black Folk*, ch. 1 (1903).

    "The history of the American Negro," wrote Du Bois, "is the history of this strife."

3   But I am not tragically colored. There is no great sorrow dammed up in my soul, nor lurking behind my eyes. I do not mind at all. I do not belong to the sobbing school of negrohood who hold that nature somehow has given them a low-down dirty deal.... No, I do not weep at the world—I am too busy sharpening my oyster knife.

    ZORA NEALE HURSTON, (1907–1960) U.S. author. "How It Feels to Be Colored Me."

I Love Myself When I Am Laughing (1979). (Essay first published 1928).

4 Body and soul, Black America reveals the extreme questions of contemporary life, questions of freedom and identity: *How can I be who I am?*

JUNE JORDAN, (b. 1939) U.S. poet, civil rights activist. "Black Studies: Bringing Back the Person," *Moving Towards Home: Political Essays* (1989). Essay originally published in *Evergreen Review* (New York, Oct. 1969).

5 If there ever are great revolutions there, they will be caused by the presence of the blacks upon American soil. That is to say, it will not be the equality of social conditions but rather their inequality which may give rise to it.

ALEXIS DE TOCQUEVILLE, (1805–1859) French social philosopher. *Democracy in America*, vol. 2, pt. 3, ch. 21 (1840).

African–American Culture

1 Look for me all around you, for with God's grace, I shall come and bring with me countless millions of Black slaves who have died in America and the West Indies and the millions in Africa to aid you in the fight for Liberty, Freedom and Life.

MARCUS GARVEY, (1887–1940) Jamaican civil rights campaigner. Quoted by Tony Martin, in *The Philosophy and Opinions of Marcus Garvey*, preface, 1986 edition, ed. Amy Jacques Garvey (1923, 1986).

2 I, too, sing America.
I am the darker brother.
They send me to eat in the kitchen when company comes.
But I laugh,
And eat well,
And grow strong.

LANGSTON HUGHES, (1902–1967) U.S. poet, author. "I, Too," *Selected Poems* (1954). *Survey Graphic* (March 1925).

3 O black and unknown bards of long ago, How came your lips to touch the sacred fire?

JAMES WELDON JOHNSON, (1871–1938) U.S. author, poet. "O Black and Unknown Bards," st. 1 (written c. 1907), publ. in *Fifty Years and Other Poems* (1917).

Opening lines.

4 There are those who believe Black people possess the secret of joy and that it is this that will sustain them through any spiritual or moral or physical devastation.

ALICE WALKER, (b. 1944) U.S. author, critic. *Possessing the Secret of Joy*, epigraph (1992).

Afterlife

1 One short sleep past, we wake eternally,
And Death shall be no more; Death, thou shalt die!

JOHN DONNE, (c. 1572–1631) British divine, metaphysical poet. "Death Be Not Proud," no. 6, *Holy Sonnets* (1609). Repr. in *Complete Poetry and Selected Prose*, ed. John Hayward (1929).

2 All argument is against it; but all belief is for it.

SAMUEL JOHNSON, (1709–1784) British author, lexicographer. Quoted in James Boswell, *Life of Dr. Johnson*, entry, March 31, 1778 (1791).

3 The dread of something after death, The undiscovered country from whose bourn
No traveller returns.

WILLIAM SHAKESPEARE, (1564–1616) British dramatist, poet. Hamlet, in *Hamlet*, act 3, sc. 1, l. 80–82 (1604).

Part of Hamlet's meditative soliloquy on the question of "To be, or not to be."

4 Each of us suffers his own fate in the after–life.

VIRGIL [PUBLIUS VERGILIUS MARO], (70–19 B.C.) Roman poet. Anchises, in *Aeneid*, bk. 6, l. 743 (19 B.C.), trans. by David West (1991).

Anchises to his son Aeneas in the Underworld.

Afternoon

1 At five in the afternoon.
It was exactly five in the afternoon.
A boy brought the white sheet
at five in the afternoon.

FEDERICO GARCÍA LORCA, (1898–1936) Spanish poet, playwright. *La Cogida y la muerte, Llanto por Ignacio Sa nchez Mejas* (1935).

On the death of a bullfighter.

Age and Aging

1 Forty years on, when afar and a sunder
Parted are those who are singing today.

E.E. BOWEN, (1836–1901) British schoolteacher. "Forty Years On" (Harrow School Song) (written 1872, published 1886).

2 A lady of a "certain age," which means
Certainly aged.

GEORGE GORDON NOEL BYRON, 6TH BARON BYRON,

(1788–1824) British poet. *Don Juan*, cto. 6, st. 69 (1819–1824).

3 But, Lord Crist! whan that it remembreth me
Upon my yowthe, and on my jolitee,

It tikleth me aboute myn herte
roote.
Unto this day it dooth myn herte
boote
That I have had my world as in my
tyme.
But age, allas! that al wole
envenyme
Hath me biraft my beautee and my
pith;
Lat go, farewel, the devel go ther-
with!
The flour is goon, ther is namoore
to telle,
The bren, as I best kan, now moste
I selle.

GEOFFREY CHAUCER, (1340–1400) British poet. *The Canterbury Tales*, "The Wife of Bath's Prologue" l. 469–78 (1387–1400). Repr. in *The Works of Geoffrey Chaucer*, ed. Alfred W. Pollard, et al. (1898).

4 Youth is a blunder; Manhood a struggle; Old Age a regret.

BENJAMIN DISRAELI, (1804–1881) British statesman, author. *Coningsby*, bk. 3, ch. 1 (1844).

5 At twenty years of age, the will reigns; at thirty, the wit; and at forty, the judgment.

BENJAMIN FRANKLIN, (1706–1790) U.S. statesman, writer. *Poor Richard's Almanac*, June (1741).

6 Ah! as the heart grows older
It will come to such sights colder
By and by, not spare a sigh
Though worlds of wanwood
leafmeal lie;
And yet you will weep and know why.

GERARD MANLEY HOPKINS, (1844–1889) British poet, Jesuit priest." Spring and Fall: to a young child," written (1880), published in *Poems* (1918).

7 No woman should ever be quite

accurate about her age. It looks so calculating.

OSCAR WILDE, (1854–1900) Anglo–Irish playwright, author. Lady Bracknell, in *The Importance of Being Earnest*, act 4 (1895).

Age: The Twenties

1   When I was one–and–twenty
I heard a wise man say,
"Give crowns and pounds and
   guineas
But not your heart away;
Give pearls away and rubies,
But keep your fancy free."
But I was one–and–twenty,
No use to talk to me.

A.E. (ALFRED EDWARD) HOUSMAN, (1859–1936) British poet. "A Shropshire Lad," no. 13 (1896). Repr. in *The Collected Poems of A.E. Housman* (1939).

2   When I was as you are now, tower-ing in the confidence of twenty–one, little did I suspect that I should be at forty–nine, what I now am.

SAMUEL JOHNSON, (1709–1784) British author, lexicographer. Quoted in James Boswell, *Life of Dr. Johnson* (1791). Letter, Jan. 9, 1758.

3   How soon hath Time, the subtle thief of youth,
Stolen on his wing my
   three–and–twentieth year!

JOHN MILTON, (1608–1674) British poet. Sonnet 7, "On His Having Arrived at the Age of Twenty–three" (written 1632, published 1645).

Also called "How Soon Hath Time."

Age: The Thirties

1   I am past thirty, and three parts iced over.

MATTHEW ARNOLD, (1822–1888) British poet, critic. *The Letters of Matthew Arnold to Arthur Hugh Clough*, ed. H.F. Lowry (1932). Letter, Feb. 12, 1853.

2   I am thirty–three—the age of the good *Sans–culotte* Jesus; an age fatal to revolutionists.

CAMILLE DESMOULINS, (1760–1794) French journalist, revolutionary leader. Quoted in *The History of the French Revolution*, bk. 6, ch. 2, Thomas Carlyle (1837).

Answer to the Revolutionary Tribunal, Paris, Apr. 2, 1784, on the eve of his execution.

3   Thirty–five is a very attractive age. London society is full of women of the highest birth who have, of their own free choice, remained thirty–five for years.

OSCAR WILDE, (1854–1900) Anglo–Irish playwright, author. Lady Brack-nell, in *The Importance of Being Earnest*, act 4 (1895).

Age: The Forties

1   At forty–five,
What next, what next?
I meet my father,
my age, still alive.

ROBERT LOWELL, (1917–1977) U.S. poet. "Middle Age," st. 2, *For The Union Dead* (1965).

Last stanza.

2   Life begins at forty.

WALTER B. PITKIN, (1878–1953) U.S. author. *Life Begins at Forty* (book title) (1932).

3   Be wise with speed;
A fool at forty is a fool indeed.

EDWARD YOUNG, (1683–1765) British poet, playwright. *Love of Fame: The Universal Passion*, satire 2, l. 282–3 (1725–1728). Repr. in *Complete Works*, ed. J. Doran (1968).

Age: The Fifties

1   Now, aged fifty, I'm just poised to shoot forth quite free straight & undeflected my bolts whatever they are.

VIRGINIA WOOLF, (1882–1941) British novelist. *The Diary of Virginia Woolf*, vol. 4, ed. Anne O. Bell (1982). Journal entry, Oct. 2, 1932.

Age: The Seventies

1   At seventy–seven it is time to be in earnest.

SAMUEL JOHNSON, (1709–1784) British author, lexicographer. *Journey to the Western Isles of Scotland*, "Col," (1775). Repr. in *Works of Samuel Johnson*, Yale Edition, vol. 9, ed. Mary Lascelles (1971).

Agents

1   It is well–known what a middleman is: he is a man who bamboozles one party and plunders the other.

BENJAMIN DISRAELI, (1804–1881) British statesman, author. *Selected Speeches of the Late Right Honourable the Earl of Beaconsfield*, vol. 1, "Maynooth," ed. T.E. Kebbes (1882). Speech, April 11, 1845.

Aggression

1   I love to see a young girl go out and grab the world by the lapels. Life's a bitch. You've got to go out and kick ass.

MAYA ANGELOU, (b. 1928) U.S. author. "Kicking Ass" (interview), *Conversations with Maya Angelou*, ed. Jeffrey M. Elliot (1989). Originally published in *Girl About Town* (Oct. 13, 1986).

Agnosticism

1   If only God would give me some clear sign! Like making a large deposit in my name at a Swiss bank.

WOODY ALLEN, (b. 1935) U.S. filmmaker. "Selections from the Allen Notebooks," *Without Feathers* (1976). Article originally published in *New Yorker* (Nov. 5, 1973).

2   Lord I disbelieve—help thou my unbelief.

E.M. (EDWARD MORGAN) FORSTER, (1879–1970) British novelist, essayist. *Two Cheers for Democracy*, "What I Believe" (1951).

A reference to Bible New Testament, Mark 9:24, "Lord, I believe, help thou mine unbelief."

Agreement

1   My idea of an agreeable person is a person who agrees with me.

BENJAMIN DISRAELI, (1804–1881) British statesman, author. Hugo Bohun, in *Lothair*, ch. 41 (1870).

Aid

1   Here is the answer which I will give to President Roosevelt.... Give us the tools and we will finish the job.

WINSTON CHURCHILL, (1874–1965) British statesman, writer. Vol. 6, *Winston S. Churchill: His Complete Speeches, 1897–1963*, ed. Robert Rhodes James (1974). Radio broadcast, Feb. 9, 1941.

2   Fool that I was, upon my eagle's wings
I bore this wren, till I was tired with soaring,

And now he mounts above me.

JOHN DRYDEN, (1631–1700) British poet, dramatist, critic. Antony, in *All for Love*, act 2, sc. 1 (1678).

3   Like a bridge over troubled water
I will lay me down.

PAUL SIMON, (b. 1949) U.S. singer, song-writer. "Bridge Over Troubled Water" (song), on the album *Bridge Over Troubled Water* (1970).

AIDS

1   Everywhere I go I see increasing evidence of people swirling about in a human cesspit of their own making.

JAMES ANDERTON, (b. 1932) British senior police officer. Quoted in *City Limits* (London, Dec. 18, 1987).

Referring to the AIDS epidemic.

2   Societies need to have one illness which becomes identified with evil, and attaches blame to its "victims."

SUSAN SONTAG, (b. 1933) U.S. essayist. *AIDS and Its Metaphors*, ch. 1 (1989).

Air

1   Wild air, world–mothering air,
Nestling me everywhere,
That each eyelash or hair
Girdles; goes home betwixt
The fleeciest, frailest–fixed
Snowflake; that's fairly mixed
With, riddles, and is rife
In every least thing's life.

GERARD MANLEY HOPKINS, (1844–1889) British poet, Jesuit priest. "The Blessed Virgin Compared to the Air We Breathe," l. 1–8 (written 1883), published in *Poems* (1918).

Air Force

1   There was only one catch and that was Catch–22, which specified that a concern for one's own safety in the face of dangers that were real and immediate was the process of a rational mind.... Orr would be crazy to fly more missions and sane if he didn't, but if he was sane he had to fly them. If he flew them he was crazy and didn't have to; but if he didn't want to he was sane and had to.

JOSEPH HELLER, (b. 1923) U.S. author. *Catch–22*, ch. 5 (1961).

Alcohol and Drunkenness

1   Inspiring bold John Barleycorn!
What dangers thou canst make us scorn!
Wi' tippenny, we fear nae evil;
Wi' usquabae, we'll face the devil!

ROBERT BURNS, (1759–1796) Scottish poet. "Tam o' Shanter," l. 105–108 (1791). Repr. in *Poetical Works*, vol. 1, ed. William Scott Douglas (1891).

Burns popularized the figure of John Barley-corn—a traditional personification of malt liquor—in various works. "Usquabae" or "usquebae" is the Gaelic word for whisky.

2   Man, being reasonable, must get drunk;
The best of life is but intoxication.

GEORGE GORDON NOEL BYRON, 6TH BARON BYRON, (1788–1824) British poet. *Don Juan*, cto. 2, st. 179 (1819–1824).

3   Alcohol is like love. The first kiss is magic, the second is intimate, the third is routine. After that you take the girl's clothes off.

RAYMOND CHANDLER, (1888–1959) U.S. author. Terry Lennox, in *The Long Goodbye*, ch. 4 (1954).

4   A sudden violent jolt of it has been known to stop the victim's watch, snap his suspenders and crack his glass eye right across.

IRVIN S. COBB, (1876–1944) U.S. author. *Attributed.*

Of moonshine corn liquor, as described to the Distillers' Code Authority, NRA.

5   Drink, and be mad, then; 'tis your country bids!
Gloriously drunk, obey th'important call!

WILLIAM COWPER, (1731–1800) British poet. *The Task,* bk. 4, l. 509–10 (1785). Repr. in *Poetical Works,* ed. H.S. Milford (1934).

6   Bring in the bottled lightning, a clean tumbler, and a corkscrew.

CHARLES DICKENS, (1812–1870) British novelist. "The Gentleman in the Small–clothes," in *Nicholas Nickleby,* ch. 49 (1839).

7   Alcohol is nicissary f'r a man so that now an' thin he can have a good opinion iv himsilf, ondisturbed be th' facts.

FINLEY PETER DUNNE, (1867–1936) U.S. journalist, humorist. "Dooley on Alcohol," *Chicago Tribune* (April 26, 1914).

8   I have fed purely upon ale; I have eat my ale, drank my ale, and I always sleep upon ale.

GEORGE FARQUHAR, (1678–1707) Irish dramatist. The landlord Boniface, in *The Beaux' Stratagem,* act 1, sc. 1 (1707). Repr. in *Complete Works,* ed. Charles Stonehill (1930).

9   The hangover became a part of the day as well allowed–for as the Spanish siesta.

F. SCOTT FITZGERALD, (1896–1940) U.S. author. "My Lost City," *The Crack–Up,*

ed. Edmund Wilson (1945). First published in *Esquire* (New York, July 1932).

10   And he smiled a kind of sickly smile, and curled up on the floor, And the subsequent proceedings interested him no more.

FRANCIS BRET HARTE, (1836–1902) U.S. author, journalist, poet. "The Society Upon the Stanislaus," st. 7 (1868).

11   Drink not the third glass, which thou canst not tame, When once it is within thee.

GEORGE HERBERT, (1593–1633) British clergyman, poet. "The Church–Porch," st. 5, *The Temple* (1633).

12   Malt does more than Milton can To justify God's ways to man.

A.E. (ALFRED EDWARD) HOUSMAN, (1859–1936) British poet, classical scholar. "A Shropshire Lad," no. 62 (1896).

Alluding to Milton's lines: See interpretation.

13   They who drink beer will think beer.

WASHINGTON IRVING, (1783–1859) U.S. author. *The Sketch Book of Geoffrey Crayon, Gent.* "Stratford–on–Avon," (1819–1820).

This quotation has also been attributed to William Warburton, Bishop of Gloucester (1698–1779).

14   If merely "feeling good" could decide, drunkenness would be the supremely valid human experience.

WILLIAM JAMES, (1843–1916) U.S. psychologist, philosopher. *The Varieties Of Religious Experience,* lecture 1, "Religion and Neurology" (1902).

15   A man who exposes himself when he is intoxicated, has not the art of getting drunk.

SAMUEL JOHNSON, (1709–1784) British author, lexicographer. Quoted in James Boswell, *Life of Dr. Johnson,* entry, April 24, 1779 (1791).

16 Drink! for you know not whence
you came, nor why:
Drink! for you know not why you
go, nor where.

OMAR KHAYYAM, (11–12th century) Persian astronomer, poet. *The Rubaiyat Khayyam*, st. 74, trans. by Edward FitzGerald, fourth edition (1879).

17 And when night
Darkens the streets, then wander
forth the sons
Of Belial, flown with insolence and
wine.

JOHN MILTON, (1608–1674) British poet. *Paradise Lost*, bk. 1, l. 500–2 (1667).

18 Candy
Is dandy
But Liquor
Is quicker.

OGDEN NASH, (1902–1971) U.S. poet. "Reflections on Ice–Breaking," *Hard Lines* (1931).

19 A torchlight procession marching
down your throat.

JOHN LOUIS O'SULLIVAN, (1813–1895) U.S. editor. Quoted in *Collections and Recollections*, ch. 19, G.W.E. Russell (1898).

Referring to whisky.

20 Drunkenness ... is temporary suicide.

**BERTRAND RUSSELL
[LORD RUSSELL, 3RD EARL],** (1872–1970) British philosopher, mathematician. *The Conquest of Happiness*, ch. 2 (1930).

21 Drunkenness is nothing but voluntary madness.

SENECA, (c. 5–65) Roman writer, philosopher, statesman. *Epistulae ad Lucilium*, epistle 83, sct. 18.

22 Drink, sir, is a great provoker of
three things ... nose–painting, sleep,
and urine. Lechery, sir, it provokes
and unprovokes: it provokes the
desire but it takes away the performance. Therefore much drink may
be said to be an equivocator with
lechery: it makes him and it mars
him; it sets him on and it takes him
off.

WILLIAM SHAKESPEARE, (1564–1616) British dramatist, poet. Porter, in *Macbeth*, act 2, sc. 3, l. 25–7 (1623).

"Nose–painting" refers to the drunkard's red nose.

23 O God, that men should put an
enemy in their mouths to steal
away their brains! That we should
with joy, pleasance, revel, and
applause transform ourselves into
beasts!

WILLIAM SHAKESPEARE, (1564–1616) British dramatist, poet. Cassio, in *Othello*, act 2, sc. 3, l. 283–6 (1623).

24 Better belly burst than good liquor
be lost.

JONATHAN SWIFT, (1667–1745) Anglo–Irish satirist. Neverout, in *Polite Conversation*, dialogue 2 (1738). Repr. in *The Prose Works of Jonathan Swift*, vol. 4, ed. Herbert Davis (1957).

Quoting a proverb first collected in James Howell's *Paroimiographia* (1659).

25 One's too many, and a hundred's
not enough.

BILLY WILDER, (b. 1906) U.S. film director. Nat the bartender (Howard Da Silva), in *The Lost Weekend* (film), spoken to his regular customer Don Birnam (Ray Milland) whose descent into alcoholic breakdown the film graphically portrays (1945).

Alienation

1 Mother died today. Or perhaps it
was yesterday, I don't know.

ALBERT CAMUS, (1913–1960) French–Algerian philosopher, author. Mersault, in *The Outsider*, pt. 1, ch. 1 (1944).

2 Although the masters make the
    rules
  For the wise men and the fools
  I got nothing, Ma, to live up to.

  **BOB DYLAN [ROBERT ALLEN ZIM-
  MERMAN],** (b. 1941) U.S. singer, songwriter. "It's Alright Ma (I'm Only Bleeding)"
  (song), on the album *Bringing it all Back
  Home* (1965).

Aliens

1 Ladies and gentlemen, I have a
  grave announcement to make.
  Incredible as it may seem, strange
  beings who landed in New Jersey
  tonight are the vanguard of an
  invading army from Mars.

  ORSON WELLES, (1915–1984) U.S. filmmaker, actor, producer. *The War of the
  Worlds* (audiocassette 1995). Radio broadcast,
  Halloween, 1938, CBS; from the original story
  by H.G. Wells (1898).

  According to the later reports, despite clear
  warnings that the broadcast was science fiction, listeners jammed switchboards and roads
  as they abandoned their homes in large numbers, with some people claiming they had
  actually seen the Martians.

Alliances

1 Alliance. In international politics,
  the union of two thieves who have
  their hands so deeply inserted in
  each other's pockets that they cannot separately plunder a third.

  AMBROSE BIERCE, (1842–1914) U.S.
  author. *The Devil's Dictionary* (1881–1906),
  repr. in *Collected Works of Ambrose Bierce*,
  vol. 7 (1911).

2 When bad men combine, the good
  must associate; else they will fall,
  one by one, an unpitied sacrifice in
  a contemptible struggle.

  EDMUND BURKE, (1729–1797) Irish
  philosopher, statesman. *Thoughts on the
  Cause of the Present Discontents*, repr. in
  Works, vol. 1 (1865). Speech, April 23, 1770.

  Arguing the need for political parties.

3 Coalitions though successful have
  always found this, that their triumph has been brief.

  BENJAMIN DISRAELI, (1804–1881)
  British statesman, author. *Selected Speeches of
  the Late Right Honourable the Earl of Beaconsfield*, ed. T.E. Kebbes (1882). Speech to House
  of Commons, Dec. 16, 1852.

4 'Tis our true policy to steer clear of
  permanent alliances with any portion of the foreign world.

  GEORGE WASHINGTON, (1732–1799)
  U.S. general, president. "Farewell Address,"
  vol. 35, *The Writings of George Washington*,
  ed. John C. Fitzpatrick (1940). Speech, Sept.
  17, 1796.

Altruism

1 He who would do good to another
    must do it in Minute Particulars:
  General Good is the plea of the
    scoundrel, hypocrite, and flatterer,
  For Art and Science cannot exist but
    in minutely organized Particulars.

  WILLIAM BLAKE, (1757–1827) British
  poet, painter, engraver. *Jerusalem*, ch. 3, plate
  55 (c. 1820), repr. in *Complete Writings*, ed.
  Geoffrey Keynes (1957).

2 I love my fellow creatures—I do all
  the good I can—
  Yet everybody says I'm such a disagreeable man!

  SIR WILLIAM SCHWENCK GILBERT,
  (1836–1911) British librettist. King Gama, in
  Princess Ida, act 1 (1884), published in *The
  Savoy Operas* (1926).

Ambition

1 No bird soars too high, if he soars
  with his own wings.

WILLIAM BLAKE, (1757–1827) British poet, painter, engraver. *The Marriage of Heaven and Hell*, plate 7, "Proverbs of Hell," (c. 1793), repr. in *Complete Writings*, ed. Geoffrey Keynes (1957).

2   'Tis not what man Does which exalts him, but what man Would do!

ROBERT BROWNING, (1812–1889) British poet. "Saul," st. 18 (1855).

3   Ambition can creep as well as soar.

EDMUND BURKE, (1729–1797) Irish philosopher, statesman. *Letters on a Regicide Peace*, letter 3 (1797), repr. in *Works*, vol. 5 (1899).

4   All ambitions are lawful except those which climb upward on the miseries or credulities of mankind. All intellectual and artistic ambitions are permissible, up to and even beyond the limit of prudent sanity. They can hurt no one.

JOSEPH CONRAD, (1857–1924) Polish–born British novelist. "A Familiar Preface," *A Personal Record* (1912).

5   Hitch your wagon to a star. Let us not fag in paltry works which serve our pot and bag alone.

RALPH WALDO EMERSON, (1803–1882) U.S. essayist, poet, philosopher. *Society and Solitude*, "Civilization" (1870).

6   Nature that fram'd us of four elements,
Warring within our breasts for regiment,
Doth teach us all to have aspiring minds.

CHRISTOPHER MARLOWE, (1564–1593) British dramatist, poet. Tamburlaine, in *Tamburlaine the Great*, pt.1, act 2, sc. 7, l. 18–20 (1590).

7   Men would be angels, angels would be gods.

ALEXANDER POPE, (1688–1744) British satirical poet. *An Essay On Man*, epistle 1, l. 126 (1733).

8   As he was valiant, I honour him. But as he was ambitious, I slew him.

WILLIAM SHAKESPEARE, (1564–1616) British dramatist, poet. Brutus, in *Julius Caesar*, act 3, sc. 2, l. 26–7 (1623).

Referring to Julius Caesar. His motivation for killing him, was "not that I loved Caesar less, but that I loved Rome more."

9   I have no spur
To prick the sides of my intent, but only
Vaulting ambition which o'er leaps itself
And falls on the other.

WILLIAM SHAKESPEARE, (1564–1616) British dramatist, poet. Macbeth, in *Macbeth*, act 1, sc. 7, l. 25–28 (1623).

Closing lines of Macbeth's soliloquy on his forthcoming murder of Duncan and its consequences.

10   When that the poor hath cried, Caesar hath wept.
Ambition should be made of sterner stuff.

WILLIAM SHAKESPEARE, (1564–1616) British dramatist, poet. Antony, in *Julius Caesar*, act 3, sc. 2, l. 92–3 (1623).

In Brutus's address to the people, after the assassination of Caesar, he had said of Caesar: "As he was ambitious, I slew him." Mark Antony's oration aims to turn the crowd's sympathies and he plays on Brutus's accusation of Caesar's ambition.

11   Man, unlike anything organic or inorganic in the universe, grows beyond his work, walks up the stairs of his concepts, emerges ahead of his accomplishments.

JOHN STEINBECK, (1902–1968) U.S. author. *The Grapes of Wrath*, ch. 14 (1939).

12 So many worlds, so much to do,
So little done, such things to be.

ALFRED TENNYSON, 1ST BARON TEN-NYSON, (1809–1892) British poet. *In Memoriam*, cto. 73, st. 1 (1850).

The lines found an echo in the words attributed to the South African statesman and business magnate, Cecil Rhodes, on the day of his death in 1902: "So much to do, so little done." Quoted in Lewis Michell, *Life of Rhodes* vol. 2, ch. 39 (1910).

13 Vain the ambition of kings
Who seek by trophies and dead things,
To leave a living name behind,
And weave but nets to catch the wind.

JOHN WEBSTER, (1580–1625) British dramatist. Romelio's song, in *The Devil's Law–Case*, act 5, sc. 4, l. 128–31 (1623). Repr. in *The Complete Works of John Webster*, ed. F.L. Lucas (1927).

American Dream

1 I will keep America moving forward, always forward—for a better America, for an endless enduring dream and a thousand points of light.

GEORGE BUSH, (b. 1924) U.S. Republican politician, president. Acceptance speech, August 18, 1988, *New Orleans, New York Times* (August 19, 1988).

The phrase "a thousand points of light," written for Bush by speechwriter Peggy Noonan, was used on various occasions during the 1988 presidential campaign. The words are not original, echoing similar phrases by Charles Dickens and Thomas Wolfe, among others. As president, Bush initiated a "Points of Light" reform program in June 1989.

Anarchism

1 With society and its public, there is no longer any other language than that of bombs, barricades, and all that follows.

ANTONIN ARTAUD, (1896–1948) French theater producer, actor, theorist. Quoted in *Writers and Revolution*, ch. 15, Renee Weingarten (1974). *Le Monde* (Paris, Sept. 11, 1970).

Remark to André Breton.

2 Anarchism is the only philosophy which brings to man the consciousness of himself; which maintains that God, the State, and society are non–existent, that their promises are null and void, since they can be fulfilled only through man's subordination. Anarchism is therefore the teacher of the unity of life; not merely in nature, but in man.

EMMA GOLDMAN, (1869–1940) U.S. anarchist. *Anarchism and Other Essays*, "Anarchism: What It Really Stands For" (1910).

Ancestry

1 Consider what you came from: you are Greeks! you were not born to live like mindless brutes but to follow paths of excellence and knowledge.

DANTE ALIGHIERI, (1265–1321) Italian poet. "Inferno," cto. 26, l. 118–20, *The Divine Comedy* (c. 1307–1321), trans. by Mark Musa (1971).

Ulysses, in Hell, repeats his exhortation to his fellows on their last, fatal voyage beyond the pillars of Hercules. The story seems to have been Dante's own invention.

2 A hairy quadruped, furnished with a tail and pointed ears, probably arboreal in its habits.

CHARLES DARWIN, (1809–1882) British naturalist. *The Descent of Man*, ch. 21 (1871).

Referring to the ancestry of humankind, according to Darwin's theory. "For my own part," Darwin wrote, "I would as soon be descended from that heroic little monkey ... or that old baboon ... as from a savage who delights to torture his enemies, offers up bloody sacrifices, practices infanticide without remorse, treats his wives like slaves, knows no decency, and is haunted by the grossest superstitions."

3   I am, in point of fact, a particularly haughty and exclusive person, of pre–Adamite ancestral descent. You will understand this when I tell you that I can trace my ancestry back to a protoplasmal primordial atomic globule.

SIR WILLIAM SCHWENCK GILBERT, (1836–1911) British librettist. Pooh–Bah, in *The Mikado*, act 1 (1885), published in *The Savoy Operas* (1926).

4   In church your grandsire cut his throat;
To do the job too long he tarried:
He should have had my hearty vote
To cut his throat before he married.

JONATHAN SWIFT, (1667–1745) Anglo–Irish satirist. *Verses on the Upright Judge* (written 1724), published in *The Poems of Jonathan Swift*, ed. H. Williams (1958).

5   I would rather make my name than inherit it.

WILLIAM MAKEPEACE THACKERAY, (1811–1863) British author. *The Virginians*, ch. 26 (1857–1859).

6   And so our mothers and grandmothers have, more often than not anonymously, handed on the creative spark, the seed of the flower they themselves never hoped to see: or like a sealed letter they could not plainly read.... Guided by my heritage of a love of beauty and a respect for strength—in search of my mother's garden, I found my own.

ALICE WALKER, (b. 1944) U.S. author, critic. "In Search of Our Mothers' Gardens," *In Search of Our Mothers' Gardens* (1983). Originally published *Ms.* (May 1974).

Anecdotes

1   When a man fell into his anecdotage it was a sign for him to retire from the world.

BENJAMIN DISRAELI, (1804–1881) British statesman, author. *Lothair*, ch. 28 (1870).

2   With a tale forsooth he cometh unto you, with a tale which holdeth children from play, and old men from the chimney corner.

SIR PHILIP SIDNEY, (1554–1586) British poet, diplomat, soldier. "An Apology for Poetry" (written 1579–1580, published 1595), ed. J. Churton Collins (1907).

Referring to poets.

3   The history of a soldier's wound beguiles the pain of it.

LAURENCE STERNE, (1713–1768) British author. *Tristram Shandy*, bk. 1, ch. 25 (1759–1767).

Angels

1   Every man hath a good and a bad angel attending on him in particular all his life long.

ROBERT BURTON, (1577–1640) British clergyman, author. *The Anatomy of Melancholy*, pt. 1, sct. 2, memb. 1, subsct. 2 (1621).

2   The angels were all singing out of tune,
And hoarse with having little else to do,
Excepting to wind up the sun and moon
Or curb a runaway young star or two.

GEORGE GORDON NOEL BYRON, 6TH
BARON BYRON, (1788–1824) British poet.
"The Vision of Judgment," st. 2 (1822).

Anger

1 Let not the sun go down upon your
wrath.

BIBLE: NEW TESTAMENT, St. Paul, in
Ephesians, 4:26.

2 The tygers of wrath are wiser than
the horses of ainstruction.

WILLIAM BLAKE, (1757–1827) British
poet, painter, engraver. The Marriage of
Heaven and Hell, plate 9, "Proverbs of Hell,"
(c. 1793), repr. in Complete Writings, ed.
Geoffrey Keynes (1957).

3 Anger is one of the sinews of the
soul; he that wants it hath a
maimed mind.

THOMAS FULLER, (1608–1661) British
cleric. The Holy State and the Profane State,
bk. 3, "Of Anger" (1642).

4 When angry, count ten, before you
speak; if very angry, an hundred.

THOMAS JEFFERSON, (1743–1826) U.S.
president. Decalogue of Canons for Observation in Practical Life, vol. 10, no. 10, The
Writings of Thomas Jefferson, ed. Paul L. Ford
(1899). Letter, Feb. 21, 1825, to Thomas
Jefferson Smith.

Animals

1 Bats have no bankers and they do
not drink
and cannot be arrested and pay no
tax
and, in general, bats have it made.

JOHN BERRYMAN, (1914–1972) U.S.
poet. 77 Dream Songs, no. 63 (1964).

2 Tyger! Tyger! burning bright
In the forests of the night,

What immortal hand or eye
Could frame thy fearful symmetry?

WILLIAM BLAKE, (1757–1827) British
poet, painter, engraver. Songs of Experience,
"The Tyger," st. 1 (1794), repr. in Complete
Writings, ed. Geoffrey Keynes (1957).

3 Rats!
They fought the dogs and killed the
cats,
And bit the babies in the cradles,
And ate the cheeses out of the vats,
And licked the soup from the
cooks' own ladles,
Split open the kegs of salted sprats,
Made nests inside men's Sunday
hats,
And even spoiled the women's
chats
By drowning their speaking
With shrieking and squeaking
In fifty different sharps and flats.

ROBERT BROWNING, (1812–1889) British
poet. "The Pied Piper of Hamelin," st. 2, Dramatic Lyrics (1842).

4 Man is the only animal that can
remain on friendly terms with the
victims he intends to eat until he
eats them.

SAMUEL BUTLER, (1835–1902) British
author. Notebooks, "Mind and Matter" (1912).

5 Fools! For I also had my hour;
One far fierce hour and sweet:
There was a shout about my ears,
And palms before my feet.

GILBERT KEITH CHESTERTON,
(1874–1936) British author. "The Donkey,"
The Wild Knight and Other Poems (1900).

6 Poor little Foal of an oppressed
race!
I love the languid patience of thy
face.

SAMUEL TAYLOR COLERIDGE,
(1772–1834) British poet and critic. "To a
Young Ass," l. 1–2, Morning Chronicle (Dec.

30, 1794). *Poems* (1796), repr. in *Poetical Works,* ed. James Dyke Campbell (1893).

7 Nothing to be done really about animals. Anything you do looks foolish. The answer isn't in us. It's almost as if we're put here on earth to show how silly they aren't.

RUSSELL HOBAN, (b. 1925) U.S. author. George Fairbairn, in *Turtle Diary,* ch. 42 (1975).

8 Be a good animal, true to your animal instincts.

D.H. (DAVID HERBERT) LAWRENCE, (1885–1930) British author. The woodkeeper Annable's motto, in *The White Peacock,* pt. 2, ch. 2 (1911).

9 Thus the orb he roamed
With narrow search, and with
inspection deep
Considered every creature, which of
all
Most opportune might serve his
wiles, and found
The serpent subtlest beast of all the
field.

JOHN MILTON, (1608–1674) British poet. *Paradise Lost,* bk. 9, l. 82–6 (1674).

Referring to Satan, searching for a place "where to lie hid."

10 Camels are snobbish
and sheep, unintelligent;
water buffaloes, neurasthenic—
even murderous.
Reindeer seem over–serious.

MARIANNE MOORE, (1887–1972) U.S. poet. "The Arctic Ox (Or Goat)," (1959).

11 The cow is of the bovine ilk; One
end is moo, the other, milk.

OGDEN NASH, (1902–1971) U.S. poet. "The Cow," (l. 1), *Free Wheeling* (1931).

12 Four legs good, two legs bad.

GEORGE ORWELL, (1903–1950) British author. *Animal Farm,* ch. 3 (1945).

By the end of the story, the animals' revolutionary maxim has changed to "Four legs good, two legs *better.*" (Ch.10).

Anniversaries

1 Let us love nobly, and live, and add
again
Years and years unto years, till we
attain
To write threescore: this is the second
of our reign.

JOHN DONNE, (c. 1572–1631) British divine, metaphysical poet. "The Anniversary," *Songs and Sonnets* (1633). Repr. in *Complete Poetry and Selected Prose,* ed. John Hayward (1929).

Closing lines.

2 The thought of our past years in me
doth breed
Perpetual benediction.

WILLIAM WORDSWORTH, (1770–1850) British poet. "Intimations of Immortality from Recollections of Early Childhood," l. 136–7, *Poems in Two Volumes* (1807).

Anthologies

1 By some might be said of me that here I have but gathered a nosegay of strange flowers, and have put nothing of mine unto it but the thread to bind them.

MICHEL DE MONTAIGNE, (1533–1592) French essayist. *Essays,* bk. 3, ch. 12 (1595), trans. by John Florio (1603).

Referring to Montaigne's own essays, which are full of classical quotations.

Anti-Christ, the

1 Here is wisdom. Let him that hath understanding count the number of

the beast: for it is the number of a man; and his number is six hundred threescore and six.

BIBLE: NEW TESTAMENT, *Revelation,* 13:18.

Who the "man" referred to by St. John the Divine was, has never been satisfactorily explained. Some cabbalists have favored the Roman Emperor Nero, who persecuted the Christians for the great fire which destroyed much of Rome (for which he himself was the most obvious suspect) in A.D. 64.

Anticipation

1 Do not count your chickens before they are hatched.

AESOP, (6th century B.C.) Greek fabulist. *Fables,* "The Milkmaid and Her Pail."

Antipathy

1 I do not like you, Sabidius; I cannot say why.
This only can I say: I do not like you.

MARCUS VALERIUS MARTIAL, (c. 40–104) Spanish–born Roman poet, epigrammatist. *Epigrams,* bk. 1, no. 32.

The original of the verse: "I do not like thee Dr. Fell, The reason why I cannot tell; But this I know, I know full well, I do not like thee Dr. Fell."—by the satirist Tom Brown (1663–1704), who, being expelled by Dr. John Fell, Dean of Christchurch, had his sentence remitted on translation of Martial's epigram.

Anxiety

1 But Jesus, when you don't have any money, the problem is food. When you have money, it's sex. When you have both, it's health, you worry about getting ruptured or something. If everything is simply

jake then you're frightened of death.

J.P. (JAMES PATRICK) DONLEAVY, (b. 1926) Irish–American author. O'Keefe, in *The Ginger Man,* ch. 5 (1955).

Apathy

1 It's no go the Government grants, it's no go the elections, Sit on your arse for fifty years and hang your hat on a pension.

LOUIS MACNEICE, (1907–1963) British poet. "Bagpipe Music," *Earth Compels* (1938).

Aphorisms and Epigrams

1 Exclusively of the abstract sciences, the largest and worthiest portion of our knowledge consists of aphorisms: and the greatest and best of men is but an aphorism.

SAMUEL TAYLOR COLERIDGE, (1772–1834) British poet, critic. *Aids to Reflection,* "Introductory Aphorisms," no. 27 (1825), repr. in *Works,* vol. I, ed. Professor Shedd (1853).

Apologies

1 Never explain—your friends do not need it and your enemies will not believe you anyhow.

ELBERT HUBBARD, (1856–1915) U.S. author. *The Motto Book* (1907), repr. in *Selected Writings,* vol. 1, "Index" (1921).

The saying found an echo in P.G. Wodehouse's short story, *The Man Upstairs* (1914): "It is a good rule in life never to apologise. The right sort of people do not want apologies, and the wrong sort take a mean advantage of them." Earlier, Benjamin Disraeli is quoted, "Never complain and never explain." (John Morley, Life of Gladstone, vol. 1, 1903).

2 Never make a defence or apology before you be accused.

KING CHARLES I, (1600–1649) British King of Britain and Ireland (1625–1649). *The Letters of Charles I*, ed. Sir Charles Petrie (1935). Letter, Sept. 3, 1636, to Lord Wentworth, later Earl of Strafford, the King's Chief Counsellor.

Appearance

1   Appearances often are deceiving.

AESOP, (6th century B.C.) Greek fabulist. *Fables*, "The Wolf in Sheep's Clothing."

2   Beyond the obvious facts that you are a bachelor, a solicitor, a Freemason, and an asthmatic, I know nothing whatever about you.

ARTHUR CONAN, SIR DOYLE, (1859–1930) British author. Sherlock Holmes, in *The Memoirs of Sherlock Holmes*, "The Norwood Butler" (1894).

3   Things are seldom what they seem, Skim milk masquerades as cream.

SIR WILLIAM SCHWENCK GILBERT, (1836–1911) British librettist. Mrs. Cripps (Little Buttercup), in *HMS Pinafore*, act 2 (1878), published in *The Savoy Operas* (1926).

4   Woman ... cannot be content with health and agility: she must make exorbitant efforts to appear something that never could exist without a diligent perversion of nature. Is it too much to ask that women be spared the daily struggle for superhuman beauty in order to offer it to the caresses of a subhumanly ugly mate?

GERMAINE GREER, (b. 1939) Australian feminist writer. *The Female Eunuch*, "Loathing and Disgust" (1970).

5   Common looking people are the best in the world: that is the reason the Lord makes so many of them.

ABRAHAM LINCOLN, (1809–1865) U.S. president. *Lincoln and the Civil War in the Diaries and Letters of John Hay*, ed. Tyler Dennett (1939). Journal entry, Dec. 23, 1863.

Spoken in a dream, in reply to one who had called Lincoln "common–looking," as reported by Lincoln's secretary John Hay. Lincoln's words on this occasion have also been given as, "The Lord prefers common–looking people. That is the reason He makes so many of them," in James Morgan *Our Presidents*, ch. 6 (1928).

6   Men seldom make passes
At girls who wear glasses.

DOROTHY PARKER, (1893–1967) U.S. humorous writer. "News Item," *Enough Rope* (1926).

7   Barring that natural expression of villainy which we all have, the man looked honest enough.

MARK TWAIN, (1835–1910) U.S. author. *A Mysterious Visit, Complete Humourous Sketches and Tales,* ed. Charles Neider (1961). (Originally published 1870).

Referring to a tax–assessor.

Appeasement

1   My good friends, this is the second time in our history that there has come back from Germany to Downing Street peace with honour. I believe it is peace for our time. We thank you from the bottom of our hearts. And now I recommend you to go home and sleep quietly in your beds.

NEVILLE CHAMBERLAIN, (1869–1940) British politician, prime minister. *The Penguin Book of Twentieth Century Speeches*, ed. Brian MacArthur (1992). Speech, Sept. 30, 1938, Downing Street, London.

The day after returning from Munich, where Chamberlain conferred with Hitler, Mussolini and Daladier, and it was agreed that Germany should annex Sudetenland while the remaining frontiers of Czechoslovakia were guaranteed, Chamberlain justified this policy: "We should seek by all means in our power to avoid war, by analysing possible causes, by trying to remove them, by discussion in a spirit of collaboration and good will. I cannot believe that such a programme would be rejected by the people of this country, even if it does mean the establishment of personal contact with the dictators" (speech, Oct. 6, 1938, House of Commons).

2   An appeaser is one who feeds a crocodile, hoping it will eat him last.

WINSTON CHURCHILL, (1874–1965) British statesman, writer. Quoted in *Reader's Digest* (Pleasantville, N.Y., Dec. 1954).

3   And that is called paying the
        Dane–geld;
    But we've proved it again and again,
    That if once you have paid him the
        Dane–geld
    You never get rid of the Dane.

RUDYARD KIPLING, (1865–1936) British author, poet. "Dane–Geld," *History of England* (1911).

4   Thus Belial, with words clothed in
        reason's garb,
    Counseled ignoble ease, and
        peaceful sloth,
    Not peace.

JOHN MILTON, (1608–1674) British poet. *Paradise Lost*, bk. 2, l. 226–8 (1667).

Referring to the debate convened by Satan in the palace of Pandemonium, to deliberate whether to launch a battle to recover heaven.

Appetite

1   It is of the nobility of man's soul that he is insatiable: for he hath a benefactor so prone to give, that he delighteth in us for asking. Do not your inclinations tell you that the WORLD is yours?

THOMAS TRAHERNE, (1636–1674) British clergyman, poet, mystic. *Centuries*, "First Century," no. 22 (written c. 1672, first published 1908).

Applause

1   We must not always judge of the generality of the opinion by the noise of the acclamation.

EDMUND BURKE, (1729–1797) Irish philosopher, statesman. "Letters on a Regicide Peace," letter 1 (1796), repr. in *The Writings and Speeches of Edmund Burke*, vol. 9, ed. Paul Langford (1991).

2   O, popular applause! what heart of man
    Is proof against thy sweet, seducing charms?

WILLIAM COWPER, (1731–1800) British poet. *The Task*, bk. 2, l. 481–2 (1785). Repr. in *Poetical Works*, ed. H.S. Milford (1934).

3   Will the people in the cheaper seats clap your hands? All the rest of you, if you'll just rattle your jewelry.

JOHN LENNON, (1940–1980) British songwriter, rock musician. Quoted in *John Winston Lennon*, pt. 1, ch. 11, R. Colman (1984). Royal Variety Performance, London, Nov. 4, 1963.

Architecture

1   Architect. One who drafts a plan of your house, and plans a draft of your money.

AMBROSE BIERCE, (1842–1914) U.S. author. *The Devil's Dictionary* (1881–1906), repr. in *Collected Works of Ambrose Bierce*, vol. 7 (1911).

2   It looks as if we may be presented with a kind of vast municipal fire station.... What is proposed is like a monstrous carbuncle on the face of a much loved and elegant friend.

CHARLES, PRINCE OF WALES, (b. 1948) Quoted in *Times* (London, May 31, 1984). Speech, May 30, 1984, to Royal Institute of British Architects.

Referring to the proposed extension to London's National Gallery, a design which, in the furore which followed Charles's attack, was rejected in favor of a more classical structure. Charles's words may have been inspired by a passage recently written by Princess Diana's step–mother, Raine Spencer, in *The Spencers on Spas* (1983): "Alas, for our towns and cities. Monstrous carbuncles of concrete have erupted in gentle Georgian squares." Prince Charles has established himself in the forefront of the traditional v. modern debate in architecture, not hiding his exasperation with postmodern and high–tech: "You have to give this much to the Luftwaffe: when it knocked down our buildings it did not replace them with anything more offensive than rubble. We did that." (speech, Dec. 2, 1987, Mansion House, London)

3   Light, God's eldest daughter, is a principal beauty in a building.

THOMAS FULLER, (1608–1661) British cleric. *The Holy State and the Profane State,* bk. 3, "Of Building" (1642).

4   I call architecture frozen music.

JOHANN WOLFGANG VON GOETHE, (1749–1832) German poet, dramatist. Quoted in *Conversations with Goethe,* Johann Peter Eckermann (1836). Entry, March 23, 1829.

A Greek myth tells that Anthion raised the walls of Thebes with the music of his lute.

5   Architecture is the art of how to waste space.

PHILIP JOHNSON, (b. 1906) U.S. architect. *The New York Times* (Dec. 27, 1964).

6   Safe upon the solid rock the ugly houses stand:
Come and see my shining palaces built upon the sand.

EDNA ST. VINCENT MILLAY, (1892–1950) U.S. poet. "Second Fig," *A Few Figs From Thistles* (1920).

7   Nor aught availed him now
To have built in heav'n high tow'rs; nor did he scape

By all his engines, but was headlong sent
With his industrious crew to build in hell.

JOHN MILTON, (1608–1674) British poet. *Paradise Lost,* bk. 1, l. 748–51 (1667).

Referring to the architect Mulciber, who had built Pandemonium, "the high capital/Of Satan and his peers" (l. 756–7).

8   No architecture is so haughty as that which is simple.

JOHN RUSKIN, (1819–1900) British art critic, author. *The Stones of Venice,* vol. 2, ch. 6 (1851–1853).

9   When we build, let us think that we build for ever.

JOHN RUSKIN, (1819–1900) British art critic, author. *Seven Lamps of Architecture,* "The Lamp of Memory," sct. 10 (1849).

Argument

1   Let the long contention cease!
Geese are swans, and swans are geese. Let them have it how they will! Thou art tired; best be still.

MATTHEW ARNOLD, (1822–1888) British poet, critic. "The Last Word " (1867).

2   As there is no worse lie than a truth misunderstood by those who hear it, so reasonable arguments, challenges to magnanimity, and appeals to sympathy or justice, are folly when we are dealing with human crocodiles and boa–constrictors.

WILLIAM JAMES, (1843–1916) U.S. psychologist, philosopher. *The Varieties of Religious Experience,* Lectures 14–15, "The Value of Saintliness" (1902).

3   There is no good in arguing with the inevitable. The only argument

available with an east wind is to put on your overcoat.

JAMES RUSSELL LOWELL, (1819–1891) U.S. poet, editor. *Democracy, Democracy and Other Addresses* (1887). Address, Oct. 6, 1884, Birmingham, England.

4 No way dude.

CHRIS MATHESON, U.S. screen actor. *Bill & Ted's Big Adventure* (film) (1989).

Running gag by characters first created for a sketch on U.S. TV comedy show. Other phrases popularized by the pair included "Radical, man" and "Excellent, dude."

5 You have not converted a man because you have silenced him.

JOHN MORLEY [1ST VISCOUNT MORLEY OF BLACKBURN], (1838–1923) British writer, Liberal politician. *On Compromise*, ch. 5 (1874).

6 The devil can cite Scripture for his purpose.

WILLIAM SHAKESPEARE, (1564–1616) British dramatist, poet. Antonio, in *The Merchant of Venice*, act 1, sc. 3, l. 97 (1600).

Referring to Shylock.

7 The lady protests too much, methinks.

WILLIAM SHAKESPEARE, (1564–1616) British dramatist, poet. Queen Gertrude, in *Hamlet*, act 3, sc. 2, l. 219 (1604).

Referring to the Player Queen in the "Mousetrap"—the play–within–a–play—who has just sworn never to re–marry if her husband died. "Protests" is used in the sense of "proclaims" rather than "complains."

8 I dislike arguments of any kind. They are always vulgar, and often convincing.

OSCAR WILDE, (1854–1900) Anglo–Irish playwright, author. Lady Bracknell, in *The Importance of Being Earnest*, act 4 (1895).

Wilde also wrote, "Arguments are extremely vulgar, for everybody in good society holds exactly the same opinions."—"The Remark-

able Rocket," published in *The Happy Prince and Other Tales* (1888).

Aristocracy

1 Nobility is a graceful ornament to the civil order. It is the Corinthian capital of polished society.

EDMUND BURKE, (1729–1797) Irish philosopher, statesman. *Reflections on the Revolution in France* (1790), repr. in *Works*, vol. 3 (1865).

2 Almost in every kingdom the most ancient families have been at first princes' bastards.

ROBERT BURTON, (1577–1640) British clergyman, author. *The Anatomy of Melancholy*, pt. 2, sct. 2, memb. 1, subsct. 1 (1621).

3 For what were all these country patriots born?
To hunt, and vote, and raise the price of corn?

GEORGE GORDON NOEL BYRON, 6TH BARON BYRON, (1788–1824) British poet. "The Age of Bronze," st. 14 (1823).

4 Democracy means government by the uneducated, while aristocracy means government by the badly educated.

GILBERT KEITH CHESTERTON, (1874–1936) British author. *The New York Times* (Feb. 1, 1931).

5 The Pedigree of Honey
Does not concern the Bee—
A Clover, any time, to him,
Is Aristocracy—

EMILY DICKINSON, (1830–1886) U.S. poet. "The Pedigree of Honey" (version 2) (written c. 1884, published 1890). Repr. in *The Complete Poems*, no. 1627, Harvard *variorum* edition (1955).

6 The aristocrat is the democrat ripe, and gone to seed.

RALPH WALDO EMERSON, (1803–1882) U.S. essayist, poet, philosopher. *Representative Men*, "Napoleon, the Man of the World" (1850).

7   That celebrated,
     Cultivated
     Underrated
     Nobleman,
     The Duke of Plaza–Toro!

SIR WILLIAM SCHWENCK GILBERT, (1836–1911) British librettist. Duke of Plaza–Toro, in *The Gondoliers*, act 1 (1889), published in *The Savoy Operas* (1926).

8   There is a natural aristocracy among men. The grounds of this are virtue and talents.

THOMAS JEFFERSON, (1743–1826) U.S. president. *The Writings of Thomas Jefferson*, vol. 9, ed. Paul L. Ford (1898). Letter, Oct. 28, 1813, to former president, John Adams.

9   A fully equipped duke costs as much to keep up as two Dreadnoughts, and dukes are just as great a terror—and they last longer.

DAVID LLOYD GEORGE, (1863–1945) British Liberal politician, prime minister. quoted in *Times* (London, Oct. 11, 1909). Speech, Oct. 9, 1909, Newcastle upon Tyne, England.

10   Lords are lordliest in their wine.

JOHN MILTON, (1608–1674) British poet. "Samson Agonistes," l. 1418 (1671).

11   Howe'er it be, it seems to me,
      'Tis only noble to be good.
      Kind hearts are more than
          coronets,
      And simple faith than Norman
          blood.

ALFRED TENNYSON, 1ST BARON TENNYSON, (1809–1892) British poet. "Lady Clara Vere de Vere," st. 7, *Poems* (1842).

Kind Hearts and Coronets is the title of an Ealing Studios movie of 1949.

12   Those comfortably padded lunatic asylums which are known, euphemistically, as the stately homes of England.

VIRGINIA WOOLF, (1882–1941) British novelist. *The Common Reader*, "Lady Dorothy Nevill," First Series (1925).

Arms

1   A well–regulated militia being necessary to the security of a free State, the right of the people to keep and bear arms shall not be infringed.

SECOND AMENDMENT, U.S. Constitution (1791).

2   When I hold you in my arms
     And I feel my finger on your trigger
     I know no one can do me no harm
     Because happiness is a warm gun.

JOHN LENNON, (1940–1980) British songwriter, rock musician. "Happiness is a Warm Gun" (song), on *Beatles White Album* (1968).

3   The main foundations of every state, new states as well as ancient or composite ones, are good laws and good arms ... you cannot have good laws without good arms, and where there are good arms, good laws inevitably follow.

NICCOLÒ MACHIAVELLI, (1469–1527) Italian political philosopher, statesman. *The Prince*, ch. 12 (written 1513–1514, published 1532), trans. by George Bull (1961).

Arms Industry

1   In the councils of government, we must guard against the acquisition of unwarranted influence, whether sought or unsought, by the military-industrial complex. The potential for the disastrous rise of mis-

placed power exists and will persist. We must never let the weight of this combination endanger our liberties or democratic processes. We should take nothing for granted.

DWIGHT D. EISENHOWER, (1890–1969) U.S. general, Republican politician, president. Farewell broadcast, *Public Papers of the Presidents of the United States* (1960). Radio and television address, Jan. 17, 1961, Washington D.C.

despite all our love of peace, not without arms. One cannot shoot with butter, but with guns.

JOSEPH GOEBBELS, (1897–1945) German Nazi leader, Minister of Propaganda. quoted in *Allgemeine Zeitung* (Jan. 18, 1936). Speech, Jan. 17, 1936, Berlin.

The origin of the "guns or butter" quote is unclear; in the summer of 1936, in a radio broadcast on the Four Year Plan, Hermann Goering announced, "Guns will make us powerful; butter will only make us fat."

Arms Race

1 The ability to get to the verge without getting into the war is the necessary art.... If you try to run away from it, if you are scared to go to the brink, you are lost.... We walked to the brink and we looked it in the face.

JOHN FOSTER DULLES, (1888–1959) U.S. politician. quoted in *Life* (New York, Jan. 16, 1956).

Adlai Stevenson characterized the Dulles–Eisenhower foreign policy as "the power of positive brinking."

2 Every gun that is made, every warship launched, every rocket fired, signifies, in the final sense, a theft from those who hunger and are not fed, those who are cold and are not clothed. The world in arms is not spending money alone. It is spending the sweat of its labourers, the genius of its scientists, the hopes of its children.

DWIGHT D. EISENHOWER, (1890–1969) U.S. general, Republican politician, president. "The Chance for Peace," *Public Papers of the Presidents of the United States* (1960). Speech, April 16, 1953, Washington D.C., to the American Society of Newspaper Editors.

3 We can do without butter, but,

Army

1 An army marches on its stomach.

NAPOLEON BONAPARTE, (1769–1821) French general and emperor. Quoted in *Mémorial de Sainte–Hélène*, vol. 4, E.A. de Las Casas (1823).

Nov. 14, 1816. The saying is also attributed to Frederick the Great.

2 A rapacious and licentious soldiery.

EDMUND BURKE, (1729–1797) Irish philosopher, statesman. "Speech on Fox's East India Bill," repr. in *Works*, vol. 2 (1899). Speech, Dec. 1, 1783.

Referring to the personal searches of women authorized by Warren Hastings, then governor–general of Bengal.

3 He learned the arts of riding, fencing, gunnery,
And how to scale a fortress—or a nunnery.

GEORGE GORDON NOEL BYRON, 6TH BARON BYRON, (1788–1824) British poet. *Don Juan*, cto. 1, st. 38 (1819–1824).

4 War is too important a matter to be left to the military.

GEORGES CLEMENCEAU, (1841–1929) French statesman. Quoted in *Soixante Années d'Histoire Française*, "Clemenceau," G. Suarez (1886).

Also attributed to Aristide Briand and Talleyrand.

5 I would rather have a plain, rus-
set–coated captain, that knows
what he fights for, and loves what
he knows, than that which you call
"a gentleman" and is nothing else.

OLIVER CROMWELL, (1599–1658) British
Parliamentarian general, Lord Protector of
England. *Oliver Cromwell's Letters and
Speeches,* Thomas Carlyle (1846). Letter, Sept.
1643.

6 Drinking is the soldier's pleasure;
Rich the treasure;
Sweet the pleasure;
Sweet is pleasure after pain.

JOHN DRYDEN, (1631–1700) British poet,
dramatist, critic. "Alexander's Feast," l. 57–60
(1697).

7 Rogues, would you live forever?

FREDERICK THE GREAT, (1712–1786)
Prussian king. *Attributed.*

Alleged call, June 18, 1757, when rallying his
troops at Kolin, Bohemia. Similar words are
attributed to Gunnery Sergeant Daniel Daly of
the U.S. Marines, who, at Belleau Wood in
France, June 4, 1918, is said to have shouted,
"Come on you sons of bitches! Do you want
to live for ever?"

8 These, in the day when heaven was
falling,
The hour when earth's foundations
fled,
Followed their mercenary calling
And took their wages and are dead.

A.E. (ALFRED EDWARD) HOUSMAN,
(1859–1936) British poet. "Epitaph on an
Army of Mercenaries," no. 37, *Last Poems*
(1922). Repr. in *The Collected Poems of A.E.
Housman* (1939).

9 Every man thinks meanly of himself
for not having been a soldier, or not
having been at sea.

SAMUEL JOHNSON, (1709–1784) British
author, lexicographer. Quoted in James
Boswell, *Life of Dr. Johnson,* entry, April 10,
1778 (1791).

10 Join the Army and See the Navy.

BERT KALMAR, Screenwriter. Sign
paraded by Brownie (Harpo Marx), in *Duck
Soup* (film) (1933). Leo McCarey.

11 We aren't no thin red 'eroes, nor
we aren't no blackguards too,
But single men in barricks, most
remarkable like you;
And if sometimes our conduck isn't
all your fancy paints,
Why, single men in barricks don't
grow into plaster saints.

RUDYARD KIPLING, (1865–1936) British
author, poet. "Tommy," *Barrack–Room Ballads* (1892).

12 When you're wounded and left on
Afghanistan's plains,
And the women come out to cut up
what remains,
Jest roll to your rifle an' blow out
your brains
An' go to your Gawd like a soldier.

RUDYARD KIPLING, (1865–1936) British
author, poet. "The Young British Soldier,"
Barrack–Room Ballads (1892).

13 Horribly stuffed with epithets of
war.

WILLIAM SHAKESPEARE, (1564–1616)
British dramatist, poet. Iago, in *Othello,* act 1,
sc. 1, l. 14 (1623).

Describing Othello.

14 Theirs not to make reply,
Theirs not to reason why,
Theirs but to do and die.

**ALFRED TENNYSON, 1ST BARON TEN-
NYSON,** (1809–1892) British poet. "The
Charge of the Light Brigade," st. 2, *Maud, and
Other Poems* (1855).

Arrogance

1 How haughtily he cocks his nose,

To tell what every schoolboy
 knows.

JONATHAN SWIFT, (1667–1745)
Anglo–Irish satirist. "The Country Life," l. 81
(1727). Repr. in *The Poems of Jonathan Swift,
D.D.*, vol. 1, ed. William Ernst Browning.

Art

1   Art! Who comprehends her? With
whom can one consult concerning
this great goddess?

LUDWIG VAN BEETHOVEN,
(1770–1827) German composer. *Beethoven's
Letters*, vol. 1, ed. A.C. Kalischer (1909). Letter, Aug. 11, 1810, to author Bettina von
Arnim.

2   What is art,
But life upon the larger scale, the
 higher,
When, graduating up in a spiral
 line
Of still expanding and ascending
 gyres,
It pushes toward the intense
 significance
Of all things, hungry for the Infinite?
Art's life,—and where we live, we
 suffer and toil.

ELIZABETH BARRETT BROWNING,
(1806–1861) British poet. "Aurora Leigh," bk.
4, l. 1151–7 (1857).

3   Religion and art spring from the
same root and are close kin. Economics and art are strangers.

WILLA CATHER, (1876–1947) U.S.
author. *On Writing*, "Four Letters: Escapism,"
(1949). Article first published in *Commonweal*
(April 17, 1936).

4   There is no more sombre enemy of
good art than the pram in the hall.

CYRIL CONNOLLY, (1903–1974) British
critic. *Enemies of Promise*, ch. 14 (1938).

5   Any work that aspires, however
humbly, to the condition of art
should carry its justification in
every line.

JOSEPH CONRAD, (1857–1924)
Polish–born British novelist. *The Nigger of the
Narcissus*, preface (1897).

Opening words. Conrad continued, "Art itself
may be defined as a single–minded attempt to
render the highest kind of justice to the visible
universe, by bringing to light the truth, manifold and one, underlying its every aspect."

6   Art for art's sake, with no purpose,
for any purpose perverts art. But art
achieves a purpose which is not its
own.

BENJAMIN CONSTANT, (1767–1834)
French politician, philosopher, author. *Journal
Intime*, journal entry, Feb. 11, 1804, *Revue
Internationale* (Jan. 10, 1887).

"Art for art's sake" became an oft–repeated
slogan. The French philosopher Victor Cousin
(1792–1867) said in a lecture at the Sorbonne
in 1818, "We must have religion for religion's
sake, morality for morality's sake, as with art
for art's sake ... the beautiful cannot be the
way to what is useful, or to what is good, or to
what is holy; it leads only to itself" (*Du vrai,
du beau, et du bien*, pt. 2, 1853). *Ars gratia
artis* was adopted in the 1930s as the motto of
Metro–Goldwyn–Mayer studios, credited to
songwriter/publicist Howard Dietz.

7   Art is significant deformity.

ROGER FRY, (1866–1934) British critic.
Quoted in *Roger Fry*, ch. 8, Virginia Woolf
(1940).

8   Art is skill, that is the first meaning
of the word.

ERIC GILL, (1882–1940) British sculptor,
engraver, writer, typographer. *Art*, ch. 1
(1934).

9   Art is the human disposition of sensible or intelligible matter for an
esthetic end.

JAMES JOYCE, (1882–1941) Irish author.
Stephen Dedalus, in *A Portrait of the Artist as
a Young Man*, ch. 5 (1916).

10   And the first rude sketch that the
         world had seen was joy to his
         mighty heart,
      Till the Devil whispered behind the
         leaves "It's pretty, but is it Art?"

RUDYARD KIPLING, (1865–1936) British
author, poet. "The Conundrum of the Work-
shops," *Barrack–Room Ballads* (1892).

Referring to "Our father Adam," who "sat
under the Tree and scratched with a stick in
the mould."

11   Art does not reproduce the visible;
      rather, it makes visible.

PAUL KLEE, (1879–1940) Swiss artist. "Creative Credo," sct. 1, *The Inward Vision* (1957).
(Originally published 1920).

12   All art is a revolt against man's fate.

ANDRI MALRAUX, (1901–1976) French
man of letters, statesman. *The Voices of
Silence*, pt. 4, ch. 7 (1951).

13   Art is man's expression of his joy in
      labour.

WILLIAM MORRIS, (1834–1896) British
artist, writer, printer. *"Art under Plutocracy,"*
(1883). Repr. in *The Collected Works of
William Morris*, vol. 23 (1910–1915).

14   We all know that Art is not truth.
      Art is a lie that makes us realize
      truth, at least the truth that is given
      us to understand. The artist must
      know the manner whereby to con-
      vince others of the truthfulness of
      his lies.

PABLO PICASSO, (1881–1973) Spanish
artist. "Picasso Speaks," *The Arts* (New York,
May 1923). Repr. in Alfred H. Barr Jr.,
Picasso: Fifty Years of His Art (1946).

15   I have seen, and heard, much of
      Cockney impudence before now;
      but never expected to hear a cox-
      comb ask two hundred guineas for
      flinging a pot of paint in the
      public's face.

JOHN RUSKIN, (1819–1900) British art
critic, author. *Fors Clavigera* (1871–1884).
Letter, June 18, 1877.

Referring to Whistler's "Nocturne in Black and
Gold: The Falling Rocket," Oscar Wilde commented that the painting was "worth looking at
for about as long as one looks at a real rocket,
that is, for somewhat less than a quarter of a
minute." Whistler took more seriously Ruskin's
remarks which he made the subject of a
law-suit. See Whistler on value.

16   Is there not
      An art, a music, and a stream of
         words
      That shalt be life, the acknowledged
         voice of life?

WILLIAM WORDSWORTH, (1770–1850)
British poet. "Home at Grasmere," l. 620–2
(written 1800, published as *The Recluse* 1888).

Art and Commerce

1   No man but a blockhead ever wrote,
     except for money.

SAMUEL JOHNSON, (1709–1784) British
author, lexicographer. Quoted in James
Boswell, *Life of Dr. Johnson*, entry, April 5,
1776 (1791).

2   In other countries, art and
     literature are left to a lot of shabby
     bums living in attics and feeding on
     booze and spaghetti, but in
     America the successful writer or
     picture–painter is indistinguishable
     from any other decent businessman.

SINCLAIR LEWIS, (1885–1951) U.S. novelist. George Follansbee Babbitt, in *Babbitt*, ch.
14, sct. 3 (1922).

Giving the annual address at the Zenith Real
Estate Board.

Art and Society

1   In free society art is not a weapon....
     Artists are not engineers of the soul.

JOHN FITZGERALD KENNEDY, (1917–1963) U.S. Democratic politician, president. Quoted in *The New York Times* (Oct. 27, 1963). Speech, Oct. 26, 1963, Amherst College, Massachusetts.

The words "Writers are the engineers of human souls" have been ascribed to Josef Stalin.

2   Note too that a faithful study of the liberal arts humanizes character and permits it not to be cruel.

OVID (PUBLIUS OVIDIUS NASO), (43 B.C.–A.D.17) Roman poet. *Epistulae Ex Ponto,* bk. 2, no. 9, l. 47.

Art: Modern Art

1   Perpetual modernness is the measure of merit in every work of art.

RALPH WALDO EMERSON, (1803–1882) U.S. essayist, poet, philosopher. *Representative Men,* "Plato" (1850).

Artists

1   The artist is extremely lucky who is presented with the worst possible ordeal which will not actually kill him. At that point, he's in business.

JOHN BERRYMAN, (1914–1972) U.S. poet. Interview in *Writers at Work,* Fourth Series, ed. George Plimpton (1976).

2   Artistic growth is, more than it is anything else, a refining of the sense of truthfulness. The stupid believe that to be truthful is easy; only the artist, the great artist, knows how difficult it is.

WILLA CATHER, (1876–1947) U.S. author. *The Song of the Lark,* pt. 6, ch. 11 (1915).

3   The artistic temperament is a disease that affects amateurs.... Artists

of a large and wholesome vitality get rid of their art easily, as they breathe easily or perspire easily. But in artists of less force, the thing becomes a pressure, and produces a definite pain, which is called the artistic temperament.

GILBERT KEITH CHESTERTON, (1874–1936) British author. *Heretics,* ch. 17 (1908).

4   It is closing time in the gardens of the West and from now on an artist will be judged only by the resonance of his solitude or the quality of his despair.

CYRIL CONNOLLY, (1903–1974) British critic. *Horizon* (London, Dec. 1949).

5   There is only one difference between a madman and me. I am not mad.

SALVADOR DALI, (1904–1989) Spanish painter. *Diary of a Genius,* May 1952 (1966).

6   Art is a jealous mistress, and, if a man have a genius for painting, poetry, music, architecture or philosophy, he makes a bad husband and an ill provider.

RALPH WALDO EMERSON, (1803–1882) U.S. essayist, poet, philosopher. *The Conduct of Life,* "Wealth" (1860).

7   Beware the artist who's an intellectual also. The artist who doesn't fit.

F. SCOTT FITZGERALD, (1896–1940) U.S. author. Amory Blaine, in *This Side of Paradise,* bk. 2, ch. 5 (1920).

8   The artist, like the God of the creation, remains within or behind or beyond or above his handiwork, invisible, refined out of existence, indifferent, paring his fingernails.

JAMES JOYCE, (1882–1941) Irish author. Stephen Dedalus, in *A Portrait of the Artist as a Young Man,* ch. 5 (1916).

9 Like any artist with no art form, she
became dangerous.

TONI MORRISON, (b. 1931) U.S. novelist,
editor. *Sula* (1973).

Asia

1 India is an abstraction.... India is no
more a political personality than
Europe. India is a geographical
term. It is no more a united nation
than the Equator.

WINSTON CHURCHILL, (1874–1965)
British statesman, writer. "On India," *Maxims
and Reflections*, ed. Colin Coote (1947).
Speech, March 18, 1931, Royal Albert Hall,
London.

2 In Xanadu did Kubla Khan
A stately pleasure–dome decree:
Where Alph, the sacred river, ran
Through caverns measureless to
 man
Down to a sunless sea.

SAMUEL TAYLOR COLERIDGE,
(1772–1834) British poet. "Kubla Khan," l.
1–5 (1816).

The poem, composed in the summer of 1797
according to the Preface—the date has been
disputed—and originally subtitled, "A Vision
in a Dream," was supposedly written under
the influence of an opium dream; the vision-
ary state was interrupted by "a person on business from Porlock" and thus was left forever
unfinished. Xanadu—now known as
Shangtu—was the site of Kublai Khan's summer residence in South–East Mongolia.

3 A puff of wind, a puff faint and
tepid and laden with strange
odours of blossoms, of aromatic
wood, comes out the still night—
the first sigh of the East on my face.
That I can never forget. It was
impalpable and enslaving, like a
charm, like a whispered promise of
mysterious delight.... The mysterious East faced me, perfumed like a
flower, silent like death, dark like a
grave.

JOSEPH CONRAD, (1857–1924)
Polish–born British novelist. Marlow, in
Youth (1902).

Of the East, Conrad wrote, "I have seen its
secret places and have looked into its very
soul."

4 The practice of politics in the East
may be defined by one word: dissimulation.

BENJAMIN DISRAELI, (1804–1881)
British statesman and author. *Contarini Fleming*, pt. 5, ch. 10 (1832).

5 Asia is not going to be civilized
after the methods of the West.
There is too much Asia and she is
too old.

RUDYARD KIPLING, (1865–1936) British
author, poet. *Life's Handicap*, "The Man Who
Was" (1891).

Assassination

1 Assassination has never changed
the history of the world.

BENJAMIN DISRAELI, (1804–1881)
British statesman, author. *Hansard*, col. 1246.
Speech, May 1, 1865, House of Commons.

Referring to Abraham Lincoln's assassination.

2 A desperate disease requires a dangerous remedy.

GUY FAWKES, (1570–1606) British
Catholic conspirator. Quoted in *The Dictio-
nary of National Biography*, vol. 6 (1917).
Remark, November 6, 1605.

On the gunpowder plot to blow up the
Houses of Parliament, November 5, 1605,
echoing the dictum of Greek physician Hippocrates.

3 In Pierre Elliot Trudeau, Canada
has at last produced a political
leader worthy of assassination.

IRVING LAYTON, (b. 1912) Canadian poet. "Obs II," *The Whole Bloody Bird* (1969).

4   Assassination's the fastest way.

MOLIÈRE [JEAN BAPTISTE POQUELIN], (1622–1673) French dramatist. Don Pedro, in *Le Sicilien,* sc. 13 (1668).

5   If it were done when 'tis done, then
      'twere well
      It were done quickly. If th'assassina-
      tion
      Could trammel up the consequence,
      and catch
      With his surcease success: that but
      this blow
      Might be the be–all and the end–all,
      here,
      But here upon this bank and shoal
      of time,
      We'd jump the life to come.

WILLIAM SHAKESPEARE, (1564–1616) British dramatist, poet. Macbeth, in *Macbeth,* act 1, sc. 7, l. 1–7 (1623).

First part of Macbeth's soliloquy on his forth-coming murder of Duncan and its conse-quences.

Astrology

1   You stars that reigned at my nativity,
      Whose influence hath allotted death
      and hell.

CHRISTOPHER MARLOWE, (1564–1593) British dramatist, poet. Faustus, in *The Tragical History of Dr. Faustus,* act 5, sc. 2, l. 155–6 (1604).

2   This is the excellent foppery of the
      world: that when we are sick in for-
      tune—often the surfeits of our own
      behaviour—we make guilty of our
      disasters the sun, the moon, and
      stars, as if we were villains on neces-
      sity, fools by heavenly compulsion,
      knaves, thieves, and treachers by
      spherical predominance, drunkards,
      liars, and adulterers by an enforced
      obedience of planetary influence....
      An admirable evasion of whoremas-
      ter man, to lay his goatish disposi-
      tion on the charge of a star!

WILLIAM SHAKESPEARE, (1564–1616) British dramatist, poet. Edmond, in *King Lear,* act 1, sc. 2, l. 116–26 (1623).

Astronomy

1   Let me arrest thy thoughts; wonder
      with me,
      Why plowing, building, ruling and
      the rest,
      Or most of those arts, whence our
      lives are blest,
      By cursed *Cain's* race invented be,
      And blest *Seth* vexed us with
      Astronomie.

JOHN DONNE, (c. 1572–1631) British divine, metaphysical poet. "The Progress of the Soul," st. 52.

Atheism

1   I had rather believe all the fables in
      the Legend, and the Talmud, and
      the Alcoran, than that this universal
      frame is without a Mind; and, there-
      fore, God never wrought miracle to
      convince atheism, because his ordi-
      nary works convince it.

FRANCIS BACON, (1561–1626) British philosopher, essayist, statesman. *Essays,* "Of Atheism," (1597–1625).

2   An atheist is a man who has no
      invisible means of support.

JOHN BUCHAN, (1875–1940) British author, statesman. Quoted in *On Being a Real Person,* ch. 10, H.E. Fosdick (1943).

3   Forth from his dark and lonely
      hiding–place,

(Portentous sight!) the owlet
  Atheism,
Sailing on obscene wings athwart
  the noon,
Drops his blue–fringed lids, and
  holds them close,
And hooting at the glorious sun in
  Heaven,
Cries out, "Where is it?"

SAMUEL TAYLOR COLERIDGE,
(1772–1834) British poet, critic. "Fears in Solitude," l. 81–6 (1798), repr. in *Poetical Works*,
ed. James Dyke Campbell (1893).

4 He was an embittered atheist (the
  sort of atheist who does not so
  much disbelieve in God as personally dislike Him).

GEORGE ORWELL, (1903–1950) British
author. *Down and Out in Paris and London*,
ch. 30 (1933).

Referring to Bozo, a London "screever" or
pavement–artist. In later years, Bozo was
heard to remark that Orwell always "had £50
in his pocket" during his "down–and–out"
experiences.

Attack

1 My centre is giving way, my right is
  in retreat; situation excellent. I shall
  attack.

FERDINAND FOCH, (1851–1929) French
general. Quoted in *Reputations Ten Years
After*, "Ferdinand Foch," B.H. Liddell Hart
(1928).

Message allegedly sent to General Joffre during Battle of the Marne, Sept. 8, 1914—
though most likely apocryphal, inspired by
Foch's repeated refrain to his troops,
Attaquez! According to Liddell Hart, his insis-
tence decimated the companies under his
command, and the eventual German with-
drawal astonished the exhausted French
troops. Other variations include "My right
gives way, my centre yields, everything's
fine—I shall attack." Hart emphasizes the
obstinacy of Foch, who is further quoted: "A
battle won is a battle which we will not
acknowledge to be lost" (a maxim taken from
French political philosopher Joseph de

Maistre: "A lost battle is a battle which one
believes lost: in a material sense no battle can
be lost").

2 Attack is the reaction; I never think
  I have hit hard unless it rebounds.

SAMUEL JOHNSON, (1709–1784) British
author, lexicographer. Quoted in James
Boswell, *Life of Dr. Johnson*, entry, April 2,
1775 (1791).

3 The game's afoot.
  Follow your spirit, and upon this
    charge
  Cry, "God for Harry! England and
    Saint George!"

WILLIAM SHAKESPEARE, (1564–1616)
British dramatist, poet. King Henry, in *Henry
V*, act 3, sc. 1, l. 32–4 (1600).

Closing words of Henry's rousing speech to
his army at Harfleur.

Audiences

1 Some writers take to drink, others
  take to audiences.

GORE VIDAL, (b. 1925) U.S. novelist,
critic. Interview in *Writers at Work*, Fifth
Series, ed. George Plimpton. First published in
Paris Review (1981).

Authority

1 Authority forgets a dying king.

ALFRED TENNYSON, 1ST BARON TEN-
NYSON, (1809–1892) British poet. *Idylls of
the King*, l. 289, "The Passing of Arthur"
(1859–1885).

Autobiography

1 An autobiography is an obituary in
  serial form with the last instalment
  missing.

QUENTIN CRISP, (b. 1908) British author.
The Naked Civil Servant, ch. 29 (1968).

2   If you really want to hear about it, the first thing you'll probably want to know is where I was born, and what my lousy childhood was like, and how my parents were occupied and all before they had me, and all that David Copperfield kind of crap, but I don't feel like going into it.

J.D. (Jerome David) Salinger, (b. 1919) U.S. author. *Catcher in the Rye*, ch. 1 (1951).

Opening words.

Autumn

1   Autumn wins you best by this its mute
Appeal to sympathy for its decay.

Robert Browning,

(1812–1889) British poet. "Paracelsus," pt. 1, l. 25–6 (1835).

2   No spring, nor summer beauty hath such grace,
As I have seen in one autumnal face.

John Donne, (c. 1572–1631) British divine, metaphysical poet. "The Autumnal," *Elegies* (1633). Repr. in *Complete Poetry and Selected Prose*, ed. John Hayward (1929).

3   Season of mists and mellow fruit fulness,
Close bosom–friend of the maturing sun;
Conspiring with him how to load and bless
With fruit the vines that round the thatch–eaves run.

John Keats, (1795–1821) British poet. "To Autumn," st. 1 (1820).

4   There is a harmony

In autumn, and a lustre in its sky,
Which through the summer is not heard or seen,
As if it could not be, as if it had not been!

Percy Bysshe Shelley, (1792–1822) British poet. "Hymn to Intellectual Beauty" (1816).

Awards

1   The cross of the Legion of Honor has been conferred on me. However, few escape that distinction.

Mark Twain, (1835–1910) U.S. author. *A Tramp Abroad*, ch. 8 (1880).

Babies

1   Out of the mouth of babes and sucklings hast thou ordained strength because of thine enemies, that thou mightest still the enemy and the avenger.

Bible: Hebrew, *Psalms*, 8:2.

2   There is no finer investment for any community than putting milk into babies.

Winston Churchill, (1874–1965) British statesman, writer. Vol. 7, *Winston S. Churchill: His Complete Speeches, 1897–1963*, ed. Robert Rhodes James (1974). Radio broadcast, March 21, 1943.

3   A loud noise at one end and no sense of responsibility at the other.

Ronald Knox, (1888–1957) British scholar, priest. *Quoted in Reith Lecture (1976).*

Ronald Reagan amended Knox's definition during his campaign for the governorship of California in 1965: "An alimentary canal with a big appetite at one end and no responsibility at the other."

Baldness

1 Bald as the bare mountain tops are bald, with a baldness full of grandeur.

MATTHEW ARNOLD, (1822–1888) British poet, critic. *Essays in Criticism*, preface to "Poems of Wordsworth," Second Series (1888).

2 There is more felicity on the far side of baldness than young men can possibly imagine.

LOGAN PEARSALL SMITH, (1865–1946) U.S. essayist, aphorist. *All Trivia*, "Last Words" (1933).

Banality

1 Men are seldom more commonplace than on supreme occasions.

SAMUEL BUTLER, (1835–1902) British author. *Notebooks*, "Material for a Projected Sequel to Alps and Sanctuaries" (1912).

Banking and Currency

1 What's breaking into a bank compared with founding a bank?

BERTOLT BRECHT, (1898–1956) German dramatist, poet. Mac, in *The Threepenny Opera*, act 3, sc. 9 (1928).

2 Put not your trust in money, but put your money in trust.

OLIVER WENDELL HOLMES, SR., (1809–1894) U.S. writer, physician. *The Autocrat of the Breakfast-Table*, ch. 2 (1858).

Barbarism

1 And now, what will become of us without the barbarians?
Those people were a kind of solution.

CONSTANTINE CAVAFY, (1863–1933) Greek poet. "Waiting for the Barbarians," (1904). Repr. in *Collected Poems*, ed. George Savidis, trans. by Edmund Keeley and Philip Sherrard (1975).

Bargaining

1 It is naught, it is naught, saith the buyer: but when he is gone his way, then he boasteth.

BIBLE: HEBREW, *Proverbs*, 20:14.

2 Necessity never made a good bargain.

BENJAMIN FRANKLIN, (1706–1790) U.S. statesman, writer. *Poor Richard's Almanack* (April 1735), *The Complete Poor Richard's Almanacks* (1970).

Bars, Pubs, and Cafés

1 At Dirty Dick's and Sloppy Joe's
We drank our liquor straight,
Some went upstairs with Margery,
And some, alas, with Kate.

W.H. (WYSTAN HUGH) AUDEN, (1907–1973) Anglo–American poet. *The Sea and the Mirror*, pt. 2, "Master and Boatswain," *For the Time Being* (1944).

2 Of all the gin joints in all the towns in all the world, she walks into mine.

JULIUS J. EPSTEIN, Screenwriter. Rick Blaine (Humphrey Bogart), in *Casablanca* (film) (1942).

3 Where village statesmen talked with looks profound,
And news much older than their ale went round.

OLIVER GOLDSMITH, (1728–1774) Anglo–Irish author, poet, playwright. "The Deserted Village," l. 223–4 (1770).

4   There is no private house in which
    people can enjoy themselves so well
    as at a capital tavern.... No, Sir;
    there is nothing which has yet been
    contrived by man by which so
    much happiness is produced as by a
    good tavern or inn.

    SAMUEL JOHNSON, (1709–1784) British
    author, lexicographer. Quoted in James
    Boswell, *Life of Dr. Johnson*, entry, March 21,
    1776 (1791).

Baseball

1   Whoever wants to know the heart
    and mind of America had better
    learn baseball, the rules and reali-
    ties of the game.

    JACQUES BARZUN, (b. 1907) U.S. scholar.
    God's Country and Mine, ch. 8 (1954).

Battles

1   All quiet along the Potomac
      to–night,
    No sound save the rush of the river,
    While soft falls the dew on the face
      of the dead,
    The picket's off duty forever.

    ETHEL LYNN BEERS, (1827–1879) U.S.
    poet. "The Picket Guard," st. 6 (1861).

    The words are based on the dispatches regu-
    larly sent by George Brinton McClellan during
    the Civil War.

2   For if the trumpet give an uncertain
    sound, who shall prepare himself to
    the battle?

    BIBLE: NEW TESTAMENT, St. Paul, in *1
    Corinthians*, 14:8.

3   How are the mighty fallen in the
    midst of the battle!... How are the
    mighty fallen, and the weapons of
    war perished!

    BIBLE: HEBREW, *Samuel*, 1:25, Part of
    David's lamentation for Saul and Jonathan.

4   It is magnificent, but it is not war.
    (*C'est magnifique, mais ce n'est pas la
    guerre.*)

    PIERRE BOSQUET, (1810–1861) French
    general. Quoted in *The Reason Why*, ch. 12,
    Cecil Woodham–Smith (1953).

    Referring to the charge of the Light Brigade at
    Balaclava, Crimea, Oct. 25, 1854. Benjamin
    Disraeli told the House of Commons that this
    military fiasco was "a feat of chivalry, fiery
    with consummate courage, and bright with
    flashing courage." *The London Times* corre-
    spondent, W.H. Russell, referred to it as a
    "glorious catastrophe."

5   We cannot dedicate, we cannot
    consecrate, we cannot hallow this
    ground. The brave men, living and
    dead, who struggled here, have con-
    secrated it far above our poor
    power to add or detract.

    ABRAHAM LINCOLN, (1809–1865) U.S.
    president. "Gettysburg Address," repr. in *Col-
    lected Works of Abraham Lincoln*, vol. 7, ed.
    Roy P. Basler (1953). Speech, Nov. 19, 1863.

    Lincoln's dedication of the national cemetery
    at Gettysburg, where fighting from July 1–3,
    1863, claimed nearly 50,000 killed or
    wounded.

6   Red lips are not so red
    As the stained stones kissed by the
      English dead.

    WILFRED OWEN, (1893–1918) British
    poet. "Greater Love," (l. 1–2) (written 1917),
    publ. in *The Poems of Wilfred Owen*, ed.
    Edmund Blunden (1931).

    Opening lines.

7   Men, you are all marksmen—don't
    one of you fire until you see the
    whites of their eyes.

    ISRAEL PUTNAM, (1718–1790) U.S. gen-
    eral. Quoted in *The History of the Siege of
    Boston*, ch. 5, R. Frothingham (1873). Com-

mand at Battle of Bunker Hill (actually Breed's Hill, Mass.), June 17, 1775.

In the first major engagement of the War of Independence, the militiamen defending Boston waited until the attackers were within 15–20 paces before loosing a volley, following which the fallen bodies lay "as thick as sheep in a fold." The command is also attributed to William Prescott (1726–1795) at Bunker Hill, Prince Charles of Prussia (18th century) at Jagerndorf, and Frederick the Great of Prussia (1712–1786) at Prague.

8   Once more unto the breach, dear
        friends, once more,
     Or close the wall up with our Eng-
        lish dead.
     In peace there's nothing so
        becomes a man
     As modest stillness and humility,
     But when the blast of war blows in
        our ears,
     Then imitate the action of the tiger.
     Stiffen the sinews, conjure up the
        blood,
     Disguise fair nature with
        hard–favoured rage.

WILLIAM SHAKESPEARE, (1564–1616) British dramatist, poet. King Henry, in *Henry V*, act 3, sc. 1, l. 1–8 (1600).

Henry's address to his troops at the siege of Harfleur.

9   Into the valley of death
     Rode the six hundred.
     Cannon to the right of them,
     Cannon to the left of them,
     Cannon in front of them
     Volleyed and thundered.
     Stormed at with shot and shell,
     Boldly they rose and well,
     Into the jaws of Death,
     Into the mouth of Hell
     Rode the six hundred.

ALFRED TENNYSON, 1ST BARON TENNYSON, (1809–1892) British poet. "The Charge of the Light Brigade," st. 2–3, *Maud, and Other Poems* (1855).

Referring to the charge of the Light Brigade at Balaclava, Crimea, Oct. 25, 1854.

Beat Generation, The

1   That isn't writing at all, it's typing.

TRUMAN CAPOTE, (1924–1984) U.S. author. Quoted in *New Republic* (Washington, DC, Feb. 9, 1959).

Remark in television discussion, referring to the Beat writers.

2   I saw the best minds of my
        generation destroyed by madness,
     starving hysterical naked,
     dragging themselves through the
        negro streets at dawn looking for
        an angry fix,
     angelheaded hipsters burning for
        the ancient heavenly connection
        to the starry dynamo in the
        machinery of night,
     who poverty and tatters and hol-
        low–eyed and high sat up smok-
        ing in the supernatural darkness
        of cold–water flats floating across
        the tops of cities contemplating
        jazz.

ALLEN GINSBERG, (b. 1926) U.S. poet. "Howl," *Howl and Other Poems* (1956).

Opening lines.

3   But then they danced down the
     street like dingledodies, and I
     shambled after as I've been doing
     all my life after people who interest
     me, because the only people for me
     are the mad ones, the ones who are
     mad to live, mad to talk, mad to be
     saved, desirous of everything at the
     same time, the ones who never
     yawn or say a commonplace thing,
     but burn, burn, burn, like fabulous
     yellow roman candles exploding
     like spiders across the stars and in
     the middle you see the blue cen-
     terlight pop and everybody goes
     "Awww!"

JACK KEROUAC, (1922–1969) U.S. author. *On the Road*, pt. 1, ch. 1 (1957).

In an interview in *Playboy*, June 1959, Kerouac explained the origin of the label "Beat Generation": "John Clellon Holmes ... and I were sitting around trying to think up the meaning of the Lost Generation and the subsequent Existentialism and I said, 'You know, this is really a beat generation' and he leapt up and said 'That's it, that's right!'" The phrase also appeared in Holmes's novel, *Go* (1952).

Beauty

1   Beauty in distress is much the most affecting beauty.

EDMUND BURKE, (1729–1797) Irish philosopher, statesman. *The Origin of our Ideas of the Sublime and Beautiful*, Introduction (1756).

2   Beauty for some provides escape,
Who gain a happiness in eyeing
The gorgeous buttocks of the ape
Or Autumn sunsets exquisitely
    dying.

ALDOUS HUXLEY, (1894–1963) British author. *Leda*, "Ninth Philosopher's Song" (1920).

3   "Beauty is truth, truth beauty,"—
    that is all
Ye know on earth, and all ye need
    to know.

JOHN KEATS, (1795–1821) British poet. "Ode on a Grecian Urn," st. 5, *Lamia, Isabella, The Eve of St. Agnes and Other Poems* (1820).

Closing lines.

4   Euclid alone
Has looked on Beauty bare. Fortunate they
Who, though once only and then
    but far away,
Have heard her massive sandal set
on stone.

EDNA ST. VINCENT MILLAY, (1892–1950) U.S. poet. "Euclid Alone Has

Looked on Beauty Bare," *The Harp-weaver and Other Poems* (1923).

5   Yet beauty, though injurious, hath
    strange power,
After offense returning, to regain
Love once possessed.

JOHN MILTON, (1608–1674) British poet. Chorus, in "Samson Agonistes," l. 1003 (1671). Repr. in *Milton's Poetical Works*, ed. Douglas Bush (1966).

6   At some point in life the world's beauty becomes enough. You don't need to photograph, paint or even remember it. It is enough.

TONI MORRISON, (b. 1931) U.S. novelist, editor. *Tar Baby*, p. 245 (1981).

7   Helen, thy beauty is to me
Like those Nicean barks of yore,
That gently, o'er a perfumed sea,
The weary, way–worn wanderer
    bore
To his own native shore.
On desperate seas long wont to
    roam,
Thy hyacinth hair, thy classic face,
Thy Naiad airs have brought me
    home
To the glory that was Greece,
And the grandeur that was Rome.

EDGAR ALLAN POE, (1809–1845) U.S. poet, critic, short–story writer. "To Helen," st. 1, 2, *The Raven and Other Poems* (1845). (Originally published 1831), subsequently revised.

8   One evening I sat Beauty on my knees—And I found her bitter—And I reviled her.

ARTHUR RIMBAUD, (1854–1891) French poet. "Une Saison en Enfer, Jadis, si je me souviens bien" (originally published 1874). Repr. in *Collected Poems*, ed. Oliver Bernard (1962).

This image was parodied by Salvador Dali in a diary entry (Aug. 1, 1953): "I seated ugliness on my knee, and almost immediately grew tired of it." (*The Diary of a Genius*, 1966).

9 The awful shadow of some unseen
  Power
  Floats though unseen among us,—
  visiting
  This various world with as incon-
  stant wing
  As summer winds that creep from
  flower to flower.

  PERCY BYSSHE SHELLEY, (1792–1822) British poet. "Hymn to Intellectual Beauty," st. 1 (1816).

  Referring to the "Spirit of Beauty."

10 Beauty seen is never lost,
   God's colors all are fast.

   JOHN GREENLEAF WHITTIER, (1807–1892) U.S. poet. "Sunset on the Bearcamp," l. 61–2 (1876). Repr. in *The Poetical Works of John Greenleaf Whittier*, ed. W. Garrett Horder (1911).

11 It is better to be beautiful than to be good. But ... it is better to be good than to be ugly.

   OSCAR WILDE, (1854–1900) Anglo–Irish author. Lord Henry, in *The Picture of Dorian Gray*, ch. 17 (1891).

Bed

1 The cool kindliness of sheets, that
  soon
  Smooth away trouble; and the
  rough male kiss
  Of blankets.

  RUPERT BROOKE, (1887–1915) British poet. "The Great Lover," *1914 and Other Poems* (1915).

2 The happiest part of a man's life is what he passes lying awake in bed in the morning.

  SAMUEL JOHNSON, (1709–1784) British author, lexicographer. Quoted in James

Boswell, *Journal of a Tour to the Hebrides*, entry, Oct. 24, 1773 (1785).

3 And so to bed.

  SAMUEL PEPYS, (1633–1703) British diarist. *The Diary of Samuel Pepys*, eds. Robert Latham and William Matthews (1977–1983). Journal entry, April 20, 1660, passim.

4 Must we to bed indeed? Well then,
  Let us arise and go like men,
  And face with an undaunted tread
  The long black passage up to bed.

  ROBERT LOUIS STEVENSON, (1850–1894) Scottish novelist, essayist, poet. "North–West Passage. Good–Night," *A Child's Garden of Verses* (1885).

Beer

1 Ale, man, ale's the stuff to drink
  For fellows whom it hurts to think.

  A.E. (ALFRED EDWARD) HOUSMAN, (1859–1936) British poet, classical scholar. "A Shropshire Lad," no. 62 (1896).

Belief

1 Every time a child says "I don't believe in fairies" there is a fairy somewhere that falls down dead.

  J.M. (JAMES MATTHEW) BARRIE, (1860–1937) British playwright. Peter, in *Peter Pan*, act 1 (performed 1904, published 1928).

2 Lord, I believe; help thou mine unbelief.

  BIBLE: NEW TESTAMENT, *Mark*, 9:24.

  Said by the father of a child brought to be healed by Jesus.

3 "One *can't* believe impossible things."
  "I daresay you haven't had much practice," said the Queen. "When I was your age, I always did it for

half–an–hour a day. Why, sometimes I've believed as many as six impossible things before breakfast."

LEWIS CARROLL [CHARLES LUTWIDGE DODGSON], (1832–1898) British writer, mathematician. Alice and the White Queen, in *Through the Looking–Glass,* "Wool and Water" (1872).

In a letter to a child–friend in 1864, Carroll wrote, "If you set to work to believe everything, you will tire out the muscles of your mind, and then you'll be so weak you won't be able to believe the simplest true things." (*A Selection from the Letters of Lewis Carroll to His Child–Friends,* ed. Evelyn M. Hatch, 1933).

4   The abdication of Belief
Makes the Behavior small—
Better an ignis fatuus
Than no illume at all.

EMILY DICKINSON, (1830–1886) U.S. poet. "Those Dying Then" (written c. 1882, published 1945). Repr. in *The Complete Poems,* no. 1551, Harvard *variorum* edition (1955).

5   With most people disbelief in a thing is founded on a blind belief in

some other thing.

GEORG CHRISTOPH LICHTENBERG, (1742–1799) German physicist, philosopher. "Notebook L," aph. 81, *Aphorisms* (written 1765–1799), trans. by R.J. Hollingdale (1990).

Benefactors

1   I have shewed you all things, how that so labouring ye ought to support the weak, and to remember the words of the Lord Jesus, how he said, It is more blessed to give than to receive.

BIBLE: NEW TESTAMENT, St. Paul, in *Acts,* 20:35.

2   No sane local official who has hung up an empty stocking over the

municipal fireplace, is going to shoot Santa Claus just before a hard Christmas.

ALFRED E. SMITH, (1873–1944) U.S. Democratic politician, governor of New York. *New Outlook* (Dec. 1933).

The phrase "Nobody shoots at Santa Claus" was used repeatedly by Smith in campaign speeches in 1936, attacking Franklin D. Roosevelt and the spendthrift policies of the New Deal.

Bereavement

1   Peace, peace! he is not dead, he
        doth not sleep—
He hath awakened from the dream
        of life—
'Tis we, who lost in stormy visions,
        keep
With phantoms an unprofitable
        strife.

PERCY BYSSHE SHELLEY, (1792–1822) British poet. "Adonais," st. 39 (1821).

Originally written for John Keats, these lines were recited by Mick Jagger on the death of fellow Rolling Stone Brian Jones, in London's Hyde Park July 5, 1969.

Betrayal

1   The Son of man goeth as it is written of him: but woe unto that man by whom the Son of man is betrayed! It had been good for that man if he had not been born.

BIBLE: NEW TESTAMENT, Jesus, in *Matthew,* 26:24.

2   Just for a handful of silver he left
        us,
Just for a riband to stick in his coat.

ROBERT BROWNING, (1812–1889) British poet. "The Lost Leader", st. 1, *Dramatic Romances and Lyrics* (1845).

Referring to Wordsworth.

3 And you too, Brutus.
  [*Et tu, Brute.*]

JULIUS CAESAR [GAIUS JULIUS CAESAR], (100–44 B.C.) Roman general, emperor. Quoted in *Lives of the Caesars*, "Julius Caesar," sct. 82, Suetonius (120 A.D.).

Spoken by Caesar in 44 B.C., on seeing that his friend Brutus was one of his assassins.

4 All things betray thee, who betrayest Me.

FRANCIS THOMPSON, (1859–1907) British poet. "The Hound of Heaven," st. 1, *Poems* (1893). *Merry England* (London, July 1890).

Bible

1 Prosperity is the blessing of the Old Testament; adversity is the blessing of the New.

FRANCIS BACON, (1561–1626) British philosopher, essayist, statesman. *Essays*, "Of Adversity," (1597–1625).

2 The pencil of the Holy Ghost hath laboured more in describing the afflictions of Job than the felicities of Solomon.

FRANCIS BACON, (1561–1626) British philosopher, essayist, statesman. *Essays*, "Of Adversity" (1597–1625).

3 Both read the Bible day and night,
  But thou read'st black where I read white.

WILLIAM BLAKE, (1757–1827) British poet, painter, engraver. *The Everlasting Gospel*, sct. A, l. 13–4 (c. 1818), repr. in *Complete Writings*, ed. Geoffrey Keynes (1957). (Written c. 1818).

4 It ain't necessarily so,
  The things that you're liable
  To read in the Bible,
  It ain't necessarily so.

IRA GERSHWIN, (1896–1983) U.S. lyricist. "It Ain't Necessarily So" (song), *Porgy and Bess* (show, 1935).

The song was recorded by, among others, Bing Crosby in 1938. Words also by Du Bose Heyward (1885–1940), music by George Gershwin (1898–1937).

5 We have used the Bible as if it was a mere special constable's handbook, an opium dose for keeping beasts of burden patient while they are being overloaded.

CHARLES KINGSLEY, (1819–1875) British author, clergyman. "Letters to the Chartists," no. 2, *The Works of Charles Kingsley* (1880–1885). *Politics for the People*, no. 4 (May 27, 1848).

Kingsley signed his numerous articles on the theme of Christian Socialism, "Parson Lot." His notion of religion as "an opium dose" recalls Marx. (See religion.).

6 The English Bible—a book which, if everything else in our language should perish, would alone suffice to show the whole extent of its beauty and power.

THOMAS BABINGTON MACAULAY, (1800–1859) British historian, Whig politician. "John Dryden," *Edinburgh Review* (Jan. 1828). *Miscellaneous Writings of Lord Macaulay*, ed. T.F. Ellis (1860).

Referring to the Catholic Church.

Bills

1 Dreading that climax of all human ills
  The inflammation of his weekly bills.

GEORGE GORDON NOEL BYRON, 6TH BARON BYRON, (1788–1824) British poet. *Don Juan*, cto. 3, st. 35 (1819–1824).

2 It is only by not paying one's bills that one can hope to live in the memory of the commercial classes.

OSCAR WILDE, (1854–1900) Anglo–Irish playwright, author. "Phrases and Philosophies for the Use of the Young," *Chameleon* (London, Dec. 1894). *Complete Works of Oscar Wilde*, ed. J.B. Foreman (1966).

Biography

1 Biography should be written by an acute enemy.

A.J. (ARTHUR JAMES) BALFOUR, (1848–1930) British Conservative politician, prime minister. Quoted in *Observer* (London, Jan. 30, 1927).

2 A well–written life is almost as rare as a well–spent one.

THOMAS CARLYLE, (1795–1881) Scottish essayist, historian. "Jean Paul Friedrich Richter," *Critical and Miscellaneous Essays* (1839–1857). (Originally published 1827).

3 Read no history: nothing but biography, for that is life without theory.

BENJAMIN DISRAELI, (1804–1881) British statesman, author. Peter Winter, in *Contarini Fleming*, pt. 1, ch. 23 (1832).

4 Great geniuses have the shortest biographies.

RALPH WALDO EMERSON, (1803–1882) U.S. essayist, poet, philosopher. *Representative Men*, "Plato; or, the Philosopher" (1850).

5 There is properly no history, only biography.

RALPH WALDO EMERSON, (1803–1882) U.S. essayist, poet, philosopher. *Essays*, "History," First Series (1841).

Thomas Carlyle similarly wrote, in his journal Jan. 13, 1832, "Biography is the only true history."

6 Biography is a very definite region bounded on the north by history, on the south by fiction, on the east by obituary, and on the west by tedium.

PHILIP GUEDALLA, (1889–1944) British author. Quoted in *Observer* (London, March 3, 1929).

7 Nobody can write the life of a man, but those who have eat and drunk and lived in social intercourse with him.

SAMUEL JOHNSON, (1709–1784) British author, lexicographer. Quoted in James Boswell, *Life of Dr. Johnson*, entry, March 31, 1772 (1791).

Johnson was referring specifically to Goldsmith's *Life of Parnell*. He later reiterated and qualified this statement: "They only who live with a man can write his life with any genuine exactness and discrimination; and few people who have lived with a man know what to remark about him." (Mar. 20, 1776).

8 Just how difficult it is to write biography can be reckoned by anybody who sits down and considers just how many people know the real truth about his or her love affairs.

REBECCA WEST [CICILY ISABEL FAIRFIELD], (1892–1983) British author. "The Art of Skepticism," *Vogue* (New York, Nov. 1, 1952).

In *Time and Tide* (1941), West wrote, "All good biography, as all good fiction, comes down to the study of original sin, of our inherent disposition to choose death when we ought to choose life." (Quoted as epigraph by Victoria Glendinning, *Rebecca West: A Life*, 1987.)

Birds

1 Ye Cupids, droop each little head,
Nor let your wings with joy be
 spread:
My Lesbia's favourite bird is dead,
Whom dearer than her eyes she
 loved.

CATULLUS [GAIUS VALERIUS CATULLUS], (84–54 B.C.) Roman poet. *Carmina*, no. 3, l. 1.

Referring to Lesbia, pseudonym for Clodia Metelli, the inspiration of much of Catullus's poetry.

2 Do you remember you shot a seagull? A man came by chance, saw it

and destroyed it, just to pass the time.

ANTON CHEKHOV, (1860–1904) Russian dramatist, author. Nina, in *The Seagull*, act 4 (1896), trans. by Elisave ta Fen (1954).

Spoken to Trepliov, who shot the bird in act 1, laying it at Nina's feet as a symbol of his ruined hopes.

3   On a tree by a river a little tom–tit
Sang "Willow, titwillow, titwillow!"
And I said to him, "Dicky–bird,
    why do you sit
Singing, "Willow, titwillow, titwil-
    low!"

SIR WILLIAM SCHWENCK GILBERT, (1836–1911) British librettist. Ko Ko, in *The Mikado*, act 2 (1885), published in *The Savoy Operas* (1926).

4   Once upon a midnight dreary,
    while I pondered, weak and
    weary,
Over many a quaint and curious
    volume of forgotten lore—
While I nodded, nearly napping,
    suddenly there came a tapping,
As of some one gently rapping, rap-
    ping at my chamber door.

EDGAR ALLAN POE, (1809–1845) U.S. poet, critic, short–story writer. "The Raven," st. 1, *The Raven and Other Poems* (1845). First published in *New York Evening Mirror* (Jan. 29, 1845).

5   Hail to thee, blithe Spirit!
    Bird thou never wert,
That from Heaven, or near it,
    Pourest thy full heart
In profuse strains of unpremedi-
    tated art.

PERCY BYSSHE SHELLEY, (1792–1822) British poet. "To a Skylark," st. 1 (written 1820).

Opening lines.

6   Pigeons on the grass alas.
Pigeons on the grass alas.

Short longer grass short longer
    longer shorter yellow
grass Pigeons large pigeons on the
    shorter longer yellow grass
alas pigeons on the grass.

GERTRUDE STEIN, (1874–1946) U.S. author. *Four Saints in Three Acts*, act 3, sc. 2, *Operas and Plays* (1932).

7   Happier of happy though I be, like
    them
I cannot take possession of the sky,
Mount with a thoughtless impulse,
    and wheel there,
One of a mighty multitude whose
    way
And motion is a harmony and
    dance
Magnificent.

WILLIAM WORDSWORTH, (1770–1850) British poet. "Home at Grasmere", l. 287–92 (written 1800, published as "The Recluse" 1888).

Birth

1   Every morn and every night
Some to misery are born.
Every morn and every night
Some are born to sweet delight.
Some are born to sweet delight,
Some are born to endless night.

WILLIAM BLAKE, (1757–1827) British poet, painter, engraver. "Auguries of Inno- cence," l. 119–24, *Poems from the Pickering Manuscript* (c. 1803), repr. in *Complete Writ- ings*, ed. Geoffrey Keynes (1957).

The last two lines of this passage were incor- porated by Jim Morrison, of The Doors rock group, in his 1967 song "End of the Night."

2   My mother groan'd! my father
    wept.
Into the dangerous world I leapt:
Helpless, naked, piping loud:
Like a fiend hid in a cloud.

WILLIAM BLAKE, (1757–1827) British poet, painter, engraver. *Songs of Experience,* "Infant Sorrow," (1794), repr. in *Complete Writings,* ed. Geoffrey Keynes (1957).

3   Piece by piece I seem
to re–enter the world: I first began
a small, fixed dot, still see
that old myself, a dark–blue
  thumbtack
pushed into the scene,
a hard little head protruding
from the pointillist's buzz and
  bloom.

ADRIENNE RICH, (b. 1929) U.S. poet. "Necessities of Life" (written 1962), published in *The Fact of a Doorframe* (1974).

Opening lines.

4   Being born is like being kidnapped. And then sold into slavery.

ANDY WARHOL, (c. 1928–1987) U.S. pop artist. *From A to B and Back Again,* ch. 6 (1975).

5   Our birth is but a sleep and a for-
getting;
The soul that rises with us, our life's
  star,
Hath had elsewhere its setting,
And cometh from afar:
Not in entire forgetfulness,
And not in utter nakedness,
But trailing clouds of glory do we
  come
From God, who is our home.

WILLIAM WORDSWORTH, (1770–1850) British poet. "Intimations of Immortality from Recollections of Early Childhood," l. 58–65, *Poems in Two Volumes* (1807).

6   Our birth is nothing but our death begun.

EDWARD YOUNG, (1683–1765) British poet, playwright. "Night 5," l. 718, *The Complaint, or Night-Thoughts on Life, Death and Immortality* (1742–1746). Repr. in *Complete Works,* ed. J. Doran (1968).

Birth Control

1   I want to tell you a terrific story about oral contraception. I asked this girl to sleep with me and she said "no."

WOODY ALLEN, (b. 1935) U.S. filmmaker. Quoted in *Woody Allen: Clown Prince of American Humor,* ch. 2, B. Adler and J. Feinman (1975).

2   The blind conviction that we have to do something about other people's reproductive behaviour, and that we may have to do it whether they like it or not, derives from the assumption that the world belongs to us, who have so expertly depleted its resources, rather than to them, who have not.

GERMAINE GREER, (b. 1939) Australian feminist writer. *Sex and Destiny,* ch. 14 (1984).

3   Contraceptives should be used on every conceivable occasion.

SPIKE MILLIGAN, (b. 1918) British comedian, humorous writer. *The Last Goon Show of Them All* (stage show) (1972). Camden Theatre, London, April 30, 1972.

4   We want better reasons for having children than not knowing how to prevent them.

DORA RUSSELL, (1894–1986) British author, campaigner. *Hypatia,* ch. 4 (1925).

Birthdays

1   Because the birthday of my life
Is come, my love is come to me.

CHRISTINA ROSSETTI, (1830–1894) British poet, lyricist. "A Birthday," l. 15–16 (written 1857), published in *Goblin Market, and Other Poems* (1862).

Last lines.

Blame

1 They have a right to censure that have a heart to help: the rest is cruelty, not justice.

WILLIAM PENN, (1644–1718) British religious leader, founder of Pennsylvania. *Some Fruits of Solitude*, pt. 1, no. 46 (1693).

Blasphemy

1 Thou shalt not take the name of the Lord thy God in vain; for the Lord will not hold him guiltless that taketh his name in vain.

BIBLE: HEBREW, *Exodus,* 20:7.

The third commandment.

2 Your blasphemy, Salman, can't be forgiven.... To set your words against the Words of God.

SALMAN RUSHDIE, (b. 1947) Indian–born British author. Mahound, in *The Satanic Verses*, "Return to Jahilia" (1988).

Speaking to Salman the Persian. Despite his crime—of pitting "his Word against mine"— Salman is spared the death–sentence.

Blindness

1 When I consider how my light is spent,
Ere half my days, in this dark world and wide,
And that one talent which is death to hide
Lodged with me useless.

JOHN MILTON, (1608–1674) British poet. Sonnet 19, "On His Blindness," l. 1–4 (written c. 1652, published 1673).

Milton became completely blind in the winter of 1651–1652. Poem is also called "When I Consider How My Light is Spent."

Blood

1 I don't mind giving them a reasonable amount, but a pint ... why that's very nearly an armful.

TONY HANCOCK, (1924–1968) British comedian. *Hancock's Half–Hour* (BBC TV series), "The Blood Donor," written by Ray Galton and Alan Simpson (1961), published in *Hancock's Half Hour* (1974). Episode broadcast, June 23, 1961.

Blues, the

1 I got the Weary Blues
And I can't be satisfied.

LANGSTON HUGHES, (1902–1967) U.S. poet, author. "The Weary Blues," *The Weary Blues* (1926). (Written 1922).

In his autobiography, Hughes claimed these lines came from "the first blues verse I'd ever heard." (*The Big Sea*, pt. 2, "Poetry is Practical," 1940).

2 It is from the blues that all that may be called American music derives its most distinctive character.

JAMES WELDON JOHNSON, (1871–1938) U.S. author, poet. *Black Manhattan*, ch. 11 (1930).

Body

1 I travel light; as light,
That is, as a man can travel who will
Still carry his body around because
Of its sentimental value.

CHRISTOPHER FRY, (b. 1907) British playwright. Thomas, in *The Lady's Not for Burning*, act 1 (1949).

2 Oh, beautiful passionate body
That never has ached with a heart!

A.C. (ALGERNON CHARLES) SWIN-
BURNE, (1837–1909) British poet, critic.
"Dolores," st. 11 (1866).

Books

1 Some books are undeservedly forgotten; none are undeservedly
remembered.

W.H. (WYSTAN HUGH) AUDEN,
(1907–1973) Anglo–American poet. *The
Dyer's Hand*, pt. 1, "Reading" (1962).

2 Some books are to be tasted, others
to be swallowed, and some few to
be chewed and digested.

FRANCIS BACON, (1561–1626) British
philosopher, essayist, statesman. *Essays*, "Of
Studies" (1597–1625).

3 Of all the ways of acquiring books,
writing them oneself is regarded as
the most praiseworthy method....
Writers are really people who write
books not because they are poor,
but because they are dissatisfied
with the books which they could
buy but do not like.

WALTER BENJAMIN, (1892–1940) Ger-
man critic, philosopher. "Unpacking my
Library" (1931), repr. in *Illuminations*, ed.
Hannah Arendt (1968).

4 The oldest books are still only just
out to those who have not read
them.

SAMUEL BUTLER, (1835–1902) British
author. *Samuel Butler's Notebooks*, p. 266
(1951).

5 'Tis pleasant, sure, to see one's
    name in print;
A book's a book, although there's
    nothing in't.

GEORGE GORDON NOEL BYRON, 6TH
BARON BYRON, (1788–1824) British poet.
"English Bards and Scotch Reviewers," l. 51–2
(1809).

6 There is no Frigate like a Book
To take us Lands away
Nor any Coursers like a Page
Of prancing Poetry.

EMILY DICKINSON, (1830–1886) U.S.
poet. "There is no Frigate Like a Book" (written
c. 1873, published 1894). Repr. in *The Complete Poems*, no. 1263, Harvard *variorum* edition (1955).

7 A book that is shut is but a block.

THOMAS FULLER, (1654–1734) British
physician. *Gnomologia*, no. 23 (1732).

8 Even bad books are books and
therefore sacred.

GÜNTHER GRASS, (b.1927) German
author. The narrator (Oskar Matzerath), in *The
Tin Drum*, bk. 1, "Rasputin and the Alphabet"
(1959), trans. by R. Manheim (1961).

9 All good books are alike in that they
are truer than if they had really happened and after you are finished
reading one you will feel that all
that happened to you and afterwards it all belongs to you; the good
and the bad, the ecstasy, the
remorse, and sorrow, the people
and the places and how the weather
was. If you can get so that you can
give that to people, then you are a
writer.

ERNEST HEMINGWAY, (1899–1961) U.S.
author. "Old Newsman Writes: A Letter from
Cuba," first published in *Esquire* (New York,
Dec. 1934). *By–Line Ernest Hemingway*, ed.
William White (1967).

10 A bad book is as much of a labour
to write as a good one; it comes as
sincerely from the author's soul.

ALDOUS HUXLEY, (1894–1963) British
author. *Point Counter Point*, ch. 13 (1928).

11 *Borrowers of books*—those mutila-
tors of collections, spoilers of the
symmetry of shelves, and creators of
odd volumes.

CHARLES LAMB, (1775–1834) British essayist, critic. *Essays of Elia,* "The Two Races of Men" (1820–23).

12 One sheds one's sicknesses in books—repeats and presents again one's emotions, to be master of them.

D.H. (DAVID HERBERT) LAWRENCE, (1885–1930) British author. *The Letters of D.H. Lawrence,* vol. 2, eds. George J. Zytaruk and James T. Boulton (1981). Letter, Oct. 26, 1913.

13 A book is a mirror: if an ape looks into it an apostle is hardly likely to look out.

GEORG CHRISTOPH LICHTENBERG, (1742–1799) German physicist, philosopher. "Notebook E," aph. 49, *Aphorisms* (written 1765–99), trans. by R.J. Hollingdale (1990).

14 All books are either dreams or swords,
You can cut, or you can drug, with words.

AMY LOWELL, (1874–1925) U.S. poet. "Sword Blades and Poppy Seed," st. 3, *Sword Blades and Poppy Seed* (1914).

15 A good book is the precious lifeblood of a master spirit, embalmed and treasured up on purpose to a life beyond life.

JOHN MILTON, (1608–1674) British poet. *Areopagitica: a Speech for the Liberty of Unlicensed Printing to the Parliament of England* (1644). Repr. in *Complete Prose Works of Milton,* ed. Ernest Sirluck (1959).

16 For books are not absolutely dead things, but do contain a potency of life in them to be as active as that soul was whose progeny they are; nay, they do preserve as in a vial the purest efficacy and extraction of that living intellect that bred them. I know they are as lively, and as vigorously productive, as those fabulous dragon's teeth; and being sown up and down, may chance to spring up armed men.

JOHN MILTON, (1608–1674) British poet. *Areopagitica: a Speech for the Liberty of Unlicensed Printing to the Parliament of England* (1644).

17 Books and marriage go ill together.

MOLIÈRE [JEAN BAPTISTE POQUELIN], (1622–1673) French dramatist. Martine, in *Les Femmes Savantes,* act 5, sc. 3, l. 66 (1672).

18 All books are divisible into two classes, the books of the hour, and the books of all time.

JOHN RUSKIN, (1819–1900) British art critic, author. *Sesame and Lilies,* lecture 1, "Of Kings' Treasuries," (1865). Repr. in *The Works of John Ruskin,* vol. 28, eds. E.T. Cook and Alexander Weddesburn (1905).

19 O let my books be then the eloquence
And dumb presagers of my speaking breast.

WILLIAM SHAKESPEARE, (1564–1616) British dramatist, poet. "Sonnet 23" (1609).

20 Books are good enough in their own way, but they are a mighty bloodless substitute for life.

ROBERT LOUIS STEVENSON, (1850–1894) Scottish novelist, essayist, poet. *Virginibus Puerisque,* "An Apology for Idlers" (1881).

21 Books, like men their authors, have no more than one way of coming into the world, but there are ten thousand to go out of it and return no more.

JONATHAN SWIFT, (1667–1745) Anglo–Irish satirist. "Epistle Dedicatory," *A Tale of a Tub* (1704). Repr. in *Jonathan Swift: A Critical Edition of the Major Works,* eds. Angus Ross and David Woolley (1984).

22 An empty book is like an infant's soul, in which anything may be

written. It is capable of all things, but containeth nothing. I have a mind to fill this with profitable wonders.

THOMAS TRAHERNE, (1636–1674) British clergyman, poet, mystic. *Centuries,* "First Century," no. 1 (written c. 1672, first published 1908).

Opening words.

23 A good book is the best of friends, the same today and for ever.

MARTIN TUPPER, (1810–1889) British author, poet, inventor. *Proverbial Philosophy,* "Of Reading," First Series (1838).

Books: Bestsellers

1 A best–seller is the gilded tomb of a mediocre talent.

LOGAN PEARSALL SMITH, (1865–1946) U.S. essayist, aphorist. *Afterthoughts,* "Art and Letters" (1931).

Cyril Connolly wrote, "A best–seller is the golden touch of mediocre talent." (*Journal and Memoir,* ch. 11, ed. David Pryce–Jones (1983)).

Books: Classics

1 The praise of ancient authors proceeds not from the reverence of the dead, but from the competition and mutual envy of the living.

THOMAS HOBBES, (1588–1679) British philosopher. *Leviathan,* "A Review and Conclusion" (1651).

2 What a sense of security in an old book which Time has criticized for us!

JAMES RUSSELL LOWELL, (1819–1891) U.S. poet, editor. "A Library of Old Authors," *My Study Windows* (1871).

3 A classic—something that everybody wants to have read and

nobody wants to read.

MARK TWAIN, (1835–1910) U.S. author. *Mark Twain's Speeches,* ed. Albert Bigelow Paine (1923). Speech, Nov. 20, 1900, Nineteenth Century Club, New York City.

Here quoting Professor Caleb Winchester. Twain varied the epigram in *Following the Equator* (1897), ch. 25; "Classic—a book which people praise and don't read."

Boredom

1 Life, friends, is boring. We must
       not say so.
    After all, the sky flashes, the great
       sea yearns,
    we ourselves flash and yearn,
    and moreover my mother told me
       as a boy
    (repeatingly) "Ever to confess
       you're bored
    means you have no
    Inner Resources." I conclude now I
       have no
    inner resources, because I am heavy
       bored.

JOHN BERRYMAN, (1914–1972) U.S. poet. *77 Dream Songs,* no. 14 (1964).

Bores

1 Bore. A person who talks when you wish him to listen.

AMBROSE BIERCE, (1842–1914) U.S. author. *The Devil's Dictionary* (1881–1906), repr. in *Collected Works of Ambrose Bierce,* vol. 7 (1911).

2 Society is now one polished horde, Formed of two mighty tribes, the
       Bores and *Bored.*

GEORGE GORDON NOËL BYRON, 6TH BARON BYRON, (1788–1824) British poet. *Don Juan,* cto. 13, st. 95 (1819–1824).

3 The age of chivalry is past. Bores have succeeded to dragons.

BENJAMIN DISRAELI, (1804–1881) British statesman, author. May Dacre, in *The Young Duke*, bk. 2, ch. 5 (1831).

4   We often forgive those who bore us, but we cannot forgive those whom we bore.

FRANÇOIS LA ROCHEFOUCAULD, DUC DE, (1613–1680) French writer, moralist. *Sentences et Maximes Morales*, no. 304 (1678).

5   A bore is a man who, when you ask him how he is, tells you.

BERT LESTON TAYLOR, (1866–1921) U.S. humorist, newspaper columnist. *The So–Called Human Race*, p. 163 (1922).

The line may have been the inspiration for Arthur Guiterman's couplet "Of Tact," in *A Poet's Proverbs* (1924): "Don't tell your friends about your indigestion: 'How are you!' Is a greeting, not a question."

6   A healthy male adult bore consumes each year one and a half times his own weight in other people's patience.

JOHN UPDIKE, (b. 1932) U.S. author, critic. *Assorted Prose*, "Confessions of a Wild Bore" (1965).

7   The secret of being a bore is to tell everything.

VOLTAIRE [FRANÇOIS MARIE AROUET], (1694–1778) French philosopher, author. "De la nature de l'homme," *Sept Discours en vers sur L'Homme* (1738).

Borrowing and Lending

1   Do not be made a beggar by banqueting upon borrowing, when thou hast nothing in thy purse: for thou shalt lie in wait for thine own life, and be talked on.

APOCRYPHA, *Ecclesiasticus*, 18:33.

2   The human species, according to the best theory I can form of it, is composed of two distinct races, *the men who borrow* and *the men who lend.*

CHARLES LAMB, (1775–1834) British essayist, critic. *Essays of Elia*, "The Two Races of Men" (1820–1823).

3   Neither a borrower nor a lender be, For loan oft loses both itself and friend, And borrowing dulls the edge of husbandry.

WILLIAM SHAKESPEARE, (1564–1616) British dramatist, poet. Polonius, in *Hamlet*, act 1, sc. 3, l. 75–7 (1604).

Giving advice to his son Laertes, departing for France.

Boston, Massachusetts

1   And this is good old Boston, The home of the bean and the cod, Where the Lowells talk to the Cabots, And the Cabots talk only to God.

JOHN COLLINS BOSSIDY, (1860–1928) U.S. Harvard alumnus, oculist. quoted in *Springfield Sunday Republican* (Dec. 14, 1924). Toast, 1910, at the Holy Cross College alumni dinner, Harvard University, Cambridge, Massachusetts.

Bourgeoisie, the

1   You must shock the Bourgeois. (*Il faut pater le bourgeois.*)

CHARLES BAUDELAIRE, (1821–1867) French poet. *Attributed.*

2   The bourgeois stands like a question mark, Speechless, like the hungry cur, The ancient world stands there behind him, A mongrel dog, afraid to stir.

ALEXANDER BLOK, (1880–1921) Russian poet. "The Twelve," sct. 9 (1918), trans. by Gerard Shelley (1942).

3 How beastly the bourgeois is
   especially the male of the species
   —presentable, eminently presentable.

   D.H. (DAVID HERBERT) LAWRENCE,
   (1885–1930) British author. "How Beastly the
   Bourgeois Is," *Pansies* (1929).

4 The bourgeoisie of the whole world,
   which looks complacently upon the
   wholesale massacre after the battle,
   is convulsed by horror at the dese-
   cration of brick and mortar.

   KARL MARX, (1818–1883) German politi-
   cal theorist, social philosopher. *Address of the
   General Council of the International Working
   Men's Association on* "The Civil War in
   France," (1871), repr. in *Selected Works*, vol.
   2 (1942).

5 The bourgeois are other people.

   JULES RENARD, (1864–1910) French novelist, playwright. *Journal 1877–1910* (1977).
   Journal entry, Jan. 28, 1890.

Boxing

1 Float like a butterfly, sting like a
   bee.

   MUHAMMAD ALI, (b. 1942) U.S. boxer.
   Quoted in *The Story of Cassius Clay*, ch. 8,
   George Edward Sullivan (1964).

   Muhammad Ali's catchphrase was said to
   have originated with his aide Drew "Bundini"
   Brown.

2 He can run. But he can't hide.

   JOE LOUIS, (1914–1981) U.S. boxer.
   Quoted in *Louis: My Life Story*, p. 176 (1947).

   To a reporter, referring to Billy Conn, his
   opponent in a World Championship match,
   June 19, 1946, which Louis won.

Boys

1 Speak roughly to your little boy,
   And beat him when he sneezes:

He only does it to annoy,
Because he knows it teases.

**LEWIS CARROLL [CHARLES
LUTWIDGE DODGSON],** (1832–1898)
British author, mathematician. The Duchess,
in *Alice's Adventures in Wonderland*, "Pig
and Pepper" (1865).

Parody of a poem attributed to both G.W.
Langford and David Bates, a Philadelphia bro-
ker. The poem appears in Bates's *The Eolian*
(1849), including the following verse: "Speak
gently to the little child! Its love be sure to
gain; Teach it in accents soft and mild; It
may not long remain."

2 Timothy Winters comes to school
   With eyes as wide as a
      football–pool,
   Ears like bombs and teeth like
      splinters:
   A blitz of a boy is Timothy Winters.

   CHARLES CAUSLEY, (b. 1917) British
   poet. "Timothy Winters," *Union Street* (1957).

3 I never see any difference in boys. I
   only know two sorts of boys. Mealy
   boys, and beef–faced boys.

   CHARLES DICKENS, (1812–1870) British
   novelist. Mr. Grimwig, in *Oliver Twist*, ch. 14
   (1838).

4 Boys are capital fellows in their own
   way, among their mates; but they
   are unwholesome companions for
   grown people.

   CHARLES LAMB, (1775–1834) British
   essayist, critic. *Essays of Elia*, "The Old and
   the New Schoolmaster," (1820–1823).

5 Every schoolboy knows it.

   JEREMY TAYLOR, (1613–1667) British
   churchman, devotional writer. *The Real Presence in the Blessed Sacrament*, sct. 5 (1654).

   What "every schoolboy knows" is that "This
   thing ... that can be understood and not
   expressed, may take a neuter gender."

6 What money is better bestowed
   than that of a schoolboy's tip? How
   the kindness is recalled by the

recipient in after days! It blesses him that gives and him that takes.

WILLIAM MAKEPEACE THACKERAY, (1811–1863) British author. *The Newcomes*, bk. 1, ch. 16 (1853–1855).

7   Oh, for boyhood's painless play,
Sleep that wakes in laughing day,
Health that mocks the doctor's rules,
Knowledge never learned of schools.

JOHN GREENLEAF WHITTIER, (1807–1892) U.S. poet. "The Barefoot Boy", l. 19–22 (1855). Repr. in *The Poetical Works of John Greenleaf Whittier*, ed. W. Garrett Horder (1911).

Bragging

1   If I cannot brag of knowing some-thing, then I brag of not knowing it; at any rate, brag.

RALPH WALDO EMERSON, (1803–1882) U.S. essayist, poet, philosopher. *Journals* (1909–1914). Journal entry, Oct.–Nov. 1866.

Brain, The

1   It's my second favorite organ.

WOODY ALLEN, (b. 1935) U.S. filmmaker. Victor Shakapopolis (Woody Allen), in *Sleeper* (film) (1973).

2   The Brain—is wider than the Sky—
For—put them side by side—
The one the other will contain
With ease—and You—beside—

EMILY DICKINSON, (1830–1886) U.S. poet. "The Brain is Wider than the Sky" (written c. 1862, published 1896). Repr. in *The Complete Poems*, no. 632, Harvard *variorum* edition (1955).

Breasts

1   Thy two breasts are like two young roes that are twins, which

feed among the lilies.

BIBLE: HEBREW, *Song of Solomon*, 4:5.

2   The straight Hellespont between
The Sestos and Abydos of her
breasts.

JOHN DONNE, (c. 1572–1631) British divine, metaphysical poet. "Love's Progress," *Elegies* (1633). Repr. in *Complete Poetry and Selected Prose*, ed. John Hayward (1929).

In classical mythology, Sestos and Abydos lay on either side of the Hellespont (the Dardanelles), and were the homes of the doomed lovers Hero and Leander.

3   Show me no more those snowy
breasts
With azure riverets branched
Where, whilst mine eye with plenty
feasts
Yet is my thirst not staunched;
O Tantalus, thy pains ne'er tell,
By me thou are prevented;
'Tis nothing to be plagued in Hell,
But thus in Heaven tormented.

MICHAEL DRAYTON, (1563–1631) British poet. "To His Coy Love," st. 2, *Odes, with Other Lyric Poesies* (1619), repr. in *Works*, vol. 2, ed. J William Hebel (1932).

4   Uncorseted, her friendly bust
Gives promise of pneumatic bliss.

T.S. (THOMAS STEARNS) ELIOT, (1888–1965) Anglo–American poet, critic. "Whispers of Immortality," st. 5, *Poems* (1919).

"Grishkin"—the character described here—is thought to be a portrayal of Serafima Astafieva (1876–1934), a Russian dancer with the Diaghilev company who opened her own ballet school in London. Ezra Pound also referred to her in his Pisan Cantos 77 and 79 (1945).

5   A full bosom is actually a millstone around a woman's neck: it endears her to the men who want to make their mammet of her, but she is never allowed to think that their popping eyes actually see her. Her

breasts ... are not parts of a person but lures slung around her neck, to be kneaded and twisted like magic putty, or mumbled and mouthed like lolly ices.

GERMAINE GREER, (b. 1939) Australian feminist writer. *The Female Eunuch,* "Curves" (1970).

Brevity

1 Brevity is the sister of talent.

ANTON CHEKHOV, (1860–1904) Russian dramatist, author. *Anton Chekhov: Letters on the Short Story,* ed. L.S. Friedland (1964). Letter, April 11, 1889.

All of Chekhov's best work has been taken to exemplify this dictum.

2 Less is more.

LUDWIG MIES VAN DER ROHE, (1886–1969) German–born U.S. architect. *New York Herald Tribune* (June 28, 1959).

For an earlier use of this aphorism, closely associated with Mies Van Der Rohe, see Browning on style.

British, The

1 Think of what our Nation stands for,
Books from Boots' and country lanes,
Free speech, free passes, class distinction,
Democracy and proper drains.

JOHN BETJEMAN, (1906–1984) British poet. "In Westminster Abbey," st. 4, *Old Lights for New Chancels* (1940).

2 Oh! what a snug little Island,
A right little, tight little Island!

THOMAS DIBDIN, (1771–1841) British actor, playwright. *The Snug Little Island* (1833).

3 The British tourist is always happy abroad as long as the natives are waiters.

ROBERT MORLEY, (1908–1992) British actor. Quoted in *Observer* (London, April 20, 1958).

4 What two ideas are more inseparable than beer and Britannia?

SYDNEY SMITH, (1771–1845) British clergyman, writer. Quoted in *The Smith of Smiths,* ch. 11, Hesketh Pearson (1934).

5 Gorgonised me from head to foot,
With a stony British stare.

ALFRED TENNYSON, 1ST BARON TENNYSON, (1809–1892) British poet. "Maud," pt. 1, sct. 13, st. 2 (1855).

Broadway

1 Give my regards to Broadway,
Remember me to Herald Square,
Tell all the gang at Forty–second Street
That I will soon be there.

GEORGE M. COHAN, (1878–1942) U.S. songwriter, performer. "Give my Regards to Broadway" *(song), Little Johnny Jones* (show, 1904).

Cohan's breakthrough hit was a failure when it opened on Broadway, though it achieved a lasting success when it returned there in 1905 following a nationwide tour. The song was one of a series of compositions on the theme of Broadway, though at the time of writing, Cohan was just twenty–six, and very much an outsider. in 1959, a statue of him was erected on Broadway. *Give my Regards to Broad Street* was the title of Paul McCartney's musical film in 1984.

Bureaucracy

1 They have given us into the hand of new unhappy lords,

Lords without anger and honour,
who dare not carry their swords.
They fight by shuffling papers; they
have bright dead alien eyes;
They look at our labour and laughter as a tired man looks at flies.

GILBERT KEITH CHESTERTON,
(1874–1936) British author. "The Secret
People," *Poems* (1915).

2   Official dignity tends to increase in
inverse ratio to the importance of
the country in which the office is
held.

ALDOUS HUXLEY, (1894–1963) British
author. *Beyond the Mexique Bay*, "Puerto
Barrios" (1934).

3   There is something about a bureau-
crat that does not like a poem.

GORE VIDAL, (b. 1925) U.S. novelist,
critic. *Sex, Death and Money*, preface (1968).

Burial

1   We therefore commit his body to
the ground; earth to earth, ashes to
ashes, dust to dust; in sure and certain hope of the Resurrection to
eternal life.

BOOK OF COMMON PRAYER, THE,
The Burial of the Dead (1662).

2   Under the wide and starry sky,
Dig the grave and let me lie.
Glad did I live and gladly die,
And I laid me down with a will.
This be the verse you grave for me:
Here he lies where he longed to be;
Home is the sailor, home from sea.
And the hunter home from the hill.

ROBERT LOUIS STEVENSON,
(1850–1894) Scottish novelist, essayist, poet.
Underwoods, "Requiem" (1887).

Inscribed on Stevenson's gravestone on Mount
Vaea, Samoa, where Stevenson spent the last
five years of his life. The inscription wrongly
transcribes the penultimate line, "Home is the
sailor, home from the sea."

Business and Commerce

1   There is no such thing as a free
lunch.

ANONYMOUS.

An axiom from economics popular in the
1960s, the words have no known source,
though have been dated to the 1840s, when
they were used in saloons where snacks were
offered to customers. Ascribed to an Italian
immigrant outside Grand Central Station,
New York, in Alistair Cooke's *America* (epilogue, 1973), the expression appears in
Robert A. Heinlein's *The Moon is a Harsh
Mistress*, ch. 11 (1966), but has become most
closely associated with economist Milton
Friedman, who made it the title of a book
in 1975.

2   Corporation. An ingenious device
for obtaining individual profit
without individual responsibility.

AMBROSE BIERCE, (1842–1914) U.S.
author. *The Devil's Dictionary* (1881–1906),
repr. in *Collected Works of Ambrose Bierce*,
vol. 7 (1911).

3   It is the interest of the commercial
world that wealth should be found
everywhere.

EDMUND BURKE, (1729–1797) Irish
philosopher, statesman. *Works*, vol. 2 (1865).
Letter, April 23, 1778, to Samuel Span Esq.

4   1. Never give anything away for
nothing.
2. Never give more than you have
to give (always catch the buyer
hungry and always make him
wait).

3. Always take everything back if you possibly can.

WILLIAM BURROUGHS, (b.1914) U.S. author. *The Naked Lunch*, introduction (1959).

The basic principles of dealing heroin.

5   After all, the chief business of the American people is business.

CALVIN COOLIDGE, (1872–1933) U.S. Republican politician, president. *Foundations of the Republic* (1926). Speech, Jan. 17, 1925, to the Society of American Newspaper Editors, Washington, DC.

6   Business? it's quite simple: it's other people's money.

ALEXANDRE DUMAS, (1824–1895) French dramatist. Giraud, in *La Question d'Argent*, act 2, sc. 7 (1857).

7   Honour sinks where commerce long prevails.

OLIVER GOLDSMITH, (1728–1774) Anglo–Irish author, poet, playwright. "The Traveller," l. 92 (1764).

8   Art is the beautiful way of doing things. Science is the effective way of doing things. Business is the economic way of doing things.

ELBERT HUBBARD, (1856–1915) U.S. author. *The Motto Book* (1907), repr. in *Selected Writings*, vol. 1, "Index" (1921).

9   When you are skinning your customers you should leave some skin on to grow again so that you can skin them again.

NIKITA KHRUSHCHEV, (1894–1971) Soviet premier. Quoted in *Observer* (London, May 28, 1961).

Advice to British businessmen.

10   In a hierarchy every employee tends to rise to his level of incompetence.

LAURENCE J. PETER, (1919–1990) U.S. Canadian author. *The Peter Principle*, ch. 1 (1969).

The so–called *Peter Principle*; compare with the *Paula Principle*: "women stay below their level of competence, because they hold back from promotion." (Liz Filkin, quoted in *Observer* (London, Oct. 19, 1986)).

11   He's a businessman.... I'll make him an offer he can't refuse.

MARIO PUZO, (b. 1920) U.S. novelist. Don Corleone, in *The Godfather*, bk. 1, ch. 1 (1969).

The line also appears in Francis Ford Coppola's film, written in collaboration with Puzo (1972).

12   Everyone lives by selling something, whatever be his right to it.

ROBERT LOUIS STEVENSON, (1850–1894) Scottish novelist, essayist, poet. *Across the Plains*, "Beggars," sct. 3 (1892).

13   Perpetual devotion to what a man calls his business is only to be sustained by neglect of many other things.

ROBERT LOUIS STEVENSON, (1850–1894) Scottish novelist, essayist, poet. *Virginibus Puerisque*, "An Apology for Idlers" (1881).

14   Being good in business is the most fascinating kind of art.... Making money is art and working is art and good business is the best art.

ANDY WARHOL, (c. 1928–1987) U.S. pop artist. *From A to B and Back Again*, ch. 6 (1975).

15   Go, go to your business, I say, pleasure, whilst I go to my pleasure, business.

WILLIAM WYCHERLEY, (1640–1716) British dramatist. Sir Jaspar Fidget, in *The Country Wife*, act 2 (1675). Repr. in *Plays of William Wycherley*, ed. W.C. Ward (1888).

Byron, Lord

1   I have not loved the world, nor the world me;

I have not flattered its rank breath,
nor bowed
To its idolatries a patient knee.

**GEORGE GORDON NOEL BYRON,
6TH BARON BYRON,** (1788–1824) British
poet. "Childe Harold's Pilgrimage," cto. 3, st.
113 (1812–1818).

In a letter April 9, 1814 to the poet Thomas
Moore, Byron wrote, "My great comfort is,
that the temporary celebrity I have wrung
from the world has been in the very teeth of
all opinions and prejudices. I have flattered no
ruling powers; I have never concealed a single
thought that tempted me." Published in
Byron's Letters and Journals, vol. 4, ed. Leslie
A. Marchand (1975).

2   If they had said that the sun or the
moon had gone out of the heavens,
it could not have struck me with
the idea of a more awful and dreary
blank in creation than the words:
"Byron is dead!"

JANE WELSH CARLYLE, (1801–1866)
Scottish poet, wife of Thomas Carlyle. *The
Love Letters of Thomas Carlyle and Jane
Welsh* (1908). Letter, May 20, 1824, to her
future husband Thomas Carlyle.

Calculation

1   I know that the right kind of leader
for the Labour Party is a kind of
desiccated calculating machine.

ANEURIN BEVAN, (1897–1960) British
Labour politician. Quoted in *Aneurin Bevan,*
vol. 2, ch. 11, Michael Foot (1973). Speech,
Sept. 29, 1954, Tribune Group, Labour Party
Conference.

Taken as referring to Hugh Gaitskell, though
Bevan later denied this.

California and the West

1   California is a fine place to live—if
you happen to be an orange.

FRED ALLEN, (1894–1957) U.S. radio
comic. *American Magazine* (Dec. 1945).

2   Out where the handclasp's a little
stronger,
Out where the smile dwells a little
longer,
That's where the West begins.

ARTHUR CHAPMAN, (1873–1935) U.S.
poet, author. "Out Where the West Begins",
st. 1 (1916).

3   California is a place in which a
boom mentality and a sense of
Chekhovian loss meet in uneasy
suspension; in which the mind is
troubled by some buried but
ineradicable suspicion that things
had better work here, because here,
beneath that immense bleached sky,
is where we run out of continent.

JOAN DIDION, (b. 1934) U.S. essayist.
Slouching Towards Bethlehem, "Notes From a
Native Daughter" (1968). (Originally pub-
lished 1965).

4   Only remember—west of the Mississippi it's a little more look, see,
act. A little less rationalize, comment, talk.

F. SCOTT FITZGERALD, (1896–1940)
U.S. author. *The Letters of F. Scott Fitzgerald,*
ed. Andrew Turnbull (1963). Letter, summer
1934, to Andrew Turnbull, Fitzgerald's biographer.

5   There is no there there.

GERTRUDE STEIN, (1874–1946) U.S.
author. *Everybody's Autobiography,* ch. 4
(1937).

Referring to Oakland, where Stein spent her
childhood.

Canada and the Canadians

1   Canada is not really a place where
you are encouraged to have large
spiritual adventures.

ROBERTSON DAVIES, (b. 1913) Canadian
novelist, journalist. *The Enthusiasms of*

Robertson Davies, "The Table Talk of Robertson Davies" (1990).

2   Long live Free Quebec!
    (Vive le Québec Libre!

CHARLES DE GAULLE, (1890–1970) French general, president. *Speeches of General de Gaulle* (1970). Speech, July 24, 1967, Montreal.

The speech by De Gaulle aroused huge controversy, appearing to advocate the cause of Quebec separatists and inflaming an already volatile situation.

Cancer

1   It was announced that the trouble was not "malignant."... It was a typical triumph of modern science to find the only part of Randolph that was not malignant and remove it.

EVELYN WAUGH, (1903–1966) British novelist. *Diaries of Evelyn Waugh*, "Irregular Notes 1960–65," ed. Michael Davie (1976). Journal entry, March 1964.

Referring to Randolph Churchill (1911–1968), son of Winston Churchill and a forthright commentator on social affairs.

Candor

1   Give me th' avowed, th' erect, the
        manly foe,
    Bold I can meet—perhaps may turn
        his blow;
    But of all plagues, good Heav'n, thy
        wrath can send,
    Save, save, oh! save me from the
        Candid Friend.

GEORGE CANNING, (1770–1827) British statesman, prime minister. *The New Morality*, l. 207–10 (1798).

2   There is an unseemly exposure of the mind, as well as of the body.

WILLIAM HAZLITT, (1778–1830) British essayist. *Sketches and Essays*, "On Disagreeable People" (1839).

The philosopher and statesman Francis Bacon had expressed a similar idea in his essay "Of Simulation and Dissimulation": "Nakedness is uncomely, as well in mind as in body."

3   Let's face it. Let's talk sense to the American people. Let's tell them the truth, that there are no gains without pains, that we are now on the eve of great decisions, not easy decisions.

ADLAI STEVENSON, (1900–1965) U.S. Democratic politician. Acceptance speech, *Speeches* (1953). July 26, 1952, Democratic National Convention, Chicago, Illinois.

Capital Punishment

1   It is a strange, strange fate, and now, as I stand face to face with death I feel just as if they were going to kill a boy. For I feel like a boy— and my hands so free from blood and my heart always so compassionate and pitiful that I cannot comprehend how anyone wants to hang me.

ROGER CASEMENT, (1864–1916) Irish colonial administrator, nationalist. Quoted in *The Lives of Roger Casement*, ch. 30, B.L. Reid (1976). (Written Aug. 1916).

Casement's final letter, written from his condemned cell in Pentonville Prison, London; he was executed after attempting to overthrow, with German help, British rule in Ireland. From an incomplete copy: the original was destroyed by the prison authorities.

2   And naked to the hangman's noose
    The morning clocks will ring
    A neck God made for other use
    Than strangling in a string.

A.E. (ALFRED EDWARD) HOUSMAN, (1859–1936) British poet. "A Shropshire Lad," no. 9 (1896). Repr. in *The Collected Poems of A.E. Housman* (1939).

3 Depend upon it, Sir, when a man knows he is to be hanged in a fortnight, it concentrates his mind wonderfully.

Samuel Johnson, (1709–1784) British author, lexicographer. quoted in James Boswell, *Life of Dr. Johnson,* entry, Sept. 19, 1777 (1791).

4 If we are to abolish the death penalty, I should like to see the first step taken by my friends the murderers.

Alphonse Karr, (1808–1890) French journalist, novelist. *Les Guépes* (Paris, Jan. 31, 1849).

An alternative source attributes these words to a voice from the hall in the French Chamber, during a debate on the death penalty, when a speech proposing abolition was being tumultuously applauded.

5 For they're hangin' Danny Deever, you can hear the Dead March play, The Regiment's in 'ollow square— they're hangin' him to–day; They've taken of his buttons off an' cut his stripes away, An' they're hangin' Danny Deever in the mornin.'

Rudyard Kipling, (1865–1936) British writer, poet. "Danny Deever," *Barrack–Room Ballads* (1892).

6 I went out to Charing Cross to see Major–General Harrison hanged, drawn and quartered—which was done there—he looking as cheerful as any man could do in that condition.

Samuel Pepys, (1633–1703) British diarist. *The Diary of Samuel Pepys,* eds. Robert Latham and William Matthews (1977–83). Journal entry, Oct. 13, 1660.

Thomas Harrison was one of the regicides responsible for Charles I's execution. It was said that he met his death with courage, making a final speech on the scaffold: "By God I have leapt over a wall, by God I have run through a troop, and by God I will go through this death, and he will make it easy."

7 The hungry judges soon the sentence sign, And wretches hang that jurymen may dine.

Alexander Pope, (1688–1744) British satirical poet. "The Rape of the Lock," cto. 3, l. 21–2 (1714).

8 Men are not hanged for stealing horses, but that horses may not be stolen.

George Savile, Lord Halifax, (1633–1695) British statesman, author. "Of Punishment," *Political, Moral, and Miscellaneous Thoughts and Reflections* (1750). Repr. in *Works,* ed. Walter Raleigh (1912); also known as George Savile, Marquess of Halifax.

9 Many a good hanging prevents a bad marriage.

William Shakespeare, (1564–1616) British dramatist, poet. Feste, in *Twelfth Night,* act 1, sc. 5, l. 18 (1623).

10 Cover her face. Mine eyes dazzle: she died young.

John Webster, (1580–1625) British dramatist. Ferdinand, in *The Duchess of Malfi,* act 4, sc. 2, l. 263 (1623). Repr. in *The Complete Works of John Webster,* ed. F.L. Lucas (1927).

Referring to the strangled duchess, his twin sister. Bosola replies, "I think not so: her infelicity/Seemed to have years too many."

11 It is sweet to dance to violins When Love and Life are fair: To dance to flutes, to dance to lutes Is delicate and rare: But it is not sweet with nimble feet To dance upon the air!

OSCAR WILDE, (1854–1900) Anglo–Irish playwright, author. "The Ballad of Reading Gaol," pt. 2, st. 9 (1898). Repr. in *Complete Works of Oscar Wilde*, ed. J.B. Foreman (1966).

Capitalism

1 The unpleasant and unacceptable face of capitalism.

EDWARD HEATH, (b. 1916) British Conservative politician, prime minister. *Hansard*, col. 1243. Speech, May 15, 1973, House of Commons, London.

Referring to the high emoluments of company directors during a period of recession.

2 The decadent international but individualistic capitalism in the hands of which we found ourselves after the war is not a success. It is not intelligent. It is not beautiful. It is not just. It is not virtuous. And it doesn't deliver the goods.

JOHN MAYNARD KEYNES, (1883–1946) British economist. *National Self–Sufficiency*, sct. 3 (1933), repr. in *Collected Works*, vol. 11 (1982).

3 Capitalists are no more capable of self–sacrifice than a man is capable of lifting himself up by his own boot-straps.

VLADIMIR ILYICH LENIN, (1870–1924) Russian revolutionary leader. *Letters From Afar*, ch. 4 (1917).

4 Capital is dead labor, which, vampire–like, lives only by sucking living labor, and lives the more, the more labor it sucks.

KARL MARX, (1818–1883) German political theorist and social philosopher. *Capital*, vol. 1, ch. 10 (1867).

Caprice

1 "Yes," I answered you last night,

"No," this morning, Sir, I say.
Colours seen by candle–light,
Will not look the same by day.

ELIZABETH BARRETT BROWNING, (1806–1861) British poet. "The Lady's 'Yes,'" st. 1, *Poems* (1844).

2 [He] has a whim of iron.

OLIVER HERFORD, (1863–1935) U.S. poet, illustrator. *Excuse It Please*, "Impossible Pudding" (1929).

Referring to King Barumph. The remark had earlier been attributed to Herford referring to his wife.

3 Unpredictability, too, can become monotonous.

ERIC HOFFER, (1902–1983) U.S. philosopher. *Reflections on the Human Condition*, aph. 224 (1955).

Cards

1 When in doubt, win the trick.

EDMOND HOYLE, (1672–1769) British writer on cards. *Hoyle's Games*, "Whist: Twenty–Four Short Rules for Learners" (c. 1756).

2 I am sorry I have not learnt to play at cards. It is very useful in life: it generates kindness, and consolidates society.

SAMUEL JOHNSON, (1709–1784) British author, lexicographer. Quoted in James Boswell, *Journal of a Tour to the Hebrides*, entry, Nov. 21, 1773 (1785).

Boswell noted that Johnson's remark would be "a valuable text for many decent old dowagers, and other good company, in various circles, to descant upon."

Cars

1 I think that cars today are almost the exact equivalent of the great Gothic cathedrals: I mean the supreme creation of an era, con-

ceived with passion by unknown artists, and consumed in image if not in usage by a whole population which appropriates them as a purely magical object.

ROLAND BARTHES, (1915–1980) French semiologist. *Mythologies,* "The New Citroën" (1957).

2 Glorious, stirring sight! The poetry of motion! The *real* way to travel! The *only* way to travel! Here today—in next week tomorrow! Villages skipped, towns and cities jumped—always somebody else's horizon! O bliss! O poop–poop! O my! O my!

KENNETH GRAHAME, (1859–1932) British essayist, writer of children's books. Toad, in *The Wind in the Willows,* ch. 2 (1908).

"Poetry in Motion" was a hit single for Johnny Tillotson in 1960, his first major success, written by Paul Kaufman and Mike Anthony.

3 The Aquarium is gone. Everywhere, giant finned cars nose forward like
   fish;
a savage servility
slides by on grease.

ROBERT LOWELL, (1917–1977) U.S. poet. "For The Union Dead," st. 17, *For The Union Dead* (1964).

Last stanza.

4 The car has become the carapace, the protective and aggressive shell, of urban and suburban man.

MARSHALL MCLUHAN, (1911–1980) Canadian communications theorist. *Understanding Media,* ch. 22 (1964).

Cartoons and Drawing

1 Boop–boop–a–doop.

MAX FLEISCHER, (1883–1972) Austrian–born U.S. film animator. Betty

Boop's catch phrase, in *Talkartoons* (animation series), *The Encyclopedia of Animated Cartoons,* ed. Jeff Lenburg (1991).

Created by Grim Natwick in 1930 for the Fleischer Studio's *Talkartoon* cartoon series, modeled on the actress Helen Kane, Betty starred in her own show from 1932 on.

Catholicism

1 Here is everything which can lay hold of the eye, ear and imagination—everything which can charm and bewitch the simple and ignorant. I wonder how Luther ever broke the spell.

JOHN ADAMS, (1735–1826) U.S. statesman, president. *The Adams Family Correspondence,* vol. 1, ed. L.H. Butterfield (1963). Letter, Oct. 9, 1774, to his wife Abigail Adams.

2 Good strong thick stupefying incense–smoke!

ROBERT BROWNING, (1812–1889) British poet. "The Bishop Orders His Tomb at Saint Praxed's Church," l. 84 (1845).

3 A little skill in antiquity inclines a man to Popery. But depth in that study brings him about again to our religion.

THOMAS FULLER, (1608–1661) British cleric. *The Holy State and the Profane State,* bk. 2, ch. 6 (1642).

4 I was a fire–breathing Catholic
   C.O.,
and made my manic statement,
telling off the state and president,
   and then
sat waiting sentence in the bull pen
beside a Negro boy with curlicues
of marijuana in his hair.

ROBERT LOWELL, (1917–1977) U.S. poet. "Memories of West Street and Lepke," *Life Studies* (1959).

Lowell was an ardent convert to Roman Catholicism in the 1940s.

5   She thoroughly understands what
no other Church has ever understood, how to deal with enthusiasts.

THOMAS BABINGTON MACAULAY,
(1800–1859) British historian, Whig politician.
"Ranke's History of the Popes, "*Critical and
Historical Essays* (1843). *Edinburgh Review*
(Oct. 1840).

Referring to the Catholic Church.

Cats

1   I tawt I taw a puddy tat a–cweepin'
up on me.

BOB CLAMPETT, U.S. animator. Tweety's
running gag, in *Looney Tunes/Merrie Melodies*
(animation series), Warner Brothers cartoon
(1944–1960s).

Created by Bob Clampett, voiced by Mel
Blanc, the little yellow canary first appeared in
the Warners' *Merrie Melodies* cartoon *Birdy
and the Beast* (1944), soon to be chased by the
lisping cat Sylvester, whose favorite line was
"Suffering Succotash!" in 1950 the lines were
incorporated into a song by Alan Livingston
and Billy May.

2   Cats seem to go on the principle
that it never does any harm to ask
for what you want.

JOSEPH WOOD KRUTCH, (1893–1970)
U.S. author, editor. *Twelve Seasons*,
"February" (1949).

3   When I play with my cat, who knows
whether she isn't amusing herself
with me more than I with her.

MICHEL DE MONTAIGNE, (1533–1592)
French essayist. *Essays*, bk. 2, ch. 12 (1595).

Causes

1   The humblest citizen of all the land,
when clad in the armor of a righteous cause, is stronger than all the
hosts of error.

WILLIAM JENNINGS BRYAN,
(1860–1925) U.S. politician. Quoted in *The
First Battle: A Story of the Campaign of 1896*,
vol. 1, ch. 10. Speech, 1896, Democratic Convention, Chicago.

2   I stick my neck out for nobody. I'm
the only cause I'm interested in.

JULIUS J. EPSTEIN, Screenwriter. Rick
Blaine (Humphrey Bogart), in *Casablanca* (film)
(1942). Michael Curtiz.

In John Huston's film *Key Largo* (1948), Bogart
also declares: "I fight nobody's battles but my
own." A similar statement was made earlier by
Clark Gable as Rhett Butler in *Gone With the
Wind* (1939).

3   I hate the idea of causes, and if I had
to choose between betraying my
country and betraying my friend, I
hope I should have the guts to
betray my country.

E.M. (EDWARD MORGAN) FORSTER,
(1879–1970) British novelist, essayist. *Two
Cheers for Democracy*, "What I Believe"
(1951).

4   There aren't any good, brave causes
left. If the big bang does come, and
we all get killed off, it won't be in
aid of the old–fashioned grand
design. It'll just be for the Brave
New–nothing–very–much–thank–y
ou. About as pointless and inglori-
ous as stepping in front of a bus.
No, there's nothing left for it, me
boy, but to let yourself be butchered
by the women.

JOHN OSBORNE, (1929–1994) British playwright. Jimmy Porter, in *Look Back in Anger*,
act 3, sc. 1 (1956).

Caution

1   Whenever our neighbour's house is
on fire, it cannot be amiss for the
engines to play a little on our own.

EDMUND BURKE, (1729–1797) Irish philosopher, statesman. *Reflections on the Revolution in France* (1790), repr. in *Works*, vol. 3 (1865).

2 In skating over thin ice, our safety is in our speed.

RALPH WALDO EMERSON, (1803–1882) U.S. essayist, poet, philosopher. *Essays*, "Prudence," First Series (1841).

3 Put all your eggs in the one basket and—WATCH THAT BASKET.

MARK TWAIN, (1835–1910) U.S. author. *Pudd'nhead Wilson*, ch. 15, "Pudd'nhead Wilson's Calendar" (1894).

Celibacy

1 Marriage has many pains, but celibacy has no pleasures.

SAMUEL JOHNSON, (1709–1784) British author, lexicographer. Nekayah, in *The History of Rasselas*, ch. 26 (1759).

Censorship

1 Tell it not in Gath, publish it not in the streets of Askelon; lest the daughters of the Philistines rejoice, lest the daughters of the uncircumcised triumph.

BIBLE: HEBREW, David, in *2 Samuel*, 1:20.

Referring to the death of Saul and Jonathan.

2 It's red hot, mate. I hate to think of this sort of book getting in the wrong hands. As soon as I've finished this, I shall recommend they ban it.

TONY HANCOCK, (1924–1968) British comedian. *Hancock's Half-Hour* (BBC TV series), "The Missing Page," written by Ray Galton and Alan Simpson (1956–1963). Episode broadcast Feb. 26, 1960.

3 As good almost kill a man as kill a good book; who kills a man kills a reasonable creature, God's image; but he who destroys a good book, kills reason itself, kills the image of God, as it were in the eye.

JOHN MILTON, (1608–1674) British poet. *Areopagitica: a Speech for the Liberty of Unlicensed Printing to the Parliament of England* (1644).

Ceremony

1 And what art thou, thou idol ceremony?
What kind of god art thou, that suffer'st more
Of mortal griefs than do thy worshippers?
What are thy rents? What are thy comings–in?
O ceremony, show me but thy worth.

WILLIAM SHAKESPEARE, (1564–1616) British dramatist, poet. King Henry, in *Henry V*, act 4, sc. 1, l. 237–41 (1600).

Part of Henry's soliloquy on the cares of kingship, after pondering, "And what have kings that privates have not too,/Save ceremony?"

Certainty

1 If a man will begin with certainties, he shall end in doubts, but if he will be content to begin with doubts, he shall end in certainties.

FRANCIS BACON, (1561–1626) British philosopher, essayist, statesman. *The Advancement of Learning*, bk. 1, ch. 5, sct. 8 (1605).

2 For every why he had a wherefore.

SAMUEL BUTLER, (1612–1680) British poet. "Hudibras," pt. 1, cto. 1, l. 132 (1663). Eds. John Wilders and Hugh de Quehen (1973).

3   In this world nothing can be said to be certain, except death and taxes.

BENJAMIN FRANKLIN, (1706–1790) U.S. statesman, writer. *Complete Works*, vol. 10, ed. John Bigelow (1887–1888). Letter, Nov. 13, 1789.

Referring to "our new Constitution" which "has an appearance that promises permanency; but in this world." See the comment by Dickens under truth for a similar observation on the inevitability of taxation.

4   I am certain of nothing but the holiness of the heart's affections, and the truth of imagination.

JOHN KEATS, (1795–1821) British poet. *Letters of John Keats*, no. 31, ed. Frederick Page (1954). Letter, Nov. 22, 1817.

5   If you do know that *here is one hand*, we'll grant you all the rest.

LUDWIG WITTGENSTEIN, (1889–1951) Austrian philosopher. *On Certainty*, sct. 1 (1969).

Opening sentence, a response to a lecture by the philosopher G.E. Moore, in which he refuted the premises of skepticism.

Change

1   When it is not necessary to change, it is necessary not to change.

LUCIUS CARY FALKLAND, 2ND VIS-COUNT, (1610–1643) British statesman, soldier, patron. "A Speech Concerning Episcopacy," *Discourses on the Infallibility of the Church of Rome* (1660). Speech, Nov. 22, 1641, to the House of Commons.

2   Most of the change we think we see in life
    Is due to truths being in and out of favor.

ROBERT FROST, (1874–1963) U.S. poet. "The Black Cottage," *North of Boston* (1914).

3   The more things change, the more they remain the same.

[Plus qu'a change, plus c'est la même chose.]

ALPHONSE KARR, (1808–1890) French journalist, novelist. *Les Guépes* (Paris, Jan. 31, 1849).

4   If we want everything to remain as it is, it will be necessary for everything to change.

GIUSEPPE TOMASI DI LAMPEDUSA, (1896–1957) Sicilian author. Prince Tancredi, in *The Leopard*, ch. 1 (1958, translated 1960).

5   Man's yesterday may ne'er be like his morrow;
    Nought may endure but Mutability.

PERCY BYSSHE SHELLEY, (1792–1822) British poet. "Mutability," st. 4 (written 1814, published 1816).

Shelley wrote another poem with this title in 1821.

6   Let the great world spin for ever down the ringing grooves of change.

ALFRED TENNYSON, 1ST BARON TENNYSON, (1809–1892) British poet. "Locksley Hall," l. 182 (1842).

Chaos

1   There is nothing stable in the world; uproar's your only music.

JOHN KEATS, (1795–1821) British poet. *Letters of John Keats*, no. 37, ed. Frederick Page (1954). Letter, Jan. 13–19, 1818, to his brothers George and Thomas Keats.

2   Lo! thy dread empire, Chaos! is restor'd;
    Light dies before thy uncreating word:
    Thy hand, great Anarch! lets the curtain fall;
    And universal darkness buries all.

ALEXANDER POPE, (1688–1744) British satirical poet. *The Dunciad*, bk. 4, l. 653–6 (1728).

Closing lines.

3   Things fall apart; the centre cannot
hold;
Mere anarchy is loosed upon the
world,
The blood–dimmed tide is loosed,
and everywhere
The ceremony of innocence is
drowned;
The best lack all conviction, while
the worst
Are full of passionate intensity.

WILLIAM BUTLER YEATS, (1865–1939)
Irish poet, playwright. "The Second Coming,"
st. 1, *Michael Robartes and the Dancer*
(1921).

Character

1   Can the Ethiopian change his skin,
or the leopard his spots? Then may
ye also do good, that are accustomed to do evil.

BIBLE: HEBREW, *Jeremiah*, 13:23.

2   Talent develops in quiet places,
character in the full current of
human life.

JOHANN WOLFGANG VON GOETHE,
(1749–1832) German poet, dramatist.
Leonore, in *Torquato Tasso*, act 1, sc. 2
(1790).

Charity

1   And though I bestow all my goods
to feed the poor, and though I give
my body to be burned, and have
not charity, it profiteth me nothing.
Charity suffereth long, and is kind;
charity envieth not; charity vaun-
teth not itself, is not puffed up.

BIBLE: NEW TESTAMENT, St. Paul, in *1
Corinthians*, 13:3–4.

2   Therefore when thou doest thine
alms, do not sound a trumpet

before thee, as the hypocrites do in
the synagogues and in the streets,
that they may have glory of men.
Verily I say unto you, they have
their reward. But when thou doest
alms, let not thy left hand know
what thy right hand doeth.

BIBLE: NEW TESTAMENT, Jesus, in
Matthew, 6:2–3.

From the Sermon on the Mount.

3   The organized charity, scrimped
and iced, In the name of a cautious,
statistical Christ.

JOHN BOYLE O'REILLY, (1844–1890)
Irish author. "In Bohemia," st. 5 (1886).

4   Charity creates a multitude of sins.

OSCAR WILDE, (1854–1900) Anglo–Irish
playwright, author. "The Soul of Man Under
Socialism" (1895) *Fortnightly Review* (London,
Feb. 1890). Repr. in *Complete Works of Oscar
Wilde*, ed. J.B. Foreman (1966).

This dictum was echoed in another line by
Wilde—"Charity ... creates a multitude of
evils," in *The Critic as Artist*, published in July
and September of the same year (1890)—but
both recall Thoreau's, "This is a charity that
hides a multitude of sins" (referring to philan-
thropists) in *Walden* (1854) "Economy," which
itself derives from the Bible, "For charity shall
cover the multitude of sins." (*1 Peter* 4:8).

Charm

1   It's a sort of bloom on a woman. If
you have it, you don't need to have
anything else; and if you don't have
it, it doesn't much matter what else
you have.

J.M. (JAMES MATTHEW) BARRIE,
(1860–1937) British playwright. Maggie Wylie,
in *What Every Woman Knows*, act 1 (performed 1908, published 1918).

2   All charming people have something to conceal, usually their total
dependence on the appreciation of
others.

CYRIL CONNOLLY, (1903–1974) British critic. *Enemies of Promise*, ch. 16 (1938).

3 What is charm then? The free giving of a grace, the spending of something given by nature in her role of spendthrift ... something extra, superfluous, unnecessary, essentially a power thrown away.

DORIS LESSING, (b. 1919) British novelist. *Particularly Cats*, ch. 9 (1967).

Chastity

1 What, then, does a chaste girl do? She does not offer, yet she does not say "No."

MARCUS VALERIUS MARTIAL, (c. 40–104) Spanish–born Roman poet, epigrammatist. *Epigrams*, bk. 4, no. 71.

2 'Tis chastity, my brother, chastity.
She that has that is clad in complete steel,
And like a quivered nymph with arrows keen
May trace huge forests and unharbored heaths,
Infamous hills and sandy perilous wilds,
Where, through the sacred rays of chastity,
No savage fierce, bandit, or mountaineer
Will dare to soil her virgin purity.

JOHN MILTON, (1608–1674) British poet. The elder brother, in "Comus," l. 420–7 (1637).

3 How happy is the blameless vestal's lot!
The world forgetting, by the world forgot.

ALEXANDER POPE, (1688–1744) British satirical poet. "Eloisa to Abelard," l. 207–8 (1717).

Chicago

1 Virgin territory for whorehouses.

AL CAPONE, (1899–1947) U.S. gangster. Quoted in *The Bootleggers*, ch. 16, Kenneth Allsop (1961).

Referring to suburban Chicago.

2 New York is one of the capitals of the world and Los Angeles is a constellation of plastic, San Francisco is a lady, Boston has become Urban Renewal, Philadelphia and Baltimore and Washington blink like dull diamonds in the smog of Eastern Megalopolis, and New Orleans is unremarkable past the French Quarter. Detroit is a one–trade town, Pittsburgh has lost its golden triangle, St. Louis has become the golden arch of the corporation, and nights in Kansas City close early. The oil depletion allowance makes Houston and Dallas naught but checkerboards for this sort of game. But Chicago is a great American city. Perhaps it is the last of the great American cities.

NORMAN MAILER, (b. 1923) U.S. author. *Miami and the Siege of Chicago*, "The Siege of Chicago," opening paragraph (1969).

3 Hog Butcher for the World,
Tool Maker, Stacker of Wheat,
Player with Railroads and the
    Nation's Freight Handler;
Stormy, husky, brawling,
City of the Big Shoulders.

CARL SANDBURG, (1878–1967) U.S. poet. "Chicago," *Chicago Poems* (1916).

Childbirth

1 Good work, Mary. We all knew you had it in you.

DOROTHY PARKER, (1893–1967) U.S. humorous writer. Quoted in *While Rome Burns*, "Our Mrs. Parker," Alexander Woollcott (1934).

Telegram to a friend who had just become a mother after a prolonged pregnancy.

2 Macduff was from his mother's
  womb
  Untimely ripped.

WILLIAM SHAKESPEARE, (1564–1616) British dramatist, poet. Macduff, in *Macbeth*, act 5, sc. 10, l. 15–16 (1623).

Macduff explains that he was born by Caesarean Section, showing Macbeth his delusion in invoking the witches' promise: "I bear a charmed life, which must not yield/To one of woman born."

Childhood

1 But childhood prolonged, cannot remain a fairyland. It becomes a hell.

LOUISE BOGAN, (1897–1970) U.S. poet and critic. "Childhood's False Eden," (1940). Repr. in *Selected Criticism: Poetry and Prose* (1955).

Referring to Katherine Mansfield.

2 There is always one moment in childhood when the door opens and lets the future in.

GRAHAM GREENE, (1904–1991) British novelist. *The Power and the Glory*, pt. 1, ch. 1 (1940).

3 I remember, I remember,
  The house where I was born,
  The little window where the sun
  Came peeping in at morn.

THOMAS HOOD, (1799–1845) British poet. "I Remember," st. 1 (1827). Repr. in *Complete Poetical Works*, ed. Walter Jerrold (1906).

4 Childhood is the kingdom where nobody dies.

Nobody that matters, that is.

EDNA ST. VINCENT MILLAY, (1892–1950) U.S. poet. "Childhood is the Kingdom Where Nobody Dies," *Wine From These Grapes* (1934).

5 The childhood shows the man,
  As morning shows the day.

JOHN MILTON, (1608–1674) British poet. *Paradise Regained*, bk. 4, l. 220–1 (1671).

6 In ancient shadows and twilights
  Where childhood had strayed,
  The world's great sorrows were
    born
  And its heroes were made.
  In the lost boyhood of Judas
  Christ was betrayed.

GEORGE WILLIAM RUSSELL [AE], (1867–1935) Irish poet, painter, journalist. "Germinal," *Vale and Other Poems* (1931).

7 Grown–ups never understand anything for themselves, and it is tiresome for children to be always and forever explaining things to them.

ANTOINE DE SAINT–EXUPÉRY, (1900–1944) French aviator, author. *The Little Prince*, ch. 1 (1943).

8 Come children, let us shut up the box and the puppets, for our play is played out.

WILLIAM MAKEPEACE THACKERAY, (1811–1863) British author. *Vanity Fair*, ch. 67 (1848).

Closing words.

9 Certainly Adam in Paradise had not more sweet and curious apprehensions of the world, than I when I was a child.

THOMAS TRAHERNE, (1636–1674) British clergyman, poet, mystic. *Centuries*, "Third Century," no. 1 (written c. 1672, first published 1908).

10 Heaven lies about us in our infancy!
Shades of the prison–house begin
to close
Upon the growing boy.

WILLIAM WORDSWORTH, (1770–1850)
British poet. *Intimations of Immortality from
Recollections of Early Childhood*, st. 5, l.
66–8, *Poems in Two Volumes* (1807).

Ambrose Bierce made a riposte to this in *The
Devil's Dictionary* (1881–1906): "Heaven lies
about us in our infancy ... and the world
begins lying about us pretty soon afterward."

Children

1 Monday's child is fair in face,
Tuesday's child is full of grace,
Wednesday's child is full of woe,
Thursday's child has far to go,
Friday's child is loving and giving,
Saturday's child works hard for its
living;
And a child that is born on a
Christmas day,
Is fair and wise, good and gay.

ANONYMOUS, quoted in *Traditions, Leg-
ends, Superstitions, and Sketches of Devonshire*, vol. 2, ed. Anna E.K.S. Bray (1838).

The penultimate line commonly refers to "the
Sabbath day."

2 Children have never been very
good at listening to their elders,
but they have never failed to imitate them.

JAMES BALDWIN, (1924–1987) U.S.
author. "The Precarious Vogue of Ingmar
Bergman," first published in *Esquire* (New
York, April 1960). Repr. in *Nobody Knows My
Name* (1961).

3 There is no sinner like a young
saint.

APHRA BEHN, (1640–1689) British playwright, poet. Willmore, in *The Rover*, act 1,
sc. 2 (1681). Published in *The Works of Aphra
Behn*, vol. 1, ed. M. Summers (1915).

4 It were better for him that a millstone were hanged about his neck,
and he cast into the sea, than that he
should offend one of these little ones.

BIBLE: NEW TESTAMENT, Jesus, in *Luke*,
17:2.

5 Suffer the little children to come
unto me, and forbid them not: for of
such is the kingdom of God.

BIBLE: NEW TESTAMENT, Jesus, in *Mark*,
10:14.

6 There is no end to the violations
committed by children on children,
quietly talking alone.

ELIZABETH BOWEN, (1899–1973)
Anglo–Irish novelist. *The House in Paris*, pt. 1,
ch. 2 (1935).

7 But the child's sob curses deeper in
the silence
Than the strong man in his wrath!

ELIZABETH BARRETT BROWNING,
(1806–1861) British poet. "The Cry of the Children," st. 13, *Poems* (1844).

Closing lines.

8 Go practise if you please
With men and women: leave a child
alone
For Christ's particular love's sake!

ROBERT BROWNING,(1812–1889) British
poet. "The Ring and the Book," bk. 3, l. 88–90
(1868–1869).

9 You may give them your love but
not your thoughts.
For they have their own thoughts.
You may house their bodies but not
their souls,
For their souls dwell in the house of
tomorrow, which you cannot visit,
not even in your dreams.

KAHLIL GIBRAN, (1883–1931) Syrian–born
U.S. poet, novelist. "On Children," *The Prophet*
(1923).

10 Alas! regardless of their doom,
The little victims play!
No sense have they of ills to come
Nor care beyond today.

THOMAS GRAY, (1716–1771) British poet. "Ode on a Distant Prospect of Eton College," st. 6 (written 1742, published 1747). Repr. in *Poetical Works*, ed. J. Rogers (1953).

Gray himself was a pupil at Eton College.

11 We in the West do not refrain from childbirth because we are concerned about the population explosion or because we feel we cannot afford children, but because we do not like children.

GERMAINE GREER, (b. 1939) Australian feminist writer. *Sex and Destiny*, ch. 1 (1984).

12 Mama may have, papa may have,
But God bless the child that's got his own!

BILLIE HOLIDAY [ELEANOR FAGAN], (1915–1959) U.S. blues singer. "God Bless the Child" (song), written in collaboration with Arthur Herzog Jr. (1941).

13 If there is anything that we wish to change in the child, we should first examine it and see whether it is not something that could better be changed in ourselves.

CARL JUNG, (1875–1961) Swiss psychiatrist. *On the Development of Personality* (1934). Repr. in *Collected Works*, vol. 17, ed. William McGuire (1954).

14 All God's children are not beautiful. Most of God's children are, in fact, barely presentable.

FRAN LEBOWITZ, (b. 1951) U.S. journalist. "Manners," *Metropolitan Life* (1978).

15 If help and salvation are to come, they can only come from the children, for the children are the makers of men.

MARIA MONTESSORI, (1870–1952) Italian educationist. *The Absorbent Mind*, ch. 1 (1949).

16 How sharper than a serpent's tooth it is
To have a thankless child.

WILLIAM SHAKESPEARE, (1564–1616) British dramatist, poet. Lear, in *King Lear*, act 1, sc. 4, l. 268–9 (1623).

17 A child should always say what's true
And speak when he is spoken to,
And behave mannerly at table;
At least as far as he is able.

ROBERT LOUIS STEVENSON, (1850–1894) Scottish novelist, essayist, poet. "The Whole Duty of Children," *A Child's Garden of Verses* (1885).

18 I have been assured by a very knowing American of my acquaintance in London, that a young healthy child, well nursed, is at a year old, a most delicious, nourishing, and wholesome food, whether *stewed, roasted, baked,* or *boiled*; and I make no doubt that it will equally serve in a *fricassee*, or a *ragout*.

JONATHAN SWIFT, (1667–1745) Anglo–Irish satirist. "A Modest Proposal for Preventing the Children of Ireland from Being a Burden to their Parents or the Country" (1729). Repr. in *The Prose Works of Jonathan Swift*, vol. 12, ed. Herbert Davies (1955).

This ironic pamphlet subverted current Whig notions of people being "the wealth of the nation" in the context of the poverty and hunger in Ireland.

19 Look for me in the nurseries of Heaven.

FRANCIS THOMPSON, (1859–1907) British poet. "To My Godchild M.W.M.," *Poems* (1913).

Words inscribed (by Eric Gill) on Thompson's tombstone, Kensal Green, London.

20 The child is father of the man.

> WILLIAM WORDSWORTH, (1770–1850) British poet. "My Heart Leaps Up When I Behold" (written 1802, published 1807).

Chivalry

1 I thought ten thousand swords must have leaped from their scabbards to avenge even a look that threatened her with insult. But the age of chivalry is gone. That of sophisters, economists and calculators has succeeded; and the glory of Europe is extinguished forever.

> EDMUND BURKE, (1729–1797) Irish philosopher, statesman. *Reflections on the Revolution in France* (1790), repr. in *Works*, vol. 3 (1865).

> Referring to Marie Antoinette.

2 The age of chivalry is never past, so long as there is a wrong left unredressed on earth, or a man or woman left to say, I will redress that wrong, or spend my life in the attempt.

> CHARLES KINGSLEY, (1819–1875) British author, clergyman. Quoted in *Charles Kingsley: His Letters and Memories of His Life*, vol. 2, ch. 28, Mrs. C. Kingsley (1879).

Choice

1 I shall be telling this with a sigh
Somewhere ages and ages hence:
Two roads diverged in a wood, and
I—
I took the one less traveled by,
And that has made all the
difference.

> ROBERT FROST, (1874–1963) U.S. poet. "The Road Not Taken," st. 4, *Mountain Interval* (1916).

2 The blame is his who chooses: God is blameless.

> PLATO, (c. 427–347 B.C.) Greek philosopher. Socrates, in *The Republic*, bk. 10, sct. 617.

Christianity and Christians

1 For God so loved the world, that he gave his only begotten Son, that whosoever believeth in him should not perish, but have everlasting life.

> BIBLE: NEW TESTAMENT, Jesus, in *John*, 3:16.

2 Think not that I am come to send peace on earth: I came not to send peace, but a sword.

> BIBLE: NEW TESTAMENT, Jesus, in *Matthew*, 10:34.

3 People in general are equally horrified at hearing the Christian religion doubted, and at seeing it practised.

> SAMUEL BUTLER, (1835–1902) British author. *Samuel Butler's Notebooks*, p. 310 (1951).

> This observation reappeared in Butler's description of a congregation of conservative farmers in *The Way of All Flesh*, ch. 15 (1903): "They would have been equally horrified at hearing the Christian religion doubted, and at seeing it practised."

4 The Christian ideal has not been tried and found wanting. It has been found difficult; and left untried.

> GILBERT KEITH CHESTERTON, (1874–1936) British author. *What's Wrong With the World*, pt. 1, ch. 5 (1910).

5 He who begins by loving Christianity better than truth, will proceed by loving his own sect or church better than Christianity, and end in loving himself better than all.

> SAMUEL TAYLOR COLERIDGE, (1772–1834) British poet, critic. *Aids to Reflection*, "Moral and Religious Aphorisms,"

no. 25 (1825), repr. in *Works*, vol. 1, ed. Professor Shedd (1853).

6 Bear the Cross cheerfully and it will bear you.

THOMAS KEMPIS, (c. 1380–1471) German monk, mystic. *The Imitation of Christ*, pt. 2, ch. 12 (written c. 1426, published 1486).

7 The Three in One, the One in
　　Three? Not so!
To my own Gods I go.
It may be they shall give me greater
　　ease
Than your cold Christ and tangled
　　Trinities.

RUDYARD KIPLING, (1865–1936) British author, poet. *Plain Tales from the Hills*, chapter heading to "Lispeth" (1888).

8 Christianity will go. It will vanish and shrink. I needn't argue with that; I'm right and I will be proved right. We're more popular than Jesus now; I don't know which will go first— rock and roll or Christianity.

JOHN LENNON, (1940–1980) British songwriter, rock musician. *Evening Standard* (London, March 4, 1966).

This remark provoked a storm of reaction, especially in the U.S., causing Lennon to explain himself at a press conference in Chicago, Aug. 11, 1966: "I'm not saying that we're better or greater, or comparing us with Jesus Christ as a person, or God as a thing, or whatever it is. I just said what I said, and it was wrong, or it was taken wrong. And now it's all this." in his autobiography, *A Moveable Feast*, ch. 18 (1964), Ernest Hemingway quoted Zelda Fitzgerald: "Ernest, don't you think Al Jolson is greater than Jesus?"

9 Two great European narcotics, alcohol and Christianity.

FRIEDRICH NIETZSCHE, (1844–1900) German philosopher. *Twilight of the Idols*, "What the Germans Lack," aph. 2 (1889).

In *The Anti-Christ*, aph. 62 (1895), Nietzsche wrote: "Wherever there are walls I shall inscribe this eternal accusation against Christianity upon them—I can write in letters which make even the blind see.... I call Christianity the one great curse, the one great intrinsic depravity, the one great instinct for revenge for which no expedient is sufficiently poisonous, secret, subterranean, petty—I call it the one immortal blemish of mankind."

Christmas

1 I'm dreaming of a white Christmas,
Just like the ones I used to know,

IRVING BERLIN, (1888–1989) U.S. songwriter. "White Christmas" (song), *Holiday Inn* (film, 1942).

The song, first recorded by Bing Crosby in *Holiday Inn* (giving Crosby sales of over 25 million), was featured again in the movie *White Christmas* (Michael Curtiz, 1954), and recorded by artists as diverse as Frank Sinatra (1944), Mantovani (1952), and The Drifters (1954).

2 And is it true? And is it true,
This most tremendous tale of all,
Seen in a stained–glass window's
　　hue,
A Baby in an ox's stall?
The Maker of the stars and sea
Become a Child on earth for me?

JOHN BETJEMAN, (1906–1984) British poet. "Christmas," st. 6, *A Few Late Chrysanthemums* (1954).

3 This is the month, and this the
　　happy morn,
Wherein the Son of heav'n's eternal
　　King,
Of wedded Maid and Virgin Mother
　　born,
Our great redemption from above
　　did bring.

JOHN MILTON, (1608–1674) British poet. *On the Morning of "Christ's Nativity,"* l. 1–4 (written 1629, published 1645).

Church, The

1 He was of the faith chiefly in the sense that the church he currently did not attend was Catholic.

KINGSLEY AMIS, (b. 1922) British novelist. *One Fat Englishman*, ch. 8 (1963).

Referring to Roger Micheldene.

2 It is indolence ... indolence and love of ease; a want of all laudable ambition, of taste for good company, or of inclination to take the trouble of being agreeable, which make men clergymen. A clergyman has nothing to do but be slovenly and selfish; read the newspaper, watch the weather, and quarrel with his wife. His curate does all the work and the business of his own life is to dine.

JANE AUSTEN, (1775–1817) British novelist. Mary Crawford, in *Mansfield Park*, ch. 11 (1814).

"It will, I believe, be everywhere found, that as the clergy are, or are not what they ought to be, so are the rest of the nation." (Edmund, in *Mansfield Park*, ch. 9).

3 And I say also unto thee, That thou art Peter, and upon this rock I will build my church; and the gates of hell shall not prevail against it.

BIBLE: NEW TESTAMENT, Jesus, in *Matthew*, 16:18.

The passage is a punning reference to the Greek word, *petros*, "stone."

4 If a man desireth the office of a bishop, he desireth a good work. A bishop then must be blameless, the husband of one wife, vigilant, sober, of good behaviour, given to hospitality, apt to teach; not given to wine, no striker, not greedy of filthy lucre; but patient, not a brawler, not covetous; one that ruleth well his own house, having his children in subjection with all gravity; (for if a man know not how to rule his own house, how

shall he take care of the church of God?).

BIBLE: NEW TESTAMENT, St. Paul, in *1 Timothy*, 3:1–5.

5 Render therefore unto Caesar the things which are Caesar's; and unto God the things that are God's.

BIBLE: NEW TESTAMENT, Jesus, in *Matthew*, 22:21.

6 The parson knows enough who knows a duke.

WILLIAM COWPER, (1731–1800) British poet. "Tirocinium," l. 403 (1785). Repr. in *Poetical Works*, ed. H.S. Milford (1934).

7 And of all plagues with which mankind are cursed, Ecclesiastic tyranny's the worst.

DANIEL DEFOE, (1660–1731) British author, poet, journalist. "The True–Born Englishman," pt. 2, l. 299–300 (1701). Repr. in *Works*, ed. Keltie (1869).

8 His creed no parson ever knew, For this was still his "simple plan," To have with clergymen to do As little as a Christian can.

FRANCIS, SIR DOYLE, (1810–1888) British poet. "The Unobtrusive Christian" (1866).

9 Those who marry God can become domesticated too—it's just as humdrum a marriage as all the others. The word "Love" means a formal touch of the lips as in the ceremony of the Mass, and "*Ave Maria*" like "dearest" is a phrase to open a letter.

GRAHAM GREENE, (1904–1991) British novelist. *A Burnt–Out Case*, pt. 1, ch. 1, sct. 2 (1961).

10 This merriment of parsons is mighty offensive.

SAMUEL JOHNSON, (1709–1784) British author, lexicographer. Quoted in James Boswell, *Life of Dr. Johnson*, entry, March 1781 (1791).

11 A Curate there is something which excites compassion in the very name of a curate!!!

SYDNEY SMITH, (1771–1845) British clergyman, writer. *The Letters of Peter Plymley*, "Persecuting Bishops" (1929). Essay first published in *Edinburgh Review* (1822).

12 I have, alas, only one illusion left, and that is the Archbishop of Canterbury.

SYDNEY SMITH, (1771–1845) British clergyman, writer. Quoted in *Memoir*, vol. 1, ch. 9, Lady Holland (1855).

13 I never saw, heard, nor read, that the clergy were beloved in any nation where Christianity was the religion of the country. Nothing can render them popular, but some degree of persecution.

JONATHAN SWIFT, (1667–1745) Anglo–Irish satirist. *Thoughts on Religion*, published in *Works*, vol. 15 (1765).

14 I don't go to church. Kneeling bags my nylons.

BILLY WILDER, (b. 1906) U.S. film director. Lorraine (Jan Sterling), in *The Big Carnival* (film) (1951).

The movie was originally released under the title *Ace in the Hole*.

Churchill, Sir Winston

1 He is a man suffering from petrified adolescence.

ANEURIN BEVAN, (1897–1960) British Labour politician. Quoted in *Aneurin Bevan*, ch. 11, Vincent Brome (1953).

On another occasion, Bevan said of Churchill, "His ear is so sensitively attuned to the bugle note of history that he is often deaf to the more raucous clamour of contemporary life." (Quoted in Michael Foot's biography, *Aneurin Bevan*, vol. 1, ch. 10, 1962).

2 It is fun to be in the same decade with you.

FRANKLIN DELANO ROOSEVELT, (1882–1945) U.S. Democratic politician, president. Quoted in *The Hinge of Fate*, ch. 4, Winston Churchill (1950). Cable, Jan. 30, 1942, to Churchill, in response to sixtieth birthday greetings.

Cinema

1 All you need for a movie is a gun and a girl.

JEAN–LUC GODARD, (b. 1930) French filmmaker, author. Quoted in *Projections*, eds. John Boorman and Walter Donohue (1992). Journal entry, May 16, 1991.

2 Photography is truth. The cinema is truth twenty–four times per second.

JEAN–LUC GODARD, (b. 1930) French filmmaker, author. *Le Petit Soldat* (film) (direction and screenplay, 1960).

3 They have slapped into the American mind more human misinformation in one evening than the Dark Ages could muster in a decade.

BEN HECHT, (1893–1964) U.S. journalist, author, screenwriter. "What the Movies Are," bk. 5, *A Child of the Century* (1954).

"Movies are one of the bad habits that corrupted our century," wrote Hecht (who enjoyed a profitable career as a Hollywood screenwriter). "Of their many sins, I offer as the worst their effect on the intellectual side of the nation. It is chiefly from that viewpoint I write of them—as an eruption of trash that has lamed the American mind and retarded Americans from becoming a cultured people."

4 You should look straight at a film; that's the only way to see one. Film

is not the art of scholars but of illiterates.

WERNER HERZOG, (b. 1942) German film director. *The New York Times* (Sept. 11, 1977).

5   The words "Kiss Kiss Bang Bang," which I saw on an Italian movie poster, are perhaps the briefest statement imaginable of the basic appeal of movies. This appeal is what attracts us, and ultimately what makes us despair when we begin to understand how seldom movies are more than this.

PAULINE KAEL, (b. 1919) U.S. film critic. *Kiss Kiss Bang Bang*, "A Note on the Title" (1968).

6   I just want to tell you all how happy I am to be back in the studio, making a picture again! You don't know much I've missed all of you.... You see, this is my life. It always will be! There's nothing else. Just us, and the cameras, and those wonderful people out there in the dark. All right, Mr. de Mille. I'm ready for my closeup.

BILLY WILDER, (b. 1906) U.S. film director. Norma Desmond (Gloria Swanson), in *Sunset Boulevard* (film) (1950). Billy Wilder.

The last lines of the film, spoken by Norma Desmond as she descends a staircase.

7   It is like writing history with lightning and my only regret is that it is all so terribly true.

WOODROW WILSON, (1856–1924) U.S. Democrat, president. Attributed in *The Image*, ch. 4, Daniel J. Boorstin (1962).

On seeing D.W. Griffith's monumental epic of the Civil War, *The Birth of a Nation*, at the White House, Feb. 18, 1915.

Circumstances

1   In the fell clutch of circumstance, I have not winced nor cried aloud:

Under the bludgeonings of chance
My head is bloody, but unbowed.

WILLIAM ERNEST HENLEY, (1849–1903) British poet, critic, editor. "Invictus: In Memoriam R.T. Hamilton Bruce," st. 2 (1875). Repr. in *Echoes* (1888).

Cities and City Life

1   That sweet city with her dreaming spires.

MATTHEW ARNOLD, (1822–1888) British poet, critic. "Thyrsis," l. 19 (1866).

Referring to Oxford, where Arnold was Professor of Poetry at the university 1857–1867.

2   One has not great hopes from Birmingham. I always say there is something direful in the sound.

JANE AUSTEN, (1775–1817) British novelist. Mrs. Elton, in *Emma*, ch. 36 (1816).

3   How doth the city sit solitary, that was full of people! how is she become as a widow! she that was great among the nations, and princess among the provinces, how is she become tributary!

BIBLE: HEBREW, Lamentations of Jeremiah, 1:1.

Referring to Jerusalem.

4   For Cambridge people rarely smile, Being urban, squat, and packed with guile.

RUPERT BROOKE, (1887–1915) British poet. "The Old Vicarage, Grantchester," *1914 and Other Poems* (1915).

5   Carthage must be destroyed.
[Delenda est Carthago.]

MARCUS PORCIUS CATO THE ELDER, (234–149 B.C.) Roman statesman. Quoted in *Parallel Lives*, "Marcus Cato," ch. 27, Plutarch.

The words are supposed to be have been repeated by Cato at the end of every speech he made in the senate, after his visit to Carthage in 175 B.C., when he became obsessed by the military threat posed by the city. It was eventually destroyed by Rome at the end of the Third Punic War in 146 B.C., though refounded a hundred years later, becoming an important center of Roman administration under Augustus.

6   It is not what they built. It is what they knocked down.
It is not the houses. It is the spaces between the houses.
It is not the streets that exist. It is the streets that no longer exist.

JAMES FENTON, (b. 1949) British poet, critic. *German Requiem* (1981).

7   There are eight million stories in the naked city. This has been one of them.

MARK HELLINGER, (1903–1947) U.S. journalist, scriptwriter, producer. *The Naked City* (film) (1948). Jules Dassin.

Afterword, spoken by Hellinger—this was his last production—and used at the end of each episode of the TV series, 1958–1962.

8   The city is not a concrete jungle, it is a human zoo.

DESMOND MORRIS, (b. 1928) British anthropologist. *The Human Zoo*, introduction (1969).

9   All great art is born of the metropolis.

EZRA POUND, (1885–1972) U.S. poet, critic. *Letters of Ezra Pound 1907–1941*, ed. D.D. Paige (1951). Letter, Nov. 7, 1913, to Harriet Monroe.

"The metropolis," Pound explained, "is that which accepts all gifts and all heights of excellence, usually the excellence that is *tabu* in its own village. The metropolis is always accused by the peasant of 'being mad after foreign notions.'" Ten years later, in the *Criterion* (Jan. 1923), Pound wrote, "All civilization has proceeded from cities and cenacles." (*Cenacle,* supping room, upper chamber).

Citizenship

1   It is not the function of our Government to keep the citizen from falling into error; it is the function of the citizen to keep the Government from falling into error.

ROBERT H. [HOUGHWOUT] JACK-SON, (1892–1954) U.S. judge. *American Communications Association v Douds* (May 1950).

2   A strict observance of the written laws is doubtless one of the high virtues of a good citizen, but it is not the highest. The laws of necessity, of self–preservation, of saving our country when in danger, are of higher obligation.

THOMAS JEFFERSON, (1743–1826) U.S. president. *The Writings of Thomas Jefferson,* vol. 9, ed. Paul L. Ford (1898). Letter, Sept. 20, 1810.

3   Before Man made us citizens, great Nature made us men.

JAMES RUSSELL LOWELL, (1819–1891) U.S. poet, editor. "On the Capture of Fugitive Slaves near Washington" (1854). Repr. in *Poetical Works of James Russell Lowell* (1978).

4   The first requisite of a good citizen in this republic of ours is that he shall be able and willing to pull his weight.

THEODORE ROOSEVELT, (1858–1919) U.S. Republican (later Progressive) politician, president. *Addresses and Presidential Messages* (1904). Speech, Nov. 11, 1902, New York City.

5   Whatever makes men good Christians, makes them good citizens.

DANIEL WEBSTER, (1782–1852) U.S. lawyer, statesman. *The Writings and Speeches of Daniel Webster,* vol. 1 (1903). Speech, Dec. 22, 1820, Plymouth, Massachusetts.

Civil Rights

1   The day that the Black man takes an uncompromising step and realizes that he is within his rights, when his own freedom is being jeopardized, to use any means necessary to bring about his freedom or put a halt to that injustice, I don't think he'll be by himself.

MALCOLM X [MALCOLM LITTLE}, (1925–1965) U.S. African–American leader. *Malcolm X Talks to Young People*, ed. Steve Clark (1991). Oxford Union Society Debate, Dec. 3, 1964.

The words "by any means necessary" became a rallying–call among radical movements since the 1960s.

2   Get up, stand up,
Stand up for your rights.
Get up, stand up,
Don't give up the fight.

PETER TOSH, (1944–1987) Jamaican reggae musician. "Get Up, Stand Up" (song), written with Bob Marley, from the album *Burnin'* (1973).

Civil War, American

1   My opinion is that the Northern states will manage somehow to muddle through.

JOHN BRIGHT, (1811–1889) British politician. Quoted in *Reminiscences*, vol. 1, ch. 5, Justin McCarthy (1899).

Bright was a vigorous supporter of the Lincoln government.

2   I, John Brown, am now quite certain that the crimes of this guilty land will never be purged away but with Blood.

JOHN BROWN, (1800–1859) U.S. abolitionist. Quoted in *John Brown and His Men*, ch. 12, R.J. Hinton (1894). Last statement, written on the day of his execution, Dec. 2, 1859.

3   "A house divided against itself cannot stand." I believe this government cannot endure permanently half slave and half free. I do not expect the Union to be dissolved—I do not expect the house to fall—but I do expect it will cease to be divided. It will become all one thing, or all the other.

ABRAHAM LINCOLN, (1809–1865) U.S. president. Collected Works of Abraham Lincoln, vol. 2, ed. Roy P. Basler (1953). Speech, June 16, 1858, Republican State Convention, Springfield, Illinois.

Lincoln quotes the words of Jesus, in Mark 3:25.

4   We here highly resolve that the dead shall not have died in vain, that this nation, under God, shall have a new birth of freedom; and that government of the people, by the people, and for the people, shall not perish from the earth.

ABRAHAM LINCOLN, (1809–1865) U.S. president. "Gettysburg Address," repr. in *Collected Works of Abraham Lincoln*, vol. 7, ed. Roy P. Basler (1953). Speech, Nov. 19, 1863.

The fighting at Gettysburg July 1–3 claimed nearly 50,000 killed or wounded.

5   With malice toward none, with charity for all, with firmness in the right, as God gives us to see the right, let us strive on to finish the work we are in, to bind up the nation's wounds, to care for him who shall have borne the battle, and for his widow and his orphan, to do all which may achieve and cherish a just and lasting peace among ourselves, and with all nations.

ABRAHAM LINCOLN, (1809–1865) U.S. president. "Second Inaugural Address," repr. in *Collected Works of Abraham Lincoln*, vol. 8, ed. Roy P. Basler (1953). Speech, March 4, 1865.

Conclusion.

6 We are constantly thinking of the great war ... which saved the Union ... but it was a war that did a great deal more than that. It created in this country what had never existed before—a national consciousness. It was not the salvation of the Union, it was the rebirth of the Union.

WOODROW WILSON, (1856–1924) U.S. Democratic politician, president. *Memorial Day address.* Address, May 31, 1915, Arlington National Cemetery.

Civilization

1 The three great elements of modern civilization, gunpowder, printing, and the Protestant religion.

THOMAS CARLYLE, (1795–1881) Scottish essayist, historian. *The State of German Literature, Critical and Miscellaneous Essays* (1839–1857).

Carlyle was alluding to an earlier observation by Francis Bacon: "Printing, gunpowder, and the magnet ... these three have changed the whole face and state of things throughout the world." (*Novum Organum*, bk. 1, aph. 129, 1620).

2 Civilization is an active deposit which is formed by the combustion of the Present with the Past. Neither in countries without a Present nor in those without a Past is it to be encountered.

CYRIL CONNOLLY, (1903–1974) British critic. *The Unquiet Grave*, pt. 2 (1944, rev. 1951).

Connolly continued—"Proust in Venice, Matisse's birdcages overlooking the flower market at Nice, Gide on the seventeenth–century quais of Toulon, Lorca in Granada, Picasso by Saint–Germain–des–Près: there lies civilization and for me it can exist only under those liberal regimes in which the Present is alive and therefore capable of assimilating the Past."

3 Increased means and increased leisure are the two civilizers of man.

BENJAMIN DISRAELI, (1804–1881) British statesman, author. *Selected Speeches of the Late Right Honourable the Earl of Beaconsfield*, vol. 2, "Conservative Principles," ed. T.E. Kebbes (1882). Speech, April 3, 1872, Manchester, England.

4 Is civilization only a higher form of idolatry, that man should bow down to a flesh–brush, to flannels, to baths, diet, exercise, and air?

MARY BAKER EDDY, (1821–1910) U.S. founder of the Christian Science movement. *Science and Health*, ch. 7 (1875).

5 We believe that civilization has been created under the pressure of the exigencies of life at the cost of satisfaction of the instincts.

SIGMUND FREUD, (1856–1939) Austrian psychiatrist. *Introductory Lectures on Psychoanalysis*, vol. 15, lecture 1, *Complete Works, Standard Edition*, eds. James Strachey and Anna Freud. (Originally published 1915).

6 Jesus wept; Voltaire smiled. From that divine tear and from that human smile is derived the grace of present civilization.

VICTOR HUGO, (1802–1885) French poet, dramatist, novelist. "Centenaire de Voltaire" (1878). Address on the centenary of Voltaire's death, May 30, 1878.

7 Civilization must be destroyed. The hairy saints
Of the North have earned this crumb by their complaints.

WALLACE STEVENS, (1879–1955) U.S. poet. *New England Verses*, "Land of Pine and Marble," *Harmonium* (1923).

Class

1 By bourgeoisie is meant the class of modern capitalists, owners of the means of social production and employers of wage labor. By proletariat, the class of modern wage

laborers who, having no means of production of their own, are reduced to selling their labor power in order to live.

FRIEDRICH ENGELS, (1820–1895) German social philosopher. *Manifesto of the Communist Party* (written in collaboration with Karl Marx), footnote (1888 edition).

2   The history of all hitherto existing society is the history of class struggles.

KARL MARX, (1818–1883) German political theorist, social philosopher. *The Communist Manifesto*, sct. 1 (1848). Repr. in *Karl Marx: Selected Works*, vol. 1 (1942).

3   I am his Highness' dog at Kew;
Pray tell me, sir, whose dog are you?

ALEXANDER POPE, (1688–1744) British satirical poet. "Epigram Engraved on the Collar of a Dog which I Gave to His Royal Highness" (1734).

Dedicated to Frederick, Prince of Wales.

Classicism and Antiquity

1   Hebraism and Hellenism between these two points of influence moves our world.

MATTHEW ARNOLD, (1822–1888) British poet, critic. *Culture and Anarchy*, ch. 4 (1869).

For Arnold, "The governing idea of Hellenism is spontaneity of consciousness, that of Hebraism, strictness of conscience."

2   Thou still unravished bride of quietness,
Thou foster–child of silence and slow time.

JOHN KEATS, (1795–1821) British poet. "Ode on a Grecian Urn," st. 1 (1820).

Cleopatra

1   Nature meant me
A wife, a silly harmless household Dove,

Fond without art; and kind without deceit.

JOHN DRYDEN, (1631–1700) British poet, dramatist, critic. Cleopatra, in *All for Love*, act 4, sc. 1 (1678).

2   Had Cleopatra's nose been shorter, the whole face of the world would have changed.

BLAISE PASCAL, (1623–1662) French scientist, philosopher. *Pensées*, no. 413, ed. Krailsheimer; no. 162, ed. Brunschvicg (1670, trans. 1688), rev. A.J. Krailsheimer (1966).

3   The barge she sat in, like a
burnished throne
Burned on the water. The poop was
beaten gold;
Purple the sails, and so perfumed
that
The winds were love–sick with them.
The oars were silver,
Which to the tune of flutes kept
stroke, and made
The water which they beat to follow
faster,
As amorous of their strokes.

WILLIAM SHAKESPEARE, (1564–1616) British dramatist, poet. Enobarbus, in *Antony and Cleopatra*, act 2, sc. 2, l. 198–204 (1623).

Describing Cleopatra's arrival at her first meeting with Antony. As for its occupant, "For her own person,/It beggared all description." T.S. Eliot wrote a pastiche of this passage in *The Waste Land*, "A Game of Chess."

Clichés

1   Man is a creature who lives not upon bread alone, but principally by catchwords; and the little rift between the sexes is astonishingly widened by simply teaching one set of catchwords to the girls and another to the boys.

ROBERT LOUIS STEVENSON, (1850–1894) Scottish novelist, essayist, poet. *Virginibus Puerisque*, "Virginibus Puerisque," sct. 2 (1881).

Clubs

1   Sir John, Sir, is a very unclubbable man.

SAMUEL JOHNSON, (1709–1784) British author, lexicographer. Quoted in James Boswell, *Life of Dr. Johnson*, entry, spring 1764 (1791).

Referring to eminent musicologist Sir John Hawkins. He was Johnson's literary executor and published an inaccurate *Life* (1787–1789) and an edition of Johnson's works.

2   Please accept my resignation. I don't care to belong to any club that will have me as a member.

GROUCHO MARX, (1895–1977) U.S. comic actor. Quoted in *The Groucho Letters*, introduction (1967).

Introduction by Arthur Sheekman, book by Groucho.

Cocktails

1   You can no more keep a martini in the refrigerator than you can keep a kiss there. The proper union of gin and vermouth is a great and sudden glory; it is one of the happiest marriages on earth, and one of the shortest–lived.

BERNARD DEVOTO, (1897–1955) U.S. historian, critic. *Harper's Magazine* (New York, Dec. 1949).

2   A medium Vodka dry Martini— with a slice of lemon peel. Shaken and not stirred, please. I would prefer Russian or Polish vodka.

IAN FLEMING, (1908–1964) British author. James Bond, in *Dr. No*, ch. 14 (1958).

Bond's favorite tipple.

Coffee

1   Dam' good coffee.

DAVID LYNCH, (b. 1946) U.S. filmmaker. Agent Dale Cooper (Kyle MacLachlan), in *Twin Peaks* (TV series), written and created by David Lynch and Mark Frost (1989–1991).

Frequent remark, together with "dam' fine cheese cake."

2   Coffee, (which makes the politician wise,
And see thro' all things with his half–shut eyes).

ALEXANDER POPE, (1688–1744) British satirical poet." Rape of the Lock", cto. 3, l. 117 (1712).

Cold War, the

1   Let us not be deceived—we are today in the midst of a cold war.

BERNARD BARUCH, (1870–1965) U.S. financier. Quoted in *The New York Times* (April 17, 1947). Speech, April 16, 1947, South Carolina Legislature, Columbia.

A year later Baruch told the Senate War Investigating Committee, "We are in the midst of a cold war which is getting warmer." Baruch claimed the expression had been suggested to him by his speechwriter (and former editor of the *New York World*), Herbert Bayard Swope.

2   A shadow has fallen upon the scenes so lately lighted by the Allied victory.... From Stettin in the Baltic to Trieste in the Adriatic, an iron curtain has descended across the Continent.

WINSTON CHURCHILL, (1874–1965) British statesman, writer. Vol. 6, *Winston S. Churchill: His Complete Speeches, 1897–1963*, ed. Robert Rhodes James (1974). Speech, March 5, 1946, Fulton, Missouri.

The phrase "iron curtain" had been used previously, notably by Joseph Goebbels in 1945, and by Churchill himself in the same year in a telegram to President Truman.

3   If we cannot end now our differences, at least we can help make the world safe for diversity.

JOHN FITZGERALD KENNEDY,
(1917–1963) U.S. Democratic politician, president. Commencement address, *Public Papers of the Presidents of the United States: John F. Kennedy, 1963*. Speech, June 10, 1963, American University, Washington D.C..

Referring to Russo–American relations.

4 Whether you like it or not, history is on our side. We will bury you.

NIKITA KHRUSHCHEV, (1894–1971) Soviet premier. Quoted in *Times* (London, Nov. 19, 1956). Remark, Nov. 18, 1956, to Western diplomats, Kremlin, Moscow.

Khrushchev later explained this remark as an idiomatic expression to mean "we will outlive you" (i.e. communism will triumph). On another occasion, Aug. 24, 1963, addressing a group of Westerners in Split, Yugoslavia, he referred to his controversial statement: "Of course we will not bury you with a shovel. Your own working class will bury you."

5 We hear the Secretary of State boasting of his brinkmanship the art of bringing us to the edge of the abyss.

ADLAI STEVENSON, (1900–1965) U.S. Democratic politician. quoted in *The New York Times* (Feb. 26, 1956), *The Papers of Adlai E. Stevenson*, vol. 5 (1974). Speech, Feb. 25, 1956, Hartford, Connecticut.

Referring to John Foster Dulles.

Coleridge, Samuel Taylor

1 He talked on for ever; and you wished him to talk on for ever.

WILLIAM HAZLITT, (1778–1830) British essayist. *Lectures on the English Poets*, "On the Living Poets" (1818).

Coleridge was the first poet Hazlitt had ever known, and produced an unforgettable effect on him: "His thoughts did not seem to come with labour and effort; but as if borne on gusts of genius, and as if the wings of his imagination lifted him off from his feet.... His mind was clothed with wings; and raised on them, he lifted philosophy to heaven."

2 You will see Coleridge—he who sits obscure

In the exceeding lustre and the pure
Intense irradiation of a mind,
Which, with its own internal lightning blind,
Flags wearily through darkness and despair—
A cloud–encircled meteor of the air,
A hooded eagle among blinking owls.

PERCY BYSSHE SHELLEY, (1792–1822) British poet. "Letter to Maria Gisborne," l. 202–8 (1820).

Color

1 The purest and most thoughtful minds are those which love colour the most.

JOHN RUSKIN, (1819–1900) British art critic, author. *The Stones of Venice*, vol. 2, ch. 5, sct. 30 (1852).

2 I think it pisses God off if you walk by the color purple in a field somewhere and don't notice it.

ALICE WALKER, (b. 1944) U.S. author, critic. Shug, in *The Color Purple* (1983).

Comebacks

1 I hate that word. It's *return*—a return to the millions of people who've never forgiven me for deserting the screen.

BILLY WILDER, (b. 1906) U.S. film director. Norma Desmond (Gloria Swanson), in *Sunset Boulevard* (film), correcting a tactless remark by Joe Gillis (William Holden) (1950).

Comedy and Comedians

1 Comedy is tragedy that happens to *other* people.

ANGELA CARTER, (1940–1992) British author. *Wise Children*, ch. 4 (1991).

2   All I need to make a comedy is a
     park, a policeman and a pretty girl.

     CHARLIE CHAPLIN, (1889–1977) British
     comic actor, filmmaker. *My Autobiography*, ch.
     10 (1964).

3   Life is a jest; and all things show it.
     I thought so once; but now I know it.

     JOHN GAY, (1685–1732) British dramatist,
     poet. "My Own Epitaph" (1720).

     Words inscribed on Gay's monument in West-
     minster Abbey.

4   We mustn't complain too much of
     being comedians—it's an hon-
     ourable profession. If only we could
     be good ones the world might gain at
     least a sense of style. We have
     failed—that's all. We are bad come-
     dians, we aren't bad men.

     GRAHAM GREENE, (1904–1991) British
     novelist. The ambassador, in *The Comedians*,
     pt. 1, ch. 5, sct. 2 (1966).

5   And I did laugh sans intermission
     An hour by his dial. O noble fool,
     A worthy fool—motley's the only
       wear.

     WILLIAM SHAKESPEARE, (1564–1616)
     British dramatist, poet. Jaques, in *As You Like It*,
     act 2, sc. 7, l. 32–4 (1623).

     Motley garments were the traditional dress of
     professional jesters, probably quartered in pri-
     mary colors, or else woven from different col-
     ored threads.

6   Though it make the unskilful laugh,
     cannot but make the judicious grieve.

     WILLIAM SHAKESPEARE, (1564–1616)
     British dramatist, poet. Hamlet, in *Hamlet*, act
     3, sc. 2, l. 25–6 (1604).

Comfort

1   Of comfort no man speak.
     Let's talk of graves, of worms and
       epitaphs,

Make dust our paper, and with rainy
  eyes
Write sorrow on the bosom of the
  earth.
Let's choose executors and talk of
  wills.

WILLIAM SHAKESPEARE, (1564–1616)
British dramatist, poet. Richard, in *Richard II*,
act 3, sc. 2, l. 140–4 (1597).

Common Sense

1   Nothing astonishes men so much as
     common sense and plain dealing.

     RALPH WALDO EMERSON, (1803–1882)
     U.S. essayist, poet, philosopher. *Essays*, "Art,"
     First Series (1841).

Commonplace, the

1   The characteristic of the hour is that
     the commonplace mind, knowing
     itself to be commonplace, has the
     assurance to proclaim the rights of
     the commonplace and to impose
     them wherever it will.

     JOSÉ ORTEGA Y GASSET, (1883–1955)
     Spanish essayist, philosopher. *The Revolt of the
     Masses*, ch. 1 (1930).

     Later in the book (ch. 14), Ortega y Gasset
     refers to commonplaces as "the tramways of
     intellectual transportation."

Communication

1   The triumphs of a mysterious
     non–meeting are desolate ones;
     unspoken phrases, silent words.

     ANNA AKHMATOVA, (1889–1966) Russian
     poet. "Two Poems," no. 2, l. 1 (1956), trans. by
     Dimitri Obolensky (1965).

2   Something there is that doesn't love
       a wall,
     And wants it down.

ROBERT FROST, (1874–1963) U.S. poet. "Mending Wall," *North of Boston* (1914).

3   Beep! Beep!

CHUCK JONES, (b. 1912) U.S. animator. The Road Runner, in *Looney Tunes/Merrie Melodies* (animation series), Warner Brothers cartoon (from 1949).

The only line of dialogue between the Road Runner and Wile E. Coyote, creations of Chuck Jones (who directed most of the episodes) and Michael Maltese, and voiced by Mel Blanc. Roadrunner was first introduced in a Warners' *Looney Tunes* cartoon called *Fast and Furry–Ous* (1949).

4   What we've got here is a failure to communicate.

DONN PEARCE, U.S. writer. Camp commandant (Strother Martin), in *Cool Hand Luke* (film) (1967).

The words appeared as a publicity slogan for the movie.

Communism

1   What is a Communist? One who has
       yearnings
For equal division of unequal
       earnings.

EBENEZER ELLIOT, (1781–1849) British pamphleteer, poet. "Epigram" (1831), published in *Poetical Works* (1840).

2   Communism, my friend, is more than Marxism, just as Catholicism ... is more than the Roman Curia. There is a *mystique* as well as a *politique*.... Catholics and Communists have committed great crimes, but at least they have not stood aside, like an established society, and been indifferent. I would rather have blood on my hands than water like Pilate.

GRAHAM GREENE, (1904–1991) British novelist. Dr. Magiot, in *The Comedians*, pt. 2, ch. 4, sct. 4 (1966).

3   I can no longer sit back and allow Communist infiltration, Communist indoctrination, Communist subversion and the international Communist conspiracy to sap and impurify all of our precious bodily fluids.

STANLEY KUBRICK, (b. 1928) U.S. filmmaker. General D. Ripper (Sterling Haydon), in *Dr. Strangelove: Or How I Learned To Stop Worrying And Love The Bomb* (film) (1963). Stanley Kubrick.

4   Communism is Soviet power plus the electrification of the whole country.

VLADIMIR ILYICH LENIN, (1870–1924) Russian revolutionary leader. (1920), repr. in *Collected Works*, vol. 31 (1966). Report on the Work of the Council of People's Commissars, Dec. 22, 1920.

The words were used as a slogan to promote the plans of the State Committee for the Electrification of Russia.

5   Communism is not love. Communism is a hammer which we use to crush the enemy.

MAO ZEDONG, (1893–1976) Chinese founder of the People's Republic of China. Quoted in *Time* (New York, Dec. 18, 1950).

6   A specter is haunting Europe—the specter of communism.

KARL MARX, (1818–1883) German political theorist, social philosopher. *The Communist Manifesto* (1848). Repr. in *Karl Marx: Selected Works*, vol. 1 (1942).

Opening sentence.

7   The theory of the Communists may be summed up in the single sentence: Abolition of private property.

KARL MARX, (1818–1883) German political theorist, social philosopher. *The Communist Manifesto*, sct. 2 (1848). Repr. in *Karl Marx: Selected Works*, vol. 1 (1942).

8   The "Communism" of the English intellectual is something explicable enough. It is the patriotism of the deracinated.

GEORGE ORWELL, (1903–1950) British author. *Inside the Whale and Other Essays,* "Inside the Whale" (1940).

9   The crusade against Communism was even more imaginary than the spectre of Communism.

A.J.P. (ALAN JOHN PERCIVALE) TAY-LOR, (1906–1990) British historian. *The Origins of the Second World War,* ch. 2 (1961).

Community

1   None of us liveth to himself, and no man dieth to himself.

BIBLE: NEW TESTAMENT, St. Paul, in *Romans,* 14:7.

Company

1   My idea of good company ... is the company of clever, well–informed people who have a great deal of conversation; that is what I call good company.

JANE AUSTEN, (1775–1817) British novelist. Anne, in *Persuasion,* ch. 16 (1818).

Mr. Elliot replies, "that is not good company; that is the best."

2   Two are better than one; because they have a good reward for their labour. For if they fall, the one will lift up his fellow: but woe to him that is alone when he falleth; for he hath not another to help him up. Again, if two lie together, then they have heat: but how can one be warm alone? And if one prevail against him, two shall withstand him; and a threefold cord is not quickly broken.

BIBLE: HEBREW, *Ecclesiastes,* 4:9–12.

3   All who joy would win
    Must share it,—Happiness was born
    a twin.

GEORGE GORDON NOEL BYRON, 6TH BARON BYRON, (1788–1824) British poet. *Don Juan,* cto. 2, st. 172 (1819–1824).

4   Tell me thy company, and I'll tell thee what thou art.

MIGUEL DE CERVANTES, (1547–1616) Spanish author. Sancho Panza, in *Don Quixote,* pt. 2, bk. 3, ch. 23 (1615), trans. by P. Motteux and J. Ozell.

Sancho is quoting a proverb.

5   Fan the sinking flame of hilarity with the wing of friendship; and pass the rosy wine.

CHARLES DICKENS, (1812–1870) British novelist. Dick Swiveller, in *The Old Curiosity Shop,* ch. 7 (1841).

6   Company, villainous company, hath been the spoil of me.

WILLIAM SHAKESPEARE, (1564–1616) British dramatist, poet. Oldcastle (Falstaff), in *Henry IV pt. 1,* act 3, sc. 3, l. 9–10 (1598).

7   You could read Kant by yourself, if you wanted; but you must share a joke with some one else.

ROBERT LOUIS STEVENSON, (1850–1894) Scottish novelist, essayist, poet. *Virginibus Puerisque,* "Virginibus Puerisque," sct. 1 (1881).

Compatibility

1   Madam your wife and I didn't hit it off the only time I ever saw her. I won't say she was silly, but I think one of us was silly, and it wasn't me.

ELIZABETH GASKELL, (1810–1865) British novelist. Squire Hamley, in *Wives and Daughters,* ch. 35 (1866).

Addressing Mr. Gibson.

2   Madam, I have been looking for a person who disliked gravy all my life; let us swear eternal friendship.

SYDNEY SMITH, (1771–1845) British clergy-man, writer. Quoted in *Memoir*, vol. 1, ch. 9, Lady Holland (1855).

3   We are so fond of one another, because our ailments are the same.

JONATHAN SWIFT, (1667–1745) Anglo–Irish satirist. *Journal to Stella* (1710–1713), published in *Works*, vol. 12 (quarto edition, 1768). Letter, Feb. 1, 1711.

Competition

1   Thou shalt not covet; but tradition Approves all forms of competition.

ARTHUR HUGH CLOUGH, (1819–1861) British poet. "The Latest Decalogue," l. 19–20 (1862). Repr. in *Collected Poems*, ed. C. Whibley (1913).

2   Take a look at them. All nice guys. They'll finish last. Nice guys. Finish last.

LEO DUROCHER, (1906–1991) U.S. base-ball coach. Quoted in *Nice Guys Finish Last*, pt. 1, Leo Durocher (1975).

Remark, July 6, 1946, referring to the New York Giants.

Complacency

1   The only thing necessary for the tri-umph of evil is for good men to do nothing.

EDMUND BURKE, (1729–1797) Irish philosopher, statesman. *Attributed.*

Ascribed in various forms to Burke, though never found in his writings. Possibly it is a dis-tillation of the words found in *Thoughts on the Cause of the Present Discontents* (1770): see Burke on alliances.

2   Everybody in America is soft, and hates conflict. The cure for this, both in politics and social life, is the same—hardihood. Give them raw truth.

JOHN JAY CHAPMAN, (1862–1933) U.S. author. *Practical Agitation*, ch. 2 (1898).

Complaint

1   If we complain about the tune, there is no reason to attack the monkey when the organ grinder is present.

ANEURIN BEVAN, (1897–1960) British Labour politician. *Hansard*, col. 680. Speech, May 16, 1957, House of Commons.

Referring to Foreign Minister Selwyn Lloyd and Prime Minister Harold Macmillan, and the lat-ter's role in the Suez fiasco the previous autumn. Though Macmillan had no direct responsibility for foreign affairs during the Suez Crisis (he was then Chancellor of the Exche-quer), he had advocated a strong response to the nationalization of the canal by Nasser, so that the subsequent replacement of Prime Min-ister Anthony Eden by Macmillan was seen by Bevan as a symbolic sacrifice.

2   It is a general popular error to sup-pose the loudest complainers for the public to be the most anxious for its welfare.

EDMUND BURKE, (1729–1797) Irish philosopher, statesman. *Observations on a Publication,* "The Present State of the Nation," (1769).

3   Depend upon it that if a man *talks* of his misfortunes there is some-thing in them that is not disagree-able to him.

SAMUEL JOHNSON, (1709–1784) British author, lexicographer. Quoted in James Boswell, *Life of Dr. Johnson*, entry, 1780 (1791).

4   When complaints are freely heard, deeply considered and speedily reformed, then is the utmost bound of civil liberty attained that wise men look for.

JOHN MILTON, (1608–1674) British poet. *Areopagitica: a Speech for the Liberty of Unli-censed Printing to the Parliament of England* (1644).

Complicity

1 We will have to repent in this generation not merely for the hateful
words and actions of the bad people but for the appalling silence of
the good people.

MARTIN LUTHER KING, JR.,
(1929–1968) U.S. clergyman, civil rights
leader. "Letter from Birmingham Jail," *Why
We Can't Wait* (1964). Open letter to clergymen, Apr. 16, 1963.

Compliments

1 A compliment is something like a
kiss through a veil.

VICTOR HUGO, (1802–1885) French poet,
dramatist, novelist. *Les Misérables*, pt. 4, bk.
8, ch. 1 (1862).

Compromise

1 All government—indeed every
human benefit and enjoyment,
every virtue and every prudent
act—is founded on compromise
and barter. We balance inconve-
niences; we give and take; we remit
some rights, that we may enjoy others; and we choose rather to be
happy citizens than subtle disputants.

EDMUND BURKE, (1729–1797) Irish
philosopher, statesman. "Second Speech on
Conciliation with America: The Thirteen Resolutions," *Works*, vol. 2 (1899). Speech, March
22, 1775, House of Commons, London.

Conditioning

1 No man ever looks at the world
with pristine eyes. He sees it edited
by a definite set of customs and
institutions and ways of thinking.

RUTH BENEDICT, (1887–1948) U.S.
anthropologist. *Patterns of Culture*, ch. 1
(1934).

Confession

1 We must not always talk in the
market–place of what happens to us
in the forest.

NATHANIEL HAWTHORNE,
(1804–1864) U.S. author. Hester Prynne, in
The Scarlet Letter, ch. 22 (1850).

2 We only confess our little faults to
persuade people that we have no
big ones.

**FRANÇOIS LA ROCHEFOUCAULD,
DUC DE,** (1613–1680) French writer, moralist. *Sentences et Maximes Morales*, no. 327
(1678).

3 There is no refuge from confession
but suicide, and suicide is
confession.

DANIEL WEBSTER, (1782–1852) U.S.
lawyer, statesman. *Argument on the Murder of
Captain White, The Writings and Speeches of
Daniel Webster*, vol. 11 (1903). Speech, April
6, 1830, in murder trial, Salem, Massachusetts.

It was during this trial that Webster famously
spoke of a "fearful concatenation of circumstances."

Conformity

1 The American ideal, after all, is that
everyone should be as much alike as
possible.

JAMES BALDWIN, (1924–1987) U.S.
author. "The Harlem Ghetto," first published
in *Commentary* (New York, Feb. 1948). Repr.
in *Notes of a Native Son*, pt. 2 (1955).

2 Conformity is the jailer of freedom
and the enemy of growth.

JOHN FITZGERALD KENNEDY,
(1917–1963) U.S. Democratic politician, pres-

ident. *Public Papers of the Presidents of the United States: John F. Kennedy, 1961.* Address, Sept. 25, 1961, to the U.N. General Assembly.

3   What are we hoping to get out of it, what's it all in aid of—is it really just for the sake of a gloved hand waving at you from a golden coach?

   JOHN OSBORNE, (1929–1994) British playwright. Jean, in *The Entertainer,* no. 10 (1957).

Confusion

1   Bewitched, bothered and bewildered am I.

   LORENZ HART, (1895–1943) U.S. songwriter. "Bewitched, Bothered and Bewildered" (song), refrain, *Pal Joey* (show, 1940).

Congress (U.S.)

1   It could probably be shown by facts and figures that there is no distinctly native American criminal class except Congress.

   MARK TWAIN, (1835–1910) U.S. author. *Following the Equator,* ch. 8, "Pudd'nhead Wilson's New Calendar" (1897).

2   This is a Senate of equals, of men of individual honor and personal character, and of absolute independence. We know no masters, we acknowledge no dictators. This is a hall for mutual consultation and discussion; not an arena for the exhibition of champions.

   DANIEL WEBSTER, (1782–1852) U.S. lawyer, statesman. "Second speech on Foote's Resolution," *The Writings and Speeches of Daniel Webster,* vol. 6 (1903). Speech, Jan. 26, 1830, U.S. Senate.

Conquest

1   I came. I saw, I conquered.
   [Veni, vidi, vici.]

   GAIUS CAESAR [GAIUS JULIUS CAESAR], (100–44 B.C.) Roman general, emperor. Quoted in *Lives of the Caesars,* "Julius Caesar," sct. 37, Suetonius (120 A.D.).

   Inscription displayed at Caesar's Pontic triumph; or according to Plutarch, written 47 B.C. in a letter to Rome, after the victory over Pharnaces at Zela which concluded the campaign.

2   Roused by the lash of his own stub born tail
   Our lion now will foreign foes assail.

   JOHN DRYDEN, (1631–1700) British poet, dramatist, critic. "Astraea Redux," l. 117–8 (1660).

3   It should be noted that when he seizes a state the new ruler ought to determine all the injuries that he will need to inflict. He should inflict them once and for all, and not have to renew them every day.

   NICCOLÒ MACHIAVELLI, (1469–1527) Italian political philosopher, statesman. *The Prince,* ch. 8 (written 1513–1514, published 1532), trans. by George Bull (1961).

   "Whoever acts otherwise," Machiavelli added, "either through timidity or bad advice, is always forced to have the knife ready in his hand.... Violence should be inflicted once and for all; people will then forget what it tastes like and so be less resentful."

Conscience

1   The Non–Conformist Conscience makes cowards of us all.

   MAX BEERBOHM, (1872–1956) British author. *Yellow Book,* "King George the Fourth" (1894).

2   Conscience is thoroughly well–bred and soon leaves off talking to those who do not wish to hear it.

   SAMUEL BUTLER, (1835–1902) British author. *Samuel Butler's Notebooks,* p. 250 (1951).

3   I cannot and will not cut my conscience to fit this year's fashions.

LILLIAN HELLMAN, (1905–1984) U.S. playwright. Quoted in *Nation* (New York, May 31, 1952). Letter, May 19, 1952, to John S. Wood, Chairman of the House un–American Activities Committee.

Refusing to testify against colleagues accused of Communist affiliations.

4 A man's conscience and his judgement is the same thing; and as the judgement, so also the conscience, may be erroneous.

THOMAS HOBBES, (1588–1679) British philosopher. *Leviathan*, pt. 2, ch. 29 (1651).

5 A clear conscience is a sure card.

JOHN LYLY, (1554–1606) British author. *Euphues: The Anatomy of Wit*, "To the Gentlemen Scholars of Oxford," (1579), ed. Edward Arber (1868).

6 Men never do evil so fully and cheerfully as when we do it out of conscience.

BLAISE PASCAL, (1623–1662) French scientist, philosopher. *Pensés*, no. 813, ed. Krailsheimer; no. 895, ed. Brunschvicg (1670, trans. 1688), rev. A.J. Krailsheimer (1966).

7 My conscience hath a thousand several tongues,
And every tongue brings in a several tale,
And every tale condemns me for a villain.

WILLIAM SHAKESPEARE, (1564–1616) British dramatist, poet. King Richard, in *Richard III*, act 5, sc. 5, l. 147 (1597).

Later, before the Battle of Bosworth, Richard rejects conscience with the words— Conscience is but a word that cowards use, Devised at first to keep the strong in awe. (Act 5, sc. 6, l. 39–40).

8 Conscience has no more to do with gallantry than it has with politics.

RICHARD BRINSLEY SHERIDAN, (1751–1816) Anglo–Irish dramatist. Isaac Mendoza, in *The Duenna*, act 2, sc. 4, l. 62–3 (1775).

Consciousness and the Subconscious

1 The ego is not master in its own house.

SIGMUND FREUD, (1856–1939) Austrian psychiatrist. *A Difficulty in the Path of Psycho-Analysis*, vol. 17, *Complete Works, Standard Edition*, eds. James Strachey and Anna Freud (1955). (Originally published 1917).

This was Freud's conclusion in the light of the discoveries made by psychoanalysis that sexual instincts could not be wholly tamed, and that mental processes were unconscious and could "only reach the ego and come under its control through incomplete and untrustworthy perceptions."

2 Man is only a reed, the weakest in nature; but he is a thinking reed. There is no need for the whole universe to take up arms to crush him: a vapor, a drop of water is enough to kill him. But even if the universe were to crush him, man would still be nobler than his slayer, because he knows that he is dying and the advantage the universe has over him. The universe knows nothing of this.

BLAISE PASCAL, (1623–1662) French scientist, philosopher. *Pensées*, no. 200, ed. Krailsheimer; no. 347, ed. Brunschvicg (1670, trans. 1688), rev. A.J. Krailsheimer (1966).

Consensus

1 We must indeed all hang together, or, most assuredly, we shall all hang separately.

BENJAMIN FRANKLIN, (1706–1790) U.S. statesman, writer. Quoted in *Ben Franklin Laughing*, P.M. Zall (1980). Remark, July 4, 1776, at the signing of the Declaration of Independence.

Replying t o John Hancock's remark that the revolutionaries should be unanimous in their action.

2　It is not much matter which we say, but mind, we must all say the same.

WILLIAM LAMB MELBOURNE, 2ND VISCOUNT, (1779–1848) British statesman, prime minister. Quoted in *The English Constitution*, ch. 1, Walter Bagehot (1867). Remark, March 1841, at a Cabinet meeting.

Consequences

1　Logical consequences are the scarecrows of fools and the beacons of wise men.

THOMAS HENRY HUXLEY, (1825–1895) British biologist. "On the Hypothesis that Animals are Automata," *Science and Culture* (1881). (Essay originally published 1874)

Conservatives

1　Conservative. A statesman who is enamored of existing evils, as distinguished from a Liberal, who wishes to replace them with others.

AMBROSE BIERCE, (1842–1914) U.S. author. *The Devil's Dictionary* (1881–1906), repr. in *Collected Works of Ambrose Bierce*, vol. 7 (1911).

2　I do not know which makes a man more conservative—to know nothing but the present, or nothing but the past.

JOHN MAYNARD KEYNES, (1883–1946) British economist. *The End of Laissez–Faire*, ch. 1 (1926).

3　What is conservatism? Is it not adherence to the old and tried, against the new and untried?

ABRAHAM LINCOLN, (1809–1865) U.S. president. *Collected Works of Abraham Lincoln*, vol. 3, ed. Roy P. Basler (1953). Speech, Feb. 27, 1860, New York City.

4　That man's the true Conservative

Who lops the mouldered branch away.

ALFRED TENNYSON, 1ST BARON TENNYSON, (1809–1892) British poet. *Hands All Round*, l. 7–8 (1885).

Consistency

1　Consistency is contrary to nature, contrary to life. The only completely consistent people are the dead.

ALDOUS HUXLEY, (1894–1963) British author. "Wordsworth in the Tropics," *Do What You Will* (1929).

Conspiracy

1　Et tu, Bruté?

WILLIAM SHAKESPEARE, (1564–1616) British dramatist, poet. Caesar, in *Julius Caesar*, act 3, sc. 1, l. 76 (1623).

Caesar's dying words. Brutus was amongst the conspirators who stabbed Caesar. in his biography *Julius Caesar*, Suetonius ascribes an utterance in Greek to Caesar from which this phrase could be derived. The words had occurred in previous dramas of the period.

2　In countries where associations are free, secret societies are unknown. In America there are factions, but no conspiracies.

ALEXIS DE TOCQUEVILLE, (1805–1859) French social philosopher. *Democracy in America*, vol. 1, ch. 12 (1835).

Constitution (U.S.)

1　The proposed Constitution ... is, in strictness, neither a national nor a federal constitution; but a composition of both.

JAMES MADISON, (1751–1836) U.S. president. *Federalist Papers* (Jan. 1788), no. 39, *The Federalist,* ed. Benjamin F. Wright (1961).

Consumer Society

1 Everything from toy guns that
spark
To flesh–colored Christs that glow
in the dark
It's easy to see without looking too
far
That not much is really sacred.

**BOB DYLAN [ROBERT ALLEN ZIM-
MERMAN],** (b. 1941) U.S. singer, songwriter.
"It's Alright Ma (I'm Only Bleeding)" (song), on
the album *Bringing it all Back Home* (1965).

2 Consumer wants can have bizarre,
frivolous, or even immoral origins,
and an admirable case can still be
made for a society that seeks to satisfy them. But the case cannot stand
if it is the process of satisfying wants
that creates the wants.

JOHN KENNETH GALBRAITH, (b. 1908)
U.S. economist. *The Affluent Society*, ch. 11,
sct. 2 (1958).

3 Conspicuous consumption of valuable goods is a means of reputability
to the gentleman of leisure.

THORSTEIN VEBLEN, (1857–1929) U.S.
social scientist. *The Theory of the Leisure
Class*, ch. 4 (1899).

4 The world is too much with us; late
and soon,
Getting and spending, we lay waste
our powers.

WILLIAM WORDSWORTH, (1770–1850)
British poet. "The World is Too Much With
Us," Sonnet 33, *Miscellaneous Sonnets* (1807).

Opening lines.

Contemplation

1 One is not idle because one is
absorbed. There is both visible and
invisible labor. To contemplate is to
toil, to think is to do. The crossed
arms work, the clasped hands act.
The eyes upturned to Heaven are
an act of creation.

VICTOR HUGO, (1802–1885) French poet,
dramatist, novelist. *Les Misérables*, pt. 2, bk.
7, ch. 8 (1862).

2 With an eye made quiet by the
power
Of harmony, and the deep power of
joy,
We see into the life of things.

WILLIAM WORDSWORTH, (1770–1850)
British poet. "Lines Composed a Few Miles
Above Tintern Abbey," l. 48–50, *Lyrical Bal-
lads* (1798).

Contemporaries

1 A man lives not only his personal
life, as an individual, but also, con-
sciously or unconsciously, the life
of his epoch and his contemporaries.

THOMAS MANN, (1875–1955) German
author, critic. *The Magic Mountain*, ch. 2, "At
Tienappels'" (1924), trans. by H.T.
Lowe–Porter (1928).

Contentment

1 For I have learned, in whatsoever
state I am, therewith to be content.

BIBLE: NEW TESTAMENT, St. Paul, in
Philippians, 4:11.

2 The year's at the spring
And day's at the morn;
Morning's at seven;
The hillside's dew–pearled;
The lark's on the wing;
The snail's on the thorn;
God's in his heaven—
All's right with the world!

ROBERT BROWNING, (1812–1889) British poet. *Pippa Passes*, pt. 1, "Morning" (1841).

Pippa's song.

3   Happy the man, and happy he
    alone,
    He who can call today his own;
    He who, secure within, can say,
    Tomorrow, do thy worst, for I have
    lived today.

JOHN DRYDEN, (1631–1700) British poet, dramatist, critic. "Imitation of Horace," bk. 3, Ode 29 (1685).

4   Few and signally blessed are those
    whom Jupiter has destined to be
    cabbage–planters. For they've always
    one foot on the ground and the
    other not far from it. Anyone is wel-
    come to argue about felicity and
    supreme happiness. But the man
    who plants cabbages I now posi-
    tively declare to be the happiest of
    mortals.

FRANÇOIS RABELAIS, (c. 1494–1553) French satirist. Panurge, in *Gargantua and Pantagruel*, bk. 4, ch. 18 (1548), trans. by J.M. Cohen (1955).

See Montaigne on death and Voltaire on self–sufficiency for developments on this theme.

5   That blessed mood
    In which the burthen of the
    mystery,
    In which the heavy and the weary
    weight
    Of all this unintelligible world
    Is lightened.

WILLIAM WORDSWORTH, (1770–1850) British poet. "Lines Composed a Few Miles Above Tintern Abbey," l. 38–42, *Lyrical Ballads* (1798).

Contracts

1   A verbal contract isn't worth the
    paper it is written on.

SAMUEL GOLDWYN, (1882–1974) U.S. film producer. Attributed in *The Great Goldwyn*, ch. 1, Alva Johnston (1937).

In Paul F. Boller, Jr. and John George, *They Never Said It*, Goldwyn's actual words are said to have been, "His verbal contract is worth more than the paper it's written on," referring to movie executive Joseph M. Schenck, who was regarded as completely trustworthy. This was possibly another of the many Goldwynisms cooked up by his own staff.

Contradiction

1   I believe that truth has only one face:
    that of a violent contradiction.

GEORGES BATAILLE, (1897–1962) French novelist, critic. *The Deadman*, preface (1967). Repr. in *Violent Silence*, ed. Paul Buck (1984).

2   But God hath chosen the foolish
    things of the world to confound the
    wise; and God hath chosen the weak
    things of the world to confound the
    things which are mighty.

BIBLE: NEW TESTAMENT, St. Paul, in *1 Corinthians*, 1:27.

3   The test of a first–rate intelligence is
    the ability to hold two opposed ideas
    in the mind at the same time, and
    still retain the ability to function.

F. SCOTT FITZGERALD, (1896–1940) U.S. author. "The Crack–Up," *The Crack–Up*, ed. Edmund Wilson (1945). First published in *Esquire* (New York, Feb. 1936).

4   Yes, they have no bananas.

JULES FURTHMAN, (1888–1960) U.S. screenwriter. The Kid (Thomas Mitchell), in *Only Angels Have Wings* (film) (1939). Directed by Howard Hawks.

Controversy

1   When a thing ceases to be a subject
    of controversy, it ceases to be a sub-
    ject of interest.

WILLIAM HAZLITT, (1778–1830) British essayist." The Spirit of Controversy," *The Atlas* (Jan. 31, 1830). *Complete Works*, vol. 20, ed. by P.P. Howe (1932).

Conversation

1   "The time has come," the Walrus said,
"To talk of many things:
Of shoes and ships and sealing wax
Of cabbages and kings
And why the sea is boiling hot
And whether pigs have wings."

LEWIS CARROLL [CHARLES LUTWIDGE DODGSON], (1832–1898) British writer, mathematician. *Through the Looking-Glass*, "Tweedledum and Twee-dledee" (1872).

Carroll's poem satirized Thomas Hood's *Dream of Eugene Aram.*

2   I find we are growing serious, and then we are in great danger of being dull.

WILLIAM CONGREVE, (1670–1729) British dramatist. Araminta, in *The Old Bachelor*, act 2, sc. 2 (1693).

The conversation turns on the subject of love.

3   And when you stick on conversation's burrs,
Don't strew your pathway with those dreadful urs.

OLIVER WENDELL HOLMES, SR., (1809–1894) U.S. writer, physician. *A Rhymed Lesson* (1848). Repr. in *The Poetical Works of Oliver Wendell Holmes*, ed. Eleanor M. Tilton (1895, rev. 1975).

4   With thee conversing I forget all time.

JOHN MILTON, (1608–1674) British poet. Eve to Adam, in *Paradise Lost*, bk. 4, l. 639 (1667).

5   There is no such thing as conversation. It is an illusion. There are intersecting monologues, that is all.

REBECCA WEST [CICILY ISABEL FAIRFIELD], (1892–1983) British author. *The Harsh Voice*, "There Is No Conversation" (1935).

Conversion

1   Almost thou persuadest me to be a Christian.

BIBLE: NEW TESTAMENT, Agrippa, in *Acts*, 26:28.

Said to Paul.

Cookery

1   First, catch your hare.

ISABELLA BEETON, (1836–1865) British writer on domestic science. *Attributed.*

This famously difficult first stage of a recipe does not appear in Mrs. Beeton's *Book of Household Management* (1859–1860), and was already proverbial when the work was published. A similar phrase, "Take your hare when it is cased [skinned] ....," formed part of a recipe in *The Art of Cookery Made Plain and Easy* (1747) by Hannah Glasse.

2   Life is too short to stuff a mushroom.

SHIRLEY CONRAN, (b. 1932) British designer, journalist. *Superwoman*, epigraph (1975).

3   Kissing don't last: cookery do!

GEORGE MEREDITH, (1828–1909) British author. Mrs. Berry, in *The Ordeal of Richard Feverel*, ch. 28 (1859).

Correspondence

1   Sir, more than kisses, letters mingle souls.
For, thus friends absent speak.

JOHN DONNE, (c. 1572–1631) British divine, metaphysical poet. "Verse Letter to Sir Henry Wotton" (1597–1598). Repr. in *Complete Poetry and Selected Prose*, ed. John Hayward (1929).

Opening lines.

2 They teach the morals of a whore, and the manners of a dancing master.

SAMUEL JOHNSON, (1709–1784) British author, lexicographer. Quoted in James Boswell, *Life of Dr. Johnson*, entry, 1754 (1791).

Referring to Lord Chesterfield's *Letters to His Son*. Of Chesterfield—Johnson's erratic patron—he remarked, "This man I thought had been a Lord among wits; but, I find, he is only a wit among Lords."

Corruption

1 O Rose, thou art sick!
The invisible worm
That flies in the night,
In the howling storm,
Has found out thy bed
Of crimson joy:
And his dark secret love
Does thy life destroy.

WILLIAM BLAKE, (1757–1827) British poet, painter, engraver. *Songs of Experience*, "The Sick Rose" (1794), repr. in *Complete Writings*, ed. Geoffrey Keynes (1957).

2 There was never any thing by the wit of man so well devised, or so sure established, which in continuance of time hath not been corrupted.

BOOK OF COMMON PRAYER, THE, *Preface* (1662).

3 Among a people generally corrupt, liberty cannot long exist.

EDMUND BURKE, (1729–1797) Irish philosopher, statesman. Letter to the Sheriffs of Bristol, April 3, 1777, repr. in *Works*, vol. 2 (1899).

4 Corruption, the most infallible symptom of constitutional liberty.

EDWARD GIBBON, (1737–1794) British historian. *The Decline and Fall of the Roman Empire*, ch. 21 (1776–1788).

5 Let no guilty man escape, if it can be avoided.... No personal considerations should stand in the way of performing a duty.

ULYSSES GRANT, (1822–1885) U.S. general, president. Quoted in *Ulysses S. Grant*, Louis A. Coolidge (1822). Endorsement to letter relating to the Whisky Ring, July 29, 1875.

In fact most of the government officials implicated in the "Whisky Ring" (a group of distillers found to have defrauded the U.S. government) did escape, including Grant's private secretary Orville Babcock; the president may have had a hand in Babcock's acquittal.

6 The sun shineth upon the dunghill, and is not corrupted.

JOHN LYLY, (1554–1606) British author. *Euphues: The Anatomy of Wit*, p. 43 (1579), ed. Edward Arber (1868).

7 People have got to know whether or not their president is a crook. Well, I'm not a crook.

RICHARD NIXON, (1913–1992) U.S. Republican politician, president. *The New York Times* (Nov. 18, 1973). Press conference Nov. 17, 1973.

8 Something is rotten in the state of Denmark.

WILLIAM SHAKESPEARE, (1564–1616) British dramatist, poet. Marcellus, in *Hamlet*, act 1, sc. 4, l. 67 (1604).

9 But the jingling of the guinea helps the hurt that Honour feels.

ALFRED TENNYSON, 1ST BARON TENNYSON, (1809–1892) British poet. "Locksley Hall," l. 105 (1842).

Cosmetics

1 Most women are not so young as they are painted.

MAX BEERBOHM, (1872–1956) British essayist, caricaturist. *The Yellow Book*, vol. 4, "A Defence of Cosmetics" (1895).

Cosmos

1 The Answer to the Great Question ... Of Life, the Universe and Everything ... Is ... Forty–two.

DOUGLAS ADAMS, (b. 1952) British author. The computer Deep Thought, in *The Hitch Hiker's Guide to the Galaxy,* ch. 27 (1979).

2 If we find the answer to that, it would be the ultimate triumph of human reason—for then we would know the mind of God.

STEPHEN HAWKING, (b. 1942) British scientist. *A Brief History of Time,* ch. 11 (1988).

Closing words, referring to the question, "why it is that we and the universe exist."

3 Nothing puzzles me more than time and space; and yet nothing troubles me less, as I never think about them.

CHARLES LAMB, (1775–1834) British essayist, critic. *Letters of Charles and Mary Lamb,* vol. 3, ed. E.W. Marrs (1978). Letter, Jan. 2, 1810, to Thomas Manning.

4 All things by immortal power,
Near and Far
Hiddenly
To each other linked are,
That thou canst not stir a flower
Without troubling of a star.

FRANCIS THOMPSON, (1859–1907) British poet. "The Mistress of Vision," *Poems* (1913).

Countryside

1 I nauseate walking; 'tis a country diversion; I loathe the country.

WILLIAM CONGREVE, (1670–1729) British dramatist. Mrs. Millamant, in *The Way of the World,* act 4, sc. 4 (1700).

2 The lowest and vilest alleys of London do not present a more dreadful record of sin than does the smiling and beautiful countryside.

SIR ARTHUR CONAN DOYLE, (1859–1930) British author. Sherlock Holmes, in *The Adventures of Sherlock Holmes,* "Copper Beeches" (1892).

3 The corn is as high as an elephant's eye,
And it looks like it's climbin' clear up to the sky.

OSCAR HAMMERSTEIN II, (1895–1960) U.S. songwriter. "Oh, What a Beautiful Mornin'" (song), *Oklahoma!* (Stage musical, 1943; film, 1955).

4 There is nothing good to be had in the country, or if there is, they will not let you have it.

WILLIAM HAZLITT, (1778–1830) British essayist. *The Round Table,* "Observations on Wordsworth's *Excursion*" (1819).

5 I have no relish for the country; it is a kind of healthy grave.

SYDNEY SMITH, (1771–1845) British clergyman, writer. *Memoir,* vol. 2, Lady Holland (1855). Letter 1838.

6 The corn was orient and immortal wheat, which never should be reaped, nor was ever sown. I thought it had stood from everlasting to everlasting.

THOMAS TRAHERNE, (1636–1674) British clergyman, poet, mystic. *Centuries,* "Third Century," no. 3 (written c. 1672, first published 1908).

Referring to Traherne's first impressions of the world.

7 Anybody can be good in the country. There are no temptations there.

OSCAR WILDE, (1854–1900) Anglo–Irish playwright, author. Lord Henry, in *The Picture of Dorian Gray,* ch. 19 (1891).

Courage

1 As to moral courage, I have rarely met with two o'clock in the morning courage; I mean instantaneous courage.

NAPOLEON BONAPARTE, (1769–1821) French general, emperor. Quoted in *Mémorial de Sainte Hélène*, vol. 1, pt. 2, E.A. de Las Casas (1823).

Said by Napoleon at the end of December 1815.

2 Courage is almost a contradiction in terms. It means a strong desire to live taking the form of a readiness to die.

GILBERT KEITH CHESTERTON, (1874–1936) British author. *Orthodoxy*, ch. 6 (1909).

3 Grace under pressure.

ERNEST HEMINGWAY, (1899–1961) U.S. author. *The New Yorker* (Nov. 30, 1929).

Definition of "guts," in an interview with Dorothy Parker. The formula was invoked by John F. Kennedy at the start of his collection of essays, *Profiles of Courage* (1956); it possibly originated in the Latin motto, *Fortiter in re, suaviter in modo*.

4 It is not book–learning young men need, nor instruction about this and that, but a stiffening of the vertebrae which will cause them to be loyal to a trust, to act promptly, concentrate their energies: do the thing—"Carry a message to Garcia!"

ELBERT HUBBARD, (1856–1915) U.S. author. "A Message to Garcia," *The Philistine* (March 1899). Repr. in *Respectfully Quoted*, ed. Suzy Platt (1989).

In the Spanish–American War, the Cuban revolutionary leader Calixto Garcîa y L'igues was able to provide vital information to the U.S. army. The task of securing the information, which assumed a mythic importance, was granted by President William Kinley to Lieutenant Rowan.

5 Courage is not simply *one* of the virtues but the form of every virtue at the testing point, which means at the point of highest reality.

C.S. (CLIVE STAPLES) LEWIS, (1898–1963) British author. quoted in *The Unquiet Grave*, pt. 3, Cyril Connolly (1944, rev. 1951).

6 But screw your courage to the sticking–place
And we'll not fail.

WILLIAM SHAKESPEARE, (1564–1616) British dramatist, poet. Lady Macbeth, in *Macbeth*, act 1, sc. 7, l. 60–1 (1623).

Exhorting Macbeth to carry out the murder of Duncan.

7 Fortune favors the brave.

VIRGIL [PUBLIUS VERGILIUS MARO], (70–19 B.C.) Roman poet. Turnus, in *Aeneid*, bk. 10, l. 284 (19 B.C.).

Turnus, King of the Rutulians, fought against and was killed by Aeneas.

8 The idea was to prove at every foot of the way up that you were one of the elected and anointed ones who had *the right stuff* and could move higher and higher and even—ultimately, God willing, one day—that you might be able to join that special few at the very top, that elite who had the capacity to bring tears to men's eyes, the very Brotherhood of the Right Stuff itself.

TOM WOLFE, (b. 1931) U.S. author, journalist. *The Right Stuff*, ch. 2 (1979).

Referring to pilots and astronauts training in the NASA space program.

Courtesy

1 It is wise to apply the oil of refined politeness to the mechanism of friendship.

COLETTE [SIDONIE GABRIELLE COLETTE], (1873–1954) French author. *The Pure and the Impure*, ch. 9 (1933, trans. 1966).

2   There can be no defence like elaborate courtesy.

E.V. (EDWARD VERRALL) LUCAS, (1868–1938) British journalist, essayist. *Reading, Writing and Remembering*, ch. 8 (1932).

Cowardice

1   Cowardice, as distinguished from panic, is almost always simply a lack of ability to suspend the functioning of the imagination.

ERNEST HEMINGWAY, (1899–1961) U.S. author. *Men at War*, introduction (1942).

In *For Whom the Bell Tolls*, ch. 30 (1940), Robert Jordan says of his father, "He was just a coward and that was the worst luck any man could have."

2   I'm a hero wid coward's legs, I'm a hero from the waist up.

SPIKE MILLIGAN, (b. 1918) British comedian, humorous writer. *Puckoon*, ch. 2 (1963).

3   Cowards die many times before their deaths;
The valiant never taste of death but once.

WILLIAM SHAKESPEARE, (1564–1616) British dramatist, poet. Julius Caesar, in *Julius Caesar*, act 2, sc. 2, l. 32–3 (1623).

Caesar disregards objections to his departure on the Ides of March for the Capitol, where he is to be assassinated.

4   My valour is certainly going, it is sneaking off! I feel it oozing out as it were, at the palms of my hands!

RICHARD BRINSLEY SHERIDAN, (1751–1816) Anglo–Irish dramatist. Acres, in *The Rivals*, act 5, sc. 2 (1775).

Cowboys

1   Hi–yo Silver! The Lone Ranger! With his faithful Indian companion, Tonto, the daring and resourceful masked rider of the plains led the fight for law and order in the West.

FRAN STRIKER, U.S. TV scriptwriters. Opening voiceover, in *The Lone Ranger* (radio and TV series).

The show ran for 16 years on radio before making its TV debut in 1949, with Clayton Moore as the Masked Man.

2   Head 'em up, move 'em out, rope 'em in, head 'em off, pull 'em down, move 'em on.

CHARLES MARQUIS WARREN, (b. 1917) U.S. writer, director, producer. *Rawhide* (TV series), created by Charles Marquis Warren (1959–1966).

The series was based on the 1866 diary of drover and pioneer cowboy George Duffield.

Creation, the

1   And Adam said, This is now bone of my bones, and flesh of my flesh: she shall be called Woman, because she was taken out of Man.

BIBLE: HEBREW, *Genesis*, 2:23.

2   And the Lord God formed man of the dust of the ground, and breathed into his nostrils the breath of life; and man became a living soul.

BIBLE: HEBREW, *Genesis*, 2:7.

3   In the beginning God created the heaven and the earth. And the earth was without form, and void; and darkness was upon the face of the deep. And the Spirit of God moved

upon the face of the waters. And
God said, Let there be light: and
there was light.

BIBLE: HEBREW, *Genesis*, 1:1–3.

Opening words of the Bible.

4   Man was kreated a little lower than
the angells and has bin gittin a little
lower ever sinse.

JOSH BILLINGS [HENRY WHEELER
SHAW], (1818–1885) U.S. humorist. *Josh
Billings, His Sayings*, ch. 28 (1865).

5   when god decided to invent
everything he took one
breath bigger than a circustent
and everything began

E.E. (EDWARD ESTLIN) CUMMINGS,
(1894–1962) U.S. poet. "When god decided
to invent," *1 x 1* (1944).

6   When God at first made man,
Having a glass of blessings standing
by;
Let us (said he) pour on him all we
can:
Let the world's riches, which
dispers'd lie,
Contract into a span.

GEORGE HERBERT, (1593–1633) British
poet, clergyman. "The Pulley," *The Temple*
(1633). Repr. in *The Works of George
Herbert*, ed. Helen Gardner (1961).

7   And God stepped out on space,
And He looked around and said,
"I'm lonely—I'll make me a world."

JAMES WELDON JOHNSON,
(1871–1938) U.S. author, poet. *The Creation*,
st. 1 (written and first publ. 1918). Repr. in
God's Trombones (1927).

8   Have We not made the earth as a
cradle and the mountains as pegs?
And We created you in pairs, and
We appointed your sleep for a rest;
and We appointed night for a gar-
ment, and We appointed day for a

livelihood. And We have built
above you seven strong ones, and
We appointed a blazing lamp and
have sent down out of the
rain–clouds water cascading that
We may bring forth thereby grain
and plants, and gardens luxuriant.

QUR'AN, "The Tiding," 78:6–16, trans. by
Arthur J. Arberry (1955).

Creativity

1   A line will take us hours maybe;
Yet if it does not seem a moment's
thought,
Our stitching and unstitching has
been naught.

WILLIAM BUTLER YEATS, (1865–1939)
Irish poet, playwright. "Adam's Curse," st. 1,
In the Seven Woods (1904).

Credulity

1   There's a sucker born every minute.

PHINEAS BARNUM, (1810–1891) U.S.
showman. *Attributed.*

Barnum doubted ever having uttered these
words, though he conceded he may have
said, "The people like to be humbugged." See
the appendix to A.H. Saxon's biography, *P.T.
Barnum: The Legend and the Man* (1989),
where it is claimed that the phrase "There's a
sucker born every minute, but none of them
ever die" originated with a notorious
con–man known as "Paper Collar Joe," (real
name, Joseph Bessimer) and was later falsely
ascribed to Barnum by show–biz rival Adam
Forepaugh in a newspaper interview. Barnum
never took pains to deny it, and even thanked
Forepaugh for the free publicity he had given
him.

2   Never give a sucker an even break.

W.C. FIELDS, (1879–1946) U.S. actor.
Poppy (film) (1936).

Fields is earlier reported to have uttered these
words on stage in the musical *Poppy* (1923),
though the phrase does not appear in the
libretto. Fields made the film *Never Give a*

Sucker an Even Break in 1941. The words have also been attributed to Edward Francis Albee.

3 A little credulity helps one on through life very smoothly.

ELIZABETH GASKELL, (1810–1865) British novelist. Miss Matty, in *Cranford*, ch. 11 (1853).

4 Man is a credulous animal, and must believe *something*; in the absence of good grounds for belief, he will be satisfied with bad ones.

BERTRAND RUSSELL [LORD RUSSELL, 3RD EARL], (1872–1970) British philosopher, mathematician. *Unpopular Essays*, "An Outline of Intellectual Rubbish" (1950).

Creeds

1 Light half–believers of our casual creeds,
Who never deeply felt, nor clearly will'd,
Whose insight never has borne fruit in deeds,
Whose vague resolves never have been fulfill'd.

MATTHEW ARNOLD, (1822–1888) British poet, critic. "The Scholar–Gipsy," l. 172–5 (1853).

2 I believe in one God, the Father almighty, maker of heaven and earth, and of all things visible and invisible.
[*Credo in unum Deum, Patrem omnipotentem, factorem coeli et terrae, visibilium omnium et invisibilium.*]

MISSAL, THE, *The Ordinary of the Mass*, "The Nicene Creed."

The Missal is book of prayers and rites used to celebrate the Roman Catholic mass during the year.

3 The dust of creeds outworn.

PERCY BYSSHE SHELLEY, (1792–1822) British poet. "First Spirit," in *Prometheus Unbound*, act 1, l. 697 (1820).

Crime and Criminals

1 My rackets are run on strictly American lines and they're going to stay that way.

AL CAPONE, (1899–1947) U.S. gangster. "Mr. Capone, Philosopher," *Cockburn Sums Up*, Claud Cockburn (1981). Interview, c. 1930.

2 The Napoleon of Crime.

SIR ARTHUR CONAN DOYLE, (1859–1930) British author. Sherlock Holmes, in *The Memoirs of Sherlock Holmes*, "The Final Problem" (1894).

Referring to "Ex–Professor Moriarty of mathematical celebrity," Holmes's arch–enemy.

3 Successful crimes alone are justified.

JOHN DRYDEN, (1631–1700) British poet, dramatist, critic. *The Medal*, l. 208 (1682).

4 Crimes, like virtues, are their own rewards.

GEORGE FARQUHAR, (1678–1707) Irish dramatist. Oriana, in *The Inconstant*, act 4, sc. 2 (1702). Repr. in *Complete Works*, ed. Charles Stonehill (1930).

5 After all, crime is only a lefthanded form of human endeavor.

JOHN HUSTON, (1906–1987) U.S. filmmaker. Emmerich (played by Louis Calhern), in *The Asphalt Jungle* (1950 film). Huston based on a novel by W.R. Burnett (1950).

6 A burglar who respects his art always takes his time before taking anything else.

O. HENRY [WILLIAM SYDNEY PORTER], (1862–1910) U.S. short–story writer. "Makes the Whole World Kin," *Sixes and Sevens* (1911).

7 From a single crime know the nation.

VIRGIL [PUBLIUS VERGILIUS MARO], (70–19 B.C.) Roman poet. *Aeneid*, bk. 2, l. 65.

8 Almost all crime is due to the repressed desire for aesthetic expression.

EVELYN WAUGH, (1903–1966) British novelist. Prison Governor Sir Wilfred Lucas–Dockery, in *Decline and Fall*, pt. 3, ch. 1 (1928).

Paul Pennyfeather, to whom these words are addressed, has just been informed that he is to be put to work in the Arts and Crafts Workshop.

Crisis

1 The time is out of joint. O curs'd spite
That ever I was born to set it right!

WILLIAM SHAKESPEARE, (1564–1616) British dramatist, poet. Hamlet, in *Hamlet*, act 1, sc. 5, l. 189–90 (1604).

Criticism

1 Why beholdest thou the mote that is in thy brother's eye, but considerest not the beam that is in thine own eye?

BIBLE: NEW TESTAMENT, Jesus, in *Matthew*, 7:3.

From the Sermon on the Mount.

2 In my conscience I believe the baggage loves me, for she never speaks well of me herself, nor suffers any body else to rail at me.

WILLIAM CONGREVE, (1670–1729) British dramatist. Bellmour, in *The Old Bachelor*, act 1, sc. 1 (1693).

Referring to Belinda.

3 Will you tell me my fault, frankly as to yourself, for I had rather wince, than die. Men do not call the surgeon to commend the bone, but to set it, Sir.

EMILY DICKINSON, (1830–1886) U.S. poet. *The Letters of Emily Dickinson*, vol. 2 (1958). Letter, July 1862, to Thomas Wentworth Higginson.

Higginson, an author, critic, and retired Unitarian minister, had received his first letter from Dickinson April 15, 1862, with four poems enclosed; the correspondence continued throughout her life. Higginson, in the role of literary mentor, eventually cooperated in producing a volume of her poems in 1890, though only after making significant textual changes.

Criticism and the Arts

1 Criticism should be a casual conversation.

W.H. (WYSTAN HUGH) AUDEN, (1907–1973) Anglo–American poet. *The Table Talk of W.H. Auden*, "November 16, 1946," comp. Alan Ansen, ed. Nicholas Jenkins (1990).

2 I would rather be attacked than unnoticed. For the worst thing you can do to an author is to be silent as to his works. An assault upon a town is a bad thing; but starving it is still worse.

SAMUEL JOHNSON, (1709–1784) British author, lexicographer. Quoted in James Boswell, *Life of Dr. Johnson*, entry, March 26, 1779 (1791).

3 Praise or blame has but a momentary effect on the man whose love of beauty in the abstract makes

him a severe critic on his own works.

JOHN KEATS, (1795–1821) British poet. *Letters of John Keats,* no. 90, ed. Frederick Page (1954). Letter, Oct. 9, 1818.

Despite Shelley's assertion in his preface to his elegy *Adonais* that Keats had suffered from the savage criticism of *Endymion* (published April 1818)—which, Shelley claimed, "produced the most violent effect on his susceptible mind," and led to Keats' last, fatal illness—Keats himself described *Endymion,* in the same letter quoted above, as "slip–shod": "Had I been nervous about its being a perfect piece, & with that view asked advice, & trembled over every page, it would not have been written."

4   Never trust the artist. Trust the tale. The proper function of a critic is to save the tale from the artist who created it.

D.H. (DAVID HERBERT) LAWRENCE, (1885–1930) British author. *Studies in Classic American Literature,* ch. 1 (1923).

5   When the reviews are bad I tell my staff that they can join me as I cry all the way to the bank.

WLADZIU VALENTINO LIBERACE, (1919–1987) U.S. entertainer. *Liberace: An Autobiography,* ch. 2 (1973).

The words became a regular part of Liberace's stage act from the 1950s.

6   For if there is anything to one's praise, it is foolish vanity to be gratified at it, and if it is abuse— why one is always sure to hear of it from one damned good–natured friend or another!

RICHARD BRINSLEY SHERIDAN, (1751–1816) Anglo–Irish dramatist. Sir Fretful Plagiary, in *The Critic,* act 1, sc. 1, l. 355–7 (1779).

On not reading the reviewers.

7   I never read a book before reviewing it; it prejudices a man so.

SYDNEY SMITH, (1771–1845) British clergyman, writer. Quoted in *The Smith of Smiths,* ch. 3, Hesketh Pearson (1934).

8   In most modern instances, interpretation amounts to the philistine refusal to leave the work of art alone. Real art has the capacity to make us nervous. By reducing the work of art to its content and then interpreting *that,* one tames the work of art. Interpretation makes art manageable, conformable.

SUSAN SONTAG, (b. 1933) U.S. essayist. "Against Interpretation," sct. 5, *Against Interpretation* (1966). Originally published in *Evergreen Review* (New York, Dec. 1964).

9   Of all the cants which are canted in this canting world—though the cant of hypocrites may be the worst—the cant of criticism is the most tormenting!

LAURENCE STERNE, (1713–1768) British author. *Tristram Shandy,* bk. 3, ch. 12 (1759–1767).

10   Writing criticism is to writing fiction and poetry as hugging the shore is to sailing in the open sea.

JOHN UPDIKE, (b. 1932) U.S. author, critic. *Hugging the Shore* (collection of essays), foreword.

Critics

1   A critic is a bundle of biases held loosely together by a sense of taste.

WHITNEY BALLIET, (b. 1926) U.S. author. *Dinosaurs in the Morning,* introductory note (1962).

2   A man must serve his time to every trade
Save censure—critics all are ready made.

GEORGE GORDON NOEL BYRON, 6TH BARON BYRON, (1788–1824) British poet. "English Bards and Scotch Reviewers," l. 63–4 (1809).

3 Though by whim, envy, or resentment led,
They damn those authors whom they never read.

CHARLES CHURCHILL, (1731–1764) British clergyman, poet. "The Candidate," l. 57 (1764).

4 Asking a working writer what he thinks about critics is like asking a lamp–post what it feels about dogs.

CHRISTOPHER HAMPTON, (b. 1946) British playwright. Sunday Times Magazine (London, Oct. 16, 1977).

5 God knows people who are paid to have attitudes toward things, professional critics, make me sick; camp following eunuchs of literature. They won't even whore. They're all virtuous and sterile. And how well meaning and high minded. But they're all camp followers.

ERNEST HEMINGWAY, (1899–1961) U.S. author. Selected Letters, ed. Carlos Baker (1981). Letter, May 23, 1925, to Sherwood Anderson.

6 A louse in the locks of literature.

ALFRED TENNYSON, 1ST BARON TENNYSON, (1809–1892) British poet. Quoted in Life and Letters of Sir Edmund Gosse, ch. 14, Evan Charteris (1931).

Referring to critic J. Churton Collins.

Crowds

1 If it has to choose who is to be crucified, the crowd will always save Barabbas.

JEAN COCTEAU, (1889–1963) French author, filmmaker. Le Coq et l'Arlequin, Le Rappel, L'Ordre (1926), repr. in Collected Works, vol. 9 (1950). (Essay originally published 1918).

Barabbas was the thief and insurrectionary leader reprieved at Christ's crucifixion, following the custom at Passover. (Matthew 27).

Cruelty

1 Come, you spirits
That tend on mortal thoughts, unsex me here,
And fill me from the crown to the toe top–full
Of direst cruelty. Make thick my blood,
Stop up th'access and passage to remorse,
That no compunctious visitings of nature
Shake my fell purpose, nor keep peace between
Th'effect and it. Come to my woman's breasts,
And take my milk for gall, you murd'ring ministers,
Wherever in your sightless substances
You wait on nature's mischief.

WILLIAM SHAKESPEARE, (1564–1616) British dramatist, poet. Lady Macbeth, in Macbeth, act 1, sc. 5, l. 39–49 (1623).

Summoning evil spirits that attend on murderous ("mortal") thoughts.

Crying

1 Oh! too convincing—dangerously dear—
In woman's eye the unanswerable tear!

GEORGE GORDON NOEL BYRON, 6TH BARON BYRON, (1788–1824) British poet. "The Corsair," cto. 2, st. 15 (1814).

2 I wept not, so to stone within I
grew.

DANTE ALIGHIERI, (1265–1321) Italian
poet. "Inferno," cto. 33, l. 49, *The Divine
Comedy* (1321).

Said by Count Ugolino.

3 I have full cause of weeping, but
this heart
Shall break into a hundred thousand flaws
Or ere I'll weep.

WILLIAM SHAKESPEARE, (1564–1616)
British dramatist, poet. Lear, in *King Lear*, act
2, sc. 2, l. 457–9 (1623).

4 Women's weapons, water–drops.

WILLIAM SHAKESPEARE, (1564–1616)
British dramatist, poet. Lear, in *King Lear*, act
2, sc. 2, l. 451 (1623).

Lear, "as full of grief as age," responds to the
treachery of the "unnatural hags" (his daughters, Goneril and Regan): "let not women's
weapons, water–drops, /Stain my man's
cheeks."

Cuba

1 They talk about who won and who
lost. Human reason won. Mankind
won.

NIKITA KHRUSHCHEV, (1894–1971)
Soviet premier. Quoted in *Observer* (London,
Nov. 11, 1962).

Referring to the Cuban missile crisis.

Culture

1 Culture, the acquainting ourselves
with the best that has been known
and said in the world, and thus with
the history of the human spirit.

MATTHEW ARNOLD, (1822–1888) British
poet, critic. *Literature and Dogma*, preface
(1873).

In *Culture and Anarchy*, ch. 1 (1869), Arnold
wrote: "Culture, then, is a study of perfection,
and perfection which insists on becoming
something rather than in having something,
in an inward condition of the mind and spirit,
not in an outward set of circumstances."

2 In the room the women come and
go
Talking of Michelangelo.

T.S. (THOMAS STEARNS) ELIOT,
(1888–1965) Anglo–American poet, critic.
"The Love Song of J. Alfred Prufrock,"
Prufrock and Other Observations (1917).

3 Every day we should hear at least
one little song, read one good
poem, see one exquisite picture,
and, if possible, speak a few sensible words.

JOHANN WOLFGANG VON GOETHE,
(1749–1832) German poet, dramatist. Serlo,
in *Wilhelm Meister's Apprenticeship*, bk. 5,
ch. 1 (1795–1796), trans. by Thomas Carlyle.

4 Letting a hundred flowers blossom
and a hundred schools of thought
contend is the policy for promoting
the progress of the arts and the sciences and a flourishing culture in
our land.

MAO ZEDONG, (1893–1976) Chinese
founder of the People's Republic of China.
Quotations from Chairman Mao Tse–Tung
(1966). Speech, Feb. 27, 1957, Peking.

5 The ideas of the ruling class are in
every epoch the ruling ideas, i.e. the
class which is the ruling *material*
force of society, is at the same time
its ruling *intellectual* force.

KARL MARX, (1818–1883) German political theorist, social philosopher. *The German
Ideology*, pt. 1, sct. B, "Ruling Class and Ruling Ideas" (1846).

The idea was carried into *The Communist
Manifesto*, sct. 2 (1848), written by Marx and
Engels.

6   We know that a man can read Goethe or Rilke in the evening, that he can play Bach and Schubert, and go to his day's work at Auschwitz in the morning.

GEORGE STEINER, (b. 1929) French–born U.S. critic, novelist. *Language and Silence,* preface (1967).

7   Whatever we have got has been by infinite labour, and search, and ranging through every corner of nature; the difference is that instead of dirt and poison, we have rather chosen to fill our hives with honey and wax, thus furnishing mankind with the two noblest of things, which are sweetness and light.

JONATHAN SWIFT, (1667–1745) Anglo–Irish satirist. Aesop, in *The Battle of the Books* (written 1697, published 1704). Repr. in *Jonathan Swift: A Critical Edition of the Major Works*, eds. Angus Ross and David Woolley (1984).

Aesop, representing the Ancients, likened them to a bee, as opposed to the spider which stood for the Moderns. The phrase "sweetness and light" was taken up by critic Matthew Arnold in *Culture and Anarchy* (see perfection).

8   Culture is an instrument wielded by teachers to manufacture teachers, who, in their turn, will manufacture still more teachers.

SIMONE WEIL, (1909–1943) French philosopher, mystic. *The Need For Roots,* pt. 2, "Uprootedness in the Towns" (1949).

Cunning

1   If ye had not plowed with my heifer, ye had not found out my riddle.

BIBLE: HEBREW, Samson, in *Judges,* 14:18.

To the men who had answered his riddle, "Out of the eater came forth meat, and out of the strong came forth sweetness."

2   The weak in courage is strong in cunning.

WILLIAM BLAKE, (1757–1827) British poet, painter, engraver. *The Marriage of Heaven and Hell,* plate 9, "Proverbs of Hell," (c. 1793), repr. in *Complete Writings,* ed. Geoffrey Keynes (1957).

3   With foxes we must play the fox.

THOMAS FULLER, (1654–1734) British physician. *Gnomologia,* no. 5797 (1732).

4   The greatest cunning is to have none at all.

CARL SANDBURG, (1878–1967) U.S. poet. "The People," *Yes* (1936).

Curiosity

1   Be not curious in unnecessary matters: for more things are shewed unto thee than men understand.

APOCRYPHA, *Ecclesiasticus,* 3:23.

2   Where the apple reddens
Never pry—
Lest we lose our Edens,
Eve and I.

ROBERT BROWNING, (1812–1889) British poet. "A Woman's Last Word," st. 5, *Men and Women,* vol. 1 (1855).

Curses

1   Ah! well a–day! what evil looks
Had I from old and young!
Instead of the cross, the Albatross
About my neck was hung.

SAMUEL TAYLOR COLERIDGE, (1772–1834) British poet, critic. "The Rime of the Ancient Mariner," pt. 2, st. 14 (1798).

The Ancient Mariner has killed the albatross, a "pious bird of good omen."

2 She left the web, she left the loom,
  She made three paces through the
    room,
  She saw the water–lily bloom,
  She saw the helmet and the plume,
  She looked down to Camelot.
  Out flew the web and floated wide;
  The mirror cracked from side to
    side;
  "The curse is come upon me,"
    cried
  The Lady of Shalott.

ALFRED TENNYSON, 1ST BARON TEN-NYSON, (1809–1892) British poet. "The Lady of Shalott," pt. 3, st. 5 (1832, rev. 1842).

The Lady of Shalott defies the injunction not to gaze upon the world unless through a mirror, as Lancelot passes.

Customs

1 Custom reconciles us to everything.

EDMUND BURKE, (1729–1797) Irish philosopher, statesman. *The Origin of our Ideas of the Sublime and Beautiful*, pt. 4, sct. 18 (1756).

2 Custom, then, is the great guide of human life.

DAVID HUME, (1711–1776) Scottish philosopher, historian. *An Enquiry Concerning Human Understanding*, sct. 5, pt. 1 (1748).

Summarizes Hume's belief in political obedience arising from habit, as opposed to consent through a "social contract."

3 And to my mind, though I am
    native here
  And to the manner born, it is a
    custom
  More honoured in the breach than
    the observance.

WILLIAM SHAKESPEARE, (1564–1616) British dramatist, poet. Hamlet, in *Hamlet*, act 1, sc. 4, l. 16–18 (1604).

The "custom" was that of fanfares accompanying the king's toast–making.

Cynics

1 Cynic. A blackguard whose faulty vision sees things as they are, not as they ought to be.

AMBROSE BIERCE, (1842–1914) U.S. author. *The Devil's Dictionary* (1881–1906), repr. in *Collected Works of Ambrose Bierce*, vol. 7 (1911).

This collection was given the title *The Cynic's Word Book* for its original 1906 publication, though Bierce's definitions first appeared in newspapers under the more famous name, *The Devil's Dictionary*, the title of the enlarged 1911 edition.

2 Cynicism is cheap—you can buy it at any Monoprix store—it's built into all poor–quality goods.

GRAHAM GREENE, (1904–1991) British novelist. *The Comedians*, pt. 1, ch. 1, sct. 3 (1966).

3 Cynicism is intellectual dandyism without the coxcomb's feathers.

GEORGE MEREDITH, (1828–1909) British author. Clara Middleton, quoting Mr. Whitford, in *The Egoist*, ch. 7 (1879).

Clara adds: "It seems to me that cynics are only happy in making the world as barren to others as they have made it for themselves."

4 Cecil Graham: What is a cynic?
  Lord Darlington: A man who
    knows the price of everything and
    the value of nothing.

OSCAR WILDE, (1854–1900) Anglo–Irish playwright, author. *Lady Windermere's Fan*, act 3 (1893).

The same formula was used in *The Picture of Dorian Gray* (1891) ch. 4: "Nowadays people know the price of everything and the value of nothing."

Damnation

1   Wandering stars, to whom is
reserved the blackness of darkness
for ever.

BIBLE: NEW TESTAMENT, *Jude*, verse
13.

Recalling the Book of Enoch, in which fallen
angels were condemned to be stars.

Dance

1   Heaven—I'm in Heaven—
And my heart beats so that I can
hardly speak;
And I seem to find the happiness I
seek
When we're out together dancing
cheek to cheek.

IRVING BERLIN, (1888–1989) U.S. songwriter. "Cheek to Cheek "(song), *Top Hat*
(film, 1935).

Written for Ginger Rogers and Fred Astaire.

2   On with the dance! let joy be
unconfined;
No sleep till morn, when Youth and
Pleasure meet
To chase the glowing hours with
flying feet.

**GEORGE GORDON NOEL BYRON, 6TH
BARON BYRON,** (1788–1824) British poet.
"Childe Harold's Pilgrimage," cto. 3, st. 2
(1812–1818).

Referring to the grand ball in Brussels interrupted by the start of the Battle of Waterloo.

3   Will you, won't you, will you, won't
you, will you join the dance?
Will you, won't you, will you, won't
you, won't you join the dance?

**LEWIS CARROLL [CHARLES
LUTWIDGE DODGSON],** (1832–1898)
British author, mathematician. The Mock Turtle's song, in *Alice's Adventures in Wonderland*, "The Lobster Quadrille" (1865).

4   Dance then wherever you may be,
I am the Lord of the Dance, said he,
And I'll lead you all, wherever you
may be
And I'll lead you all in the dance,
said he.

SYDNEY CARTER, (b. 1915) British songwriter. "Lord of the Dance," *Nine Carols or
Ballads* (1967).

5   How inimitably graceful children
are in general before they learn to
dance!

SAMUEL TAYLOR COLERIDGE,
(1772–1834) British poet, critic. *Table Talk*,
"1 Jan. 1832," *Specimens of the Table Talk of
Samuel Taylor Coleridge*, ed. Henry Nelson
Coleridge (1835). Repr. in *Collected Works*,
vol. 14, ed. Kathleen Coburn (1990).

6   The real American type can never
be a ballet dancer. The legs are too
long, the body too supple and the
spirit too free for this school of
affected grace and toe walking.

ISADORA DUNCAN, (1878–1927) U.S.
dancer. *My Life*, ch. 30 (1927).

7   We look at the dance to impart the
sensation of living in an affirmation
of life, to energize the spectator
into keener awareness of the vigor,
the mystery, the humor, the variety,
and the wonder of life. This is the
function of the American dance.

MARTHA GRAHAM, (1894–1991) U.S.
dancer, choreographer. "The American
Dance," *Modern Dance*, ed. Virginia Stewart
(1935).

8   Stately as a galleon, I sail across the
floor,
Doing the military two–step, as in
the days of yore.

JOYCE GRENFELL, (1910–1979) British
actress, writer. "Stately as a Galleon" (song),
Stately as a Galleon (1977).

9   My men, like satyrs grazing on the
     lawns,
     Shall with their goat feet dance an
     antic hay.

CHRISTOPHER MARLOWE, (1564–1593)
British dramatist, poet. Piers Gaveston, in
Edward II, act 1, sc. 1 (1593).

"Antic hay" refers to a playful dance.

10   Dancing is a wonderful training for
     girls, it's the first way you learn to
     guess what a man is going to do
     before he does it.

CHRISTOPHER MORLEY, (1890–1957)
U.S. novelist, journalist, poet. *Kitty Foyle*, ch.
11 (1939).

Dandies and Dandyism

1   The dandy should aspire to be
     uninterruptedly sublime. He
     should live and sleep in front of a
     mirror.

CHARLES BAUDELAIRE, (1821–1867)
French poet. *My Heart Laid Bare, Intimate
Journals*, sct. 27 (1887), trans. by Christopher
Isherwood (1930), rev. Don Bachardy (1989).

2   I cannot talk with civet in the
     room,
     A fine puss–gentleman that's all
     perfume.

WILLIAM COWPER, (1731–1800) British
poet. "Conversation," l. 283–4 (1782). Repr.
in *Poetical Works*, ed. H.S. Milford (1934).

Danger

1   But oh, beamish nephew, beware of
     the day,
     If your Snark be a Boojum! for then
     You will softly and suddenly vanish
     away,
     And never be met with again!

LEWIS CARROLL [CHARLES
LUTWIDGE DODGSON], (1832–1898)
British author, mathematician. *The Hunting of
the Snark*, "Fit 3: The Baker's Tale" (1876).

2   Out of this nettle danger we pluck
     this flower safety.

WILLIAM SHAKESPEARE, (1564–1616)
British dramatist, poet. Hotspur, in *Henry IV,
pt. 1*, act 2, sc. 4, l. 9–10 (1598).

Daughters

1   Oh my son's my son till he gets him
     a wife,
     But my daughter's my daughter all
     her life.

DINAH MULOCK CRAIK, (1826–1887)
British writer, poet. "Young and Old."

Days

1   All moanday, tearsday, wailsday,
     thumpsday, frightday, shatterday
     till the fear of the Law.

JAMES JOYCE, (1882–1941) Irish author.
Finnegans Wake, pt. 2 (1939).

2   What are days for?
     Days are where we live.
     They come, they wake us
     Time and time over.
     They are to be happy in:
     Where can we live but days?

PHILIP LARKIN, (1922–1986) British poet.
"Days," st. 1, *The Whitsun Weddings* (1964).
Written Aug. 3, 1953.

Dead, the

1   Man is a noble animal, splendid in
     ashes, and pompous in the grave.

THOMAS BROWNE, (1605–1682) British
doctor, author. *Urn Burial*, ch. 5 (1658).

2   An orphan's curse would drag to
    hell
    A spirit from on high;
    But oh! more horrible than that
    Is a curse in a dead man's eye!

    SAMUEL TAYLOR COLERIDGE,
    (1772–1834) British poet, critic. "The Rime of
    the Ancient Mariner," pt. 4, st. 9 (1798).

3   He'd make a lovely corpse.

    CHARLES DICKENS, (1812–1870) British
    novelist. Mrs. Gamp, in *Martin Chuzzlewit*,
    ch. 25 (1843–1844).

    Mrs. Gamp, the "night–nurse," referring to her
    patient.

4   And what the dead had no speech
        for, when living,
    They can tell you, being dead: the
        communication
    Of the dead is tongued with fire
        beyond the language of the living.

    T.S. (THOMAS STEARNS) ELIOT,
    (1888–1965) Anglo–American poet, critic.
    "Little Gidding," pt. 1, *Four Quartets* (1942).

5   Felix Randal the farrier, O he is
        dead then? My duty all is ended,
    Who have watched his mould of
        man, big–boned and hardy–hand-
        some,
    Pining, pining, till time when rea-
        son rambled in it and some
    Fatal four disorders, fleshed there,
        all contended?

    GERARD MANLEY HOPKINS,
    (1844–1889) British poet, Jesuit priest. "Felix
    Randal," *Poems* (1918).

6   The tumult and the shouting dies;
    The Captains and the Kings depart:
    Still stands Thine ancient sacrifice,
    An humble and a contrite heart.
    Lord God of Hosts, be with us yet,
    Lest we forget—lest we forget!

    RUDYARD KIPLING, (1865–1936) British
    writer, poet. "Recessional," st. 2 (1897). Repr.

in *The Definitive Edition of Rudyard Kipling's
Verse* (1940).

"Lest we forget" was adopted as an epitaph by
the War Graves Commission—for which
Kipling worked—after World War I.

7   Lie lightly on her, turf and dew:
    She put so little weight on you.

    MARCUS VALERIUS MARTIAL, (c.
    40–104) Spanish–born Roman poet, epigram-
    matist. *Epigrams*, bk. 5, no. 34.

    Referring to the death of a little girl of six, and
    parodied in the epitaph for Vanbrugh, the
    architect of Blenheim Palace, "Lie heavy on
    him, earth! For he Laid many heavy loads on
    thee."

8   Either he's dead or my watch has
    stopped.

    GROUCHO MARX, (1895–1977) U.S.
    comic actor. *A Day at the Races* (film) (1937),
    screenplay by Robert Pirosh, George Seaton
    and George Oppenheimer.

9   May they rest in peace.
    [*Requiescant in pace.*]

    MISSAL, THE, Order of Mass for the Dead.

    The Missal is book of prayers and rites used to
    celebrate the Roman Catholic mass during the
    year.

10 This parrot is no more! It has
    ceased to be! It's expired and gone
    to meet its maker! This is a late par-
    rot! It's a stiff!... THIS IS AN
    EX–PARROT!

    MONTY PYTHON'S FLYING CIRCUS,
    Monty Python's Flying Circus (TV series),
    episode 8 (series first broadcast 1969–1974).

    John Cleese, in *Dead Parrot Sketch*. Monty
    Python episodes were written and performed
    by Graham Chapman (1941–1989); John
    Cleese (b. 1939); Terry Gilliam (b. 1940); Eric
    Idle (b. 1943); Terry Jones (b. 1942); and
    Michael Palin (b. 1943).

11 How do they know?

    DOROTHY PARKER, (1893–1967) U.S.
    humorous writer. Quoted in *Writers at Work*,
    First Series, ed. Malcolm Cowley (1958).

Remark on hearing the announcement that Calvin Coolidge had died (1933).

12 After life's fitful fever he sleeps well.
Treason has done his worst. Nor
   steel nor poison,
Malice domestic, foreign levy,
   nothing
Can touch him further.

WILLIAM SHAKESPEARE, (1564–1616) British dramatist, poet. Macbeth, in *Macbeth*, act 3, sc. 2, l. 25–8 (1623).

Referring to Duncan.

13 He has outsoared the shadow of
   our night;
Envy and calumny and hate and
   pain,
And that unrest which men miscall
   delight,
Can touch him not and torture not
   again;
From the contagion of the world's
   slow stain
He is secure, and now can never
   mourn
A heart grown cold, a head grown
   grey in vain.

PERCY BYSSHE SHELLEY, (1792–1822) British poet. "Adonais," st. 40 (1821).

Written for poet John Keats, died aged 25.

14 Illiterate him, I say, quite from your
memory.... There is nothing on
earth so easy as to *forget,* if a person
chooses to set about it. I'm sure I
have as much forgot your poor,
dear uncle, as if he had never
existed—and I thought it my duty
to do so.

RICHARD BRINSLEY SHERIDAN, (1751–1816) Anglo–Irish dramatist. Mrs. Malaprop, in *The Rivals*, act 1, sc. 2 (1775).

The first appearance of Mrs. Malaprop in the play, which is peppered with her "malapropisms." Her name is from the French, *mal à propos,* or "inappropriate."

15 To the living we owe respect, but to
the dead we owe only the truth.

VOLTAIRE [FRANÇOIS MARIE AROUET], (1694–1778) French philosopher, author. *Première Lettre sur Oedipe,* preface (footnote) (2nd edition, 1719). *Works,* vol. 1 (1785).

16 No motion has she now, no force;
She neither hears nor sees;
Rolled round in earth's diurnal
   course,
With rocks, and stones, and trees.

WILLIAM WORDSWORTH, (1770–1850) British poet. "A Slumber Did My Spirit Seal," st. 2 (1800).

This verse has been the subject of a literary dispute centering on Wordsworth's pantheism: is the death of the girl (Lucy) terrible because she is as inanimate as the earth's inert objects, or consoling because she is one with nature?

Death and Dying

1 See in what peace a Christian can
die.

JOSEPH ADDISON, (1672–1719) British essayist. Quoted in *Conjectures on Original Composition,* Edward Young (1759), ed. Edith Morley (1918).

Dying words.

2 It's not that I'm afraid to die, I just
don't want to be there when it happens.

WOODY ALLEN, (b. 1935) U.S. filmmaker. *Without Feathers,* "Death (A Play)," (1976).

3 Truth sits upon the lips of dying
men.

MATTHEW ARNOLD, (1822–1888) British poet, critic. "Sohrab and Rustum," l. 656 (1853).

4 It is as natural to die as to be born;
and to a little infant, perhaps, the
one is as painful as the other.

FRANCIS BACON, (1561–1626) British philosopher, essayist, statesman. *Essays,* "Of Death" (1597–1625).

5   To die will be an awfully big adventure.

J.M. (JAMES MATTHEW) BARRIE, (1860–1937) British playwright. Peter, in *Peter Pan,* act 3 (performed 1904, published 1928).

Closing words of play.

6   And I looked, and behold a pale horse: and his name that sat on him was Death.

BIBLE: NEW TESTAMENT, St. John the Divine, in *Revelation,* 6:8.

7   Lord, make me to know mine end, and the measure of my days, what it is; that I may know how frail I am.

BIBLE: HEBREW, *Psalms,* 39:4.

8   O death, where is thy sting? O grave, where is thy victory?

BIBLE: NEW TESTAMENT, St. Paul, in *1 Corinthians,* 15:55.

9   The last enemy that shall be destroyed is death.

BIBLE: NEW TESTAMENT, St. Paul, in *1 Corinthians,* 15:26.

10   Yea, though I walk through the valley of the shadow of death, I will fear no evil: for thou art with me; thy rod and thy staff they comfort me.

BIBLE: HEBREW, *Psalms,* 23:4.

11   We all labour against our own cure, for death is the cure of all diseases.

THOMAS BROWNE, (1605–1682) British doctor, author. *Religio Medici,* pt. 2, ch. 9 (1643).

12   For 'tis not in mere death that men die most.

ELIZABETH BARRETT BROWNING, (1806–1861) British poet. *Aurora Leigh,* bk. 3, l. 12 (1857).

13   To live in hearts we leave behind
Is not to die.

THOMAS CAMPBELL, (1777–1844) Scottish poet. "Hallowed Ground," (1825). Repr. in *Complete Poetical Works,* ed. J.L. Robertson (1907).

14   He had been, he said, an unconscionable time dying; but he hoped that they would excuse it.

KING CHARLES II, (1630–1685) British King of Great Britain. Quoted in *History of England,* vol. 1, ch. 4, Lord Macaulay (1849).

See also last words.

15   This world nys but a thurghfare
ful of wo,
And we been pilgrymes, passynge to
and fro;
Deeth is an ende of every worldly
soore.

GEOFFREY CHAUCER, (1340–1400) British poet. *The Canterbury Tales,* Egeus, in "The Knight's Tale," l. 2847–9 (c. 1387–1400), repr. in *The Works of Geoffrey Chaucer,* ed. Alfred W. Pollard, et al. (1898).

16   Death is a displaced name for a linguistic predicament.

PAUL DE MAN, (1919–1983) Belgian–born U.S. literary critic. Quoted in *Signs of the Times,* ch. 4, David Lehman (1991).

Lehman called this, "the ultimate statement of the deconstructive credo."

17   Because I could not stop for
Death—
He kindly stopped for me—
The Carriage held but just Ourselves—
And Immortality.

EMILY DICKINSON, (1830–1886) U.S. poet. "Because I Could Not Stop for Death," st. 1 (written c. 1863, published 1890). Repr. in *The Complete Poems,* no. 712, Harvard *variorum* edition (1955).

18 As virtuous men pass mildly away,
And whisper to their souls to go,
Whilst some of their sad friends do
   say
The breath goes now, and some say
   no.

JOHN DONNE, (c. 1572–1631) British divine,
metaphysical poet. "Valediction: Forbidding
Mourning," *Songs and Sonnets* (1633). Repr. in
Complete Poetry and Selected Prose, ed. John
Hayward (1929).

19 Death, be not proud, though some
   have called thee
Mighty and dreadful, for thou art
   not so,
For, those, whom thou think'st, thou
   dost overthrow,
Die not, poor death, nor yet canst
   thou kill me.

JOHN DONNE, (c. 1572–1631) British divine,
metaphysical poet. "Death Be Not Proud," *Holy
Sonnets* (1609). Repr. in *Complete Poetry and
Selected Prose*, ed. John Hayward (1929).

20 When one man dies, one chapter is
not torn out of the book, but translated into a better language.

JOHN DONNE, (c. 1572–1631) British divine,
metaphysical poet. *Devotions Upon Emergent
Occasions*, meditation 17 (1624). Repr. in *Complete Poetry and Selected Prose*, ed. John Hayward (1929).

21 Like pilgrims to th'appointed place
   we tend;
The world's an inn, and death the
   journey's end.

JOHN DRYDEN, (1631–1700) British poet,
dramatist, critic. Egeus, in *Palamon and Arcite*,
bk. 3, l. 887–8 (1700).

Dryden's dramatic poem was adapted from
Chaucer's *Knight's Tale*.

22 Death destroys a man: the idea of
Death saves him.

E.M. (EDWARD MORGAN) FORSTER,
(1879–1970) British novelist, essayist. Helen
Schlegel, in *Howards End*, ch. 27 (1927).

23 This is the end, the redemption
from Wilderness, way for the Won-
derer, House sought for All, black
handkerchief washed clean by
weeping—page beyond Psalm—
Last change of mine and Naomi—
to God's perfect Darkness— Death,
stay thy phantoms!

ALLEN GINSBERG, (b. 1926) U.S. poet.
"Kaddish," sct. 1, *Kaddish and Other Poems*
(1960).

24 Death's at the bottom of everything, Martins. Leave death to the
professionals.

GRAHAM GREENE, (1904–1991) British
novelist. Major Calloway (Trevor Howard), in
The Third Man (film) (1950).

25 We sometimes congratulate ourselves at the moment of waking
from a troubled dream; it may be
so the moment after death.

NATHANIEL HAWTHORNE,
(1804–1864) U.S. author. *Passages from the
American Notebooks* (1868). Journal entry,
Oct. 25, 1836.

26 Death cancels everything but truth;
and strips a man of everything but
genius and virtue. It is a sort of natural canonization. It makes the
meanest of us sacred—it installs the
poet in his immortality, and lifts
him to the skies.

WILLIAM HAZLITT, (1778–1830) British
essayist. *The Spirit of the Age*, "Lord Byron"
(1825).

Referring to the death of Byron.

27 Turn up the lights; I don't want to
go home in the dark.

O. HENRY [WILLIAM SYDNEY
PORTER], (1862–1910) U.S. short–story
writer. Quoted in *O. Henry Biography*, ch. 9,
Charles Alphonso Smith (1916).

Last words, quoting a 1907 song by Harry
Williams.

28 I will be conquered; I will not capitulate.

SAMUEL JOHNSON, (1709–1784) British author, lexicographer. Quoted in James Boswell, *Life of Dr. Johnson,* entry, Nov. 1784 (1791).

In his last illness.

29 It matters not how a man dies, but how he lives. The act of dying is not of importance, it lasts so short a time.

SAMUEL JOHNSON, (1709–1784) British author, lexicographer. Quoted in James Boswell, *Life of Dr. Johnson,* entry, Oct. 26, 1769 (1791).

30 Teach me to live that I may dread The grave as little as my bed.

THOMAS KEN, (1637–1711) British churchman, hymn–writer. "Evening Hymn," st. 3 (1695).

31 Death never takes the wise man by surprise,
He is always ready to go.

JEAN DE LA FONTAINE, (1621–1695) French poet, fabulist. "La Mort et le Mourant," bk. 8, *Fables* (1678–1679).

32 We are all dead men on leave.

EUGENE LEVINÉ, Russian Jew, friend of Rosa Luxemburg's lover, Jogiches. Quoted in *Men in Dark Times,* "Rosa Luxemburg: 1871–1919," sct. 3, Hannah Arendt (1968).

33 A man's dying is more the survivors' affair than his own.

THOMAS MANN, (1875–1955) German author, critic. *The Magic Mountain,* ch. 6, "A Soldier, And Brave," (1924), trans. by H.T. Lowe–Porter (1928).

34 The grave's a fine and private place, But none, I think, do there embrace.

ANDREW MARVELL, (1621–1678) British metaphysical poet. "To His Coy Mistress," l. 31–2 (written c. 1650, published 1681).

35 Whom the gods love dies young.

MENANDER, (c. 342–c. 291 B.C.) Greek playwright. *The Double Deceiver,* fragment 25, *Menandri Reliquiae Selectae,* ed. F.H. Sandbach (1990).

36 Death devours all lovely things; Lesbia with her sparrow Shares the darkness—presently Every bed is narrow.

EDNA ST. VINCENT MILLAY, (1892–1950) U.S. poet. "Passer Mortuus Est," *Second April* (1921).

37 A man should ever, as much as in him lieth, be ready booted to take his journey.

MICHEL DE MONTAIGNE, (1533–1592) French essayist. *Essays,* bk. 1, ch. 19 (1580), trans. by John Florio (1603).

Referring to the possibility of death.

38 I want Death to find me planting my cabbages, neither worrying about it nor the unfinished gardening.

MICHEL DE MONTAIGNE, (1533–1592) French essayist. *Essays,* bk. 1, ch. 20 (1580).

39 Dying
Is an art, like everything else.
I do it exceptionally well.
I do it so it feels like hell.
I do it so it feels real.
I guess you could say I've a call.

SYLVIA PLATH, (1932–1963) U.S. poet. "Lady Lazarus," *Encounter* (London, Oct. 1963). *Ariel* (1965).

40 Good God! how often are we to die before we go quite off this stage? In every friend we lose a part of ourselves, and the best part.

ALEXANDER POPE, (1688–1744) British satirical poet. *The Correspondence of Alexander Pope,* vol. 3, ed. George Sherburn (1956). Letter, Dec. 5, 1732, to poet and author Jonathan Swift.

Written the day after the death of playwright John Gay.

41   When I am dead, my dearest,
      Sing no sad songs for me;
      Plant thou no roses at my head,
      Nor shady cypress tree:
      Be the green grass above me
      With showers and dewdrops wet;
      And if thou wilt, remember,
      And if thou wilt, forget.

CHRISTINA ROSSETTI, (1830–1894)
British poet, lyricist. "Song: 'When I am
Dead'," st. 1 (written 1848), published in
Goblin Market, and Other Poems (1862).

42   Ay, but to die, and go we know not
          where;
      To lie in cold obstruction, and to
          rot;
      This sensible warm motion to
          become
      A kneaded clod, and the dilated
          spirit
      To bathe in fiery floods, or to reside
      In thrilling region of thick–ribb'd
          ice;
      To be imprisoned in the viewless
          winds,
      And blown with restless violence
          round about
      The pendent world; or to be worse
          than worst
      Of those that lawless and incertain
          thought
      Imagine howling—'tis too horrible!
      The weariest and most loath'd
          worldly life
      That age, ache, penury, and impris-
          onment
      Can lay on nature is a paradise
      To what we fear of death.

WILLIAM SHAKESPEARE, (1564–1616)
British dramatist, poet. Claudio, in *Measure
for Measure*, act 3, sc.1, l. 118–32 (1623).

43   But I will be

      A bridegroom in my death, and run
          into't
      As to a lover's bed.

WILLIAM SHAKESPEARE, (1564–1616)
British dramatist, poet. Antony, in *Antony and
Cleopatra*, act 4, sc. 15, l. 99–101 (1623).

Defeated and dishonored by Octavius Caesar,
Antony longs to join Cleopatra, whom he
believes to be dead, though he botches his act
of suicide.

44   He that dies pays all debts.

WILLIAM SHAKESPEARE, (1564–1616)
British dramatist, poet. Stefano, in *The Tempest*, act 3, sc. 2, l. 134 (1623).

45   Men must endure
      Their going hence even as their
          coming hither.
      Ripeness is all.

WILLIAM SHAKESPEARE, (1564–1616)
British dramatist, poet. Edgar, in *King Lear*, act
5, sc. 2, l. 9 (1623).

Addressed to his father Gloucester, who
wishes only for death.

46   Nothing in his life
      Became him like the leaving it. He
          died
      As one that had been studied in his
          death
      To throw away the dearest thing he
          owed
      As 'twere a careless trifle.

WILLIAM SHAKESPEARE, (1564–1616)
British dramatist, poet. Malcolm, in *Macbeth*,
act 1, sc. 4, l. 7–11 (1623).

Referring to Cawdor.

47   To die, to sleep—
      No more, and by a sleep to say we
          end
      The heartache and the thousand
          natural shocks
      That flesh is heir to—'tis a consum-
          mation
      Devoutly to be wished. To die, to
          sleep.

To sleep, perchance to dream. Ay,
there's the rub,
For in that sleep of death what
dreams may come
When we have shuffled off this
mortal coil
Must give us pause.

WILLIAM SHAKESPEARE, (1564–1616)
British dramatist, poet. Hamlet, in *Hamlet*, act
3, sc. 1, l. 62–70 (1604).

Part of Hamlet's meditative soliloquy on the
question of "To be, or not to be." Sleep was
proverbially the image of death; "rub" means
snag (a term from the game of bowls); "coil"
means turmoil.

48   Death is the veil which those who
live call life:
They sleep, and it is lifted.

PERCY BYSSHE SHELLEY, (1792–1822)
British poet. The earth, in *Prometheus
Unbound*, act 3, sc. 3 (1820).

in 1818, two years before the publication of
this work, Shelley started an untitled sonnet,
"Lift not the painted veil which those who
live/ Call Life ...."

49   Twilight and evening bell,
And after that the dark!
And may there be no sadness of
farewell,
When I embark.

**ALFRED TENNYSON, 1ST BARON TEN-
NYSON,** (1809–1892) British poet. "Crossing
the Bar," st. 3, *Demeter and Other Poems*
(1889).

Tennyson's last poem describes a crossing
made from Lymington to the Isle of Wight,
where he lived; the poet requested his publisher to include the stanzas at the end of each
section of his works.

50   Do not go gentle into that good
night,
Old age should burn and rage at
close of day;
Rage, rage, against the dying of the
light.

DYLAN THOMAS, (1914–1953) Welsh
poet. "Do Not Go Gentle into that Good
Night," *Collected Poems* (1952).

51   Though lovers be lost love shall not;
And death shall have no dominion.

DYLAN THOMAS, (1914–1953) Welsh
poet. "And Death Shall Have No Dominion,"
25 Poems (1936).

St. Paul used these words in Romans 6:9,
"Christ being raised form the dead dieth no
more; death hath no more dominion over
him."

52   Whoever has lived long enough to
find out what life is, knows how
deep a debt of gratitude we owe to
Adam, the first great benefactor of
our race. He brought death into the
world.

**MARK TWAIN [SAMUEL LANGHORNE
CLEMENS],** (1835–1910) U.S. author. *Pud-
d'nhead Wilson*, ch. 3, "Pudd'nhead Wilson's
Calendar" (1894).

Twain offered further thanks to Adam in *Following the Equator*, ch. 33 (1897): "Let us be
grateful to Adam, our benefactor. He cut us
out of the 'blessing' of idleness and won for us
the 'curse' of labor."

53   I know death hath ten thousand
several doors
For men to take their exits.

JOHN WEBSTER, (1580–1625) British
dramatist. The Duchess, in *The Duchess of
Malfi*, act 4, sc. 2, l. 219–20 (1623). Repr. in
The Complete Works of John Webster, ed. F.L.
Lucas (1927).

See Swift on books.

54   Come lovely and soothing death,
Undulate round the world, serenely
arriving, arriving,
In the day, in the night, to all, to
each,
Sooner or later, delicate death.

WALT WHITMAN, (1819–1892) U.S.
poet. "When Lilacs Last in the Dooryard
Bloomed," st. 14 (1881).

55 Against you I will fling myself,
    unvanquished and unyielding, O
    Death!

VIRGINIA WOOLF, (1882–1941) British
novelist. Bernard, in *The Waves* (1931).

Final words of the novel, chosen by her husband Leonard Woolf as her epitaph at her burial–place and former home, Monk's House,
Rodmell, Sussex, England. Virginia Woolf
committed suicide by drowning March 28,
1941.

56 The good die first
    And they whose hearts are dry as
        summer dust
    Burn to the socket.

WILLIAM WORDSWORTH, (1770–1850)
British poet. the old man, in "The Ruined Cottage," l. 77–9, part of *The Excursion*, bk. 1
(1814).

Debauchery

1 They were as fed horses in the
   morning: every one neighed after
   his neighbour's wife.

BIBLE: HEBREW, *Jeremiah,* 5:8.

Referring to the corruption of morals in
Jerusalem.

2 I may not here omit those two main
   plagues, and common dotages of
   human kind, wine and women,
   which have infatuated and besotted
   myriads of people. They go commonly together.

ROBERT BURTON, (1577–1640) British
clergyman, author. *The Anatomy of Melancholy,* pt. 1, sct. 2, memb. 3, subsct. 13
(1621).

3 My problem lies in reconciling my
   gross habits with my net income.

ERROL FLYNN, (1909–1959) U.S. screen
actor. Quoted in *Great Lovers of the Movies,*
"Errol Flynn," Jane Mercer (1975).

Debt

1 Well, they hired the money, didn't
   they?

CALVIN COOLIDGE, (1872–1933) U.S.
Republican politician, president. Quoted in
The Wit and Wisdom of Calvin Coolidge, ed.
John H. McKee (1933). Comment, 1925.

On a proposal to restructure European war
debts. in *They Never Said It* (Paul F. Boller, Jr.
and John George, 1989), it is noted that
Coolidge's biographer, Claud M. Fuess, failed
to find any evidence that Coolidge spoke
these words, though his wife observed, "I
don't know whether he said it, but it is just
what he might have said."

2 In the midst of life we are in debt.

ETHEL WATTS MUMFORD,
(1878–1940) U.S. novelist, humorous writer.
The Altogether New Cynic's Calendar (1907).

The line parodies *The Book of Common
Prayer* (See life and death.).

3 To John I owed great obligation;
   But John, unhappily, thought fit
   To publish it to all the nation:
   Sure John and I are more than quit.

MATTHEW PRIOR, (1664–1721) British
poet, diplomat. "EpigramAnother," *Poems*
(1718). Repr. in *The Writings of Matthew
Prior* (1905).

Decay

1 For the world hath lost his youth,
   and the times begin to wax old.

APOCRYPHA, *2 Esdras,* 14:10.

2 Thy decay
   Is still impregnate with divinity.

**GEORGE GORDON NOEL BYRON, 6TH
BARON BYRON,** (1788–1824) British poet.
"Childe Harold's Pilgrimage," cto. 4, st. 55
(1812–1818).

Referring to Italy.

3 All human things are subject to
   decay,
   And when fate summons, mon-
   archs must obey.

   JOHN DRYDEN, (1631–1700) British poet,
   dramatist, critic. "Mac Flecknoe," l. 1–2
   (1682).

Deception

1 You may fool all the people some of
   the time; you can even fool some of
   the people all the time; but you
   can't fool all of the people all the
   time.

   ABRAHAM LINCOLN, (1809–1865) U.S.
   president. Quoted in *"Abe" Lincoln's Yarns
   and Stories*, p. 184, Alexander McClure
   (1904).

   The famous aphorism has also been attributed
   to the showman Phineas T. Barnum.

2 For I have sworn thee fair, and
   thought thee bright,
   Who art as black as hell, as dark as
   night.

   WILLIAM SHAKESPEARE, (1564–1616)
   British dramatist, poet. "Sonnet 151" (1609).

Decisions

1 Let your yea be yea; and your nay,
   nay.

   BIBLE: NEW TESTAMENT, *James,* 5:12.

2 The die is cast.

   **GAIUS CAESAR [GAIUS JULIUS CAE-
   SAR],** (100–44 B.C.) Roman general,
   emperor. *Parallel Lives,* "Caesar," sct. 32,
   Plutarch.

   Julius Caesar on crossing the Rubicon in 49
   B.C., an action which provoked the start of
   the first Civil War.

Decolonization

1 Many politicians of our time are in
   the habit of laying it down as a
   self–evident proposition that no
   people ought to be free till they are
   fit to use their freedom. The maxim
   is worthy of the fool in the old story
   who resolved not to go into the
   water until he had learnt to swim. If
   men are to wait for liberty till they
   become wise and good in slavery,
   they may indeed wait forever.

   THOMAS BABINGTON MACAULAY,
   (1800–1859) British historian, Whig politician.
   "Milton," *Edinburgh Review* (Aug. 1825). *Critical and Historical Essays* (1843).

Decorum

1 Let them cant about decorum
   Who have characters to lose!

   ROBERT BURNS, (1759–1796) Scottish
   poet. "The Jolly Beggars," (1799). Repr. in
   Poetical Works, vol. 2, ed. William Scott Douglas (1891).

2 Impropriety is the soul of wit.

   W. SOMERSET MAUGHAM, (1874–1965)
   British author. *The Moon and Sixpence,* ch. 4
   (1919).

Defeat

1 I give the fight up: let there be an
   end,
   A privacy, an obscure nook for me.
   I want to be forgotten even by God.

   ROBERT BROWNING, (1812–1889) British
   poet. "Paracelsus," pt. 5, l. 363–5 (1835).

2 Victory has a hundred fathers but
   defeat is an orphan.

GALEAZZO CIANO, (1903–1944) Italian Fascist leader. *Diario 1939–1943* (1946). Journal entry, Sept. 9, 1942.

President Kennedy is credited with the same comment in the wake of the Bay of Pigs invasion, April 1961.

3   Man is not made for defeat. A man can be destroyed but not defeated.

ERNEST HEMINGWAY, (1899–1961) U.S. author. *The Old Man and the Sea* (1952).

Quoted at the end of A.E. Hotchner's biography, *Papa Hemingway* (1966 edition).

4   For by superior energies; more
         strict
     Affiance in each other; faith more
         firm
     In their unhallowed principles, the
         bad
     Have fairly earned a victory o'er the
         weak,
     The vacillating, inconsistent good.

WILLIAM WORDSWORTH, (1770–1850) British poet. "The Excursion," bk. 4, l. 305–9 (1814).

Defense

1   Self–defence is Nature's eldest law.

JOHN DRYDEN, (1631–1700) British poet, dramatist, critic. "Absalom and Achitophel," pt. 1, l. 458 (1681).

Defiance

1   And yet ... it moves!
     (Eppursi muove!)

GALILEI GALILEO, (1564–1642) Italian astronomer, mathematician, physicist. Quoted in *Querelles littéraires*, vol. 3, Abbé Irailh (1761).

Allegedly muttered to a companion in 1633, as Galileo rose from signing a recantation—forced on him by the Inquisition in Rome—of the Copernican theory that the sun, not the earth, was the center of the solar system.

Deliberation

1   The woman that deliberates is lost.

JOSEPH ADDISON, (1672–1719) British essayist. Marcia, in *Cato*, act 4, sc. 1 (1713). Repr. in *Works of Addison*, ed. R. Hurd (1883).

2   And men say
     Our second thoughts are wiser
         every way.

EURIPIDES, (480–406 B.C.) Greek dramatist. Nurse, in *Hippolytus*, l. 435, *Collected Plays of Euripides*, ed. and trans. by Gilbert Murray (1954).

3   Thus conscience does make
         cowards of us all,
     And thus the native hue of resolution
     Is sicklied o'er with the pale cast of
         thought,
     And enterprises of great pith and
         moment
     With this regard their currents turn
         awry,
     And lose the name of action.

WILLIAM SHAKESPEARE, (1564–1616) British dramatist, poet. Hamlet, in *Hamlet*, act 3, sc. 1, l. 85–90 (1604).

Part of Hamlet's meditative soliloquy on the question of "To be, or not to be." William Hazlitt echoed these words in *Characteristics* (1823) no. 228, "Reflection makes men cowards."

Delusions of Grandeur

1   There is less in this than meets the eye.

TALLULAH BANKHEAD, (1903–1968) U.S. screen actor. Quoted in *Shouts and Murmurs*, ch. 4, Alexander Woollcott (1922).

Remark to Woollcott, referring to a revival of Maeterlinck's play *Aglavaine and Selysette*.

2 I recoil, overcome with the glory of my rosy hue and the knowledge that I, a mere cock, have made the sun rise.

EDMOND ROSTAND, (1868–1918) French poet, playwright. Chantecler, in *The Chantecler*, act 2, sc. 3 (1910).

Demagogues

1 In every age the vilest specimens of human nature are to be found among demagogues.

THOMAS BABINGTON MACAULAY, (1800–1859) British historian, Whig politician. *History of England*, vol. 1, ch. 5 (1849).

Democracy

1 Remember, democracy never lasts long. It soon wastes, exhausts, and murders itself. There never was a democracy yet that did not commit suicide.

JOHN ADAMS, (1735–1826) U.S. statesman, president. *The Works of John Adams*, vol. 6, ed. Charles Francis Adams (1851). Letter, April 15, 1814.

2 The worst thing I can say about democracy is that it has tolerated the Right Honourable Gentleman for four and a half years.

ANEURIN BEVAN, (1897–1960) British Labour politician. *Hansard*, col. 1191. Speech, July 23, 1929, to House of Commons.

Referring to Neville Chamberlain, prime minister 1937–1940. Bevan did not hide his low opinion of Chamberlain. "He has the lucidity which is the by–product of a fundamentally sterile mind," he wrote. "He does not have to struggle ... with the crowded pulsations of a fecund imagination. On the contrary he is almost devoid of imagination." (Quoted in Michael Foot, *Aneurin Bevan*, vol. 1, ch. 8, 1962).

3 The tendency of democracies is, in all things, to mediocrity.

JAMES FENIMORE COOPER, (1789–1851) U.S. novelist. *The American Democrat*, "On the Disadvantages of Democracy" (1838).

4 That fatal drollery called a representative government.

BENJAMIN DISRAELI, (1804–1881) British statesman, author. *Tancred*, bk. 2, ch. 13 (1847).

5 Nor is the people's judgement always true:
The most may err as grossly as the few.

JOHN DRYDEN, (1631–1700) British poet, dramatist, critic. "Absalom and Achitophel," pt. 1, l. 781–2 (1681).

6 Democracy don't rule the world,
You'd better get that in your head;
This world is ruled by violence
But I guess that's better left unsaid.

BOB DYLAN [ROBERT ALLEN ZIMMERMAN], (b. 1941) U.S. singer, songwriter. "Union Sundown" (song), on the album *Infidels* (1983).

7 I swear to the Lord
I still can't see
Why Democracy means
Everybody but me.

LANGSTON HUGHES, (1902–1967) U.S. poet, author. "The Black Man Speaks," *Jim Crow's Last Stand* (1943).

8 As I would not be a *slave*, so I would not be a *master*. This expresses my idea of democracy.

ABRAHAM LINCOLN, (1809–1865) U.S. president. *Collected Works of Abraham Lincoln*, vol. 2, ed. Roy P. Basler (1953). Autograph fragment, c. Aug. 1, 1858.

9 No man is good enough to govern another man without that other's consent.

ABRAHAM LINCOLN, (1809–1865) U.S. president. *Collected Works of Abraham Lincoln*, ed. Roy P. Basler (1953). Speech, Oct. 16, 1854, Peoria, Illinois.

The first of the Lincoln–Douglas debates.

10 Man's capacity for justice makes democracy possible, but man's inclination to injustice makes democracy necessary.

REINHOLD NIEBUHR, (1892–1971) U.S. theologian, historian. *The Children of Light and the Children of Darkness*, foreword (1944).

11 Not only does democracy make every man forget his ancestors, but also clouds their view of their descendants and isolates them from their contemporaries. Each man is for ever thrown back on himself alone, and there is danger that he may be shut up in the solitude of his own heart.

ALEXIS DE TOCQUEVILLE, (1805–1859) French social philosopher. *Democracy in America*, vol. 2, pt. 2, ch. 2 (1840).

12 There is a limit to the application of democratic methods. You can inquire of all the passengers as to what type of car they like to ride in, but it is impossible to question them as to whether to apply the brakes when the train is at full speed and accident threatens.

LEON TROTSKY, (1879–1940) Russian revolutionary. *The History of the Russian Revolution*, vol. 3, ch. 6 (1933).

13 Democracy means simply the bludgeoning of the people by the people for the people.

OSCAR WILDE, (1854–1900) Anglo-Irish playwright, author. "The Soul of Man Under Socialism," *Fortnightly Review* (London, Feb. 1891). (1895), repr. in *Complete Works of Oscar Wilde*, ed. J.B. Foreman (1966).

14 The world must be made safe for democracy. Its peace must be planted upon the tested foundations of political liberty.

WOODROW WILSON, (1856–1924) U.S. Democratic politician, president. *Selected Addresses* (1918). Speech to Congress, April 2, 1917.

Proposing a state of war against Germany, which was declared April 6. Wilson ran his reelection campaign in 1916 on the boast of having "kept us out of war." See Wilson on war.

Democratic Party (U.S.)

1 The Democratic Party is like a mule. It has neither pride of ancestry nor hope of posterity.

IGNATIUS DONNELLY, (1831–1901) U.S. author, politician. Quoted in *Dictionary of Political Quotations*, ed. Robert Stewart (1984). Speech, Sept. 13, 1860, Minnesota State Legislature.

Departure

1 I sprang to the stirrup, and Joris, and he;
I galloped, Dirck galloped, we galloped all three.

ROBERT BROWNING, (1812–1889) British poet. "How They Brought the Good News from Ghent to Aix," st. 1, *Dramatic Romances* (1845).

Opening lines.

2 Parting is all we know of heaven, And all we need of hell.

EMILY DICKINSON, (1830–1886) U.S. poet. "My Life Closed Twice Before its Close" (published 1896). Repr. in *The Complete Poems*, no. 1732, Harvard *variorum* edition (1955).

3   In every parting there is an image
     of death.

> GEORGE ELIOT [MARY ANN (OR
> MARIAN) EVANS], (1819–1880) British
> novelist. *Amos Barton*, ch. 10, *Scenes of Cleri-*
> *cal Life* (1858). First published in *Blackwood's*
> *Magazine* (1857).

4   Beam me up, Scotty.

> GENE RODDENBERRY, (1921–1991) U.S.
> writer. Attributed to *Star Trek* (television series)
> (1966–69).

> The words as they appear here were never actu-
> ally spoken in the series: the nearest is "Beam
> us up, Mr. Scott," said by Captain James T. Kirk
> to his chief engineer. The script was written by
> Gene Roddenberry.

5   Parting is such sweet sorrow
     That I shall say good night till it be
       morrow.

> WILLIAM SHAKESPEARE, (1564–1616)
> British dramatist, poet. Juliet, in *Romeo and*
> *Juliet*, act 2, sc. 1, l. 229–30 (1599).

Depression

1   I am—yet what I am, none cares or
     knows; My friends forsake me like a
     memory lost: I am the self–con-
     sumer of my woes.

> JOHN CLARE, (1793–1864) British poet. "I
> Am," (1844–1846), first publ. *Bedford Times*
> (Jan. 1848). Repr. in *The Poems of John Clare*,
> ed. J.W. Tibble (1935).

> Opening lines of poem, written at Northampton
> Asylum.

2   Be near me when my light is low,
     When the blood creeps, and the
       nerves prick
     And tingle; and the heart is sick,
     And all the wheels of Being slow.

> ALFRED TENNYSON, 1ST BARON TEN-
> NYSON, (1809–1892) British poet. "In Memo-
> riam A.H.H.," cto. 50, st. 1 (1850).

Depression (1930s)

1   Once I built a railroad, made it run,
     Made it race against time ...
     Now it's done,
     Buddy, can you spare a dime?

> YIP HARBURG, (1898–1981) U.S. song-
> writer. "Brother Can You Spare a Dime?"
> (Song), *Americana* (show, 1932).

> Born Isidore Hochberg, name changed to
> Edgar Y. Harburg.

2   I see one–third of a nation
     ill–housed, ill–clad, ill–nourished.

> FRANKLIN DELANO ROOSEVELT,
> (1882–1945) U.S. Democratic politician, pres-
> ident. *Public Papers and Addresses of Franklin*
> *D. Roosevelt*, vol. 6 (1941). Second inaugural
> addresss, Jan. 20, 1937.

Design

1   Art has to move you and design
     does not, unless it's a good design
     for a bus.

> DAVID HOCKNEY, (b. 1937) British artist.
> quoted in *Guardian* (London, Oct. 26, 1988).
> Press conference, Oct. 25, 1988, Tate Gallery,
> London.

Desire

1   Man is a creation of desire, not a
     creation of need.

> GASTON BACHELARD, (1884–1962)
> French scientist, philosopher, literary theorist.
> *The Psychoanalysis of Fire*, ch. 2, "Fire and
> Reverie" (1938).

2   What is it men in women do
     require?
     The lineaments of Gratified Desire.
     What is it women do in men
       require?
     The lineaments of Gratified Desire.

WILLIAM BLAKE, (1757–1827) British poet, painter, engraver. *Manuscript Notebook (1793)*, no. 46, "The Question Answered," published in *Complete Writings*, ed. Geoffrey Keynes (1957).

3 The man's desire is for the woman; but the woman's desire is rarely other than for the desire of the man.

SAMUEL TAYLOR COLERIDGE, (1772–1834) British poet, critic. *Table Talk*, "23 July 1827," *Specimens of the Table Talk of Samuel Taylor Coleridge*, ed. Henry Nelson Coleridge (1835). Repr. in *Collected Works*, vol. 14, ed. Kathleen Coburn (1990).

4 The reason can give nothing at all Like the response to desire.

WALLACE STEVENS, (1879–1955) U.S. poet. "Dezembrum," *Parts of a World* (1942).

Concluding lines.

Despair

1 Let the day perish wherein I was born, and the night in which it was said, There is a man child conceived.

BIBLE: HEBREW, *Job*, 3:3.

A similar imprecation is found in *Jeremiah* 20:14–15.

2 There shall be weeping and gnashing of teeth.

BIBLE: NEW TESTAMENT, Jesus, in *Matthew*, 8:12.

Referring to "the children of the kingdom ... cast out into outer darkness." The words are also used in the parable of the talents, in *Matthew* 25:30, said of the "unprofitable servant."

3 The name of the slough was Despond.

JOHN BUNYAN, (1628–1688) British Baptist preacher, author. *The Pilgrim's Progress*, pt. 1 (1678).

Referring to the "miry slough" in which Christian and Pliable waded.

4 Abandon all hope, you who enter here!

DANTE ALIGHIERI, (1265–1321) Italian poet. "Inferno," cto. 3, l. 9, *The Divine Comedy* (1321).

Inscription at the entrance to Hell.

5 Despair is the price one pays for setting oneself an impossible aim. It is, one is told, the unforgivable sin, but it is a sin the corrupt or evil man never practises. He always has hope. He never reaches the freezing–point of knowing absolute failure. Only the man of goodwill carries always in his heart this capacity for damnation.

GRAHAM GREENE, (1904–1991) British novelist. *The Heart of the Matter*, bk. 1, pt. 1, ch. 2, sct. 4 (1948).

6 Don't despair, not even over the fact that you don't despair.

FRANZ KAFKA, (1883–1924) Czech novelist, short–story writer. *The Diaries of Franz Kafka: 1910–1923*, ed. Max Brod (1948). Journal entry, July 21, 1913.

7 O God, O God,
How weary, stale, flat, and unprofitable
Seem to me all the uses of this world!

WILLIAM SHAKESPEARE, (1564–1616) British dramatist, poet. Hamlet, in *Hamlet*, act 1, sc. 2, l. 132–4 (1604).

Hamlet's first soliloquy of the play, voicing his dismay at the marriage of his mother to Claudius so soon after his father's death.

Destiny

1   *Ça ira.*
(It will go its own way.)

BENJAMIN FRANKLIN, (1706–1790) U.S. statesman, writer. *Attributed.*

Said about the American Revolution while Franklin was in Paris 1776–1777. The remark was popularized and made the refrain of a revolutionary song—the *Carillon National*— by Ladé during the French Revolution of 1789.

2   We are not permitted to choose the frame of our destiny. But what we put into it is ours.

DAG HAMMARSKJÖLD, (1905–1961) Swedish statesman, Secretary–General of the United Nations. "Night Is Drawing Nigh," *Markings* (1963). Notebook entry, 1950.

3   'Tis all a Chequer–board of Nights and Days
Where Destiny with Men for Pieces plays:
Hither and thither moves, and mates, and slays,
And one by one back in the Closet lays.

OMAR KHAYYAM, (11–12th century) Persian astronomer, poet. *The Rubaiyat of Omar Khayyam,* st. 49, trans. by Edward FitzGerald, first edition (1859).

4   "Take thy beak from out my heart, and take thy form from off my door!"
Quoth the Raven, "Nevermore."

EDGAR ALLAN POE, (1809–1845) U.S. poet, critic, short–story writer. "The Raven," st. 17 (1845). First published in *New York Evening Mirror* (Jan. 29, 1845).

5   There's a divinity that shapes our ends,
Rough–hew them how we will.

WILLIAM SHAKESPEARE, (1564–1616) British dramatist, poet. Hamlet, in *Hamlet,* act 5, sc. 2, l. 10–11 (1604).

Destructiveness

1   The passion for destruction is also a creative passion.

MIKHAIL BAKUNIN, (1814–1876) Russian political theorist. "Die Reaktion in Deutschland," *Jahrbuch fur Wissenshaft und Kunst* (1842).

The phrase in Bakunin's article, "Reaction in Germany" (written under the pseudonym "Jules Elysard"), was later adopted as an anarchist slogan...

2   If destruction be our lot, we must ourselves be its author and finisher. As a nation of freemen, we must live through all time, or die by suicide.

ABRAHAM LINCOLN, (1809–1865) U.S. president. "The Perpetuation of Our Political Institutions," *Collected Works of Abraham Lincoln,* vol. 1, ed. Roy P. Basler (1953). Speech, Jan. 27, 1837, Springfield, Illinois.

Detectives

1   Down these mean streets a man must go who is not himself mean, who is neither tarnished nor afraid.... He is the hero, he is everything. He must be a complete man and a common man and yet an unusual man. He must be, to use a rather weathered phrase, a man of honor, by instinct, by inevitability, without thought of it, and certainly without saying it. He must be the best man in his world and a good enough man for any world.

RAYMOND CHANDLER, (1888–1959) U.S. author. "The Simple Art of Murder," first published in *Atlantic Monthly* (Boston, Dec. 1944). Repr. in *Pearls are a Nuisance* (1950).

2   "It is of the highest importance in the art of detection to be able to recognise out of a number of facts which are incidental and which are

vital.... I would call your attention to the curious incident of the dog in the night–time."
"The dog did nothing in the night–time."
"That was the curious incident."

ARTHUR CONAN, SIR DOYLE, (1859–1930) British author. Sherlock Holmes talking to Inspector Gregory, in *The Memoirs of Sherlock Holmes*, "Silver Blaze" (1893).

3　This is the city. Los Angeles, California. I work here. I carry a badge. My name's Friday. The story you are about to see is true; the names have been changed to protect the innocent.

JACK WEBB, (1920–1987) U.S. actor, producer. Sergeant Joe Friday (Jack Webb), in *Dragnet* (radio and TV series), introduction, written, produced, directed by, and starring, Jack Webb (1949–1971).

Originally produced for radio, then successfully on TV for another 18 years, the crime serial *Dragnet* started every episode with the above monologue. Friday speech's was also characterized by such expressions as, "Just the facts, ma'am," "that's my job," and "I carry a badge." Created by Jack Webb and Richard L. Breen.

Determination

1　If I cannot prevail upon heaven, I shall move hell.

VIRGIL [PUBLIUS VERGILIUS MARO], (70–19 B.C.) Roman poet. Juno, in *Aeneid*, bk. 7, l. 312 (19 B.C.), trans. by Kate Hughes (1995).

Spoken by Juno on realizing that she will be unable to prevent Aeneas from gaining Latium.

Devil, the

1　Be sober, be vigilant; because your adversary the devil, as a roaring lion, walketh about, seeking whom he may devour.

BIBLE: NEW TESTAMENT, *1 Peter*, 5:8.

2　An apology for the Devil—it must be remembered that we have only heard one side of the case. God has written all the books.

SAMUEL BUTLER, (1835–1902) British author. *Notebooks*, "Higgledy–Piggledy" (1912).

3　And Satan trembles when he sees The weakest saint upon his knees.

WILLIAM COWPER, (1731–1800) British poet. *Olney Hymns*, no. 29, "Exhortation to Prayer," (1779). Repr. in *Poetical Works*, ed. H.S. Milford (1934).

4　If the devil doesn't exist and, therefore, man has created him, he has created him in his own image and likeness.

FEODOR DOSTOYEVSKY, (1821–1881) Russian novelist. Ivan Karamazov, in *The Brothers Karamazov*, bk. 5, ch. 4 (published 1879–1888), trans. by David Magarshak (1958).

5　Better to reign in Hell than serve in Heaven.

JOHN MILTON, (1608–1674) British poet. Satan, in *Paradise Lost*, bk. 1, l. 263 (1667).

6　The Prince of Darkness is a gentleman.

WILLIAM SHAKESPEARE, (1564–1616) British dramatist, poet. Edgar, in *King Lear*, act 3, sc. 4, l. 134 (1623).

Spoken by Edgar in the guise of Poor Tom.

Diaries

1　A man who keeps a diary pays Due toll to many tedious days; But life becomes eventful—then

His busy hand forgets the pen.
Most books, indeed, are records less
Of fulness than of emptiness.

WILLIAM ALLINGHAM, (1824–1889)
Irish poet, diarist. *A Diary*, ch. 6, eds. H.
Allingham and D. Radford (1907). Journal
entry, March 24–28, 1864.

Dictators

1   Dictators ride to and fro upon
tigers which they dare not dis-
mount. And the tigers are getting
hungry.

WINSTON CHURCHILL, (1874–1965)
British statesman, writer. *Step By Step.* Letter,
Nov. 11, 1937.

Quoting a "Hindustani" proverb, though cited
as Chinese in the *Concise Oxford Dictionary
of Proverbs*, ed. John Simpson (1982).

Dictionaries

1   Dictionaries are like watches, the
worst is better than none, and the
best cannot be expected to go quite
true.

SAMUEL JOHNSON, (1709–1784) British
author, lexicographer. Quoted in James
Boswell, *Life of Dr. Johnson* (1791). Letter,
August 21, 1784.

2   Lexicographer: a writer of dictionaries, a harmless drudge, that
busies himself in tracing the original, and detailing the signification
of words.

SAMUEL JOHNSON, (1709–1784) British
author, lexicographer. *Dictionary of the English Language* (1755).

"Every other author may aspire to praise,"
wrote Johnson in his Preface, "the lexicographer can only hope to escape reproach, and
even this negative recompense has been yet
granted to very few." Under the entry for *Dull*,
Johnson gave the following illustration: "To
make dictionaries is *dull* work."

Dignity

1   Perhaps the only true dignity of
man is his capacity to despise
himself.

GEORGE SANTAYANA, (1863–1952) U.S.
philosopher, poet. *Spinoza's Ethics*, introduction (1910).

Dilemmas

1   To be, or not to be; that is the question:
Whether 'tis nobler in the mind to
suffer
The slings and arrows of outrageous fortune,
Or to take arms against a sea of
troubles,
And, by opposing, end them.

WILLIAM SHAKESPEARE,(1564–1616)
British dramatist, poet. Hamlet, in *Hamlet*, act
3, sc. 1, l. 58–62 (1604).

Dinner Parties

1   I'm a man more dined against than
dining.

MAURICE BOWRA, (1898–1971) British
scholar, warden of Wadham College, Oxford.
Quoted in *Summoned by Bells*, ch. 9, John
Betjeman (1960).

2   This was a good enough dinner, to
be sure; but it was not a dinner to
ask a man to.

SAMUEL JOHNSON, (1709–1784) British
author, lexicographer. quoted in James
Boswell, *Life of Dr. Johnson*, entry, Aug. 5,
1763 (1791).

3   At a dinner party one should eat
wisely but not too well, and talk
well but not too wisely.

W. SOMERSET MAUGHAM, (1874–1966) British author. *A Writer's Notebook*, entry, 1896 (1949).

4 He showed me his bill of fare to tempt me to dine with him; said I, I value not your bill of fare, give me your bill of company.

JONATHAN SWIFT, (1667–1745) Anglo–Irish satirist. *Journal to Stella* (1710–1713), published in *Works*, vol. 12 (quarto edition, 1768). Letter, Sept. 2, 1711.

5 After a good dinner one can forgive anybody, even one's own relations.

OSCAR WILDE, (1854–1900) Anglo–Irish playwright, author. Lady Caroline, in *A Woman of No Importance*, act 2.

Diplomacy

1 Consul. In American politics, a person who having failed to secure an office from the people is given one by the Administration on condition that he leave the country.

AMBROSE BIERCE, (1842–1914) U.S. author. *The Devil's Dictionary* (1881–1906), repr. in *Collected Works of Ambrose Bierce*, vol. 7 (1911).

2 Diplomacy is to do and say
The nastiest things in the nicest way.

ISAAC GOLDBERG, (1887–1938) U.S. critic. *The Reflex* (Oct. 1927).

3 The hand that signed the treaty bred a fever,
And famine grew, and locusts came;
Great is the hand that holds dominion over
Man by a scribbled name.

DYLAN THOMAS, (1914–1953) Welsh poet. "The Hand That Signed The Paper," *25 Poems* (1936). First published *New Verse 18* (Dec. 1935).

Disability

1 Now she's like everyone else.

CHARLES DE GAULLE, (1890–1970) French general, president. Quoted in *De Gaulle*, Jean Lacouture (1965).

Remark at the funeral of his handicapped daughter (1948).

Disagreement

1 Gentlemen, include me out!

SAMUEL GOLDWYN, (1882–1974) U.S. film producer. Attributed in *The Goldwyn Touch*, ch. 10, Michael Freedland (1986).

Remark Oct 1933, on resigning from the Motion Picture Producers and Distributors of America over a labor dispute. Goldwyn himself denied ever having used the words, as he denied most "Goldwynisms," claiming instead to have said, "Gentlemen, I'm withdrawing from the association."

Disappointment

1 I have many years ago magnified in my own mind, and repeated to you, a ninth Beatitude, added to the eight in the Scripture: *Blessed is he who expects nothing, for he shall never be disappointed.*

ALEXANDER POPE, (1688–1744) British satirical poet. *The Correspondence of Alexander Pope*, vol. 2, ed. George Sherburn (1956). Letter, Oct. 16, 1727, to playwright John Gay.

2 In this world there are two tragedies. One is not getting what one wants, and the other is getting it. The last is much the worst.

OSCAR WILDE, (1854–1900) Anglo–Irish playwright, author. Dumby, in *Lady Windermere's Fan*, act 3 (1893).

George Bernard Shaw expressed a similar idea in *Man and Superman* (published ten years after *Lady Windermere's Fan*), in which Mendoza says: "There are two tragedies in life. One is to lose your heart's desire. The other is to gain it." (Act 4).

Disarmament

1 If you carry this resolution you will send Britain's Foreign Secretary naked into the conference chamber.

ANEURIN BEVAN, (1897–1960) British Labour politician. Quoted in *Daily Herald* (London, Oct. 4, 1957). Speech, Oct. 2, 1957, Brighton.

Opposing a motion in favor of unilateral nuclear disarmament.

Disasters

1 Calamities are of two kinds: misfortune to ourselves, and good fortune to others.

AMBROSE BIERCE, (1842–1914) U.S. author. *The Devil's Dictionary* (1881–1906), repr. in *Collected Works of Ambrose Bierce*, vol. 7 (1911).

2 1992 is not a year I shall look back on with undiluted pleasure. In the words of one of my more sympathetic correspondents, it has turned out to be an Annus Horribilis.

ELIZABETH II, (b. 1926) British monarch, Queen of Great Britain and Northern Ireland. quoted in *Times* (London, Nov. 25, 1992). Speech, Nov. 24, 1992, Guildhall, London.

The Queen's reference to John Dryden's long poem, "Annus Mirabilis" (1667), was lost on much of the nation, producing headlines such as "Queen's Bum Year" in the tabloid press. Dryden had described the events of 1666 a "year of marvels" which included the Great Fire of London; a few days before the Queen's speech, which commemmorated her 40 years on the throne, a fire had gutted some of the State Apartments in Windsor Castle. Other personal disasters included the separation of the Prince and Princess of Wales, and a fierce press campaign against the royal family.

3 Our sympathy is cold to the relation of distant misery.

EDWARD GIBBON, (1737–1794) British historian. *The Decline and Fall of the Roman Empire*, ch. 49 (1776–1788).

4 Aprés nous le déluge.
["After us, the flood."]

MADAME DE POMPADOUR, (1721–1764) French mistress of Louis XV of France. Quoted in *Mémoires de Madame du Hausset*, p. 19 (1824).

Remark November 5, 1757, to Louis XV after the defeat of the French army by Frederick the Great at the Battle of Rossbach. The phrase has also been attributed to Louis XV, but in any case may already have been current as a proverb.

Disciples

1 Behold, I send you forth as sheep in the midst of wolves: be ye therefore wise as serpents, and harmless as doves.

BIBLE: NEW TESTAMENT, Jesus, in *Matthew,* 10:16.

On sending forth the Apostles.

2 Ye are the salt of the earth: but if the salt have lost his savour, wherewith shall it be salted?

BIBLE: NEW TESTAMENT, Jesus, in *Matthew,* 5:13.

From the Sermon on the Mount.

3 Every great man nowadays has his disciples, and it is usually Judas who writes the biography.

OSCAR WILDE, (1854–1900) Anglo–Irish playwright, author. "The Butterfly's Boswell," *Court and Society Review* (London, April 20, 1887). Repr. in *Complete Works of Oscar Wilde*, ed. J.B. Foreman (1966).

Also in *The Critic as Artist*, pt. 1, in *Intentions* (1891).

Discipline

1 An Englishman, even if he is alone, forms an orderly queue of one.

GEORGE MIKES, (1912–1987) Hungarian–born British humorist. *How To Be An Alien*, ch. 1, sct. 14 (1946).

Mikes elaborated further in *How To Be Decadent* (1977): "in shops the English stand in queues; in government offices they sit in queues; in churches they kneel in queues; at sale times, they lie in queues all night."

Discovery

1 They are ill discoverers that think there is no land, when they can see nothing but sea.

FRANCIS BACON, (1561–1626) British philosopher, essayist, statesman. *The Advancement of Learning*, bk. 2, ch. 7, sct. 5 (1605).

Discretion

1 Hear no evil, see no evil, speak no evil.

ANONYMOUS, (17th century).

Bartlett's Familiar Quotations (16th edition, 1992) describes these words as the legend carved over door of Sacred Stable, Nikko, Japan (17th century), relating to the "Three Wise Monkeys." Similar phrases are to be found in all cultures. in English, the closest and earliest is in the work by Brian Melbancke, *Philotimus: The War Betwixt Nature and Fortune* (1583): "Thus you are hearing, and seeing and saying nothing."

2 As a jewel of gold in a swine's snout, so is a fair woman which is without discretion.

BIBLE: HEBREW, *Proverbs*, 11:22.

Disgrace

1 Let us not speak of them; but look, and pass on.

DANTE ALIGHIERI, (1265–1321) Italian poet. "Inferno," cto. 3, l. 51, *The Divine Comedy* (1321).

Said by Virgil, of the souls of the Futile in the vestibule to Hell.

2 Unhappy as the event must be ... we may draw from it this useful lesson: that loss of virtue in a female is irretrievable; that one false step involves her in endless ruin; that her reputation is no less brittle than it is beautiful; and that she cannot be too much guarded in her behaviour towards the undeserving of the other sex.

JANE AUSTEN, (1775–1817) British novelist. Mary Bennet, in *Pride and Prejudice*, ch. 47 (1813).

On the elopement of Lydia Bennet with Wickham.

3 Oh! no! we never mention her,
   Her name is never heard;
   My lips are now forbid to speak
   That once familiar word.

THOMAS BAYLY, (1797–1839) British writer, poet. "Oh! No! We Never Mention Her " (1844).

4 She is absolutely inadmissible into society. Many a woman has a past, but I am told that she has at least a dozen, and that they all fit.

OSCAR WILDE, (1854–1900) Anglo–Irish playwright, author. The Duchess of Berwick, in *Lady Windermere's Fan*, act 1 (1893).

Referring to Mrs. Erlynne.

Dismissal

1 Go, you are dismissed.
   [*Ite missa est.*]

MISSAL, THE, *The Ordinary of the Mass.*

Missal is book of prayers and rites used to celebrate the Roman Catholic mass during the year.

Dissatisfaction

1   The idiot who praises, with
enthusiastic tone,
All centuries but this, and every
country but his own.

SIR WILLIAM SCHWENCK GILBERT,
(1836–1911) British librettist. Ko Ko, in *The Mikado*, act 1 (1885), published in *The Savoy Operas* (1926).

2   No, no, we are not satisfied, and we
will not be satisfied until justice
rolls down like waters and righteousness like a mighty stream.

MARTIN LUTHER KING, JR.,
(1929–1968) U.S. clergyman, civil rights leader. "I Have a Dream," *A Testament of Hope: Essential Writings*, ed. James Melvin Washington (1986). Speech, Aug. 28, 1963, at civil rights march, Washington, DC.

King was quoting the Hebrew Bible, Amos 5:24.

Dissent

1   If a house be divided against itself,
that house cannot stand.

BIBLE: NEW TESTAMENT, Jesus, in *Mark*, 3:25.

2   One does not arrest Voltaire.

CHARLES DE GAULLE, (1890–1970) French general, president. Quoted in *Encounter* (London, June 1975).

Referring to the Maoist and Communist activities of Jean–Paul Sartre during the 1960s.

3   Assent—and you are sane—
Demur—you're straightway dan-
gerous—
And handled with a Chain—

EMILY DICKINSON, (1830–1886) U.S. poet. "Much Madness is Divinest Sense" (written c. 1862, published 1890). Repr. in *The Complete Poems*, no. 435, Harvard *variorum* edition (1955).

4   The dissident does not operate in
the realm of genuine power at all.
He is not seeking power. He has no
desire for office and does not gather
votes. He does not attempt to
charm the public, he offers nothing
and promises nothing. He can offer,
if anything, only his own skin—and
he offers it solely because he has no
other way of affirming the truth he
stands for. His actions simply artic-
ulate his dignity as a citizen, regardless of the cost.

VACLAV HAVEL, (b. 1936) Czechoslova-kian playwright, president. "An Anatomy of Reticence," pt. 1, sct. 10, *Living in Truth* (1986).

5   If all mankind minus one, were of
one opinion, and only one person
were of the contrary opinion,
mankind would be no more justified in silencing that one person,
than he, if he had the power, would
be justified in silencing mankind.

JOHN STUART MILL, (1806–1873) British philosopher, economist. *On Liberty*, ch. 2 (1859).

6   Discussion in America means
dissent.

JAMES THURBER, (1894–1961) U.S. humorist, illustrator. "The Duchess and the Bugs," *Lanterns and Lances* (1961).

Dissipation

1   Gentleman–rankers out on the
spree,
Damned from here to Eternity.

RUDYARD KIPLING, (1865–1936) British author, poet. "Gentleman–Rankers," *Bar-rack–Room Ballads* (1892).

2   My only books Were woman's
looks And folly's all they taught me.

THOMAS MOORE, (1779–1852) Irish poet. "The time I've lost in wooing," st. 1, *Irish Melodies* (1807). Repr. in *Moore's Poetical Works,* ed. A.D. Godley (1910).

3   We have heard the chimes at midnight, Master Shallow.

WILLIAM SHAKESPEARE, (1564–1616) British dramatist, poet. Sir John Falstaff, in *Henry IV pt. 2,* act 3, sc. 2, l. 211 (1600).

Referring to the youthful antics of Falstaff and Justice Shallow. *Chimes at Midnight* was the title of Orson Welles's 1966 film based on Shakespeare's portrayal of Falstaff, with Welles himself in the central role.

Diversity

1   In my Father's house are many mansions.

BIBLE: NEW TESTAMENT, Jesus, in *John,* 14:2.

2   Variety's the very spice of life That gives it all its flavour.

WILLIAM COWPER, (1731–1800) British poet. *The Task,* bk. 2, l. 606–7 (1785). Repr. in *Poetical Works,* ed. H.S. Milford (1934).

3   Our flag is red, white and blue, but our nation is a rainbow—red, yellow, brown, black and white—and we're all precious in God's sight.

JESSE JACKSON, (b. 1941) U.S. clergyman, civil rights leader. Quoted in *The Harper Book of American Quotations,* ed. Gorton Carruth and Eugene Ehrlich (1988). Speech, July 16, 1984, Democratic National Convention, San Francisco.

Jackson added, "My constituency is the desperate, the damned, the disinherited, the disrespected and the despised."

4   The diversity in the faculties of men, from which the rights of property originate, is not less an insuperable obstacle to a uniformity of interests. The protection of these faculties is the first object of government.

JAMES MADISON, (1751–1836) U.S. Democratic–Republican politician, president. *Federalist Papers,* Nov. 1787, no. 10, *The Federalist,* ed. Benjamin F. Wright (1961).

Divorce

1   That's the only good thing about divorce. You get to sleep with your mother.

ANITA LOOS, (1893–1981) U.S. novelist, screenwriter. Little Mary (Virginia Weidler), in *The Women* (film) (1932).

Adapted from the hit Broadway play by Claire Boothe (later Claire Boothe Luce), the movie achieved some notoriety with a cast of 130 women and no men.

Doctors

1   Honour a physician with the honour due unto him for the uses which ye may have of him: for the Lord hath created him. For of the most High cometh healing, and ye shall receive honour of the king. The skill of the physician shall lift up his head: and in the sight of great men he shall be in admiration.

APOCRYPHA, *Ecclesiasticus,* 38:1–3.

2   A skilful leech is better far Than half a hundred men of war.

SAMUEL BUTLER, (1612–1680) British poet. "Hudibras," pt. 1, cto. 2, l. 245 (1663). Eds. John Wilders and Hugh de Quehen (1973).

3   Surgeons must be very careful When they take the knife! Underneath their fine incisions Stirs the Culprit—*Life!*

EMILY DICKINSON, (1830–1886) U.S. poet. "Surgeons Must be Very Careful" (written c. 1859, published 1891). Repr. in *The*

Complete Poems, no. 108, Harvard variorum edition (1955).

4   When the artless doctor sees
    No one hope, but of his fees,
    And his skill runs on the lees;
    Sweet Spirit, comfort me!
    When his potion and his pill,
    Has, or none, or little skill,
    Meet for nothing, but to kill;
    Sweet Spirit, comfort me!

ROBERT HERRICK, (1591–1674) British poet, clergyman. "His Litany to the Holy Spirit," st. 4–5, Noble Numbers (1647). Repr. in The Poems of Robert Herrick, ed. L.C. Martin (1956).

5   Emily, I've a little confession to make. I really am a horse doctor. But marry me, and I'll never look at another horse.

ROBERT PIROSH, Screenwriter. Dr. Hackenbush (Groucho Marx), in A Day at the Races (film), proposing to Mrs. Upjohn (Margaret Dumont) (1937). Sam Wood.

6   Is it not also true that no physician, in so far as he is a physician, considers or enjoins what is for the physician's interest, but that all seek the good of their patients? For we have agreed that a physician strictly so called, is a ruler of bodies, and not a maker of money, have we not?

PLATO, (c. 427–347 B.C.) Greek philosopher. Socrates, in The Republic, bk. 1, sct. 342.

7   Cured yesterday of my disease,
    I died last night of my physician.

MATTHEW PRIOR, (1664–1721) British poet, diplomat. "The Remedy Worse than the Disease" (written 1714, published 1727). Repr. in The Literary Works of Matthew Prior, eds. H.B. Wright and M.K. Spears (1959).

8   There are worse occupations in this world than feeling a woman's pulse.

LAURENCE STERNE, (1713–1768) British author. A Sentimental Journey, "The Pulse, Paris" (1768).

9   The best doctors in the world are Doctor Diet, Doctor Quiet, and Doctor Merryman.

JONATHAN SWIFT, (1667–1745) Anglo–Irish satirist. Lord Smart, in Polite Conversation, dialogue 2 (1738). Repr. in The Prose Works of Jonathan Swift, vol. 4, ed. Herbert Davis (1957).

Swift was repeating an adage first recorded by the physician William Bullein in his Government of Health, folio 50, (1558).

Doctrine

1   What makes all doctrines plain and clear?
    About two hundred pounds a year.
    And that which was proved true before
    Prove false again? Two hundred more.

SAMUEL BUTLER, (1612–1680) British poet. "Hudibras," pt. 3, cto. 1, l. 1277–80 (1678). Eds. John Wilders and Hugh de Quehen (1973).

Dogmatism

1   Any stigma, as the old saying is, will serve to beat a dogma.

PHILIP GUEDALLA, (1889–1944) British author. "Ministers of State," Masters and Men (1923).

2   Dogmatism is puppyism come to its full growth.

DOUGLAS JERROLD, (1803–1857) British playwright, humorist. "Man Made of Money," The Wit and Opinions of Douglas Jerrold (1859).

3   The greater the ignorance the greater the dogmatism.

WILLIAM, SIR OSLER, (1849–1919)
Canadian physician. *Montreal Medical Journal*
(Sept. 1902).

Dogs

1   Dog. A kind of additional or sub-sidiary Deity designed to catch the overflow and surplus of the world's worship.

AMBROSE BIERCE, (1842–1914) U.S.
author. *The Devil's Dictionary* (1881–1906),
repr. in *Collected Works of Ambrose Bierce*,
vol. 7 (1911).

2   The great pleasure of a dog is that you may make a fool of yourself with him and not only will he not scold you, but he will make a fool of himself too.

SAMUEL BUTLER, (1835–1902) British
author. *Notebooks*, "Higgledy–Piggledy"
(1912).

3   Near this spot are deposited the remains of one who possessed Beauty without Vanity, Strength without Insolence, Courage without Ferocity, and all the Virtues of Man without his Vices. This praise, which would be unmeaning Flat-tery, if inscribed over human ashes, is but a just Tribute to the Memory of BOATSWAIN, a Dog.

JOHN CAM HOBHOUSE, (1786–1869)
British statesman. Quoted in *The Late Lord
Byron*, ch. 10, Doris Langley Moore (1961,
rev. 1976).

Inscription on the monument raised for Lord
Byron's dog, Boatswain, in the grounds of
Newstead Abbey, Byron's seat in Notting-
hamshire. The lines are commonly attributed
to Byron, but a draft of a letter written by Hobhouse in 1830 shows that Byron decided to
use Hobhouse's epitaph instead of his own,
which ran, "To mark a friend's remains these
stones arise/I never knew but one—and here
he lies."

4   A door is what a dog is perpetually on the wrong side of.

OGDEN NASH,(1902–1971) U.S. poet. "A
Dog's Best Friend Is his Illiteracy," *The Private
Dining Room* (1953).

5   I always disliked dogs, those protec-tors of cowards who lack the courage to fight an assailant them-selves.

J. AUGUST STRINDBERG, (1849–1912)
Swedish dramatist, novelist, poet. "A Madman's Defense," pt. 3, ch. 1 (1968).

6   If you pick up a starving dog and make him prosperous, he will not bite you. This is the principal dif-ference between a dog and a man.

MARK TWAIN, (1835–1910) U.S. author.
Pudd'nhead Wilson, ch. 16, "Pudd'nhead
Wilson's Calendar" (1894).

Doubts

1   No, when the fight begins within
     himself,
A man's worth something.

ROBERT BROWNING, (1812–1889) British
poet. "Bishop Blougram's Apology," l. 693–4,
Men and Women, vol. 1 (1855).

2   Between the conception
And the creation
Between the emotion
And the response
Falls the Shadow.

T.S. (THOMAS STEARNS) ELIOT,
(1888–1965) Anglo–American poet, critic.
"The Hollow Men," sct. 5, *Poems 1909–1925*
(1925).

3   Half the failures of this world arise from pulling in one's horse as he is leaping.

JULIUS HARE, (1795–1855) British cleric,
writer. *Guesses at Truth*, First Series (1827).

4   Life is doubt,
    And faith without doubt is nothing
      but death.

MIGUEL DE UNAMUNO, (1864–1936)
Spanish philosophical writer. "Salmo II," *Poesias* (1907).

Drawing

1   An active line on a walk, moving
    freely without a goal. A walk for a
    walk's sake.

PAUL KLEE, (1879–1940) Swiss artist. *Pedagogical Sketchbook*, ch. 1 (1925).

Dreams and Dreaming

1   The armored cars of dreams,
    contrived to let us do so many a
    dangerous thing.

ELIZABETH BISHOP, (1911–1979) U.S.
poet. "Sleeping Standing Up," st. 2, *Poems: North and South a Cold Spring* (1955).

2   A man that is born falls into a
    dream like a man who falls into the
    sea. If he tries to climb out into the
    air as inexperienced people endeav-
    our to do, he drowns.

JOSEPH CONRAD, (1857–1924)
Polish–born British novelist. Marlow, in *Lord Jim*, ch. 20 (1900).

3   The interpretation of dreams is the
    royal road to a knowledge of the
    unconscious activities of the mind.

SIGMUND FREUD, (1856–1939) Austrian
psychiatrist. *The Interpretation of Dreams*, ch.
7 (1900). Repr. in *Complete Works, Standard Edition*, vol. 5–6, eds. James Strachey and Anna Freud (1955).

4   Climb every mountain, ford every
      stream
    Follow every rainbow, till you find
      your dream!

OSCAR HAMMERSTEIN II, (1895–1960)
U.S. songwriter. "Climb Every Mountain" (song), *The Sound of Music* (stage musical, 1959; film, 1965).

5   As Gregor Samsa awoke one morn-
    ing from uneasy dreams he found
    himself transformed in his bed into
    a gigantic insect.

FRANZ KAFKA, (1883–1924) Czech novel-
ist, short–story writer. *Metamorphosis*, ch. 1, *Metamorphosis and Other Stories* (1961). (Originally published 1916).

Opening sentence.

6   Wouldn't it be loverly.

ALAN JAY LERNER, (1918–1986) U.S.
songwriter. "Wouldn't it be Loverly" (song), *My Fair Lady* (show, 1956; film, 1964).

Sung by Eliza Doolittle.

7   But oh as to embrace me she
      inclined
    I waked, she fled, and day brought
      back my night.

JOHN MILTON, (1608–1674) British poet.
"Methought I saw my late espoused saint," Sonnet 23 (1658). Repr. in *Milton's Poetical Works*, ed. Douglas Bush (1966).

Last lines.

8   Those who have likened our life to
    a dream were more right, by
    chance, than they realized. We are
    awake while sleeping, and waking
    sleep.

MICHEL DE MONTAIGNE, (1533–1592)
French essayist. *Essays*, bk. 2, ch. 12 (1588).

See Poe on dreams, Calderón on life.

9   All that we see or seem
    Is but a dream within a dream.

EDGAR ALLAN POE, (1809–1845) U.S.
poet, critic, short–story writer. *A Dream within a Dream* (1849).

10   Oh, Jerry, don't let's ask for the
     moon—we have the stars.

CASEY ROBINSON, Screenwriter. Charlotte Vale (Bette Davis), in *Now, Voyager* (film) (1950). Irving Rapper.

The movie's title is taken from Walt Whitman's *Leaves of Grass.*

11 I keep picturing all these little kids playing some game in this big field of rye and all.... If they're running and they don't look where they're going I have to come out from somewhere and *catch* them. That's all I'd do all day. I'd just be the catcher in the rye and all. I know it's crazy.

J.D. (JEROME DAVID) SALINGER, (b. 1919) U.S. author. The narrator (Holden Caulfield), in *The Catcher in the Rye*, ch. 22 (1951).

12 But I, being poor, have only my
    dreams;
I have spread my dreams under
    your feet;
Tread softly because you tread on
    my dreams.

WILLIAM BUTLER YEATS, (1865–1939) Irish poet, playwright. "He Wishes for the Cloths of Heaven," *The Wind Among the Reeds* (1899).

13 In dreams begins responsibility.

WILLIAM BUTLER YEATS, (1865–1939) Irish poet, playwright. *Responsibilities*, epigraph (1914).

Dress

1 You look rather rash my dear your colors don't quite match your face.

DAISY ASHFORD, (1881–1972) British writer. Mr. Salteena, in *The Young Visiters*, ch. 2, "Starting Gaily" (published 1919).

Written when the author was aged nine.

2 How did you get into that dress— with a spray gun?

EDMUND BELOIN, U.S. screenwriter. Hot Lips Barton (Bob Hope), in *Road To Rio* (film) (1947).

Spoken to Lucia Maria De Andrade (Dorothy Lamour).

3 I have heard with admiring submission the experience of the lady who declared that the sense of being perfectly well dressed gives a feeling of inward tranquility which religion is powerless to bestow.

RALPH WALDO EMERSON, (1803–1882) U.S. essayist, poet, philosopher. *Letters and Social Aims*, "Social Aims" (1876).

4 Englishwomen's shoes look as if they had been made by someone who had often heard shoes described, but had never seen any.

MARGARET HALSEY, (b. 1910) U.S. author. *With Malice Toward Some*, pt. 2 (1938).

5 Clothes make the poor invisible.... America has the best–dressed poverty the world has ever known.

MICHAEL HARRINGTON, (1928–1989) U.S. social scientist, author. *The Other America*, ch. 1, sct. 1 (1962).

6 A sweet disorder in the dress
Kindles in clothes a wantonness.

ROBERT HERRICK, (1591–1674) British poet, clergyman. "Delight in Disorder," *Hesperides* (1648). Repr. in *The Poems of Robert Herrick*, ed. L.C. Martin (1956).

7 Whenas in silks my Julia goes,
Then, then (methinks) how sweetly
    flows
That liquefaction of her clothes.
Next, when I cast mine eyes and see
That brave vibration each way free;
O how that glittering taketh me!

ROBERT HERRICK, (1591–1674) British poet, clergyman. "Upon Julia's Clothes," *Hesperides* (1648). Repr. in *The Poems of Robert Herrick*, ed. L.C. Martin (1956).

8 Brevity is the soul of lingerie.

DOROTHY PARKER, (1893–1967) U.S. humorous writer. Quoted in *While Rome Burns,* "Our Mrs. Parker," Alexander Woollcott (1934).

Caption published in *Vogue* (1916): an allusion to Shakespeare on brevity.

9 Where's the man could ease a heart
Like a satin gown?

DOROTHY PARKER, (1893–1967) U.S. humorous writer. "The Satin Dress," st. 1, *Enough Rope* (1926).

10 I hold that gentleman to be the best–dressed whose dress no one observes.

ANTHONY TROLLOPE, (1815–1882) British novelist. *Thackeray,* ch. 9 (1879).

Drugs

1 Opiate. An unlocked door in the prison of Identity. It leads into the jail yard.

AMBROSE BIERCE, (1842–1914) U.S. author. *The Devil's Dictionary* (1881–1906), repr. in *Collected Works of Ambrose Bierce,* vol. 7 (1911).

2 I'll die young but it's like kissing God.

LENNY BRUCE, (1925–1966) U.S. comic. Quoted in *Playpower,* ch. 4, Richard Neville (1970).

On his drug addiction.

3 Junk is the ideal product ... the ultimate merchandise. No sales talk necessary. The client will crawl through a sewer and beg to buy.

WILLIAM BURROUGHS, (b. 1914) U.S. author. *The Naked Lunch,* introduction (1959).

4 I experimented with marijuana a time or two. And I didn't like it, and I didn't inhale.

BILL CLINTON, (b. 1946) U.S. Democratic politician, president. Quoted in *Washington Post* (March 30, 1992).

Said during a television debate with Jerry Brown, a rival candidate for the Democratic Party nomination. Under close questioning to ascertain whether the two men had ever broken state, federal or international laws, Clinton admitted his misdemeanor while a Rhodes Scholar at Oxford University.

5 Everything one does in life, even love, occurs in an express train racing toward death. To smoke opium is to get out of the train while it is still moving. It is to concern oneself with something other than life or death.

JEAN COCTEAU, (1889–1963) French author, filmmaker. *Opium* (1929).

6 Thou hast the keys of Paradise, O just, subtle, and mighty opium!

THOMAS DE QUINCEY, (1785–1859) British author. *The Confessions of an English Opium–Eater,* pt. 2, "The Pleasures of Opium" (1822).

7 I'd love to turn you on.

JOHN LENNON, (1940–1980) British songwriter, rock musician. "A Day in the Life" (song), on the album *Sgt. Pepper's Lonely Hearts Club Band* (1967).

8 Is marijuana addictive? Yes, in the sense that most of the really pleasant things in life are worth endlessly repeating.

RICHARD NEVILLE, (b. 1941) Australian journalist. "Johnny Pot Wears Gold Sandals and a Black Derby Hat," *Playpower* (1971).

9 I'm waiting for my man
Twenty–six dollars in my hand
Up to Lexington 1–2–5
Feeling sick and dirty more dead
     than alive
I'm waiting for my man.

LOU REED, (b. 1944) U.S. rock musician. "I'm Waiting for the Man" (song), from the album *The Velvet Underground and Nico* (1967).

Dullness

1 Authors have established it as a kind of rule, that a man ought to be dull sometimes; as the most severe reader makes allowances for many rests and nodding–places in a voluminous writer.

JOSEPH ADDISON, (1672–1719) British essayist. *Spectator* (London, July 23, 1711), no. 124, *The Spectator*, ed. D.F. Bond (1965).

2 There is no such thing on earth as an uninteresting subject; the only thing that can exist is an uninterested person.

GILBERT KEITH CHESTERTON, (1874–1936) British author. *Heretics*, ch. 3 (1905).

3 What can he mean by coming among us? He is not only dull himself, but the cause of dullness in others.

SAMUEL FOOTE, (1720–1777) British dramatist. Quoted in *Life of Samuel Johnson*, entry for 1783, James Boswell (1791).

Referring to "a law–lord, who, it seems, once took a fancy to associate with the wits of London."

4 It is to be noted that when any part of this paper appears dull there is a design in it.

RICHARD STEELE, (1672–1729) British dramatist, essayist, editor. *Tatler* (London, July 7, 1709), no. 38, *The Tatler*, vol. 1, ed. G.A. Aitken (1898).

Duty

1 Pressed into service means pressed out of shape.

ROBERT FROST, (1874–1963) U.S. poet. "The Self–Seeker," *North of Boston* (1914).

2 A sense of duty is useful in work but offensive in personal relations. People wish to be liked, not to be endured with patient resignation.

BERTRAND RUSSELL [LORD RUSSELL, 3RD EARL], (1872–1970) British philosopher, mathematician. *The Conquest of Happiness*, ch. 9 (1930).

3 There is no duty we so much underrate as the duty of being happy.

ROBERT LOUIS STEVENSON, (1850–1894) Scottish novelist, essayist, poet. *Virginibus Puerisque*, "An Apology for Idlers" (1881).

4 Not once or twice in our rough island story
The path of duty was the way to glory.

ALFRED TENNYSON, 1ST BARON TENNYSON, (1809–1892) British poet. "Ode on the Death of the Duke of Wellington," st. 8 (1852).

Dystopia

1 It was a bright, cold day in April and the clocks were striking thirteen.

GEORGE ORWELL, (1903–1950) British author. *Nineteen Eighty–Four*, pt. 1, ch. 1 (1949).

Opening words.

Earth

1 Let me enjoy the earth no less
Because the all–enacting Might
That fashioned forth its loveliness
Had other aims than my delight.

THOMAS HARDY, (1840–1928) British novelist, poet. "Let Me Enjoy the Earth," *Time's Laughing Stocks* (1909).

2 To see the earth as we now see it,
small and beautiful in that eternal
silence where it floats, is to see
ourselves as riders on the earth
together, brothers on that bright
loveliness in the unending night—
brothers who *see* now they are
truly brothers.

ARCHIBALD MACLEISH, (1892–1982)
U.S. poet. "Riders on Earth Together, Broth-
ers in Eternal Cold," *The New York Times*
(Dec. 25, 1968). Repr. as "Bubble of Blue
Air" in *Riders on Earth* (1978).

Of the first pictures of the earth from the
moon.

East and West

1 Oh, East is East, and West is West,
and never the twain shall meet,Till
Earth and Sky stand presently at
God's great Judgement Seat; But
there is neither East nor West,
Border, nor Breed, nor Birth,
When two strong men stand face
to face, though they come from
the ends of the earth.

RUDYARD KIPLING, (1865–1936)
British writer, poet. *"The Ballad of East and
West,"* Barrack–Room Ballads (1892).

Opening lines.

Easter

1 The dripping blood our only
drink,
The bloody flesh our only food:
In spite of which we like to think
That we are sound, substantial
flesh and blood—
Again, in spite of that, we call this
Friday good.

T.S. (THOMAS STEARNS) ELIOT,
(1888–1965) Anglo–American poet, critic.
"East Coker," pt. 4 (1940). *Four Quartets*
(1942).

Eccentricity

1 Anybody who hates dogs and
babies can't be all bad.

LEO ROSTEN, (b. 1908) U.S. author.
Quoted in *Saturday Review* (June 12, 1976).
Speech Feb. 16, 1939 in honor of W.C. Fields,
Masquers' Club Dinner, Hollywood.

Referring to W.C. Fields, and often erroneously ascribed to him, with the words "Anyone who hates children and dogs can't be all
bad."

2 So long as a man rides his
Hobby–Horse peaceably and quietly along the King's highway, and
neither compels you or me to get
up behind him—pray, Sir, what
have either you or I to do with it?

LAURENCE STERNE, (1713–1768) British
author. *Tristram Shandy*, bk. 1, ch. 7
(1759–1767).

Ecology

1 O if we but knew what we do
When we delve or hew—
Hack and rack the growing green!
Since country is so tender
To touch, her being so slender,
That, like this sleek and seeing ball
But a prick will make no eye at all,
Where we, even where we mean
To mend her we end her,
When we hew or delve:
After–comers cannot guess the
   beauty been.

GERARD MANLEY HOPKINS,
(1844–1889) British poet, Jesuit priest. "Binsey
Poplars," st. 2 (written 1879), published in
Poems (1918).

Economics

1 In the usual (though certainly not
in every) public decision on eco-

nomic policy, the choice is between courses that are almost equally good or equally bad. It is the narrowest decisions that are most ardently debated. If the world is lucky enough to enjoy peace, it may even one day make the discovery, to the horror of doctrinaire free–enterprisers and doctrinaire planners alike, that what is called capitalism and what is called socialism are both capable of working quite well.

JOHN KENNETH GALBRAITH, (b. 1908) U.S. economist. *The American Economy: Its Substance and Myth* (1949). Repr. in *Years of the Modern*, ed. J.W. Chase.

Economizing

1   Mere parsimony is not economy.... Expense, and great expense, may be an essential part in true economy.

EDMUND BURKE, (1729–1797) Irish philosopher, statesman. *A Letter to a Noble Lord* (1796), repr. in *Works*, vol. 5 (1899).

Economy, the

1   This island is made mainly of coal and surrounded by fish. Only an organizing genius could produce a shortage of coal and fish at the same time.

ANEURIN BEVAN, (1897–1960) British Labour politician. Quoted in *Daily Herald* (London, May 25, 1945). Speech, May 24, 1945, Blackpool.

Bevan's speech occurred on the day when Churchill announced the formation of a Conservative "caretaker" government in the wake of V.E. Day and the dissolution of the wartime coalition. The Conservatives were to be ejected from office two months later following a landslide victory for the Labour Party.

2   For at least another hundred years we must pretend to ourselves and

to every one that fair is foul and foul is fair; for foul is useful and fair is not. Avarice and usury and precaution must be our gods for a little longer still.

JOHN MAYNARD KEYNES, (1883–1946) British economist. *Essays in Persuasion*, ch. 5, "The Future" (1931).

Keynes argued that the "detestable ... love of money" and other vices of greed must continue until the economy has grown enough to satisfy human wants and provide the potential for removing poverty.

Ecstasy

1   To burn always with this hard, gemlike flame, to maintain this ecstasy, is success in life.

WALTER PATER, (1839–1894) British essayist, critic. *Studies in the History of the Renaissance*, "Conclusion" (1873).

Referring to "the focus where the greatest number of vital forces unite in their purest energy."

Eden

1   And out of the ground made the Lord God to grow every tree that is pleasant to the sight, and good for food: the tree of life also in the midst of the garden, and the tree of knowledge of good and evil. And a river went out of Eden to water the garden.

BIBLE: HEBREW, *Genesis*, 2:9–10.

Editing

1   Art, it seems to me, should simplify ... finding what conventions of form and what detail one can do without and yet preserve the spirit of the whole—so that all that one has suppressed and cut away is

there to the reader's consciousness as much as if it were in type on the page.

WILLA CATHER, (1876–1947) U.S. author. *On Writing*, "On the Art of Fiction" (1949). (Written 1920).

2 What I have crossed out I didn't like. What I haven't crossed out I'm dissatisfied with.

CECIL B. DE MILLE, (1881–1959) U.S. film director, producer. Quoted in *Halliwell's Filmgoer's Companion* (1984).

Note attached to rejected script.

3 Read your own compositions, and when you meet with a passage which you think is particularly fine, strike it out.

SAMUEL JOHNSON, (1709–1784) British author, lexicographer. Quoted in James Boswell, *Life of Dr. Johnson*, entry, April 30, 1773 (1791).

Quoting a college tutor.

Editors

1 Editor: a person employed by a newspaper, whose business it is to separate the wheat from the chaff, and to see that the chaff is printed.

ELBERT HUBBARD, (1856–1915) U.S. author. *Roycroft Dictionary of Epigrams* (1914).

This definition was picked up by Adlai Stevenson, and included in *The Stevenson Wit* (1966).

Education

1 Train up a child in the way he should go: and when he is old, he will not depart from it.

BIBLE: HEBREW, *Proverbs*, 22:6.

2 What sculpture is to a block of marble, education is to an human soul.

JOSEPH ADDISON, (1672–1719) British essayist. *Spectator* (London, Nov. 6, 1711), no. 215, *The Spectator*, ed. D.F. Bond (1965).

3 There's a new tribunal now Higher than God's—the educated man's!

ROBERT BROWNING, (1812–1889) British poet. "The Ring and the Book," bk. 10, l. 1976–7 (1868–1869).

4 Better build schoolrooms for "the boy" Than cells and gibbets for "the man."

ELIZA COOK, (1818–1889) British poet. "A Song for the Ragged Schools," st. 12 (1853).

5 We are not to give credit to the many, who say that none ought to be educated but the free; but rather to the philosophers, who say that the well–educated alone are free.

EPICTETUS,

(c. 55–c. 135) Greek stoic philosopher. *Discourses*, bk. 2, ch. 1, trans. by Elizabeth Carter (1758).

6 Education is the art of making man ethical.

GEORG HEGEL, (1770–1831) German philosopher. *The Philosophy of Right*, no. 58 (1821, trans. 1942).

7 The only fence against the world is a thorough knowledge of it.

JOHN LOCKE, (1632–1704) British philosopher. *Some Thoughts Concerning Education*, sct. 88 (1693).

8 If education is always to be conceived along the same antiquated lines of a mere transmission of

knowledge, there is little to be hoped from it in the bettering of man's future. For what is the use of transmitting knowledge if the individual's total development lags behind?

Maria Montessori, (1870–1952) Italian educator. *The Absorbent Mind*, ch. 1 (1949).

9 'Tis education forms the common mind,
Just as the twig is bent, the tree's inclined.

Alexander Pope, (1688–1744) British satirical poet. "Epistle to Cobham," l. 149–50 (1734).

10 We are born weak, we need strength; helpless, we need aid; foolish, we need reason. All that we lack at birth, all that we need when we come to man's estate, is the gift of education.

Jean–Jacques Rousseau, (1712–1778) Swiss–born French philosopher, political theorist. *Emile*, bk. 1 (1762).

11 So that with much ado I was corrupted, and made to learn the dirty devices of this world.
Which now I unlearn, and become, as it were, a little child again that I may enter into the Kingdom of God.

Thomas Traherne, (1636–1674) British clergyman, poet, mystic. *Centuries of Meditations*, "Third Century," no. 3 (written c. 1672, first published 1908).

Effort

1 Inscribe all human effort with one word,
Artistry's haunting curse, the Incomplete!

Robert Browning, (1812–1889) British poet. "The Ring and the Book," bk. 11, l. 1560 (1868–1869).

2 You can't always get what you want
But if you try sometimes
You just might find
You get what you need.

Mick Jagger, (b. 1943) British rock musician. "You Can't Always Get What You Want" (song), on the album *Let It Bleed* (1970).

3 I wish to preach, not the doctrine of ignoble ease, but the doctrine of the strenuous life.

Theodore Roosevelt, (1858–1919) U.S. Republican (later Progressive) politician, president. *The Penguin Book of Twentieth Century Speeches*, ed. Brian MacArthur (1992). Speech, April 10, 1899, Chicago.

Roosevelt devoted much of his life to "strenuous" pursuits, building up a slender frame by vigorous exercise, and enduring extreme conditions as rancher and soldier.

Elation

1 Yabba dabba do!

William Denby Hanna, (b. 1910) U.S. animator. Fred Flintstone, in *The Flintstones* (TV cartoon).

Fred Flintstone (voiced by Alan Reed) and the other characters were adapted from *The Honeymooners* (TV sitcom), whose protagonists, Jackie Gleason and Art Carney, bore a striking resemblance to Fred and Barney. Hanna–Barbera production (from 1960).

Elections

1 I just received the following wire from my generous Daddy—"Dear Jack, Don't buy a single vote more than is necessary. I'll be damned if I'm going to pay for a landslide."

John Fitzgerald Kennedy, (1917–1963) U.S. Democratic politician, president. Quoted in *The Wit of President Kennedy*, Bill Adler (1964). Speech, 1958, Gridiron Dinner, Washington D.C..

2 A funny thing happened to me on the way to the White House.

ADLAI STEVENSON, (1900–1965) U.S. Democratic politician. Quoted in *Portrait: Adlai E. Stevenson*, ch. 1, Alden Whitman (1965). Speech, Dec. 13, 1952, Washington D.C..

After his defeat in the Presidential election, in which Eisenhower won a landslide victory.

Elegance

1 Elegance does not consist in putting on a new dress.

COCO CHANEL, (1883–1971) French *couturière*. Quoted in *Coco Chanel: Her Life, Her Secrets*, ch. 21, Marcel Haedrich (1971).

Elite, the

1 For many are called, but few are chosen.

BIBLE: NEW TESTAMENT, Jesus, in *Matthew*, 22:14.

In the parable of the marriage of the king's son.

Eloquence

1 To acquire immunity to eloquence is of the utmost importance to the citizens of a democracy.

BERTRAND RUSSELL [LORD RUSSELL, 3RD EARL], (1872–1970) British philosopher, mathematician. *Power*, ch. 18, sct. 4 (1938).

Embarrassment

1 Well, la–de–da!

WOODY ALLEN, (b. 1935) U.S. filmmaker. Annie, in *Annie Hall* (film) (1977).

2 Man is the only animal that blushes. Or needs to.

MARK TWAIN, (1835–1910) U.S. author. *Following the Equator*, ch. 27, "Pudd'nhead Wilson's New Calendar" (1897).

Emigrants and Refugees

1 Emigration, forced or chosen, across national frontiers or from village to metropolis, is the quintessential experience of our time.

JOHN BERGER, (b. 1926) British author, critic. *And Our Faces, My Heart, Brief As Photos*, pt. 2 (1984).

2 One must apply one's reason to everything here, learning to obey, to shut up, to help, to be good, to give in, and I don't know what else. I'm afraid I shall use up all my brains too quickly, and I haven't got so very many. Then I shall not have any left for when the war is over.

ANNE FRANK, (1929–1945) German Jewish refugee, diarist. *The Diary of a Young Girl* (1947, trans. 1952). Entry, Dec. 22, 1942.

3 As a lone ant from a broken ant–hill
from the wreckage of Europe, ego scriptor.

EZRA POUND, (1885–1972) U.S. poet, critic. "Canto 76," *The Pisan Cantos* (1948).

Empires

1 The day of small nations has long passed away. The day of Empires has come.

JOSEPH CHAMBERLAIN, (1836–1914) British politician. Quoted in *Times* (London, May 13, 1904). Speech, May 12, 1904, Birmingham, England.

2 The conquest of the earth, which mostly means the taking it away from those who have a different complexion or slightly flatter noses than ourselves, is not a pretty thing when you look into it.

JOSEPH CONRAD, (1857–1924) Polish–born British novelist. *The Heart of Darkness*, ch. 1 (1902).

3 How is the Empire?

GEORGE V, KING, (1865–1936) British King of Great Britain and Ireland. *Attributed.*

Attributed last words, as reported to the nation, Jan. 21, 1936—the day after the king's death—in a broadcast tribute by Prime Minister Stanley Baldwin, though other accounts deny these were the king's last words: Lord Dawson, the king's physician, recorded in his diary the king's actual last words were "God damn you." See George V on places.

4 And the end of the fight is a tombstone white with the name of the late deceased,
And the epitaph drear: "A Fool lies here who tried to hustle the East."

RUDYARD KIPLING, (1865–1936) British author, poet. *The Naulahka*, heading of ch. 5 (1892).

5 Take up the White Man's burden—
Send forth the best ye breed—
Go, bind your sons to exile
To serve your captives' need.

RUDYARD KIPLING, (1865–1936) British author, poet. "The White Man's Burden," *The Five Nations* (1903). Poem first published (1899).

Addressed to the American people on the occasion of their occupation of the Philippines at the end of the Spanish–American War of 1898. The poem's title has become a euphemism for the kind of patriarchal imperialism then current.

6 Imperialism is capitalism at that stage of development at which the dominance of monopolies and finance capitalism is established; in which the export of capital has acquired pronounced importance; in which the division of the world among the international trusts has begun, in which the division of all territories of the globe among the biggest capitalist powers has been completed.

VLADIMIR ILYICH LENIN, (1870–1924) Russian revolutionary leader. *Imperialism, the Highest Stage of Capitalism*, ch. 7 (1916).

7 The reluctant obedience of distant provinces generally costs more than it [the territory] is worth. Empires which branch out widely are often more flourishing for a little timely pruning.

THOMAS BABINGTON MACAULAY, (1800–1859) British historian, Whig politician. "War of the Succession in Spain," *Edinburgh Review* (Jan. 1833). *Critical and Historical Essays* (1843).

8 To found a great empire for the sole purpose of raising up a people of customers, may at first sight appear a project fit only for a nation of shopkeepers. It is, however, a project altogether unfit for a nation of shopkeepers, but extremely fit for a nation that is governed by shopkeepers.

ADAM SMITH, (1723–1790) Scottish economist. *The Wealth of Nations*, vol. 2, bk. 4, ch. 7 (1776).

Stevenson's *Book of Quotations* cites a similar remark made slightly earlier by English economist Josiah Tucker in *Four Tracts on Political and Commercial Subjects* (1766) but Adam Smith's version was probably the source for its wider dissemination, and the origin of Napoleon's more famous utterance, "England is a nation of shopkeepers." (See quotes under "England and the English.").

9 To plunder, butcher, steal, these things they misname empire: they

make a desolation and they call it peace.

TACITUS, (c. 55–c. 120) Roman historian. *Agricola*, sct. 30.

Ascribed by Tacitus to a Scottish chief, Calgacus, on the Roman victory at Mons Graupius, near Inverness.

End of the World

1   Amen. Even so, come, Lord Jesus.

BIBLE: NEW TESTAMENT, St. John the Divine, in *Revelation*, 22:20.

From the penultimate verse in the New Testament; the last is: "The grace of our Lord Jesus Christ be with you all. Amen."

2   And ye shall hear of wars and rumours of wars: see that ye be not troubled: for all these things must come to pass, but the end is not yet. For nation shall rise against nation, and kingdom against kingdom: and there shall be famines, and pestilences, and earthquakes, in divers places.

BIBLE: NEW TESTAMENT, Jesus, in *Matthew*, 24:6–7.

3   This is the way the world ends
This is the way the world ends
This is the way the world ends
Not with a bang but a whimper.

T.S. (THOMAS STEARNS) ELIOT, (1888–1965) Anglo–American poet, critic. "The Hollow Men," *Poems 1909–1925* (1925).

Concluding lines.

4   Some say the world will end in fire,
Some say in ice.
From what I've tasted of desire
I hold with those who favor fire.
But if it had to perish twice,
I think I know enough of hate
To say that for destruction ice
Is also great

And would suffice.

ROBERT FROST, (1874–1963) U.S. poet. "Fire and Ice," *New Hampshire* (1923).

5   God seems to have left the receiver off the hook, and time is running out.

ARTHUR KOESTLER, (1905–1983) Hungarian–born British author. *The Ghost in the Machine*, ch. 18 (1967).

6   The world began without man, and it will end without him.

CLAUDE LEVI–STRAUSS, (b. 1908) French anthropologist. *Tristes Tropiques*, pt. 9, ch. 40 (1955).

Ends and Means

1   The end may justify the means as long as there is something that justifies the end.

LEON TROTSKY, (1879–1940) Russian revolutionary. Quoted in *Antonio Gramsci: an Introduction to his Thought*, preface, Alberto Pozzolini (1970).

Endurance

1   Lord, how long?

BIBLE: HEBREW, *Isaiah*, 6:11.

Asking how long will the chastisement of the people last. God replies, "Until the cities be wasted without inhabitant, and the houses without man, and the land be utterly desolate, and the Lord have removed man far away, and there be a great forsaking in the midst of the land."

2   Now this is not the end. It is not even the beginning of the end. But it is, perhaps, the end of the beginning.

WINSTON CHURCHILL, (1874–1965) British statesman, writer. *The End of the Beginning* (1943). Speech, Nov. 10, 1942, the Mansion House, London.

On the Eighth Army's victory against Rommel at El Alamein, Egypt. In his *History of the Second*

World War, vol. 4 (1951), Churchill wrote, "It may almost be said, 'Before Alamein we never had a victory. After Alamein we never had a defeat.'"

3 Since every man who lives is born
    to die,
    And none can boast sincere felicity,
    With equal mind, what happens, let
    us bear,
    Nor joy nor grieve too much for
    things beyond our care.

JOHN DRYDEN, (1631–1700) British poet, dramatist, critic. Egeus, in *Palamon and Arcite*, bk. 3, l. 883 (1700).

Dryden's dramatic poem was adapted from Chaucer's *Knight's Tale*.

4 There is nothing happens to any
    person but what was in his power
    to go through with.

MARCUS AURELIUS, (121–180) Roman emperor, philosopher. *Meditations*, bk. 5, sct. 18, trans. by Jeremy Collier.

5 Till the sun grows cold,
    And the stars are old,
    And the leaves of the Judgment
    Book unfold.

BAYARD TAYLOR, (1825–1875) U.S. poet, author, translator. "Bedouin Song," refrain.

Enemies

1 And I will call for a sword against
    him throughout all my mountains,
    saith the Lord God: every man's
    sword shall be against his brother.

BIBLE: HEBREW, *Ezekiel*, 38:21.

God, prophesying the time when Gog, prince of Magog, shall come against Israel.

2 I wish my deadly foe no worse
    Than want of friends, and empty
    purse.

NICHOLAS BRETON, (c.1545–1626) British author, poet. "A Farewell to Town," (1577). Repr. in *Works in Verse and Prose of Nicholas Breton*, vol. 1 (1879).

3 You shall judge of a man by his foes
    as well as by his friends.

JOSEPH CONRAD, (1857–1924) Polish–born British novelist. Marlow, in *Lord Jim*, ch. 34 (1900).

4 Treating your adversary with
    respect is giving him an advantage
    to which he is not entitled.

SAMUEL JOHNSON, (1709–1784) British author, lexicographer. Quoted in James Boswell, *Journal of a Tour to the Hebrides*, entry, Aug. 15, 1773 (1785).

5 Forgive your enemies, but never
    forget their names.

JOHN FITZGERALD KENNEDY, (1917–1963) U.S. Democratic politician, president. Attributed in *The Harper Book of American Quotations*, eds. Gorton Carruth and Eugene Ehrlich (1988).

The quote has also been ascribed to Robert Kennedy.

6 I am the enemy you killed, my
    friend. I knew you in this dark; for
    so you frowned Yesterday through
    me as you jabbed and killed. I par-
    ried; but my hands were loath and
    cold. Let us sleep now.

WILFRED OWEN, (1893–1918) British poet. "Strange Meeting," (written 1918), publ. in *The Poems of Wilfred Owen*, ed. Edmund Blunden (1931).

Closing lines of poem, of which variant versions exist.

Engineering

1 For 'tis the sport to have the engi-
    neer
    Hoised with his own petard.

WILLIAM SHAKESPEARE, (1564–1616) British dramatist, poet. Hamlet, in *Hamlet*, act 3, sc. 4, l. 190–1 (1604).

Referring to the untrustworthiness of Rosencrantz and Guildenstern. (These lines do not appear in the 1623 Folio edition.) A "petard" was an explosive device used by engineers of the time, and thus the expression has passed into common usage to mean "caught in one's own trap."

England and the English

1   He was born an Englishman and remained one for years.

BRENDAN BEHAN, (1923–1964) Irish playwright. Pat, in *The Hostage*, act 1 (1958).

Referring to Monsewer, who later "found out he was an Irishman."

2   England! awake! awake! awake!
Jerusalem thy sister calls!
Why wilt thou sleep the sleep of
   death,
And close her from thy ancient walls?

WILLIAM BLAKE, (1757–1827) British poet, painter, engraver. *Jerusalem*, plate 77, "To the Christians," (c. 1820), repr. in *Complete Writings*, ed. Geoffrey Keynes (1957).

3   The harlot's cry from street to street
Shall weave old England's winding
   sheet.

WILLIAM BLAKE, (1757–1827) British poet, painter, engraver. *Auguries of Innocence*, l. 115–6, Keynes (1957).

4   Oh, to be in England
Now that April's there,
And whoever wakes in England
Sees, some morning, unaware,
That the lowest boughs and the
   brushwood sheaf
Round the elm–tree bole are in tiny
   leaf,
While the chaffinch sings on the
   orchard bough
In England—now!

ROBERT BROWNING, (1812–1889) British poet. "Home Thoughts, From Abroad," st. 1, *Dramatic Romances and Lyrics* (1845).

5   I am sure my bones would not rest in an English grave, or my clay mix with the earth of that country. I believe the thought would drive me mad on my death–bed could I suppose that any of my friends would be base enough to convey my carcass back to her soil. I would not even feed her worms if I could help it.

GEORGE GORDON NOEL BYRON, 6TH BARON BYRON,(1788–1824) British poet. *Byron's Letters and Journals*, vol. 6, ed. Leslie Marchand (1976). Letter, June 7, 1819, to publisher John Murray.

After Byron's death from a fever in Greece, his body was brought back to England where it was interred together with his ancestors near his home at Newstead Abbey, having been refused burial at Westminster Abbey.

6   In England there are sixty different religions, and only one sauce.

FRANCESCO CARACCIOLO, (1752–1799) Neapolitan naval commander. *Attributed.*

7   I know an Englishman,
Being flattered, is a lamb; threatened, a lion.

GEORGE CHAPMAN, c. 1559–1634 British dramatist, poet, translator. Archbishop of Cologne, in *Alphonsus, Emperor of Germany*, act 1, sc. 2, l. 208–9 (1654). Repr. in *Plays and Poems of George Chapman: The Tragedies*, ed. Thomas Marc Parrott (1910).

On the proposal to make Richard, Earl of Cornwall, Holy Roman Emperor. The ascription of the play to Chapman has been questioned.

8   In Bengal to move at all
Is seldom, if ever, done,
But mad dogs and Englishmen
Go out in the midday sun.

NOËL COWARD, (1899–1973) British playwright, actor, composer. "Mad Dogs and Englishmen" (song) (1930), published in *Collected Sketches and Lyrics* (1931).

9 England is the paradise of women, the purgatory of men, and the hell of horses.

JOHN FLORIO, (c. 1553–1625) British author, translator. Silvestro, in *Second Frutes*, ch. 12 (1591).

10 It is not that the Englishman can't feel—it is that he is afraid to feel. He has been taught at his public school that feeling is bad form. He must not express great joy or sorrow, or even open his mouth too wide when he talks—his pipe might fall out if he did.

E.M. (EDWARD MORGAN) FORSTER, (1879–1970) British novelist, essayist. "Notes on the English Character," repr. in *Abinger Harvest* (1936). (Originally published 1920).

11 Not Angles, but angels.
[Non Angli sed Angeli.]

GREGORY THE GREAT, POPE, (c. 540–604) *Attributed.*

Probably an oral rendition of words that appear in Bede's *History of the English Church and People* (bk. 2, sct. 1; completed 731), in which Gregory—before he was Pope—was presented with some slaves in the market–place in Rome, with "fair complexions, fine–cut features, and beautiful hair." On being told they were Angles, he said, "That is appropriate, for they have angelic faces, and it is right that they should become joint–heirs with the angels in heaven." According to Bede, this encounter led him to take in hand the conversion of Britain immediately on succeeding to the Papacy.

12 The English (it must be owned) are rather a foul–mouthed nation.

WILLIAM HAZLITT, (1778–1830) British essayist. *Table Talk*, "On Criticism" (1821–1822).

13 The Englishman never enjoys himself except for a noble purpose.

A.P. (SIR ALAN PATRICK) HERBERT, (1890–1971) British author, politician. Mr. Justice Plush, in *Uncommon Law*, "Is Fox–Hunting Fun?" (1935).

14 And what should they know of England who only England know?

RUDYARD KIPLING, (1865–1936) British author, poet. "The English Flag," l. 2, *Barrack–Room Ballads* (1892).

15 An acre in Middlesex is better than a principality in Utopia.

THOMAS BABINGTON MACAULAY, (1800–1859) British historian, Whig politician. *Lord Bacon, Edinburgh Review* (July 1837). *Critical and Historical Essays* (1843).

16 On the Continent people have good food; in England people have good table manners.

GEORGE MIKES, (1912–1987) Hungarian–born British humorist. *How To Be An Alien*, ch. 1, sct. 1 (1946).

Commenting in 1977 on his oft–quoted remark above; "Since then, food in England has improved, table manners have deteriorated. In those days food was hardly ever discussed, it was taboo, like sex." (*How To Be Decadent*).

17 Let not England forget her precedence of teaching nations how to live.

JOHN MILTON, (1608–1674) British poet. *The Doctrine and Discipline of Divorce*, "To the Parliament of England" (1643).

18 England is a nation of shopkeepers.

NAPOLEON BONAPARTE, (1769–1821) French general, emperor. Quoted in *Napoleon in Exile*, vol. 2, p. 81, Barry E. O'Meara (1822).

Remark made while in exile on St. Helena. It is thought that Napoleon heard the phrase from Bernard de Vieuzac Barée, who may have adopted it from economist Adam Smith. (See Smith on empire.).

19 Every Englishman is convinced of one thing, viz.: That to be an Eng-

lishman is to belong to the most exclusive club there is.

OGDEN NASH, (1902–1971) U.S. poet. "England Expects," *I'm a Stranger Here Myself* (1938).

20 But Lord! to see the absurd nature of Englishmen, that cannot forbear laughing and jeering at everything that looks strange.

SAMUEL PEPYS, (1633–1703) British diarist. *The Diary of Samuel Pepys,* eds. Robert Latham and William Matthews (1977–1983). Journal entry, Nov. 27, 1662.

21 This royal throne of kings, this
   sceptred isle,
   This earth of majesty, this seat of
   Mars,
   This other Eden, demi–paradise,
   This fortress built by nature for
   herself
   Against infection and the hand of
   war,
   This happy breed of men, this little
   world,
   This precious stone set in the silver
   sea,
   Which serves it in the office of a
   wall,
   Or as a moat defensive to a house
   Against the envy of less happier
   lands;
   This bless'd plot, this earth, this
   realm, this England.

WILLIAM SHAKESPEARE, (1564–1616) British dramatist, poet. John of Gaunt, in *Richard II,* act 2, sc. 1, l. 40–50 (1597).

Contrasting England, "this other Eden," with its present state of degeneration—"leased out ... like to a tenement or pelting farm."

22 This Englishwoman is so refined
   She has no bosom and no behind.

STEVIE SMITH, (1902–1971) British poet, novelist. "This Englishwoman," *A Good Time Was Had By All* (1937).

The title of Stevie Smith's first book of poems is given as the original source of the expres-

sion "A good time was had by all" in Eric Partridge, *A Dictionary of Catch Phrases,* ed. Paul Beale (1985).

23 I cannot but conclude the bulk of your natives to be the most pernicious race of little, odious vermin that Nature ever suffered to crawl upon the surface of the earth.

JONATHAN SWIFT, (1667–1745) Anglo–Irish satirist. The king of Brobdingnag, in *Gulliver's Travels,* "A Voyage to Brobdingnag," ch. 6 (1726).

Addressing Gulliver.

English Language

1 We have really everything in common with America nowadays, except, of course, language.

OSCAR WILDE, (1854–1900) Anglo–Irish playwright, author. *The Canterville Ghost,* ch. 1, *Court and Society Review* (London, Feb. 23 and March 2, 1887). Repr. in *Complete Works of Oscar Wilde,* ed. J.B. Foreman (1966).

The words, or similar ones, have often been attributed to George Bernard Shaw, though they are not to be found in Shaw's published writings. Bertrand Russell made a similar point in *Saturday Evening Post,* June 3, 1944: "It is a misfortune for Anglo–American friendship that the two countries are supposed to have a common language."

Enlightenment

1 Time advances: facts accumulate; doubts arise. Faint glimpses of truth begin to appear, and shine more and more unto the perfect day. The highest intellects, like the tops of mountains, are the first to catch and to reflect the dawn. They are bright, while the level below is still in darkness. But soon the light, which at first illuminated only the loftiest eminences, descends on the plain, and penetrates to the deepest

valley. First come hints, then fragments of systems, then defective systems, then complete and harmonious systems. The sound opinion, held for a time by one bold speculator, becomes the opinion of a small minority, of a strong minority, of a majority of mankind. Thus, the great progress goes on.

THOMAS BABINGTON MACAULAY, (1800–1859) British historian, Whig politician. "Sir James Mackintosh," *Edinburgh Review* (July 1835). *Critical and Historical Essays* (1843).

Ennui

1   What'll we do with ourselves this afternoon? And the day after that, and the next thirty years?

F. SCOTT FITZGERALD, (1896–1940) U.S. author. Daisy Buchanan, in *The Great Gatsby*, ch. 7 (1925).

2   What a day–to–day affair life is.

JULES LAFORGUE, (1860–1887) French symbolist poet. "Complainte sur certains ennuis," *Les Complaintes* (1885).

3   Alas, the flesh is weary, and I've read all the books.

STÉPHANE MALLARMÉ, (1842–1898) French symbolist poet." Brise Marine", st. 1, *Mallarmé, The Poems*, trans. by and ed. Keith Bosley (1977). *Posies* (1887).

4   She, while her lover pants upon her breast,
     Can mark the figures on an Indian chest.

ALEXANDER POPE, (1688–1744) British satirical poet. "Epistle to a Lady," l. 167–8 (1735).

5   There's nothing in this world can make me joy.
     Life is as tedious as a twice–told tale,

Vexing the dull ear of a drowsy man.

WILLIAM SHAKESPEARE, (1564–1616) British dramatist, poet. Louis the Dauphin, in *King John*, act 3, sc. 4, l. 107–9 (1623).

Enterprise

1   Look with favor on a bold enterprise.

VIRGIL [PUBLIUS VERGILIUS MARO], (70–19 B.C.) Roman poet. "Georgics," bk. 1, l. 40 (29 B.C.), trans. by Kate Hughes (1995).

The words "annuit coeptis" were inscribed on the reverse side of the Great Seal of the United States of America, June 29, 1782.

Entertainment

1   Th' only way t' entertain some folks is t' listen t' 'em.

KIN HUBBARD (F. [FRANK] McKINNEY HUBBARD), (1868–1930) U.S. humorist, journalist. *Abe Martin's Wisecracks*, ed. E.V. Lucas (1930).

Enthusiasm

1   Does it *really* matter what these affectionate people do—so long as they don't do it in the streets *and frighten the horses!*

MRS. PATRICK CAMPBELL, (1865–1940) British actress. Quoted in *Mrs. Patrick Campbell*, p. 78, Alan Dent (1961).

Referring to rumors of a homosexual liaison between two actors.

2   Life is too short to be little. Man is never so manly as when he feels deeply, acts boldly, and expresses himself with frankness and with fervour.

BENJAMIN DISRAELI, (1804–1881) British statesman, author. *Coningsby*, bk.7, ch. 2 (1844).

3 Nothing great was ever achieved without enthusiasm.

RALPH WALDO EMERSON, (1803–1882) U.S. essayist, poet, philosopher. *Essays,* "Circles," First Series (1841).

4 Oh heavens, how I long for a little ordinary human enthusiasm. Just enthusiasm—that's all. I want to hear a warm, thrilling voice cry out Hallelujah! Hallelujah! I'm alive!

JOHN OSBORNE, (1929–1994) British playwright. Jimmy, in *Look Back in Anger,* act 1 (1956).

Environment

1 I live not in myself, but I become
   Portion of that around me; and to
   me
   High mountains are a feeling, but
   the hum
   Of human cities torture.

GEORGE GORDON NOEL BYRON, 6TH BARON BYRON, (1788–1824) British poet. "Childe Harold's Pilgrimage," cto. 3, st. 72 (1812–18).

2 That which is not good for the bee–hive cannot be good for the bees.

MARCUS AURELIUS, (121–180) Roman emperor, philosopher. *Meditations,* bk. 6, sct. 54, trans. by Jeremy Collier.

Envy

1 For not many men, the proverb
   saith,
   Can love a friend whom fortune
   prospereth
   Unenvying; and about the envious
   brain
   Cold poison clings, and doubles all
   the pain

Life brings him.

AESCHYLUS, (525–456 B.C.) Greek dramatist. Agamemnon, in *Agamemnon,* l. 832–6, trans. by Gilbert Murray.

See Vidal on success.

2 Thou shalt not covet thy neighbour's house, thou shalt not covet thy neighbour's wife, nor his manservant, nor his maidservant, nor his ox, nor his ass, nor any thing that is thy neighbour's.

BIBLE: HEBREW, *Exodus,* 20:17.

The tenth commandment.

3 Fools may our scorn, not envy, raise.
   For envy is a kind of praise.

JOHN GAY, (1685–1732) British dramatist, poet. "The Hound and the Huntsman," *Fables* (1727).

Ephemerality

1 We are such stuff
   As dreams are made on, and our
   little life
   Is rounded with a sleep.

WILLIAM SHAKESPEARE, (1564–1616) British dramatist, poet. Prospero, in *The Tempest,* act 4, sc. 1, l. 156–8 (1623).

Epics

1 Arms, and the man I sing.
   [Arma virumque cano.]

VIRGIL [PUBLIUS VERGILIUS MARO], (70–19 B.C.) Roman poet. *Aeneid,* bk. 1, l. 1 (19 B.C.), trans. by John Dryden (1697).

Opening line of the Aeneid, from which George Bernard Shaw took the title of his satire (1894).

Epiphany

1   By an epiphany he meant a sudden spiritual manifestation, whether in vulgarity of speech or of gesture or in a memorable phase of the mind itself. He believed that it was for the man of letters to recover these epiphanies with extreme care, seeing that they are the most delicate and evanescent of moments.

JAMES JOYCE, (1882–1941) Irish author. *Stephen Hero*, ch. 25 (written c. 1914, published 1944).

Linked to its religious connotation (from the Greek *epiphaneia*, meaning "manifestation, appearance"), the term "epiphany" was coined by Joyce to describe the sudden revelation of a particular moment, occasioned by an encounter, remark or coincidence, that encapsulates a truth—when "the soul of the commonest object ... seems to us radiant."

Epitaphs

1   Posterity will ne'er survey
A nobler grave than this:
Here lie the bones of Castlereagh:
Stop, traveller, and piss.

GEORGE GORDON NOEL BYRON, 6TH BARON BYRON, (1788–1824) British poet. "Epitaph for Castlereagh" (1822).

Robert Stewart, Viscount Castlereagh, a Tory foreign secretary, was held responsible for many of his government's repressive measures abroad; he committed suicide August 12, 1822.

2   Here lies W.C. Fields. I would rather be living in Philadelphia.

W.C. FIELDS, (1879–1946) U.S. actor. *Vanity Fair* (New York, June 1925).

Suggested epitaph as told to *Vanity Fair*. Fields, who was born in Philadelphia, may have had in mind an anecdote about George Washington, who was reported to have uttered a similar sentiment regarding the choice of New York as federal capital in 1789. The words have become associated with Fields in the form, "On the whole, I'd rather be in Philadelphia"—though they do not appear in any form on Fields's gravestone. Ronald Reagan quipped, "All in all, I'd rather be in Philadelphia" following an assassination attempt in 1981.

3   Here Skugg
Lies snug
As a bug
In a rug

BENJAMIN FRANKLIN, (1706–1790) U.S. statesman, writer. *Papers of Benjamin Franklin*, vol. 19, ed. W.B. Willcox (1975). Letter, Sept. 26, 1772.

On the death of a squirrel.

4   The body
Of
Benjamin Franklin
Printer (Like the cover of an old book
Its contents torn out
And stripped of its lettering and gilding)
Lies here, food for worms. But the work shall not be lost
For it will (as he believed) appear once more
In a new and more elegant edition
Revised and corrected
by The Author.

BENJAMIN FRANKLIN, (1706–1790) U.S. statesman, writer. "Epitaph on Himself," *Complete Works*, vol. 10, ed. John Bigelow (1887–1888).

The lines, which were composed in 1728, when Franklin was 22, were not used on his monument. In his *Autobiography*, Franklin wrote, "I should have no objection to go over the same life from its beginning to the end: requesting only the advantage authors have, of correcting in a second edition the faults of the first."

5   And were an epitaph to be my story
I'd have a short one ready for my own.
I would have written of me on my stone:

I had a lover's quarrel with the world.

ROBERT FROST, (1874–1963) U.S. poet. "The Lesson for Today," *A Witness Tree* (1942).

6   In lapidary inscriptions a man is not upon oath.

SAMUEL JOHNSON, (1709–1784) British author, lexicographer. Quoted in James Boswell, *Life of Dr. Johnson*, entry, 1775 (1791).

7   Excuse my dust.

DOROTHY PARKER, (1893–1967) U.S. humorous writer. Quoted in *While Rome Burns*, "Our Mrs. Parker," Alexander Woollcott (1934).

Suggested epitaph.

8   GOOD FREND FOR JESVS SAKE FORBEARE
TO DIGG THE DUST ENCLOASED
HEARE
BLESE BE YE MAN YT SPARES THES STONES
AND CURST BE HE YT MOVES MY BONES

WILLIAM SHAKESPEARE, (1564–1616) British dramatist, poet. *Epitaph on Shakespeare's tomb at Holy Trinity Church, Stratford–upon–Avon.*

Critics have disputed whether Shakespeare wrote his own epitaph, or merely chose it.

9   When I die, my epitaph should read: *She Paid the Bills.* That's the story of my private life.

GLORIA SWANSON, (1897–1983) U.S. screen actor. Quoted in *Saturday Evening Post* (New York, July 22, 1950).

10   Where fierce indignation can no longer tear his heart.
[Ubi saeva indignatio ulterius cor lacerare nequit.]

JONATHAN SWIFT, (1667–1745) Anglo–Irish satirist. *Epitaph, Jonathan Swift: A*

Critical Edition of the Major Works, eds. Angus Ross and David Woolley (1984).

In accordance with his will, inscribed on Swift's tomb in St Patrick's Cathedral, Dublin, where he had served as Dean for 30 years.

11   Under bare Ben Bulben's head
In Drumcliff churchyard Yeats is laid.
An ancestor was rector there
Long years ago, a church stands near,
By the road an ancient cross.
No marble, no conventional phrase;
On limestone quarried near the spot
By his command these words are cut:
Cast a cold eye
On life, on death.
Horseman pass by!

WILLIAM BUTLER YEATS, (1865–1939) Irish poet, playwright. "Under Ben Bulben," pt. 6, *Last Poems* (1939).

The last three lines are engraved on Yeats's gravestone, in Drumcliff, north of Sligo.

Equality

1   It is the nature of our desires to be boundless, and many live only to gratify them. But for this purpose the first object is, not so much to establish an equality of fortune, as to prevent those who are of a good disposition from desiring more than their own, and those who are of a bad one from being able to acquire it; and this may be done if they are kept in an inferior station, and not exposed to injustice.

ARISTOTLE, (384–322 B.C.) Greek philosopher. *Politics*, bk. 2, ch. 7, sct. 1267b (c. 343 B.C.), trans. by William Ellis (1912).

2 All animals are equal but some animals are more equal than others.

GEORGE ORWELL, (1903–1950) British author. *Animal Farm*, ch. 10 (1945).

The animals' Commandment. The original version in the book was "All animals are equal." The wording derives from Thomas Jefferson's Preamble to the American Declaration of Independence.

Eroticism

1 Pornography is about dominance. Erotica is about mutuality.

GLORIA STEINEM, (b. 1934) U.S. feminist writer, editor. "Erotica vs Pornography," *Outrageous Acts and Everyday Rebellions* (1983). Adapted from articles in *Ms.* (New York, Aug. 1977 and Nov. 1978).

Errors

1 There is no original truth, only original error.

GASTON BACHELARD, (1884–1962) French scientist, philosopher, literary theorist. "A Retrospective Glance at the Lifework of a Master of Books," *Fragments of a Poetics of Fire* (1988).

2 Let them alone: they be blind leaders of the blind. And if the blind lead the blind, both shall fall into the ditch.

BIBLE: NEW TESTAMENT, Jesus, in *Matthew*, 15:14.

Referring to the Pharisees.

3 Errors look so very ugly in persons of small means—one feels they are taking quite a liberty in going astray; whereas people of fortune may naturally indulge in a few delinquencies.

GEORGE ELIOT [MARY ANN (OR MARIAN) EVANS], (1819–1880) British novelist. "Janet's Repentance," ch. 25, *Scenes*

of Clerical Life (1858). First published in *Blackwood's Magazine* (1857).

4 It is worse than a crime: it is a mistake.

JOSEPH FOUCHÉ, (1759–1820) French minister of police under Napoleon. *Attributed.*

Remark, March 21, 1804, on the execution of the abducted royalist émigré the Duc d'Enghien, at Vincennes.

5 While Man's desires and aspirations stir,
He cannot choose but err.

JOHANN WOLFGANG VON GOETHE, (1749–1832) German poet, dramatist. the Lord, in *Faust*, pt. 1, "Prologue in Heaven," l. 317–8 (1808), trans. by Bayard Taylor (1870–1871).

Other translations render this line more prosaically: "Men err as long as they strive."

6 The greatest blunders, like the thickest ropes, are often compounded of a multitude of strands. Take the rope apart, separate it into the small threads that compose it, and you can break them one by one. You think, "That is all there was!" But twist them all together and you have something tremendous.

VICTOR HUGO, (1802–1885) French poet, dramatist, novelist. *Les Misérables*, pt. 2, bk. 5, ch. 10 (1862).

7 For to err in opinion, though it be not the part of wise men, is at least human.

PLUTARCH, (c. 46–c. 120) Greek essayist, biographer. "Against Colotes," *Morals*.

The phrase was already proverbial in Plutarch's time.

Escape

1 I long for scenes where man has never trod A place where woman never smiled or wept There to abide with my Creator God And sleep as I in childhood sweetly slept, Untroubling and untroubled where I lie The grass below, above, the vaulted sky.

JOHN CLARE, (1793–1864) British poet. "I Am," (1844–1846), first publ. in *Bedford Times* (Jan. 1848). Repr. in *The Poems of John Clare*, ed. J.W. Tibble (1935).

Closing lines, written at Northampton Asylum.

Escapism

1   It is the hour to be drunken! To escape being the martyred slaves of time, be ceaselessly drunk. On wine, on poetry, or on virtue, as you wish.

CHARLES BAUDELAIRE, (1821–1867) French poet. "Enivrez–vous," *Figaro* (Paris, Feb. 7, 1864). *Complete Works*, vol. 1, "Shorter Prose Poems," ed. Yves-Gérard le Dantec; rev. Claude Pichois (1953).

Espionage

1   And ye shall know the truth, and the truth shall make you free.

BIBLE: NEW TESTAMENT, Jesus, in *John*, 8:32.

These words are inscribed on the wall of the main lobby at the CIA headquarters, Langley, Virginia.

Eternity

1   Eternity is in love with the productions of time.

WILLIAM BLAKE, (1757–1827) British poet, painter, engraver. *The Marriage of Heaven and Hell*, plate 7, "Proverbs of Hell," (c. 1793), repr. in *Complete Writings*, ed. Geoffrey Keynes (1957).

2   Eternity. It is the sea mingled with the sun.

... L'éternité

ARTHUR RIMBAUD, (1854–1891) French poet. *Une Saison en Enfer*, "Delires II: Faim," (originally published 1874). Repr. in *Collected Poems*, ed. Oliver Bernard (1962).

Europe

1   When an American heiress wants to buy a man, she at once crosses the Atlantic. The only really materialistic people I have ever met have been Europeans.

MARY McCARTHY, (1912–1989) U.S. author, critic. "America the Beautiful," *On the Contrary* (1961). First published in *Commentary* (New York, Sept. 1947).

Europe and the United States

1   Can we never extract the tapeworm of Europe from the brain of our countrymen?

RALPH WALDO EMERSON, (1803–1882) U.S. essayist, poet, philosopher. *The Conduct of Life*, "Culture" (1860).

2   The immense popularity of American movies abroad demonstrates that Europe is the unfinished negative of which America is the proof.

MARY McCARTHY, (1912–1989) U.S. author, critic. "America the Beautiful," first published in *Commentary* (New York, Sept. 1947). *On the Contrary* (1961).

Europe, Eastern

1   There is no Soviet domination of Eastern Europe and there never will be under a Ford administration.... The United States does not concede that those countries are under the domination of the Soviet Union.

GERALD FORD, (b. 1913) U.S. Republican politician, president. Published in S. Kraus, *Great Debates* (1979). T.V. debate, Oct. 6, 1976, with presidential contender Jimmy Carter.

On questioning, Ford admitted he may not have been as precise as he might have been.

Euthanasia

1   Just as I shall select my ship when I am about to go on a voyage, or my house when I propose to take a residence, so I shall choose my death when I am about to depart from life.

SENECA, (c. 5–65) Roman writer, philosopher, statesman. *Epistulae ad Lucilium*, epistle 70, sct. 11.

2   O, let him pass. He hates him
That would upon the rack of this
   tough world
Stretch him out longer.

WILLIAM SHAKESPEARE, (1564–1616) British dramatist, poet. Kent, in *King Lear*, act 5, sc. 3, l. 289–91 (1623).

On Lear's death.

Evangelism

1   Let us pray for the whole state of Christ's Church Militant here in earth.

BOOK OF COMMON PRAYER, THE, *Holy Communion*, "Prayer for the Church Militant" (1662).

Evening

1   The curfew tolls the knell of parting day,
The lowing herd wind slowly o'er the lea,

The ploughman homeward plods his weary way,
And leaves the world to darkness and to me.
Now fades the glimmering landscape on the sight,
And all the air a solemn stillness holds,
Save where the beetle wheels his droning flight,
And drowsy tinklings lull the distant folds.

THOMAS GRAY, (1716–1771) British poet. "Elegy Written in a Country Churchyard," st. 1–2 (1751). Repr. in *Poetical Works*, ed. J. Rogers (1953).

Events

1   A pseudo–event ... comes about because someone has planned it, planted, or incited it. Typically, it is not a train wreck or an earthquake, but an interview.

DANIEL J. BOORSTIN, (b. 1914) U.S. historian. *The Image*, ch. 1 (1961).

2   I claim not to have controlled events, but confess plainly that events have controlled me.

ABRAHAM LINCOLN, (1809–1865) U.S. Republican politician, president. *Collected Works of Abraham Lincoln*, vol. 7, ed. Roy P. Basler (1953). Letter, April 4, 1864.

Evil

1   For we wrestle not against flesh and blood, but against principalities, against powers, against the rulers of the darkness of this world, against spiritual wickedness in high places.

BIBLE: NEW TESTAMENT, St. Paul, in *Ephesians*, 6:12.

St. Paul's words were used by William Blake as an epigraph to *The Four Zoas* (c. 1800).

2   The face of "evil" is always the face of total need.

WILLIAM BURROUGHS, (b. 1914) U.S. author. "Deposition: Testimony Concerning a Sickness" (1959). *Evergreen Review* (Jan./Feb. 1960).

The essay was later published as the introduction to *The Naked Lunch* in the 1962 edition.

3   The belief in a supernatural source of evil is not necessary; men alone are quite capable of every wickedness.

JOSEPH CONRAD, (1857–1924) Polish–born British novelist. "Dame de compagnie," pt. 2, ch. 4, *Under Western Eyes* (1911).

4   Evil be to him who evil thinks.
    (Honi soit qui mal y pense.)

EDWARD III, (1312–1377) British King of England. Motto of the Order of the Garter, quoted in *Historiae Anglicae,* Polydore Vergil (1535).

Alleged remark at the falling of the Countess of Salisbury's garter, presumably when the Order of the Garter was founded in 1344. No contemporary evidence whatsoever exists for the attribution, but the traditional tale was current in Henry VIII's reign, when Vergil was writing.

5   But evil is wrought by want of thought
    As well as want of heart!

THOMAS HOOD, (1799–1845) British poet. *The Lady's Dream,* st. 16 (written 1827, published 1844). Repr. in *Complete Poetical Works,* ed. Walter Jerrold (1906).

6   There is hardly a man clever enough to recognize the full extent of the evil he does.

FRANÇOIS LA ROCHEFOUCAULD, DUC DE, (1613–1680) French writer, moralist. *Sentences et Maximes Morales,* no. 269 (1678).

7   When choosing between two evils, I always like to pick the one I never tried before.

MAE WEST, (1892–1980) U.S. screen actor. As Frisco Doll, in the film *Klondike Annie* (1936).

Evolution

1   From the war of nature, from famine and death, the most exalted object which we are capable of conceiving, namely, the production of the higher animals, directly follows. There is grandeur in this view of life, with its several powers, having been breathed into a few forms or into one; and that, whilst this planet has gone cycling on according to the fixed law of gravity, from so simple a beginning endless forms most beautiful and most wonderful have been, and are being, evolved.

CHARLES DARWIN, (1809–1882) British naturalist. *The Origin of Species,* ch. 14 (1859).

Closing words of 1859 edition.

2   Natural selection, the blind, unconscious, automatic process which Darwin discovered, and which we now know is the explanation for the existence and apparently purposeful form of all life, has no purpose in mind. It has no mind and no mind's eye. It does not plan for the future. It has no vision, no foresight, no sight at all. If it can be said to play the role of the watchmaker in nature, it is the *blind* watchmaker.

RICHARD DAWKINS, (b. 1941) British biologist. *The Blind Watchmaker,* ch. 1 (1986).

3   The question is this—Is man an ape or an angel? My Lord, I am on the side of the angels. I repudiate with indignation and abhorrence the contrary view, which is I believe, foreign to the conscience of humanity.

BENJAMIN DISRAELI, (1804–1881) British statesman, author. *Selected Speeches of the Late Right Honourable the Earl of Beaconsfield,* vol. 2, "Church Policy," ed. T.E. Kebbes (1882). Speech, Nov. 25, 1864, Diocesan Conference, Oxford.

4   While Darwinian Man, though well–behaved,
At best is only a monkey shaved!

SIR WILLIAM SCHWENCK GILBERT, (1836–1911) British librettist. Lady Psyche, in *Princess Ida,* act 2 (1884), published in *The Savoy Operas* (1926).

5   If the question is put to me would I rather have a miserable ape for a grandfather or a man highly endowed by nature and possessed of great means of influence and yet who employs those faculties and that influence for the mere purpose of introducing ridicule into a grave scientific discussion—I unhesitatingly affirm my preference for the ape.

THOMAS HENRY HUXLEY, (1825–1895) British biologist. Quoted in *Harvest of a Quiet Eye,* ed. Alan L. Mackay (1977). Speech, June 30, 1860, University Museum, Oxford.

When asked by Samuel Wilberforce, Bishop of Oxford, whether he traced his descent from an ape on his mother's or his father's side, during a meeting of the British Association (commemorated by a plate in the University Museum). Huxley was the foremost scientific supporter of Darwin's theory of evolution, and became known as "Darwin's Bulldog." The precise wording of his retort to Wilberforce, which was remembered afterwards, varies according to different versions.

6   Organic life, we are told, has developed gradually from the proto-zoon to the philosopher, and this development, we are assured, is indubitably an advance. Unfortunately it is the philosopher, not the protozoon, who gives us this assurance.

BERTRAND RUSSELL [LORD RUSSELL, 3RD EARL], (1872–1970) British philosopher, mathematician. *Mysticism and Logic,* ch. 6 (1917).

Examinations

1   Examinations, sir, are pure humbug from beginning to end. If a man is a gentleman, he knows quite enough, and if he is not a gentleman, whatever he knows is bad for him.

OSCAR WILDE, (1854–1900) Anglo–Irish playwright, author. Lord Fermor, in *The Picture of Dorian Gray,* ch. 3 (1891).

Lord Illingworth makes the same declaration in *A Woman of No Importance* (act 3), first performed three years after the publication of *Dorian Gray.*

Examples

1   But Cristes loore and his apostles twelve
He taughte, but first he folwed it hymselve.

GEOFFREY CHAUCER, (1340–1400) British poet. *The Canterbury Tales,* "General Prologue," l. 527–8 (1387–1400), repr. in *The Works of Geoffrey Chaucer,* ed. Alfred W. Pollard, et al. (1898).

Referring to the Parson.

2   Caesar had his Brutus; Charles the First his Cromwell, and George the Third ... ("Treason," cried the Speaker) ... *may profit by their example.* If *this* be treason, make the most of it.

PATRICK HENRY, (1736–1799) U.S. statesman. Quoted in *Patrick Henry*, sct. 2, William Wirt (1818). Speech, May 1765, Williamsburg, Virginia.

3   Few things are harder to put up with than the annoyance of a good example.

MARK TWAIN, (1835–1910) U.S. author. *Pudd'nhead Wilson*, ch. 19, "Pudd'nhead Wilson's Calendar" (1894).

4   In this country it's a good thing to kill an admiral now and then to encourage the others [*pour encourager les autres*].

VOLTAIRE [FRANÇOIS MARIE AROUET], (1694–1778) French philosopher, author. English bystanders, in *Candide*, ch. 23 (1759).

At the execution of an admiral. On March 14, 1757, Admiral John Byng was executed for failing to relieve the island of Minorca, besieged by the French.

Exasperation

1   Lord Ronald said nothing; he flung himself from the room, flung himself upon his horse and rode madly off in all directions.

STEPHEN LEACOCK, (1869–1944) Canadian humorist, economist. "Gertrude the Governess," *Nonsense Novels* (1911).

Excellence

1   The highest good.
    [*summum bonum.*]

MARCUS TULLIUS CICERO, (106–43 B.C.) Roman orator and philosopher. *De Officiis*, bk. 1, ch. 5 (44 B.C.).

2   Sublimity is the echo of great mind.

LONGINUS, (3rd century A.D.) Greek critic. *On The Sublime*, sct. 9.

Also translated, "great writing is the echo of great mind."

3   The best is the enemy of the good.

VOLTAIRE [FRANÇOIS MARIE AROUET], (1694–1778) French philosopher, author. "Dramatic Art," *Philosophical Dictionary* (1764).

Excess

1   The road of excess leads to the palace of wisdom.

WILLIAM BLAKE, (1757–1827) British poet, painter, engraver. *The Marriage of Heaven and Hell*, plate 7, "Proverbs of Hell," (c. 1793), repr. in *Complete Writings*, ed. Geoffrey Keynes (1957).

2   My candle burns at both ends;
    It will not last the night;
    But ah, my foes, and oh, my
        friends—
    It gives a lovely light.

EDNA ST. VINCENT MILLAY, (1892–1950) U.S. poet. "First Fig," *A Few Figs From Thistles* (1920).

3   The superfluous, a very necessary thing.

VOLTAIRE [FRANÇOIS MARIE AROUET], (1694–1778) French philosopher, author. *Le Mondain*, l. 22 (1736).

4   Moderation is a fatal thing.... Nothing succeeds like excess.

OSCAR WILDE, (1854–1900) Anglo–Irish playwright, author. Lord Illingworth, in *A Woman of No Importance*, act 3. (1893).

Excrement and Excretion

1   Where there is a stink of shit there is a smell of being.

ANTONIN ARTAUD, (1896–1948) French theater producer, actor, theorist. "The Pursuit of Fecality," *To Have Done with the Judgment of God* (1947). Repr. in *Selected Writings*, ed. Susan Sontag (1976).

2   When he urinated, it sounded like night prayer.

F. SCOTT FITZGERALD, (1896–1940) U.S. author. *The Crack–Up*, "Notebook M," ed. Edmund Wilson (1945).

Excuses

1   Two wrongs don't make a right, but they make a good excuse.

THOMAS SZASZ, (b. 1920) U.S. psychiatrist. "Social Relations," *The Second Sin* (1973).

Exile

1   By the rivers of Babylon, there we sat down, yea, we wept: when we remembered Zion.

BIBLE: HEBREW, *Psalms*, 137:1.

2   An exile, saddest of all prisoners,
Who has the whole world for a
   dungeon strong,
Seas, mountains, and the horizon's
   verge for bars.

GEORGE GORDON NOEL BYRON, 6TH BARON BYRON, (1788–1824) British poet. "The Prophecy of Dante," cto. 4, l. 131–3 (1819).

3   For the weariest road that man may
   wend
Is forth from the home of his
   father.

EURIPIDES, (480–406 B.C.) Greek dramatist. "Others," in *Medea*, l. 650, *Collected Plays of Euripides*, ed. and trans. by Gilbert Murray (1954).

4   I have loved justice and hated iniquity: therefore I die in exile.

POPE GREGORY VII, (c. 1020–1085) Italian cleric, pope. Quoted in *The Life and Pontificate of Gregory VII*, vol. 2, bk. 3, ch. 20, J.W. Bowden (1840).

Attributed last words in Salerno, Italy, where he had taken refuge after being ousted from Rome by the Holy Roman Emperor Henry IV.

Existence

1   It is living and ceasing to live that are imaginary solutions. Existence is elsewhere.

ANDRÉ BRETON, (1896–1966) French surrealist. "Manifesto of Surrealism," (1924). Repr. in *Manifestos of Surrealism* (1969).

2   One must *be* something to be able to *do* something.

JOHANN WOLFGANG VON GOETHE, (1749–1832) German poet, dramatist. Quoted in *Conversations with Goethe*, entry, Oct. 20, 1828, Johann Peter Eckermann (1836).

3   As far as we can discern, the sole purpose of human existence is to kindle a light in the darkness of mere being.

CARL JUNG, (1875–1961) Swiss psychiatrist. *Memories, Dreams, Reflections*, ch. 11 (1962).

4   The cradle rocks above an abyss, and common sense tells us that our existence is but a brief crack of light between two eternities of darkness.

VLADIMIR NABOKOV, (1899–1977) Russian–born U.S. novelist, poet. *Speak, Memory*, ch. 1, sct. 1 (1955, rev. 1966).

Autobiography, opening words.

Expatriates

1   Ship me somewhere east of Suez, where the best is like the worst,

Where there aren't no Ten Com-
mandments an' a man can raise a
thirst.

Rudyard Kipling, (1865–1936) British
writer, poet. "Mandalay," *Barrack–Room Ballads* (1892).

Experience

1 To most men, experience is like the
stern lights of a ship, which illu-
mine only the track it has passed.

Samuel Taylor Coleridge,
(1772–1834) British poet, critic. *Table Talk,*
"1820," *Letters and Conversations of S.T.
Coleridge,* vol. 1, "Thomas Allsop" (1836).
Repr. in *Collected Works,* vol. 14, ed. Kathleen Coburn (1990).

2 I have but one lamp by which my
feet are guided; and that is the lamp
of experience. I know no way of
judging the future but by the
past.

Patrick Henry, (1736–1799) U.S.
statesman. Quoted in *Sketches of the Life and
Character of Patrick Henry,* William Wirt
(1836). Speech, March 23, 1775, to the Virginia Convention, Richmond, Virginia.

3 Experience is not a matter of having
actually swum the Hellespont, or
danced with the dervishes, or slept
in a doss–house. It is a matter of
sensibility and intuition, of seeing
and hearing the significant things,
of paying attention at the right
moments, of understanding and
co–ordinating. Experience is not
what happens to a man; it is what
a man does with what happens to
him.

Aldous Huxley, (1894–1963) British
author. *Texts and Pretexts,* introduction
(1932).

4 Not the fruit of experience, but
experience itself, is the end.

Walter Pater, (1839–1894) British
essayist, critic. *Studies in the History of the
Renaissance,* "Conclusion" (1873).

5 Men may rise on stepping–stones
Of their dead selves to higher
things.

**Alfred Tennyson, 1st Baron
Tennyson,** (1809–1892) British poet. "In
Memoriam," pt. 1, st.1 (1850).

6 We should be careful to get out of
an experience only the wisdom that
is in it—and stop there; lest we be
like the cat that sits down on a hot
stove–lid. She will never sit down
on a hot stove–lid again—and that
is well; but also she will never sit
down on a cold one anymore.

Mark Twain, (1835–1910) U.S. author.
Following the Equator, ch. 11, "Pudd'nhead
Wilson's New Calendar" (1897).

7 Experience is the name every one
gives to their mistakes.

Oscar Wilde, (1854–1900) Anglo–Irish
playwright, author. Dumby, in *Lady Windermere's Fan,* act 3 (1893).

Wilde used the same formulation in *The Picture of Dorian Gray,* ch. 4 (1891).

Experts

1 Physician, heal thyself.

Bible: New Testament, Jesus, in
Luke, 4:23.

Jesus preaches to the people of Nazareth: "Ye
will surely say unto me this proverb, Physician,
heal thyself: whatsoever we have heard done
in Capernaum, do also here in thy country."

2 All other men are specialists, but
his specialism is omniscience.

Arthur Conan, Sir Doyle,
(1859–1930) British author. Sherlock Holmes,
in *His Last Bow,* "The Bruce–Partington Plans"
(1917).

Referring to his brother, Mycroft.

Exploration

1   We shall not cease from exploration
And the end of all our exploring
Will be to arrive where we started
And know the place for the first
    time.

T.S. (THOMAS STEARNS) ELIOT,
(1888–1965) Anglo–American poet, critic.
"Little Gidding," pt. 5, *Four Quartets* (1942).

2   Dr. Livingstone, I presume?

SIR HENRY MORTON STANLEY,
(1841–1904) British explorer, journalist. *How
I Found Livingstone*, ch. 11 (1872).

Greeting to the missing explorer and missionary, Dr. David Livingstone, at Ujiji, Lake Tan-
ganyika, November 10, 1871. Stanley had
been dispatched to find Livingstone by the
New York Herald, a task he accomplished
after an eight–month voyage. In Sheridan's
play, *School for Scandal*, act 5, sc. 1, one
character (Sir Oliver Surface) meets up with
another with the line, "Mr. Stanley, I presume?"

Extremism

1   So over violent, or over civil
That every man with him was God
  or Devil.

JOHN DRYDEN, (1631–1700) British
poet, dramatist, critic. "Absalom and Achitophel," pt. 1, l. 557–8 (1681).

2   I would remind you that extremism
in the defense of liberty is no vice!
And let me remind you also that
moderation in the pursuit of justice
is no virtue!

BARRY GOLDWATER, (b. 1909) U.S.
Republican politician. Quoted in *The New
York Times* (July 17, 1964). Speech, July 16,
1964, accepting presidential nomination,
Republican National Convention, San Fran-
cisco.

Goldwater later attributed these words to
Cicero. On Oct. 31, 1964, the Democratic
contender for the presidency, Lyndon B. Johnson, replied in a speech in New York:
"Extremism is an unpardonable vice. Moderation in the affairs of the nation is the highest
virtue." Johnson won a sweeping victory
against Goldwater in the presidential election
three days later.

3   The question is not whether we will
be extremist but what kind of
extremist will we be.

MARTIN LUTHER KING, JR.,
(1929–1968) U.S. clergyman, civil rights
leader. "Letter from Birmingham Jail," *Why
We Can't Wait* (1964). Open letter to clergymen, Apr. 16, 1963.

Faces

1   My face looks like a wedding–cake
left out in the rain.

W.H. (WYSTAN HUGH) AUDEN,
(1907–1973) Anglo–American poet. Quoted
in *W.H. Auden*, pt. 2, ch. 6, Humphrey Carpenter (1981).

In *The Dyer's Hand*, pt. 3, "Hic et Ille" (1962),
Auden wrote: "Every European visitor to the
United States is struck by the comparative rar-
ity of what he would call a face.... To have a
face, in the European sense of the word, it
would seem that one must not only enjoy and
suffer but also desire to preserve the memory
of even the most humiliating and unpleasant
experiences of the past."

2   There is a garden in her face
Where roses and white lilies grow;
A heavenly paradise is that place
Wherein all pleasant fruits do flow.

THOMAS CAMPION,(1567–1620) British
poet, musician. "There is a garden in her
face," st. 1, *The Third and Fourth Books of
Airs* (c. 1617). Repr. in *Works of Thomas
Campion*, ed. W.R. Davis (1967).

3   He ... had a face like a blessing.

MIGUEL DE CERVANTES, (1547–1616)
Spanish author. Peter, in *Don Quixote*, pt. 1,
ch. 4 (1605), trans. by P. Motteux.

Peter's description of the shepherd and
scholar Chrysostome (Gris .stomo).

4   I am the family face;
    Flesh perishes, I live on,
    Projecting trait and trace
    Through time to times anon,
    And leaping from place to place
    Over oblivion.

    THOMAS HARDY, (1840–1928) British
    novelist, poet. "Heredity," *Moments of Vision*
    (1917).

5   Was this the face that launch'd a
        thousand ships,
    And burnt the topless towers of
        Ilium?

    CHRISTOPHER MARLOWE, (1564–1593)
    British dramatist, poet. Faustus, in *The Tragi-
    cal History of Dr. Faustus*, act 5, sc. 1, l. 96–7
    (1604).

    Referring to Helen of Troy, conjured up by
    Faustus.

6   I never forget a face, but in your
    case I'll be glad to make an excep-
    tion.

    GROUCHO MARX, (1895–1977) U.S.
    comic actor. Quoted in *People I have Loved,
    Known or Admired,* "Groucho," Leo Rosten
    (1970).

7   At fifty, everyone has the face he
    deserves.

    GEORGE ORWELL, (1903–1950) British
    author. *The Collected Essays, Journalism and
    Letters of George Orwell,* vol. 4, eds. Sonia
    Orwell and Ian Angus (1968). Journal entry,
    April 17, 1949.

    Last entry in Orwell's notebook. Albert
    Camus, in *The Fall* (1956), expressed much
    the same when he wrote: "After a certain age
    every man is responsible for his face."

8   There's no art
    To find the mind's construction in
        the face.

    WILLIAM SHAKESPEARE, (1564–1616)
    British dramatist, poet. Duncan, in *Macbeth,*
    act 1, sc. 4, l. 12–13 (1623).

    Referring to the original Thane of Cawdor, in
    whom Duncan had put his misplaced trust.

9   But Lancelot mused a little space;
    He said, "She has a lovely face;
    God in his mercy lend her grace,
    The Lady of Shalott."

    **ALFRED TENNYSON, 1ST BARON
    TENNYSON,** (1809–1892) British poet.
    "The Lady of Shalott," pt. 4, st. 6 (1832, rev.
    1842).

    Last lines of the poem: spoken of the dead
    Lady of Shalott, who invoked a curse by gaz-
    ing upon Lancelot, unbeknown to him.

Facts

1   But Facts are cheels that winna
    ding,
    An' downa be disputed.

    ROBERT BURNS, (1759–1796) Scottish
    poet. "A Dream," st. 4 (1786). Repr. In *Poeti-
    cal Works,* vol. 1, ed. William Scott Douglas
    (1891).

    Alan L. Mackay, in *The Harvest of a Quiet
    Eye* (1977), offers the translation, "Facts are
    entities which cannot be manipulated or dis-
    puted."

2   Not many people know that.

    **MICHAEL CAINE [MAURICE JOSEPH
    MICKLEWHITE],** (b. 1933) British stage
    and screen actor. Catch–phrase and book
    title (1984).

    Caine's catch–phrase, which found its way
    into his films and was made the title of his
    memoirs, is said to have been his comment
    when habitually offering information gar-
    nered from *The Guinness Book of Records.*

3   Now, what I want is, Facts. Teach
    these boys and girls nothing but
    Facts. Facts alone are wanted in
    life. Plant nothing else, and root
    out everything else. You can only
    form the minds of reasoning ani-
    mals upon Facts: nothing else will
    ever be of any service to them. This
    is the principle on which I bring
    up my own children, and this is
    the principle on which I bring up
    these children. Stick to Facts, sir!

CHARLES DICKENS, (1812–1870) British novelist. Mr. Gradgrind, in *Hard Times*, bk. 1, ch. 1 (1854).

Opening lines. Thomas Gradgrind is described as "a man of realities. A man of facts and calculations." (bk.1, ch. 2).

4   Sit down before fact as a little child, be prepared to give up every preconceived notion, follow humbly wherever and to whatever abysses nature leads, or you shall learn nothing.

THOMAS HENRY HUXLEY, (1825–1895) British biologist. *Life and Letters of Thomas Henry Huxley*, vol. 1, Leonard Huxley (1900). Letter, Sept. 23, 1860, to Charles Kingsley.

5   A fact is like a sack—it won't stand up if it's empty. To make it stand up, first you have to put in it all the reasons and feelings that caused it in the first place.

LUIGI PIRANDELLO, (1867–1936) Italian author, playwright. The father, in *Six Characters in Search of an Author*, act 1 (1921).

The notion of an empty bag, or sack is proverbial: Benjamin Franklin noted in *Poor Richard's Almanac*: "An empty bag cannot stand upright." (Jan. 1740).

6   Obviously the facts are never just coming at you but are incorporated by an imagination that is formed by your previous experience. Memories of the past are not memories of facts but memories of your imaginings of the facts.

PHILIP ROTH, (b. 1933) U.S. novelist. *The Facts* (1988).

Opening letter to Zuckerman, Roth's fictional alter ego.

7   The squirming facts exceed the squamous mind, If one may say so.

WALLACE STEVENS, 1879–1955 U.S. poet. "Connoisseur of Chaos," *Parts of a World* (1942).

8   It is the spirit of the age to believe that any fact, no matter how suspect, is superior to any imaginative exercise, no matter how true.

GORE VIDAL, (b. 1925) U.S. novelist, critic. "French Letters: Theories of the New Novel," *Encounter* (London, Dec. 1967).

Failure

1   Ever tried. Ever failed. No matter. Try again. Fail again. Fail better.

SAMUEL BECKETT, (1906–1989) Irish dramatist, novelist. *Worstward Ho* (1984).

2   She knows there's no success like failure
And that failure's no success at all.

BOB DYLAN [ROBERT ALLEN ZIMMERMAN], (b. 1941) U.S. singer, songwriter. "Love Minus Zero/No Limit" (song), on the album *Bringing it All Back Home* (1965).

3   If at first you don't succeed, try again. Then quit. No use being a damn fool about it.

W.C. FIELDS, (1879–1946) U.S. screen actor. Quoted in *Halliwell's Filmgoer's Companion*, ed. John Walker (1995).

4   And nothing to look backward to with pride,
And nothing to look forward to with hope.

ROBERT FROST, (1874–1963) U.S. poet. "The Death of the Hired Man," *North of Boston* (1914).

5   He was a self–made man who owed his lack of success to nobody.

JOSEPH HELLER, (b. 1923) U.S. novelist. *Catch–22*, ch. 3 (1961).

Referring to Colonel Cargill.

6   There is no loneliness greater than the loneliness of a failure. The failure is a stranger in his own house.

ERIC HOFFER, (1902–1983) U.S. philosopher. *The Passionate State of Mind*, aph. 223 (1955).

7   There is not a fiercer hell than the failure in a great object.

JOHN KEATS, (1795–1821) British poet. *Endymion*, preface (1818).

8   I don't say he's a great man. Willy Loman never made a lot of money. His name was never in the paper. He's not the finest character that ever lived. But he's a human being, and a terrible thing is happening to him. So attention must be paid.

ARTHUR MILLER, (b. 1915) U.S. dramatist. Linda, in *Death of a Salesman*, act 1 (1949).

Referring to her husband Willy Loman.

9   What do I get—a couple of bucks and a one–way ticket to Palookaville. It was you, Charley. You was my brother. You should've looked out for me. Instead of making me take them dives for the short–end money.... You don't understand! I could've been a contender. I could've had class and been somebody. Real class. Instead of a bum, which is what I am. It was you, Charley.

BUDD SCHULBERG, Screenwriter. Terry Mallon (Marlon Brando), in *On The Waterfront* (film), Spoken to his brother Charley (Rod Steiger), whom he blames for his failed boxing career. (1954).

Fairies

1   Up the airy mountain,
    Down the rushy glen,
    We daren't go a–hunting
    For fear of little men.

WILLIAM ALLINGHAM, (1824–1889) Irish poet, diarist. "The Fairies," *Day and Night Songs* (1855).

2   When the first baby laughed for the first time, the laugh broke into a thousand pieces and they all went skipping about, and that was the beginning of fairies. And now when every new baby is born its first laugh becomes a fairy. So there ought to be one fairy for every boy or girl.

J.M. (JAMES MATTHEW) BARRIE, (1860–1937) British playwright. Peter, in *Peter Pan*, act 1 (performed 1904, published 1928).

3   The land of faery
    Where nobody gets old and godly
        and grave,
    Where nobody gets old and crafty
        and wise,
    Where nobody gets old and bitter
        of tongue.

WILLIAM BUTLER YEATS, (1865–1939) Irish poet, playwright. *The Land of Heart's Desire* (1894).

Faith

1   The Sea of Faith
    Was once, too, at the full, and
        round earth's shore
    Lay like the folds of a bright girdle
        furled.
    But now I only hear
    Its melancholy, long, withdrawing
        roar,
    Retreating, to the breath
    Of the night–wind, down the vast
        edges drear
    And naked shingles of the world.

MATTHEW ARNOLD, (1822–1888) British poet, critic. "Dover Beach," st. 3 (1867).

2   Faith is the substance of things hoped for, the evidence of things not seen.

BIBLE: NEW TESTAMENT, St. Paul, in *Hebrews*, 11:1.

3   Faith. Belief without evidence in what is told by one who speaks without knowledge, of things without parallel.

AMBROSE BIERCE, (1842–1914) U.S. author. *The Devil's Dictionary* (1881–1906), repr. in *Collected Works of Ambrose Bierce*, vol. 7 (1911).

4   Faith—is the Pierless Bridge
Supporting what We see
Unto the Scene that We do not—

EMILY DICKINSON, (1830–1886) U.S. poet. "Faith is the Pierless Bridge" (written c. 1864, published 1929). Repr. in *The Complete Poems*, no. 915, Harvard *variorum* edition (1955).

5   Reason is our soul's left hand, Faith her right,
By these we reach divinity.

JOHN DONNE, (c. 1572–1631) British divine, metaphysical poet. "Verse Letter to the Countess of Bedford" (written c. 1607–1608, published 1633). Repr. in *Complete Poetry and Selected Prose*, ed. John Hayward (1929).

6   If you have abandoned one faith, do not abandon all faith. There is always an alternative to the faith we lose. Or is it the same faith under another mask?

GRAHAM GREENE, (1904–1991) British novelist. Dr. Magiot, in *The Comedians*, pt. 2, ch. 4, sct. 4 (1966).

Closing words of Dr. Magiot's last letter.

7   Absolute faith corrupts as absolutely as absolute power.

ERIC HOFFER, (1902–1983) U.S. philosopher. *Reflections on the Human Condition*, aph. 13 (1973).

8   Faith is the highest passion in a human being. Many in every generation may not come that far, but none comes further.

SOREN KIERKEGAARD, (1813–1855) Danish philosopher. *Fear and Trembling*, "Epilogue" (1843, trans. 1985).

9   It is as absurd to argue men, as to torture them, into believing.

CARDINAL JOHN HENRY NEWMAN, (1801–1890) British churchman, theologian. "The Usurpation of Reason," *Oxford University Sermons* (1843). Sermon, Dec. 11, 1831, Oxford, England.

10   My faith
is a great weight
hung on a small wire,
as doth the spider
hang her baby on a thin web.

ANNE SEXTON, (1928–1974) U.S. poet. "Small Wire," *The Awful Rowing Toward God* (1975).

11   And here's to you, Mrs. Robinson
Jesus loves you more than you will know.
God bless you please, Mrs. Robinson
Heaven holds a place for those who pray.

PAUL SIMON, (b. 1941) U.S. rock musician. "Mrs. Robinson" (song), from Mike Nichols' film *The Graduate* (1967), released on the soundtrack and, in a different version, on the album *Bookends* (1968).

Fallibility

1   For I know that in me (that is, in my flesh) dwelleth no good thing: for to will is present with me; but how to perform that which is good I find not. For the good that I would I do not: but the evil which I would not, that I do.

BIBLE: NEW TESTAMENT, St. Paul, in *Romans*, 7:18–19.

See Ovid's coment on "weakness."

2   We have left undone those things which we ought to have done; and we have done those things which we ought not to have done.

BOOK OF COMMON PRAYER, THE, *Morning Prayer,* "General Confession," (1662).

3   I beseech you, in the bowels of Christ, think it possible you may be mistaken.

OLIVER CROMWELL, (1599–1658) British Parliamentarian general, Lord Protector of England. *Oliver Cromwell's Letters and Speeches,* Thomas Carlyle (1845). Letter, Aug. 3, 1650, to the General Assembly of the Scottish Kirk.

4   I don't like people who have never fallen or stumbled. Their virtue is lifeless and it isn't of much value. Life hasn't revealed its beauty to them.

BORIS PASTERNAK, (1890–1960) Russian poet, novelist, translator. Zhivago, in *Doctor Zhivago,* ch. 13, sct. 12 (1957).

Fame

1   There be of them, that have left a name behind them, that their praises might be reported. And some there be, which have no memorial; who are perished, as though they had never been; and are become as though they had never been born; and their children after them.

APOCRYPHA, *Apocrypha, Ecclesiasticus* 44:8–9.

2   The celebrity is a person who is known for his well-knownness.

DANIEL J. BOORSTIN, (b. 1914) U.S. historian. *The Image,* ch. 2 (1961).

"In our world of big names," Boorstin wrote, "our true heroes tend to be anonymous. In this life of illusion and quasi-illusion, the person of solid virtues who can be admired for something more substantial than his well-known-ness often proves to be the unsung hero: the teacher, the nurse, the mother, the honest cop, the hard worker at lonely, underpaid, unglamorous, unpublicized jobs."

3   Fame is a fickle food
Upon a shifting plate.

EMILY DICKINSON, (1830–1886) U.S. poet. "Fame is a Fickle Food" (published 1914). Repr. in *The Complete Poems,* no. 1659, Harvard *variorum* edition (1955).

4   It is a mark of many famous people that they cannot part with their brightest hour.

LILLIAN HELLMAN, (1905–1984) U.S. playwright. "Theatre," *Pentimento* (1973).

5   Fame is no plant that grows on mortal soil.

JOHN MILTON, (1608–1674) British poet. Phoebes, in "Lycidas," l. 78 (1637). Repr. in *Milton's Poetical Works,* ed. Douglas Bush (1966).

6   Not to know me argues yourselves unknown.

JOHN MILTON, (1608–1674) British poet. Satan, in *Paradise Lost,* bk. 4, l. 830 (1667).

Speaking to "two fair angels."

7   Time hath ...
A wallet at his back, wherein he
    puts
Alms for oblivion, a great–sized
    monster
Of ingratitudes.

WILLIAM SHAKESPEARE, (1564–1616) British dramatist, poet. Ulysses, in *Troilus and Cressida,* act 3, sc. 3, l. 139–142 (1609).

8   Censure is the tax a man pays to the public for being eminent.

JONATHAN SWIFT, (1667–1745) Anglo–Irish satirist. "Various Thoughts Moral and Diverting," *Miscellanies in Prose and Verse* (1711). Repr. in *Jonathan Swift: A Critical Edition of the Major Works,* eds. Angus Ross and David Woolley (1984).

9   Celebrity is a mask that eats into the face. As soon as one is aware of being "somebody," to be watched

and listened to with extra interest, input ceases, and the performer goes blind and deaf in his overanimation. One can either see or be seen.

JOHN UPDIKE, (b. 1932) U.S. author, critic. *Self–Consciousness: Memoirs*, ch. 6 (1989).

10   In the future everybody will be world famous for fifteen minutes.

ANDY WARHOL, (c. 1928–1987) U.S. pop artist. *Andy Warhol* (exhibition catalog) (1968).

In *Andy Warhol's Exposures,* "Studio 54" (1954), the artist wrote, "I'm bored with that line. I never use it any more. My new line is, 'In fifteen minutes everybody will be famous.'"

Familiarity

1   Familiarity breeds contempt.

AESOP, (6th century B.C.) Greek fabulist. *Fables,* "The Fox and the Lion."

Families

1   A brother offended is harder to be won than a strong city: and their contentions are like the bars of a castle.

BIBLE: HEBREW, *Proverbs,* 18:19.

2   The awe and dread with which the untutored savage contemplates his mother–in–law are amongst the most familiar facts of anthropology.

SIR JAMES FRAZER, (1854–1941) Scottish classicist, anthropologist. *The Golden Bough,* ch. 18 (1922 edition).

3   The roaring of the wind is my wife and the stars through the window pane are my children. The mighty

abstract idea I have of beauty in all things stifles the more divided and minute domestic happiness.

JOHN KEATS, (1795–1821) British poet. *Letters of John Keats,* no. 94, ed. Frederick Page (1954). Letter, Oct. 14–31, 1818, to his brother and sister–in–law.

George and Georgiana Keats, married in June of that year and recently settled in the United States, had urged the poet to think of starting a family.

4   A poor relation is the most irrelevant thing in nature, a piece of impertinent correspondency, an odious approximation, a haunting conscience, a preposterous shadow, lengthening in the noon–tide of our prosperity.... He is known by his knock.

CHARLES LAMB, (1775–1834) British essayist, critic. *Last Essays of Elia,* "Poor Relations" (1833).

Opening lines of essay.

5   For there is no friend like a sister
In calm or stormy weather;
To cheer one on the tedious way,
To fetch one if one goes astray,
To lift one if one totters down,
To strengthen whilst one stands.

CHRISTINA ROSSETTI, (1830–1894) British poet, lyricist. "Goblin Market," l. 562–567 (written 1859), published in *Goblin Market, and Other Poems* (1862).

Last lines.

6   A boy's best friend is his mother.

JOSEPH STEFANO, U.S. screenwriter. Norman Bates (Anthony Perkins), in *Psycho* (film) (1960).

7   The family is the basic cell of government.

GLORIA STEINEM, (b. 1934) U.S. feminist writer, editor. Quoted in *The Quotable Woman,* ed. Elaine Partnow (1982). Speech,

July 1981, National Women's Political Causus Conference, Albuquerque, New Mexico.

8   Relations are simply a tedious pack of people, who haven't got the remotest knowledge of how to live, nor the smallest instinct about when to die.

OSCAR WILDE, (1854–1900) Anglo–Irish playwright, author. Algernon, in *The Importance of Being Earnest*, act 1 (1895).

Fanatics

1   A fanatic is one who can't change his mind and won't change the subject.

WINSTON CHURCHILL, (1874–1965) British statesman, writer. Quoted in *The New York Times* (July 5, 1954).

2   From fanaticism to barbarism is only one step.

DENIS DIDEROT, (1713–1784) French philosopher. "Essay on Merit and Virtue" (1745). Repr. in *Complete Works*, eds. J. Asszat and M. Tourneux (1875–1877).

Diderot's essay is a translation of Shaftesbury's *Essay on the Merit of Virtue* (1699).

3   A fanatic is a man that does what he thinks the Lord would do if He knew the facts of the case.

FINLEY PETER DUNNE, (1867–1936) U.S. journalist, humorist. *Dooley's Opinions*, "Casual Observations" (1890).

4   The worst of madmen is a saint run mad.

ALEXANDER POPE, (1688–1744) British satirical poet. *Imitations of Horace*, bk. 1, epistle 6, "To Mr. Murray" l. 27 (1738).

Fantasy

1   O power of fantasy that steals our minds from things outside, to leave us unaware, although a thousand trumpets may blow loud—what stirs you if the senses show you nothing? Light stirs you, formed in Heaven, by itself, or by His will Who sends it down to us.

DANTE ALIGHIERI, (1265–1321) Italian poet. "Purgatory," cto. 17, l. 13–18, *The Divine Comedy* (c. 1307–1321), trans. by Mark Musa (1981).

2   The dream of reason produces monsters. Imagination deserted by reason creates impossible, useless thoughts. United with reason, imagination is the mother of all art and the source of all its beauty.

FRANCISCO JOSÉ DE GOYA Y LUCIENTES, (1746–1828) Spanish painter. *Caprichos*, no. 43 (1799).

Caption in the series of eighty etchings completed in 1798, satirical and grotesque in form.

3   There is a fifth dimension beyond those known to man. It is a dimension vast as space and timeless as infinity. It is the middle ground between light and shadow, between the pit of his fears and the summit of his knowledge. This is the dimension of imagination. It is an area called the Twilight Zone.

ROD SERLING, (1924–1975) U.S. TV writer, producer. *The Twilight Zone* (TV series), preamble, written, created, and narrated by Rod Serling (1959–1964).

4   The Right Honourable gentleman is indebted to his memory for his jests, and to his imagination for his facts.

RICHARD BRINSLEY SHERIDAN, (1751–1816) Anglo–Irish dramatist. Quoted in *Memoirs of the Life of Richard Brinsley Sheridan*, vol. 2, Thomas Moore (1825).

Reply to Dundas.

Farewells

1 Th–th–th–th–that's all, folks!

TEX AVERY [FRED AVERY],
(1907–1980) U.S. animator. Porky Pig, in
Looney Tunes/Merrie Melodies (animation
series), Warner Brothers cartoon (1935–1965).

Porky's famous sign–off line (created and
voiced by Mel Blanc from 1938) was used at
the end of various other Warner Brothers' cartoons; also at the end of Peter Bogdanovich's
1972 screwball comedy *What's Up Doc?* (see
Avery's comment on "greetings"). Porky Pig
first appeared in the *Looney Tunes* cartoon *I
Haven't Got A Hat* (1935).

2 All farewells should be sudden,
when forever.

**GEORGE GORDON NOEL BYRON, 6TH
BARON BYRON,** (1788–1824) British poet.
Sardanapalus, in *Sardanapalus*, act 5, sc. 1
(1821).

3 Hasta la vista, baby.

JAMES CAMERON, Writer. The Terminator
(Arnold Schwarzenegger), in *Terminator 2:
Judgment Day* (film) (1991).

4 And forever, brother, hail and
farewell.
*[Atque in perpetuum, frater, ave
atque vale.]*

**CATULLUS [GAIUS VALERIUS CAT-
ULLUS],** (84–54 B.C.) Roman poet. *Carmina*,
no. 101, l. 10.

5 When I died last, and, dear, I die
As often as from thee I go
Though it be but an hour ago,
And lovers' hours be full eternity.

JOHN DONNE, (c. 1572–1631) British
divine, metaphysical poet. "The Legacy,"
Songs and Sonnets (1633). Repr. in *Complete
Poetry and Selected Prose*, ed. John Hayward
(1929).

6 I always made an awkward bow.

JOHN KEATS, (1795–1821) British poet.
Letters of John Keats, no. 242, ed. Frederick
Page (1954). Letter, Nov. 30, 1820.

Last words of the last letter sent by Keats, following his remark, "I can scarcely bid you
goodbye, even in a letter." Two weeks earlier,
desperately ill with tuberculosis, the poet had
arrived in Rome, where he was to die Feb. 23,
1821.

7 Every parting gives a foretaste of
death, every reunion a hint of the
resurrection.

ARTHUR SCHOPENHAUER, (1788–1860)
German philosopher. *Parerga and Paralipom-
ena*, vol. 2, ch. 26, sct. 310 (1851), trans. by
E.F.J. Payne.

8 Come,
Let's have one other gaudy night.
  Call to me
All my sad captains. Fill our bowls
  once more.
Let's mock the midnight bell.

WILLIAM SHAKESPEARE, (1564–1616)
British dramatist, poet. Antony, in *Antony and
Cleopatra*, act 3, sc. 13, l. 184–7 (1623).

The poet Thom Gunn took the phrase "my sad
captains" for a poem and volume of verse
published 1961.

9 Farewell, a long farewell, to all my
greatness!

WILLIAM SHAKESPEARE, (1564–1616)
British dramatist, poet. Cardinal Wolsey, in
Henry VIII, act 3, sc. 2, l. 352 (1623).

Opening lines of Wolsey's soliloquy on his
downfall.

Farmers and Farming

1 How can he get wisdom that holdeth the plough, and that glorieth in
the goad, that driveth oxen, and is
occupied in their labours, and
whose talk is of bullocks?

APOCRYPHA, *Ecclesiasticus*, 38:25.

2 Our farmers round, well pleased
with constant gain,

Like other farmers, flourish and
complain.

GEORGE CRABBE, (1754–1832) British
poet, clergyman. "Baptisms," pt. 1, l. 273–4,
The Parish Register (1807). Repr. in *Poetical
Works*, eds. A.J. and R.M. Carlyle (1908,
rev.1924).

3   Bowed by the weight of centuries
he leans Upon his hoe and gazes on
the ground, The emptiness of ages
in his face, And on his back the
burden of the world.

EDWIN MARKHAM, (1852–1940) U.S.
poet. "The Man with the Hoe," st. 1, *The Man
with the Hoe and Other Poems* (1899).

4   And he gave it for his opinion, that
whoever could make two ears of
corn, or two blades of grass, to
grow upon a spot of ground where
only one grew before, would
deserve better of mankind, and do
more essential service to his country, than the whole race of politicians put together.

JONATHAN SWIFT, (1667–1745)
Anglo–Irish satirist. *Gulliver's Travels*, "A Voyage to Brobdingnag," ch. 7 (1726).

The king of Brobdingnag addressing Gulliver.
The physicist Henry Augustus Rowland
(1848–1901) is quoted in D.S. Greenberg, *The
Politics of Pure Science* (1967) as saying, "He
who makes two blades of grass grow where
one grew before is the benefactor of mankind,
but he who obscurely worked to find the laws
of such growth is the intellectual superior as
well as the greater benefactor of mankind."

5   No race can prosper till it learns
there is as much dignity in tilling a
field as in writing a poem.

BOOKER T. WASHINGTON,
(1856–1915) U.S. educator. *Up From Slavery*
(1901). Address, Sept. 18, 1895, Atlanta Expo-
sition.

6   When *tillage* begins, other arts follow. The farmers, therefore, are the
founders of human civilization.

DANIEL WEBSTER, (1782–1852) U.S.
lawyer, statesman. *Remarks on the Agriculture
of England, The Writings and Speeches of
Daniel Webster* (1903). Speech, Jan. 13,
1840, Boston.

Fascism

1   AS A MIND, who the hell else is
there left for me to take an interest
IN??

EZRA POUND, (1885–1972) U.S. poet,
critic. Quoted in *A Serious Character*, pt. 3,
ch. 13, Humphrey Carpenter (1988). Letter,
Aug. 28, 1934.

Referring to Mussolini. In the opening lines of
Canto 74, first of Pound's *Pisan Cantos* (written in 1948 while he was awaiting trial for
treason), Pound spoke of "the enormous
tragedy of the dream in the peasant's bent
shoulders." Interviewed in May 1945, he had
described Mussolini as "a very human, imper-
fect character who lost his head."

2   Fascism is not defined by the number of its victims, but by the way it
kills them.

JEAN–PAUL SARTRE, (1905–1980)
French philosopher, author. *Libération*
(Paris, June 22, 1953).

On the execution of Julius and Ethel Rosen-
berg.

Fashion

1   For the fashion of this world passeth away.

BIBLE: NEW TESTAMENT, St. Paul, in *1
Corinthians*, 7:31.

2   Fashion is architecture: it is a matter of proportions.

COCO CHANEL, (1883–1971) French *couturière*. Quoted in *Coco Chanel: Her Life, Her
Secrets*, ch. 21, Marcel Haedrich (1971).

3   You know, one had as good be out
of the world, as out of the fashion.

COLLEY CIBBER, (1671–1757) British actor–manager, playwright. Narcissa, in *Love's Last Shift*, act 2, sc. 1 (1696). Repr. in *Dramatic Works* (1966).

The proverb can be dated back to 1639.

4 The same costume will be Indecent 10 years before its time, Shameless 5 years before its time, *Outré* (daring) 1 year before its time, Smart, Dowdy 1 year after its time, Hideous 10 years after its time, Ridiculous 20 years after its time, Amusing 30 years after its time, Quaint 50 years after its time, Charming 70 years after its time, Romantic 100 years after its time, Beautiful 150 years after its time.

JAMES LAVER, (1899–1975) British art critic, author. *Taste and Fashion*, ch. 18 (1937).

"The erogenous zone," Laver wrote, "is always shifting, and it is the business of fashion to pursue it, without ever catching it up."

5 They come to see; they come that they themselves may be seen.

OVID (PUBLIUS OVIDIUS NASO), (43 B.C.–A.D.17) Roman poet. *Ars Amatoria*, bk. 1, l. 99.

Father–Son Relationships

1 I sighed as a lover, I obeyed as a son.

EDWARD GIBBON, (1737–1794) British historian. *Memoirs of my Life*, p. 55 (1796), published as *Autobiography*, Routledge (1971).

Of his father's refusal to accept Gibbon's attachment to Suzanne Curchod, daughter of a pastor in Lausanne.

2 What harsh judges fathers are to all young men!

TERENCE, (c. 190–159 B.C.) Roman dramatist. *Heauton Timorumenos* [*The Self–Tormentor*], l. 213.

Fathers

1 It is a wise father that knows his own child.

WILLIAM SHAKESPEARE, (1564–1616) British dramatist, poet. Launcelot, in *The Merchant of Venice*, act 2, sc. 2, l. 72–3 (1600).

Launcelot repeats a proverbial saying as he attempts to make himself known to his blind father Gobbo.

2 An unforgiving eye, and a damned disinheriting countenance!

RICHARD BRINSLEY SHERIDAN, (1751–1816) Anglo–Irish dramatist. Careless, in *The School for Scandal*, act 4, sc. 1, l. 91 (1777).

Describing the portrait of Sir Oliver Surface.

Fatigue

1 I am poured out like water, and all my bones are out of joint: my heart is like wax; it is melted in the midst of my bowels.

BIBLE: HEBREW, *Psalms*, 22:14.

2 A small man can be just as exhausted as a great man.

ARTHUR MILLER, (b. 1915) U.S. dramatist. Linda, in *Death of a Salesman*, act 1 (1949).

Referring to her husband Willy Loman.

3 Not tonight, Josephine.

NAPOLEON BONAPARTE, (1769–1821) French general, emperor. *Attributed*.

Legendary reply to the Empress Joséphine.

Faults and Fault–Finding

1 It is easier to discover a deficiency in individuals, in states, and in Providence, than to see their real import and value.

Georg Hegel, (1770–1831) German philosopher. *The Philosophy of History,* "Introduction," sct. 3 (1837).

2   If we had no faults of our own, we should not take so much pleasure in noticing those in others.

François La Rochefoucauld, Duc De, (1613–1680) French writer, moralist. *Sentences et Maximes Morales,* no. 31 (1678).

3   Through my fault, my most grievous fault.
[*Mea culpa, mea maxima culpa.*]

Missal, The, *The Ordinary of the Mass.*

Missal is book of prayers and rites used to celebrate the Roman Catholic mass during the year.

Favors

1   Too great a hurry to discharge an obligation is a kind of ingratitude.

François La Rochefoucauld, Duc De, (1613–1680) French writer, moralist. *Sentences et Maximes Morales,* no. 226 (1678).

2   I do not ask you much;
I beg cold comfort, and you are so strait
And so ingrateful you deny me that.

William Shakespeare, (1564–1616) British dramatist, poet. John, in *King John,* act 5, sc. 7, l. 41–3 (1623).

The words of the dying king to his son (Prince Henry) and the English nobles. The phrase "cold comfort" was already current.

Fear

1   No passion so effectually robs the mind of all its powers of acting and reasoning as fear.

Edmund Burke, (1729–1797) Irish philosopher, statesman. *The Origin of our Ideas of the Sublime and Beautiful,* pt. 2, ch. 2 (1756).

2   If hopes were dupes, fears may be liars.

Arthur Hugh Clough, (1819–1861) British poet. "Say Not the Struggle Nought Availeth," (1862). Repr. in *Collected Poems,* ed. C. Whibley (1913).

3   How does one kill fear, I wonder? How do you shoot a spectre through the heart, slash off its spectral head, take it by its spectral throat?

Joseph Conrad,(1857–1924) Polish–born British novelist. Marlow, in *Lord Jim,* ch. 33 (1900).

4   I will show you fear in a handful of dust.

T.S. (Thomas Stearns) Eliot, (1888–1965) Anglo–American poet, critic. *The Waste Land,* pt. 1, "The Burial of the Dead" (1922).

5   I will show you fear in a handful of dust.

T.S. (Thomas Stearns) Eliot, (1888–1965) Anglo–American poet, critic. *The Waste Land,* pt. 1, "The Burial of the Dead" (1922).

6   Let me assert my firm belief that the only thing we have to fear is fear itself.

Franklin Delano Roosevelt, (1882–1945) U.S. Democratic politician, president. *The Penguin Book of Twentieth Century Speeches,* ed. Brian MacArthur (1992). First inaugural address, March 4, 1933.

Roosevelt had used the expression on previous occasions, and it has numerous earlier attributions, including the Duke of Wellington, Montaigne, Thoreau and the Bible. Sir Winston Churchill is associated with the words in his wartime broadcasts.

7   Fear is the main source of superstition, and one of the main sources of cruelty. To conquer fear is the

beginning of wisdom, in the pursuit of truth as in the endeavour after a worthy manner of life.

BERTRAND RUSSELL [LORD RUSSELL, 3RD EARL], (1872–1970) British philosopher, mathematician. *Unpopular Essays,* "An Outline of Intellectual Rubbish" (1950).

8   Present fears
Are less than horrible imaginings.

WILLIAM SHAKESPEARE, (1564–1616) British dramatist, poet. Macbeth, in *Macbeth,* act 1, sc. 3, l. 136–37 (1623).

Macbeth muses on the Witches' prophesy that he will be king, "Whose horrid image doth unfix my hair And make my seated heart knock at my ribs Against the use of nature."

Feelings

1   The deepest feeling always shows itself in silence;
not in silence, but restraint.

MARIANNE MOORE, (1887–1972) U.S. poet. "Silence," *Selected Poems* (1935).

Fellowship

1   We must love one another or die.

W.H. (WYSTAN HUGH) AUDEN, (1907–1973) Anglo–American poet. "September 1, 1939," st. 8, *Another Time* (1940).

Auden later repudiated the line, insisting that it be altered for a 1955 anthology to "We must love one another and die." He referred to the poem as "the most dishonest poem I have ever written."

2   Be my brother, or I will kill you.

SÉBASTIEN–ROCH NICOLAS DE CHAMFORT, (1741–1794) French writer, wit. Quoted in *Complete Works,* vol. 1, "Note on the Life and Writings of Chamfort," trans. by P.R. Anguis (1824).

Chamfort's interpretation of the revolutionary slogan, "Fraternity or death!"

3   All for one and one for all.

ALEXANDRE DUMAS, (1802–1870) French dramatist. Musketeers' motto, in *The Three Musketeers,* ch. 9 (1844).

4   The world has narrowed to a neighborhood before it has broadened to brotherhood.

LYNDON BAINES JOHNSON, (1908–1973) U.S. Democratic politician, president. *Public Papers of the Presidents of the United States, Lyndon B. Johnson: 1963–64.* Speech, Dec. 17, 1963, New York City.

5   The brotherhood of man is evoked by particular men according to their circumstances. But it seldom extends to all men. In the name of our freedom and our brotherhood we are prepared to blow up the other half of mankind and to be blown up in our turn.

R.D. (RONALD DAVID) LAING, (1927–1989) British psychiatrist. *The Politics of Experience,* ch. 4 (1967).

Fellowship, Human

1   I believe in the brotherhood of man, all men, but I don't believe in brotherhood with anybody who doesn't want brotherhood with me. I believe in treating people right, but I'm not going to waste my time trying to treat somebody right who doesn't know how to return the treatment.

MALCOLM X [MACOLM LITTLE], (1925–1965) U.S. African–American leader. Speech, Dec. 12, 1964, New York City.

Feminism

1   Feminism is hated because women are hated. Anti-feminism is a direct

expression of misogyny; it is the political defense of women hating.

ANDREA DWORKIN, (b. 1946) U.S. feminist critic. *Right–Wing Women*, ch. 6 (1978).

2   Women's liberation, if it abolishes the patriarchal family, will abolish a necessary substructure of the authoritarian state, and once that withers away Marx will have come true willy–nilly, so let's get on with it.

GERMAINE GREER, (b. 1939) Australian feminist writer. *The Female Eunuch*, "Revolution" (1970).

3   The people I'm furious with are the Women's Liberationists. They keep getting up on soapboxes and proclaiming women are brighter than men. That's true, but it should be kept quiet or it ruins the whole racket.

ANITA LOOS, (1893–1981) U.S. screenwriter. Quoted in *Observer* (London, Dec. 30, 1973).

4   Madonna is the true feminist. She exposes the puritanism and suffocating ideology of American feminism, which is stuck in an adolescent whining mode. Madonna has taught young women to be fully female and sexual while still exercising control over their lives.

CAMILLE PAGLIA, (b. 1947) U.S. author, critic, educator. "Madonna 1: Animality and Artifice," *The New York Times* (Dec. 14, 1991). Repr. in *Sex, Art, and American Culture* (1992).

5   The connections between and among women are the most feared, the most problematic, and the most potentially transforming force on the planet.

ADRIENNE RICH, (b. 1929) U.S. poet. "Disloyal To Civilization: Feminism, Racism,

Gynophobia," *On Lies, Secrets, and Silence* (1980). Originally published in *Chrysalis*, no. 7 (1979).

6   Womanist is to feminist as purple is to lavender.

ALICE WALKER, (b. 1944) U.S. author, critic. *In Search of Our Mothers' Gardens*, epigraph (1983).

7   People call me a feminist whenever I express sentiments that differentiate me from a doormat or a prostitute.

REBECCA WEST [CICILY ISABEL FAIRFIELD], (1892–1983) British author. Attributed in 1913, quoted in *Penguin Dictionary of Twentieth–Century Quotations*, J.M. and M.J. Cohen (1993).

8   If the abstract rights of man will bear discussion and explanation, those of women, by a parity of reasoning, will not shrink from the same test: though a different opinion prevails in this country.

MARY WOLLSTONECRAFT, (1759–1797) British feminist writer. "Dedication," *A Vindication of the Rights of Women* (1792).

Festivals

1   The second day of July 1776, will be the most memorable epoch in the history of America. I am apt to believe that it will be celebrated by succeeding generations as the great anniversary festival. It ought to be commemorated, as the day of deliverance, by solemn acts of devotion to God Almighty. It ought to be solemnized with pomp and parade, with shows, games, sports, guns, bells, bonfires and illuminations, from one end of this continent to the other, from this time forward forever more

JOHN ADAMS, (1735–1826) U.S. statesman, president. *The Adams Family Correspon-*

dence, vol. 2, ed. L.H. Butterfield (1963). Letter, July 3, 1776, to his wife Abigail Adams.

2   What, to the American slave, is your Fourth of July? I answer: A day that reveals to him, more than all other days in the year, the gross injustice and cruelty to which he is the constant victim. To him your celebration is a sham.

FREDERICK DOUGLASS, (c.1817–1895) U.S. abolitionist. "What to the Slave Is the Fourth of July?" *The Frederick Douglass Papers*, ed. John W. Blassingame, first series (1982). Speech, July 5, 1852, Rochester, NY.

Fiction

1   Although our productions have afforded more extensive and unaffected pleasure than those of any other literary corporation in the world, no species of composition has been so much decried.... "And what are you reading, Miss—?" "Oh! it is only a novel!" replies the young lady; while she lays down her book with affected indifference, or momentary shame. "It is only *Cecilia*, or *Camilla*, or *Belinda*"; or, in short, only some work in which the greatest powers of the mind are displayed, in which the most thorough knowledge of human nature, the happiest delineation of its varieties, the liveliest effusions of wit and humour, are conveyed to the world in the best chosen language.

JANE AUSTEN, (1775–1817) British novelist. *Northanger Abbey*, ch. 5 (1818).

2   Our interest's on the dangerous edge of things.
The honest thief, the tender murderer,
The superstitious atheist.

ROBERT BROWNING, (1812–1889) British poet. "Bishop Blougram's Apology," l. 396–8, *Men and Women*, vol. 1 (1855).

These lines were cited by Graham Greene as the epigraph he would choose for all of his novels.

3   But I hate things *all fiction* ... there should always be some foundation of fact for the most airy fabric— and pure invention is but the talent of a liar.

GEORGE GORDON NOEL BYRON, 6TH BARON BYRON, (1788–1824) British poet. *Byron's Letters and Journals*, vol. 5, ed. Leslie A. Marchand (1973–1981). Letter, April 2, 1817, to publisher John Murray.

4   When the characters are really alive before their author, the latter does nothing but follow them in their action, in their words, in the situations which they suggest to him.

LUIGI PIRANDELLO, (1867–1936) Italian author, playwright. The father, in *Six Characters in Search of an Author*, act 3 (1921).

5   Undermining experience, embellishing experience, rearranging and enlarging experience into a species of mythology.

PHILIP ROTH, (b. 1933) U.S. novelist. *The Facts* (1988).

Describing the life of a fiction writer, in opening letter to Zuckerman.

6   Persons attempting to find a motive in this narrative will be prosecuted; persons attempting to find a moral in it will be banished; persons attempting to find a plot in it will be shot.

MARK TWAIN, (1835–1910) U.S. author. *Huckleberry Finn*, "Notice—By Order of the Author" (1884).

7   The good ended happily, and the bad unhappily. That is what Fiction means.

Oscar Wilde, (1854–1900) Anglo–Irish playwright, author. Miss Prism, in *The Importance of Being Earnest*, act 2 (1895).

Speaking of her own novel.

Fiction: Suspense and Mystery

1 Detection is, or ought to be, an exact science, and should be treated in the same cold and unemotional manner. You have attempted to tinge it with romanticism, which produces much the same effect as if you worked a love–story or an elopement into the fifth proposition of Euclid.

Arthur Conan, Sir Doyle, (1859–1930) British author. Sherlock Holmes, in *The Sign of Four*, ch. 1 (1890).

Addressing Dr. Watson. Watson had written what he called "a small brochure, with the somewhat fantastic title of 'A Study in Scarlet,'"—the name of the tale in which Conan Doyle first introduced Sherlock Holmes.

2 The detective novel is the art–for–art's–sake of our yawning Philistinism, the classic example of a specialized form of art removed from contact with the life it pretends to build on.

V.S. (Victor Sawdon) Pritchett, (b. 1900) British author, critic. "The Roots of Detection," *Books in General* (1953). *New Statesman* (London, June 16, 1951).

Fidelity

1 Be thou faithful unto death, and I will give thee a crown of life.

Bible: New Testament, St. John the Divine, in *Revelation*, 2:10.

2 Ah, love, let us be true
To one another! for the world, which seems

To lie before us like a land of
dreams,
So various, so beautiful, so new,
Hath really neither joy, nor love,
nor light,
Nor certitude, nor peace, nor help
for pain;
And we are here as on a darkling
plain
Swept with confused alarms of
struggle and flight,
Where ignorant armies clash by
night.

Matthew Arnold, (1822–1888) British poet, critic. "Dover Beach," st. 4 (1867).

3 Fidelity. A virtue peculiar to those who are about to be betrayed.

Ambrose Bierce, (1842–1914) U.S. author. *The Devil's Dictionary* (1881–1906), repr. in *Collected Works of Ambrose Bierce*, vol. 7 (1911).

4 I have been faithful to thee, Cynara! in my fashion.

Ernest Dowson, (1867–1900) British poet. "Cynara" *(full title:* "Non sum qualis eram bonae sub regno Cynarae"), refrain (1896).

The title ("I am not as I was when dear Cynara was my queen") is from Horace, *Odes*, book 4.

5 We only part to meet again.
Change, as ye list, ye winds: my heart shall be
The faithful compass that still points to thee.

John Gay, (1685–1732) British dramatist, poet. "Sweet William's Farewell to Black–Eyed Susan" (1720).

Fighting

1 Put up again thy sword into his place: for all they that take the sword shall perish with the sword.

BIBLE: NEW TESTAMENT, Jesus, in
Matthew, 26:52.

2   There are not fifty ways of fighting,
there's only one, and that's to win.
Neither revolution nor war consists
in doing what one pleases.

ANDRÉ MALRAUX, (1901–1976) French
man of letters, statesman. *Man's Hope*, pt. 2,
sct. 2, ch. 12 (1937).

First Ladies of the United States

1   I do not think it altogether inappropriate to introduce myself to
this audience. I am the man who
accompanied Jacqueline Kennedy
to Paris, and I have enjoyed it.

JOHN FITZGERALD KENNEDY,
(1917–1963) U.S. Democratic politician, pres-
ident. *Public Papers of the Presidents of the
United States: John F. Kennedy, 1961.* Speech,
June 2, 1961, SHAPE Headquarters, Paris,
France.

Referring to the massive media publicity
attracted by the Kennedys' visit to Paris—
focused particularly on Jackie Kennedy.

2   You will feel that you are no longer
clothing yourself, you are dressing a
public monument.

ELEANOR ROOSEVELT, (1884–1962) U.S.
columnist, lecturer, wife of Franklin Roosevelt. Quoted in *Herald Tribune* (New York,
Oct. 27, 1960).

Warning to wives of future presidents.

Fish

1   But somewhere, beyond Space and
Time,
Is wetter water, slimier slime!
And there (they trust) there swim-
meth One

Who swam ere rivers were begun,
Immense, of fishy form and mind,
Squamous, omnipotent, and kind.

RUPERT BROOKE, (1887–1915) British
poet. "Heaven," *1914 and Other Poems*
(1915).

Fishing

1   Fly fishing may be a very pleasant
amusement; but angling or float
fishing I can only compare to a
stick and a string, with a worm at
one end and a fool at the other.

SAMUEL JOHNSON, (1709–1784) British
author, lexicographer. Attributed in *Instructions to Young Sportsmen*, Hawker (1859).

Never found in Johnson's works, the remark is
also attributed to Jonathan Swift.

Fitzgerald, F. Scott

1   I am not a great man, but sometimes I think the impersonal and
objective equality of my talent and
the sacrifices of it, in pieces, to preserve its essential value has some
sort of epic grandeur.

F. SCOTT FITZGERALD, (1896–1940)
U.S. author. *The Crack–Up,* ed. Edmund Wilson (1945). Letter, spring 1940, to his daughter Frances Scott Fitzgerald.

The words "some sort of epic grandeur" were
used by Matthew J. Bruccoli as a title for his
1981 biography of Fitzgerald.

Flattery

1   Women who are either indisputably beautiful, or indisputably
ugly, are best flattered upon the
score of their understandings; but
those who are in a state of mediocrity are best flattered upon their

beauty, or at least their graces: for every woman who is not absolutely ugly, thinks herself handsome.

PHILIP DORMER STANHOPE, 4TH EARL CHESTERFIELD, (1694–1773) British statesman, man of letters. *The Letters of the Earl of Chesterfield to His Son*, vol. 1, no. 161, ed. Charles Strachey (1901). Letter, Sept. 5, 1748, first published (1774).

2 Flattery'll get you anywhere.

CHARLES LEDERER, U.S. screenwriter. Dorothy (Jane Russell) to Malone, in *Gentlemen Prefer Blondes* (film) (1953). Howard Hawks.

Flirtation

1 We have progressively improved into a less spiritual species of tenderness—but the seal is not yet fixed though the wax is preparing for the impression.

GEORGE GORDON NOEL BYRON, 6TH BARON BYRON, (1788–1824) British poet. *Byron's Letters and Journals*, vol. 3, ed. Leslie Marchand (1974). Letter, Oct. 14, 1813.

Of his dealings with Lady Frances Webster.

2 O Polly, you might have toyed and kissed,
By keeping men off, you keep them on.

JOHN GAY, (1685–1732) British dramatist, poet. Mrs. Peach, in *The Beggar's Opera*, act 1, sc. 8, air 9 (1728), ed. F.W. Bateson (1934).

3 Drink to me only with thine eyes,
And I will pledge with mine;
Or leave a kiss but in the cup,
And I'll not look for wine.

BEN JONSON, (c. 1572–1637) British dramatist, poet. *The Forest*, no. 9, "Song to Celia," (1616). Repr. in *The Complete Poems*, ed. George Parfitt (1975).

The sense of these lines is borrowed from the Greek sophist Philostratus, epistle 24.

Flowers

1 Ah, Sun–flower, weary of time,
Who countest the steps of the Sun,
Seeking after that sweet golden clime
Where the traveller's journey is done:
Where the Youth pined away with desire,
And the pale Virgin shrouded in snow
Arise from their graves, and aspire
Where my Sun–flower wishes to go.

WILLIAM BLAKE, (1757–1827) British poet, painter, engraver. *Songs of Experience*, "Ah! Sun–flower," (1794), repr. in *Complete Writings*, ed. Geoffrey Keynes (1957).

2 Half–opening her lips to the frost's morning sigh, how strangely the rose has smiled on a swift–fleeting day of September!
   How audacious it is to advance in stately manner before the blue–tit fluttering in the shrubs that have long lost their leaves, like a queen with the spring's greeting on her lips;
   to bloom with steadfast hope that, parted from the cold flower–bed, she may be the last to cling, intoxicated, to a young hostess's breast.

AFANASI FET, (1820–1892) Russian poet. "The September Rose," (1890), trans. by Dimitri Obolensky (1965).

3 A perfect beauty of a sunflower! a perfect excellent lovely sunflower existence! a sweet natural eye to the new hip moon, woke up alive and excited grasping in the sunset shadow sunrise golden monthly breeze

ALLEN GINSBERG, (b. 1926) U.S. poet. "Sunflower Sutra," *Howl and Other Poems* (1956).

4 Fair daffodils, we weep to see
You haste away so soon:
As yet the early–rising sun

Has not attained his noon.

ROBERT HERRICK, (1591–1674) British poet, clergyman. "To Daffodils," st. 1, *Hesperides* (1648). Repr. in *The Poems of Robert Herrick*, ed. L.C. Martin (1956).

5   When you take a flower in your hand and really look at it, it's your world for the moment. I want to give that world to someone else. Most people in the city rush around so, they have no time to look at a flower. I want them to see it whether they want to or not.

GEORGIA O'KEEFFE, (1887–1986) U.S. artist. Quoted in "Portrait of an Artist," Laurie Lisle (1986). *New York Post* (May 16, 1946).

6   Where have all the flowers gone?

PETE SEEGER, (b. 1919) U.S. folk singer, songwriter. "Where Have All the Flowers Gone?" (song title) (1961).

7   Rose is a rose is a rose is a rose.

GERTRUDE STEIN, (1874–1946) U.S. author. "Sacred Emily" (written 1913), published in *Geography and Plays* (1922).

Thought to refer to the artist Sir Francis Rose, one of whose paintings was hung in her Paris drawing–room.

8   To me the meanest flower that blows can give
Thoughts that do often lie too deep for tears.

WILLIAM WORDSWORTH, (1770–1850) British poet. "Intimations of Immortality from Recollections of Early Childhood," l. 206–7 (written 1802–1804), published in *Poems in Two Volumes* (1807).

Closing lines of poem.

Food and Eating

1   Let us eat and drink; for tomorrow we shall die.

BIBLE: HEBREW, *Isaiah,* 22:13.

Almost the same words are found in *1 Corinthians* 15:32, and both verses are frequently confused with *Ecclesiastes* 8:15: "A man hath no better thing under the sun, than to eat, and to drink, and to be merry."

2   Edible. Good to eat and wholesome to digest, as a worm to a toad, a toad to a snake, a snake to a pig, a pig to a man, and a man to a worm.

AMBROSE BIERCE, (1842–1914) U.S. author. *The Devil's Dictionary* (1881–1906), repr. in *Collected Works of Ambrose Bierce*, vol. 7 (1911).

3   Tell me what you eat and I'll tell you who you are.

JEAN–ANTHELME BRILLAT–SAVARIN, (1755–1826) French jurist, gastronome. *La Physiologie du Goethe,* introduction, aph. 4 (1826).

Brillat–Savarin's aphorism was echoed by the philosopher Ludwig Feuerbach, quoted in 1850: "Man is what he eats"—itself probably the precursor of the expression, "You are what you eat."

4   Some hae meat and canna eat,
And some wad eat that want it;
But we hae meat, and we can eat,
And sae the Lord be thanket.

ROBERT BURNS, (1759–1796) Scottish poet. "The Selkirk Grace," (c. 1790). *Poetical Works,* vol. 2, ed. William Scott Douglas (1891).

5   The healthy stomach is nothing if it is not conservative. Few radicals have good digestions.

SAMUEL BUTLER, (1835–1902) British author. *Notebooks,* ch. 6 (1912).

6   My dear, if Mr. Carlyle's digestion had been stronger, there is no saying what he might have been!

JANE WELSH CARLYLE, (1801–1866) Scottish poet, wife of Thomas Carlyle. Quoted in *Autobiography and Letters of Mrs. Margaret Oliphant* (1899). Letter, May [?] 1866.

In answer to a remark by Margaret Oliphant that "Mr. Carlyle seemed the only virtuous philosopher we had."

7 A cheese may disappoint. It may be dull, it may be naive, it may be oversophisticated. Yet it remains cheese, milk's leap toward immortality.

CLIFTON FADIMAN, (b. 1904) U.S. essayist. *Any Number Can Play*, p. 105 (1957).

8 He who does not mind his belly, will hardly mind anything else.

SAMUEL JOHNSON, (1709–1784) British author, lexicographer. Quoted in James Boswell, *Life of Dr. Johnson*, entry, Aug. 5, 1763 (1791).

Boswell further described Johnson's dedication to eating thus: "I never knew any man who relished good eating more than he did. When at table he was totally absorbed in the business of the moment.... To those whose sensations were delicate, this could not but be disgusting; and it was doubtless not very suitable to the character of a philosopher.... But it must be owned that Johnson, though he could be rigidly *abstemious*, was not a *temperate* man."

9 Time for a little something.

A.A. (ALAN ALEXANDER) MILNE, (1882–1958) British author.Winnie–the–Pooh, in *Winnie–the–Pooh*, ch. 6 (1926).

10 One should eat to live, not live to eat.

MOLIÈRE [JEAN BAPTISTE POQUELIN], (1622–1673) French dramatist. Valière, in *The Miser*, act 3, sc. 1, l. 149 (1669).

11 I eats my spinach.

POPEYE, Popeye's catch phrase, *The Encyclopedia of Animated Cartoons*, ed. Jeff Lenburg (1991). (Created 1929).

Originally created by cartoonist E.C. Segar (1894–1938) for a syndicated strip called *Thimble Theatre* which began life in the *Evening News* in Dec. 1919, Popeye's character was prefigured many times in marginal

form during the 1920s before his first official appearance in Jan. 17, 1929. First film appearance was in 1932 for the Fleischer Studio's *Talkartoon* series, opposite Betty Boop.

12 You needn't tell me that a man who doesn't love oysters and asparagus and good wines has got a soul, or a stomach either. He's simply got the instinct for being unhappy highly developed.

[H.H. (HECTOR HUGH) MUNRO] SAKI, (1870–1916) Scottish author. Clovis, in "The Match–Maker," *The Chronicles of Clovis* (1911).

13 Let onion atoms lurk within the bowl,
   And, scarce suspected, animate the whole.

SYDNEY SMITH, (1771–1845) British clergyman, writer. *Memoir*, vol. 1, ch. 11, "Recipe for Salad," Lady Holland (1855).

14 The only emperor is the emperor of ice–cream.

WALLACE STEVENS, (1879–1955) U.S. poet. "The Emperor of Ice–Cream," *Harmonium* (1923).

Fools and Follies

1 Answer a fool according to his folly, lest he be wise in his own conceit.

BIBLE: HEBREW, *Proverbs*, 26:5.

2 As a dog returneth to his vomit, so a fool returneth to his folly.

BIBLE: HEBREW, *Proverbs*, 26:11.

3 A fool sees not the same tree that a wise man sees.

WILLIAM BLAKE, (1757–1827) British poet, painter, engraver. *The Marriage of Heaven and Hell*, plate 7, "Proverbs of Hell," (c. 1793), repr. in *Complete Writings*, ed. Geoffrey Keynes (1957).

4 If the fool would persist in his folly he would become wise.

WILLIAM BLAKE, (1757–1827) British poet, painter, engraver. *The Marriage of Heaven and Hell,* plate 7, "Proverbs of Hell," (c. 1793), repr. in *Complete Writings,* ed. Geoffrey Keynes (1957).

5 They never open their mouths without subtracting from the sum of human knowledge.

THOMAS BRACKETT REED, (1839–1902) U.S. lawyer, politician. Quoted in *The Life of Thomas Brackett Reed,* ch. 21, Samuel W. McCall (1914).

Referring to two colleagues in the House of Representatives.

6 Lord, what fools these mortals be!

WILLIAM SHAKESPEARE, (1564–1616) British dramatist, poet. Robin Goodfellow (Puck), in *A Midsummer Night's Dream,* act 3, sc. 2, l. 115, 1594–95.

Referring to the antics of the Athenian lovers, upon whom he has sprinkled his love potion. Seneca wrote similar words in *Epistulae ad Lucilium,* epistle 1, sct. 3.

7 The dullness of the fool is the whetstone of the wits.

WILLIAM SHAKESPEARE, (1564–1616) British poet, dramatist. Celia, in *As You Like It,* act 1, sc. 2, l. 52–3 (1623).

Shakespeare was possibly making a punning reference to *The Whetstone of Witte*—a famous treatise on algebra by Robert Recorde published in 1557. The book's title was a literal translation of *Cos Ingenii* (*cos* being the Latin for "whetstone," while *Coss* or *the Cossic Art* was also the old name for algebra).

8 Let us be thankful for the fools. But for them the rest of us could not succeed.

MARK TWAIN, (1835–1910) U.S. author. *Following the Equator,* ch. 28, "Pudd'nhead Wilson's New Calendar" (1897).

Force

1 The great questions of the day will not be settled by means of speeches and majority decisions ... but by iron and blood.

OTTO VON BISMARCK, (1815–1898) Prussian statesman. *Bismarck: Life and Works,* vol. 4 (1878). Speech, Sept. 30, 1862.

"Iron and blood," or "blood and iron," were favorite expressions of Bismarck's.

2 The use of force alone is but *temporary.* It may subdue for a moment; but it does not remove the necessity of subduing again: and a nation is not governed, which is perpetually to be conquered.

EDMUND BURKE, (1729–1797) Irish philosopher, statesman. *Second Speech on Conciliation with America: The Thirteen Resolutions, Works,* vol. 2 (1899). Speech, March 22, 1775, House of Commons, London.

3 Who breaks a butterfly on a wheel?

ALEXANDER POPE, (1688–1744) British satirical poet. Lord Hervey, in "Epistle to Dr. Arbuthnot," l. 308 (1735).

The line has passed into common usage, and achieved notoriety in the 1960s when it was used to head the London *Times* leader July 1, 1967, on Mick Jagger and Keith Richard's arrest on drugs charges—an article which was thought to have contributed to their acquittal.

4 Where force is necessary, there it must be applied boldly, decisively and completely. But one must know the limitations of force; one must know when to blend force with a manoeuver, a blow with an agreement.

LEON TROTSKY, (1879–1940) Russian revolutionary. *What Next?* Ch. 14 (1932).

5 Other nations use "force"; we Britons alone use "Might."

EVELYN WAUGH, (1903–1966) British novelist. Mr. Baldwin, in *Scoop*, bk. 2, ch. 5, sct. 1 (1938).

Ford, Gerald R.

1   I am a Ford, not a Lincoln.

GERALD FORD, (b. 1913) U.S. Republican politician, president. Quoted in *A Ford, Not a Lincoln*, ch. 2, Richard Reeves (1975). Address, Dec. 6, 1973, on taking vice–presidential oath.

Ford explained, "My addresses will never be as eloquent as Lincoln's. But I will do my best to equal his brevity and plain speaking." Eight months later, Ford was sworn in as president. He told Congress, "The truth is I am the people's man" (Aug. 12, 1974).

Foreign Countries

1   I have been a stranger in a strange land.

BIBLE: HEBREW, *Exodus*, 2:22.

Moses, referring to his time in Egypt.

2   Should we have stayed at home and thought of here?
Where should we be today?
Is it right to be watching strangers in a play
in this strangest of theatres?

ELIZABETH BISHOP, (1911–1979) U.S. poet. "Questions of Travel," *Questions of Travel* (1965).

Bishop, an avid traveler, spent the last 16 years of her life in Brazil.

3   "Abroad," that large home of ruined reputations.

GEORGE ELIOT [MARY ANN (OR MARIAN) EVANS], (1819–1880) British novelist. *Felix Holt*, epilogue (1866).

4   Abroad is bloody.

GEORGE VI, (1895–1952) British King of Great Britain and Northern Ireland.

Attributed in *A Certain World*, "Royalty," W.H. Auden (1970).

See Mitford on foreigners.

5   On the road to Mandalay,
Where the flyin'–fishes play,
An' the dawn comes up like thunder outer China 'crost the Bay!

RUDYARD KIPLING, (1865–1936) British writer, poet. "Mandalay," refrain, *Barrack–Room Ballads* (1892).

6   Toto, I've a feeling we're not in Kansas anymore.... Now I know we're not in Kansas.

NOEL LANGLEY, (1898–1981) U.S. author. Dorothy, in *The Wizard of Oz* (film, 1939).

On arriving in the Land of Oz. The words do not appear in Baum's original book, *The Wonderful Wizard of Oz* (1900).

7   As the traveler who has once been from home is wiser than he who has never left his own doorstep, so a knowledge of one other culture should sharpen our ability to scrutinize more steadily, to appreciate more lovingly, our own.

MARGARET MEAD, (1901–1978) U.S. anthropologist. *Coming of Age in Samoa*, introduction (1928).

8   Furthermost Thule.
[Ultima Thule.]

VIRGIL [PUBLIUS VERGILIUS MARO], (70–19 B.C.) Roman poet. "Georgics," bk. 1, l. 30 (29 B.C.), trans. by Kate Hughes (1995).

Used to denote a far–off land or an unattainable goal: Thule was thought to be six days' travel north of England—possibly Iceland.

Foreign Policy

1   Much of what Mr. Wallace calls his global thinking is, no matter how you slice it, still "globaloney." Mr.

Wallace's warp of sense and his woof of nonsense is very tricky cloth out of which to cut the pattern of a post–war world.

CLARE BOOTHE LUCE, (1903–1987) U.S. playwright, diplomat. *Congressional Record*, vol. 89. Speech, Feb. 9, 1943, to Congress.

Referring to Vice President Henry Wallace's views on foreign policy, in Clare Boothe Luce's maiden speech in the House.

2   Our policy is directed not against any country or doctrine, but against hunger, poverty, desperation and chaos. Its purpose should be the revival of a working economy in the world so as to permit the emergence of political and social conditions in which free institutions can exist.

GEORGE MARSHALL, (1880–1959) U.S. general, Democratic politician. Quoted in *The Harper Book of American Quotations*, eds. Gorton Carruth and Eugene Ehrlich (1988). Speech, June 5, 1947, Harvard University.

Describing what became known as the Marshall Plan for recovery in post–war Europe.

3   We owe it, therefore, to candor and to the amicable relations existing between the United States and those powers to declare that we should consider any attempt on their part to extend their system to any portion of this hemisphere as dangerous to our peace and safety. With the existing colonies or dependencies of any European power we have not interfered and shall not interfere. But with the Governments who have declared their independence and maintain it, and whose independence we have, on great consideration and on just principles, acknowledged, we could not view any interposition for the purpose of oppressing them, or controlling in any other manner

their destiny, by any European power in any other light than as the manifestation of an unfriendly disposition toward the United States.

JAMES MONROE, (1758–1831) U.S. president. *The Monroe Doctrine*. Seventh annual message to Congress, Dec. 2, 1823.

The Monroe Doctrine was formulated with the help of John Quincy Adams and formed the basis of U.S. foreign policy in the ambit of central and South America. Theodore Roosevelt's corollary in 1904 that disturbances in Latin America might compel U.S. intervention to preempt European involvement was invoked by presidents Taft and Wilson to justify operations in the Caribbean.

4   In the field of world policy I would dedicate this nation to the policy of the good neighbor.

FRANKLIN DELANO ROOSEVELT, (1882–1945) U.S. Democratic politician, president. *The Penguin Book of Twentieth Century Speeches*, ed. Brian MacArthur (1992). First inaugural address, March 4, 1933.

5   Speak softly and carry a big stick.

THEODORE ROOSEVELT, (1858–1919) U.S. Republican (later Progressive) politician, president. *The Works of Theodore Roosevelt*, vol. 13. Speech, April 2, 1903, Chicago.

A favorite adage, referring to military preparation and the Monroe Doctrine.

6   We cannot be any stronger in our foreign policy for all the bombs and guns we may heap up in our arsenals than we are in the spirit which rules inside the country. Foreign policy, like a river, cannot rise above its source.

ADLAI STEVENSON, (1900–1965) U.S. Democratic politician. "What I Think" (1956). Speech, Dec. 4, 1954, New Orleans.

Foreigners

1   Frogs are slightly better than Huns or Wops, but abroad is unutter-

ably bloody and foreigners are fiends.

NANCY MITFORD, (1904–1973) British author. Uncle Matthew, in *The Pursuit of Love*, ch. 15 (1945).

"Uncle Matthew's four years in France and Italy between 1914 and 1918 had given him no great opinion of foreigners."

Forgiveness

1   Father, forgive them; for they know not what they do.

BIBLE: NEW TESTAMENT, Jesus, in *Luke*, 23:34.

Praying for those who crucified him.

2   Once a woman has forgiven her man, she must not reheat his sins for breakfast.

MARLENE DIETRICH, (1904–1992) German–born U.S. film actress. "Forgiveness," *Marlene Dietrich's ABC* (1962).

3   Nobuddy ever fergits where he buried a hatchet.

KIN HUBBARD (F. [FRANK] McKIN-NEY HUBBARD), (1868–1930) U.S. humorist, journalist. "Abe Martin's Broadcast" (1930). *Indianapolis News* (Jan. 4, 1925).

4   We pardon to the extent that we love.

FRANÇOIS LA ROCHEFOUCAULD, DUC DE, (1613–1680) French writer, moralist. *Sentences et Maximes Morales*, no. 330 (1678).

5   How shall I lose the sin, yet keep
    the sense,
    And love th'offender, yet detest
    th'offence?

ALEXANDER POPE, (1688–1744) British satirical poet. "Eloisa to Abelard," l. 191–2 (1717).

6   The stupid neither forgive nor forget; the naïve forgive and forget; the wise forgive but do not forget.

THOMAS SZASZ, (b. 1920) U.S. psychiatrist. "Personal Conduct," *The Second Sin* (1973).

7   Forgive! How many will say, "for
    give," and find
    A sort of absolution in the sound
    To hate a little longer!

ALFRED TENNYSON, 1ST BARON TENNYSON, (1809–1892) British poet. "Sea Dreams," l. 60–3 (1864).

France and the French

1   Fifty million Frenchmen can't be wrong.

ANONYMOUS, Popular saying.

Dating from World War I—when it was used by U.S. soldiers—or before, the saying was associated with nightclub hostess Texas Quinan in the 1920s. It was the title of a song recorded by Sophie Tucker in 1927, and of a Cole Porter musical in 1929.

2   France, famed in all great arts, in none supreme.

MATTHEW ARNOLD, (1822–1888) British poet, critic. *To a Republican Friend Continued* (1849).

3   All Gaul is divided into three parts.

GAIUS CAESAR [GAIUS JULIUS CAESAR], (100–44 B.C.) Roman general, emperor. *The Gallic War*, bk. 1, l. 1 (52–51 B.C.).

First line of the book—indelibly associated with the study of Latin at school.

4   France was long a despotism tempered by epigrams.

THOMAS CARLYLE, (1795–1881) Scottish essayist, historian. *History of the French Revolution*, pt. 1, bk. 1, ch. 1 (1837).

5   How can anyone govern a nation that has two hundred and forty–six different kinds of cheese?

CHARLES DE GAULLE, (1890–1970) French general, president. Quoted in *Newsweek* (New York, Oct. 1, 1962).

7　They order, said I, this matter better in France.

LAURENCE STERNE, (1713–1768) British author. *A Sentimental Journey* (1768).

Opening words.

8　[France is] a country where the money falls apart but you can't tear the toilet paper.

BILLY WILDER, (b. 1906) U.S. film director. Quoted in *Billy Wilder in Hollywood*, ch. 18, Maurice Zolotow (1977).

Free Will

1　Do what thou wilt shall be the whole of the law.

ALEISTER CROWLEY, (1875–1947) British occultist. *The Confessions of Aleister Crowley*, prelude (1929). Ed. (1970).

The maxim is repeated throughout Crowley's works, as representing the key to his philosophy. It has a precedent of a sort in St. Augustine's "Love and do what you will." [*Dilige et quod vis fac.*].

2　In their rules there was only one clause: DO WHAT YOU WILL because people who are free, well–born, well–bred, and easy in honest company have a natural spur and instinct which drives them to virtuous deeds and deflects them from vice; and this they called honor.

FRANÇOIS RABELAIS, (c. 1494–1553) French satirist. *Gargantua and Pantagruel*, bk. 1, ch. 57 (1548), trans. by J.M. Cohen (1955).

Rules of monastic life, laid down by Gargantua.

3　We defy augury. There's a special providence in the fall of a sparrow. If it be now, 'tis not to come. If it be not to come, it will be now. If it be not now, yet it will come. The readiness is all.

WILLIAM SHAKESPEARE, (1564–1616) British dramatist, poet. Hamlet, in *Hamlet*, act 5, sc. 2, l. 165–8 (1604).

Responding to Horatio's offer to forestall Hamlet's duel with Laertes, of which Hamlet has a premonition that all is not well.

Freedom

1　The caged bird sings
with a fearful trill
of things unknown
but longed for still
and his tune is heard
on the distant hill
for the caged bird
sings of freedom.

MAYA ANGELOU, (b. 1928) U.S. author. *Caged Bird, Shaker, Why Don't You Sing?* (1983).

2　I am truly free only when all human beings, men and women, are equally free. The freedom of other men, far from negating or limiting my freedom, is, on the contrary, its necessary premise and confirmation.

MIKHAIL BAKUNIN, (1814–1876) Russian political theorist. *God and the State* (1871). Repr. in *Bakunin on Anarchism*, ed. Sam Dolgoff (1980).

3　Yet, Freedom! yet thy banner, torn, but flying,
Streams like the thunderstorm *against* the wind.

GEORGE GORDON NOEL BYRON, 6TH BARON BYRON, (1788–1824) British poet. "Childe Harold's Pilgrimage," cto. 4, st. 98 (1812–18).

4　No man has received from nature the right to give orders to others.

Freedom is a gift from heaven, and every individual of the same species has the right to enjoy it as soon as he is in enjoyment of his reason.

DENIS DIDEROT, (1713–1784) French philosopher. *"Political Authority,"* vol. 1, *Encyclopedia* (1751). Repr. in *Selected Writings,* ed. Lester G. Crocker (1966).

5   The history of the world is none other than the progress of the consciousness of freedom.

GEORG HEGEL, (1770–1831) German philosopher. *The Philosophy of History,* "Introduction," sct. 3 (1837).

6   It is often safer to be in chains than to be free.

FRANZ KAFKA, (1883–1924) Czech novelist, short–story writer. The Advocate, in *The Trial,* ch. 8 (1925, trans. 1935).

An echo of Rousseau's famous dictum.

7   Freedom is never voluntarily given by the oppressor; it must be demanded by the oppressed.

MARTIN LUTHER KING, JR., (1929–1968) U.S. clergyman, civil rights leader. "Letter from Birmingham Jail," *Why We Can't Wait* (1963). Open letter to clergymen, Apr. 16, 1963.

8   Freedom's just another word for nothing left to lose.

KRIS KRISTOFFERSON, (b. 1936) U.S. singer, songwriter, actor. "Me and Bobby McGhee" *(song)* (1969).

The song was a success for Janis Joplin.

9   Freedom is always and exclusively freedom for the one who thinks differently.

ROSA LUXEMBURG, (1870–1919) German revolutionary. *The Russian Revolution,* ch. 6 (1922, trans. 1961). Prison notes, 1918.

10   You can't separate peace from freedom because no one can be at peace unless he has his freedom.

MALCOLM X [MALCOLM LITTLE], (1925–1965) U.S. African–American leader. *Malcolm X Speaks,* ch. 12 (1965). "Prospects for Freedom in 1965," speech, Jan. 7, 1965, New York City.

11   Emancipate yourselves from mental slavery.
None but ourselves can free our minds.

BOB MARLEY, (1945–1981) Jamaican reggae musician. "Redemption Song" (song), from the album *Uprising* (1980).

12   None can love freedom heartily, but good men; the rest love not freedom, but licence.

JOHN MILTON, (1608–1674) British poet. *The Tenure of Kings and Magistrates* (1649). Repr. in *Complete Prose Works of Milton,* ed. Ernest Sirluck (1959).

13   Freedom is the freedom to say that two plus two make four. If that is granted, all else follows.

GEORGE ORWELL, (1903–1950) British author. *Nineteen Eighty–Four,* pt. 2, ch. 7 (1949).

Winston Smith, in his diary.

14   We look forward to a world founded upon four essential human freedoms. The first is freedom of speech and expression—everywhere in the world. The second is freedom of every person to worship God in his own way—everywhere in the world. The third is freedom from want ... everywhere in the world. The fourth is freedom from fear ... anywhere in the world.

FRANKLIN DELANO ROOSEVELT, (1882–1945) U.S. Democratic politician, president. Annual message to Congress, *The Penguin Book of Twentieth Century Speeches,* ed. Brian MacArthur (1992). Speech, Jan. 6, 1941, Washington, D.C..

15   Man is born free, and everywhere he is in chains.

JEAN–JACQUES ROUSSEAU, (1712–1778) Swiss–born French philosopher, political theorist. *The Social Contract*, ch. 1 (1762).

Opening sentence of work. More than a hundred years earlier John Milton had written in his pamphlet *The Tenure of Kings and Magistrates* (1649): "No man who knows aught, can be so stupid to deny that all men naturally were born free."

16 Freedom! A wanton slut on a profligate's breast!

MARINA TSVETAEVA, (1892–1941) Russian poet. "You came out of a severe, well–proportioned church" (1917), trans. by Dimitri Obolensky (1965).

17 It is by the goodness of God that in our country we have those three unspeakably precious things: freedom of speech, freedom of conscience, and the prudence never to practice either of them.

MARK TWAIN, (1835–1910) U.S. author. *Following the Equator*, ch. 20, "Pudd'nhead Wilson's New Calendar" (1897).

18 There is an untroubled harmony in everything, a full consonance in nature; only in our illusory freedom do we feel at variance with it.

FYODOR TYUTCHEV, (1803–1873) Russian poet. *The Last Love*, "There is melody in the waves of the sea," (1865), trans. by Dimitri Obolensky (1965).

Freedom of Speech

1 The most stringent protection of free speech would not protect a man in falsely shouting fire in a theater and causing a panic.

OLIVER WENDELL HOLMES, JR., (1841–1935) U.S. jurist. *Schenk v. United States, Baer v. United States*, 249 U.S. 52 (1919). Supreme Court opinion.

2 Every man has a right to utter what he thinks truth, and every other

man has a right to knock him down for it. Martyrdom is the test.

SAMUEL JOHNSON, (1709–1784) British author, lexicographer. Quoted in James Boswell, *Life of Dr. Johnson*, entry, 1780 (1791).

As quoted by Mr. Langton.

3 Give me the liberty to know, to utter, and to argue freely according to conscience, above all liberties.

JOHN MILTON, (1608–1674) British poet. *Areopagitica: a Speech for the Liberty of Unlicensed Printing to the Parliament of England* (1644).

4 The sound of tireless voices is the price we pay for the right to hear the music of our own opinions. But there is also, it seems to me, a moment at which democracy must prove its capacity to act. Every man has a right to be heard; but no man has the right to strangle democracy with a single set of vocal chords.

ADLAI STEVENSON, (1900–1965) U.S. Democratic politician. *The Papers of Adlai E. Stevenson*, vol. 4 (1974). Speech, Aug. 28, 1952, New York City.

In the *New York Times*, Jan. 19, 1962, Stevenson was reported as saying, "the first principle of a free society is an untrammeled flow of words in an open forum."

5 In America the majority raises formidable barriers around the liberty of opinion; within these barriers an author may write what he pleases, but woe to him if he goes beyond them.

ALEXIS DE TOCQUEVILLE, (1805–1859) French social philosopher. *Democracy in America*, vol. 1, ch. 15 (1835).

6 I disapprove of what you say, but I will defend to the death your right to say it.

VOLTAIRE [FRANÇOIS MARIE AROUET], (1694–1778) French philosopher, author. Quoted in *The Friends of Voltaire*, S.G. Tallentyre (1907).

Paraphrase of Voltaire's sentiments in his *Essay on Tolerance*. Voltaire wrote in February 1770 to M. le Riche: "Monsieur l'Abbé, I detest what you write, but I would give my life to make it possible for you to continue to write."

Freud, Sigmund

1   For one who lived among enemies
     so long:
     If often he was wrong and at times
       absurd,
     To us he is no more a person
     Now but a whole climate of opin-
       ion.

W.H. (WYSTAN HUGH) AUDEN, (1907–1973) Anglo–American poet. "In Memory of Sigmund Freud," *Another Time* (1940).

2   The trouble with Freud is that he
     never played the Glasgow Empire
     Saturday night.

KEN DODD, (b. 1931) British comic. Quoted in *Times* (London, Aug. 7, 1965). Television interview, *The Laughter Makers*.

Friendlessness

1   Friendless. Having no favors to
     bestow. Destitute of fortune.
     Addicted to utterance of truth and
     common sense.

AMBROSE BIERCE, (1842–1914) U.S. author. *The Devil's Dictionary* (1881–1906), repr. in *Collected Works of Ambrose Bierce*, vol. 7 (1911).

Friendliness

1   The social, friendly, honest man,
     Whate'er he be,
     'Tis he fulfils great Nature's plan,

And none but he.

ROBERT BURNS, (1759–1796) Scottish poet. "Epistle to John Lapraik No.2," st. 15 (1786). Repr. in *Poetical Works*, vol. 1, ed. William Scott Douglas (1891).

Friends and Friendship

1   Forsake not an old friend; for the
     new is not comparable to him: a
     new friend is as new wine; when it
     is old, thou shalt drink it with plea-
     sure.

APOCRYPHA, *Ecclesiasticus*, 9:10.

2   I am distressed for thee, my brother
     Jonathan: very pleasant hast thou
     been unto me: thy love to me was
     wonderful, passing the love of
     women.

BIBLE: HEBREW, David, in *2 Samuel*, 1:26.

King David's lament for Saul and Jonathan.

3   Saul and Jonathan were lovely and
     pleasant in their lives, and in their
     death they were not divided: they
     were swifter than eagles, they were
     stronger than lions.

BIBLE: HEBREW, David, in *2 Samuel*, 1:23.

4   O God, protect me from my
     friends, that they have not power
     over me. Thou hast giv'n me power
     to protect myself from thy bitterest
     enemies.

WILLIAM BLAKE, (1757–1827) British poet, painter, engraver. Palamabron, in *Milton*, bk. 1 (c. 1810), repr. in *Complete Writings*, ed. Geoffrey Keynes (1957).

The saying has earlier proverbial antecedents in several languages: Queen Elizabeth I, quoted in J.E. Neale, *Elizabeth I and Her Parliament* ch. 4 (1957), said: "There is an Italian proverb which saith, 'From my enemy let me defend myself; but from a pretensed friend, good Lord deliver me.'"

5   Thy friendship oft has made my heart to ache:
Do be my enemy for friendship's sake.

WILLIAM BLAKE, (1757–1827) British poet, painter, engraver. *Manuscript Notebook (1808–1811),* no. 39, published in *Complete Writings,* ed. Geoffrey Keynes (1957).

Referring to his patron William Hayley.

6   A man's friendships are, like his will, invalidated by marriage—but they are also no less invalidated by the marriage of his friends.

SAMUEL BUTLER, (1835–1902) British author. *The Way of All Flesh,* ch. 75 (1903).

7   Only solitary men know the full joys of friendship. Others have their family—but to a solitary and an exile his friends are everything.

WILLA CATHER, (1876–1947) U.S. author. *Shadows on the Rock,* bk. 3, ch. 5 (1931).

8   My true friends have always given me that supreme proof of devotion, a spontaneous aversion for the man I loved.

COLETTE [SIDONIE GABRIELLE COLETTE], (1873–1954) French author. *Break of Day* (1928).

Of her younger friends, Colette wrote, "I instinctively like to acquire and store up what promises to outlast me."

9   The man that hails you Tom or Jack,
And proves by thumps upon your back
How he esteems your merit,
Is such a friend, that one had need
Be very much his friend indeed
To pardon or to bear it.

WILLIAM COWPER, (1731–1800) British poet. "Friendship," l. 169–74 (written 1781, published 1800). Repr. in *Poetical Works,* ed. H.S. Milford (1934).

10   You got a lotta nerve
To say you are my friend
When I was down
You just stood there grinning.

BOB DYLAN [ROBERT ALLEN ZIMMERMAN], (b. 1941) U.S. singer, song-writer. "Positively 4th Street" (song) (1965), re-released on *Bob Dylan's Greatest Hits* (1967).

11   A friend is a person with whom I may be sincere. Before him, I may think aloud.

RALPH WALDO EMERSON, (1803–1882) U.S. essayist, poet, philosopher. *Essays,* "Friendship," First Series (1841).

12   A friend may well be reckoned the masterpiece of Nature.

RALPH WALDO EMERSON, (1803–1882) U.S. essayist, poet, philosopher. *Essays,* "Friendship," First Series (1841).

13   Louis, I think this is the beginning of a beautiful friendship.

JULIUS J. EPSTEIN, Screenwriter. Rick Blaine (Humphrey Bogart), in *Casablanca* (film), spoken to Capt. Louis Renault (Claude Rains) in the last line of the film (1942).

Ingrid Bergman recounts in her autobiography 1980, the uncertainty over how the film was going to end, whether or not she was to get on the plane, until they shot the above scene. "Hold it!" she exclaimed, "That's it! We don't have to shoot the other ending. That's just perfect, a wonderful closing line."

14   It is in the thirties that we want friends. In the forties we know they won't save us any more than love did.

F. SCOTT FITZGERALD, (1896–1940) U.S. author. *The Crack-Up,* "Notebook O," ed. Edmund Wilson (1945).

15 You know you don't have to act with me, Steve. You don't have to say anything, and you don't have to do anything. Not a thing. Oh, maybe just whistle. You know how to whistle, don't you, Steve? You just put your lips together, and blow.

JULES FURTHMAN, (1888–1960) U.S. screenwriter. Marie Browning (Lauren Bacall), in *To Have And To Have Not* (film), spoken to Harry Morgan (Humphrey Bogart) (1944).

The film is best remembered for the on– and offscreen romance between Bogart and Bacall, which resulted in marriage the following year.

16 Friendship is but another name for an alliance with the follies and the misfortunes of others. Our own share of miseries is sufficient: why enter then as volunteers into those of another?

THOMAS JEFFERSON, (1743–1826) U.S. president. *The Papers of Thomas Jefferson*, vol. 10, Julian P. Boyd (1954). Letter, Oct. 12, 1786, to Maria Cosway.

17 If a man does not make new acquaintance as he advances through life, he will soon find himself left alone. A man, Sir, should keep his friendship in constant repair.

SAMUEL JOHNSON, (1709–1784) British author, lexicographer. Quoted in James Boswell, *Life of Dr. Johnson*, note to entry, 1755 (1791).

Records Johnson's opinion "at a subsequent period of his life" to 1755.

18 In the misfortunes of our best friends we always find something not altogether displeasing to us.

FRANÇOIS LA ROCHEFOUCAULD, DUC DE, (1613–1680) French writer, moralist. *Sentences et Maximes Morales*, no. 583 (1678).

19 If a man urge me to tell wherefore I loved him, I feel it cannot be expressed but by answering: Because it was he, because it was myself.

MICHEL DE MONTAIGNE, (1533–1592) French essayist. *Essays*, bk. 1, ch. 27 (1580), trans. by John Florio (1603).

Referring to Étienne de la Boétie.

20 God gives us our relatives—thank God we can choose our friends.

ETHEL WATTS MUMFORD, (1878–1940) U.S. novelist, humorous writer. *The Cynic's Calendar* (1903).

21 The friends thou hast, and their adoption tried,
Grapple them to thy soul with hoops of steel,
But do not dull thy palm with entertainment
Of each new–hatched unfledged comrade.

WILLIAM SHAKESPEARE, (1564–1616) British dramatist, poet. Polonius, in *Hamlet*, act 1, sc. 3, l. 62–5 (1604).

Advice to his son Laertes, departing for France.

22 So long as we are loved by others I should say that we are almost indispensable; and no man is useless while he has a friend.

ROBERT LOUIS STEVENSON, (1850–1894) Scottish novelist, essayist, poet. *Across the Plains*, "Lay Morals" (1892).

23 The holy passion of friendship is of so sweet and steady and loyal and enduring a nature that it will last through a whole lifetime, if not asked to lend money.

MARK TWAIN, (1835–1910) U.S. author. *Pudd'nhead Wilson*, ch. 8, "Pudd'nhead Wilson's Calendar" (1894).

24 Whenever a friend succeeds, a little something in me dies.

> GORE VIDAL, (b. 1925) U.S. novelist, critic. Quoted in *Sunday Times Magazine* (London, Sept. 16, 1973).

25 We shelter children for a time; we live side by side with men; and that is all. We owe them nothing, and are owed nothing. I think we owe our friends more, especially our female friends.

> FAY WELDON, (b. 1933) British novelist. The narrator (Praxis Duveen), in *Praxis*, ch. 19 (1978).

26 Laughter is not at all a bad beginning for a friendship, and it is far the best ending for one.

> OSCAR WILDE, (1854–1900) Anglo–Irish playwright, author. Lord Henry, in *The Picture of Dorian Gray*, ch. 1 (1891).

Friendship and Love

1 Friendship is Love without his wings!

> GEORGE GORDON NOEL BYRON, 6TH BARON BYRON, (1788–1824) British poet. "L'Amitié est L'Amour Sans Ailes" (written 1806, published 1833).

2 A woman can only become a man's friend in three stages: first, she's an agreeable acquaintance, then a mistress, and only after that a friend.

> ANTON CHEKHOV, (1860–1904) Russian dramatist, author. Astrov, in *Uncle Vanya*, act 2 (1897), trans. by Elisaveta Fen (1954).
>
> Vanya (Voynitsky) replies to this, "That's a crude sort of philosophy."

3 Friendship is a disinterested commerce between equals; love, an abject intercourse between tyrants and slaves.

> OLIVER GOLDSMITH, (1728–1774) Anglo–Irish author, poet, playwright. Mr. Honeywood, in *The Good Natur'd Man*, act 1 (1768).

Frigidity

1 She looked as though butter wouldn't melt in her mouth—or anywhere else.

> ELSA LANCHESTER, (1902–1986) British–born U.S. actor. *Attributed.*
>
> Referring to actress Maureen O'Hara.

Fulfillment

1 Ask, and it shall be given you; seek, and ye shall find; knock, and it shall be opened unto you. For every one that asketh receiveth; and he that seeketh findeth; and to him that knocketh it shall be opened.

> BIBLE: NEW TESTAMENT, Jesus, in *Matthew*, 7:7–8.
>
> From the Sermon on the Mount.

Fun

1 For present joys are more to flesh and blood
Than a dull prospect of a distant good.

> JOHN DRYDEN, (1631–1700) British poet, dramatist, critic. "The Hind and the Panther," pt. 3, l. 364–5 (1687).

2 People must not do things for fun. We are not here for fun. There is no reference to fun in any act of Parliament.

> A.P. (SIR ALAN PATRICK) HERBERT, (1890–1971) British author, politician. Lord Light, in *Uncommon Law*, "Is it a Free Country?" (1935).

3   Nothing is more hopeless than a scheme of merriment.

> **SAMUEL JOHNSON,** (1709–1784) British author, lexicographer. *The Idler*, no. 58, first published in *Universal Chronicle* (London, May 26, 1759). Repr. in *Works of Samuel Johnson*, Yale Edition, vol. 2, eds. W.J. Bate, John M. Bullitt and L.F. Powell (1963).

Fundamentalism

1   Except a man be born again, he cannot see the kingdom of God.

> **BIBLE: NEW TESTAMENT,** Jesus, in *John*, 3:3.

> Spoken to the Pharisee Nicodemus.

Futility

1   I have measured out my life with coffee spoons.

> **T.S. (THOMAS STEARNS) ELIOT,** (1888–1965) Anglo–American poet, critic. "The Love Song of J. Alfred Prufrock," *Prufrock and Other Observations* (1917).

2   It is the superfluous things for which men sweat.

> **SENECA,** (c. 5–65) Roman writer, philosopher, statesman. *Epistulae ad Lucilium*, epistle 4, l. 11.

3   Tomorrow, and tomorrow, and tomorrow
    Creeps in this petty pace from day to day
    To the last syllable of recorded time,
    And all our yesterdays have lighted fools
    The way to dusty death.

> **WILLIAM SHAKESPEARE,** (1564–1616) British dramatist, poet. Macbeth, in *Macbeth*, act 5, sc. 5, l. 18–22 (1623).

> On hearing of the death of Lady Macbeth.

Future, the

1   We yearned for the future. How did we learn it, that talent for insatiability?

> **MARGARET ATWOOD,** (b. 1939) Canadian novelist, poet, critic. *The Handmaid's Tale*, ch. 1 (1986).

2   Take therefore no thought for the morrow: for the morrow shall take thought for the things of itself. Sufficient unto the day is the evil thereof.

> **BIBLE: NEW TESTAMENT,** Jesus, in *Matthew*, 6:34.

> From the Sermon on the Mount.

3   Future. That period of time in which our affairs prosper, our friends are true and our happiness is assured.

> **AMBROSE BIERCE,** (1842–1914) U.S. author. *The Devil's Dictionary* (1881–1906), repr. in *Collected Works of Ambrose Bierce*, vol. 7 (1911).

Gardens and Gardening

1   God Almighty first planted a garden. And indeed, it is the purest of human pleasures.

> **FRANCIS BACON,** (1561–1626) British philosopher, essayist, statesman. *Essays*, "Of Gardens" (1597–1625).

2   I just come and talk to the plants, really—very important to talk to them, they respond I find.

> **CHARLES, PRINCE OF WALES,** (b. 1948) Quoted in *Daily Telegraph* (London, Dec. 22, 1986). Television interview, Sept. 21, 1986.

> Charles's half–joking remark helped to establish his reputation as a new–age eccentric. Responding humorously to this, he was later

quoted as saying, "Only the other day I was inquiring of an entire bed of old–fashioned roses, forced to listen to my ramblings on the meaning of the universe as I sat cross–legged in the lotus position in front of them." (*Daily Telegraph*, Nov. 15, 1988).

3 Annihilating all that's made
To a green thought in a green shade.

ANDREW MARVELL, (1621–1678) British metaphysical poet. *The Garden*, st. 6 (written c. 1650, published 1681).

Gender

1 There is no female mind. The brain is not an organ of sex. As well speak of a female liver.

CHARLOTTE PERKINS GILMAN, (1860–1935) U.S. feminist, writer. *Women and Economics*, ch. 8 (1898).

2 The mind is not sex–typed.

MARGARET MEAD, (1901–1978) U.S. anthropologist. *Blackberry Winter*, ch. 5 (1972).

3 As the French say, there are three sexes—men, women, and clergy-men.

SYDNEY SMITH, (1771–1845) British clergyman, writer. *Memoir*, vol. 1, ch. 11, Lady Holland (1855).

4 Well, nobody's perfect.

BILLY WILDER, (b. 1906) U.S. film director. Osgood E. Fielding III (Joe E. Brown), in *Some Like It Hot* (film), final words of film, on Osgood's discovery that his bride–to–be (Jack Lemmon) is a man (1959).

Generals

1 Rides in the whirlwind and directs the storm.

JOSEPH ADDISON, (1672–1719) British essayist. *The Campaign*, l. 292 (1705). Repr. in *Works of Addison*, ed. R. Hurd (1883).

2 In defeat unbeatable: in victory unbearable.

WINSTON CHURCHILL, (1874–1965) British statesman, writer. Quoted in *Ambrosia and Small Beer*, ch. 5, Edward Marsh (1964).

Referring to Viscount Montgomery, victor at El Alamein and later chief of the imperial general staff.

3 Humility must always be the portion of any man who receives acclaim earned in the blood of his followers and the sacrifices of his friends.

DWIGHT D. EISENHOWER, (1890–1969) U.S. general, Republican politician, president. Speech, July 12, 1945, Guildhall, London.

4 In enterprise of martial kind,
When there was any fighting,
He led his regiment from behind—
He found it less exciting.

SIR WILLIAM SCHWENCK GILBERT, (1836–1911) British librettist. Duke of Plaza–Toro, in *The Gondoliers*, act 1 (1889), published in *The Savoy Operas* (1926).

5 I came through and I shall return.

DOUGLAS MACARTHUR, (1880–1964) U.S. general. Quoted in *The New York Times* (March 21, 1942). Statement, March 20, 1942, Adelaide, Australia.

On arriving in Australia from the Philippines, which he had been ordered to evacuate, following an unsuccessful defense of the Bataan peninsula. Promoted to Supreme Commander of the South West Pacific area, MacArthur pursued a brilliant "leap–frogging" strategy which enabled him to return to the Philippines in October 1944. His men celebrated his victory with the song, "By the grace of God and a few Marines/MacArthur returned to the Philippines."

Generations

1 One generation passeth away, and another generation cometh: but the earth abideth for ever. The sun also

ariseth, and the sun goeth down, and hasteth to the place where he arose.

BIBLE: HEBREW, *Ecclesiastes,* 1:4–5. Ernest Hemingway took the title *The Sun Also Rises* (1926) from this passage.

2 Come mothers and fathers
Throughout the land
And don't criticize
What you can't understand
Your sons and your daughters
Are beyond your command
Your old road is rapidly agin.'

BOB DYLAN [ROBERT ALLEN ZIM-MERMAN], (b. 1941) U.S. singer, song-writer. "The Times They Are A–Changin'" (song), on the album *The Times They Are A–Changin'* (1964).

3 Generations have trod, have trod, have trod;
And all is seared with trade;
bleared, smeared with toil;
And wears man's smudge and shares man's smell: the soil
Is bare now, nor can foot feel, being shod.

GERARD MANLEY HOPKINS, (1844–1889) British poet, Jesuit priest. "God's Grandeur" (written 1877), published in *Poems* (1918).

4 From the earliest times the old have rubbed it into the young that they are wiser than they, and before the young had discovered what non-sense this was they were old too, and it profited them to carry on the imposture.

W. SOMERSET MAUGHAM, (1874–1966) British author. Ashenden, in *Cakes and Ale,* ch. 11 (1930).

5 Every generation revolts against its fathers and makes friends with its grandfathers.

LEWIS MUMFORD, (1895–1990) U.S. social philosopher. *The Brown Decades,* p. 3 (1931).

6 People try to put us down
(Talkin' 'bout my generation)
Just because we get around
(Talkin' 'bout my generation)
Things they do look awful c–c–cold
(Talkin' 'bout my generation)
Hope I die before I get old.

PETE TOWNSHEND, (b. 1945) British rock musician. "My Generation" (song), on the album *My Generation* (1965).

7 The old believe everything; the middle–aged suspect everything; the young know everything.

OSCAR WILDE, (1854–1900) Anglo–Irish playwright, author. *Phrases and Philosophies for the Use of the Young,* repr. in *Complete Works of Oscar Wilde,* ed. J.B. Foreman (1966). *Chameleon* (London, Dec. 1894).

Generosity

1 Generosity lies less in giving much than in giving at the right moment.

JEAN DE LA BRUYÈRE, (1645–1696) French writer, moralist. *Characters,* "Of the Heart," aph. 47 (1688).

2 The sage does not hoard. Having bestowed all he has on others, he has yet more; Having given all he has to others, he is richer still.

LAO–TZU, (6th century B.C.) Chinese philosopher. *Tao–te–ching,* bk. 2, ch. 81, trans. by T.C. Lau (1963).

3 Give all thou canst; high Heaven rejects the lore
Of nicely–calculated less or more.

WILLIAM WORDSWORTH, (1770–1850) British poet. "Tax Not the Royal Saint," or "Inside of King's College Chapel, Cambridge," Sonnet 43, *Ecclesiastical Sonnets* (1822).

Genius

1 We know that the nature of genius is to provide idiots with ideas twenty years later.

LOUIS ARAGON, (1897–1982) French poet. *Treatise on Style,* pt. 1, "The Pen" (1928).

2 Since when was genius found respectable?

ELIZABETH BARRETT BROWNING, (1806–1861) British poet. *Aurora Leigh,* bk. 6, l. 275 (1857).

3 Genius (which means transcendent capacity of taking trouble, first of all).

THOMAS CARLYLE, (1795–1881) Scottish essayist, historian. *The History of Frederick II of Prussia,* bk. 4, ch. 3 (1858–1865).

The words are often misquoted as "Genius is an infinite capacity for taking pains."

4 What makes men of genius, or rather, what they make, is not new ideas, it is that idea—possessing them—that what has been said has still not been said enough.

EUGÈNE DELACROIX, (1798–1863) French artist. *The Journal of Eugène Delacroix,* trans. by Walter Pach (1937). Journal entry, May 15, 1824.

5 Mediocrity knows nothing higher than itself, but talent instantly recognizes genius.

ARTHUR CONAN, SIR DOYLE, (1859–1930) British author. *The Valley of Fear,* ch. 1 (1915).

6 Great wits are sure to madness near allied,
And thin partitions do their bounds divide.

JOHN DRYDEN, (1631–1700) British poet, dramatist, critic. *Absalom and Achitophel,* pt. 1, l. 163–4 (1681).

7 Genius is one per cent inspiration, ninety–nine per cent perspiration.

THOMAS ALVA EDISON, (1847–1931) U.S. inventor. *Harper's* (New York, Sept. 1932). Remark by Edison c. 1903.

Edison, one of the most inspired and productive inventors of his time, received only three months of formal schooling.

8 A man of genius makes no mistakes. His errors are volitional and are the portals of discovery.

JAMES JOYCE, (1882–1941) Irish author. Stephen Dedalus, in *Ulysses,* ch. 9 of 1984 (Garland)edition (1922).

9 Who in the same given time can produce more than others has *vigor;* who can produce more and better, has *talents;* who can produce what none else can, has *genius.*

JOHANN KASPAR LAVATER, (1741–1801) Swiss divine, poet. *Aphorisms on Man,* no. 23 (1788).

10 The genius of Einstein leads to Hiroshima.

PABLO PICASSO, (1881–1973) Spanish artist. Quoted in *Life with Picasso,* pt. 2, Françoise Gilot and Carlton Lake (1964).

Remark to Françoise Gilot in 1946.

11 I have nothing to declare except my genius.

OSCAR WILDE, (1854–1900) Anglo–Irish playwright, author. Attributed in *Oscar Wilde,* ch. 6, Richard Ellman (1987).

Remark at the New York Customs, Jan. 3, 1882, though there is no contemporary evidence for it.

12 I put all my genius into my life; I put only my talent into my works.

OSCAR WILDE,(1854–1900) Anglo–Irish playwright, author. Quoted in *Journals 1889–1949,* André Gide (1951). Journal entry, June 29, 1913.

Also quoted in Gide's *Oscar Wilde* "In Memoriam" (1910).

Genocide

1   Genocide begins, however improbably, in the conviction that classes of biological distinction indisputably sanction social and political discrimination.

ANDREA DWORKIN, (b. 1946) U.S. feminist critic. "Biological Superiority: The World's Most Dangerous and Deadly Idea," sct. 3, *Letters from a War–Zone* (1987). (Essay originally published 1978).

Gentlemen

1   I am parshial to ladies if they are nice[.] I suppose it is my nature. I am not quite a gentleman but you would hardly notice it.

DAISY ASHFORD, (1881–1972) British writer. Alfred Salteena, in *The Young Visiters*, ch. 1: "Quite a Young Girl" (published 1919).

Written when the author was aged nine.

2   And though that he were worthy,
    he was wys,
    And of his port as meeke as is a
      mayde.
    He never yet no vileynye ne sayde
    In al his lyf unto no maner wight;
    He was a verray parfit, gentil
      knight.

GEOFFREY CHAUCER, (1340–1400) British poet. *The Canterbury Tales*, "General Prologue," l. 68–72 (1387–1400), repr. in *The Works of Geoffrey Chaucer*, ed. Alfred W. Pollard, et al. (1898).

Referring to the Knight.

3   I can make him a lord, but I cannot make him a gentleman.

GEORGE I, KING, (1660–1727) British King of Great Britain and Ireland. Attributed in

Correspondence of Horace Walpole, vol. 24, ed. W.S. Lewis and Ralph S. Brown, Jr. (1941).

George I's remark—as reported by Horace Walpole—referred to William Bateman (d. 1744), MP and merchant, whom he created 1st Viscount Bateman in the Irish peerage, apparently in order to avoid making him a Knight of the Bath.

4   He is every other inch a gentleman.

REBECCA WEST [CICILY ISABEL FAIRFIELD], (1892–1983) British author. Quoted in *Rebecca West*, pt. 3, ch. 5, Victoria Glendinning (1987).

Referring to novelist Michael Arlen. Alexander Woollcott is also credited with this remark about Arlen, in *Wit's End*, ed. Robert E. Drennan (1968).

Gentleness

1   Blessed are the meek: for they shall inherit the earth.

BIBLE: NEW TESTAMENT, Jesus, in *Matthew*, 5:5.

The third of the Beatitudes, from the Sermon on the Mount. The words recall those in *Proverbs* 37:11, "But the meek shall inherit the earth; and shall delight themselves in the abundance of peace." In his Notebooks, the author Samuel Butler wrote, "I really do not see much use in exalting the humble and meek; they do not remain humble and meek long when they are exalted." (*Samuel Butler's Notebooks*, p. 220, 1951).

2   For God's sake (I never was more serious) don't make me ridiculous any more by terming me gentle–hearted in print ... substitute drunken dog, ragged head, seld–shaven, odd–eyed, stuttering, or any other epithet which truly and properly belongs to the gentleman in question.

CHARLES LAMB, (1775–1834) British essayist, critic. *Complete Works*, vol. 3. Letter, Aug. 1800, to Samuel Talyor Coleridge.

Referring to lines Coleridge had inserted in his poem *This Lime Tree Bower My Prison*: For

thee, my gentle–hearted Charles, to whom /
No sound is dissonant which tells of life.

Germany and the Germans

1 Don't mention the war.

JOHN CLEESE, (b. 1939) British comic
actor, author. Basil, in *Fawlty Towers* (TV
series), broadcast 1975, published in *The
Complete Fawlty Towers* (1988).

On the pending arrival of German guests at
Basil's hotel.

2 All free men, wherever they may
live, are citizens of Berlin, and
therefore, as a free man, I take pride
in the words, *Ich bin ein Berliner.*

JOHN FITZGERALD KENNEDY,
(1917–1963) U.S. Democratic politician, president. Quoted in *Kennedy*, pt. 5, ch. 21,
Theodore C. Sorenson (1965). Speech, June
26, 1963, West Berlin, Germany.

The words recall Cicero: *Civis Romanus
sum*—"I am a Roman citizen." (*In Verrem*,
speech 5).

3 Whenever the literary German
dives into a sentence, that is the last
you are going to see of him till he
emerges on the other side of his
Atlantic with his verb in his mouth.

MARK TWAIN, (1835–1910) U.S. author. *A
Connecticut Yankee in King Arthur's Court*,
ch. 22 (1889).

Twain's bewilderment with the German language was a recurring subject: it is "the language which enables a man to travel all day
in one sentence without changing cars."
Speakng the language was the main difficulty:
"I can *understand* German as well as the
maniac that invented it, but I *talk* it best
through an interpreter." (Quoted in *Greatly
Exaggerated*, ed. Alex Ayres, 1988).

Getting Ahead

1 No man rises so high as he knows
not whither he goes.

OLIVER CROMWELL, (1599–1658) British
Parliamentarian general, Lord Protector of
England. Quoted in *Essays in English History*,
"Cromwell and the Historians," A.J.P. Taylor
(1976).

2 Bold knaves thrive without one
grain of sense,
But good men starve for want of
impudence.

JOHN DRYDEN, (1631–1700) British poet,
dramatist, critic. *Constantine the Great: Epilogue.*

3 It's them as take advantage that get
advantage i' this world.

**GEORGE ELIOT [MARY ANN (OR
MARIAN) EVANS],** (1819–1880) British
novelist. Mrs. Poyser, in *Adam Bede*, bk. 4,
ch. 32 (1859).

4 Be nice to people on your way up
because you'll meet them on your
way down.

WILSON MIZNER, (1876–1933) U.S.
dramatist, wit. Quoted in *The Legendary
Mizners*, ch. 4, Alva Johnson (1953).

Also attributed to the comic Jimmy Durante.

5 If you want to get along, go along.

SAM RAYBURN,(1882–1961) U.S. legislator, Democratic politician. Quoted in *Forge of
Democracy*, ch. 6, Neil MacNeil (1963).

6 Never burn bridges. Today's
junior prick, tomorrow's senior
partner.

KEVIN WADE, U.S. screenwriter. Katharine
Parker (Sigourney Weaver), in *Working Girl*
(film) (1988).

Ghosts

1 you want to know
whether i believe in ghosts
of course i do not believe in them
if you had known

as many of them as i have
you would not
believe in them either

DON MARQUIS, (1878–1937) U.S.
humorist, journalist. *Archy and mehitabel,*
"ghosts" (1927).

Gifts and Giving

1   Give not that which is holy unto the
dogs, neither cast ye your pearls
before swine, lest they trample
them under their feet, and turn
again and rend you.

BIBLE: NEW TESTAMENT, Jesus, in
Matthew, 7:6.

From the Sermon on the Mount.

2   God loveth a cheerful giver.

BIBLE: NEW TESTAMENT, St. Paul, in *2
Corinthians,* 9:7.

3   One must be poor to know the luxury of giving!

**GEORGE ELIOT [MARY ANN (OR
MARIAN) EVANS],** (1819–1880) British
novelist. *Middlemarch,* bk. 2, ch. 17
(1871–1872).

4   Why is it no one ever sent me yet
One perfect limousine, do you
      suppose?
Ah no, it's always just my luck to
      get
One perfect rose.

DOROTHY PARKER, (1893–1967) U.S.
humorous writer. "One Perfect Rose," st. 3,
Enough Rope (1926).

5   Trust not the horse, O Trojans. Be
it what it may, I fear the Grecians
even when they offer gifts.

**VIRGIL [PUBLIUS VERGILIUS
MARO],** (70–19 B.C.) Roman poet. Laocöen,
in *Aeneid,* bk. 2, l. 48–9.

Girls

1   Three little maids from school are
we,
Pert as a school–girl well can be,
Filled to the brim with girlish glee,
Three little maids from school!

SIR WILLIAM SCHWENCK GILBERT,
(1836–1911) British librettist. Trio of girls, in
The Mikado, act 1 (1885), published in *The
Savoy Operas* (1926).

2   Thank heaven for little girls!
For little girls get bigger every day.

ALAN JAY LERNER, (1918–1986) U.S.
songwriter. "Thank Heaven for Little Girls"
(song), *Gigi* (film 1958).

The song was sung and recorded by Maurice
Chevalier, whose signature tune it became.

3   Between the age limits of nine and
fourteen there occur maidens who,
to certain bewitched travelers, twice
or many times older than they,
reveal their true nature which is not
human, but nymphic (that is,
demoniac); and these chosen creatures I propose to designate as
"nymphets."

VLADIMIR NABOKOV, (1899–1977)
Russian–born U.S. novelist, poet. Humbert
Humbert (narrator), in *Lolita,* pt. 1, ch. 5
(1955).

This passage was cut in the 1962 film directed
by Stanley Kubrick.

Give and Take

1   The Lord gave, and the Lord hath
taken away.

BIBLE: HEBREW, Job, in *Job,* 1:21.

2   Before he left, Aunt William
pressed a sovereign into his hand
guiltily, as if it were conscience

money. He, on his side, took it as though it were a doctor's fee, and both ignored the transaction.

ADA LEVERSON, (1862–1933) British novelist. *The Twelfth Hour*, ch. 4, "Aunt William" (1907).

Glamour

1   It was a blonde. A blonde to make a bishop kick a hole in a stained–glass window.

RAYMOND CHANDLER, (1888–1959) U.S. author. Philip Marlowe, in *Farewell, My Lovely*, ch. 13 (1940).

Referring to Helen Grayle.

Glory

1   The strongest poison ever known Came from Caesar's laurel crown.

WILLIAM BLAKE, (1757–1827) British poet, painter, engraver. "Auguries of Innocence," l. 97–8, *Poems from the Pickering Manuscript* (c. 1803), repr. in *Complete Writings*, ed. Geoffrey Keynes (1957).

2   The deed is everything, the glory naught.

JOHANN WOLFGANG VON GOETHE, (1749–1832) German poet, dramatist. Faust, in *Faust*, pt. 2, act 4, sc. 1, "High Mountains" (1832), trans. by Bayard Taylor (1870–1871).

3   The paths of glory lead but to the grave.

THOMAS GRAY, (1716–1771) British poet. "Elegy Written in a Country Churchyard," st. 9 (1751). Repr. in *Poetical Works*, ed. J. Rogers (1953).

4   Oh, the brave Music of a *distant* Drum!

OMAR KHAYYAM, (11–12th century) Persian astronomer and poet. *The Rubaiyat of*

Omar Khayyam, st. 12, trans. by Edward FitzGerald, first edition (1859).

5   Is it not passing brave to be a King, And ride in triumph through Persepolis?

CHRISTOPHER MARLOWE, (1564–1593) British dramatist, poet. Tamburlane, in *Tamburlaine the Great*, pt. 1, act 2, sc. 5, l. 758–9 (1590).

6   I have touched the highest point of all my greatness,
And from that full meridian of my glory
I haste now to my setting. I shall fall
Like a bright exhalation in the evening,
And no man see me more.

WILLIAM SHAKESPEARE, (1564–1616) British dramatist, poet. Wolsey, in *King Henry VIII*, act 3, sc. 2, l. 224–6 (1623).

7   Avoid shame but do not see glory— nothing so expensive as glory.

SYDNEY SMITH, (1771–1845) British clergyman, writer. Quoted in *Memoir*, vol. 1, ch. 4, Lady Holland (1855).

8   Glories, like glow–worms, afar off shine bright,
But looked to near, have neither heat nor light.

JOHN WEBSTER, (1580–1625) British dramatist. Bosola's song, in *The Duchess of Malfi*, act 4, sc. 2, l. 143–4 (1623). Repr. in *The Complete Works of John Webster*, ed. F.L. Lucas (1927).

God

1   The bastard! He doesn't exist!

SAMUEL BECKETT, (1906–1989) Irish dramatist, novelist. Hamm, in *Endgame* (1957, trans. 1958).

Hamm's exclamation after attempting to pray. Clov replies, "Not yet."

2   For the Lord thy God is a jealous
    God among you.

BIBLE: HEBREW, *Deuteronomy,* 6:15.

The words are also found in *Exodus* 20:5,
referring to the second commandment: "Thou
shalt not make unto thee any graven image ...
for I the Lord thy God am a jealous God, visiting the iniquity of the fathers upon the children unto the third and fourth generation of
them that hate me."

3   I am Alpha and Omega, the begin-
    ning and the end, the first and the
    last.

BIBLE: NEW TESTAMENT, *Revelation,*
22:13.

4   The Lord is my shepherd; I shall
    not want. He maketh me to lie
    down in green pastures: he leadeth
    me beside the still waters.

BIBLE: HEBREW, *Psalms,* 23:1–2.

5   The peace of God, which passeth all
    understanding.

BIBLE: NEW TESTAMENT, St. Paul, in
Philippians, 4:7.

The words are also used in the Book of Common Prayer, *Holy Communion* (1662). An
allusion to them is attributed to King James I
of England, speaking of poet John Donne: "Dr.
Donne's verses are like the peace of God:
they pass all understanding."

6   And lips say "God be pitiful,"
    Who ne'er said, "God be praised."

ELIZABETH BARRETT BROWNING,
(1806–1861) British poet. "The Cry of the
Human," st. 1, *Poems* (1844).

7   As you know, God is generally on
    the side of the big squadrons
    against the small ones.

ROGER BUSSY–RABUTIN, COMTE DE,
(1618–1693) French soldier, writer. *Letters,*
vol. 4 (1697). Letter, Oct. 18, 1677.

In his *Notebooks,* written 1735–1750, Voltaire
argued instead, "God is not on the side of the
big battalions, but on the side of those who

shoot best." (vol. 2 "The Piccini Notebooks,"
ed.1968) (See also Anouilh on the rich.).

8   God moves in a mysterious way,
    His wonders to perform;
    He plants his footsteps in the sea,
    And rides upon the storm.

WILLIAM COWPER, (1731–1800) British
poet. *Olney Hymns,* no. 35, "Light Shining Out
of Darkness" (1779). Repr. in *Poetical Works,*
ed. H.S. Milford (1934).

9   God is subtle, but he is not
    malicious.
    [Raffiniert ist der Herr Gott, aber
    boshaft ist er nicht.]

ALBERT EINSTEIN, (1879–1955)
German–born U.S. theoretical physicist.
Quoted in *Einstein,* ch. 14, R.W. Clark (1973).

Remark made in April 1921, during Einstein's
first visit to Princeton University. The words
were later carved above the fireplace of the
Common Room of Fine Hall in the former Mathematical Institute; in 1946 Einstein gave a freer
translation: "God is slick, but he ain't mean."

10 The psychoanalysis of individual
    human beings, however, teaches us
    with quite special insistence that the
    god of each of them is formed in the
    likeness of his father, that his per-
    sonal relation to God depends on his
    relation to his father in the flesh and
    oscillates and changes along with
    that relation, and that at bottom
    God is nothing other than an exalted
    father.

SIGMUND FREUD, (1856–1939) Austrian
psychiatrist. *Totem and Taboo,* vol. 13, pt. 4,
sct. 6, *Complete Works, Standard Edition,* eds.
James Strachey and Anna Freud (1953). (Originally published 1913).

11 Forgive, O Lord, my little jokes on
    Thee
    And I'll forgive Thy great big one on
    me.

ROBERT FROST, (1874–1963) U.S. poet.
"Cluster of Faith," *In the Clearing* (1962).

12   Here is God's purpose—
     for God, to me, it seems,
     is a verb
     not a noun,
     proper or improper.

     R. BUCKMINSTER FULLER, (1895–1983)
     U.S. architect, engineer. *No More Second-
     hand God* (1963). Untitled poem written
     1940.

13   Throw away thy rod,
     Throw away thy wrath;
     O my God,
     Take the gentle path.

     GEORGE HERBERT, (1593–1633) British
     clergyman, poet. "Discipline," *The Temple*
     (1633).

14   The world is charged with the
        grandeur of God.
     It will flame out, like shining from
        shook foil.

     GERARD MANLEY HOPKINS,
     (1844–1889) British poet, Jesuit priest. "God's
     Grandeur" (written 1877), published in *Poems*
     (1918).

15   Thou art indeed just, Lord, if I
        cotend
     With thee; but, sir, so what I plead
        is just.
     Why do sinners' ways prosper? and
        why must
     Disappointment all I endeavour
        end?

     GERARD MANLEY HOPKINS,
     (1844–1889) British poet, Jesuit priest. "Thou
     art indeed just, Lord" (written 1889), pub-
     lished in *Poems* (1918).

16   An honest God is the noblest work
     of man.

     ROBERT GREEN INGERSOLL,
     (1833–1899) U.S. lawyer, orator. "The Gods"
     (1872), publ. in *The Gods, and Other Essays*
     (1876).

17   Young man—Young man—Your
     arm's too short to box with God.

JAMES WELDON JOHNSON, (1871–1938)
U.S. author, poet. "The Prodigal Son," *God's
Trombones* (1927).

18   For man proposes, but God disposes.

     THOMAS À KEMPIS, (c. 1380–1471) Ger-
     man monk, mystic. *The Imitation of Christ,* pt.
     1, ch. 19 (written c. 1426, published 1486).

19   God is only a great imaginative expe-
     rience.

     D.H. (DAVID HERBERT) LAWRENCE,
     (1885–1930) British author. *Phoenix: The
     Posthumous Papers of D.H. Lawrence,* pt. 4, ed.
     E. McDonald (1936). "Introduction to *The
     Dragon of the Apocalypse* by Frederick Carter"
     first published in *London Mercury* (July 1930).

20   God is a concept by which we
        measure our pain.

     JOHN LENNON, (1940–1980) British song-
     writer, rock musician. "God" (song), on the
     album *John Lennon/Plastic Ono Band* (1970).

21   Just are the ways of God,
     And justifiable to men;
     Unless there be who think not God at
        all.

     JOHN MILTON, (1608–1674) British poet.
     Chorus, in" Samson Agonistes," l. 293–5 (1671).
     Repr. In *Milton's Poetical Works,* ed. Douglas
     Bush (1966).

22   If triangles had a god, they would
     give him three sides.

     CHARLES DE MONTESQUIEU,
     (1689–1755) French philosopher, lawyer. *Per-
     sian Letters,* no. 59 (1721), trans. by C.J. Betts
     (1973).

23   God is really only another artist. He
     invented the giraffe, the elephant,
     and the cat. He has no real style. He
     just keeps on trying other things.

     PABLO PICASSO, (1881–1973) Spanish
     artist. Quoted in *Life with Picasso,* pt. 1,
     Françoise Gilot and Carlton Lake (1964).

24   God owns heaven
     but He craves the earth.

ANNE SEXTON, (1928–1974) U.S. poet. "The Earth," st. 2, *The Awful Rowing Toward God* (1975).

25 If you talk to God, you are praying; if God talks to you, you have schizophrenia.

THOMAS SZASZ, (b. 1920) U.S. psychiatrist. "Schizophrenia," *The Second Sin* (1973).

26 If God did not exist, it would be necessary to invent him.

VOLTAIRE [FRANÇOIS MARIE AROUET], (1694–1778) French philosopher, author. "A l'auteur du livre des trois imposteurs," no. 96, *Atres* (1770).

See Ovid on gods and goddesses, for an anticipation of this thought.

Gods and Goddesses

1 The gods help them that help themselves.

AESOP, (6th century B.C.) Greek fabulist. *Fables,* "Hercules and the Wagoner."

2 And there appeared a great wonder in heaven; a woman clothed with the sun, and the moon under her feet, and upon her head a crown of twelve stars.

BIBLE: NEW TESTAMENT, St. John the Divine, in *Revelation,* 12:1.

3 Thou shalt have no other gods before me.

BIBLE: HEBREW, *Exodus,* 20:3.

The first commandment.

4 I think there are innumerable gods. What we on earth call God is a little tribal God who has made an awful mess. Certainly forces operating through human consciousness control events.

WILLIAM BURROUGHS, (b. 1914) U.S. author. Interview in *Writers at Work,* Third Series, ed. George Plimpton (1967).

5 A civilization is destroyed only when its gods are destroyed.

E.M. (EMIL MIHAI) CIORAN, (1911–1995) Romanian–born French philosopher. "The New Gods," *The New Gods* (1969, trans. 1974).

6 When men make gods, there is no God!

EUGENE O'NEILL, (1888–1953) U.S. dramatist. Lazarus, in *Lazarus Laughed,* act 2, sc. 2 (1927).

7 It is convenient that there be gods, and, as it is convenient, let us believe there are.

OVID (PUBLIUS OVIDIUS NASO), (43 B.C.–A.D.17) Roman poet. *Ars Amatoria,* bk. 1, l. 637.

8 The gods thought otherwise.

VIRGIL [PUBLIUS VERGILIUS MARO], (70–19 B.C.) Roman poet. *Aeneid,* bk. 2, l. 428 (19 B.C.).

Golf

1 If you watch a game, it's fun. If you play it, it's recreation. If you work at it, it's golf.

BOB HOPE, (b. 1903) U.S. comedian. Quoted in *Reader's Digest* (Pleasantville, N.Y., Oct. 1958).

Good Deeds

1 No people do so much harm as those who go about doing good.

MANDELL CREIGHTON, (1843–1901) British prelate, historian. Quoted in *The Life and Letters of Mandell Creighton,* vol. 2 (1904).

2   The last temptation is the greatest
    treason:
    To do the right deed for the wrong
    reason.

    T.S. (THOMAS STEARNS) ELIOT,
    (1888–1965) Anglo–American poet, critic.
    Thomas à Becket, in *Murder in the Cathedral,*
    pt. 1 (1935).

3   The greatest pleasure I know, is to
    do a good action by stealth, and to
    have it found out by accident.

    CHARLES LAMB, (1775–1834) British
    essayist, critic. *Athenaeum* (London, Jan. 4,
    1834), "Table Talk by the Late Elia."

4   Always do right—this will gratify
    some and astonish the rest.

    MARK TWAIN, (1835–1910) U.S. author.
    Message, Feb. 16, 1901, to the Young Peo-
    ple's Society, New York City.

    President Truman is reported to have had this
    remark framed behind his desk in the Oval
    Office.

5   That best portion of a good man's
    life;
    His little, nameless, unremembered
    acts
    Of kindness and of love.

    WILLIAM WORDSWORTH, (1770–1850)
    British poet. "Lines Composed a Few Miles
    Above Tintern Abbey," l. 34–6, *Lyrical Ballads*
    (1798).

Goodness

1   Be good, sweet maid, and let who
    will be clever.

    CHARLES KINGSLEY, (1819–1875) British
    author, clergyman. "A Farewell," st. 3 (1858).
    Repr. in *The Works of Charles Kingsley*
    (1880–1885).

2   Be good and you will be lonesome.

    MARK TWAIN, (1835–1910) U.S. author.
    Following the Equator, frontispiece (1897).

    Caption for author's photograph.

3   To be good, according to the vulgar
    standard of goodness, is obviously
    quite easy. It merely requires a cer-
    tain amount of sordid terror, a cer-
    tain lack of imaginative thought,
    and a certain low passion for mid-
    dle–class respectability.

    OSCAR WILDE, (1854–1900) Anglo–Irish
    playwright, author. Gilbert, in *The Critic as
    Artist,* pt. 2, *Intentions* (1891). Repr. in *Com-
    plete Works of Oscar Wilde,* ed. J.B. Foreman
    (1966).

Gossip

1   Not only idle, but tattlers also and
    busybodies, speaking things which
    they ought not.

    BIBLE: NEW TESTAMENT, St. Paul, in *1
    Timothy,* 5:13.

2   The Athenians and strangers which
    were there spent their time in noth-
    ing else, but either to tell, or to hear
    some new thing.

    BIBLE: NEW TESTAMENT, *Acts,* 17:21.

3   Alas! they had been friends in
    youth;
    But whispering tongues can poison
    truth.

    SAMUEL TAYLOR COLERIDGE,
    (1772–1834) British poet, critic." Christabel,"
    pt. 2, l. 408–9 (1816) repr. in *Poetical Works,*
    ed. James Dyke Campbell (1893).

4   They come together like the Coro-
    ner's Inquest, to sit upon the mur-
    dered reputations of the week.

    WILLIAM CONGREVE, (1670–1729)
    British dramatist. Fainall, in *The Way of the
    World,* act 1, sc. 1 (1700).

5   While the town small–talk flows
    from lip to lip;
    Intrigues half–gathered, conversa-
    tion–scraps,

Kitchen–cabals, and
nursery–mishaps.

GEORGE CRABBE, (1754–1832) British
clergyman, poet. "The Vicar," l. 70–2, *The
Borough*, letter 3 (1810). Repr. in *Poetical
Works*, eds. A.J. and R.M. Carlyle (1908,
rev.1924).

6 Gossip is the opiate of the
oppressed.

ERICA JONG, (b. 1942) U.S. author. The
narrator (Isadora Wing), in *Fear of Flying*, ch.
6 (1973).

7 And all who told it added something new,
And all who heard it, made enlarge-
ments too.

ALEXANDER POPE, (1688–1744) British
satirical poet. "The Temple of Fame," l. 470–1
(1715).

8 At ev'ry word a reputation dies.

ALEXANDER POPE, (1688–1744) British
satirical poet. "The Rape of the Lock," cto. 3,
l. 16 (1714).

9 How awful to reflect that what people say of us is true!

LOGAN PEARSALL SMITH, (1865–1946)
U.S. essayist, aphorist. *Afterthoughts*, "Life
and Human Nature" (1931).

10 It takes your enemy and your
friend, working together, to hurt
you to the heart: the one to slander
you and the other to get the news to
you.

MARK TWAIN, (1835–1910) U.S. author.
Following the Equator, ch. 45, "Pudd'nhead
Wilson's New Calendar" (1897).

11 There is only one thing in the world
worse than being talked about, and
that is not being talked about.

OSCAR WILDE, (1854–1900) Anglo–Irish
playwright, author. Lord Henry, in *The Picture
of Dorian Gray*, ch. 1 (1891).

Government

1 A government of laws, and not of
men.

JOHN ADAMS, (1735–1826) U.S. statesman, president. *Novanglus Papers*, *Boston
Gazette*, no. 7 (1774). *The Works of John
Adams*, vol. 4, ed. Charles Francis Adams
(1851).

This phrase, taken from one of the articles
published in the *Boston Gazette*, was attributed by Adams to English political theorist
and republican, James Harrington
(1611–1677), whose actual words were, "the
empire of laws and not of men" (*Oceana*,
1656). The words were incorporated by
Adams into the Massachusetts Constitution
(1780).

2 The happiness of society is the end
of government.

JOHN ADAMS, (1735–1826) U.S. statesman, president. *Thoughts on Government*
(1776).

The purpose of government to secure, among
other rights, the pursuit of happiness, is one of
the "self–evident truths" enshrined in the Declaration of Independence. See Jefferson on
independence.

3 Royalty is a government in which
the attention of the nation is con-
centrated on one person doing
interesting actions. A Republic is a
government in which that attention
is divided between many, who are
all doing uninteresting actions.
Accordingly, so long as the human
heart is strong and the human reason weak, Royalty will be strong
because it appeals to diffused feeling, and Republics weak because
they appeal to the understanding.

WALTER BAGEHOT, (1826–1877) British
economist, critic. *The English Constitution*,
ch. 2 (1867).

Bagehot returned to this theme in ch. 3: "The
best reason why Monarchy is a strong government is, that it is an intelligible government.
The mass of mankind understand it, and they

hardly anywhere in the world understand any other."

4   The object of government in peace and in war is not the glory of rulers or of races, but the happiness of the common man.

WILLIAM BEVERIDGE, (1879–1963) British economist. *Social Insurance and Allied Services*, pt. 7 (1942).

5   Nothing turns out to be so oppressive and unjust as a feeble government.

EDMUND BURKE, (1729–1797) Irish philosopher, statesman. "Reflections on the Revolution in France" (1790), repr. in *Works*, vol. 3 (1865).

6   Men are to be guided only by their self–interests. Good government is a good balancing of these; and, except a keen eye and appetite for self–interest, requires no virtue in any quarter. To both parties it is emphatically a machine: to the discontented, a "taxing–machine;" to the contented, a "machine for securing property." Its duties and its faults are not those of a father, but of an active parish–constable.

THOMAS CARLYLE, (1795–1881) Scottish essayist, historian. "Signs of the Times," first published in *Edinburgh Review*, no. 98 (1829). *Critical and Miscellaneous Essays* (1839–1857).

7   Good government is the outcome of private virtue.

JOHN JAY CHAPMAN, (1862–1933) U.S. author. *Practical Agitation*, ch. 2 (1898).

8   Truth is the glue that holds government together.

GERALD FORD, (b. 1913) U.S. Republican politician, president. *Public Papers of the Presidents* (1974). Speech, Aug. 9, 1974.

On succeeding Richard Nixon as president. Ford had used the words on several previous occasions.

9   I would not give half a guinea to live under one form of government rather than another. It is of no moment to the happiness of an individual.

SAMUEL JOHNSON, (1709–1784) British author, lexicographer. Quoted in James Boswell, *Life of Dr. Johnson*, entry, March 31, 1772 (1791).

10 Of the best rulers The people only know that they exist; The next best they love and praise The next they fear; And the next they revile. When they do not command the people's faith, Some will lose faith in them, And then they resort to oaths! But of the best when their task is accomplished, their work done, The people all remark, "We have done it ourselves."

LAO–TZU, (6th century B.C.) Chinese philosopher. *The Wisdom of Laotse*, ch. 17, ed. and trans. by Lin Yutang (1948).

11 Freedom of men under government is to have a standing rule to live by, common to every one of that society, and made by the legislative power vested in it; a liberty to follow my own will in all things, when the rule prescribes not, and not to be subject to the inconstant, unknown, arbitrary will of another man.

JOHN LOCKE, (1632–1704) British philosopher. *Second Treatise on Civil Government* (written 1681, publ. 1690).

12 Nothing is so galling to a people not broken in from the birth as a paternal, or in other words a meddling government, a government

which tells them what to read and say and eat and drink and wear.

THOMAS BABINGTON MACAULAY, (1800–1859) British historian, Whig politician. "Southey's Colloquies on Society," *Edinburgh Review* (Jan. 1830). *Critical and Historical Essays* (1843).

13   Every country has the government it deserves.

JOSEPH DE MAISTRE, (1753–1821) French diplomat, philosopher. *Lettres et Opuscules Inedits*, vol. 1, no. 53 (1851). Letter, Aug. 15, 1811.

Thomas Carlyle, in *Past and Present*, bk. 4, ch. 4 (1843), wrote: "In the long–run every Government is the exact symbol of its People, with their wisdom and unwisdom; we have to say, Like People like Government."

14   Every government is a parliament of whores. The trouble is, in a democracy the whores are us.

P.J. O'ROURKE, (b. 1947) U.S. journalist. *Parliament of Whores*, "At Home In the Parliament of Whores" (1991).

15   For forms of Government let fools contest;
Whate'er is best administered is best.

ALEXANDER POPE, (1688–1744) British satirical poet. *An Essay on Man*, epistle 3, l. 303–4 (1733).

16   Governments need to have both shepherds and butchers.

VOLTAIRE [FRANÇOIS MARIE AROUET], (1694–1778) French philosopher, author. "The Piccini Notebooks" (c. 1735–1750). Repr.in *Voltaire's Notebooks*, vol. II, ed. T. Besterman (1968).

17   The people's government, made for the people, made by the people, and answerable to the people.

DANIEL WEBSTER, (1782–1852) U.S. lawyer, statesman." Second speech on Foote's Resolution," vol. 6, *The Writings and*

Speeches of Daniel Webster (1903). Speech, Jan. 26, 1830, U.S. Senate.

Grammar, Spelling and Punctuation

1   When I split an infinitive, God damn it, I split it so it will stay split.

RAYMOND CHANDLER, (1888–1959) U.S. author. *Life of Raymond Chandler*, ch. 7, F. MacShane (1976). Letter, Jan. 18, 1947, to his editor Edward Weeks.

2   Colorless green ideas sleep furiously.

NOAM CHOMSKY, (b. 1928) U.S. linguist, political analyst. *Syntactic Structures*, ch. 2 (1957).

Example of the independence of syntax from meaning. Chomsky gave the following example of a sentence lacking both meaning and syntactic form: "Furiously sleep ideas green colorless."

3   This is the sort of English up with which I will not put.

WINSTON CHURCHILL, (1874–1965) British statesman, writer. Quoted in *The Complete Plain Words*, "The Handling of Words," Ernest Gowers (1954).

Said to be a marginal comment by Churchill against a sentence that clumsily avoided ending with a preposition.

4   My spelling is Wobbly. It's good spelling but it Wobbles, and the letters get in the wrong places.

A.A. (ALAN ALEXANDER) MILNE, (1882–1958) British author.Winnie–the–Pooh, in *Winnie–the–Pooh*, ch. 6 (1926).

5   Grammar, which can govern even Kings.

MOLIÈRE [JEAN BAPTISTE POQUELIN], (1622–1673) French dramatist. Philaminte, in *Les Femmes Savantes*, act 2, sc. 6 (1672).

Gratitude

1 In most of mankind gratitude is merely a secret hope of further favors.

FRANÇOIS LA ROCHEFOUCAULD, DUC DE, (1613–1680) French writer, moralist. *Sentences et Maximes Morales*, no. 298 (1678).

2 My life has crept so long on a broken wing
Through cells of madness, haunts of horror and fear,
That I come to be grateful at last for a little thing.

ALFRED TENNYSON, 1ST BARON TENNYSON, (1809–1892) British poet. "Maud: A Monodrama," pt. 3, sct. 6, st. 1, *Maud, and Other Poems* (1855).

Graves

1 Personally I have no bone to pick with graveyards, I take the air there willingly, perhaps more willingly than elsewhere, when take the air I must.

SAMUEL BECKETT, (1906–1989) Irish dramatist, novelist. *First Love* (1970, trans. 1973).

2 If I should die, think only this of me:
That there's some corner of a foreign field
That is for ever England.

RUPERT BROOKE, (1887–1915) British poet. "The Soldier," *1914 and Other Poems* (1915). Originally published in *New Numbers*, no. 4 (1914).

Brooke, who died of blood–poisoning while serving during World War I, is buried on the island of Skyros, Greece.

3 Beneath those rugged elms, that yew–tree's shade,
Where heaves the turf in many a mouldering heap,
Each in his narrow cell for ever laid,
The rude forefathers of the hamlet sleep.

THOMAS GRAY, (1716–1771) British poet. "Elegy Written in a Country Churchyard," st. 4 (1751). Repr. in *Poetical Works*, ed. J. Rogers (1953).

Greatness

1 The dullard's envy of brilliant men is always assuaged by the suspicion that they will come to a bad end.

MAX BEERBOHM, (1872–1956) British essayist and caricaturist. *Zuleika Dobson*, ch. 4 (1911).

2 It is the nature of all greatness not to be exact.

EDMUND BURKE, (1729–1797) Irish philosopher, statesman. "First Speech on Conciliation with America: American Taxation," *Works*, vol. 2 (1899). Speech, April 19, 1774, House of Commons, London.

3 The great must submit to the dominion of prudence and of virtue, or none will long submit to the dominion of the great.

EDMUND BURKE, (1729–1797) Irish philosopher, statesman. *The Writings and Speeches of Edmund Burke*, vol. 9, ed. Paul Langford (1991). Letter, May 26, 1795.

4 What millions died that Caesar might be great!

THOMAS CAMPBELL, (1777–1844) Scottish poet. "The Pleasures of Hope," pt. 2, l. 174 (1799). Repr. in *Complete Poetical Works*, ed. J.L. Robertson (1907).

5 No great man lives in vain. The history of the world is but the biography of great men.

THOMAS CARLYLE, (1795–1881) Scottish essayist, historian. *On Heroes and Hero–Worship*, "The Hero as Divinity" (1841).

In *Critical and Miscellaneous Essays*, "On History" (1839–1857), Carlyle wrote, "History is the essence of innumerable biographies."

6 No sadder proof can be given by a man of his own littleness than disbelief in great men.

THOMAS CARLYLE, (1795–1881) Scottish essayist, historian. *On Heroes and Hero–Worship*, "The Hero as Divinity" (1841).

7 It is a melancholy truth that even great men have their poor relations.

CHARLES DICKENS, (1812–1870) British novelist. *Bleak House*, ch. 28 (1852).

8 To be great is to be misunderstood.

RALPH WALDO EMERSON, (1803–1882) U.S. essayist, poet, philosopher. *Essays*, "Self–Reliance," First Series (1841).

9 Great men are rarely isolated mountain–peaks; they are the summits of ranges.

THOMAS WENTWORTH HIGGINSON, (1823–1911) U.S. clergyman, writer. "A Plea for Culture," *Atlantic Essays* (1871).

10 A great man's greatest good luck is to die at the right time.

ERIC HOFFER, (1902–1983) U.S. philosopher. *The Passionate State of Mind*, aph. 276 (1955).

11 There is a sacred horror about everything grand. It is easy to admire mediocrity and hills; but whatever is too lofty, a genius as well as a mountain, an assembly as well as a masterpiece, seen too near, is appalling.

VICTOR HUGO, (1802–1885) French poet, dramatist, novelist. *Ninety–Three*, pt. 2, bk. 3, ch. 1 (1879).

12 Greatness, in order to gain recognition, must all too often consent to ape greatness.

JEAN ROSTAND, (1894–1977) French biologist, writer. *Pensées d'un Biologiste* (1939). Repr. in *The Substance of Man* (1962).

13 In my stars I am above thee, but be not afraid of greatness. Some are born great, some achieve greatness, and some have greatness thrust upon 'em.

WILLIAM SHAKESPEARE, (1564–1616) British dramatist, poet. Malvolio, in *Twelfth Night*, act 2, sc. 5, l. 139–41 (1623).

Reading out Maria's letter, purportedly from the countess Olivia.

14 Madness in great ones must not unwatched go.

WILLIAM SHAKESPEARE, (1564–1616) British dramatist, poet. Claudius, in *Hamlet*, act 3, sc. 1, l. 191 (1604).

15 Great men hallow a whole people, and lift up all who live in their time.

SYDNEY SMITH, (1771–1845) British clergyman, writer. Quoted in *Memoir*, vol. 1, ch. 7, Lady Holland (1855).

16 None think the great unhappy, but the great.

EDWARD YOUNG, (1683–1765) British poet, playwright. *Love of Fame: The Universal Passion*, satire 1, l. 238 (1725–1728). Repr. in *Complete Works*, ed. J. Doran (1968).

Greece and the Greeks

1 The Cretans are always liars, evil beasts, slow bellies.

BIBLE: NEW TESTAMENT, St. Paul, in *Titus*, 1:12.

Cited by Paul, this remark is attributed to Epimenides.

2 The isles of Greece, the isles of
   Greece!
   Where burning Sappho loved and
   sung.
   Where grew the arts of war and
   peace,
   Where Delos rose, and Phoebus
   sprung!
   Eternal summer gilds them yet,
   But all, except their sun, is set.

   **GEORGE GORDON NOEL BYRON, 6TH
   BARON BYRON,** (1788–1824) British poet.
   Don Juan, cto. 3, st. 86, verse 1 (1819–1824).

3 Ancient sculpture is the true school
   of modesty. But where the Greeks
   had modesty, we have cant; where
   they had poetry, we have cant;
   where they had patriotism, we have
   cant; where they had anything that
   exalts, delights, or adorns humanity, we have nothing but cant, cant,
   cant.

   THOMAS LOVE PEACOCK, (1785–1866)
   British author. *Crotchet Castle*, ch. 7 (1831).

Greed

1 For what shall it profit a man, if he
   shall gain the whole world, and lose
   his own soul?

   BIBLE: NEW TESTAMENT, Jesus, in
   Mark, 8:36.

2 Greed is all right, by the way.... I
   think greed is healthy. You can be
   greedy and still feel good about
   yourself.

   IVAN F. BOESKY, (b. 1937) U.S. financier.
   Commencement Address. Speech, May 18,
   1986, School of Business Administration, University of California, Berkeley.

   Boesky's remarks were featured in Oliver
   Stone's film *Wall Street* (1987), spoken by
   Gordon Gecko (played by Michael Douglas).
   Boesky himself was later convicted of conspir-

ing to file false documents with the federal
government, involving insider trading violations, and agreed to pay $100 million in fines
and illicit profits.

3 There is enough in the world for
   everyone's need, but not enough
   for everyone's greed.

   FRANK BUCHMAN, (1878–1961) U.S.
   evangelist. *Remaking the World* (1947).

4 So for a good old–gentlemanly vice,
   I think I must take up with avarice.

   **GEORGE GORDON NOEL BYRON, 6TH
   BARON BYRON,** (1788–1824) British poet.
   Don Juan, cto.1, st. 216 (1819–1824).

5 Avarice, the spur of industry.

   DAVID HUME, (1711–1776) Scottish
   philosopher, historian. "Of Civil Liberty,"
   Essays Moral, Political, and Literary (1742).

Greetings

1 Eh, what's up Doc?

   TEX AVERY [FRED AVERY],
   (1907–1980) U.S. animator. Bugs Bunny's
   running gag, in *Looney Tunes/Merrie
   Melodies* (animation series), Warner Brothers
   cartoon (1938–1964).

   The rabbit made his first appearance in a
   Warner Brothers' *Looney Tunes* cartoon in
   1937, voiced by Mel Blanc. In 1940 Tex
   Avery gave him his name (after West Coast
   mobster Bugsy Siegel) and his famous catch-
   phrase, and directed the first official Bugs
   Bunny cartoon, *A Wild Hare* (1940). "What's
   Up Doc?" was also the title of Peter Bogdanovich's 1972 screwball comedy with Bar-
   bra Streisand and Ryan O'Neal.

2 Is this really you, here, Ser
   Brunetto?

   DANTE ALIGHIERI, (1265–1321) Italian
   poet. "Inferno," cto. 15, l. 30, *The Divine
   Comedy* (c. 1307–1321), trans. by Mark Musa
   (1971).

   Dante's words on meeting Brunetto Latini,
   Florentine statesman and scholar, a friend and

mentor of Dante in his youth, among the "Sodomites" in the seventh circle of Hell.

3   Hello, good evening, and welcome.

DAVID FROST, (b. 1939) British TV presenter. *The Frost Report* (TV show) (1966–1967).

The words were used to open each show 1966–1967, as well as subsequent Frost series.

Grief

1   Jesus wept.

BIBLE: NEW TESTAMENT, *John*, 11:35.

The shortest verse in the Bible; refers to Jesus' grief at the death of Lazarus, whom he raised from the dead after four days.

2   Weeping may endure for a night, but joy cometh in the morning.

BIBLE: HEBREW, *Psalms*, 30:5.

3   I tell you, hopeless grief is passionless.

ELIZABETH BARRETT BROWNING, (1806–1861) British poet. "Grief," l. 1, *Poems* (1844).

4   This is the Hour of Lead—
Remembered, if outlived,
As Freezing persons, recollect the Snow—
First—Chill—then Stupor—then the letting go—

EMILY DICKINSON, (1830–1886) U.S. poet. "After Great Pain, a Formal Feeling Comes" (written c. 1862, published 1929). Repr. in *The Complete Poems*, no. 341, Harvard *variorum* edition (1955).

5   In all the silent manliness of grief.

OLIVER GOLDSMITH, (1728–1774) Anglo–Irish author. *The Deserted Village*, l. 384 (1770).

6   Margaret, are you grieving

Over Goldengrove unleaving?

GERARD MANLEY HOPKINS, (1844–1889) British poet, Jesuit priest. "Spring and Fall: to a young child" (written 1880), published in *Poems* (1918).

7   No one ever told me that grief felt so like fear.

C.S. (CLIVE STAPLES) LEWIS, (1898–1963) British author. *A Grief Observed* (1961).

Opening words of Lewis's book of mourning for his dead wife.

8   Nothing becomes so offensive so quickly as grief. When fresh it finds someone to console it, but when it becomes chronic, it is ridiculed, and rightly.

SENECA, (c. 5–65) Roman writer, philosopher, statesman. *Epistulae ad Lucilium*, epistle 68, l. 13.

9   Grief fills the room up of my absent child,
Lies in his bed, walks up and down with me,
Puts on his pretty looks, repeats his words,
Remembers me of all his gracious parts,
Stuffs out his vacant garments with his form;
Then have I reason to be fond of grief.

WILLIAM SHAKESPEARE, (1564–1616) British dramatist, poet. Constance, in *King John*, act 3, sc. 4, l. 93–5 (1623).

On her separation from her son Arthur, taken prisoner by John.

10 Ah, woe is me! Winter is come and gone,
But grief returns with the revolving year.

PERCY BYSSHE SHELLEY, (1792–1822) British poet. "Adonais," st. 18 (1821).

Grotesque, the

1 Her skin was white as leprosy,
The nightmare Life–in–Death was
she,
Who thicks man's blood with cold.

SAMUEL TAYLOR COLERIDGE,
(1772–1834) British poet, critic. "The Rime of
the Ancient Mariner," pt. 3, st. 11 (1798).

Describing the skeleton–ship's crew.

2 I have found that anything that
comes out of the South is going to
be called grotesque by the Northern
reader, unless it is grotesque, in
which case it is going to be called
realistic.

FLANNERY O'CONNOR, (1925–1964) U.S.
author. "Some Aspects of the Grotesque in
Southern Fiction," *Mystery and Manners,* eds.
Sally and Robert Fitzgerald (1972). First published in *Cluster Review* (Macon University,
1965).

The essay was originally a paper read at Wes-
leyan College for Women, Macon, Georgia, fall
1960.

Guests

1 One might well say that mankind is
divisible into two great classes: hosts
and guests.

MAX BEERBOHM, (1872–1956) British
essayist and caricaturist. *And Even Now,* "Hosts
and Guests" (1920). (Essay written 1918).

2 Some men are like musical glasses;
to produce their finest tones, you
must keep them wet.

SAMUEL TAYLOR COLERIDGE,
(1772–1834) British poet, critic. *Table Talk,* "20
Jan. 1834," *Specimens of the Table Talk of
Samuel Taylor Coleridge,* ed. Henry Nelson
Coleridge (1835). Repr. in *Collected Works,*
vol. 14, ed. Kathleen Coburn (1990).

3 Some people can stay longer in an
hour than others can in a week.

WILLIAM DEAN HOWELLS,
(1837–1920) U.S. novelist, critic. *Attributed.*

4 Makin' a long stay short is a great
aid t' popularity.

**KIN HUBBARD (F. [FRANK] McKIN-
NEY HUBBARD),** (1868–1930) U.S.
humorist, journalist. *Abe Martin's Wisecracks,*
ed. E.V. Lucas (1930).

5 Not many sounds in life ... exceed
in interest a knock at the door.

CHARLES LAMB, (1775–1834) British
essayist, critic. *Essays of Elia,* "Valentine's
Day" (1820–1823).

6 My father used to say,
"Superior people never make long
visits,
have to be shown Longfellow's
grave
or the glass flowers at Harvard."

MARIANNE MOORE, (1887–1972) U.S.
poet. "Silence," *Selected Poems* (1935).

Guilt

1 My guiding principle is this: Guilt is
never to be doubted.

FRANZ KAFKA, (1883–1924) Czech novelist, short–story writer. The officer, in "In
The Penal Settlement," *Metamorphosis and
Other Stories* (1961). (Originally published
1919).

2 True guilt is guilt at the obligation
one owes to oneself to be oneself.
False guilt is guilt felt at not being
what other people feel one ought to
be or assume that one is.

R.D. (RONALD DAVID) LAING,
(1927–1989) British psychiatrist. *The Self and
Others,* ch. 10 (1961).

3 Out, damned spot; out I say.

WILLIAM SHAKESPEARE, (1564–1616)
British dramatist, poet. Lady Macbeth, in *Macbeth,* act 5, sc. 1, l. 33 (1623).

Lady Macbeth, sleepwalking, sees the murdered Duncan's blood on her hands.

Gulf War, the

1   The great, the jewel and the mother of battles has begun.

SADDAM HUSSEIN, (b. 1937) Iraqi president. Quoted in *Independent* (London, Jan. 19, 1991). Speech, Jan. 6, 1991.

Said at the start of the Gulf War.

Habit

1   Certes, they been lyk to houndes, for an hound whan he comth by the roser, or by other bushes, though he may nat pisse, yet wole he heve up his leg and make a contenaunce to pisse.

GEOFFREY CHAUCER, (1340–1400) British poet. *The Canterbury Tales,* "The Parson's Tale," *Sequitur de Luxuria* (c. 1387–1400), repr. in *The Works of Geoffrey Chaucer,* ed. Alfred W. Pollard, etc. (1898).

2   Habit with him was all the test of truth,
     "It must be right: I've done it from my youth."

GEORGE CRABBE, (1754–1832) British clergyman, poet. "The Vicar," l. 138–9, *The Borough,* letter 3 (1810). Repr. in *Poetical Works,* eds. A.J. and R.M. Carlyle (1908, rev.1924).

3   Habit is thus the enormous fly–wheel of society, its most precious conservative agent. It alone is what keeps us all within the bounds of ordinance, and saves the children of fortune from the envious uprisings of the poor.

WILLIAM JAMES, (1843–1916) U.S. psychologist, philosopher. *Principles of Psychology,* vol. 1, ch. 4 (1890).

4   To fall into a habit is to begin to cease to be.

MIGUEL DE UNAMUNO, (1864–1936) Spanish philosophical writer. *The Tragic Sense of Life,* ch. 9 (1913, trans. 1921).

Hair

1   But if a woman have long hair, it is a glory to her: for her hair is given her for a covering.

BIBLE: NEW TESTAMENT, St. Paul, in *1 Corinthians,* 11:15.

2   The hoary head is a crown of glory, if it be found in the way of righteousness.

BIBLE: HEBREW, *Proverbs,* 16:31.

3   I'm gonna wash that man right out of my hair.

OSCAR HAMMERSTEIN II, (1895–1960) U.S. songwriter. "I'm Gonna Wash That Man Right Out Of My Hair" (song), *South Pacific* (stage musical, 1949; film, 1958).

4   Sabrina fair,
     Listen where thou art sitting
     Under the glassy, cool, translucent wave,
     In twisted braids of lilies knitting
     The loose train of thy amber–dropping hair.

JOHN MILTON, (1608–1674) British poet. Attendant Spirit's song, in "Comus," l. 859–63 (1637). Repr. in *Milton's Poetical Works,* ed. Douglas Bush (1966).

5   Fair tresses man's imperial race ensnare,
     And beauty draws us with a single hair.

ALEXANDER POPE, (1688–1744) British satirical poet. "The Rape of the Lock," cto. 2, l. 27–8 (1714).

Happiness

1 If happiness, then, is activity expressing virtue, it is reasonable for it to express the supreme virtue, which will be the virtue of the best thing.

ARISTOTLE, (384–322 B.C.) Greek philosopher. *Nicomachean Ethics*, bk. 10, ch. 7, trans. by Terence Irwin (1985).

2 The said truth is that it is the greatest happiness of the greatest number that is the measure of right and wrong.

JEREMY BENTHAM, (1748–1832) British philosopher, political theorist, jurist. *Fragment of Government* (1776). Repr. (1948).

The formula was repeated with minor variations in Bentham's later writings. He ascribed the originator of this definition to be either clergyman and scientist Joseph Priestley (1733–1804) or Italian legal reformer Cesare Beccaria (1738–1794), though the Scottish philosopher Francis Hutcheson had said much the same in his *Inquiry into the Original of our Ideas of Beauty and Virtue* (1725): "That action is best which procures the greatest happiness for the greatest numbers."

3 What though my wing'd hours of bliss have been,
Like angel–visits, few and far between?

THOMAS CAMPBELL, (1777–1844) Scottish poet. "The Pleasures of Hope," pt. 2, l. 375–376 (1799). Repr. in *Complete Poetical Works*, ed. J.L. Robertson (1907).

The image is borrowed from the Scottish poet Robert Blair (1699–1746): "The good he scorned Stalked off reluctant, like an ill–used ghost, Not to return; or if it did, its visits Like those of angels, short, and far between." "The Grave," l. 586–589 (1743).

4 Happiness is a mystery, like religion, and should never be rationalised.

GILBERT KEITH CHESTERTON, (1874–1936) British author. *Heretics*, ch. 7 (1905).

5 Happiness makes up in height what it lacks in length.

ROBERT FROST, (1874–1963) U.S. poet. "A Witness Tree" (1942).

6 Oh, what a beautiful mornin',
Oh, what a beautiful day!
I got a beautiful feelin'
Ev'rything's goin' my way.

OSCAR HAMMERSTEIN II, (1895–1960) U.S. songwriter. "Oh, What a Beautiful Mornin'" (song), *Oklahoma!* (Stage musical, 1943; film, 1955).

7 The search for happiness is one of the chief sources of unhappiness.

ERIC HOFFER, (1902–1983) U.S. philosopher. *The Passionate State of Mind*, aph. 280 (1955).

8 The great end of all human industry is the attainment of happiness. For this were arts invented, sciences cultivated, laws ordained, and societies modelled, by the most profound wisdom of patriots and legislators. Even the lonely savage, who lies exposed to the inclemency of the elements and the fury of wild beasts, forgets not, for a moment, this grand object of his being.

DAVID HUME, (1711–1776) Scottish philosopher, historian. "The Stoic," pt. 1, *Essays Moral, Political, and Literary* (1742). Repr. in *The Philosophical Works of David Hume*, vol. 3 (1826).

9 Sir, that all who are happy, are equally happy, is not true. A peasant and a philosopher may be equally *satisfied*, but not equally *happy*. Happiness consists in the multiplicity of agreeable consciousness.

SAMUEL JOHNSON, (1709–1784) British author, lexicographer. Quoted in James Boswell, *Life of Dr. Johnson*, entry, Feb. 1766 (1791).

Johnson was arguing against the proposition by David Hume (in the essay *The Sceptic*) that "a little miss, dressed in a new gown for a dancing–school ball, receives as complete enjoyment as the greatest orator, who triumphs in the splendor of his eloquence."

10 Ask yourself whether you are happy, and you cease to be so.

JOHN STUART MILL, (1806–1873) British philosopher, economist. *Autobiography*, ch. 5 (1873).

11 Happiness is the only sanction of life; where happiness fails, existence remains a mad and lamentable experiment.

GEORGE SANTAYANA, (1863–1952) U.S. philosopher, poet. *The Life of Reason*, "Reason in Common Sense," ch. 10 (1905–1906).

12 But O, how bitter a thing it is to look into happiness through another man's eyes.

WILLIAM SHAKESPEARE, (1564–1616) British dramatist, poet. Orlando, in *As You Like It*, act 5, sc. 2, l. 41–2 (1623).

13 We are never happy; we can only remember that we were so once.

ALEXANDER SMITH, (1830–1867) Scottish poet. *Dreamthorp*, "On Death and the Fear of Dying" (1863).

14 Happiness is an imaginary condition, formerly often attributed by the living to the dead, now usually attributed by adults to children, and by children to adults.

THOMAS SZASZ, (b. 1920) U.S. psychiatrist. "Emotions," *The Second Sin* (1973).

15 You never enjoy the world aright, till the sea itself floweth in your veins, till you are clothed with the heavens and crowned with the stars: and perceive yourself to be the sole heir of the whole world.

THOMAS TRAHERNE, (1636–1674) British clergyman, poet, mystic. *Centuries*, "First Century," no. 29 (written c. 1672, first published 1908).

Hard Times

1 For men must work, and women must weep,
And there's little to earn, and many to keep,
Though the harbour bar be moaning.

CHARLES KINGSLEY, (1819–1875) British author, clergyman. "The Three Fishers," st. 1 (1851). Repr. in *The Works of Charles Kingsley* (1880–1885).

Haste

1 Now, *here*, you see, it takes all the running *you* can do, to keep in the same place. If you want to get somewhere else, you must run at least twice as fast as that.

LEWIS CARROLL [CHARLES LUTWIDGE DODGSON], (1832–1898) British author, mathematician. The Red Queen, in *Through the Looking–Glass*, "The Garden of Live Flowers" (1872).

The passage is usually quoted with reference to rapidly changing political situations.

2 Ther nis no werkman, whatsoevere he be,
That may bothe werke wel and hastily.

GEOFFREY CHAUCER, (1340–1400) British poet. *The Canterbury Tales*, Januarie, in "The Merchant's Tale," l. 1832–3 (c. 1387–1400), repr. in *The Works of Geoffrey Chaucer*, ed. Alfred W. Pollard, etc. (1898).

3 Whoever is in a hurry, shows that the thing he is about is too big for him.

PHILIP DORMER STANHOPE, 4TH EARL CHESTERFIELD, (1694–1773) British statesman, man of letters. *The Letters of the Earl of Chesterfield to His Son*, vol. 1, no. 190, ed. Charles Strachey (1901). Letter, Aug. 30, 1749, first published (1774).

4   'T were better to be eaten to death with a rust than to be scoured to nothing with perpetual motion.

WILLIAM SHAKESPEARE, (1564–1616) British dramatist, poet. Sir John Falstaff, in *Henry IV pt. 2*, act 1, sc. 2, l. 219–21 (1600).

5   He sows hurry and reaps indigestion.

ROBERT LOUIS STEVENSON, (1850–1894) Scottish novelist, essayist, poet. *Virginibus Puerisque*, "An Apology for Idlers" (1881).

Referring to "industrious fellows."

Hate

1   Now hatred is by far the longest pleasure;
Men love in haste, but they detest at leisure.

GEORGE GORDON NOEL BYRON, 6TH BARON BYRON, (1788–1824) British poet. *Don Juan*, cto. 13, st. 6 (1819–1824).

2   I never hated a man enough to give him diamonds back.

ZSA ZSA GABOR, (b. 1919) Hungarian–born U.S. screen actor. Quoted in *Observer* (London, Aug. 28, 1957).

3   What we need is hatred. From it our ideas are born.

JEAN GENET, (1910–1986) French playwright, novelist. *The Blacks*, Epigraph (1959, trans. 1960).

4   Dear Bathurst was a man to my very heart's content: he hated a fool, and he hated a rogue, and he hated a whig; he was a very good hater.

SAMUEL JOHNSON, (1709–1784) British author, lexicographer. Quoted in *Anecdotes of the Late Samuel Johnson*, Hester Piozzi (1786). Repr. in *Johnsonian Miscellanies*, vol. 1, ed. George Birkbeck Hill (1891).

5   The most deadly fruit is borne by the hatred which one grafts on an extinguished friendship.

GOTTHOLD EPHRAIM LESSING, (1729–1881) German dramatist, critic. Philotas, in *Philotas*, act 3 (1759).

6   Always remember, others may hate you. Those who hate you don't win unless you hate them. And then you destroy yourself.

RICHARD NIXON, (1913–1992) U.S. Republican politician, president. Speech, Aug. 9, 1974.

To members of his administration, on leaving office.

7   The greatest hatred, like the greatest virtue and the worst dogs, is silent.

JEAN PAUL RICHTER, (1763–1825) German novelist. *Hesperus*, ch. 12 (1795).

8   *Hatred* is an affair of the heart; *contempt* that of the head.

ARTHUR SCHOPENHAUER, (1788–1860) German philosopher. *Parerga and Paralipomena*, vol. 2, ch. 24, sct. 324 (1851), trans. by E.F.J. Payne.

9   It is human nature to hate the man whom you have hurt.

TACITUS, (c. 55–c. 120) Roman historian. *Agricola*, sct. 42.

10   An intellectual hatred is the worst,
So let her think opinions are accursed.

WILLIAM BUTLER YEATS, (1865–1939) Irish poet, playwright. "A Prayer for My Daughter," st. 8, *Michael Robartes and the Dancer* (1920).

Hats

1 There is not so variable a thing in nature as a lady's head–dress.

JOSEPH ADDISON, (1672–1719) British essayist. *Spectator* (London, June 22, 1711), no. 98, *The Spectator*, ed. D.F. Bond (1965).

2 Well, you look so pretty in it
Honey, can I jump on it sometime?
Yes, I just wanna see
If it's really that expensive kind
You know it balances on your head
Just like a mattress balances
On a bottle of wine
Your brand new leopard–skin
     pill–box hat.

BOB DYLAN [ROBERT ALLEN ZIMMERMAN], (b. 1941) U.S. singer, songwriter. "Leopard–Skin Pill–Box Hat" (song), on the album *Blonde on Blonde* (1968).

Health

1 A sound mind in a sound body, is a short, but full description of a happy state in this World: he that has these two, has little more to wish for; and he that wants either of them, will be little the better for anything else.

JOHN LOCKE, (1632–1704) British philosopher. *Some Thoughts Concerning Education* (1693).

Opening sentence The famous prescription, *mens sana in corpore sano,* goes back to Juvenal (c. 60–130 A.D.).

Heart

1 There are strings in the human heart that had better not be wibrated.

CHARLES DICKENS, (1812–1870) British novelist. Mr. Tappertit, in *Barnaby Rudge,* ch. 22 (1841).

Heartbreak

1 Had we never lov'd sae kindly,
Had we never lov'd sae blindly,
Never met—or never parted—
We had ne'er been broken–
     hearted.

ROBERT BURNS, (1759–1796) Scottish poet. "Ae Fond Kiss, and Then We Sever," st. 4, *Johnson's Musical Museum,* vol. 4 (1792). Repr. in *Poetical Works,* vol. 1, ed. William Scott Douglas (1891).

Walter Scott described these lines—addressed to "Clarinda" (Agnes Maclehose), parting for the West Indies as "worth a thousand romances," and Byron chose the stanza as the motto for his poem "The Bride of Abydos."

2 How else but through a broken heart
May Lord Christ enter in?

OSCAR WILDE, (1854–1900) Anglo–Irish playwright, author. "The Ballad of Reading Gaol," pt. 5, st. 14 (1898). Repr. in *Complete Works of Oscar Wilde,* ed. J.B. Foreman (1966).

Heaven

1 And God shall wipe away all tears from their eyes; and there shall be no more death, neither sorrow, nor crying, neither shall there be any more pain: for the former things are passed away.

BIBLE: NEW TESTAMENT, St. John the Divine, in *Revelation,* 21:4.

2 And I heard a voice from heaven, as the voice of many waters, and as the voice of a great thunder: and I

heard the voice of harpers harping with their harps.

BIBLE: NEW TESTAMENT, St. John the Divine, in *Revelation*, 14:2.

3 But as it is written, eye hath not seen, nor ear heard, neither have entered into the heart of man, the things which God hath prepared for them that love him.

BIBLE: NEW TESTAMENT, St. Paul, in *1 Corinthians*, 2:9.

4 All places are distant from heaven alike.

ROBERT BURTON, (1577–1640) British clergyman, author. *The Anatomy of Melancholy*, pt. 2, sct. 3, memb. 4, subsct. 1 (1621).

5 Our remedies oft in ourselves do lie,
Which we ascribe to heaven.

WILLIAM SHAKESPEARE, (1564–1616) British dramatist, poet. Helena, in *All's Well That Ends Well*, act 1, sc. 1, l. 212–3 (1623).

6 My idea of heaven is eating *paté de foie gras* to the sound of trumpets.

SYDNEY SMITH, (1771–1845) British clergyman, writer. Quoted in *The Smith of Smiths*, ch. 10, Hesketh Pearson (1934).

7 O world invisible, we view thee, O world intangible, we touch thee, O world unknowable, we know thee, Inapprehensible, we clutch thee!

FRANCIS THOMPSON, (1859–1907) British poet. "The Kingdom of God (In No Strange Land)," st. 1, *Collected Works of Francis Thompson,* vol. 2, ed. Wilfred Meynell (1913). Athenaeum (London, Aug. 8, 1909).

Opening lines.

8 Heaven–gates are not so highly arched
As princes' palaces: they that enter there

Must go upon their knees.

JOHN WEBSTER, (1580–1625) British dramatist. The Duchess, in *The Duchess of Malfi*, act 4, sc. 2, l. 232–4 (1623). Repr. in *The Complete Works of John Webster*, ed. F.L. Lucas (1927).

Hedonism

1 A man hath no better thing under the sun, than to eat, and to drink, and to be merry.

BIBLE: HEBREW, *Ecclesiastes*, 8:15. Compare with *Luke* 12:19: "And I will say to my soul, Soul, thou hast much goods laid up for many years; take thine ease, eat, drink, and be merry."

2 Life admits not of delays; when pleasure can be had, it is fit to catch it: every hour takes away part of the things that please us, and perhaps part of our disposition to be pleased.

SAMUEL JOHNSON, (1709–1784) British author, lexicographer. Quoted in James Boswell, *Life of Dr. Johnson* (1791). Letter, Sept. 1, 1777, to Boswell.

3 Ah, make the most of what we yet may spend,
Before we too into the Dust descend.

OMAR KHAYYAM, (11–12th century) Persian astronomer, poet. *The Rubaiyat of Omar Khayyam*, st. 23, trans. by Edward FitzGerald, first edition (1859).

4 God forgive me, I do still see that my nature is not to be quite conquered, but will esteem pleasure above all things; though, yet in the middle of it, it hath reluctancy after my business, which is neglected by my following my pleasure. However, music and women I cannot but give way to, whatever my business is.

SAMUEL PEPYS, (1633–1703) British diarist. *The Diary of Samuel Pepys*, eds. Robert Latham and William Matthews (1977–1983). Journal entry, March 9, 1666.

Hell

1   Here sighs and cries and shrieks of lamentation echoed throughout the starless air of Hell; at first these sounds resounding made me weep: tongues confused, a language strained in anguish with cadences of anger, shrill outcries and raucous groans that joined with sounds of hands, raising a whirling storm that turns itself forever through that air of endless black, like grains of sand swirling when a whirlwind blows.

DANTE ALIGHIERI, (1265–1321) Italian poet. "Inferno," cto. 3, l. 22–31, *The Divine Comedy* (c. 1307–1321), trans. by Mark Musa (1971).

Of the Vestibule to Hell.

2   I AM THE WAY INTO THE SOR-ROWFUL CITY. I AM THE WAY INTO ETERNAL GRIEF, I AM THE WAY TO A FORSAKEN RACE.... ABANDON EVERY HOPE, ALL YOU WHO ENTER.

DANTE ALIGHIERI, (1265–1321) Italian poet. "Inferno," cto. 3, l. 1–3 and 9, *The Divine Comedy* (c. 1307–1321), trans. by Mark Musa (1971).

Inscription at the entrance to Hell.

3   There sighs, lamentations and loud wailings resounded through the starless air, so that at first it made me weep; strange tongues, horrible language, words of pain, tones of anger, voices loud and hoarse, and with these the sound of hands, made a tumult which is whirling through that air forever dark, as sand eddies in a whirlwind.

DANTE ALIGHIERI, (1265–1321) Italian poet. "Inferno," cto. 3, l. 22, *The Divine Comedy* (1321).

4   Hell is oneself,
Hell is alone, the other figures in it
Merely projections. There is noth-
    ing to escape from
And nothing to escape to. One is
    always alone.

T.S. (THOMAS STEARNS) ELIOT, (1888–1965) Anglo–American poet, critic. Edward, in *The Cocktail Party*, act 1, sc. 3 (1950).

5   The safest road to Hell is the grad-ual one—the gentle slope, soft underfoot, without sudden turn-ings, without milestones, without signposts.

C.S. (CLIVE STAPLES) LEWIS, (1898–1963) British author. Screwtape, in *The Screwtape Letters*, letter 12 (1942).

6   Hell hath no limits, nor is circum-scrib'd
In one self place; for where we are is
    Hell,
And where Hell is, there must we
    ever be.

CHRISTOPHER MARLOWE, (1564–1593) British dramatist, poet. Mephistopheles, in *The Tragical History of Dr. Faustus*, act 2, sc. 1, l. 121–3 (1604).

7   I believe that I am in hell, therefore I am there.

ARTHUR RIMBAUD, (1854–1891) French poet. *Une Saison en Enfer*, "Nuit de l'Enfer," (originally published 1874). Repr. in *Collected Poems*, ed. Oliver Bernard (1962).

8   The gates of Hell are open night and
        day;
Smooth the descent, and easy is the
    way:
But, to return, and view the cheer-
    ful skies;

In this, the task and mighty labour lies.

VIRGIL [PUBLIUS VERGILIUS MARO], (70–19 B.C.) Roman poet. the Sibyl of Cumae, in *Aeneid*, bk. 6, l. 126–9, trans. by John Dryden.

Spoken to Aeneas, in his quest to find his father.

Hemingway, Ernest

1 He is gentle, as all real men are gentle; without tenderness, a man is uninteresting.

MARLENE DIETRICH, (1904–1992) German–born U.S. film actress. Quoted in *Papa Hemingway*, pt. 1, ch. 1, A.E. Hotchner (1966 edition).

2 I started out very quiet and I beat Turgenev. Then I trained hard and I beat de Maupassant. I've fought two draws with Stendhal, and I think I had an edge in the last one. But nobody's going to get me in any ring with Tolstoy unless I'm crazy or I keep getting better.

ERNEST HEMINGWAY, (1899–1961) U.S. author. *The New Yorker* (May 13, 1950).

Heresy

1 It may be you fear more to deliver judgment upon me than I fear judgment.

GIORDANO BRUNO, (1548–1600) Italian philosopher. Quoted in *Life of Giordano Bruno*, ch. 11, I. Frith (1887).

Said to the inquisitors who had condemned him to death.

Heritage

1 Stands the Church clock at ten to three?

And is there honey still for tea?

RUPERT BROOKE, (1887–1915) British poet. "The Old Vicarage," *Grantchester, 1914 and Other Poems* (1915).

Concluding lines.

Hermits

1 And he was driven from men, and did eat grass as oxen, and his body was wet with the dew of heaven, till his hairs were grown like eagles' feathers, and his nails like birds' claws.

BIBLE: HEBREW, *Daniel*, 4:33.

Referring to Nebuchadnezzar, king of Babylon.

Heroes and Heroines

1 I'm not the heroic type. I was beaten up by Quakers.

WOODY ALLEN, (b. 1935) U.S. filmmaker. Victor Shakapopolis (Woody Allen), in *Sleeper* (film) (1973).

2 Unhappy the land that is in need of heroes.

BERTOLT BRECHT, (1898–1956) German dramatist, poet. Galileo, in *Life of Galileo*, sc. 13.

Responding to Andrea's remark, "Unhappy the land that has no heroes."

3 One who never turned his back but marched breast forward,
Never doubted clouds would break,
Never dreamed, though right were worsted, wrong would triumph.
Held we fall to rise, are baffled to fight better,
Sleep to wake.

ROBERT BROWNING, (1812–1889) British poet. *Asolando*, "Epilogue," st. 3 (1889).

4 The drying up a single tear has
more
Of honest fame than shedding seas
of gore.

**GEORGE GORDON NOEL BYRON, 6TH
BARON BYRON,** (1788–1824) British poet.
Don Juan, cto. 8, st. 3 (1819–1824).

5 I am convinced that a light supper,
a good night's sleep, and a fine
morning, have sometimes made a
hero of the same man, who, by an
indigestion, a restless night, and
rainy morning, would have proved
a coward.

**PHILIP DORMER STANHOPE, 4TH
EARL CHESTERFIELD,** (1694–1773)
British statesman, man of letters. *The Letters of
the Earl of Chesterfield to His Son*, vol. 1, no.
149, ed. Charles Strachey (1901). Letter, April
26, 1748, first published (1774).

6 Never in the field of human conflict
was so much owed by so many to
so few.

WINSTON CHURCHILL, (1874–1965)
British statesman, writer. Vol. 6, *Winston S.
Churchill: His Complete Speeches,
1897–1963*, ed. Robert Rhodes James (1974).
Speech, Aug. 20, 1940, House of Commons,
London.

Referring to the pilots who fought the Battle of
Britain.

7 To have no heroes is to have no
aspiration, to live on the momen-
tum of the past, to be thrown back
upon routine, sensuality, and the
narrow self.

CHARLES HORTON COOLEY,
(1864–1929) U.S. sociologist. *Human Nature
and the Social Order*, ch. 8 (1902).

8 No bastard ever won a war by dying
for his country. He won it by making the other poor dumb bastard
die for his country.

FRANCIS FORD COPPOLA, (b. 1939)
U.S. film director, writer. General George S.

Patton Jr. (George C. Scott), in *Patton* (film),
opening speech in which General Patton
addresses the audience as though they were his
troops (1970).

9 Every hero becomes a bore at last.

RALPH WALDO EMERSON, (1803–1882)
U.S. essayist, poet, philosopher. *Representative
Men*, "Uses of Great Men" (1850).

10 Show me a hero and I will write you
a tragedy.

F. SCOTT FITZGERALD, (1896–1940) U.S.
author. *The Crack–Up*, "Notebook E," ed.
Edmund Wilson (1945).

11 I offer neither pay, nor quarters, nor
food; I offer only hunger, thirst,
forced marches, battles and death.
Let him who loves his country with
his heart, and not merely with his
lips, follow me.

GIUSEPPE GARIBALDI, (1807–1882) Ital-
ian patriot, soldier. Quoted in *Garibaldi's
Defence of the Roman Republic*, G.M.
Trevelyan (1907–1911). Speech, July 2, 1849.

To the Garibaldi legion besieged in Rome.

12 The world doesn't make any heroes
anymore.

GRAHAM GREENE, (1904–1991) British
novelist. Major Calloway, in *The Third Man*
(film) (1950).

13 The greatest obstacle to being heroic
is the doubt whether one may not be
going to prove one's self a fool; the
truest heroism is to resist the doubt;
and the profoundest wisdom, to
know when it ought to be resisted,
and when to be obeyed.

NATHANIEL HAWTHORNE, (1804–1864)
U.S. author. *The Blithedale Romance*, ch. 2
(1852).

14 The boy stood on the burning deck
Whence all but he had fled.

FELICIA HEMANS, (1793–1835) British
poet. "Casabianca," st. 1 (1849).

15 So long as men worship the Caesars and Napoleons, Caesars and Napoleons will duly rise and make them miserable.

ALDOUS HUXLEY, (1894–1963) British author. *Ends and Means*, ch. 8 (1937).

16 I do honour the very flea of his dog.

BEN JONSON, (c. 1572–1637) British dramatist, poet. Cob, in *Every Man in His Humour*, act 4, sc. 4, l. 19 (performed 1598, published 1616). Repr. in *The Complete Plays*, vol. 1, ed. G.A. Wilkes (1981).

17 Claret is the liquor for boys; port for men; but he who aspires to be a hero must drink brandy.

SAMUEL JOHNSON, (1709–1784) British author, lexicographer. Quoted in James Boswell, *Life of Dr. Johnson*, entry, April 7, 1779 (1791).

18 Heroes are created by popular demand, sometimes out of the scantiest materials, or none at all.

GERALD W. JOHNSON, (1890–1980) U.S. author. *American Heroes and Hero–Worship*, ch. 1 (1943).

19 It was involuntary. They sank my boat.

JOHN FITZGERALD KENNEDY, (1917–1963) U.S. Democratic politician, president. *A Thousand Days*, ch. 4, Arthur M. Schlesinger Jr. (1965).

On being asked by a small boy how he became a war hero.

20 What is our task? To make Britain a fit country for heroes to live in.

DAVID LLOYD GEORGE, (1863–1945) British Liberal politician, Prime Minister. Quoted in *Times* (London, Nov. 25, 1918). Speech, Nov. 24, 1918, Wolverhampton, England.

The words were frequently recalled in the years of low wages and unemployment that followed.

21 And how can man die better

Than facing fearful odds,
For the ashes of his fathers,
And the temples of his Gods?

THOMAS BABINGTON MACAULAY, (1800–1859) British historian, Whig politician. "Horatius," st. 27, *Lays of Ancient Rome* (1842).

22 Ultimately a hero is a man who would argue with the gods, and so awakens devils to contest his vision. The more a man can achieve, the more he may be certain that the devil will inhabit a part of his creation.

NORMAN MAILER, (b. 1923) U.S. author. *The Presidential Papers*, preface (1963).

23 We few, we happy few, we band of brothers.
For he today that sheds his blood with me
Shall be my brother; be he ne'er so vile,
This day shall gentle his condition.
And gentlemen in England now abed
Shall think themselves accursed they were not here,
And hold their manhoods cheap whiles any speaks
That fought with us upon Saint Crispin's day.

WILLIAM SHAKESPEARE, (1564–1616) British dramatist, poet. King Henry, in *King Henry V*, act 4, sc. 3, l. 60–7 (1600).

Henry's speech before the battle of Agincourt.

24 Is it a bird? Is it a plane? No, it's SUPERMAN!

JOE SHUSTER, (b. 1914) Canadian–born U.S. cartoonist. Crowd, in *Superman* (cartoon, radio and TV series) (from June 1930).

Superman was first concocted by Siegel and Schuster as a prototype in a fanzine; re–launched in *Action Comics* June 1938, the character was adapted for radio in 1940, later appearing on TV and cinema screens. At the start of each radio and TV broadcast, a voiceover announced: "Faster than a speeding bullet! More powerful than a locomotive! Able to leap tall buildings at a single bound!... Strange visitor from another planet, who came to earth with powers and abilities far beyond those of mortal men. Superman! Who can change the course of mighty rivers, bend steel with his bare hands, and who ... fights a never ending battle for truth, justice and the American way!"

25   The opportunities for heroism are limited in this kind of world: the most people can do is sometimes not to be as weak as they've been at other times.

ANGUS WILSON, (1913–1991) British author. Interview in *Writers at Work*, First Series, ed. Malcolm Cowley (1958).

Hipness

1   Hip is the sophistication of the wise primitive in a giant jungle.

NORMAN MAILER, (b. 1923) U.S. author. *Advertisements for Myself*, sct. 3, "The White Negro" (1959). First published in *Dissent* (summer 1957).

Hippies

1   We are stardust,
We are golden,
And we got to get ourselves
Back to the garden.

JONI MITCHELL, (b. 1943) Canadian–born U.S. singer, songwriter. "Woodstock" (song) (1969).

Mitchell never actually appeared at The Woodstock Festival.

Historians

1   To give an accurate and exhaustive account of that period would need a far less brilliant pen than mine.

MAX BEERBOHM, (1872–1956) British essayist, caricaturist. *The Yellow Book*, vol. 4, "1880" (1895).

2   And hiving wisdom with each studious year,
In meditation dwelt, with learning wrought,
And shaped his weapon with an edge severe,
Sapping a solemn creed with solemn sneer.

GEORGE GORDON NOEL BYRON, 6TH BARON BYRON, (1788–1824) British poet. "Childe Harold's Pilgrimage, "cto. 3, st. 107 (1812–1818).

Referring to historian Edward Gibbon.

History

1   Histories make men wise; poets witty; the mathematics subtle; natural philosophy deep; moral grave; logic and rhetoric able to contend.

FRANCIS BACON, (1561–1626) British philosopher, essayist, statesman. *Essays*, "Of Studies" (1597–1625).

2   Happy is the nation without a history.

CESARE BECCARIA, (1735–1794) Italian jurist, philosopher. *On Crimes and Punishments*, Introduction (1764).

Thomas Carlyle attributes a similar utterance to Charles de Montesquieu, in *History of Frederick the Great* (1858–1865) bk. 16, ch. 1: "Happy the people whose annals are blank in history–books!"

3   History. An account, mostly false, of events, mostly unimportant, which are brought about by rulers, mostly knaves, and soldiers, mostly fools.

AMBROSE BIERCE, (1842–1914) U.S. author. *The Devil's Dictionary* (1881–1906), repr. in *Collected Works of Ambrose Bierce*, vol. 7 (1911).

4 That great dust-heap called "history."

AUGUSTINE BIRRELL, (1850–1933) British essayist, politician. "Carlyle," *Obiter Dicta*, first series (1884).

5 Universal history is the history of a few metaphors.

JORGE LUIS BORGES, (1899–1986) Argentinian author. "Pascal's Sphere," *Other Inquisitions* (1960), trans. (1964). (Essay first published 1951).

6 All true histories contain instruction; though, in some, the treasure may be hard to find, and when found, so trivial in quantity that the dry, shrivelled kernel scarcely compensates for the trouble of cracking the nut.

ANNE BRONTË (1820–1849) British novelist, poet. *Agnes Grey*, ch. 1 (1847).

Opening words.

7 Happy the people whose annals are vacant.

THOMAS CARLYLE, (1795–1881) Scottish essayist, historian. *History of the French Revolution*, vol. 1, bk. 2, ch. 1 (1837).

Quoting "a paradoxical philosopher" in reply to an aphorism of Montesquieu's, "Happy the people whose annals are tiresome."

8 History, a distillation of rumour.

THOMAS CARLYLE, (1795–1881) Scottish essayist, historian. *History of the French Revolution*, pt. 1, bk. 7, ch. 5 (1837).

9 Only the history of free peoples is worth our attention; the history of men under a despotism is merely a collection of anecdotes.

SÉBASTIEN–ROCH NICOLAS DE CHAMFORT, (1741–1794) French writer, wit. *Maxims and Considerations*, vol. 2, no. 487 (1796), trans. by E. Powys Mathers (1926).

10 A people without history

Is not redeemed from time, for history is a pattern
Of timeless moments.

T.S. (THOMAS STEARNS) ELIOT, (1888–1965) Anglo–American poet, critic. "Little Gidding," pt. 5, *Four Quartets* (1942).

11 Hegel remarks somewhere that all great, world–historical facts and personages occur, as it were, twice. He has forgotten to add: the first time as tragedy, the second as farce.

T.S. (THOMAS STEARNS) ELIOT, (1888–1965) Anglo–American poet, critic. "Little Gidding," pt. 5, *Four Quartets* (1942).

12 History ... is, indeed, little more than the register of the crimes, follies, and misfortunes of mankind.

EDWARD GIBBON, (1737–1794) British historian. *The Decline and Fall of the Roman Empire*, ch. 3 (1776–1788).

13 But what experience and history teach is this—that peoples and governments have never learned anything from history, or acted on principles deduced from it.

GEORG HEGEL, (1770–1831) German philosopher. *The Philosophy of History*, introduction (1837).

14 Hegel remarks somewhere that all great, world–historical facts and personages occur, as it were, twice. He has forgotten to add: the first time as tragedy, the second as farce.

KARL MARX, (1818–1883) German political theorist, social philosopher. *The Eighteenth Brumaire of Louis Bonaparte*, pt. 1 (1852), repr. in *Selected Works*, vol. 2 (1942).

This opening sentence of the essay is usually paraphrased, "History repeats itself, first as tragedy, second as farce."

15 Whosoever, in writing a modern history, shall follow truth too near

the heels, it may haply strike out his teeth.

SIR WALTER RALEIGH, (1552–1618) British author, soldier, explorer. *The History of the World*, preface (1614).

Ralegh's *History* was banned by James I soon after its publication, precisely because, it was alleged, Ralegh followed too closely the "heels of truth"—according to biographer Robert Lacey in *Sir Walter Ralegh*, ch. 41 (1973), Ralegh "took every opportunity he could in his book to pour scorn on famous sodomites, and James took the point."

16 The principal office of history I take to be this: to prevent virtuous actions from being forgotten, and that evil words and deeds should fear an infamous reputation with posterity.

TACITUS, (c. 55–c. 120) Roman historian. *The Histories*, bk. 3, sct. 65.

17 The one duty we owe to history is to rewrite it.

OSCAR WILDE, (1854–1900) Anglo–Irish playwright, author. Gilbert, in *The Critic as Artist*, pt. 1, *Intentions* (1891). Repr. in *Complete Works of Oscar Wilde*, ed. J.B. Foreman (1966).

Hitler, Adolf

1 Whatever may be the reason, whether it was that Hitler thought he might get away with what he had got without fighting for it, or whether it was that after all the preparations were not sufficiently complete—however, one thing is certain: he missed the bus.

NEVILLE CHAMBERLAIN, (1869–1940) British politician, prime minister. Quoted in *Times* (London, Apr. 5, 1940). Speech, Apr. 4, 1940, Central Hall, London.

2 If Hitler invaded hell I would make at least a favourable reference to the devil in the House of Commons.

WINSTON CHURCHILL, (1874–1965) British statesman, writer. *The Grand Alliance*, vol. 3, ch. 20, *The Second World War* (1950).

3 After fifteen years of work I have achieved, as a common German soldier and merely with my fanatical will–power, the unity of the German nation, and have freed it from the death sentence of Versailles.

ADOLF HITLER, (1889–1945) German dictator. *Proclamation (Dec. 21, 1941)*.

Addressing troops after taking over as commander–in–chief of the army.

Hobos

1 The hunchback in the park
A solitary mister
Propped between trees and water.

DYLAN THOMAS, (1914–1953) Welsh poet. "The Hunchback in the Park."

Holland and the Dutch

1 Where the broad ocean leans against the land.

OLIVER GOLDSMITH, (1728–1774) Anglo–Irish poet, essayist, playwright. "The Traveller," l. 284 (1764).

Hollywood and Writers

1 I went out there for a thousand a week, and I worked Monday, and I got fired Wednesday. The guy that hired me was out of town Tuesday.

NELSON ALGREN, (1909–1981) U.S. author. Interview in *Writers at Work*, First Series, ed. Malcolm Cowley (1958).

2 If my books had been any worse, I should not have been invited to

Hollywood, and ... if they had been any better, I should not have come.

RAYMOND CHANDLER, (1888–1959) U.S. author. *Raymond Chandler Speaking,* eds. Dorothy Gardiner and Katherine S. Walker (1962). Letter, Dec. 12, 1945, *Atlantic Monthly* (Boston).

To *Atlantic Monthly* editor, Charles W. Morton, responding to criticism of Chandler's article *Writers in Hollywood.*

Hollywood, California

1　Hollywood is a place where people from Iowa mistake each other for stars.

FRED ALLEN, (1894–1957) U.S. radio comic. Quoted in *No People Like Show People,* ch. 8, Maurice Zolotow (1951).

2　In Beverly Hills ... they don't throw their garbage away. They make it into television shows.

WOODY ALLEN, (b. 1935) U.S. filmmaker. Alvy Singer (Allen), in the film *Annie Hall* (1977). Repr. in *Four Films of Woody Allen* (1982).

3　Much more frequent in Hollywood than the emergence of Cinderella is her sudden vanishing. At our party, even in those glowing days, the clock was always striking twelve for someone at the height of greatness; and there was never a prince to fetch her back to the happy scene.

BEN HECHT, (1893–1964) U.S. journalist, author, screenwriter. "My Poverty Row," bk. 5, *A Child of the Century* (1954).

4　Strip away the phony tinsel of Hollywood and you find the real tinsel underneath.

OSCAR LEVANT, (1906–1972) U.S. pianist, composer. *Inquisition in Eden* (1965).

5　A trip through a sewer in a glass–bottomed boat.

WILSON MIZNER, (1876–1933) U.S. dramatist, wit. Quoted in *The Legendary Mizners,* ch. 4, Alva Johnson (1953).

Mizner's description of Hollywood was reworked by Mayor James J. Walker: "A reformer is a guy who rides through a sewer in a glass–bottomed boat." (Speech as mayor of New York, 1928).

6　Working for Warner Brothers is like fucking a porcupine: it's a hundred pricks against one.

WILSON MIZNER, (1876–1933) U.S. dramatist, wit. Quoted in *Bring on the Empty Horses,* "Degrees of Friendliness," David Niven (1975).

7　Hollywood's a place where they'll pay you a thousand dollars for a kiss, and fifty cents for your soul. I know, because I turned down the first offer often enough and held out for the fifty cents.

MARILYN MONROE, (1926–1962) U.S. screen actor. Quoted in *Marilyn Monroe In Her Own Words,* "Acting" (1990).

8　The lunatics have taken charge of the asylum.

RICHARD ROWLAND, *A Million and One Nights,* vol. 2, ch. 79, Terry Ramsaye (1926).

Remark in 1920, on the formation of United Artists film production company by D.W. Griffith, Mary Pickford, Douglas Fairbanks, and Charlie Chaplin.

Homeless, the

1　The foxes have holes, and the birds of the air have nests; but the Son of man hath not where to lay his head.

BIBLE: NEW TESTAMENT, Jesus, in *Matthew,* 8:20.

2　And meanwhile we have gone on living,
　Living and partly living,
　Picking together the pieces,

Gathering faggots at nightfall,
Building a partial shelter,
For sleeping and eating and drink-
ing and laughter.

T.S. (THOMAS STEARNS) ELIOT,
(1888–1965) Anglo–American poet, critic.
"The Chorus of Women of Canterbury," in
Murder in the Cathedral, pt. 1 (1935).

Homosexuality

1 I became one of the stately homos
of England.

QUENTIN CRISP, (b. 1908) British author.
Naked Civil Servant, ch. 24 (1968).

Parody of opening lines of Felicia Hemans's
poem, *The Homes of England*: "The stately
homes of England, How beautiful they
stand!"

2 I am the Love that dare not speak
its name.

LORD ALFRED DOUGLAS, (1870–1945)
British poet, lover of Oscar Wilde. "Two
Loves" (1896) quoted in H. Montgomery
Hyde, *Oscar Wilde*, ch. 6 (1976).

Concluding line of poem contributed by Douglas to the undergraduate magazine *The
Chameleon* (1896). During Oscar Wilde's first
trial for "indecent acts" (*Regina v. Wilde and
Taylor*, April 30, 1895), Wilde responded to
questioning about the meaning of these words
with a statement that provoked "a spontaneous outburst of applause from the public
gallery": "'The Love that dare not speak its
name' in this century is such a great affection
of an elder for a younger man as there was
between David and Jonathan, such as Plato
made the very basis of his philosophy, and
such as you find in the sonnets of Michelangelo and Shakespeare. It is that deep, spiritual
affection that is as pure as it is perfect.... It is
in this century misunderstood ... and on
account of it I am placed where I am now."

3 Understand that sexuality is as wide
as the sea. Understand that your
morality is not law. Understand
that we are you. Understand that if
we decide to have sex whether safe,
safer, or unsafe, it is our decision

and you have no rights in our lovemaking.

DEREK JARMAN, (1942–1994) British filmmaker, artist, author. "1940's," *At Your Own
Risk: A Saint's Testament* (1992).

4 There is probably no sensitive heterosexual alive who is not preoccupied with his latent homosexuality.

NORMAN MAILER, (b. 1923) U.S. author.
Advertisements for Myself, "The Homosexual
Villain" (1959).

5 I have heard some say ... that such
practices are allowed in France and
in other NATO countries. We are
not French, and we are not other
nationals. We are British, thank God!

**BERARD LAW, 1ST VISCOUNT MONT-
GOMERY OF ALAMEIN MONT-
GOMERY,** (1887–1976) British soldier.
Hansard, col. 648. Speech, May 26, 1965, to
House of Lords, debating Sexual Offences Bill.

6 And the wild regrets, and the
bloody sweats,
None knew so well as I:
For he who lives more lives than
one
More deaths than one must die.

OSCAR WILDE, (1854–1900) Anglo–Irish
playwright, author. "The Ballad of Reading
Gaol," pt. 3, st. 37 (1898). Repr. in *Complete
Works of Oscar Wilde*, ed. J.B. Foreman
(1966).

In 1895, Wilde was tried twice for "indecent
acts" and sentenced to two years' hard labor
in Reading Gaol. Almost universally
ostracised on his release, he spent the remaining three years of his life under an assumed
name in voluntary exile in Europe.

Honesty

1 A few honest men are better than
numbers.

OLIVER CROMWELL, (1599–1658) British
Parliamentarian general, Lord Protector of
England. Quoted in *Oliver Cromwell's Letters*

and Speeches, Thomas Carlyle, 2nd ed. (1846).
Letter, September 1643.

2   Go, and catch a falling star,
    Get with child a mandrake root,
    Tell me, where all past years are,
    Or who cleft the devil's foot,
    Teach me to her mermaids singing,
    Or to keep off envy's stinging,
    And find
    What wind
    Serves to advance an honest mind.

    JOHN DONNE, (c. 1572–1631) British
    divine, metaphysical poet. "Song: Go, and
    Catch a Falling Star," Songs and Sonnets
    (1633). Repr. in Complete Poetry and Selected
    Prose, ed. John Hayward (1929).

3   Honest men are the soft easy cush-
    ions on which knaves Repose and
    fatten.

    THOMAS OTWAY, (1652–1685) British
    dramatist. Pierre, in Venice Preserved, act 1, sc.
    1 (1682). Repr. in Works of Thomas Otway, ed.
    J.C. Ghosh (1932).

Honor

1   The louder he talked of his honor,
    the faster we counted our spoons.

    RALPH WALDO EMERSON, (1803–1882)
    U.S. essayist, poet, philosopher. The Conduct
    of Life, "Worship" (1870).

2   I could not love thee, Dear, so much,
    Loved I not honour more.

    RICHARD LOVELACE, (1618–1658) British
    poet. "To Lucasta, Going to the Wars," st. 3
    (1649). Repr. in Poems, ed. C.H. Wilkinson
    (1930).

Hope

1   Still nursing the unconquerable hope,
    Still clutching the inviolable shade.

    MATTHEW ARNOLD, (1822–1888) British
    poet, critic. "The Scholar–Gipsy," st. 22
    (1853).

2   Hope deferred maketh the heart
    sick: but when the desire cometh, it
    is a tree of life.

    BIBLE: HEBREW, Proverbs, 13:12.

3   But what is Hope? Nothing but the
    paint on the face of Existence; the
    least touch of truth rubs it off, and
    then we see what a hollow–cheeked
    harlot we have got hold of.

    **GEORGE GORDON NOEL BYRON, 6TH
    BARON BYRON,** (1788–1824) British poet.
    Byron's Letters and Journals, vol. 4, ed. Leslie
    Marchand (1975). Letter, Oct. 28, 1815, to the
    poet Thomas Moore.

4   "Hope" is the thing with feathers—
    That perches in the soul—
    And sings the tunes without the
        words—
    And never stops—at all—

    EMILY DICKINSON, (1830–1886) U.S.
    poet. "Hope is the Thing with Feathers," st. 1
    (written c. 1861, published 1891). Repr. in
    The Complete Poems, no. 254, Harvard vario-
    rum edition (1955).

5   The miserable have no other
        medicine
    But only hope.

    WILLIAM SHAKESPEARE, (1564–1616)
    British dramatist, poet. Claudio, in Measure
    for Measure, act 3, sc. 1, l. 2–3 (1623).

Horror

1   The horror! The horror!

    JOSEPH CONRAD, (1857–1924)
    Polish–born British novelist. Kurtz, in The
    Heart of Darkness, ch. 3 (1902).

    Kurtz's dying words.

2   Where there is no imagination there is no horror.

ARTHUR CONAN, SIR DOYLE, (1859–1930) British author. Sherlock Holmes, in *A Study in Scarlet*, ch. 5 (1887).

3   I am Dracula. And I bid you welcome.

BRAM STOKER, (1847–1912) British author. Count Dracula, in *Dracula*, ch. 2 (1897).

The line is remembered in the mouth of Bela Lugosi in the film *Dracula*, directed by Todd Browning, 1931.

Horses

1   They say princes learn no art truly, but the art of horsemanship. The reason is, the brave beast is no flatterer. He will throw a prince as soon as his groom.

BEN JONSON, (c. 1572–1637) British dramatist, poet. *Timber, or Discoveries Made upon Men and Matter*, para. 95, "Illiteratus Princeps" (1641), ed. Felix E. Schelling (1892).

The aphorism is attributed to the Greek philosopher Carneades by Montaigne (in *Essays*, bk. 3, ch. 7 "Of the Incommodity of Greatness," 1588): "Princes' children learnt nothing aright but to manage and ride horses; forsomuch as in all other exercises every man yieldeth and giveth them the victory; but a horse, who is neither a flatterer nor a courtier, will as soon throw the child of a king as the son of a base porter."

2   The horse, the horse! The symbol of surging potency and power of movement, of action, in man.

D.H. (DAVID HERBERT) LAWRENCE, (1885–1930) British author. *Apocalypse*, ch. 10 (1931).

3   A horse! A horse! My kingdom for a horse!

WILLIAM SHAKESPEARE, (1564–1616) British dramatist, poet. Richard, in *Richard III*, act 5, sc. 7, l. 7 and 13 (1597).

Richard's last words at the Battle of Bosworth.

Hostages

1   Hostage is a crucifying aloneness. It is a silent, screaming slide into the bowels of ultimate despair. Hostage is a man hanging by his fingernails over the edge of chaos, feeling his fingers slowly straightening. Hostage is the humiliating stripping away of every sense and fibre of body and mind and spirit that make us what we are. Hostage is a mutant creation filled with fear, self–loathing, guilt and death–wishing. But he is a man, a rare, unique and beautiful creation of which these things are no part.

BRIAN KEENAN, (b. 1950) Irish teacher, hostage in Lebanon. Quoted in *Independent* (London, Aug. 31, 1990). News conference, Aug. 30, 1990, Dublin.

On his 4½–year ordeal as a hostage.

Houses and Homes

1   Houses are built to live in, and not to look on: therefore let use be preferred before uniformity.

FRANCIS BACON, (1561–1626) British philosopher, essayist, statesman. *Essays*, "Of Building" (1597–1625).

Bacon adds, "except where both may be had."

2   You are a king by your own fireside, as much as any monarch in his throne.

MIGUEL DE CERVANTES, (1547–1616) Spanish author. *Don Quixote*, preface (1605), trans. by P. Motteux.

3   Many a man who thinks to found a home discovers that he has merely opened a tavern for his friends.

NORMAN DOUGLAS, (1868–1952) British author. Mr. Keith, in *South Wind*, ch. 24 (1917).

4 Home is the place where, when you have to go there,
They have to go to take you in.

ROBERT FROST, (1874–1963) U.S. poet. "Husband," in "The Death of the Hired Man," l. 118–9, *North of Boston* (1914).

"Wife" replies: "I should have called it Something you somehow haven't to deserve."

5 I want a house that has got over all its troubles; I don't want to spend the rest of my life bringing up a young and inexperienced house.

JEROME K. JEROME, (1859–1927) British author. *They and I,* ch. 11 (1909).

6 A house is a machine for living in.

LE CORBUSIER [CHARLE ...DOUARD JEANNE], (1887–1965) Swiss–born French architect. *Toward a New Architecture,* ch. 1, "Eyes Which Do Not See: Airplanes" (1923, trans. 1946).

7 If you want a golden rule that will fit everything, this is it: Have nothing in your houses that you do not know to be useful or believe to be beautiful.

WILLIAM MORRIS, (1834–1896) British artist, writer, printer. "The Decorative Arts: Their Relation to Modern Life and Progress," publ. as "The Lesser Arts" in *Hopes and Fears for Art* (1882). Lecture, 1877.

Morris's first public lecture.

Housework

1 The works of women are symbolical.
We sew, sew, prick our fingers, dull our sight,
Producing what? A pair of slippers, sir,
To put on when you're weary or a stool
To stumble over and vex you ...
"curse that stool!"

Or else at best, a cushion, where you lean
And sleep, and dream of something we are not,
But would be for your sake. Alas, alas!
This hurts most, this ... that, after all, we are paid
The worth of our work, perhaps.

ELIZABETH BARRETT BROWNING, (1806–1861) British poet. "Aurora Leigh," bk. 1, l. 456 (1857).

2 I make no secret of the fact that I would rather lie on a sofa than sweep beneath it. But you have to be efficient if you're going to be lazy.

SHIRLEY CONRAN, (b. 1932) British designer, journalist. "The Reason Why," *Superwoman* (1975).

3 The labor of women in the house, certainly, enables men to produce more wealth than they otherwise could; and in this way women are economic factors in society. But so are horses.

CHARLOTTE PERKINS GILMAN, (1860–1935) U.S. feminist, writer. *Women and Economics,* ch. 1 (1898).

Human Nature

1 There is a great deal of human nature in man.

CHARLES KINGSLEY, (1819–1875) British author, clergyman. *At Last,* ch. 2 (1872).

Quoting the words of "the wise Yankee."

2 His life was gentle, and the elements
So mixed in him that nature might stand up
And say to all the world "This was a man."

WILLIAM SHAKESPEARE, (1564–1616)
British dramatist, poet. Antony, in *Julius Cae-sar*, act 5, sc. 5, l. 72–4 (1623).

Referring to Brutus. Antony bases the end of his panegyric on the Platonic notion that the four natural elements (earth, air, fire and water) are represented in man.

Human Rights

1   We hold these truths to be self–evi-dent, that all men are created equal, that they are endowed by their Cre-ator with certain unalienable rights, that among these are life, liberty, and the pursuit of happiness. That to secure these rights, governments are instituted among men, deriving their just powers from the consent of the governed. That whenever any form of government becomes destructive of these ends, it is the right of the people to alter or to abolish it, and to institute new gov-ernment, laying its foundation on such principles and organizing its powers in such form, as to them shall seem most likely to effect their safety and happiness.

THOMAS JEFFERSON, (1743–1826) U.S. president. *American Declaration of Indepen-dence* (1776) published in *The Papers of Thomas Jefferson*, vol. 1, ed. Julian P. Boyd (1950).

It is unknown how much of these lines was Jefferson's sole responsibility. In June 1776 he had composed a rough draft: "We hold these truths to be sacred and undeniable; that all men are created equal and independent, that from that equal creation they derive rights inherent and inalienable, among which are the preservation of life, and liberty, and the pursuit of happiness."

Humankind

1   I love men, not for what unites them, but for what divides them, and I want to know most of all what gnaws at their hearts.

GUILLAUME APOLLINAIRE, (1880–1918) Italian–born French poet, critic. *Anecdotiques* (1926). *Mercure de France* (Paris) no. 33 (April 1, 1911).

2   Drinking when we are not thirsty and making love at any time, madam, is all that distinguishes us from the other animals.

PIERRE DE BEAUMARCHAIS, (1732–1799) French dramatist. Antonio, in *Le Mariage de Figaro*, act 2, sc. 21 (1784).

3   When I consider thy heavens, the work of thy fingers, the moon and the stars, which thou hast ordained; what is man, that thou art mindful of him? and the son of man, that thou visitest him? For thou hast made him a little lower than the angels, and hast crowned him with glory and honour.

BIBLE: HEBREW, *Psalms*, 8:2.

"Man was kreated a little lower than the angells and has bin gittin a little lower ever sinse." (*Josh Billings, His Sayings*, ch. 28, 1865).

4   Ye shall be as gods, knowing good and evil.

BIBLE: HEBREW, *Genesis*, 3:5.The serpent's temptation, spoken to Eve.

5   Cruelty has a Human Heart, And jealousy a Human Face; Terror the Human Form Divine, And secrecy the Human Dress.

WILLIAM BLAKE, (1757–1827) British poet, painter, engraver. *Songs of Experience*, "A Divine Image," (1794), repr. in *Complete Writ-ings*, ed. Geoffrey Keynes (1957).

This poem, etched on a copper plate in his usual manner, does not appear in any copy of the *Songs of Experience*, and so was probably rejected by him.

6   Humanity i love you because

when you're hard up you pawn your intelligence to buy a drink

E.E. (EDWARD ESTLIN) CUMMINGS, (1894–1962) U.S. poet. "La Guerre no.2," *XLI Poems* (1925).

7 Consider your breed; you were not made to live like beasts, but to follow virtue and knowledge.

DANTE ALIGHIERI, (1265–1321) Italian poet. Ulysses, in *The Divine Comedy*, "Inferno," cto. 18, l. 118–20 (1321).

Urging his companions to a journey that would prove disastrous.

8 Man with all his noble qualities, with sympathy which feels for the most debased, with benevolence which extends not only to other men but to the humblest living creature, with his god–like intellect which has penetrated into the movements and constitution of the solar system—with all these exalted powers—man still bears in his bodily frame the indelible stamp of his lowly origin.

CHARLES DARWIN, (1809–1882) British naturalist. *The Descent of Man*, ch. 21 (1871).

Closing words of book.

9 What is man, when you come to think upon him, but a minutely set, ingenious machine for turning, with infinite artfulness, the red wine of Shiraz into urine?

ISAK DINESEN [KAREN BLIXEN], (1885–1962) Danish author. *Seven Gothic Tales*, "The Dreamers" (1934).

10 Man is more interesting than men. God made *him* and not them in his image. Each one is more precious than all.

ANDRÉ GIDE, (1869–1951) French author. "Literature and Ethics," journal entry, 1901, *Journals 1889–1949*, ed. Justin O'Brien (1951).

11 Man cannot live on the human plane, he must be either above or below it.

ERIC GILL, (1882–1940) British sculptor, engraver, writer, typographer. *Autobiography*, "Conclusion" (1944).

12 Man ... knows only when he is satisfied and when he suffers, and only his sufferings and his satisfactions instruct him concerning himself, teach him what to seek and what to avoid. For the rest, man is a confused creature; he knows not whence he comes or whither he goes, he knows little of the world, and above all, he knows little of himself.

JOHANN WOLFGANG VON GOETHE, (1749–1832) German poet, dramatist. Quoted in *Conversations with Goethe*, entry, April 10, 1829, Johann Peter Eckermann (1836).

13 The only thing that separates us from the animals is our ability to accessorize.

ROBERT HARLING, U.S. writer. Clairee Belcher (Olympia Dukakis), in *Steel Magnolias* (film) (1989).

14 Man is the only animal that laughs and weeps; for he is the only animal that is struck with the difference between what things are and what they ought to be.

WILLIAM HAZLITT, (1778–1830) British essayist. *Lectures on the English Comic Writers*, Lecture 1 (1819).

This passage was copied and inserted in the notebooks of Adlai Stevenson.

15 Out of timber so crooked as that from which man is made nothing entirely straight can be carved.

IMMANUEL KANT, (1724–1804) German philosopher. *Idee zu einer Allgemeinen Gesichte in Weltburgerlicher Absicht*, proposition 6 (1784).

Quoted by Isaiah Berlin as epigraph to *The Crooked Timber of Humanity* (1990).

16 Ah! what is man? Wherefore does he why? Whence did he whence? Whither is he withering?

DAN LENO, (1860–1904) British comedian. *Dan Leno Hys Booke*, ch. 1 (1901).

17 Every man bears the whole stamp of the human condition.

MICHEL DE MONTAIGNE, (1533–1592) French essayist. *Essays*, bk. 3, ch. 1 (1588).

18 *I teach you the Superman [‹bermensch]. Man is something that should be overcome.*

FRIEDRICH NIETZSCHE, (1844–1900) German philosopher. *Thus Spoke Zarathustra*, pt. 1, "Zarathustra's Prologue," sct. 3 (1883–1892).

19 Man is the only one that knows nothing, that can learn nothing without being taught. He can neither speak nor walk nor eat, and in short he can do nothing at the prompting of nature only, but weep.

PLINY THE ELDER, (23–79) Roman scholar. *Natural History*, bk. 7, sct. 4.

20 Know then thyself, presume not to God to scan;
The proper study of Mankind is Man.
Plac'd on this isthmus of a middle state,
A being darkly wise, and rudely great.

ALEXANDER POPE, (1688–1744) British satirical poet. "An Essay on Man," epistle 2, l. 1–4 (1733).

For an earlier version of this view, see Charron's comment under "social sciences."

21 Man is a useless passion.

JEAN–PAUL SARTRE, (1905–1980) French philosopher, author. *Being and Nothingness*, "Doing and Having," sct. 3 (1943).

22 All the world's a stage,
And all the men and women merely players.
They have their exits and their entrances,
And one man in his time plays many parts,
His acts being seven ages. At first the infant,
Mewling and puking in the nurse's arms.
Then the whining schoolboy, with his satchel
And shining morning face, creeping like snail
Unwillingly to school. And then the lover,
Sighing like furnace, with a woeful ballad
Made to his mistress' eyebrow. Then, a soldier,
Full of strange oaths, and bearded like the pard,
Jealous in honour, sudden, and quick in quarrel,
Seeking the bubble reputation
Even in the cannon's mouth. And then the justice,
In fair round belly with good capon lined,
With eyes severe and beard of formal cut,
Full of wise saws and modern instances;
And so he plays his part. The sixth age shifts
Into the lean and slippered pantaloon,
With spectacles on nose and pouch on side,
His youthful hose, well saved, a world too wide
For his shrunk shank, and his big, manly voice,
Turning again toward childish treble, pipes

And whistles in his sound. Last
  scene of all,
That ends this strange, eventful
  history,
Is second childishness and mere
  oblivion,
Sans teeth, sans eyes, sans taste,
  sans everything.

WILLIAM SHAKESPEARE, (1564–1616)
British dramatist, poet. Jaques, in *As You Like
It*, act 2, sc. 7, l. 139–66 (1623).

23 What a piece of work is a man!
How noble in reason, how infinite
in faculty, in form and moving how
express and admirable, in action
how like an angel, in apprehension
how like a god—the beauty of the
world, the paragon of animals!

WILLIAM SHAKESPEARE, (1564–1616)
British dramatist, poet. Hamlet, in *Hamlet*, act
2, sc. 2, l. 304–8 (1604).

"And yet to me," Hamlet adds, "what is this
quintessence of dust?" The passage was set to
music in the 1968 stage show *Hair*.

24 The whole race is a poet that writes
down The eccentric propositions of
its fate.

WALLACE STEVENS, 1879–1955 U.S.
poet. "Men Made Out of Words," *Transport to
Summer* (1947).

Concluding lines.

25 We're all of us guinea pigs in the
laboratory of God. Humanity is just
a work in progress.

TENNESSEE WILLIAMS, (1914–1983)
U.S. dramatist. The Gipsy, in *Camino Real*,
Block 12 (1953).

Humility

1 And the Devil did grin, for his
  darling sin
Is pride that apes humility.

SAMUEL TAYLOR COLERIDGE,
(1772–1834) British poet, critic. "The Devil's
Thoughts" (1799–1827), repr. in *Poetical
Works*, ed. James Dyke Campbell (1893).

2 We are so very 'umble.

CHARLES DICKENS, (1812–1870) British
novelist. Uriah Heep, in *David Copperfield*,
ch. 17 (1849–1850).

Humor

1 Mirth is like a flash of lightning,
that breaks through a gloom of
clouds, and glitters for a moment;
cheerfulness keeps up a kind of
daylight in the mind, and fills it
with a steady and perpetual
serenity.

JOSEPH ADDISON, (1672–1719) British
essayist. *Spectator* (London, May 17, 1712),
no. 381, *The Spectator*, ed. D.F. Bond (1965).

2 Among those whom I like or
admire, I can find no common
denominator, but among those
whom I love, I can: all of them
make me laugh.

W.H. (WYSTAN HUGH) AUDEN,
(1907–1973) Anglo–U.S. poet. *The Dyer's
Hand*, pt. 7, "Notes on the Comic" (1962).

3 All my humor is based upon
destruction and despair. If the
whole world were tranquil, without
disease and violence, I'd be standing on the breadline right in back of
J. Edgar Hoover.

LENNY BRUCE, (1925–1966) U.S. satirical
comedian. *The Essential Lenny Bruce*, "Performing and the Art of Comedy," ed. John
Cohen (1967).

The passage also appears as the book's epigraph.

4 A difference of tastes in jokes is a
great strain on the affections.

GEORGE ELIOT [MARY ANN (OR MARIAN) EVANS], (1819–1880) British novelist. *Daniel Deronda*, bk. 2, ch. 15 (1874–1876).

5   Good taste and humour are a contradiction in terms, like a chaste whore.

MALCOLM MUGGERIDGE, (1903–1990) British journalist. Quoted in *Time* (New York, Sept. 14, 1953).

Defending his editorship of the humorous magazine *Punch*.

6   Humor is emotional chaos remembered in tranquility.

JAMES THURBER, (1894–1961) U.S. humorist, illustrator. Max Eastman in *Enjoyment of Laughter* (1936) records the earlier remark by Thurber: "Humor is a kind of emotional chaos told about calmly and quietly in retrospect. There is always a laugh in the utterly familiar."

Hunger

1   A dog starved at his master's gate
Predicts the ruin of the state.

WILLIAM BLAKE, (1757–1827) British poet, painter, engraver. "Auguries of Innocence," l. 9–10, *Poems from the Pickering Manuscript* (c. 1803), repr. in *Complete Writings*, ed. Geoffrey Keynes (1957).

2   There's no sauce in the world like hunger.

MIGUEL DE CERVANTES, (1547–1616) Spanish author. Teresa Panza (Sancho's wife), in *Don Quixote*, pt. 2, ch. 5 (1615), trans. by P. Motteux.

This well–worn proverb was attributed to Socrates by Cicero in *De Finibus*, bk. 2, sct. 90.

3   Please, sir, I want some more.

CHARLES DICKENS, (1812–1870) British novelist. Oliver, in *Oliver Twist*, ch. 2 (1838).

Oliver, suffering from slow starvation in the workhouse, asks for more food.

4   A hungry man is not a free man.

ADLAI STEVENSON, (1900–1965) U.S. Democratic politician. "Farm Policy," *The Speeches of Adlai Stevenson* (1952). Speech, Sept. 6, 1952, Kasson, Minnesota.

5   In the Lord's Prayer, the first petition is for daily bread. No one can worship God or love his neighbor on an empty stomach.

WOODROW WILSON, (1856–1924) U.S. Democratic politician, president. Speech, May 23, 1912, New York City.

Hunting

1   Each outcry of the hunted hare
A fibre from the brain does tear.

WILLIAM BLAKE, (1757–1827) British poet, painter, engraver. "Auguries of Innocence," l. 13–14, Keynes (1957).

2   There is a passion *for hunting something* deeply implanted in the human breast.

CHARLES DICKENS, (1812–1870) British novelist. *Oliver Twist*, ch. 10 (1838).

Referring to chasing pickpockets.

3   It is very strange, and very melancholy, that the paucity of human pleasures should persuade us ever to call hunting one of them.

SAMUEL JOHNSON, (1709–1784) British author, lexicographer. Quoted in *Anecdotes of Samuel Johnson* (1786). Repr. in *Johnsonian Miscellanies*, vol. 1, p. 288, ed. George Birkbeck Hill (1897).

4   One knows so well the popular idea of health. The English country gentleman galloping after a fox—the unspeakable in full pursuit of the uneatable.

OSCAR WILDE, (1854–1900) Anglo–Irish playwright, author. Lord Illingworth, in *A Woman of No Importance*, act 1 (1893).

Husbands

1 Every man who is high up likes to think he has done it all himself; and the wife smiles, and lets it go at that. It's our only joke. Every woman knows that.

J.M. (JAMES MATTHEW) BARRIE, (1860–1937) British playwright. Maggie Shand, in *What Every Woman Knows*, act 4 (performed 1908, published 1918).

2 Husbands, love your wives, and be not bitter against them.

BIBLE: NEW TESTAMENT, St. Paul, in *Colossians*, 3:19.

3 I *N* take thee *M* to my wedded husband, to have and to hold from this day forward, for better for worse, for richer for poorer, in sickness and in health, to love, cherish, and to obey, till death us do part, according to God's holy ordinance; and thereto I give thee my troth.

BOOK OF COMMON PRAYER, THE, *Solemnization of Matrimony,* "Betrothal" (1662).

"N" and "M" refer to "name" and "names" respectively, standing for the Latin *nomen* and *nomina* (rendered as "M," for two "N's" contracted). In general practise, the man promises only "to love and to cherish" his wife and uses the words "I plight thee my troth."

4 You—poor and obscure, and small and plain as you are—I entreat to accept me as a husband.

CHARLOTTE BRONTË (1816–1855) British novelist. Mr. Rochester, in *Jane Eyre*, ch. 23 (1847).

Mr. Rochester's first proposal to Jane.

5 I revere the memory of Mr. F. as an estimable man and most indulgent husband, only necessary to mention Asparagus and it appeared or to hint at any little delicate thing to

drink and it came like magic in a pint bottle; it was not ecstasy but it was comfort.

CHARLES DICKENS, (1812–1870) British novelist. Flora Finching, in *Little Dorrit*, bk. 1, ch. 24 (1857).

6 A good husband makes a good wife.

JOHN FLORIO, (c. 1553–1625) British author, translator. Silvestro, in *Second Frutes*, ch. 12 (1591).

The adage is also found in Robert Burton *Anatomy of Melancholy*, pt. 3, sct. 3 (1621).

7 Those men are most apt to be obsequious and conciliating abroad, who are under the discipline of shrews at home.

WASHINGTON IRVING, (1783–1859) U.S. author. *The Sketch Book of Geoffrey Crayon, Gent.* "Rip Van Winkle" (1819–1820).

8 A little in drink, but at all times your faithful husband.

RICHARD STEELE, (1672–1729) British dramatist, essayist, editor. *The Correspondence of Sir Richard Steele*, ed. R. Blanchard (1941). Midnight letter to his wife, Sept. 27, 1708.

9 In marriage, a man becomes slack and selfish, and undergoes a fatty degeneration of his moral being.

ROBERT LOUIS STEVENSON, (1850–1894) Scottish novelist, essayist, poet. *Virginibus Puerisque*, "Virginibus Puerisque" sct. 1 (1881).

Hygiene

1 Bathe twice a day to be really clean, once a day to be passably clean, once a week to avoid being a public menace.

ANTHONY BURGESS, (1917–1993) British author, critic. *Inside Mr. Enderby*, ch. 2, sct.1 (1963).

"Grim apothegm" quoted from a women's magazine.

Hypocrisy

1   The smylere with the knyf under the cloke.

GEOFFREY CHAUCER, (1340–1400) British poet. *The Canterbury Tales*, "The Knight's Tale," l. 1999 (c. 1387–1400), repr. in *The Works of Geoffrey Chaucer*, ed. Alfred W. Pollard, et al. (1898).

2   With affection beaming in one eye, and calculation shining out of the other.

CHARLES DICKENS, (1812–1870) British novelist. *Martin Chuzzlewit*, ch. 8 (1844).

Referring to Mrs. Todgers.

3   An open foe may pove a curse, But a pretended friend is worse.

JOHN GAY, (1685–1732)

British dramatist, poet. "The Shepherd's Dog and the Wolf," pt. 1, l. 33–4, *Fables* (1727).

4   A favourite has no friend!

THOMAS GRAY, (1716–1771) British poet. "Ode on the Death of a Favourite Cat," st. 6 (1748). Repr. in *Poetical Works*, ed. J. Rogers (1953).

5   No man is a hypocrite in his pleasures.

SAMUEL JOHNSON, (1709–1784) British author, lexicographer. Quoted in James Boswell, *Life of Dr. Johnson*, entry, June 19, 1784 (1791).

6   Hypocrisy is a tribute that vice pays to virtue.

FRANÇOIS LA ROCHEFOUCAULD, DUC DE, (1613–1680) French writer, moralist. *Sentences et Maximes Morales*, no. 218 (1678).

7   Hypocrisy is the most difficult and nerve-racking vice that any man can pursue; it needs an unceasing vigilance and a rare detachment of spirit. It cannot, like adultery or gluttony, be practised at spare moments; it is a whole-time job.

W. SOMERSET MAUGHAM, (1874–1966) British author. *Cakes and Ale*, ch. 1 (1930).

8   For neither man nor angel can discern
Hypocrisy, the only evil that walks Invisible, except to God alone.

JOHN MILTON, (1608–1674) British poet. *Paradise Lost*, bk. 3, l. 682–4 (1667).

9   His honour rooted in dishonour sto,
And faith unfaithful kept him falsely true.

ALFRED TENNYSON, 1ST BARON TENNYSON, (1809–1892) British poet. *Idylls of the King*, "Lancelot and Elaine," l. 871 (1859–1885).

Referring to Lancelot.

Idealism

1   Idealism is the despot of thought, just as politics is the despot of will.

MIKHAIL BAKUNIN, (1814–1876) Russian political theorist. *A Circular Letter to my Friends in Italy* (1871).

2   Ah, but a man's reach should exceed his grasp,
Or what's a heaven for?

ROBERT BROWNING, (1812–1889) British poet. "Andrea del Sarto," l. 97–8, *Men and Women*, vol. 2 (1855).

3   It's really a wonder that I haven't dropped all my ideals because they seem so absurd and impossible to carry out. Yet, I keep them, because in spite of everything I still believe that people are really good at heart.

on a foundation consisting of confusion, misery, and death. I see the world gradually being turned into a wilderness, I hear the ever–approaching thunder, which will destroy us too, I can feel the sufferings of millions and yet, if I look up into the heavens, I think that it will all come right, that this cruelty too will end, and that peace and tranquility will return again.

ANNE FRANK, (1929–1945) German Jewish refugee, diarist. *The Diary of a Young Girl* (1947, trans. 1952). Journal entry, July 15, 1944.

On Aug. 4, 1944, Anne along with the other occupants of the secret annex in which they had been hiding were arrested by the Nazis and sent to concentration camps in Germany.

4 We for a certainty are not the first
Have sat in taverns while the tempest hurled
Their hopeful plans to emptiness, and cursed
Whatever brute and blackguard made the world.

A.E. (ALFRED EDWARD) HOUSMAN, (1859–1936) British poet, classical scholar. *Last Poems*, no. 9 (1922).

5 Some day the soft Ideal that we wooed
Confronts us fiercely, foe–beset, pursued,
And cries reproachful: "Was it then my praise,
And not myself was loved? Prove now thy truth;
I claim of thee the promise of thy youth."

JAMES RUSSELL LOWELL, (1819–1891) U.S. poet, editor." Ode Recited at the Harvard Commemoration (Commemoration Ode)," l. 130–4 (1865). Repr. in *Poetical Works of James Russell Lowell* (1978).

6 Sad that our finest aspiration
Our freshest dreams and meditations,

In swift succession should decay,
Like Autumn leaves that rot away.

ALEXANDER PUSHKIN, (1799–1837) Russian poet. *Eugene Onegin*, ch. 8, st. 10 (1831), trans. by Oliver Elton (1943).

7 Saddle your dreams afore you ride 'em.

MARY WEBB, (1881–1927) British author. *Precious Bane*, bk. 1, ch. 6 (1924).

8 We are all in the gutter, but some of us are looking at the stars.

OSCAR WILDE, (1854–1900) Anglo–Irish playwright, author. Lord Darlington, in *Lady Windermere's Fan*, act 3 (1893).

Ideas

1 One of the greatest pains to human nature is the pain of a new idea.

WALTER BAGEHOT, (1826–1877) British economist, critic. *Physics and Politics*, ch. 5 (1872).

2 Such as take lodgings in a head
That's to be let unfurnished.

SAMUEL BUTLER, (1612–1680) British poet." Hudibras," pt. 1, cto. 1, l. 159–160 (1663). Eds. John Wilders and Hugh de Quehen (1973).

3 My ideas are my whores.

DENIS DIDEROT, (1713–1784) French philosopher. *Rameau's Nephew* (written 1762, published 1821). Repr. in *Selected Writings*, ed. Lester G. Crocker (1966).

Admission by the interlocutor (*Moi*), to the amoral figure of Rameau's nephew (*Lui*).

4 No idea is so antiquated that it was not once modern. No idea is so modern that it will not someday be antiquated.

ELLEN GLASGOW, (1874–1945) U.S. novelist. *The Quotable Woman*, ed. Elaine Partnow (1982). Address, 1936, to the Modern Language Association.

5 An invasion of armies can be resisted, but not the invasion of ideas.

VICTOR HUGO, (1802–1885) French poet, dramatist, novelist. *Histoire d'un Crime*, conclusion (written 1852, published 1877).

6 Ideas that enter the mind under fire remain there securely and for ever.

LEON TROTSKY, (1879–1940) Russian revolutionary. *My Life*, ch. 35 (1930).

7 Say it! No ideas but in things.

WILLIAM CARLOS WILLIAMS, (1883–1963) U.S. poet. *Paterson*, bk. 1, "The Delineaments of the Giants,: sct. 1 (1946, rev. 1963). Repr. in *Collected Earlier Poems* (1966).

Identity

1 *I* is another.

ARTHUR RIMBAUD, (1854–1891) French poet. *Collected Poems*, ed. Oliver Bernard (1962). Letter, May 13, 1871.

Idleness

1 Idleness is an appendix to nobility.

ROBERT BURTON, (1577–1640) British clergyman, author. *The Anatomy of Melancholy*, pt. 1, sct. 2, memb. 2, subsct. 6 (1621).

2 It is impossible to enjoy idling thoroughly unless one has plenty of work to do. There is no fun in doing nothing when you have nothing to do. Wasting time is merely an occupation then, and a most exhausting one. Idleness, like kisses, to be sweet must be stolen.

JEROME K. JEROME, (1859–1927) British author. "On Being Idle," *Idle Thoughts of an Idle Fellow* (1889).

3 Perhaps man is the only being that can properly be called idle.

SAMUEL JOHNSON, (1709–1784) British author, lexicographer. *The Idler*, no. 1, *Universal Chronicle* (London, April 15, 1758). Repr. in *Works of Samuel Johnson,* Yale Edition, vol. 2, eds. W.J. Bate, John M. Bullitt and L.F. Powell (1963).

"As peace is the end of war," Johnson wrote, "so to be idle is the ultimate purpose of the busy."

4 They shift coffee–houses and chocolate–houses from hour to hour, to get over the insupportable labour of doing nothing.

RICHARD STEELE, (1672–1729) British dramatist, essayist, editor. *Spectator* (London, Sept. 9, 1712), no. 479, *The Spectator*, ed. D.F. Bond (1965).

Last words of article, referring to "loungers ... satisfied with being merely part of the number of mankind, without distinguishing themselves from amongst them."

5 It is better to have loafed and lost than never to have loafed at all.

JAMES THURBER, (1894–1961) U.S. humorist, illustrator. "The Courtship of Arthur and Al," *Fables for our Time* (1940).

6 For Satan finds some mischief still For idle hands to do.

ISAAC WATTS, (1674–1748) British hymn–writer. "Against Idleness and Mischief," st. 3, *Divine Songs for Children* (1715).

A similar thought was expressed in one of the *Scottish Proverbs* collected by John Ray in 1719; variations of the saying have been traced back as far as St Jerome (c. 342–420).

Ignorance

1 Ignorance is an evil weed, which dictators may cultivate among their dupes, but which no democracy can afford among its citizens.

WILLIAM BEVERIDGE, (1879–1963) British economist. *Full Employment in a Free Society*, pt. 4 (1944).

2 Ignorance is not innocence but sin.

ROBERT BROWNING, (1812–1889) British poet. *The Inn Album*, cto. 5 (1875).

3 Where ignorance is bliss,
'Tis folly to be wise.

THOMAS GRAY, (1716–1771) British poet. *Ode on a Distant Prospect of Eton College*, l. 99–100 (written 1742, published 1747). Repr. in *Poetical Works*, ed. J. Rogers (1953).

Last lines.

4 Nothing in all the world is more dangerous than sincere ignorance and conscientious stupidity.

MARTIN LUTHER KING, JR., (1929–1968) U.S. clergyman, civil rights leader. *Strength to Love*, ch. 4, sct. 3 (1963).

5 Better be ignorant of a matter than half know it.

PUBLILIUS SYRUS, (1st century B.C.) Roman writer of mimes. *Sententiae*, no. 865.

6 One's ignorance is one's chief asset.

WALLACE STEVENS, (1879–1955) U.S. poet. *Opus Posthumous*, "Adagia," (1959).

Illegitimacy

1 There are no illegitimate children, only illegitimate parents—if the term is to be used at all.

BERNADETTE DEVLIN MCALISKEY, (b. 1947) Northern Irish politician. Reported in *Irish Times* (Dublin, July 31, 1971).

The words are not original: the lawyer L. ;on Yankwich said the same during a hearing at the State District Court, Southern District of California, in June 1928; and he was quoting the journalist O.O. McIntyre.

Illness and Convalescence

1 "Healing,"
Papa would tell me,
"is not a science,

but the intuitive art
of wooing Nature."

W.H. (WYSTAN HUGH) AUDEN, (1907–1973) Anglo–American poet. "The Art of Healing," *Collected Poems* (1976).

2 Illness is the night–side of life, a more onerous citizenship. Everyone who is born holds dual citizenship, in the kingdom of the well and in the kingdom of the sick. Although we all prefer to use only the good passport, sooner or later each of us is obliged, at least for a spell, to identify ourselves as citizens of that other place.

SUSAN SONTAG, (b. 1933)U.S. essayist. *Illness As Metaphor*, preface (1978).

Opening words.

Illusion

1 The Good of man is the active exercise of his soul's faculties in conformity with excellence or virtue.... Moreover this activity must occupy a complete lifetime; for one swallow does not make spring, nor does one fine day; and similarly one day or a brief period of happiness does not make a man supremely blessed and happy.

ARISTOTLE, (384–322 B.C.) Greek philosopher. *Nicomachean Ethics*, bk. 1, ch. 7, sct. 1098a.

The words "One swallow does not make a summer" also appear as the title of Aesop's Fable no. 190.

2 Is this a dagger which I see before me,
The handle toward my hand?
Come, let me clutch thee.
I have thee not, and yet I see thee still.

Art thou not, fatal vision, sensible
To feeling as to sight? Or art thou
   but
A dagger of the mind, a false creation
Proceeding from the
   heat–oppress'd brain?

WILLIAM SHAKESPEARE, (1564–1616)
British dramatist, poet. Macbeth, in *Macbeth*,
act 2, sc. 1, l. 33–39 (1623).

Soliloquy preceding the murder of Duncan.

3   Were such things here as we do
      speak about,
    Or have we eaten on the insane
      root
    That takes the reason prisoner?

WILLIAM SHAKESPEARE, (1564–1616)
British dramatist, poet. Banquo, in *Macbeth*,
act 1, sc. 3, l. 81–3 (1623).

Addressing Macbeth, referring to the Witches
which have just vanished.

Image

1   Isn't life a series of images that
    change as they repeat themselves?

ANDY WARHOL, (c. 1928–1987) U.S. pop
artist. Quoted in *Warhol*, "Too Much Work
1980–84," Victor Bokris (1989).

Imagination

1   Only in men's imagination does
    every truth find an effective and
    undeniable existence. Imagination,
    not invention, is the supreme mas-
    ter of art as of life.

JOSEPH CONRAD, (1857–1924) Polish–born
British novelist. *A Personal Record*, ch. 1
(1912).

2   Imagination has seized power.
    [L'imagination prend le pouvoir.]

GRAFFITO, *Paris '68*, ch. 2, Marc Rohan
(1988).

3   His imagination resembled the
    wings of an ostrich. It enabled him
    to run, though not to soar.

THOMAS BABINGTON MACAULAY,
(1800–1859) British historian, Whig politician.
"John Dryden," *Edinburgh Review* (Jan. 1828).
Miscellaneous Writings of Lord Macaulay, ed.
T.F. Ellis (1860).

Referring to Dryden.

4   The great instrument of moral
    good is the imagination.

PERCY BYSSHE SHELLEY, (1792–1822)
British poet. *A Defence of Poetry* (written
1821, published 1840).

This axiom constituted the cornerstone of
Shelley's philosophy.

5   To regard the imagination as meta-
    physics is to think of it as part of
    life, and to think of it as part of life
    is to realize the extent of artifice.
    We live in the mind.

WALLACE STEVENS, (1879–1955) U.S.
poet. "Imagination as Value," lecture, 1948,
The Necessary Angel (1951). (Originally published 1949).

Imitation

1   When people are free to do as they
    please, they usually imitate each
    other.

ERIC HOFFER, (1902–1983) U.S. philosopher. *The Passionate State of Mind*, aph. 33
(1955).

Hoffer adds, "A society which gives unlimited
freedom to the individual, more often than not
attains a disconcerting sameness. On the other
hand, where communal discipline is strict but
not ruthless ... originality is likely to thrive."

2   To do the opposite of something is
    also a form of imitation, namely an
    imitation of its opposite.

GEORG CHRISTOPH LICHTENBERG,
(1742–1799) German physicist, philosopher.
"Notebook D," aph. 96, *Aphorisms* (written
1765–1799), trans. by R.J. Hollingdale (1990).

3　Artistic genius is an expansion of monkey imitativeness.

W. WINWOOD READE, (1838–1875) British traveler, author. *The Martyrdom of Man,* ch. 3 (1872).

Immigration and Immigrants

1　"Keep, ancient lands, your storied pomp!" cries she With silent lips. "Give me your tired, your poor, Your huddled masses yearning to breathe free, The wretched refuse of your teeming shore. Send these, the homeless, tempest–tossed, to me; I lift my lamp beside the golden door."

EMMA LAZARUS, (1849–1887) U.S. poet. "The New Colossus" (1883). Repr. in *Selection from her Poetry and Prose.*

Written for inscription on the Statue of Liberty.

2　It is like watching a nation busily engaged in heaping up its own funeral pyre.... As I look ahead, I am filled with foreboding. Like the Roman, I seem to see "the River Tiber foaming with much blood."

J. ENOCH POWELL, (b. 1912) British Conservative politician. Quoted in *Observer* (London, April 21, 1968). Speech, April 20, 1968, to West Midlands Conservatives, Birmingham.

The day after making this notorious warning on the consequences of large–scale immigration into Britain from Commonwealth countries, Powell was dropped from the Shadow Cabinet. According to *Brewer's Quotations* (Nigel Rees, 1994), Powell afterwards commented that he should have quoted the remark in Latin to emphasize that he was not predicting a bloodbath, only evoking the Sybil's prophesy in Virgil's *Aeneid,* bk. 6, l. 86: "*Et Thybrim multo spumantem sanguine cerno.*" The phrase "rivers of blood" was also used by, among others, Thomas Jefferson and Winston Churchill.

3　There can be no fifty–fifty Americanism in this country. There is room

here for only 100% Americanism, only for those who are Americans and nothing else.

THEODORE ROOSEVELT, (1858–1919) U.S. Republican (later Progressive) politician, president. *Roosevelt Policy,* vol. 3 (1919). Speech, July 19, 1918, State Republican Party Convention, Saratoga, New York.

Roosevelt had earlier drawn attention to "hyphenated Americans" in a speech, Oct. 12, 1915: "Americanism is a matter of the spirit and the soul. Our allegiance must be purely to the United States."

Immortality

1　For the wages of sin is death; but the gift of God is eternal life through Jesus Christ our Lord.

BIBLE: NEW TESTAMENT, St. Paul, in *Romans,* 6:23.

2　If you were to destroy the belief in immortality in mankind, not only love but every living force on which the continuation of all life in the world depended, would dry up at once.

FEODOR DOSTOYEVSKY, (1821–1881) Russian novelist. Mr. Miusov, in *The Brothers Karamazov,* bk. 2, ch. 6 (published 1879–1880), trans. by David Magarshak (1958).

3　For them that think death's honesty Won't fall upon them naturally Life sometimes Must get lonely.

BOB DYLAN [ROBERT ALLEN ZIMMERMAN], (b. 1941) U.S. singer, songwriter. "It's Alright Ma (I'm Only Bleeding)" (song), on the album *Bringing it all Back Home* (1965).

4　If you would not be forgotten, as soon as you are dead and rotten, either write things worth reading or do things worth the writing.

BENJAMIN FRANKLIN, (1706–1790) U.S. statesman, writer. *Poor Richard's Almanac,* May (1738).

This aphorism has also been credited to Pliny.

5   He had decided to live for ever or die in the attempt.

JOSEPH HELLER, (b. 1923) U.S. author. *Catch–22,* ch. 3 (1961).

Referring to Yossarian.

6   Perhaps too my name will be joined to theirs.

OVID (PUBLIUS OVIDIUS NASO), (43 B.C.–A.D.17) Roman poet. *Ars Amatoria,* bk. 3, l. 339.

Referring to the names of the great poets.

7   But thy eternal summer shall not fade.

WILLIAM SHAKESPEARE, (1564–1616) British dramatist, poet. Sonnet 18, "Shall I Compare Thee to a Summer's Day?" (1609).

Impatience

1   Too slow, the wagons of years,
    The oxen of days—too glum.
    Our god is the god of speed,
    Our heart—our battle–drum.

VLADIMIR MAYAKOVSKY, (1893–1930) Russian poet, dramatist. *Our March,* sts. 2 and 6 (1917), trans. by Dorian Rottenberg (1972).

Impotence

1   This is the monstruosity in love, lady—that the will is infinite and the execution confined; that the desire is boundless and the act a slave to limit.

WILLIAM SHAKESPEARE, (1564–1616) British dramatist, poet. Troilus, in *Troilus and Cressida,* act 3, sc. 2, l. 77–80 (1609).

Troilus, in *Troilus and Cressida,* on the discrepancy between lovers' aspirations and their realization, shortly before the first sexual encounter between himself and Cressida.

Impulse

1   The awful daring of a moment's surrender
    Which an age of prudence can never retract.

T.S. (THOMAS STEARNS) ELIOT, (1888–1965)

Anglo–American poet, critic. *The Waste Land,* pt. 5, "What the Thunder Said" (1922).

2   The most decisive actions of our life—I mean those that are most likely to decide the whole course of our future—are, more often than not, unconsidered.

ANDRÉ GIDE, (1869–1951) French author. Hildebrant, in *The Counterfeiters,* pt. 3, ch. 16 (1925).

Inconsistency

1   A man so various, that he seemed to be
    Not one, but all mankind's epitome.
    Stiff in opinions, always in the wrong;
    Was everything by starts, and nothing long:
    But in the course of one revolving moon
    Was chemist, fiddler, statesman and buffoon.

JOHN DRYDEN, (1631–1700) British poet, dramatist, critic. "Absalom and Achitophel," pt. 1, l. 545–50 (1681).

Describing Zimri, who in the poem represents George Villiers, 2nd Duke of Buckingham. A Privy Councillor and favorite of Charles II, the flamboyant Villiers had himself parodied Dryden in his comedy, *The Rehearsal* (1671). In 1978, Labour prime minister James Callaghan had quoted these words to tease Margaret

Thatcher—then leader of the Conservative opposition—who had been trained as a chemist.

2   Like the British Constitution, she owes her success in practice to her inconsistencies in principle.

THOMAS HARDY, (1840–1928) British novelist, poet. Mrs. Napper, in *The Hand of Ethelberta*, ch. 9 (1876).

Speaking of Ethelberta.

Indecision

1   My mind is not a bed to be made and re–made.

JAMES AGATE, (1877–1947) British drama critic. *Ego 6* (1944). Journal entry, June 9, 1943.

2   We know what happens to people who stay in the middle of the road. They get run over.

ANEURIN BEVAN, (1897–1960) British Labour politician. Quoted in *Observer* (London, Dec. 6, 1953).

3   How long halt ye between two opinions?

BIBLE: HEBREW, Elijah, in *1 Kings*, 18:21.

Spoken to the children of Israel.

4   Neither have they hearts to stay,
Nor wit enough to run away.

SAMUEL BUTLER, (1612–1680) British poet. "Hudibras," pt. 3, cto. 3, l. 569–570 (1678). Eds. John Wilders and Hugh de Quehen (1973).

5   There is no more miserable human being than one in whom nothing is habitual but indecision, and for whom the lighting of every cigar, the drinking of every cup, the time of rising and going to bed every day, and the beginning of every bit of work, are subjects of express volitional deliberation.

WILLIAM JAMES, (1843–1916) U.S. psychologist, philosopher. *Principles of Psychology*, vol. 1, ch. 4 (1890).

Independence

1   Who to himself is law, no law doth need, Offends no law, and is a king indeed.

GEORGE CHAPMAN, (c. 1559–1634) British dramatist, poet, translator. Bussy d'Ambois, in *Bussy d'Ambois*, act 2, sc. 1, l. 203–4 (1607, rev. 1641). Repr. in *Plays and Poems of George Chapman: The Tragedies,* ed. Thomas Marc Parrott (1910).

Addressing Henry III of France, in self–vindication after killing two men in a quarrel.

2   When, in the course of human events, it becomes necessary for one people to dissolve the political bands which have connected them with another, and to assume the powers of the earth, the separate and equal station to which the laws of nature and of nature's God entitle them, a decent respect to the opinions of mankind requires that they should declare the causes which impel them to the separation.

THOMAS JEFFERSON, (1743–1826) U.S. president. "American Declaration of Independence" (1776), published in *The Papers of Thomas Jefferson*, vol. 1, ed. Julian P. Boyd (1950).

Opening lines.

Indifference

1   Lukewarmness I account a sin, As great in love as in religion.

ABRAHAM COWLEY, (1618–1667) British essayist, poet. *The Mistress*, "The Request" (1647).

2   Men are accomplices to that which
     leaves them indifferent.

     GEORGE STEINER, (b. 1929)
     French–born U.S. critic, novelist. "A Kind of
     Survivor,"
     Language and Silence (1967).

Individuality

1   Comrades! We must abolish the
     cult of the individual decisively,
     once and for all.

     NIKITA KHRUSHCHEV, (1894–1971)
     Soviet premier. Quoted in *Manchester
     Guardian* (June 11, 1956). Speech, Feb. 25,
     1956, to the secret session of the 20th Con-
     gress of the Communist Party.

     Khrushchev used the occasion to identify
     Stalin as the chief exponent of the cult of
     the individual (also translated "cult of the
     personality") by "the glorification of his
     own person." He expanded: "Everyone can
     err, but Stalin considered that he never
     erred, that he was always right. He never
     acknowledged to anyone that he made any
     mistake, large or small, despite the fact that
     he made not a few mistakes in the matter of
     theory and in his practical activity."
     (Quoted in *Stalin,* pt. 2, ch. 6, ed. T.H.
     Rigby, 1966)

2   The definition of the individual
     was: a multitude of one million
     divided by one million.

     ARTHUR KOESTLER, (1905–1983) Hun-
     garian–born British author. *Darkness at
     Noon,* "The Grammatical Fiction" (1940).

     The teaching of the Party.

3   I am not a number—I am a free
     man!

     PATRICK MCGOOHAN, (b. 1928)
     U.S.–born British actor. Number Six (Patrick
     McGoohan), in *The Prisoner* (TV series), cre-
     ated by Patrick McGoohan, George Mark-
     stein and David Tomblin (1967–1968).

     Preamble to each episode. Elsewhere in the
     series, Number Six (who is never named),
     states, "I will not be pushed, stamped, filed,
     indexed, briefed, debriefed, or numbered.
     My life is my own."

4   Principally I hate and detest that
     animal called man; although I
     heartily love John, Peter, Thomas,
     and so forth.

     JONATHAN SWIFT, (1667–1745)
     Anglo–Irish satirist. *The Correspondence of
     Jonathan Swift,* vol. 3, ed. H. Williams (1963).
     Letter, Sept. 29, 1725, to Alexander Pope.

Inequality

1   The rich man in his castle,
     The poor man at his gate,
     God made them, high or lowly,
     And order'd their estate.

     CECIL F. ALEXANDER, (1818–1895) Irish
     poet, hymn writer. "All Things Bright and
     Beautiful," *Hymns for Little Children* (1848).

2   When Adam delved and Eve span,
     Who was then the gentleman?

     JOHN BALL, (hanged 1381) British priest,
     agitator. *Attributed.*

     Verse preached to rebels at Blackheath, out-
     side London, June 12, 1381, during the Peas-
     ants' Revolt. The lines, which have been
     traced back to c. 1340, are said to have
     breathed "a spirit fatal to the whole system of
     the Middle Ages" (J.R. Green, *A Short History
     of the English People,* 1874).

3   For unto every one that hath shall
     be given, and he shall have abun-
     dance; but from him that hath not
     shall be taken away even that which
     he hath.

     BIBLE: NEW TESTAMENT, Jesus, in
     Matthew, 25:29.

     In the parable of the talents.

4   We accept and welcome ... as con-
     ditions to which we must accom-
     modate ourselves, great inequality
     of environment; the concentration
     of business, industrial and com-
     mercial, in the hands of a few; and
     the law of competition between

these, as being not only beneficial, but essential for the future progress of the race.

ANDREW CARNEGIE, (1835–1919) U.S. industrialist, philanthropist. "The Gospel of Wealth," quoted in *Life of Andrew Carnegie*, vol. 1, ch. 17, Burton J. Hendrick (1932). First published in *North American Review*, Cedar Falls, Iowa, (June 1889).

5 My old grannum (rest her soul) was wont to say, there were but two families in the world, have–much and have–little.

MIGUEL DE CERVANTES, (1547–1616) Spanish author. Sancho Panza, in *Don Quixote*, pt. 2, ch. 20 (1615), trans. by P. Motteux.

6 Two nations between whom there is no intercourse and no sympathy; who are as ignorant of each other's habits, thoughts, and feelings, as if they were dwellers in different zones, or inhabitants of different planets.... The rich and the poor.

BENJAMIN DISRAELI, (1804–1881) British statesman, author. Stephen Morley, in *Sybil*, bk. 2, ch. 5 (1845).

7 There is no good ... in living in a society where you are merely the equal of everybody else.... The true pleasure of life is to live with your inferiors.

WILLIAM MAKEPEACE THACKERAY, (1811–1863) British author. *The Newcomes*, bk. 1, ch. 9 (1855).

Inertia

1 Nothing happens, nobody comes, nobody goes, it's awful.

SAMUEL BECKETT, (1906–1989) Irish dramatist, novelist. Estragon, in *Waiting for Godot*, act 1 (1952, trans. 1954).

2 It is not necessary that you leave the house. Remain at your table and lis-

ten. Do not even listen, only wait. Do not even wait, be wholly still and alone. The world will present itself to you for its unmasking, it can do no other, in ecstasy it will writhe at your feet.

FRANZ KAFKA, (1883–1924) Czech novelist, short story writer. "The Collected Aphorisms," vol. 1, no. 109, *Shorter Works*, ed. and trans. by Malcolm Pasley (1973). Written Oct. 1917–Feb. 1918.

3 Fix'd like a plan on his peculiar spot,
To draw nutrition, propagate, and rot.

ALEXANDER POPE, (1688–1744) British satirical poet. *An Essay on Man*, epistle 2, l. 63–4 (1733).

3 Perhaps man is the only being that can properly be called idle.

SAMUEL JOHNSON, (1709–1784) British author, lexicographer. *The Idler*, no. 1, *Universal Chronicle* (London, April 15, 1758). Repr. in *Works of Samuel Johnson*, Yale Edition, vol. 2, eds. W.J. Bate, John M. Bullitt and L.F. Powell (1963).

"As peace is the end of war," Johnson wrote, "so to be idle is the ultimate purpose of the busy."

4 They shift coffee–houses and chocolate–houses from hour to hour, to get over the insupportable labour of doing nothing.

RICHARD STEELE, (1672–1729) British dramatist, essayist, editor. *Spectator* (London, Sept. 9, 1712), no. 479, *The Spectator*, ed. D.F. Bond (1965).

Last words of article, referring to "loungers ... satisfied with being merely part of the number of mankind, without distinguishing themselves from amongst them."

5 It is better to have loafed and lost than never to have loafed at all.

JAMES THURBER, (1894–1961) U.S. humorist, illustrator. "The Courtship of Arthur and Al," *Fables for our Time* (1940).

6　For Satan finds some mischief still
　　For idle hands to do.

ISAAC WATTS, (1674–1748) British
hymn–writer. *Against Idleness and Mischief,*
st. 3, *Divine Songs for Children* (1715).

A similar thought was expressed in one of the
Scottish Proverbs collected by John Ray in
1719; variations of the saying have been
traced back as far as St Jerome (c. 342–420).

Infallibility

1　Faultless to a fault.

ROBERT BROWNING, (1812–1889) British
poet. "The Ring and the Book, "bk. 9, l. 1177
(1868–1869).

2　We are none of us infallible—not
　　even the youngest of us.

WILLIAM HEPWORTH THOMPSON,
(1810–1886) British academic, Master of Trinity College, Cambridge. Quoted in *Collections
and Recollections,* ch. 18, G.W.E. Russell
(1898).

Referring to G.W. Balfour, then a junior fellow
at Trinity College, Cambridge, later politician
and Secretary for Ireland. A similar remark has
been attributed to the Master of Balliol,
Oxford, Benjamin Jowett (1817–1893): "Even
the youngest among us is not infallible."

Infatuation

1　If all else perished, and *he*
　　remained, I should still continue to
　　be; and if all else remained, and he
　　were annihilated, the universe
　　would turn to a mighty stranger. I
　　should not seem a part of it.... My
　　love for Heathcliff resembles the
　　eternal rocks beneath—a source of
　　little visible delight, but necessary.
　　Nelly, I *am* Heathcliff—he's always,
　　always in my mind—not as a plea-
　　sure, any more than I am always a
　　pleasure to myself—but as my own
　　being.

EMILY BRONTË (1818–1848) British novelist,
poet. Catherine, in *Wuthering Heights,* ch. 9
(1847).

2　When Love's delirium haunts the
　　glowing mind,
　　Limping Decorum lingers far behind.

**GEORGE GORDON NOEL BYRON, 6TH
BARON BYRON,** (1788–1824) British poet.
*Answer To Some Elegant Verses Sent By A
Friend,* l. 11–12 (1806).

3　Mad about the boy,
　　I know it's stupid to be mad about
　　　the boy,
　　I'm so ashamed of it
　　But must admit
　　The sleepless nights I've had about
　　　the boy.
　　On the Silver Screen
　　He melts my foolish heart in every
　　　single scene.

NOËL COWARD, (1899–1973) British playwright, actor, composer. "Mad About the Boy"
(song), *Words and Music* (musical revue) (1932).

4　Take me to you, imprison me, for I,
　　Except you enthrall me, never shall
　　　be free,
　　Nor ever chaste, except you ravish me.

JOHN DONNE, (c. 1572–1631) British divine,
metaphysical poet. *Holy Sonnets,* no. 14 (1633).
Repr. in *Complete Poetry and Selected Prose,*
ed. John Hayward (1929).

Last lines of sonnet.

5　I know I am but summer to your
　　　heart,
　　And not the full four seasons of the
　　　year.

EDNA ST. VINCENT MILLAY,
(1892–1950) U.S. poet. "I Know I Am But Summer to Your Heart," *The Harp–weaver and
Other Poems* (1923).

6　Lolita, light of my life, fire of my
　　loins. My sin, my soul. Lo–lee–ta: the
　　tip of the tongue taking a trip of

three steps down the palate to tap, at three, on the teeth. Lo. Lee. Ta.

VLADIMIR NABOKOV, (1899–1977) Russian–born U.S. novelist, poet. Humbert Humbert (narrator), in *Lolita*, pt. 1, ch. 1 (1955).

Opening paragraph of novel.

7 She never told her love,
But let concealment, like a worm
i'th'bud,
Feed on her damask cheek.

WILLIAM SHAKESPEARE, (1564–1616) British dramatist, poet. Viola, in *Twelfth Night*, act 2, sc. 4, l. 110–12 (1623).

Viola, disguised as Cesario, voices her love to Orsino, by pretending she is describing her sister's love.

8 It is best to love wisely, no doubt: but to love foolishly is better than not to be able to love at all.

WILLIAM MAKEPEACE THACKERAY, (1811–1863) British author. *Pendennis*, ch. 6 (1848–1850).

9 Deep in her breast lives the silent wound.

VIRGIL [PUBLIUS VERGILIUS MARO], (70–19 B.C.) Roman poet. *Aeneid*, bk. 4, l. 67 (19 B.C.), trans. by H. Rushton Fairclough (1967).

Referring to Dido, Queen of Carthage, deserted by Aeneas.

Infidelity

1 I had been happy, if the general camp,
Pioneers and all, had tasted her sweet body,
So I had nothing known.

WILLIAM SHAKESPEARE, (1564–1616) British dramatist, poet. Othello, in *Othello*, act 3, sc. 3, l. 350–2 (1623).

On Desdemona's imagined infidelity.

2 You may build castles in the air, and fume, and fret, and grow thin and lean, and pale and ugly, if you please. But I tell you, no man worth having is true to his wife, or can be true to his wife, or ever was, or will be so.

JOHN VANBRUGH, (1663–1726) British playwright, architect. Berinthia, in *The Relapse; or, Virtue in Danger*, act 3, sc. 2 (1708). Repr. in *The Plays of Sir John Vanbrugh*, ed. W.C. Ward (1893).

3 Those who are faithful know only the trivial side of love: it is the faithless who know love's tragedies.

OSCAR WILDE, (1854–1900) Anglo–Irish playwright, author. Lord Henry, in *The Picture of Dorian Gray*, ch. 1 (1891).

Infinity

1 There is no more steely barb than that of the Infinite.

CHARLES BAUDELAIRE, (1821–1867) French poet. "The Artist 'Confiteor,'" *La Presse* (Paris, Aug. 26, 1862). *Complete Works*, vol. 1, "Shorter Prose Poems," ed. Gérard le Dantec; rev. Claude Pichois (1953).

Inflation

1 The best way to destroy the capitalist system is to debauch the currency. By a continuing process of inflation governments can confiscate, secretly and unobserved, an important part of the wealth of their citizens.

JOHN MAYNARD KEYNES, (1883–1946) British economist. *Essays in Persuasion*, ch. 2 (1931).

Keynes attributed this view to Lenin (also referred to in *Economic Consequences of the Peace*, ch. 6, 1919), though the words have never been found in Lenin's writings.

Influence

1   The ideas of economists and political philosophers, both when they are right and when they are wrong, are more powerful than is commonly understood. Indeed the world is ruled by little else. Practical men, who believe themselves to be quite exempt from any intellectual influence, are usually the slaves of some defunct economist. Madmen in authority, who hear voices in the air, are distilling their frenzy from some academic scribbler of a few years back.

JOHN MAYNARD KEYNES, (1883–1946)

British economist. *The General Theory of Employment, Interest and Money,* ch. 24 (1936).

The economist James M. Buchanan commented, "Why does Camelot lie in ruins? Intellectual error of monumental proportion has been made, and not exclusively by the politicians. Error also lies squarely with the economists. The 'academic scribbler' who must bear substantial responsibility is Lord Keynes ..." (*The Consequences of Keynes,* written with Richard E. Wagner and John Burton, 1978).

2   A cock has great influence on his own dunghill.

PUBLILIUS SYRUS, (1st century B.C.) Roman writer of mimes. *Sententiae,* no. 357.

Ingratiation

1   The art of pleasing consists in being pleased.

WILLIAM HAZLITT, (1778–1830) British essayist. *The Round Table,* "On Manner" (1817).

2   You might as well fall flat on your face as lean over too far backward.

JAMES THURBER, (1894–1961) U.S. humorist, illustrator. *Fables for our Time,* "The

Bear who Let it Alone" (1940). Originally published in *The New Yorker* (April 29, 1939).

Ingratitude

1   He receives comfort like cold porridge.

WILLIAM SHAKESPEARE, (1564–1616) British dramatist, poet. Sebastian, in *The Tempest,* act 2, sc. 1, l. 10–11 (1623).

Inheritance

1   My sword I give to him that shall succeed me in my pilgrimage, and my courage and skill to him that can get it.

JOHN BUNYAN, (1628–1688) British Baptist preacher, author. Valiant–for–Truth makes his farewell, in *The Pilgrim's Progress,* pt. 2 (1684).

2   All heiresses are beautiful.

JOHN DRYDEN, (1631–1700) British poet, dramatist, critic. Albanat, in *King Arthur,* act 1, sc. 1 (1691).

3   And all to leave what with his toil he won
To that unfeathered two–legged
   thing, a son.

JOHN DRYDEN, (1631–1700) British poet, dramatist, critic. "Absalom and Achitophel," pt. 1, l. 169–70 (1681).

Referring to Achitophel, who in the poem represents the statesman Anthony Ashley Cooper, Earl of Shaftesbury.

4   Say not you know another entirely till you have divided an inheritance with him.

JOHANN KASPAR LAVATER, (1741–1801) Swiss divine, poet. *Aphorisms on Man,* no. 157 (1788).

5   But thousands die without or this or that,

Die, and endow a college, or a cat:
To some, indeed, Heaven grants the
  happier fate,
T'enrich a bastard, or a son they hate.

ALEXANDER POPE, (1688–1744) British satirical poet. "Epistle to Lord Bathurst," l. 95–8 (1733).

6 The weeping of an heir is laughter in disguise.

PUBLILIUS SYRUS, (1st century B.C.) Roman writer of mimes. *Sententiae*, no. 221.

Montaigne, in his *Essays*, bk. 1, ch. 37, attributes this aphorism to the second–century Roman grammarian Aulus Gellius.

Inhumanity

1 Man's inhumanity to Man
  Makes countless thousands mourn!

ROBERT BURNS, (1759–1796) Scottish poet. "Man was made to Mourn," st. 7 (1786). Repr. in *Poetical Works*, vol. 1, ed. William Scott Douglas (1891).

Injury

1 Young men soon give, and soon forget, affronts;
  Old age is slow in both.

JOSEPH ADDISON, (1672–1719) British essayist. Syphax, in *Cato*, act 2, sc. 5 (1713), *Works of Addison*, ed. R. Hurd (1883).

2 No man lives without jostling and being jostled; in all ways he has to *elbow* himself through the world, giving and receiving offence.

THOMAS CARLYLE, (1795–1881) Scottish essayist, historian. "Sir Walter Scott," first published in *London and Westminster Review* (Nov. 12, 1838). *Critical and Miscellaneous Essays* (1839–1857).

3 There is nothing that people bear more impatiently, or forgive less, than contempt: and an injury is much sooner forgotten than an insult.

PHILIP DORMER STANHOPE, 4TH EARL CHESTERFIELD, (1694–1773) British statesman, man of letters. *The Letters of the Earl of Chesterfield to His Son*, vol. 1, no. 113, ed. Charles Strachey (1901). Letter, Oct. 9, 1746, first published (1774).

4 He threatens many that hath injured one.

BEN JONSON, (c. 1572–1637) British dramatist, poet. Silius, in *Fall of Sejanus*, act 2, l. 476 (performed 1603, published 1616). Repr. in *The Complete Plays*, vol. 2, ed. G.A. Wilkes (1981).

Injustice

1 Indeed I tremble for my country when I reflect that God is just; that his justice cannot sleep forever.

THOMAS JEFFERSON, (1743–1826) U.S. president. *Notes on the State of Virginia*, query 18 (written 1781, published 1784–1785). Repr. in *The Writings of Thomas Jefferson*, vol. 3, ed. Paul L. Ford (1894).

Referring to the practice of slavery. The words are inscribed on the northeast quadrant of the Jefferson Memorial, Washington D.C..

2 A rape! a rape!...
  Yes, you have ravished justice;
  Forced her to do your pleasure.

JOHN WEBSTER, (1580–1625) British dramatist. Vittoria, in *The White Devil*, act 3, sc. 2, l. 273–4 (1612). Repr. in *The Complete Works of John Webster*, ed. F.L. Lucas (1927).

Innocence

1 Every harlot was a virgin once.

WILLIAM BLAKE, (1757–1827) British poet, painter, engraver. *The Gates of Paradise*, epilogue, l. 3 (c. 1818), repr. in *Complete Writings*, ed. Geoffrey Keynes (1957).

2 He was as fressh as is the month of May.

GEOFFREY CHAUCER, (1340–1400)
British poet. *The Canterbury Tales*, "General
Prologue," l. 92 (1387–1400), repr. in *The
Works of Geoffrey Chaucer*, ed. Alfred W.
Pollard, etc. (1898).

Referring to the Squire.

3   Innocence always calls mutely for
protection when we would be so
much wiser to guard ourselves
against it: innocence is like a dumb
leper who has lost his bell, wandering the world, meaning no harm.

GRAHAM GREENE, (1904–1991) British
novelist. *The Quiet American*, pt. 1, ch. 3, sct.
3 (1955).

Later in the book, the narrator describes
Pyle—"the quiet American" of the title, a fum-
bling idealist in Cold–War Vietnam—in similar terms: "What's the good? He'll always be
innocent, you can't blame the innocent, they
are always guiltless. All you can do is control
them or eliminate them. Innocence is a kind
of insanity." (pt. 3, ch. 2, sct. 1).

4   All things truly wicked start from
an innocence.

ERNEST HEMINGWAY, (1899–1961) U.S.
author. *A Moveable Feast*, ch. 17 (1964).

5   An innocent man is a sin before
God. Inhuman and therefore
untrustworthy. No man should live
without absorbing the sins of his
kind, the foul air of his innocence,
even if it did wilt rows of angel
trumpets and cause them to fall
from their vines.

TONI MORRISON, (b. 1931) U.S. novelist,
editor. *Tar Baby*, p. 245 (1981).

6   Children, I grant, should be innocent; but when the epithet is
applied to men, or women, it is but
a civil term for weakness.

MARY WOLLSTONECRAFT, (1759–1797)
British feminist writer. *A Vindication of the
Rights of Women*, ch. 2 (1792).

Innovation

1   As the births of living creatures, at
first, are ill–shapen: so are all *Innovations*, which are the births of
time.

FRANCIS BACON, (1561–1626) British
philosopher, essayist, statesman. *Essays*, "Of
Innovations" (1597–1625).

In his *Annotations to Bacon* (c. 1798), William
Blake commented: "What a cursed fool is this,
Ill Shapen! Are infants or small plants ill
shapen because they are not yet come to their
maturity? What a contemptible fool is this
Bacon!" (In *Complete Writings*, ed. Keynes,
1957).

2   Neither do men put new wine into
old bottles: else the bottles break,
and the wine runneth out, and the
bottles perish: but they put new
wine into new bottles, and both are
preserved.

BIBLE: NEW TESTAMENT, Jesus, in
Matthew, 9:17.

3   To innovate is not to reform.

EDMUND BURKE, (1729–1797) Irish
philosopher, statesman. *Letter to a Noble Lord*
(1796), repr. in *Works*, vol. 5 (1899).

4   Pure innovation is more gross than
error.

GEORGE CHAPMAN, (1559–1634) British
dramatist, poet, translator. *King Henry*, in
Bussy D'Ambois, act 1, sc. 2, l. 38 (1607).

Innuendo

1   Nudge, nudge, wink, wink, say no
more, know what I mean ...

MONTY PYTHON'S FLYING CIRCUS,
Monty Python's Flying Circus (TV series)
(1969–1974), quoted in Jonathon Green, *Says
Who?* (1988).

Phrase spoken by Eric Idle in the character of an insinuating bore. Monty Python episodes were written and performed by Graham Chapman (1941–1989); John Cleese (b. 1939); Terry Gilliam (b. 1940); Eric Idle (b. 1943); Terry Jones (b. 1942); and Michael Palin (b. 1943).

2   That's what I always say. Love flies out the door when money comes innuendo.

ARTHUR SHEERMAN, U.S. screenwriter. *Monkey Business* (film) (1931). Norman McLeod.

3   Nor do they trust their tongue
     alone,
But speak a language of their own;
Can read a nod, a shrug, a look,
Far better than a printed book;
Convey a libel in a frown,
And wink a reputation down.

JONATHAN SWIFT, (1667–1745) Anglo–Irish satirist. *The Journal of a Modern Lady*, l. 188–93 (1729). Repr. in *The Poems of Jonathan Swift*, ed. H. Williams (1958).

Insanity

1   There is in every madman a misunderstood genius whose idea, shining in his head, frightened people, and for whom delirium was the only solution to the strangulation that life had prepared for him.

ANTONIN ARTAUD, (1896–1948) French theater producer, actor, theorist. *Van Gogh, the Man Suicided by Society* (1947). Repr. in *Selected Writings*, pt. 33, ed. Susan Sontag (1976).

2   Insanity is often the logic of an accurate mind overtasked.

OLIVER WENDELL HOLMES, SR., (1809–1894) U.S. writer, physician. *The Autocrat of the Breakfast–Table*, ch. 2 (1858).

Insects

1   His Labor is a Chant—
His Idleness—a Tune—
Oh, for a Bee's experience
Of Clovers, and of Noon!

EMILY DICKINSON, (1830–1886) U.S. poet. *His Feet Are Shod With Gauze*, st. 2 (written c. 1864, published 1890). Repr. in *The Complete Poems*, no. 916, Harvard *variorum* edition (1955).

2   I saw the spiders marching through
     the air,
Swimming from tree to tree that
     mildewed day
In latter August when the hay
Came creaking to the barn.

ROBERT LOWELL, (1917–1977) U.S. poet. *Mr. Edwards and the Spider*, st. 1, *Poems 1938–1949* (1950).

3   How doth the little busy bee
Improve each shining hour,
And gather honey all the day
From every opening flower!

ISAAC WATTS, (1674–1748) British hymn–writer. *Against Idleness and Mischief*, st. 1, *Divine Songs for Children* (1715).

Lewis Carroll parodied the song in *Alice's Adventures in Wonderland*: "How doth the little crocodile Improve his shining tail, And pour the waters of the Nile On every golden scale!" (Ch. 2, 1865).

Insecurity

1   My apprehensions come in crowds;
I dread the rustling of the grass;
The very shadows of the clouds
Have power to shake me as they
     pass:
I question things and do not find
One that will answer to my mind;
And all the world appears unkind.

WILLIAM WORDSWORTH, (1770–1850) British poet. *The Affliction of Margaret,* st. 10, *Poems in Two Volumes* (1807).

Insignificance

1 We are merely the stars'
   tennis–balls, struck and bandied
   Which way please them.

JOHN WEBSTER, (1580–1625) British dramatist. Bosola, in *The Duchess of Malfi,* act 5, sc. 4, l. 53–4 (1623). Repr. in *The Complete Works of John Webster,* ed. F.L. Lucas (1927).

See Shakespeare's comment on "life and death," expressing a similar idea.

Inspiration

1 Stung by the splendour of a sudden
   thought.

ROBERT BROWNING, (1812–1889) British poet. *A Death in the Desert,* l. 59 (1864).

2 We have watered our houses in
   Helicon.

GEORGE CHAPMAN, (c. 1559–1634) British dramatist, poet, translator. Lodovico, in *May–Day,* act 3, sc. 3, l. 9–10 (1611). Repr. in *Plays and Poems of George Chapman: The Comedies,* ed. Thomas Marc Parrott (1914).

Refers to a mountain–range in Boeotia (central Greece), sacred to the Muses. The line has often appeared with *horses* printed for "houses."

3 You beat your pate, and fancy wit
   will come:
   Knock as you please, there's
   nobody at home.

ALEXANDER POPE, (1688–1744) British satirical poet. "Another Epigram," *Miscellanies,* vol. 3 (1732).

4 Everyone has left me

except my muse,
that good nurse.
She stays in my hand,
a mild white mouse.

ANNE SEXTON, (1928–1974) U.S. poet. *Flee on Your Donkey,* st. 3, *Live or Die* (1966).

The title quotes Rimbaud's *Fêtes de la Faim* (1872).

5 O for a muse of fire, that would
   ascend
   The brightest heaven of invention.

WILLIAM SHAKESPEARE, (1564–1616) British dramatist, poet. Chorus, in *Henry V,* prologue, l. 1–2 (1600).

6 Why does my Muse only speak
   when she is unhappy?
   She does not, I only listen when I
   am unhappy
   When I am happy I live and despise
   writing
   For my Muse this cannot but be
   dispiriting.

STEVIE SMITH, (1902–1971) British poet, novelist. *My Muse, Selected Poems* (1962).

Instinct

1 The natural man has only two primal passions, to get and to beget.

SIR WILLIAM OSLER, (1849–1919) Canadian physician. *Science and Immortality,* ch. 2 (1904).

Institutions

1 The whole history of civilisation is
   strewn with creeds and institutions
   which were invaluable at first, and
   deadly afterwards.

WALTER BAGEHOT, (1826–1877) British economist, critic. *Physics and Politics,* ch. 2, sct. 3 (1872).

2   Prisons are built with stones of law, brothels with bricks of religion.

    WILLIAM BLAKE, (1757–1827) British poet, painter, engraver. *The Marriage of Heaven and Hell*, plate 8, "Proverbs of Hell," (c. 1793), repr. in *Complete Writings*, ed. Geoffrey Keynes (1957).

3   Nouns of number, or multitude, such as *Mob, Parliament, Rabble, House of Commons, Regiment, Court of King's Bench, Den of Thieves*, and the like.

    WILLIAM COBBETT, (1762–1835) British journalist, reformer. *English Grammar*, letter 17 (1817).

4   An institution is the lengthened shadow of one man.

    RALPH WALDO EMERSON, (1803–1882) U.S. essayist, poet, philosopher. *Essays*, "Self–reliance," First Series (1841).

5   In any great organization it is far, far safer to be wrong with the majority than to be right alone.

    JOHN KENNETH GALBRAITH, (b. 1908) U.S. economist. *Guardian* (London, July 28, 1989).

Insults

1   You dirty, double–crossing rat.

    JAMES CAGNEY, (1899–1986) U.S. screen actor. *Blonde Crazy* (film) (1931).

    Popularized in the form "You dirty rat": which Cagney vehemently denied ever saying, in his autobiography *Cagney by Cagney* (1976).

Insurance

1   Down went the owners—greedy men whom hope of gain allured: Oh, dry the starting tear, for they were heavily insured.

    SIR WILLIAM SCHWENCK GILBERT, (1836–1911) British librettist. "Etiquette," *The "Bab" Ballads* (1866–1871).

Integrity

1   I cannot and will not recant anything, for to go against conscience is neither right nor safe. Here I stand, I can do no other, so help me God. Amen.

    MARTIN LUTHER, (1483–1546) German leader of the Protestant Reformation. Speech, April 18, 1521, at the Diet of Worms, Germany.

    Luther was summoned to Worms by the Holy Roman Emperor Charles V in an attempt to effect a conciliation between Luther and the established Church. The words, "Here I stand, I can do no other"—added in Luther's handwriting to the original printed version of the speech—were later inscribed on the monument to Luther at Worms: *Hier steh' ich, ich kann nicht anders.*

2   Few men have virtue to withstand the highest bidder.

    GEORGE WASHINGTON, (1732–1799) U.S. general, president. Quoted in *Maxims of Washington*, "Virtue and Vice," (1942). Letter, Aug. 17, 1779.

Intellect and Intellectuals

1   A spirit of national masochism prevails, encouraged by an effete corps of impudent snobs who characterize themselves as intellectals.

    SPIRO T. AGNEW, (b. 1918) U.S. Republican politician, vice president. *Collected Speeches of Spiro Agnew* (1971). Speech, Oct. 19, 1969, New Orleans, Louisiana.

2   To the man–in–the–street, who, I'm sorry to say, Is a keen observer of life, The word "Intellectual" suggests straight away

A man who's untrue to his wife.

W.H. (WYSTAN HUGH) AUDEN,
(1907–1973) Anglo–U.S. poet. *New Year Letter*, note to l. 1277 (1961), repr. in *Collected Poems* (1976).

3 I've been called many things, but never an intellectual.

TALLULAH BANKHEAD, (1903–1968) U.S. screen actor. *Tallulah,* ch. 15 (1952).

4 The intellectual is a middle–class product; if he is not born into the class he must soon insert himself into it, in order to exist. He is the fine nervous flower of the bourgeoisie.

LOUISE BOGAN, (1897–1970) U.S. poet, critic. "Some Notes on Popular and Unpopular Art," (1943). Repr. in *Selected Criticism: Poetry and Prose* (1955).

5 An intellectual is someone whose mind watches itself. I am happy to be both halves, the watcher and the watched.

ALBERT CAMUS, (1913–1960) French–Algerian philosopher, author. *Notebooks (1935–42)* (1962).

6 I now know all the people worth knowing in America, and I find no intellect comparable to my own.

MARGARET FULLER, (1810–1850) U.S. writer, lecturer. Quoted in *Memoirs of Margaret Fuller Ossoli*, vol. 1, pt. 4, Ralph Waldo Emerson (1884), repr. (1972).

reported to have been uttered at Emerson's table. Emerson wrote only this section: other sections of Memoirs are by William Henry Channing and James Freeman Clarke.

7 And still they gazed, and still the
    wonder grew,
 That one small head could carry all
    he knew.

OLIVER GOLDSMITH, (1728–1774) Anglo–Irish poet, essayist, playwright. *The Deserted Village,* l. 215–6 (1770).

Referring to the village schoolmaster.

8 To be wholly devoted to some intellectual exercise is to have succeeded in life.

ROBERT LOUIS STEVENSON, (1850–1894) Scottish novelist, essayist, poet. *Weir of Hermiston,* ch. 2 (1896).

9 The good are so harsh to the clever,
 The clever so rude to the good!

ELIZABETH WORDSWORTH, (1840–1932) British educator. *Good and Clever* (1890).

Intelligence

1 These little grey cells. It is "up to them."

AGATHA CHRISTIE, (1890–1976) British mystery writer. Hercule Poirot, in *The Mysterious Affair at Styles,* ch. 10 (1920).

Christie's first detective novel introduced both Belgian sleuth Hercule Poirot and Poirot's famous reference to the efficacy of brain–power—the "little grey cells"—to solve mysteries, a faith he drew attention to in almost every subsequent appearance.

2 One definition of man is "an intelligence served by organs."

RALPH WALDO EMERSON, (1803–1882) U.S. essayist, poet, philosopher. "Works and Days," *Society and Solitude* (1870).

Emerson may have taken this definition from Louis De Bonald's *Th ;orie de Pouvoir Politique et Religieux* (1796). The French writers Edmond and Jules de Goncourt, in an entry July 30, 1861, in *The Goncourt Journals* (1888–1896), wrote "Man is a mind betrayed, not served, by his organs," and Aldous Huxley proposed rather that "Man is an intelligence, not served by, but in servitude to his organs" (in *Themes and Variations,* "Variations on a Philosopher," 1950).

3 The height of cleverness is being able to conceal it.

FRANÇOIS LA ROCHEFOUCAULD, DUC DE, (1613–1680) French writer, moralist. *Sentences et Maximes Morales*, no. 245 (1678).

4 There are three kinds of intelligence: one kind understands things for itself, the other appreciates what others can understand, the third understands neither for itself nor through others. This first kind is excellent, the second good, and the third kind useless.

NICCOLₑ + MACHIAVELLI, (1469–1527) Italian political philosopher, statesman. *The Prince*, ch. 22 (written 1513–1514, published 1532), trans. by George Bull (1961).

Intelligibility

1 This particularly rapid, unintelligible patter
Isn't generally heard, and if it is it
  doesn't matter!

SIR WILLIAM SCHWENCK GILBERT, (1836–1911) British librettist. Despard, in *Ruddigore*, act 2 (1887), published in *The Savoy Operas* (1926).

2 Never be lucid, never state,
If you would be regarded great,
The simplest thought or sentiment
(For thought, we know, is decadent).

DYLAN THOMAS, (1914–1953) Welsh poet. "A Letter to My Aunt Discussing the Correct Approach to Modern Poetry," *The Poems*, ed. Daniel Jones (1971). (Written 1933).

3 Nowadays to be intelligible is to be found out.

OSCAR WILDE, (1854–1900) Anglo–Irish playwright, author. Lord Darlington, in *Lady Windermere's Fan*, act 1 (1893).

International Relations

1 Peace, commerce and honest friendship with all nations; entangling alliances with none.

THOMAS JEFFERSON, (1743–1826) U.S. president. *First Inaugural Address, The Writings of Thomas Jefferson*, vol. 3, ed. Andrew A. Lipscomb (1904). Speech, March 4, 1801.

2 There can be no greater error than to expect, or calculate, upon real favors from nation to nation. It is an illusion which experience must cure, which a just pride ought to discard.

GEORGE WASHINGTON, (1732–1799) U.S. general, president. *Farewell Address*, vol. 35, *The Writings of George Washington*, ed. John C. Fitzpatrick (1940). Speech, Sept. 17, 1796.

Internationalism

1 A steady patriot of the world alone,
The friend of every country but his
  own.

GEORGE CANNING, (1770–1827) British statesman, prime minister. *The New Morality*, l. 113–4 (1798).

Referring to the Jacobin. See Disraeli's comment on "liberals."

2 Our country is the world—our countrymen are all mankind.

WILLIAM LLOYD GARRISON, (1805–1879) U.S. abolitionist. *Liberator* (Boston, Dec. 15, 1837).

Prospectus of Garrison's anti–slavery newspaper.

Interpretation

1 Interpretation is the revenge of the intellect upon art. Even more. It is the revenge of the intellect upon the world. To interpret is to impoverish, to deplete the world—in order to set up a shadow world of "meanings."

SUSAN SONTAG, (b. 1933) U.S. essayist. "Against Interpretation," sct. 4, *Against Interpretation* (1966). Originally published in *Evergreen Review* (New York, Dec. 1964).

Intervention

1 It is an honor for a man to cease from strife: but every fool will be meddling.

BIBLE: HEBREW, *Proverbs*, 20:3.

2 "If everybody minded their own business," the Duchess said in a hoarse growl, "the world would go round a deal faster than it does."

LEWIS CARROLL [CHARLES LUTWIDGE DODGSON], (1832–1898) British author, mathematician. *Alice's Adventures in Wonderland*, "Pig and Pepper," (1865).

3 Those who in quarrels interpose, Must often wipe a bloody nose.

JOHN GAY, (1685–1732) British dramatist, poet. "The Mastiffs," pt. 1, l. 1–2, *Fables* (1727).

Interviews

1 I cried, "Come, tell me how you live!" And thumped him on the head.

LEWIS CARROLL [CHARLES LUTWIDGE DODGSON], (1832–1898) British author, mathematician. The White Knight's song, in *Through the Looking–Glass*, "It's My Own Invention," (1865).

The song, titled in an earlier version *Upon the Lonely Moor* (1856), is a parody of Wordsworth's *Resolution and Independence*, which includes the lines, "My question eagerly I did renew, 'How is it that you live, and what is it you do?.'"

2 It is not every question that deserves an answer.

PUBLILIUS SYRUS, (1st century B.C.) Roman writer of mimes. *Sententiae*, no. 581.

Introspection

1 The mind can weave itself warmly in the cocoon of its own thoughts,

and dwell a hermit anywhere.

JAMES RUSSELL LOWELL, (1819–1891) U.S. poet, editor. *On a Certain Condescension in Foreigners*, vol. 3, *Literary Essays* (1890). Originally published in *Atlantic Monthly* (Boston, Jan. 1869).

Invention

1 This is the patent age of new inventions
For killing bodies, and for saving souls,
All propagated with the best intentions.

GEORGE GORDON NOEL BYRON, 6TH BARON BYRON, (1788–1824) British poet. *Don Juan*, cto. 1, st. 132 (1819–1824).

Involvement

1 Am I my brother's keeper?

BIBLE: HEBREW, Cain, in *Genesis*, 4:9.

On being asked the whereabouts of Abel, whom he has slain.

2 No man is an island entire of itself; every man is a piece of the Continent, a part of the main.... Any man's death diminishes me because I am involved in Mankind; and therefore never send to know for whom the bell tolls; it tolls for thee.

JOHN DONNE, (c. 1572–1631) British divine, metaphysical poet. *Devotions Upon Emergent Occasions*, meditation 17 (1624). Repr. in *Complete Poetry and Selected Prose*, ed. John Hayward (1929).

"To be no part of any body, is to be nothing." (letter, Sept. 1608, to Sir Henry Goodyer, published in *Complete Poetry and Selected Prose*, ed. John Hayward, 1929).

Ireland and the Irish

1 Pat: He was an Anglo–Irishman.

Meg: In the blessed name of God, what's that?
Pat: A Protestant with a horse.

BRENDAN BEHAN, (1923–1964) Irish playwright. *The Hostage*, act 1 (1958).

Referring to Monsewer: See Behan on England and the English.

2   For the great Gaels of Ireland
Are the men that God made mad,
For all their wars are merry
And all their songs are sad.

GILBERT KEITH CHESTERTON, (1874–1936) British author. *Ballad of the White Horse*, bk. 2.

3   Consider Ireland.... You have a starving population, an absentee aristocracy, and an alien Church, and in addition the weakest executive in the world. That is the Irish Question.

BENJAMIN DISRAELI, (1804–1881) British statesman, author. *Hansard*, col. 1016. Speech to House of Commons (Feb. 16, 1844).

4   The Irish are a fair people; they never speak well of one another.

SAMUEL JOHNSON, (1709–1784) British author, lexicographer. Quoted in James Boswell, *Life of Dr. Johnson*, entry, Feb. 1775 (1791).

5   Ireland is the old sow that eats her farrow.

JAMES JOYCE, (1882–1941) Irish author. Stephen Dedalus, in *A Portrait of the Artist as a Young Man*, ch. 5 (1916).

6   It is a symbol of Irish art. The cracked lookingglass of a servant.

JAMES JOYCE, (1882–1941) Irish author. Stephen Dedalus, in *Ulysses*, ch. 1 of 1984 edition (1922).

Referring to Buck Mulligan's purloined mirror.

7   When the soul of a man is born in this country there are nets flung at it to hold it back from flight. You talk to me of nationality, language, religion. I shall try to fly by those nets.

JAMES JOYCE, (1882–1941) Irish author. Stephen Dedalus, in *A Portrait of the Artist as a Young Man*, ch. 5 (1916).

Speaking to the young patriot Davin.

8   Och, Dublin City, there is no doubtin', Bates every city upon the say; 'Tis there you'll see O'Connell spoutin', An' Lady Morgan makin' tay; For 'tis the capital of the finest nation, Wid charmin' pisintry on a fruitful sod, Fightin' like divils for conciliation An' hatin' each other for the love of God.

CHARLES JAMES LEVER, (1809–1872) Irish novelist. "Dublin City" (song), attributed.

The novelist Lady Sydney Morgan, in an entry for Oct. 30, 1826, in her *Memoirs* (vol. 2, 1862), mentions this compliment paid to her by a street ballad singer, which has been attributed to Lever.

9   The moment the very name of Ireland is mentioned, the English seem to bid adieu to common feeling, common prudence, and common sense, and to act with the barbarity of tyrants, and the fatuity of idiots.

SYDNEY SMITH, (1771–1845) British clergyman, writer. *The Letters of Peter Plymley*, no. 2 (1807).

10   Out of Ireland have we come,
Great hatred, little room
Maimed us at the start.
I carry from my mother's womb
A fanatic's heart.

WILLIAM BUTLER YEATS, (1865–1939) Irish poet, playwright. *Remorse for Intemperate Speech, Words for Music Perhaps and Other Poems* (1932).

Irreverence

1 Conventionality is not morality. Self–righteousness is not religion. To attack the first is not to assail the last. To pluck the mask from the face of the Pharisee is not to lift an impious hand to the Crown of Thorns.

CHARLOTTE BRONTË(1816–1855) British novelist. *Jane Eyre*, Preface (1847).

Isolation

1 We allow our ignorance to prevail upon us and make us think we can survive alone, alone in patches, alone in groups, alone in races, even alone in genders.

MAYA ANGELOU, (b. 1928) U.S. author. *New York Times* (March 11, 1990). Address, March 1990, Centenary College of Louisiana.

2 I stood
Among them, but not of them; in a shroud
Of thoughts which were not their thoughts.

GEORGE GORDON NOEL BYRON, 6TH BARON BYRON, (1788–1824) British poet. *Childe Harold's Pilgrimage*, cto. 3, st. 113 (1812–1818).

3 Life is for each man a solitary cell whose walls are mirrors.

EUGENE O'NEILL, (1888–1953) U.S. dramatist. Lazarus, in *Lazarus Laughed*, act 2, sc. 1 (1927).

4 We're all of us sentenced to solitary confinement inside our own skins, for life!

TENNESSEE WILLIAMS, (1914–1983) U.S. dramatist. Val Xavier, in *Orpheus Descending*, act 2, sc. 1 (1957).

Israel

1 The fathers have eaten sour grapes, and the children's teeth are set on edge.

BIBLE: HEBREW, *Ezekiel*, 18:2.

Proverbial reproach by God, concerning the land of Israel. The same image is used in *Jeremiah* 31:29.

2 In Israel, in order to be a realist you must believe in miracles.

DAVID BEN GURION, (1886–1973) Israeli statesman. *Interview on CBS–TV, Oct. 5, 1956.*

3 In Israel, in order to be a realist you must believe in miracles.

DAVID BEN GURION, (1886–1973) Israeli statesman. *interview on CBS–TV, Oct. 5, 1956.*

4 We have always said that in our war with the Arabs we had a secret weapon—no alternative.

GOLDA MEIR, (1898–1978) Israeli politician, prime minister. *Life* (New York, Oct. 3, 1969).

Italy and the Italians

1 For wheresoe'er I turn my ravished eyes,
Gay gilded scenes and shining prospects rise,
Poetic fields encompass me around,
And still I seem to tread on classic ground.

JOSEPH ADDISON, (1672–1719) British essayist. *Letter from Italy* (1704). Repr. in *Works of Addison*, ed. R. Hurd (1883).

2 Open my heart and you will see, Graved inside of it, "Italy."

ROBERT BROWNING, (1812–1889) British poet. *De Gustibus*, st. 2 (1855).

After Mary Tudor (Mary I), who is reported to have said, "When I am dead and opened, you shall find 'Calais' lying in my heart."

3   I love the language, that soft bastard Latin,
Which melts like kisses from a
    female mouth,
And sounds as if it should be writ
    on satin
With syllables which breathe of the
    sweet South.

GEORGE GORDON NOEL BYRON, 6TH BARON BYRON, (1788–1824) British poet. *Beppo*, st. 44 (1818).

4   Italia! oh Italia! thou who hast
The fatal gift of beauty.

GEORGE GORDON NOEL BYRON, 6TH BARON BYRON, (1788–1824) British poet. *Childe Harold's Pilgrimage*, cto. 4, st. 42 (1812–1818).

A loose translation of the sonnet *Italia* by the 17th–century Italian poet Vincenzo da Filicaja.

5   Italia! oh Italia! thou who hast
The fatal gift of beauty.

GEORGE GORDON NOEL BYRON, 6TH BARON BYRON, (1788–1824) British poet. *Childe Harold's Pilgrimage*, cto. 4, st. 42 (1812–1818).

A loose translation of the sonnet *Italia* by the 17th–century Italian poet Vincenzo da Filicaja.

6   A man who has not been in Italy, is always conscious of an inferiority.

SAMUEL JOHNSON, (1709–1784) British author, lexicographer. Quoted in James Boswell, *Life of Dr. Johnson*, entry, April 11, 1776 (1791).

Remark over supper with James Boswell and the Corsican patriot Pasquale Paoli.

7   Christ never came this far, nor did time, nor the individual soul, nor hope, nor the relation of cause to effect, nor reason nor history.

CARLO LEVI, (1902–1975) Italian writer, painter. *Christ Stopped at Eboli*, ch. 1 (1945, trans. 1948).

of Basilicata, in southern Italy. The book, describing Levi's internment in a small village as a consequence of his anti–Fascist activities, was the first to publicize the true plight of the Italian South.

8   Italy is a geographical expression.

PRINCE METTERNICH, (1773–1859) Austrian statesman. *Memoirs*, vol. 7 (1883). Letter, Nov. 19, 1849.

The Prussian statesman Otto von Bismarck used the same term, in a marginal comment on a letter of Nov. 1876, to the Russian Chancellor Gorchakov: "Whoever speaks of Europe is wrong: it is a geographical expression."

9   Thou Paradise of exiles, Italy!

PERCY BYSSHE SHELLEY, (1792–1822) British poet. *Julian and Maddalo*, l. 57 (1819).

10   Lump the whole thing! Say that the Creator made Italy from designs by Michael Angelo!

MARK TWAIN, (1835–1910) U.S. author. Dan, in *The Innocents Abroad*, ch. 27 (1869).

Twain's surfeit of and exasperation with Michelangelo during his visit to Rome was eloquently expressed: "I used to worship the mighty genius of Michael Angelo.... But I do not want Michael Angelo for breakfast—for luncheon—for dinner—for tea—for supper— for between meals.... Here—here it is frightful. He designed St Peter's; he designed the Pope ... the eternal bore designed the Eternal City, and unless all men and books do lie, he painted everything in it!... I never felt so fervently thankful, so soothed, so tranquil, so filled with the blessed peace, as I did yesterday when I learned that Michael Angelo was dead."

Ivory Towers

1   The only refuge left to us was the poet's ivory tower, which we climbed, ever higher, to isolate ourselves from the mob.

GÉRARD DE NERVAL, (1808–1855) French poet, author. the narrator, in *Sylvie*, ch. 1, *Revue des Deux Mondes* (Paris, Aug. 15, 1853). Repr. in *Les Filles du Feu* (1854).

Thought to be the earliest source for the expression *ivory tower*.

James, Henry

1 Few writers have had less journalistic talent than James, and this is his defect, for the supreme masters have one trait in common with the childish scribbling mass, the vulgar curiosity of a police–court reporter.

W.H. (WYSTAN HUGH) AUDEN, (1907–1973) Anglo–American poet. *The Dyer's Hand*, pt. 7, "The American Scene," (1962).

2 The work of Henry James has always seemed divisible by a simple dynastic arrangement into three reigns: James I, James II, and the Old Pretender.

PHILIP GUEDALLA, (1889–1944) British author. "Some Critics," *Supers and Supermen* (1920).

3 Poor Henry, he's spending eternity wandering round and round a stately park and the fence is just too high for him to peep over and they're having tea just too far away for him to hear what the countess is saying.

W. SOMERSET MAUGHAM, (1874–1966) British author. Edward Driffield, in *Cakes and Ale*, ch. 11 (1930).

In a notebook entry, Maugham wrote of James in 1937, "He did not live, he observed life from a window, and too often was inclined to content himself with no more than what his friends told him they saw when *they* looked out of a window.... In the end the point of Henry James is neither his artistry nor his seriousness, but his personality, and this was curious and charming and a trifle absurd." (*A Writer's Notebook*, 1949).

4 Mr. Henry James writes fiction as if it were a painful duty.

OSCAR WILDE, (1854–1900) Anglo–Irish playwright, author. Vivian, in *The Decay of Lying, Intentions* (1891). Repr. In *Complete Works of Oscar Wilde*, ed. J.B. Foreman (1966).

Jealousy

1 Set me as a seal upon thine heart, as a seal upon thine arm: for love is strong as death; jealousy is cruel as the grave: the coals thereof are coals of fire, which hath a most vehement flame.

BIBLE: HEBREW, *Song of Solomon*, 8:6.

2 Jealousy is all the fun you *think* they had.

ERICA JONG, (b. 1942) U.S. author. *How To Save Your Own Life*, epigraph to "Bennett tells all in Woodstock ... " (1977).

3 Jealousy contains more of self-love than of love.

FRANÇOIS LA ROCHEFOUCAULD, DUC DE, (1613–1680) French writer, moralist. *Sentences et Maximes Morales*, no. 324 (1678).

4 Nor jealousy
Was understood, the injured lover's hell.

JOHN MILTON, (1608–1674) British poet. *Paradise Lost*, bk. 5, l. 449 (1674). Repr. in *Paradise Lost*, ed. Scott Elledge (1993).

5 O curse of marriage,
That we can call these delicate creatures ours
And not their appetites! I had rather be a toad,
And live upon the vapour of a dungeon
Than keep a corner in the thing I love

For others' uses.

WILLIAM SHAKESPEARE, (1564–1616) British dramatist, poet. Othello, in *Othello*, act 3, sc. 3, l. 272–7 (1623).

Jesus Christ

1   Behold the man!

BIBLE: NEW TESTAMENT, Pilate, in *John*, 19:5.

The words of Pontius Pilate to Jesus, wearing the crown of thorns and purple robe, are best known in the Latin form in which they appear in the Vulgate: *Ecce homo.*

2   He is despised and rejected of men; a man of sorrows, and acquainted with grief: and we hid as it were our faces from him; he was despised, and we esteemed him not. Surely he hath borne our griefs, and carried our sorrows: yet we did esteem him stricken, smitten of God, and afflicted.

BIBLE: HEBREW, *Isaiah*, 53:3–4.

The passage is traditionally considered to fore-tell Christ's passion.

3   I am the bread of life: he that cometh to me shall never hunger; and he that believeth on me shall never thirst.

BIBLE: NEW TESTAMENT, Jesus, in *John*, 6:35.

4   Thinking as I do that the Creator of this world is a very cruel being, & being a worshipper of Christ, I cannot help saying: "the Son, O how unlike the Father!" First God Almighty comes with a thump on the head. Then Jesus Christ comes with a balm to heal it.

WILLIAM BLAKE, (1757–1827) British poet, painter, engraver. "A Vision of the Last Judgement " (1810), repr. in *Complete Writings*, ed. Geoffrey Keynes (1957).

5   A lot of people say to me, "Why did you kill Christ?" "I dunno ... it was one of those parties, got out of hand, you know." We killed him because he didn't want to become a doctor, that's why we killed him.

LENNY BRUCE, (1925–1966) U.S. satirical comedian. *The Essential Lenny Bruce*, "The Jews," ed. John Cohen (1967).

6   Jesus died for somebody's sins but not mine.

PATTI SMITH, (b. 1946) U.S. rock musician, poet. "Gloria," on the album *Horses* (1975).

Opening line of album; song originally by Van Morrison.

7   Thou has conquered, O pale Galilean.

A.C. (ALGERNON CHARLES) SWINBURNE, (1837–1909) British poet, critic. "Hymn to Proserpine" (1866).

"Thou hast conquered, Galilean" were alleged by some early Christian historians to have been the dying words of the Roman emperor Julian the Apostate (c. 332–363), uttered after his victory against the Persians in 363. Swinburne also used the words in his poem "The Last Oracle."

Jewelry

1   Don't ever wear artistic jewelry; it wrecks a woman's reputation.

COLETTE [SIDONIE GABRIELLE COLETTE], (1873–1954) French author. Aunt Alicia, in *Gigi* (1944, trans.1953).

When asked (by Gilberte) "What is an artistic jewel?" Aunt Alicia replied, "It all depends. A mermaid in gold, with eyes of chrysoprase. An Egyptian scarab. A large engraved amethyst. A not very heavy bracelet said to have been chased by a master–hand. A lyre or star, mounted as a brooch. A studded tortoise. In a word, all of them frightful. Never wear baroque pearls, not even as hat–pins. Beware above all things, of family jewels!"

2   Diamonds are a girl's best friend.

LEO ROBIN, (b. 1900) U.S. songwriter. "Diamonds Are a Girl's Best Friend" (song), *Gentleman Prefer Blondes* (stage show 1949; film 1953).

Johnson, Samuel

1   If you were to make little fishes talk, they would talk like whales.

OLIVER GOLDSMITH, (1728–1774) Anglo–Irish author, poet, playwright. Quoted in James Boswell, *Life of Dr. Johnson*, entry, April 27, 1773 (1791).

Remark to Johnson.

2   Beyond all question, I might have had a wiser friend than he. The atmosphere in which alone he breathed was dense; his awful dread of death showed how much muddy imperfection was to be cleansed out of him, before he could be capable of spiritual existence; he meddled only with the surface of life, and never cared to penetrate further than to ploughshare depth; his very sense and sagacity were but a one–eyed clear–sightedness.... Dr. Johnson's morality was as English an article as a beefsteak.

NATHANIEL HAWTHORNE, (1804–1864) U.S. author. "Lichfield and Uttoxeter," *Our Old Home* (1863).

Henry James said that this formed part of a graceful tribute to Johnson who "certainly has nowhere else been more tenderly spoken of."

Jokes and Jokers

1   My life has been one great big joke,
A dance that's walked
A song that's spoke,
I laugh so hard I almost choke
When I think about myself.

MAYA ANGELOU, (b. 1928) U.S. author. "When I Think About Myself," *Just Give Me a Cool Drink of Water 'fore I Diiie* (1971).

2   His hilarity was like a scream from a crevasse.

GRAHAM GREENE, (1904–1991) British novelist. *The Heart of the Matter*, bk. 3, pt. 1, ch. 1, sct. 1 (1948).

Referring to Major Scobie.

3   Indeed—very good. I shall—have to repeat—that—on the Golden Floor.

A.E. (ALFRED EDWARD) HOUSMAN, (1859–1936) British poet. Quoted in *A.E. Housman, The Scholar Poet*, ch. 12, Richard Perceval Graves (1979). Doctor's letter, May 12, 1976, to Richard Perceval Graves.

Last words spoken to his doctor, who had just recounted the reply of an actor when asked what members of his profession did in their spare time: "Well, I suppose you could say we spend half our time lying on the sands looking at the stars, and the other half lying on the Stars looking at the sands!"

4   A dirty joke is a sort of mental rebellion.

GEORGE ORWELL, (1903–1950) British author. "The Art of Donald McGill," *Horizon* (London, Sept. 1941). Repr. in *Collected Essays* (1961).

5   Alas, poor Yorick. I knew him, Horatio—a fellow of infinite jest, of most excellent fancy.

WILLIAM SHAKESPEARE, (1564–1616) British dramatist, poet. Hamlet, in *Hamlet*, act 5, sc. 1, l. 180–1 (1604).

Said of Hamlet's father's jester, whose skull has just been dug up. "Where be your gibes now, your gambols, your songs, your flashes of merriment that were wont to set the table on a roar?"

6   Alas, poor Yorick. I knew him, Horatio—a fellow of infinite jest, of most excellent fancy.

WILLIAM SHAKESPEARE, (1564–1616) British dramatist, poet. Hamlet, in *Hamlet*, act 5, sc. 1, l. 180–1 (1604).

Said of Hamlet's father's jester, whose skull has just been dug up. "Where be your gibes now, your gambols, your songs, your flashes of merriment that were wont to set the table on a roar?"

7 He jests at scars that never felt a
wound.

WILLIAM SHAKESPEARE, (1564–1616)
British dramatist, poet. Romeo, in *Romeo and
Juliet*, act 2, sc. 1, l. 43 (1599).

Spoken of Mercutio, who mocked Romeo's
love–lorn state, in "the balcony scene."

8 'Tis no extravagant arithmetic to
say, that for every ten jokes,—thou
hast got an hundred enemies; and
till thou hast gone on, and raised a
swarm of wasps about thine ears,
and art half stung to death by them,
thou wilt never be convinced it is
so.

LAURENCE STERNE, (1713–1768) British
author. *Tristram Shandy*, bk. 1, ch. 12
(1759–1767).

9 All human race would fain be wits.
And millions miss, for one that hits.

JONATHAN SWIFT, (1667–1745)
Anglo–Irish satirist. "On Poetry: A Rhapsody,"
l. 1–2 (1733), published in *Jonathan Swift: A
Critical Edition of the Major Works*, eds.
Angus Ross and David Woolley (1984).

Journalism and Journalists

1 Literature is the art of writing
something that will be read twice;
journalism what will be grasped at
once.

CYRIL CONNOLLY, (1903–1974) British
critic. *Enemies of Promise*, ch. 3 (1938).

2 A petty reason perhaps why novelists more and more try to keep a
distance from journalists is that
novelists are trying to write the
truth and journalists are trying to
write fiction.

GRAHAM GREENE, (1904–1991) British
novelist. *Yours, Etc: Letters to the Press,
1945–1989* (1989). Letter, Jan. 18, 1981, to
critic Stephen Pile, *Sunday Times* (London).

3 The man must have a rare recipe
for melancholy, who can be dull in
Fleet Street.

CHARLES LAMB, (1775–1834) British
essayist, critic. *Letters of Charles and Mary
Lamb*, vol. 2, ed. E.W. Marrs (1976). Letter,
Feb. 15, 1802, to Thomas Manning.

4 The journalists have constructed
for themselves a little wooden
chapel, which they also call the
Temple of Fame, in which they put
up and take down portraits all day
long and make such a hammering
you can't hear yourself speak.

GEORG CHRISTOPH LICHTENBERG,
(1742–1799) German physicist, philosopher.
"Notebook D," aph. 20, *Aphorisms* (written
1765–1799), trans. by R.J. Hollingdale (1990).

5 Every journalist who is not too stupid or too full of himself to notice
what is going on knows that what
he does is morally indefensible. He
is a kind of confidence man, prey-
ing on people's vanity, ignorance,
or loneliness, gaining their trust
and betraying them without
remorse.

JANET MALCOLM, (b. 1934) U.S. author.
The Journalist and the Murderer, pt. 1 (1990).

Opening paragraph of the book, which dis-
cusses the case of journalist Joe McGinniss.
The latter won the trust of an alleged murderer, then wrote a best–seller, *Fatal Vision*
(1984), proclaiming his guilt.

Joy

1 He who binds to himself a joy
Does the winged life destroy;
But he who kisses the joy as it flies
Lives in Eternity's sunrise.

WILLIAM BLAKE, (1757–1827) British
poet, artist. "Eternity", from the Note–Book, c.
1793, published in *Complete Writings*, ed.
Geoffrey Keynes (1957).

2   Breathless, we flung us on the
     windy hill,
     Laughed in the sun, and kissed the
     lovely grass.

RUPERT BROOKE, (1887–1915) British
poet. "The Hill," *Collected Poems*
(1966).(1910).

4   Grief can take care of itself, but to
     get the full value of a joy you must
     have somebody to divide it with.

MARK TWAIN, (1835–1910) U.S. author.
Following the Equator, ch. 12, "Pudd'nhead
Wilson's New Calendar" (1897).

Joyce, James

1   Welcome, O life! I go to encounter
     for the millionth time the reality of
     experience and to forge in the
     smithy of my soul the uncreated
     conscience of my race.... Old father,
     old artificer, stand me now and ever
     in good stead.

JAMES JOYCE, (1882–1941) Irish author.
Stephen Dedalus, in *A Portrait of the Artist as
a Young Man,* ch. 5 (1916).

Departing from Ireland, in the closing lines of
the book. "Old artificer" refers to Daedalus,
the mythical craftsman, whose flight from
Crete ended in the drowning of his son.
Joyce's own experience on fleeing Ireland was
characterized by debt and penury.

2   Never did I read such tosh. As for
     the first two chapters we will let
     them pass, but the 3rd 4th 5th
     6th—merely the scratching of pim-
     ples on the body of the bootboy at
     Claridges.

VIRGINIA WOOLF, (1882–1941) British
novelist. *Letters,* vol. 2, "The Question of
Things Happening," ed. Nigel Nicolson
(1976). Letter, April 24, 1922, to Lytton Strachey.

Referring to Joyce's *Ulysses.*

Judaism and Jewish People

1   Yes, I am a Jew, and when the
     ancestors of the right honourable
     gentleman were brutal
     savages in an unknown island,
     mine were priests in the temple of
     Solomon.

BENJAMIN DISRAELI, (1804–1881)
British statesman, author. Quoted in *The Fine
Art of Political Wit,* ch. 4, Leon Harris (1964).

Disraeli's attributed reply to a taunt by Irish
political leader Daniel O'Connell bears
resemblance to the reputed retort to a senator
of German extraction by Senator Judah P.
Benjamin of Louisiana: "The gentleman will
please remember that when his half–civilized
ancestors were hunting the wild boar in the
forests of Silesia, mine were the princes of the
earth."

2   Is discord going to show itself while
     we are still fighting, is the Jew once
     again worth less than another? Oh,
     it is sad, very sad, that once more,
     for the umpteenth time, the old
     truth is confirmed: "What *one*
     Christian does is his own responsi-
     bility, what *one* Jew does is thrown
     back at all Jews."

ANNE FRANK, (1929–1945) German Jewish refugee, diarist. *The Diary of a Young Girl*
(1947, trans. 1952). Journal entry, May 22,
1944.

On anti–semitism in Holland.

3   *I determine who is a Jew.*

KARL LUEGER, (1844–1910) Austrian
lawyer, politician. quoted in *Hitler, a Study in
Tyranny,* ch. 1, sct. 4, Alan Bullock (1962).

The statement has also been attributed to Nazi
leader Hermann Goering.

4   From the outset, the Christian was
     the theorizing Jew, the Jew is there-
     fore the practical
     Christian, and the practical
     Christian has become a Jew again.

Karl Marx, (1818–1883) German political theorist, social philosopher. "On the Jewish Question," sct. 2 (1843), repr. in Karl Marx and Friedrich Engels: *Collected Works*, vol. 3 (1975).

5   In my blood there is no Jewish blood.
In their callous rage, all antisemites
    must hate me now as a Jew.
For that reason I am a true Russian.

Yevgeny Yevtushenko, (b. 1933) Russian poet. "Babi Yar," (1961) trans. by George Reavey.

Last lines of the poem which described the massacre of 96,000 Jews in the Ukraine by the Nazis. The poem caused controversy by implying that the Soviet régime was antisemitic.

Judges

1   Judges don't age. Time decorates them.

Enid Bagnold, (1889–1981) British novelist, playwright. Judge, in *The Chalk Garden*, act 2 (1953).

2   A day in thy courts is better than a thousand.

Bible: Hebrew, *Psalms*, 84:10.

3   The cold neutrality of an impartial judge.

Edmund Burke, (1729–1797) Irish philosopher, statesman. *To His Constituents*, "Translator's Preface," J.P. Brissot (1794).

4   My object all sublime
    I shall achieve in time—
To let the punishment fit the
    crime—
    The punishment fit the crime;
And make each prisoner pent
Unwillingly represent
A source of innocent merriment!
Of innocent merriment!

Sir William Schwenck Gilbert, (1836–1911) British librettist. Mikado, in *The Mikado*, act 2 (1885), published in *The Savoy Operas* (1926).

Judgment

1   Judge none blessed before his death: for a man shall be known in his children.

Apocrypha, *Ecclesiasticus*, 11:28.

2   Thou art weighed in the balances, and art found wanting.

Bible: Hebrew, *2 Samuel*, 5:27.

Daniel interprets for Belshazzar the "writing on the wall."

3   Thou art weighed in the balances, and art found wanting.

Bible: Hebrew, *2 Samuel*, 5:27.

Daniel interprets for Belshazzar the "writing on the wall."

4   We are ashamed to seem evasive in the presence of a straightforward man, cowardly in the presence of a brave one, gross in the eyes of a refined one, and so on. We always imagine, and in imagining share, the judgments of the other mind.

Charles Horton Cooley, (1864–1929) U.S. sociologist. *Human Nature and the Social Order*, ch. 5 (1902).

5   You say that you are my judge; I do not know if you are; but take good heed not to judge me ill, because you would put yourself in great peril.

Joan of Arc, (c.1412–1431) French patriot, martyr. Quoted in *The Trial of Jeanne d'Arc*, ed. W.P. Barrett (1931).

6   Everyone complains of his memory, none of his judgment.

FRANÇOIS LA ROCHEFOUCAULD, DUC DE, (1613–1680) French writer, moralist. *Sentences et Maximes Morales,* no. 89 (1678).

7   Speak of me as I am. Nothing
    extenuate,
    Nor set down aught in malice.

WILLIAM SHAKESPEARE, (1564–1616) British dramatist, poet. Othello, in *Othello,* act 5, sc. 2, l. 351–2 (1623).

Spoken to his arresting officers.

Judgment Day

1   And I saw the dead, small and
    great, stand before God; and the
    books were opened: and another
    book was opened, which is the
    book of life: and the dead were
    judged out of those things which
    were written in the books, according to their works.

BIBLE: NEW TESTAMENT, St. John the Divine, in *Revelation,* 20:12.

Juries

1   "Write that down," the King said to
    the jury, and the jury eagerly wrote
    down all three dates on their slates,
    and then added them up, and
    reduced the answer to shillings and
    pence.

LEWIS CARROLL [CHARLES LUTWIDGE DODGSON], (1832–1898) British author, mathematician. *Alice's Adventures in Wonderland,* "Who Stole the Tarts?" (1865).

2   Our civilization has decided ... that
    determining the guilt or innocence
    of men is a thing too important to
    be trusted to trained men.... When
    it wants a library catalogued, or the
    solar system discovered, or any tri-
    fle of that kind, it uses up its specialists. But when it wishes anything
    done which is really serious, it collects twelve of the ordinary men
    standing round. The same thing
    was done, if I remember right, by
    the Founder of Christianity.

GILBERT KEITH CHESTERTON, (1874–1936) British author. *Tremendous Trifles,* "The Twelve Men" (1909).

Justice

1   Blessed are they which do hunger
    and thirst after righteousness: for
    they shall be filled.

BIBLE: NEW TESTAMENT, Jesus, in *Matthew,* 5:6.

The fourth of the Beatitudes, from the Sermon on the Mount.

2   It is better that ten guilty persons
    escape than that one innocent suffer.

WILLIAM BLACKSTONE, (1723–1780) British jurist. *Commentaries on the Laws of England,* bk. 4, ch. 27 (1765–1769).

3   A good parson once said that where
    mystery begins religion ends. Cannot I say, as truly at least, of human
    laws, that where mystery begins justice ends?

EDMUND BURKE, (1729–1797) Irish philosopher, statesman. *A Vindication of Natural Society* (1756), repr. in *Works,* vol. 1 (1865).

4   Justice consists in doing no injury
    to men; decency in giving them no
    offence.

MARCUS TULLIUS CICERO, (106–43 B.C.) Roman orator, philosopher. *De Officiis,* bk. 1, ch. 28, sct. 99 (44 B.C.).

5   Let justice be done, though the
    world perish. *(Fiat justitia et pereat mundus.)*

FERDINAND I, (1503–1564) Hungarian King of Bohemia and Hungary, Holy Roman Emperor 1558–1564. *Motto.*

The Latin maxim—adopted as Ferdinand's motto in the early 1530s—has been ascribed to Lucius Calpurnius Piso Caesoninus (d. 43 B.C.) in the form, "Let justice be done, though heaven should fall." *(Fiat justitia ruat coelum.)*

6　Justice should not only be done, but should manifestly and undoubtedly be seen to be done.

GORDON, 1ST BARON OF BURY HEWART, (1870–1943) British judge. "Rex v. Surrey Justices," vol. 1, *King's Bench Reports* (1924). Remark, Nov. 9, 1923.

Ruling on the quashing of a conviction on technical grounds.

7　The love of justice is, in most men, nothing more than the fear of suffering injustice.

FRANÇOIS LA ROCHEFOUCAULD, DUC DE, (1613–1680) French writer, moralist. *Sentences et Maximes Morales*, no. 78 (1678).

The aphorism was repeated with a slight variation by the French writer, Lautréamont, in *Poèsies*, ch. 2 (1870): "Love of justice is for most men only the courage to suffer injustice."

8　Yet I shall temper so Justice with mercy.

JOHN MILTON, (1608–1674) British poet. *Paradise Lost*, bk. 10, l. 77–8 (1674). Repr. in *Paradise Lost*, ed. Scott Elledge (1993).

The words of Jesus to God.

9　What I say is that "just" or "right" means nothing but what is in the interest of the stronger party.

PLATO, (c. 427–347 B.C.) Greek philosopher. Thrasymachus, in *The Republic*, bk. 1, sct. 338 (trans. by F.M. Cornford).

10　This even–handed justice Commends th'ingredience of our poisoned chalice

To our own lips.

WILLIAM SHAKESPEARE, (1564–1616) British dramatist, poet. Macbeth, in *Macbeth*, act 1, sc. 7, l. 10–12 (1623).

Part of Macbeth's soliloquy on his forthcoming murder of Duncan and its consequences.

Keats, John

1　Such writing is a sort of mental masturbation.... I don't mean that he is *indecent* but viciously soliciting his own ideas into a state which is neither poetry nor anything else but a Bedlam vision produced by raw pork and opium.

GEORGE GORDON NOEL BYRON, 6TH BARON BYRON, (1788–1824) British poet. *Byron's Letters and Journals*, vol. 7, ed. Leslie A. Marchand (1973–1981). Letter, Nov. 9, 1820, to the publisher John Murray.

Byron had previously called Keats's work "the Onanism of Poetry," but later retracted his attack, limiting his criticism to the younger poet's style.

2　Here Lies One Whose Name was writ in Water.

JOHN KEATS, (1795–1821) British poet. *Life, Letters and Literary Remains of John Keats*, vol. 2, p. 91 (1848)."Epitaph for Himself" (1821).

Keats's epitaph is inscribed on his grave in the English cemetery in Rome. A few days before he died, the poet stipulated that there should be no mention of his name or country on the headstone. It is reported that he had in mind lines from the play by Francis Beaumont and John Fletcher, *Philaster, or Love Lies A–Bleeding* (1609): "All your better deeds/Shall be in water writ, but this in marble." See Shakespeare on virtue for another possible source.

3　"If I should die," said I to myself, "I have left no immortal work behind me—nothing to make my friends proud of my memory—but I have loved the principle of beauty in all things, and if I had had time I would have made myself remembered."

JOHN KEATS, (1795–1821) British poet. *Letters of John Keats*, no. 186, ed. Frederick Page (1954). Letter, Feb. 1820, to Fanny Brawne.

Of Keats's thoughts during his illness.

4   I weep for Adonais—he is dead!
O, weep for Adonais! though our tears
Thaw not the frost which binds so dear a head!

PERCY BYSSHE SHELLEY, (1792–1822) British poet. "Adonais," st. 1 (1821).

Opening lines. This elegy written for poet John Keats, died aged 25, is framed in the tradition of Greek poetry, fitting for one whom Shelley regarded as deriving his inspiration from ancient Greece. The name "Adonais" was probably chosen in allusion to the beautiful youth Adonis, killed by a boar while hunting.

Kennedy Family

1   One would never have guessed that the world had such a capacity for genuine grief. The most we can do is exploit our memories of his excellence.

JOHN CHEEVER, (1912–1982) U.S. author. *John Cheever: The Journals*, "The Sixties," ed. Robert Gottlieb (1991). Journal entry, 1963.

Referring to the assassination of John F. Kennedy.

2   Ask every person if he's heard the story, And tell it strong and clear if he has not, That once there was a fleeting wisp of glory Called Camelot ... Don't let it be forgot That once there was a spot For one brief shining moment that was known As Camelot.

ALAN JAY LERNER, (1918–1986) U.S. composer, lyricist. "Camelot" (song), *Camelot* (musical show, 1960; filmed, 1967).

The song was named by Jackie Kennedy in an interview shortly after John F. Kennedy's assassination as one of which her husband was particularly fond. Official biographer William Manchester called his book *One Brief Shining Moment* (1983).

Killing

1   Thou shalt not kill.

BIBLE: HEBREW, *Exodus*, 20:13.

The sixth commandment.

2   Thou shalt not kill; but need'st not strive
Officiously to keep alive.

ARTHUR HUGH CLOUGH, (1819–1861) British poet. "The Latest Decalogue," (1862). Repr. in *Collected Poems*, ed. C. Whibley (1913).

3   Kill a man one is a murderer; kill a million, a conqueror; kill them all, a God.

JEAN ROSTAND, (1894–1977) French biologist, writer. *Pensées d'un Biologiste* (1939). Repr. in *The Substance of Man* (1962).

4   The urge to kill, like the urge to beget,
Is blind and sinister. Its craving is set
Today on the flesh of a hare: tomorrow it can
Howl the same way for the flesh of a man.

ANDREI VOZNESENSKY, (b. 1933) Russian poet. "Hunting a Hare," st. 5 (1964), trans. by W.H. Auden.

5   Yet each man kills the thing he loves,
By each let this be heard,
Some do it with a bitter look,
Some with a flattering word.
The coward does it with a kiss,
The brave man with a sword!

OSCAR WILDE, (1854–1900) Anglo–Irish playwright, author. *The Ballad of Reading Gaol*, pt. 1, st. 7 (1898). Repr. in *Complete Works of Oscar Wilde*, ed. J.B. Foreman (1966).

The lines are often interpreted as referring to Lord Alfred Douglas, with whom Wilde had a liaison which led to Wilde's trial and imprisonment for homosexual offenses. Wilde reproached Douglas for the latter's behavior towards him during and after the trial.

Kindness

1 I want a kinder, gentler nation.

GEORGE BUSH, (b. 1924) U.S. Republican politician, president. *acceptance speech, The New York Times* (Aug. 19, 1988). Republican National Convention, New Orleans, August 18, 1988.

In her memoirs, *What I Saw at the Revolution* (1990), speechwriter Peggy Noonan suggests that Bush added the word "gentler" to her original draft. Charlie Chaplin had used a similar form of words at the end of *The Great Dictator* (1940), when he urged, "More than cleverness, we need kindness and gentleness."

2 When kindness has left people, even for a few moments, we become afraid of them as if their reason had left them. When it has left a place where we have always found it, it is like shipwreck; we drop from security into something malevolent and bottomless.

WILLA CATHER, (1876–1947) U.S. author. *My Mortal Enemy* (1926), p.62, of Hamish & Hamish edition (1963).

3 Yet do I fear thy nature,
It is too full o'th' milk of human
   kindness
To catch the nearest way.

WILLIAM SHAKESPEARE, (1564–1616) British dramatist, poet. Lady Macbeth, in *Macbeth*, act 1, sc. 5, l. 15–17 (1623).

Lady Macbeth reacts to Macbeth's letter informing her of the Witches' prophesy that he will be king. Fearing Macbeth is too gentle to murder the king ("catch the nearest way").

4 Yet do I fear thy nature,
It is too full o'th' milk of human
   kindness
To catch the nearest way.

WILLIAM SHAKESPEARE, (1564–1616) British dramatist, poet. Lady Macbeth, in *Macbeth*, act 1, sc. 5, l. 15–17 (1623).

Lady Macbeth reacts to Macbeth's letter informing her of the Witches' prophesy that he will be king.

Kissing

1 What of soul was left, I wonder, when the kissing had to stop?

ROBERT BROWNING, (1812–1889) British poet. "A Toccata of Galuppi's," st. 14, *Men and Women*, vol. 1 (1855).

2 Give me a thousand kisses, and then a hundred,
Then another thousand, then a second hundred,
And then yet another thousand, then a hundred.

CATULLUS [GAIUS VALERIUS CATULLUS], (84–54 B.C.) Roman poet. "Carmina," no. 5, l. 7–9.

3 Mr. Grenville squeezed me by the hand again, kissed the ladies, and withdrew. He kissed likewise the maid in the kitchen, and seemed upon the whole a most loving, kissing, kind–hearted gentleman.

WILLIAM COWPER, (1731–1800) British poet. *Letters and Prose Writings of William Cowper*, vol. 2, eds. J. King and C. Ryskamp (1981). Letter, March 29, 1874.

4 What did that mean, to kiss? You put your face up like that to say goodnight and then his mother put her face down. That was to kiss. His mother put her lips on his cheek; her lips were soft and they wetted his cheek; and they made a tiny lit-

tle noise: kiss. Why did people do
that with their two faces?

JAMES JOYCE, (1882–1941) Irish author.
Stephen Dedalus, in *A Portrait of the Artist as a
Young Man*, ch. 1 (1916).

Knowledge

1 For in much wisdom is much grief:
and he that increaseth knowledge
increaseth sorrow.

BIBLE: HEBREW, *Ecclesiastes*, 1:18.

2 For in much wisdom is much grief:
and he that increaseth knowledge
increaseth sorrow.

BIBLE: HEBREW, *Ecclesiastes*, 1:18.

3 Knowledge puffeth up, but charity
edifieth. And if any man think that
he knoweth any thing, he knoweth
nothing yet as he ought to know.

BIBLE: NEW TESTAMENT, St. Paul, in *1
Corinthians*, 8:1–2.

4 Everyman, I will go with thee, and
be thy guide,
In thy most need to go by thy side.

ANONYMOUS, Knowledge, in *Everyman*, act
1, l. 522 (c. 1509–1519).

5 All men by nature desire knowledge.

ARISTOTLE, (384–322 B.C.) Greek philosopher. *Metaphysics*, bk. 1, ch. 1.

6 For also knowledge itself is power.

FRANCIS BACON, (1561–1626) British
philosopher, essayist, statesman. *Religious
Meditations*, "Of Heresies" (1597).

7 I have as vast contemplative ends, as
I have moderate civil ends; for I have
taken all knowledge to be my
province.

FRANCIS BACON, (1561–1626) British
philosopher, essayist, statesman. *The Letters
and Life of Francis Bacon*, vol. 1, p. 109, ed. J.
Spedding (1861). Letter, 1592, *To My Lord
Treasurer Burghley*.

8 Sorrow is knowledge: they who
know the most
Must mourn the deepest o'er the
fatal truth,
The Tree of Knowledge is not that
of Life.

**GEORGE GORDON NOEL BYRON, 6TH
BARON BYRON,** (1788–1824) British poet.
Manfred, in *Manfred*, act 1, sc. 1 (1817).

Manfred's opening speech. According to
Michael Foot's biography, *The Politics of Paradise: A Vindication of Byron*, ch. 5 (1988),
this speech was considered by Nietzsche to
be "immortal," for stating the terrible fact that
a man might bleed to death through the truth
that he recognizes.

9 For out of olde feldes, as men seith,
Cometh al this new corn fro yeer to
yere;
And out of olde bokes, in good
feith,
Cometh al this newe science that
men lere.

GEOFFREY CHAUCER, (1340–1400)
British poet. *The Parlement of Foules*, "The
Proem," l. 22–5 (c. 1380–1386), repr. in *The
Works of Geoffrey Chaucer*, ed. Alfred W.
Pollard, et al. (1898).

10 Knowledge, a rude unprofitable
mass,
The mere materials with which wisdom builds,
Till smoothed and squared and fit-
ted to its place,
Does but encumber whom it seems
to enrich.
Knowledge is proud that he has
learned so much;
Wisdom is humble that he knows
no more.

WILLIAM COWPER, (1731–1800) British poet. *The Task*, bk. 6, l. 92–7 (1785). Repr. in *Poetical Works*, ed. H.S. Milford (1934).

11   For lust of knowing what should
      not be known,
      We take the Golden Road to
      Samarkand.

JAMES ELROY FLECKER, (1884–1915) British poet. Ishak, in *Hassan*, act 5, sc. 2 (1922).

12   It is the province of knowledge to
      speak, and it is the privilege of wis-
      dom to listen.

OLIVER WENDELL HOLMES, SR., (1809–1894) U.S. writer, physician. *The Poet at the Breakfast–Table*, ch. 10 (1872).

13   To know yet to think that one does
      not know is best; Not to know yet
      to think that one knows will lead to
      difficulty.

LAO–TZU, (6th century B.C.) Chinese philosopher. *Tao–te–ching*, bk. 2, ch. 71, trans. by T.C. Lau (1963).

14   People of quality know everything
      without ever having learned any-
      thing.

MOLIÈRE [JEAN BAPTISTE POQUELIN], (1622–1673) French dramatist. Mascarille, in *Les Précieuses Ridicules*, sc. 9 (1659).

15   Children with Hyacinth's tempera-
      ment don't know better as they
      grow older; they merely know
      more.

[H.H. (HECTOR HUGH) MUNRO] SAKI, (1870–1916) Scottish author. "Hyacinth," *The Toys of Peace* (1919).

16   Happy the man who has been able
      to know the reasons for things.

VIRGIL [PUBLIUS VERGILIUS MARO], (70–19 B.C.) Roman poet.

Georgics, bk. 2, l. 490 (19 B.C.), trans. by Kate Hughes (1995).

Thought to refer to the poet and philosopher Lucretius.

Korean War, The

1   The wrong war, at the wrong place,
     at the wrong time, and with the
     wrong enemy.

OMAR BRADLEY, (1893–1981) U.S. general. *The Military Situation in the Far East*, Senate Hearings (1951). Speech, May 15, 1951, to Senate Committees on Armed Services and Foreign Relations.

As Chairman of the Joint Chiefs of Staff, Bradley was giving testimony before a Senate inquiry into General MacArthur's proposal to carry the Korean conflict into China; Bradley opposed the scheme, arguing that "Red China is not the powerful nation seeking to dominate the world."

Labor

1   The labourer is worthy of his hire.

BIBLE: NEW TESTAMENT, Jesus, in *Luke*, 10:7.

Instructing his disciples to accept any hospitality offered to them.

2   I tell you, sir, the only safeguard of
     order and discipline in the modern
     world is a standardized worker with
     interchangeable parts. That would
     solve the entire problem of man-
     agement.

JEAN GIRAUDOUX, (1882–1944) French author, diplomat. The President, in *The Madwoman of Chaillot*, act 1 (1945).

3   Labor is prior to, and independent
     of, capital. Capital is only the fruit
     of labor, and could never have
     existed if labor had not first existed.
     Labor is the superior of capital, and

deserves much the higher consideration.

ABRAHAM LINCOLN, (1809–1865) U.S. president. *First Annual Message to Congress, Collected Works of Abraham Lincoln,* vol. 5, ed. Roy P. Basler (1953). Speech, Dec. 3, 1861.

4   Men of England, wherefore plough
    For the lords who lay ye low?

PERCY BYSSHE SHELLEY, (1792–1822) British poet. "Song to the Men of England," st. 1 (written 1819).

Opening lines.

Ladies

1   What Soft—Cherubic Creatures—
    These Gentlewomen are—
    One would as soon assault a Plush—
    Or violate a Star—

EMILY DICKINSON, (1830–1886) U.S. poet. "What Soft Cherubic Creatures," st. 1 (written c. 1862, published 1896). Repr. in *The Complete Poems,* no. 401, Harvard *variorum* edition (1955).

2   Ermined and minked and
    Persian–lambed,
    Be–puffed (be–painted, too, alas!)
    Be–decked, be–diamonded
      be–damned!
    The Women of the Better Class.

OLIVER HERFORD, (1863–1935) U.S. poet, illustrator. *The Women of the Better Class,* st. 4.

3   To behold her is an immediate check to loose behaviour; to love her is a liberal education.

RICHARD STEELE, (1672–1729) British dramatist, essayist, editor. *Tatler* (London, Aug. 2, 1709), vol. 1, no. 49, *The Tatler,* ed. G.A. Aitken (1898).

Referring to Lady Elizabeth Hastings.

4   Women of quality are so civil, you can hardly distinguish love from good breeding.

WILLIAM WYCHERLEY, (1640–1716) British dramatist. Horner, in *The Country Wife,* act 1 (1675). Repr. in *Plays of William Wycherley,* ed. W.C. Ward (1888).

Land, the

1   The land was ours before we were
      the land's.
    She was our land more than a hun-
      dred years
    Before we were her people.

ROBERT FROST, (1874–1963) U.S. poet. "The Gift Outright," *The Witness Tree* (1942).

Frost recited this poem at the inauguration of President Kennedy, Jan. 20, 1961.

2   This land is your land, this land is my land, From California to the New York Island. From the red-wood forest to the Gulf Stream waters This land was made for you and me.

WOODY GUTHRIE, (1912–1967) U.S. singer, songwriter. "This Land Is Your Land" (song) (1956).

"This land is your land & this land is my land—sure," Bob Dylan wrote in *Tarantula* (1970),"but the world is run by those that never listen to music anyway."

3   We abuse land because we regard it as a commodity belonging to us. When we see land as a community to which we belong, we may begin to use it with love and respect.

ALDO LEOPOLD, (1886–1948) U.S. forester. *A Sand Country Almanac,* foreword (1949).

Landscapes

1   'Tis distance lends enchantment to
      the view,
    And robes the mountain in its
      azure hue.

THOMAS CAMPBELL, (1777–1844) Scottish poet. "The Pleasures of Hope," pt. 1, l. 7–8 (1799). Repr. in *Complete Poetical Works*, ed. J.L. Robertson (1907).

Language

1   Ye knowe eek, that in forme of speche is chaunge
    Withinne a thousand yeer, and wordes tho
    That hadden prys, now wonder nyce and straunge
    Us thinketh hem; and yet they spake hem so,
    And spedde as wel in love as men now do;
    Eek for to winne love in sondry ages,
    In sondry londes, sondry ben usages.

    GEOFFREY CHAUCER, (1340–1400) British poet. *Troilus and Criseyde*, bk. 2, l. 22–8 (c. 1385), repr. in *The Works of Geoffrey Chaucer*, ed. Alfred W. Pollard, et al. (1898).

2   The common faults of American language are an ambition of effect, a want of simplicity, and a turgid abuse of terms.

    JAMES FENIMORE COOPER, (1789–1851) U.S. novelist. *The American Democrat*, "On Language" (1838).

3   And who, in time, knows whither we may vent
    The treasure of our tongue, to what strange shores
    This gain of our best glory shall be sent,
    T'enrich unknowing nations with our stores?
    What worlds in th'yet unformed Occident
    May come refined with th'accents that are ours?

    SAMUEL DANIEL, (c.1562–1619) British poet, dramatist. "Musophilus," l. 957–962, *Poetical Essays* (1599). Repr. in *Complete Works*, ed. A.B. Grosart (1963).

4   Curiously enough, it seems to be only in describing a mode of language which does not mean what it says that one can actually say what one means.

    PAUL DE MAN, (1919–1983) Belgian–born U.S. literary critic. *The Rhetoric of Temporality*, sct. 2, "Blindness and Insight" (1971, rev. 1983). Essay originally published in *Interpretation*, ed. Charles Singelton (1969).

5   There's a cool web of language winds us in,
    Retreat from too much joy or too much fear.

    ROBERT GRAVES, (1895–1985) British poet, novelist. "The Cool Web," *Poems* (1927).

6   Man acts as though *he* were the shaper and master of language, while in fact *language* remains the master of man.

    MARTIN HEIDEGGER, (1889–1976) German philosopher. "Building Dwelling Thinking," *Poetry, Language, Thought* (1971). Lecture, Aug. 5, 1951.

7   Language most shews a man: Speak, that I may see thee.

    BEN JONSON, (c. 1572–1637) British dramatist, poet. *Timber, or Discoveries Made upon Men and Matter*, para. 121, "Explorata: Oratio Imago Animi" (1641), ed. Felix E. Schelling (1892).

8   I speak Spanish to God, Italian to women, French to men and German to my horse.

    KING CHARLES V, (1500–1558) Spanish King of Spain and Holy Roman Emperor. *Attributed.*

9   Language is a form of human reason, which has its internal logic of which man knows nothing.

    CLAUDE LÉVI–STRAUSS, (b. 1908) French anthropologist. *The Savage Mind*, ch. 9 (1962).

10 Don't you see that the whole aim of Newspeak is to narrow the range of thought? In the end we shall make thoughtcrime literally impossible, because there will be no words in which to express it.

GEORGE ORWELL, (1903–1950) British author. Symes, in *Nineteen Eighty–Four*, pt. 1, ch. 5 (1949).

11 The genius of democracies is seen not only in the great number of new words introduced but even more in the new ideas they express.

ALEXIS DE TOCQUEVILLE, (1805–1859) French social philosopher. *Democracy in America*, vol. 2, pt. 1, ch. 16 (1840).

Language: English

1 If English is spoken in heaven ... God undoubtedly employs Cranmer as his speechwriter. The angels of the lesser ministries probably use the language of the New English Bible and the Alternative Service Book for internal memos.

CHARLES, PRINCE OF WALES, (b. 1948) Quoted in *Times* (London, Dec. 20, 1989).

Remark when judging a reading competition.

2 The English language is nobody's special property. It is the property of the imagination: it is the property of the language itself.

DEREK WALCOTT, (b. 1930) West Indian poet, playwright. Interview in *Writers at Work*, Eighth Series, ed. George Plimpton (1988).

Last Judgment, the

1 I shall tell you a great secret, my friend. Do not wait for the last judgment. It takes place every day.

ALBERT CAMUS, (1913–1960) French–Algerian philosopher, author. The narrator, Jean–Baptiste Clamence, in *The Fall* (1956).

Last Words

1 Farewell, my friends. I go to glory.

ISADORA DUNCAN, (1878–1927) U.S. dancer. Quoted in *Isadora Duncan's End*, ch. 25, Mary Desti (1929).

Duncan was accidentally strangled when her long scarf caught in the wheel of her car; her parting words were spoken in French.

2 All my possessions for a moment of time.

ELIZABETH I, (1533–1603) British Queen of England. *Alleged last words.*

3 Let not poor Nelly starve.

KING CHARLES II, (1630–1685) British King of Great Britain and Ireland. quoted in *The History of My Own Time*, vol. 1, bk. 3, Gilbert Burnet (1724).

Said on his deathbed, referring to his mistress, Nell Gwynne.

4 Just before she died she asked, "What *is* the answer?" No answer came. She laughed and said, "In that case, what is the question?" Then she died.

GERTRUDE STEIN, (1874–1946) U.S. author. Quoted in *Gertrude Stein, A Biography of Her Work*, ch. 6, Donald Sutherland (1951).

Sutherland concludes the biography, "Those were her last words, but they say what she had always been saying."

Laughter

1 If we may believe our logicians, man is distinguished from all other creatures by the faculty of laughter. He has a heart capable of mirth, and naturally disposed to it.

JOSEPH ADDISON, (1672–1719) British essayist. *Spectator* (London, Sept. 26, 1712), no. 494, *The Spectator*, ed. D.F. Bond (1965).

2   I hasten to laugh at everything for fear of being obliged to weep at it.

PIERRE DE BEAUMARCHAIS, (1732–1799) French dramatist. Figaro, in *Le Barbier de Séville*, act 1, sc. 2 (1775).

Byron expressed a similar idea in *Don Juan* cto. 4, st. 4: "And if I laugh at any mortal thing, 'Tis that I may not weep."

3   Nothing can confound
     A wise man more than laughter
        from a dunce.

GEORGE GORDON NOEL BYRON, 6TH BARON BYRON, (1788–1824) British poet. *Don Juan*, cto. 16, st. 88 (1819–1824).

4   No man who has once heartily and wholly laughed can be altogether irreclaimably bad.

THOMAS CARLYLE, (1795–1881) Scottish essayist, historian. *Sartor Resartus*, bk. 1, ch. 4 (1833–1834).

5   Of all days, the day on which one has not laughed is the one most surely wasted.

SÉBASTIEN–ROCH NICOLAS DE CHAMFORT, (1741–1794) French writer, wit. *Maxims and Considerations*, vol. 1, no. 80 (1796), trans. by E. Powys Mathers (1926).

6   In my mind, there is nothing so illiberal, and so ill–bred, as audible laughter.

PHILIP DORMER STANHOPE, 4TH EARL CHESTERFIELD, (1694–1773) British statesman, man of letters. *The Letters of the Earl of Chesterfield to His Son*, vol. 1, no. 144, ed. Charles Strachey (1901). Letter, March 9, 1748, first published (1774).

In a later letter, Dec. 12, 1765, Chesterfield wrote: "Observe it, the vulgar often laugh, but never smile, whereas well–bred people often smile, and seldom or never laugh. A witty thing never excited laughter, it pleases only the mind and never distorts the counte-

nance." (*Lord Chesterfield's Letters to His Godson*, no. 135, ed. Earl of Carnarvon, 1889).

7   For public opinion does not admit that lofty rapturous laughter is worthy to stand beside lofty lyrical emotion and that there is all the difference in the world between it and the antics of a clown at a fair.

NIKOLAI VASILYEVICH GOGOL, (1809–1852) Russian author, dramatist. *Dead Souls*, pt. 1, ch. 7 (1842), trans. by David Magarshak (1961).

8   The loud laugh that spoke the vacant mind.

OLIVER GOLDSMITH, (1728–1774) Anglo–Irish author, poet, playwright. "The Deserted Village," l. 122 (1770).

9   We should laugh before being happy, for fear of dying without having laughed.

JEAN DE LA BRUYÈRE, (1645–1696) French writer, moralist. *Characters*, "Of the Heart," aph. 63 (1688).

10   Present mirth hath present laughter
     What's to come is still unsure.

WILLIAM SHAKESPEARE, (1564–1616) British dramatist, poet. Feste, in *Twelfth Night*, act 2, sc. 3, l. 47–8 (1623).

Sung to Sir Toby Belch and Sir Andrew Aguecheek. The lines gave Noël Coward a title for his play, *Present Laughter*.

Lawrence, D.H. (David Herbert)

1   Primarily I am a passionately religious man, and my novels must be written from the depth of my religious experience.

D.H. (DAVID HERBERT) LAWRENCE, (1885–1930) British author. *The Letters of D.H. Lawrence*, vol. 2, eds. George J. Zytaruk and James T. Boulton (1981). Letter, April 22, 1914, to writer and critic Edward Garnett.

Laws and the Law

1   The law is not a "light" for you or any man to see by; the law is not an instrument of any kind. The law is a causeway upon which so long as he keeps to it a citizen may walk safely.

ROBERT BOLT, (1924–1995) British playwright. Sir Thomas More, in *A Man For All Seasons*, act 2 (1960).

2   Laws, like houses, lean on one another.

EDMUND BURKE, (1729–1797) Irish philosopher, statesman. *Tracts Relating to Popery Laws*, ch. 3, pt. 1 (1765), repr. in *The Writings and Speeches of Edmund Burke*, vol. 9, ed. Paul Langford (1991).

3   There is but one law for all, namely that law which governs all law, the law of our Creator, the law of humanity, justice, equity—the law of nature and of nations.

EDMUND BURKE, (1729–1797) Irish philosopher, statesman. *Speeches ... in the Trial of Warren Hastings*, vol. 4, ed. E.A. Bond (1859). Speech, May 28, 1794 at Westminster Hall, London.

Spoken at the impeachment of Warren Hastings.

4   The Law is the true embodiment
Of everything that's excellent.
It has no kind of fault or flaw,
And I, my Lords, embody the Law.

SIR WILLIAM SCHWENCK GILBERT, (1836–1911) British librettist. Lord Chancellor, in *Iolanthe*, act 1 (1882), published in *The Savoy Operas* (1926).

5   Law grinds the poor, and rich men rule the law.

OLIVER GOLDSMITH, (1728–1774) Anglo–Irish author, poet, playwright. "The Traveller," l. 386 (1764).

6   I know no method to secure the repeal of bad or obnoxious laws so effective as their stringent execution.

ULYSSES S. GRANT, (1822–1885) U.S. general, president. Quoted in *The Life and Campaigns of General U.S. Grant*, ch. 29, P.C. Headley (1869). Inaugural address, March 4, 1869.

7   Law and order exist for the purpose of establishing justice, and ... when they fail to do this purpose they become dangerously structured dams that block the flow of social progress.

MARTIN LUTHER KING, JR., (1929–1968) U.S. clergyman, civil rights leader. "Letter from Birmingham Jail," *Why We Can't Wait* (1963). Open letter to clergymen, Apr. 16, 1963.

8   The law is a sort of hocus–pocus science, that smiles in yer face while it picks yer pocket: and the glorious uncertainty of it is of more use to the professors than the justice of it.

CHARLES MACKLIN, (1690–1797) Irish actor, dramatist. Sir Archy MacSarcasm, in *Love à la Mode*, act 2, sc. 1 (1759).

The part of Sir Archy was played by Macklin himself, at Drury Lane, London, Dec. 12, 1759.

9   The good of the people is the greatest law.

MARCUS TULLIUS CICERO, (106–43 B.C.) Roman orator, philosopher. *De Legibus*, bk. 3, ch. 3, sct. 8 (52–45 B.C.).

Lawyers

1   Woe unto you, lawyers! for ye have taken away the key of knowledge: ye entered not in yourselves, and them that were entering in ye hindered.

BIBLE: NEW TESTAMENT, Jesus, in *Luke*, 11:52.

2   I would be loath to speak ill of any person who I do not know deserves it, but I am afraid he is an *attorney*.

SAMUEL JOHNSON, (1709–1784) British author, lexicographer. Quoted in *Anecdotes of the Late Samuel Johnson*, Hester Piozzi (1786). Repr. in *Johnsonian Miscellanies*, vol. 1, p. 327, ed. George Birkbeck Hill (1891).

Also quoted in Boswell's *Life of Samuel Johnson* (1791) for the year 1770.

3   A lawyer with his briefcase can steal more than a hundred men with guns.

MARIO PUZO, (b. 1920) U.S. novelist. Don Corleone, in *The Godfather*, bk. 1, ch. 1 (1969).

A favorite saying of Don Corleone.

4   I said there was a society of men among us, bred up from their youth in the art of proving by words multiplied for the purpose, that white is black, and black is white, according as they are paid. To this society all the rest of the people are as slaves.

JONATHAN SWIFT, (1667–1745) Anglo–Irish satirist. Gulliver, in *Gulliver's Travels,*. "A Voyage to the Country of the Houyhnhnms," ch. 5 (1726).

Describing his native land.

Laziness

1   Go to the ant, thou sluggard; consider her ways, and be wise.

BIBLE: HEBREW, *Proverbs*, 6:6.

The words were rendered by Samuel Johnson in the opening lines of *The Ant*: "Turn on the prudent ant thy heedful eyes, Observe her labours, sluggard, and be wise."

Leadership

1   Don't follow leaders
    Watch the parkin' meters.

BOB DYLAN [ROBERT ALLEN ZIMMERMAN], (b. 1941) U.S. singer, songwriter. "Subterranean Homesick Blues" (song), on the album *Bringing it all Back Home* (1965).

2   Though God hath raised me high, yet this I count the glory of my crown: that I have reigned with your loves.... And though you have had, and may have, many mightier and wiser princes sitting in this seat; yet you never had, nor shall have any that will love you better.

ELIZABETH I, (1533–1603) British Queen of England. "The Golden Speech," *Historical Collections of the Four Last Parliaments of Queen Elizabeth*, ed. Heywood Townshend (1680). Speech, Nov. 30, 1601, House of Commons.

3   The art of leadership ... consists in consolidating the attention of the people against a single adversary and taking care that nothing will split up that attention.... The leader of genius must have the ability to make different opponents appear as if they belonged to one category.

ADOLF HITLER, (1889–1945) German dictator. *Mein Kampf*, vol. 1, ch. 3 (1925).

4   The final test of a leader is that he leaves behind him in other men the conviction and the will to carry on.... The genius of a good leader is to leave behind him a situation which common sense, without the grace of genius, can deal with successfully.

WALTER LIPPMANN, (1889–1974) U.S. journalist. "Roosevelt Is Gone," *New York Herald Tribune* (April 14, 1945). Repr. in *The Essential Lippman*, pt. 10, sct. 5 (1982).

5 The ripest fruit of all,
   That perfect bliss and sole felicity,
   The sweet fruition of an earthly
      crown.

Christopher Marlowe,
(1564–1593) British dramatist, poet. Tamburlaine, in *Tamburlaine the Great*, pt. 1, act 2, sc. 7, l. 28–9 (1590).

6 A little touch of Harry in the
   night.

William Shakespeare, (1564–1616) British dramatist, poet. Chorus, in *Henry V*, act 4, l. 47 (1600).

Referring to Henry's eve–of–battle tour of his army's camp, rallying his men: "The royal captain of this ruined band/Walking from watch to watch, from tent to tent,/... /That every wretch, pining and pale before,/Beholding him, plucks comfort from his looks."

7 To be
   Omnipotent but friendless is to
      reign.

Percy Bysshe Shelley, (1792–1822) British poet. Asia, in *Prometheus Unbound*, act 2, sc. 4, l. 47–8 (1820).

8 No one would have doubted his
   ability to reign had he never been
   emperor.

Tacitus, (c. 55–c. 120) Roman historian. *The Histories*, bk. 1, sct. 49.

This summary of the character of the Emperor Galba is regarded as a masterpiece of epigrammatic writing. (*Omnium consensu capax imperii nisi imperasset.*).

Learning

1 Paul, thou art beside thyself; much
   learning doth make thee mad.

Bible: New Testament, *Acts*, 26:24.

Said by Festus, the Roman Procurator.

2 With just enough of learning to
   misquote.

George Gordon Noel Byron, 6th Baron Byron, (1788–1824) British poet. "English Bards and Scotch Reviewers," l. 66 (1809).

Referring to critics.

3 Never seem wiser, nor more
   learned, than the people you are
   with. Wear your learning, like
   your watch, in a private pocket:
   and do not merely pull it out and
   strike it; merely to show that you
   have one.

Philip Dormer Stanhope, 4th Earl Chesterfield, (1694–1773) British statesman, man of letters. *The Letters of the Earl of Chesterfield to His Son*, vol. 1, no. 142, ed. Charles Strachey (1901). Letter, Feb. 22, 1748, first published (1774).

4 Learned without sense, and venerably dull.

Charles Churchill, (1731–1764) British clergyman, poet. "The Rosciad," l. 592 (1761).

Referring to Irish playwright and actor, Arthur Murphy.

5 I've studied now Philosophy
   And Jurisprudence, Medicine—
   And even, alas! Theology—
   From end to end with labor keen;
   And here, poor fool! with all my
      lore
   I stand, no wiser than before.

Johann Wolfgang Von Goethe, (1749–1832) German poet, dramatist. Faust, in *Faust*, pt. 1, "Night" (1808), trans. by Bayard Taylor (1870–1871).

6 Their learning is like bread in a
   besieged town: every man gets a little, but no man gets a full meal.

Samuel Johnson, (1709–1784) British author, lexicographer. Quoted in James Boswell, *Life of Dr. Johnson*, entry, April 18, 1775 (1791).

Referring to the Scots.

Leisure

1 The wisdom of a learned man cometh by opportunity of leisure: and he that hath little business shall become wise.

APOCRYPHA, *Ecclesiasticus,* 38:24.

2 Leisure is the mother of Philosophy.

THOMAS HOBBES, (1588–1679) British philosopher. *Leviathan,* pt. 4, ch. 46 (1651).

3 Life isn't all beer and skittles, but beer and skittles, or something better of the same sort, must form a good part of every Englishman's education.

THOMAS HUGHES, (1822–1896) British author. *Tom Browne's Schooldays,* pt. 1, ch. 2 (1857).

4 To be able to fill leisure intelligently is the last product of civilization.

BERTRAND RUSSELL [LORD RUSSELL, 3RD EARL], (1872–1970) British philosopher, mathematician. *The Conquest of Happiness,* ch. 14 (1930).

"At present," Russell added, "very few people have reached this level."

5 A day
Spent in a round of strenuous idleness.

WILLIAM WORDSWORTH, (1770–1850) British poet. "The Prelude," bk. 4, l. 376–7 (1850).

Lesbianism

1 You're neither unnatural, nor abominable, nor mad; you're as much a part of what people call nature as anyone else; only you're unexplained as yet you've not got your niche in creation.

RADCLYFFE HALL, (1883–1943) British novelist. Puddle, in *The Well of Loneliness,* bk. 2, ch. 20, sct. 3 (1928).

Words that Puddle (the tutor, Miss Puddleton) resolves to say to the book's heroine, Stephen Gordon, a young lesbian. Later in the book, Stephen says, "I am one of those whom God marked on the forehead. Like Cain, I am marked and blemished. If you come to me ... the world will abhor you, will persecute you, will call you unclean." (ch. 37, sct. 3) The book was temporarily suspended in the U.S., and, after a notorious trial, banned in Britain, where the editor of the *Sunday Express* wrote that he "would sooner give a healthy boy or girl a dose of prussic acid than a copy of it."

Liberals

1 Ultraliberalism today translates into a whimpering isolationism in foreign policy, a mulish obstructionism in domestic policy, and a pusillanimous pussyfooting on the critical issue of law and order.

SPIRO T. AGNEW, (b. 1918) U.S. Republican politician, vice president. *Collected Speeches of Spiro Agnew* (1971). Speech, Sept. 10, 1970, Springfield, Illinois.

2 The liberals can understand everything but people who don't understand them.

LENNY BRUCE, (1925–1966) U.S. satirical comedian. *The Essential Lenny Bruce,* "Politics," ed. John Cohen (1967).

3 Cosmopolitan critics, men who are the friends of every country save their own.

BENJAMIN DISRAELI, (1804–1881) British statesman, author.Speech, Nov. 9, 1877, Guildhall, London.

See Gilbert' comment on "dissatisfaction" and Canning's comment on "internationalism."

4 Liberalism, austere in political trifles, has learned ever more artfully to unite a constant protest against

the government with a constant submission to it.

ALEXANDER HERZEN, (1812–1870) Russian journalist, political thinker. *My Past and Thoughts*, vol. 4, "Ends & Beginnings," (1921), trans. by Constance Garnett (1924–1927). Letter, 1862, to Ivan Turgenev.

5 I have almost reached the regrettable conclusion that the Negro's great stumbling block in his stride toward freedom is not the White Citizen's Counciler or the Ku Klux Klanner, but the white moderate.

MARTIN LUTHER KING, JR., (1929–1968) U.S. clergyman, civil rights leader. "Letter from Birmingham Jail," *Why We Can't Wait* (1964). Open letter to clergymen, Apr. 16, 1963.

6 We who are liberal and progressive know that the poor are our equals in every sense except that of being equal to us.

LIONEL TRILLING, (1905–1975) U.S. critic. "The Princess Casamassima," *The Liberal Imagination* (1950).

7 A liberal is a conservative who has been arrested.

TOM WOLFE, (b. 1931) U.S. author, journalist. *The Bonfire of the Vanities*, ch. 24 (1987).

Liberty

1 The condition upon which God hath given liberty to man is eternal vigilance; which condition if he break, servitude is at once the consequence of his crime, and the punishment of his guilt.

JOHN PHILPOT CURRAN, (1750–1817) Irish lawyer, politician. *Speeches of the Right Hon. John Philpot Curran*, ed. Thomas Davis (1847). Speech, July 10, 1790, Dublin.

On the Right of Election of the Lord Mayor of Dublin. See Orwell on liberty.

2 I know not what course others may take; but as for me, give me liberty, or give me death.

PATRICK HENRY, (1736–1799) U.S. statesman. Quoted in *Patrick Henry*, pt. 4, William Wirt (1818). Speech, March 23, 1775, Virginia House of Delegates, Richmond.

3 It is true that liberty is precious so precious that it must be rationed.

VLADIMIR ILYICH LENIN, (1870–1924) Russian revolutionary leader. Attributed in *Soviet Communism: A New Civilisation?* Sidney and Beatrice Webb (1936).

4 O liberty! O liberty! What crimes are committed in thy name!

MADAME ROLAND [MARIE–JEANNE PHILIPO, (1754–1793) French revolutionary. Quoted in *Histoire des Girondins*, bk. 51, ch. 8, Alphonse de Lamartine (1847). Remark at her execution, Nov. 8, 1793.

Madame Roland's remark at the guillotine was apparently addressed to a huge statue of Liberty erected nearby.

5 No man who knows aught, can be so stupid to deny that all men naturally were born free.

JOHN MILTON, (1608–1674) British poet. *The Tenure of Kings and Magistrates* (1649). Repr. in *Complete Prose Works of Milton*, ed. Ernest Sirluck (1959).

Libraries

1 The true university of these days is a collection of books.

THOMAS CARLYLE, (1795–1881) Scottish essayist, historian. *On Heroes and Hero–Worship*, "The Hero as Man of Letters" (1841).

2 With awe, around these silent walks I tread;
These are the lasting mansions of the dead.

GEORGE CRABBE, (1754–1832) British clergyman, poet. "The Library," l. 105–6

(1808). Repr. in *Poetical Works*, eds. A.J. and R.M. Carlyle (1908, rev.1924).

3   A man should keep his little brain attic stocked with all the furniture that he is likely to use, and the rest he can put away in the lumber room of his library, where he can get it if he wants it.

SIR ARTHUR CONAN DOYLE, (1859–1930) British author. Sherlock Holmes, in *The Adventures of Sherlock Holmes*, "The Five Orange Pips" (1892).

4   I've been drunk for about a week now, and I thought it might sober me up to sit in a library.

F. SCOTT FITZGERALD, (1896–1940) U.S. author. *The Great Gatsby*, ch. 3 (1925).

The words of an unnamed guest at one of Gatsby's parties.

5   Libraries are reservoirs of strength, grace and wit, reminders of order, calm and continuity, lakes of mental energy, neither warm nor cold, light nor dark. The pleasure they give is steady, unorgastic, reliable, deep and long–lasting. In any library in the world, I am at home, unselfconscious, still and absorbed.

GERMAINE GREER, (b. 1939) Australian feminist writer. *Daddy, We Hardly Knew You*, "Still in Melbourne, January 1987" (1989).

6   No place affords a more striking conviction of the vanity of human hopes than a public library.

SAMUEL JOHNSON, (1709–1784) British author, lexicographer. *Rambler*, no. 106 (London, March 23, 1751), repr. in *Works of Samuel Johnson*, Yale Edition, vol. 4, eds. W.J. Bate and Albrecht B. Strauss (1969).

7   Some on commission, some for the love of learning, Some because they have nothing better to do Or because they hope these walls of books will deaden The drumming of the demon in their ears.

LOUIS MACNEICE, (1907–1963) British poet. "The British Museum Reading Room," l. 4–7, *Plant and Phantom* (1941).

8   What do we, as a nation, care about books? How much do you think we spend altogether on our libraries, public or private, as compared with what we spend on our horses?

JOHN RUSKIN, (1819–1900) British art critic, author. "Of Kings' Treasuries," lecture 1, *Sesame and Lilies* (1865). Repr. in *The Works of John Ruskin*, vol. 28, eds. E.T. Cook and Alexander Weddesburn (1905).

9   My library
Was dukedom large enough.

WILLIAM SHAKESPEARE, (1564–1616) British dramatist, poet. Prospero, in *The Tempest*, act 1, sc. 2, l. 109–10 (1623).

Lies and Lying

1   Husband a lie, and trump it up in some extraordinary emergency.

JOSEPH ADDISON, (1672–1719) British essayist. *Spectator* (London, Oct. 11, 1712), no. 507, *The Spectator*, ed. D.F. Bond (1965).

2   It contains a misleading impression, not a lie. It was being economical with the truth.

ROBERT, SIR ARMSTRONG, (b. 1927) British civil servant. Quoted in *Daily Telegraph* (London, Nov. 19, 1986). Remark, Nov. 18, 1986, Supreme Court, New South Wales.

Referring to a letter written by Armstrong when the British government was attempting to suppress publication of *Spycatcher* by ex–secret service agent Peter Wright. As Armstrong made clear, he was quoting Edmund Burke in *Two Letters on Proposals for Peace*, pt. 1 (1796): "Falsehood and delusion are allowed in no case whatsoever: But, as in the exercise of all the virtues, there is an economy of truth." See also Mark Twain's comment on "truth."

3 Thou shalt not bear false witness against thy neighbour.

BIBLE: HEBREW, *Exodus*, 20:16.

The ninth commandment.

4 I do not mind lying, but I hate inaccuracy.

SAMUEL BUTLER, (1835–1902) British author. *Notebooks*, "Truth and Convenience: Falsehood" (1912).

5 The best liar is he who makes the smallest amount of lying go the longest way.

SAMUEL BUTLER, (1835–1902) British author. *The Way of all Flesh*, ch. 39 (1903).

5 And, after all, what is a lie? 'Tis but The truth in masquerade.

GEORGE GORDON NOEL BYRON, 6TH BARON BYRON, (1788–1824) British poet. *Don Juan*, cto. 11, st. 37 (1819–1824).

6 I am a lie who always speaks the truth.

JEAN COCTEAU, (1889–1963) French author, filmmaker. *Opéra* "Le Paquet Rouge" (1925).

7 The great mass of people ... will more easily fall victim to a big lie than to a small one.

ADOLF HITLER, (1889–1945) German dictator. *Mein Kampf*, vol. 1, ch. 10 (1925).

8 The most dangerous untruths are truths slightly distorted.

GEORG CHRISTOPH LICHTENBERG, (1742–1799) German physicist, philosopher. "Notebook H," aph. 7, *Aphorisms* (written 1765–99), trans. by R.J. Hollingdale (1990).

9 Every word she writes is a lie, including "and" and "the."

MARY MCCARTHY, (1912–1989) U.S. author, critic. Quoted in *The New York Times* (Feb. 16, 1980). Interview on *Dick Cavett Show* (Jan. 1980).

Quoting herself, referring to Lillian Hellman in the 1930s. McCarthy's remark resulted in a row and prolonged law–suit which probably contributed to the wasting illness that eventually killed her—see Carol Brightman, *Writing Dangerously: Mary McCarthy and Her World* (1993).

10 No man lies so boldly as the man who is indignant.

FRIEDRICH NIETZSCHE, (1844–1900) German philosopher. *Beyond Good and Evil*, ch. 2, aph. 26 (1886).

11 A little ina ccuracy sometimes saves tons of explanation.

[H.H. (HECTOR HUGH) MUNRO] SAKI, (1870–1916) Scottish author. "Clovis on the Alleged Romance of Business," *The Square Egg* (1924).

12 I will name you the degrees. The first, the Retort Courteous; the second, the Quip Modest; the third, the Reply Churlish; the fourth, the Reproof Valiant; the fifth, the Countercheck Quarrelsome; the sixth, the Lie with Circumstance; the seventh, the Lie Direct.

WILLIAM SHAKESPEARE, (1564–1616) British dramatist, poet. Touchstone, in *As You Like It*, act 5, sc. 4, l. 89–94 (1623).

13 Lord, Lord, how this world is given to lying!

WILLIAM SHAKESPEARE, (1564–1616) British dramatist, poet. Sir John Oldcastle (Falstaff), in *Henry IV pt. 1*, act 5, sc. 4, l. 142–43 (1598).

Oldcastle (Falstaff) laments the dishonesty of the world when his false claim to have dispatched Hotspur is shown up.

14 Lying is like alcoholism. You are always recovering.

STEVEN SODERBERGH, (b. 1963) U.S. filmmaker. Graham Dalton (James Spader), in *Sex, Lies and Videotape* (film) (1989).

Quoted in Norman K. Denzin's *Images of Postmodern Society*, ch. 8 (1991).

15 The cruellest lies are often told in silence. A man may have sat in a room for hours and not opened his mouth, and yet come out of that room a disloyal friend or a vile calumniator.

ROBERT LOUIS STEVENSON, (1850–1894) Scottish novelist, essayist, poet. *Virginibus Puerisque,* "Virginibus Puerisque" sct. 4 (1881).

16 He will lie even when it is inconvenient, the sign of a true artist.

GORE VIDAL, (b. 1925) U.S. novelist, critic. *Two Sisters,* attributed (1970).

The *Penguin Dictionary of Twentieth–Century Quotations,* eds. J.M. and M.J. Cohen (1993) has cited this well–known quote in *Two Sisters* but it has not been found there.

Life

1 For what is your life? It is even a vapor, that appeareth for a little time, and then vanisheth away.

BIBLE: New Testament, *James,* 4:14.

2 The days of our years are threescore years and ten; and if by reason of strength they be fourscore years, yet is their strength labor and sorrow; for it is soon cut off, and we fly away.

BIBLE: HEBREW, *Psalms,* 90:10.

The Book of Common Prayer (1662) has a variant version (*Psalms* 87:10).

3 Life is divided up into the horrible and the miserable.

WOODY ALLEN, (b. 1935) U.S. filmmaker. Alvy Singer (Allen), in *Annie Hall* (film) (1977).

repr. in *Four Films of Woody Allen* (1982).

4 Life loves the liver of it.

MAYA ANGELOU, (b. 1928) U.S. author. "The Black Scholar Interviews Maya Angelou," *Conversations with Maya Angelou,* ed. Jeffrey M. Elliot (1989). Originally published Jan.–Feb. 1977).

5 There's night and day, brother, both sweet things; sun, moon, and stars, brother, all sweet things; there's likewise a wind on the heath. Life is very sweet, brother; who would wish to die?

GEORGE BORROW, (1803–1881) British author. Jasper, in *Lavengro,* ch. 25 (1851).

6 Life is like playing a violin solo in public and learning the instrument as one goes on.

SAMUEL BUTLER, (1835–1902) British author. *Samuel Butler's Notebooks,* p. 310 (1951). Speech, Feb. 27, 1895, Somerville Club, London.

7 Between two worlds life hovers like a star,
'Twixt night and morn, upon the horizon's verge.

GEORGE GORDON NOEL BYRON, 6TH BARON BYRON, (1788–1824) British poet. *Don Juan,* cto. 15, st. 99 (1819–1824).

8 What is life? A frenzy. What is life? An illusion, a shadow, a fiction. And the greatest good is trivial; for all life is a dream and all dreams are dreams.

PEDRO CALDERÓN DE LA BARCA, (1600–1681) Spanish playwright. Sigismundo, in *La Vida es Sueño,* "2nd Day," l. 2182–7 (1636).

See Poe on dreams for a similar idea.

9 Living is a sickness to which sleep provides relief every sixteen hours. It's a palliative. The remedy is death.

SÉBASTIEN–ROCH NICOLAS DE CHAMFORT, (1741–1794) French writer, wit. *Maxims and Considerations*, vol. 1, no. 113 (1796), trans. by E. Powys Mathers (1926).

10 Life is a tragedy when seen in close–up, but a comedy in long–shot.

CHARLIE CHAPLIN, (1889–1977) British comic actor, filmmaker. Quoted in obituary, *Guardian* (London, Dec. 28, 1977).

11 Life is a horizontal fall.

JEAN COCTEAU, (1889–1963) French author, filmmaker. *Opium* (1929).

12 Life is an incurable disease.

ABRAHAM COWLEY, (1618–1667) British essayist, poet." To Dr. Scarborough," st. 6 (1656).

13 The dreamcrossed twilight between birth and dying.

T.S. (THOMAS STEARNS) ELIOT, (1888–1965) Anglo–American poet, critic. "Ash–Wednesday," pt. 6 (1930).

14 What is life but the angle of vision? A man is measured by the angle at which he looks at objects. What is life but what a man is thinking all day? This is his fate and his employer. Knowing is the measure of the man. By how much we know, so much we are.

RALPH WALDO EMERSON, (1803–1882) U.S. essayist, poet, philosopher. *Natural History of Intellect*, pt. 1 (1893). Repr. in *The Complete Works of Ralph Waldo Emerson*, vol. 12 (1921).

15 Life is an end in itself, and the only question as to whether it is worth living is whether you have had enough of it.

OLIVER WENDELL HOLMES, JR., (1841–1935) U.S. jurist. *Collected Legal Papers by Oliver Wendell Holmes* (1937). Speech, March 7, 1900, Bar Association Dinner, Boston.

16 Life is just one damned thing after another.

ELBERT HUBBARD, (1856–1915) U.S. author. *The Philistine* (Dec. 1909).

The quote has also been attributed to Frank Ward O'Malley. Edna St. Vincent Millay wrote in a letter, Oct. 24, 1930: "It's not true that life is one damn thing after another—it's one damned thing over and over." (*Letters of Edna St. Vincent Millay*, ed. Allen R. Macdougall, 1952).

17 It is quite true what Philosophy says: that Life must be understood backwards. But that makes one forget the other saying: that it must be lived—forwards. The more one ponders this, the more it comes to mean that life in the temporal existence never becomes quite intelligible, precisely because at no moment can I find complete quiet to take the backward–looking position.

SOREN KIERKEGAARD, (1813–1855) Danish philosopher. *The Diary of Soren Kierkegaard*, pt. 5, sct. 4, no. 136, ed. Peter Rohde (1960). Journal entry, 1843.

18 Life is what happens while you are making other plans.

JOHN LENNON, (1940–1980) British songwriter, rock musician. "Beautiful Boy" (song), on the album *Starting Over* (1980).

The line has also been attributed to Betty Talmadge (divorced wife of Senator Herman Talmadge) and Thomas La Mance (unknown).

19 Life well spent is long.

LEONARDO DA VINCI, (1452–1519) Italian artist, scientist. *Leonardo da Vinci's Notebooks*, bk. 1, ch. 1, ed. and trans. by Edward McCurdy (1906).

20 My art and profession is to live.

MICHEL DE MONTAIGNE, (1533–1592) French essayist. *Essays*, bk. 2, ch. 6 (1580–1588), trans. by John Florio (1603).

21   The value of life lies not in the length of days but in the use you make of them; he has lived for a long time who has little lived.

MICHEL DE MONTAIGNE, (1533–1592) French essayist. *Essays*, bk. 1, ch. 20 (1595).

22   What a life! True life is elsewhere. We are not in the world.

ARTHUR RIMBAUD, (1854–1891) French poet. *Une Saison en Enfer*, "Délires I," (originally published 1874). Repr. in *Collected Poems*, ed. Oliver Bernard (1962).

23   Out, out, brief candle.
Life's but a walking shadow, a poor player
That struts and frets his hour upon the stage,
And then is heard no more. It is a tale
Told by an idiot, full of sound and fury,
Signifying nothing.

WILLIAM SHAKESPEARE, (1564–1616) British dramatist, poet. Macbeth, in *Macbeth*, act 5, sc. 5, l. 22–7 (1623).

On hearing of the death of Lady Macbeth.

24   There is one thing that matters to set a chime of words tinkling in the minds of a few fastidious people.

LOGAN PEARSALL SMITH, (1865–1946) U.S. essayist, aphorist. Quoted by Cyril Connolly in obituary, *New Statesman* (London, March 9, 1946).

In answer to the question asked two weeks before his death whether he had discovered any meaning in life.

25   The force that through the green fuse drives the flower
Drives my green age; that blasts the roots of trees
Is my destroyer.

DYLAN THOMAS, (1914–1953) Welsh poet. "The Force that through the Green Fuse Drives the Flower," *18 Poems* (1934).

26   Along a parabola life like a rocket flies,
Mainly in darkness, now and then on a rainbow.

ANDREI VOZNESENSKY, (b. 1933) Russian poet. "Parabolic Ballad," st. 1 (1960), trans. by W.H. Auden.

Opening line of poem.

27   Life, Lady Stutfield, is simply a *mauvais quart d'heure* made up of exquisite moments.

OSCAR WILDE, (1854–1900) Anglo–Irish playwright, author. Mrs. Allonby, in *A Woman of No Importance*, act 2 (1893).

Life and Death

1   In the midst of life we are in death.

BOOK OF COMMON PRAYER, THE, *Burial of the Dead*, "Interment" (1662).

2   Man that is born of woman hath but a short time to live, and is full of misery. He cometh up, and is cut down, like a flower; he fleeth as it were a shadow, and never continueth in one stay.

BOOK OF COMMON PRAYER, THE, *Burial of the Dead*, "First Anthem" (1662).

Derived from *Job* 14:1–2.

3   But there is good news yet to hear and fine things to be seen
Before we go to Paradise by way of Kensal Green.

G.K. GILBERT KEITH CHESTERTON, (1874–1936) British author. "The Rolling English Road," *The Flying Inn*, ch. 21 (1914).

Kensal Green is one of London's largest cemeteries, resting–place of some of the country's most illustrious dead.

4   The aims of life are the best defense against death.

PRIMO LEVI, (1919–1987) Italian author. *The Drowned and the Saved*, ch. 6 (1988).

5   The ceaseless labor of your life is to build the house of death.

MICHEL DE MONTAIGNE, (1533–1592) French essayist. *Essays*, bk. 1, ch. 20 (1595).

6   The boundaries which divide Life from Death are at best shadowy and vague. Who shall say where the one ends, and where the other begins?

EDGAR ALLAN POE, (1809–1845) U.S. poet, critic, short–story writer. "The Premature Burial" (1844).

7   As flies to wanton boys, are we to th' gods;
They kill us for their sport.

WILLIAM SHAKESPEARE, (1564–1616) British dramatist, poet. Gloucester, in *King Lear*, act 4, sc. 1, l. 37–8 (1623).

8   Life is the desert, life the solitude, Death joins us to the great majority.

EDWARD YOUNG, (1683–1765) British poet, playwright. Don Alonzo, in *The Revenge*, act 4, sc. 1 (1721). Repr. in *Complete Works*, ed. J. Doran (1968).

Light

1   God's first creature, which was light.

FRANCIS BACON, (1561–1626) British philosopher, essayist, statesman. *New Atlantis*, sct. 14 (1627).

2   Ye are the light of the world.

BIBLE: NEW TESTAMENT, Jesus, in *Matthew*, 5:14.

From the Sermon on the Mount.

3   More light!
[Mehr Licht!]

JOHANN WOLFGANG VON GOETHE, (1749–1832) German poet, dramatist. *Attributed last words.*

According to *Oxford Dictionary of Quotations*, ed. Angela Partington (1992), Goethe's actual last words were: "Open the second shutter, so that more light can come in."

Lincoln, Abraham

1   Lincoln, six feet one in his stocking feet,
The lank man, knotty and tough as a hickory rail,
Whose hands were always too big for white–kid gloves,
Whose wit was a coonskin sack of dry, tall tales,
Whose weathered face was homely as a plowed field.

STEPHEN VINCENT BENÉT, (1898–1943) U.S. novelist, poet. "John Brown's Body" (1928).

Literature

1   Literature is the effort of man to indemnify himself for the wrongs of his condition.

RALPH WALDO EMERSON, (1803–1882) U.S. essayist, poet, philosopher. "Walter Savage Landor," *The Natural History of Intellect* (1893). *The Dial*, vol. 12, 1841.

2   [The] attempt to devote oneself to literature alone is a most deceptive thing, and...often, paradoxically, it is literature that suffers for it.

VACLAV HAVEL, (b. 1936) Czechoslovakian playwright, president. *Disturbing the Peace*, ch. 3 (1986, trans. 1990).

3   All modern American literature comes from one book by Mark Twain called *Huckleberry Finn*.... American writing comes from that. There was nothing before. There has been nothing as good since.

ERNEST HEMINGWAY, (1899–1961) U.S. author. *The Green Hills of Africa*, ch. 1 (1935).

"How simple the writing of literature would be," Hemingway said on accepting the Nobel Prize for Literature in Dec. 1954, "if it were only necessary to write in another way what has been well written. It is because we have had such great writers in the past that a writer is driven far out past where he can go, out to where no one can help him." (Carlos Baker, *Hemingway: the Writer as Artist*, ch. 13, ed.1963).

4   The thing that teases the mind over and over for years, and at last gets itself put down rightly on paper—whether little or great, it belongs to Literature.

SARAH ORNE JEWETT, (1849–1909) U.S. author. *The Country of the Pointed Firs and Other Stories*, preface (1896). Letter to author Willa Cather.

5   Our American professors like their literature clear and cold and pure and very dead.

SINCLAIR LEWIS, (1885–1951) U.S. novelist. Quoted in *Literature 1901–1967*, H. Frenz (1969). Speech, Dec. 12, 1930, to Swedish Academy, Stockholm; accepting the Nobel Prize for Literature.

6   Everything in the world exists to end up in a book.

STÉPHANE MALLARMÉ, (1842–1898) French symbolist poet. *Variations on a Subject*, "As to the Book: The Book, a Spiritual Instrument," *Mallarmé: The Poems*, trans. by and ed. Keith Bosley (1977). (Originally published 1886–1896).

7   Literature, the most seductive, the most deceiving, the most dangerous of professions.

JOHN MORLEY [1ST VISCOUNT MORLEY OF BLACKBURN], (1838–1923) British writer, Liberal politician. *Life of Burke*, ch. 1 (1879).

8   Literature is news that STAYS news.

EZRA POUND, (1885–1972) U.S. poet, critic. *ABC of Reading*, ch. 2 (1934).

"If a nation's literature declines, the nation atrophies and decays," Pound wrote in ch. 3.

9   Hemingway, remarks are not literature.

GERTRUDE STEIN, (1874–1946) U.S. author. *The Autobiography of Alice B. Toklas*, ch. 7 (1933).

Referring to a comment about a book *The Enormous Room* ("the greatest book he had ever read"), incorporated by Hemingway in a manuscript of short stories which he showed to Stein.

10   As life grows more terrible, its literature grows more terrible.

WALLACE STEVENS, (1879–1955) U.S. poet. *Opus Posthumous*, "Adagia" (1959).

11   All the rest is mere fine writing.

PAUL VERLAINE, (1844–1896) French poet. "L'Art Poetique," *Jadis et Naguère* (1884).

12   *Middlemarch*, the magnificent book which with all its imperfections is one of the few English novels for grown–up people.

VIRGINIA WOOLF, (1882–1941) British novelist. *The Common Reader*, "George Eliot," First Series (1925).

Literature and Society

1   The writer in western civilization has become not a voice of his tribe, but of his individuality. This is a very narrow–minded situation.

AHARON APPELFELD, (b. 1932) Israeli novelist. *International Herald Tribune* (Paris, Aug. 10, 1989).

2   Creative writers are always greater than the causes that they represent.

E.M. (EDWARD MORGAN) FORSTER, (1879–1970) British novelist, essayist. *Two Cheers for Democracy*, "Gide and George," (1951).

3 Literature is the one place in any society where, within the secrecy of our own heads, we can hear *voices talking about everything in every possible way*. The reason for ensuring that that privileged arena is preserved is not that writers want the absolute freedom to say and do whatever they please. It is that we, all of us, readers and writers and citizens and generals and goodmen, need that little, unimportant–looking room. We do not need to call it sacred, but we do need to remember that it is necessary.

SALMAN RUSHDIE, (b. 1947) Indian–born British author. "Is Nothing Sacred?" *Guardian* (London, Feb. 7, 1990).Herbert Read Memorial Lecture, Feb. 6, 1990, at ICA, London.

In the wake of the *fatwa* issued twelve months earlier by the Ayatollah Khomeini (see Khomeini on censorship), Rushdie's lecture was read by Harold Pinter.

4 The literary "fellow travelers" of the Revolution.

LEON TROTSKY, (1879–1940) Russian revolutionary. *Literature and Revolution*, ch. 2 (1923).

Living Together

1 It is better to dwell in a corner of the housetop, than with a brawling woman in a wide house.

BIBLE: HEBREW, *Proverbs*, 21:9 and 25:24.

2 I cannot live with You—
It would be Life—
And Life is over there—
Behind the Shelf

EMILY DICKINSON, (1830–1886) U.S. poet. "I Cannot Live With You" (written c. 1862, published 1890). Repr. in *The Complete Poems*, no. 640, Harvard *variorum* edition (1955).

3 Do you think your mother and I should have lived comfortably so long together, if ever we had been married? Baggage!

JOHN GAY, (1685–1732) British dramatist, poet. Peachum, in *The Beggar's Opera*, act 1, sc. 8 (1728), ed. F.W. Bateson (1934).

4 Come live with me, and be my love,
And we will all the pleasures prove
That valleys, groves, hills, and
    fields,
Woods or steepy mountain yields.

CHRISTOPHER MARLOWE, (1564–1593) British dramatist, poet. "The Passionate Shepherd to his Love" (c. 1589).

A close version of this poem appears in *The Passionate Pilgrim*, an anthology of 1599, together with a quatrain, *Love's Answer*. Other variations were written by Robert Herrick and by John Donne (*The Bait*). Walter Ralegh wrote the famous *Answer to Marlow*, with the conclusion: "But could youth last, and love still breed,/Had joys no date, nor age no need,/Then these delights my mind might move, To live with thee, and be thy love."

Logic

1 Contrariwise, if it was so, it might be; and if it were so, it would be; but as it isn't, it ain't. That's logic.

LEWIS CARROLL [CHARLES LUTWIDGE DODGSON], (1832–1898) British author, mathematician. Tweedledee, in *Through the Looking–Glass*, "Tweedledum and Tweedledee," (1872).

2 Logic takes care of itself; all we have to do is to look and see how it does it.

LUDWIG WITTGENSTEIN, (1889–1951) Austrian philosopher. *Notebooks 1914–1916*, ed. Anscombe (1961). Entry, Oct. 13, 1914.

Also published in *Tractatus Logico–Philosophicus*, sct. 5:473 (1921, trans. 1922).

London

1   I wander thro' each charter'd street,
Near where the charter'd Thames
   does flow,
And mark in every face I meet
Marks of weakness, marks of woe.

WILLIAM BLAKE, (1757–1827) British
poet, painter, engraver. *Songs of Experience,*
"London," (1794), repr. in *Complete Writings,*
ed. Geoffrey Keynes (1957).

2   London is a modern Babylon.

BENJAMIN DISRAELI, (1804–1881)
British statesman and author. *Tancred,* bk. 5,
ch. 5 (1847).

3   London, that great cesspool into
which all the loungers and idlers of
the Empire are irresistibly drained.

SIR ARTHUR CONAN DOYLE,
(1859–1930) British author. Dr. Watson, in *A
Study in Scarlet,* ch. 1 (1887).

4   Crowds without company, and dissipation without pleasure.

EDWARD GIBBON, (1737–1794) British
historian. *Memoirs of My Life,* ch. 5 (1796),
published as *Autobiography,* Routledge
(1971).

5   You find no man, at all intellectual,
who is willing to leave London. No,
Sir, when a man is tired of London,
he is tired of life; for there is in
London all that life can afford.

SAMUEL JOHNSON, (1709–1784) British
author, lexicographer. Quoted in James
Boswell, *Life of Dr. Johnson,* entry, Sept. 20,
1777 (1791).

6   I have passed all my days in London, until I have formed as many
and intense local attachments as
any of you mountaineers can have
done with dead nature. The lighted
shops of the Strand and Fleet Street,
the innumerable trades, tradesmen,
and customers, coaches, waggons,
playhouses, all the bustle and
wickedness round about Covent
Garden, the very women of the
town, the watchmen, drunken
scenes, rattles, life awake, if you
awake, at all hours of the night, the
impossibility of being dull in Fleet
Street, the crowds, the very dirt and
mud, the sun shining upon houses
and pavements, the print shops, the
old book stalls, parsons cheap'ning
books, coffee houses, steam of soups
from kitchens, pantomimes, London
itself a pantomime and a masquerade, all these things work themselves
into my mind and feed me, without
a power of satiating me. The wonder
of these sights impels me into
night–walks about her crowded
streets, I often shed tears in the
Strand from fullness of joy at so
much life.

CHARLES LAMB, (1775–1834) British essayist, critic. *Complete Works,* vol. 3 (1882). Letter, Jan. 30, 1801, to William Wordsworth.

See Lamb's comments on "mountains."

7   Behold now this vast city; a city of
refuge, the mansion house of liberty,
encompassed and surrounded with
his protection; the shop of war hath
not there more anvils and hammers
waking, to fashion out the plates and
instruments of armed justice in
defence of beleaguered truth, than
there be pens and hands there, sitting by their studious lamps, musing, searching, revolving new
notions.

JOHN MILTON, (1608–1674) British poet.
Areopagitica: a Speech for the Liberty of Unlicensed Printing to the Parliament of England
(1644).

Describing London during the English Civil War.

8   Dear, damned, distracting town, farewell!

ALEXANDER POPE, (1688–1744) British satirical poet. "A Farewell to London," l. 1 (1715).

9   You are now
    In London, that great sea, whose
        ebb and flow
    At once is deaf and loud, and on
        the shore
    Vomits its wrecks, and still howls
        on for more.
    Yet in its depth what treasures!

PERCY BYSSHE SHELLEY, (1792–1822) British poet. "Letter to Maria Gisborne," l. 192–6 (1820).

10 The capital is become an overgrown monster; which like a dropsical head, will in time leave the body and extremities without nourishment and support.

TOBIAS SMOLLETT, (1721–1771) Scottish novelist, surgeon. *Humphrey Clinker,* vol. 1, letter from Matthew Bramble, May 29 (1771).

11 Earth has not anything to show
        more fair:
    Dull would he be of soul who could
        pass by
    A sight so touching in its majesty:
    This city now doth, like a garment,
        wear
    The beauty of the morning; silent,
        bare,
    Ships, towers, domes, theatres and
        temples lie
    Open unto the fields and to the sky;
    All bright and glittering in the
        smokeless air.

WILLIAM WORDSWORTH, (1770–1850) British poet. "Composed Upon Westminster Bridge" (written 1802, published 1807).

Loneliness

1   No one ever discovers the depths of his own loneliness.

GEORGES BERNANOS, (1888–1948) French novelist, political writer. *The Diary of a Country Priest,* ch. 7 (1936).

2   Alone, alone, all, all alone,
    Alone on a wide wide sea!
    And never a saint took pity on
    My soul in agony.

SAMUEL TAYLOR COLERIDGE, (1772–1834) British poet. "The Rime of the Ancient Mariner," pt. 4, st. 3 (1798).

Loquacity

1   The habit of common and continuous speech is a symptom of mental deficiency. It proceeds from not knowing what is going on in other people's minds.

WALTER BAGEHOT, (1826–1877) British economist, critic. *Hartley Coleridge,* vol. 1, *Literary Studies* (1878). (Article originally published 1852).

2   I prefer tongue–tied knowledge to ignorant loquacity.

MARCUS TULLIUS CICERO, (106–43 B.C.) Roman orator and philosopher. *De Oratore,* bk. 3, sct. 142 (55 B.C.).

3   Blessed is the man who, having nothing to say, abstains from giving us wordy evidence of the fact.

GEORGE ELIOT [MARY ANN (OR MARIAN) EVANS], (1819–1880) British novelist. *Impressions of Theophrastus Such,* ch. 4 (1879).

4   They never taste who always drink;
    They always talk who never think.

MATTHEW PRIOR, (1664–1721) British poet, diplomat. "Upon this Passage in Scaligerana" (1740). Repr. in *The Literary Works of Matthew Prior,* eds. H.B. Wright and M.K. Spears (1959).

5   His enemies might have said before
     that he talked rather too much; but
     now he has occasional flashes of
     silence, that make his conversation
     perfectly delightful.

SYDNEY SMITH, (1771–1845) British clergyman, writer. Quoted in *Memoir*, vol. 1, ch. 11, Lady Holland (1855).

Referring to historian Thomas Macaulay, whom Smith called "a book in breeches." Thomas Carlyle was quoted as saying, "Macaulay is well for a while, but one wouldn't *live* under Niagara." (R.M. Milnes, *Notebook*, 1838).

Los Angeles

1   I don't wanna live in a city where
     the only cultural advantage is that
     you can make a right turn on a red
     light.

WOODY ALLEN, (b. 1935) U.S. filmmaker. Alvy Singer (Allen), in *Annie Hall* (film), comparing Los Angeles unfavorably to Manhattan (1977).

repr. in *Four Films of Woody Allen* (1982).

2   I used to like this town.... Los
     Angeles was just a big dry sunny
     place with ugly homes and no
     style, but good–hearted and peace-
     ful.... Now ... we've got the big
     money, the sharpshooters, the per-
     centage workers, the fast dollar
     boys, the hoodlums out of New
     York and Chicago and Detroit—
     and Cleveland. We've got the flash
     restaurants and night clubs they
     run, and the hotels and apartment
     houses they own, and the grifters
     and con men and female bandits
     that live in them. The luxury
     trades, the pansy decorators, the
     Lesbian dress designers, the
     riff–raff of a big hardboiled city
     with no more personality than a
     paper cup.

RAYMOND CHANDLER, (1888–1959) U.S. author. Philip Marlowe, in *The Little Sister*, ch. 26 (1949).

Loss

1   The art of losing isn't hard to
         master;
     so many things seem filled with the
         intent
     to be lost that their loss is no
         disaster.

ELIZABETH BISHOP, (1911–1979) U.S. poet. "One Art," *Geography III* (1976).

Love

1   Love is a great beautifier.

LOUISA MAY ALCOTT, (1832–1888) U.S. author. *Little Women*, pt. 2, ch. 1 (1869).

2   For a crowd is not company; and
     faces are but a gallery of pictures;
     and talk but a tinkling cymbal,
     where there is no love.

FRANCIS BACON, (1561–1626) British philosopher, essayist, statesman. *Essays*, "Of Friendship" (1597–1625).

3   Love ceases to be a pleasure, when
     it ceases to be a secret.

APHRA BEHN, (1640–1689) British playwright, poet. "Four O'Clock. General Conversation," *The Lover's Watch* (1686). Repr. in *The Works of Aphra Behn*, vol. 6, ed. M. Summers (1915).

4   There is no fear in love; but perfect
     love casteth out fear: because fear
     hath torment. He that feareth is not
     made perfect in love.

BIBLE: NEW TESTAMENT, 1 John, 4:18.

5   Love seeketh only self to please,
     To bind another to its delight,
     Joys in another's loss of ease,

And builds a Hell in Heaven's
despite.

WILLIAM BLAKE, (1757–1827) British
poet, painter, engraver. *Songs of Experience,*
"The Clod & the Pebble," st. 1 (1794), repr. in
Complete Writings, ed. Geoffrey Keynes
(1957).

Reply of the Pebble to the Clod of Clay's
verse: "Love seeketh not itself to please,/Nor
for itself hath any care,/But for another gives
its ease,/And builds a Heaven in Hell's
despair."

6   To fall in love is to create a religion
that has a fallible god.

JORGE LUIS BORGES, (1899–1986)
Argentinian author. "The Meeting in a
Dream," *Other Inquisitions* (1960, trans.
1964). (Essay first published 1952).

7   All the little emptiness of love!

RUPERT BROOKE, (1887–1915) British
poet. "Peace", *1914 and Other Poems* (1915).
New Numbers, no. 4 (1914).

8   How do I love thee? Let me count
the ways.
I love thee to the depth and breadth
and height
My soul can reach, when feeling
out of sight
For the ends of Being and Ideal
Grace.
I love thee to the level of every day's
Most quiet need, by sun and
candle–light.
I love thee freely, as men strive for
Right;
I love thee purely, as they turn
from Praise;
I love thee with a passion put to use
In my old griefs, and with my
childhood's faith;
I love thee with a love I seemed to
lose
With my lost saints, I love thee
with the breath,
Smiles, tears, of all my life! and, if
God choose,

I shall but love thee better after
death.

ELIZABETH BARRETT BROWNING,
(1806–1861) British poet. "Sonnets" *from the
Portuguese,* Sonnet 14 (1850).

9   O lyric Love, half angel and half
bird
And all a wonder and a wild desire.

ROBERT BROWNING, (1812–1889) British
poet. *The Ring and the Book,* bk. 1, l. 1391–2
(1868–1869).

10   We loved, sir—used to meet:
How sad and bad and mad it was—
But then, how it was sweet!

ROBERT BROWNING, (1812–1889) British
poet. "Confessions," st. 9 (1864).

11   Whoso loves
Believes the impossible.

ELIZABETH BARRETT BROWNING,
(1806–1861) British poet. *Aurora Leigh,* bk. 5,
l. 408 (1857).

12   Love is a thyng as any spirit free.
Wommen, of kynde, desiren
libertee,
And nat to been constreyned as a
thral;
And so doon men, if I sooth seyen
shal.

GEOFFREY CHAUCER, (1340–1400)
British poet. *The Canterbury Tales,* "The
Franklin's Tale," l. 767–70 (c. 1387–1400),
repr. in *The Works of Geoffrey Chaucer,* ed.
Alfred W. Pollard, et al. (1898).

13   The lyf so short, the craft so longe
to lerne,
Th' assay so hard, so sharp the conquerynge,
The dredful joye, alwey that slit so
yerne;
Al this mene I be love.

GEOFFREY CHAUCER, (1340–1400)
British poet. *The Parlement of Foules,* "The
Proem," l. 1–2 (1380–1386), repr. in *The*

Works of Geoffrey Chaucer, ed. Alfred W. Pollard, etc. (1898).

See Hippocrates on doctors.

14 If there's delight in love, 'tis when I
    see
    That heart, which others bleed for,
    bleed for me.

WILLIAM CONGREVE, (1670–1729) British dramatist. Song sung by Mrs. Hodgson, in *The Way of the World*, act 3, sc. 12 (1700).

15 It has been said that love robs those
    who have it of their wit, and gives it
    to those who have none.

DENIS DIDEROT, (1713–1784) French philosopher. *Paradox of the Actor* (written 1770–1773, originally published 1830). Repr. in *Selected Writings*, ed. Lester G. Crocker (1966).

16 Love, all alike, no season knows, nor
    clime,
    Nor hours, days, months, which are
    the rags of time.

JOHN DONNE, (c. 1572–1631) British divine, metaphysical poet. "The Sun Rising," *Songs and Sonnets* (1633). Repr. in *Complete Poetry and Selected Prose*, ed. John Hayward (1929).

17 Love was as subtly catched, as a dis
    ease;
    But being got it is a treasure sweet,
    Which to defend is harder than to
    get:
    And ought not be profaned on either
    part,
    For though 'tis got by *chance*,'tis
    kept by *art*.

JOHN DONNE, (c. 1572–1631) British divine, metaphysical poet. *The Expostulation, Elegies* (1633). Repr. in *Complete Poetry and Selected Prose*, ed. John Hayward (1929).

Last lines of poem.

18 I don't want to live—I want to love
    first, and live incidentally.

ZELDA FITZGERALD, (1900–1948) U.S. writer, wife of F. Scott Fitzgerald. quoted in *Zelda*, pt. 1, ch. 4, Nancy Milford (1970). Letter, March 1919, to F. Scott Fitzgerald.

19 Love gives naught but itself and
    takes naught but from itself.
    Love possesses not nor would it be
    possessed;
    For love is sufficient unto love.

KAHLIL GIBRAN, (1883–1931) Syrian–born U.S. poet, novelist. *The Prophet* (1923).

20 Today I begin to understand what
    love must be, if it exists.... When we
    are parted, we each feel the lack of
    the other half of ourselves. We are
    incomplete like a book in two vol-
    umes of which the first has been
    lost. That is what I imagine love to
    be: incompleteness in absence.

EDMOND LOUIS ANTOINE HUOT DE GONCOURT, (1822–1896) French writer, journalist. *The Goncourt Journals* (1956), repr. in *Pages from the Goncourt Journal*, ed. Robert Baldick (1962). Journal entry, Nov. 15, 1859.

21 Love, love, love—all the wretched
    cant of it, masking egotism, lust,
    masochism, fantasy under a
    mythology of sentimental postures,
    a welter of self–induced miseries
    and joys, blinding and masking the
    essential personalities in the frozen
    gestures of courtship, in the kissing
    and the dating and the desire, the
    compliments and the quarrels
    which vivify its barrenness.

GERMAINE GREER, (b. 1939) Australian feminist writer. *The Female Eunuch*, "Obsession" (1970).

22 "You must sit down, says Love, and
    taste my meat:"
    So I did sit and eat.

GEORGE HERBERT, (1593–1633) British poet, clergyman."Love," st. 3, *The Temple*

(1633). Repr. in *The Works of George Herbert*, ed. Helen Gardner (1961).

23   Love's like the measles—all the worse when it comes late in life.

DOUGLAS JERROLD, (1803–1857) British playwright, humorist. "A Philanthropist," *The Wit and Opinions of Douglas Jerrold* (1859).

There is an echo of this in Jerome K. Jerome's *Idle Thoughts of an Idle Fellow*, "On Being in Love" (1889): "Love is like the measles; we all have to go through it. Also like the measles, we take it only once."

24   Love is the wisdom of the fool and the folly of the wise.

SAMUEL JOHNSON, (1709–1784) British author, lexicographer. Quoted in William Cooke, *Life of Samuel Foote*, vol. 2, repr. in *Johnsonian Miscellanies*, vol. 2, p. 393, ed. George Birkbeck Hill (1897).

25   Come, my Celia, let us prove,
While we can, the sports of love.

BEN JONSON, (c. 1572–1637) British dramatist, poet. Volpone, in *Volpone*, act 3, sc. 7 (written c. 1605, published 1616). Repr. in *The Complete Plays*, ed. G.A. Wilkes (1981–1982).

The lines also appear (with slight variations) in Jonson's *The Forest*, no. 5: "Song to Celia."

26   Where love reigns, there is no will to power; and where the will to power is paramount, love is lacking. The one is but the shadow of the other.

CARL JUNG, (1875–1961) Swiss psychiatrist. *On the Psychology of th Unconscious* (1917), repr. in *Collected Works*, vol. 7, ed. William McGuire (1953).(Revised 1926 and 1943).

27   True love is like ghosts, which everyone talks about but few have seen.

FRANÇOIS LA ROCHEFOUCAULD, DUC DE, (1613–1680) French writer, moralist. *Sentences et Maximes Morales*, no. 76 (1678).

28   I shall always be a priest of love.

D.H. (DAVID HERBERT) LAWRENCE, (1885–1930) British author. *The Letters of D.H. Lawrence*, vol. 1, ed. James T. Boulton (1979). Letter, Dec. 25, 1912.

29   All you need is love.

JOHN LENNON, (1940–1980) British songwriter, rock musician. "All You Need Is Love" (song), on the album *Yellow Submarine* (1968).

30   Love's boat has been shattered against the life of everyday. You and I are quits, and it's useless to draw up a list of mutual hurts, sorrows, and pains.

VLADIMIR MAYAKOVSKY, (1893–1930) Russian poet, dramatist. "Unfinished poem," *The Heritage of Russian Verse*, ed. and trans. by Dimitri Obolensky (1965). Letter, Apr. 12, 1930.

Mayakovsky's last poem was found in his papers after his suicide.

31   What thou art is mine;
Our state cannot be severed, we are one,
One flesh; to lose thee were to lose myself.

JOHN MILTON, (1608–1674) British poet. Adam, in *Paradise Lost*, bk. 9, l. 957–9 (1674). Repr. in *Paradise Lost*, ed. Scott Elledge (1993).

Addressing Eve, after she has confessed her sin.

32   Love means never having to say you're sorry.

ERICH SEGAL, (b. 1937) U.S. author. *Love Story* (film) (1970).

The words (spoken by Ali McGraw) were used to promote the movie; in Segal's novelization of the film (he also wrote the screenplay), the words appear as "Love means not ever having to say you're sorry." (ch. 13). Many variations have been coined over the years, for example, "Vasectomy means not ever having to say you're sorry." (Attributed to Larry Adler).

33 Men have died from time to time, and worms have eaten them, but not for love.

WILLIAM SHAKESPEARE, (1564–1616) British dramatist, poet. Rosalind, in *As You Like It*, act 4, sc. 1, l. 99–101 (1623).

34 Familiar acts are beautiful through love.

PERCY BYSSHE SHELLEY, (1792–1822) British poet. The earth, in *Prometheus Unbound*, act 4, l. 403 (1820).

35 'Tis better to have loved and lost Than never to have loved at all.

ALFRED TENNYSON, 1ST BARON TEN-NYSON, (1809–1892) British poet." In Memoriam A.H.H.", cto. 27, st. 4 (1850).

36 Love conquers everything *[Amor vincit omnia]*: let us, too, yield to love.

VIRGIL [PUBLIUS VERGILIUS MARO], (70–19 B.C.) Roman poet. Gallus, in *Eclogues*, no. 10, l. 69 (37 B.C.), trans. by Kate Hughes (1995).

37 A pity beyond all telling Is hid in the heart of love.

WILLIAM BUTLER YEATS, (1865–1939) Irish poet. "The Pity of Love", *The Rose* (1893).

Love and Marriage

1 Where there's marriage without love, there will be love without marriage.

BENJAMIN FRANKLIN, (1706–1790) U.S. statesman, writer. *Poor Richard's Almanac*, May (1734).

2 A man in love is incomplete until he has married—then he's finished.

ZSA ZSA GABOR, (b. 1919) Hungarian-born U.S. screen actor. Quoted in *Newsweek* (New York, March 28, 1960).

Love at First Sight

1 For which he wex a litel red for shame,
Whan he the peple upon him herde cryen,
That to beholde it was a noble game,
How sobreliche he caste doun his yen.
Criseyda gan al his chere aspyen,
And let so softe it in her herte sinke
That to herself she seyde, "Who yaf me drinke?"

GEOFFREY CHAUCER, (1340–1400) British poet. *Troilus and Criseyde*, bk. 2, l. 645–51 (c. 1385), repr.in *The Works of Geoffrey Chaucer*, ed. Alfred W. Pollard, et al. (1898).

2 Where both deliberate, the love is slight:
Who ever loved, that loved not at first sight?

CHRISTOPHER MARLOWE, (1564–1593) British dramatist, poet. *Hero and Leander*, "First Sestiad" l. 175–6 (1598).

The words are recalled in Shakespeare's *As You Like It*, act 3, sc. 5, l. 175–6, which appeared a year after Marlowe's poem: "Dead shepherd, now I find thy saw of might: 'Who ever loved that loved not at first sight?'."

Love, Ended

1 Alas, my Love! ye do me wrong To cast me off discourteously: And I have loved you so long, Delighting in your company.

Greensleeves was all my joy, Greensleeves was my delight; Greensleeves was my heart of gold, And who but Lady Greensleeves.

ANONYMOUS, "Greensleeves," st. 1 and refrain, *A Handful Of Pleasant Delights* (1584).

2 And I shall find some girl perhaps,
And a better one than you,
With eyes as wise, but kindlier,
And lips as soft, but true,
And I daresay she will do.

RUPERT BROOKE, (1887–1915) British
poet. "The Chilterns," *Collected Poems* (1966).

3 So, we'll go no more a–roving
So late into the night,
Though the heart be still as loving,
And the moon be still as bright.
For the sword outwears its sheath,
And the soul wears out the breast.
And the heart must pause to breathe
And love itself have rest.

**GEORGE GORDON NOEL BYRON, 6TH
BARON BYRON,** (1788–1824) British poet.
"So We'll Go No More A–Roving" (1817)

4 Heaven has no rage like love to
hatred turned,
Nor Hell a fury, like a woman
scorned.

WILLIAM CONGREVE, (1670–1729) British
dramatist. Zara, in *The Mourning Bride*, act 3
(1697).

Concluding lines of the play.

5 Since there's no help, come let us
kiss and part,
Nay, I have done: you get no more
of me,
And I am glad, yea glad with all my
heart,
That thus so cleanly I myself can
free.
Shake hands for ever, cancel all our
vows,
And when we meet at any time again
Be it not seen in either of our brows
That we one jot of former love
retain;
Now at the last gasp of Love's latest
breath,
When his pulse failing, Passion
speechless lies,

When Faith is kneeling by his bed
of death,
And Innocence is closing up his
eyes,
Now if thou wouldst, when all have
given him over,
From death to life, thou might'st
him yet recover.

MICHAEL DRAYTON, (1563–1631) British
poet." Idea," Sonnet 61, *Idea: in Sixty–three
Sonnets* (1619), repr. in *Works*, vol. 2, ed. J.
William Hebel (1932).

6 When love grows diseased, the best
thing we can do is to put it to a violent death; I cannot endure the torture of a lingering and consumptive
passion.

GEORGE ETHEREGE, (1635–1691) British
dramatist, diplomat. Dorimant, in *The Man of
Mode*, act 2, sc. 2 (1676).

7 Let's call the whole thing off.

IRA GERSHWIN, (1896–1983) U.S. lyricist.
"Let's Call the Whole Thing Off" (song), *Shall
We Dance* (film, 1937).

8 There are few people who are not
ashamed of their love affairs when
the infatuation is over.

**FRANÇOIS LA ROCHEFOUCAULD,
DUC DE,** (1613–1680) French writer, moralist. *Sentences et Maximes Morales*, no. 71
(1678).

9 After all, my erstwhile dear,
My no longer cherished,
Need we say it was not love,
Now that love is perished?

EDNA ST. VINCENT MILLAY,
(1892–1950) U.S. poet. "Passer Mortuus Est,"
Second April (1921).

10 I was never one to patiently pick up
broken fragments and glue them
together again and tell myself that
the mended whole was as good as
new. What is broken is broken—

and I'd rather remember it as it was at its best than mend it and see the broken places as long as I lived.... I wish I could care what you do or where you go, but I can't. My dear, I don't give a damn.

MARGARET MITCHELL, (1900–1949) U.S. novelist. Rhett Butler, in *Gone with the Wind*, vol. 2, pt. 5, ch. 63 (1936).

In the 1939 movie (screenplay by Sidney Howard), the final words of Rhett's farewell to Scarlett O'Hara are "Frankly, my dear, I don't give a damn!"—with the emphasis on "give" to soften the impact of the "damn."

11 And the best and the worst of this is
    That neither is most to blame,
    If you have forgotten my kisses
    And I have forgotten your name.

A.C. (ALGERNON CHARLES) SWIN-BURNE, (1837–1909) British poet, critic. "An Interlude," st. 14 (1866).

Love, First Love

1 In her first passion woman loves
       her lover,
    In all the others all she loves is love.

GEORGE GORDON NOEL BYRON, 6TH BARON BYRON, (1788–1824) British poet. *Don Juan*, cto. 3, st. 3 (1819–1824).

Love, Unrequited

1 My love is of a birth as rare
    As 'tis for object strange and high:
    It was begotten by Despair
    Upon Impossibility.

ANDREW MARVELL, (1621–1678) British metaphysical poet. "The Definition of Love" (written c. 1650, published 1681).

Lovers

1 My beloved is white and ruddy, the
    chiefest among ten thousand. His

head is as the most fine gold, his locks are bushy, and black as a raven. His eyes are as the eyes of doves by the rivers of waters, washed with milk, and fitly set. His cheeks are as a bed of spices, as sweet flowers: his lips like lilies, dropping sweet smelling myrrh. His hands are as gold rings set with the beryl, his belly is as bright ivory overlaid with sapphires. His legs are as pillars of marble, set upon sockets of fine gold: his countenance is as Lebanon, excellent as the cedars. His mouth is most sweet: yea, he is altogether lovely. This is my beloved, and this is my friend, O daughters of Jerusalem.

BIBLE: HEBREW, *Song of Solomon*, 5:10–16.

2 Stay me with flagons, comfort me
    with apples: for I am sick of love.

BIBLE: HEBREW, *Song of Solomon*, 2:5.

3 Nay but you, who do not love her,
    Is she not pure gold, my mistress?

ROBERT BROWNING, (1812–1889) British poet. "Song," l. 1–2 (1842).

4 Never the time and the place
    And the loved one all together!

ROBERT BROWNING, (1812–1889) British poet." Never the Time and the Place", l. 1–2, *Jocoseria* (1883).

5 O my luve's like a red, red rose
       That's newly sprung in June;
    O my luve's like the melodie
       That's sweetly play'd in tune.

ROBERT BURNS, (1759–1796) Scottish poet. "A Red, Red Rose," st. 1 and 5, *Johnson's Musical Museum*, vol. 5 (1796). *Poetical Works*, vol. 2, ed. William Scott Douglas (1891).

6 My sweetest Lesbia let us live and
    love,

And though the sager sort our deeds
  reprove,
Let us not weigh them: Heav'n's
  great lamps do dive
Into their west, and straight again
  revive,
But soon as once set is our little
  light,
Then must we sleep one ever–during
  night.

CATULLUS [GAIUS VALERIUS CATUL-LUS], (84–54 B.C.) Roman poet. "Carmina," no. 5, l.1–7, trans. by Thomas Campion (1601).

Lesbia was the pseudonym for Clodia Metelli, the inspiration for much of Catullus's poetry.

7   All mankind love a lover.

RALPH WALDO EMERSON, (1803–1882) U.S. essayist, poet, philosopher. *Essays*, "Love," First Series (1841).

8   O'er her warm cheek and rising
       bosom move
     The bloom of young desire and pur-
       ple light of love.

THOMAS GRAY, (1716–1771) British poet. "The Progress of Poesy", pt. 1, sct. 3, l. 16–7 (written 1754, published 1757). Repr. in *Poetical Works*, ed. J. Rogers (1953).

9   A lover without indiscretion is no
     lover at all. Circumspection and
     devotion are a contradiction in terms.

THOMAS HARDY, (1840–1928) British novelist, poet. Ladywell, in *The Hand of Ethelberta*, ch. 20 (1875).

10   Bid me to live, and I will live
     Thy Protestant to be:
     Or bid me love, and I will give
     A loving heart to thee.

ROBERT HERRICK, (1591–1674) British poet, clergyman." To Anthea, Who May Command Him Anything,"st. 1, *Hesperides* (1648). Repr. in *The Poems of Robert Herrick*, ed. L.C. Martin (1956).

11   We can recognize the dawn and the
     decline of love by the uneasiness we
     feel when alone together.

JEAN DE LA BRUYÈRE, (1645–1696) French writer, moralist. *Characters*, "Of the Heart," aph. 33 (1688).

12   Queen Guenever, for whom I make
     here a little mention, that while she
     lived she was a true lover, and
     therefore she had a good end.

THOMAS MALORY, (c. 1430–1471) British author. *Le Morte d'Arthur*, bk. 18, ch. 25 (1485).

13   These two
     Imparadised in one another's arms,
     The happier Eden, shall enjoy their
       fill
     Of bliss on bliss.

JOHN MILTON, (1608–1674) British poet. The devil, in *Paradise Lost*, bk. 4, l. 505–8 (1667).

Referring to Adam and Eve.

14   Scratch a lover, and find a foe.

DOROTHY PARKER, (1893–1967) U.S. humorous writer. "Ballade of a Great Weariness" *Enough Rope* (1926).

15   And this maiden she lived with no
     other thought
     Than to love and be loved by me.

EDGAR ALLAN POE, (1809–1845) U.S. poet, critic, short–story writer. "Annabel Lee" st. 1 (1845). First published in *New York Tribune* (Oct. 9, 1849).

The poem is addressed to Poe's 13–year–old cousin and wife, Virginia Clemm, who died in 1847 aged 24.

16   *I* was a child and *she* was a child,
     In this kingdom by the sea;
     But we loved with a love which was
       more than love —
     I and my Annabel Lee.

EDGAR ALLAN POE, (1809–1845) U.S. poet, critic, short–story writer. *Annabel Lee*, st. 2 (written 1845). First published in *New York Tribune* (Oct. 9, 1849).

17   We that are true lovers run into
     strange capers.

WILLIAM SHAKESPEARE, (1564–1616) British dramatist, poet. Touchstone, in *As You Like It*, act 2, sc. 4, l. 50–1 (1623).

18 She bid me take love easy, as the
leaves grow on the tree;
But I, being young and foolish,
    with her would not agree.

WILLIAM BUTLER YEATS, (1865–1939) Irish poet, playwright. "Down by the Salley Gardens," *Crossways* (1889).

Loyalty

1 Intreat me not to leave thee, or to
return from following after thee:
for whither thou goest, I will go;
and where thou lodgest, I will
lodge: thy people shall be my people, and thy God my God.

BIBLE: HEBREW, Ruth, in *Ruth*, 1:16.

Spoken to her mother–in–law Naomi.

2 That is no use at all. What I want is
men who will support me when I
am in the wrong.

WILLIAM LAMB MELBOURNE, 2ND VISCOUNT, (1779–1848) British statesman, prime minister. Quoted in *Lord M*, ch. 4, David Cecil (1954).

Reply to a politician's pledge: "I will support you as long as you are in the right."

3 Freely we serve,
Because we freely love, as in our
    will
To love or not; in this we stand or
    fall.

JOHN MILTON, (1608–1674) British poet. The angel Raphael, in *Paradise Lost*, bk. 5, l. 538–40 (1674). Repr. in *Paradise Lost*, ed. Scott Elledge (1993).

Addressing Adam.

4 Histories are more full of examples
of the fidelity of dogs than of
friends.

ALEXANDER POPE, (1688–1744) British satirical poet. *The Correspondence of Alexander Pope*, vol. 1, ed. George Sherburn (1956). Letter, Oct. 19, 1709.

5 Had I but served my God with half
    the zeal
I served my King, He would not in
    mine age
Have left me naked to mine ene-
    mies.

WILLIAM SHAKESPEARE, (1564–1616) British dramatist, poet. Cardinal Wolsey, in *Henry VIII*, act 3, sc. 2, l. 456–8 (1623).

These words, spoken in the play to Thomas Cromwell, were in fact recorded as Wolsey's dying words in Raphael Holinshed *Chronicles* (1577), one of Shakespeare's main sources, where they appear in the form, "If I had served God as diligently as I have done the King, He would not have given me over in my grey hairs."

Luck

1 The race is not to the swift, nor
the battle to the strong, neither yet
bread to the wise, nor yet riches
to men of understanding, nor
yet favour to men of skill; but
time and chance happeneth to
them all.

BIBLE: HEBREW, *Ecclesiastes*, 9:11.

2 In short, Luck's always to blame.

JEAN DE LA FONTAINE, (1621–1695) French poet, fabulist. "La Fortune et le Jeune Enfant," bk. 5, *Fables* (1678–1679).

3 Fortune's a right whore.
If she give ought, she deals it in
    small parcels,
That she may take away all at one
    swoop.

JOHN WEBSTER, (1580–1625) British dramatist. Lodovico, in *The White Devil*, act 1, sc. 1, l. 4–6 (1612). Repr. in *The Complete Works of John Webster*, ed. F.L. Lucas (1927).

Lust

1 Abstinence sows sand all over
The ruddy limbs and flaming hair,
But desire gratified
Plants fruits of life and beauty
there.

WILLIAM BLAKE, (1757–1827) British
poet, painter, engraver. *Manuscript Notebook
(1793)*, "Poems and Fragments," no. 40, published in *Complete Writings*, ed. Geoffrey
Keynes (1957).

2 I've looked on a lot of women with
lust. I've committed adultery in my
heart many times. This is something God recognizes I will do—
and I have done it—and God for-
gives me for it.

JIMMY CARTER, (b. 1924) U.S. Democratic politician, president. Interview in *Playboy*
(Chicago, Nov. 1976).

Said during the presidential campaign against
Gerald Ford.

3 What most men desire is a virgin
who is a whore.

EDWARD DAHLBERG, (1900–1977) U.S.
author, critic. *Reasons of the Heart*, "On Lust"
(1965).

4 The infernal storm, eternal in its
rage, sweeps and drives the spirits
with its blast; it whirls them, lash-
ing them with punishment. When
they are swept back past their place
of judgment then come the shrieks,
laments, and anguished cries; there
they blaspheme God's almighty
power.

DANTE ALIGHIERI, (1265–1321) Italian
poet. "Inferno," cto. 5, l. 31–6, *The Divine
Comedy* (c. 1307–1321), trans. by Mark Musa
(1971).

The whirlwind of the Lustful, in the second
circle of Hell.

5 Down, wanton, down! Have you no
shame

That at the whisper of Love's
name,
Or Beauty's, presto! up you raise
Your angry head and stand at
gaze?

ROBERT GRAVES, (1895–1985) British
poet, novelist. "Down, Wanton, Down!"
Collected Poems (1965).

6 There goes a saying, and 'twas
shrewdly said,
Old fish at table, but young flesh
in bed.

ALEXANDER POPE, (1688–1744) British
satirical poet. "January and May", l.
101–2. *Poetical Miscellanies* (1709).

A translation of Chaucer *The Merchant's
Tale*, written aged sixteen or seventeen.

Luxury

1 The saddest thing I can imagine is
to get used to luxury.

CHARLIE CHAPLIN, (1889–1977) British
comic actor, filmmaker. *My Autobiography*,
ch. 22 (1960).

2 The lust for comfort, that stealthy
thing that enters the house a guest,
and then becomes a host, and then
a master.

KAHLIL GIBRAN, (1883–1931)
Syrian–born U.S. poet, novelist. "On
Houses," *The Prophet* (1923).

3 Give us the luxuries of life, and
we will dispense with its neces-
saries.

JOHN LOTHROP MOTLEY,
(1814–1877) U.S. historian. Quoted in *The
Autocrat of the Breakfast–Table*, ch. 6,
Oliver Wendell Holmes Sr. (1858).

Machinery

1 One machine can do the work of
fifty ordinary men. No machine

can do the work of one extraordinary man.

ELBERT HUBBARD, (1856–1915) U.S. author. *One Thousand and One Epigrams* (1911).

2   From coupler–flange to
    spindle–guide I see Thy Hand, O God—
    Predestination in the stride o' yon
       connectin'–rod.

RUDYARD KIPLING, (1865–1936) British author, poet." McAndrew's Hymn," *The Seven Seas* (1896).

3   Machines are worshipped because they are beautiful and valued because they confer power; they are hated because they are hideous and loathed because they impose slavery.

BERTRAND RUSSELL [LORD RUSSELL, 3RD EARL], (1872–1970) British philosopher, mathematician. *Sceptical Essays,* "Machines and Emotions" (1928).

Madness

1   We all are born mad. Some remain so.

SAMUEL BECKETT, (1906–1989) Irish dramatist, novelist. Estragon, in *Waiting for Godot,* act 2 (1952, trans. 1954).

2   He is mad past recovery, but yet he has lucid intervals.

MIGUEL DE CERVANTES, (1547–1616) Spanish author. Don Lorenzo, in *Don Quixote,* pt. 2, ch. 18 (1615), trans. by P. Motteux. Describing Don Quixote.

3   Victor Hugo was a madman who thought he was Victor Hugo.

JEAN COCTEAU, (1889–1963) French author, filmmaker. *Opium* (1929). Quoting himself from a previous occasion.

4   Much Madness is divinest Sense—
    To a discerning Eye—

Much Sense—the starkest Madness—

EMILY DICKINSON, (1830–1886) U.S. poet. "Much Madness is Divinest Sense" (written c. 1862, published 1890). Repr. in *The Complete Poems,* no. 435, Harvard *variorum* edition (1955).

5   One thing in any case is certain: man is neither the oldest nor the most constant problem that has been posed for human knowledge.

MICHEL FOUCAULT, (1926–1984) French philosopher. *The Order of Things,* ch. 10, sct. 6 (1966, trans. 1970).

6   Madness need not be all breakdown. It may also be break–through. It is potential liberation and renewal as well as enslavement and existential death.

R.D. (RONALD DAVID) LAING, (1927–1989) British psychiatrist. *The Politics of Experience,* ch. 6 (1967).

7   I guess the definition of a lunatic is a man surrounded by them.

EZRA POUND, (1885–1972) U.S. poet, critic. Quoted in *Charles Olson and Ezra Pound,* Catherine Seelye (1975). Said to poet and critic Charles Olson in 1945, when Olson visited Pound in Howard Hall, the institution for the criminally insane in which Pound was detained pending a judgment on his wartime broadcasts from Rome.

8   O what a noble mind is here o'erthrown!

WILLIAM SHAKESPEARE, (1564–1616) British dramatist, poet. Ophelia, in *Hamlet,* act 3, sc. 1, l. 153 (1604). Referring to Hamlet's bizarre behavior, part of his "antic disposition."

9   Though this be madness, yet there is
    method in't.

WILLIAM SHAKESPEARE, (1564–1616) British dramatist, poet. Polonius, in *Hamlet,* act 2, sc. 2, l. 206–7 (1604). Referring to the logic in Hamlet's "mad" discourse. The expression, "there is method in my/his/her madness" has entered common usage.

10 We all go a little mad sometimes.

JOSEPH STEFANO, U.S. screenwriter. Norman Bates (Anthony Perkins), in *Psycho* (1960).

11 To think the world therefore a general Bedlam, or place of madmen, and oneself a physician, is the most necessary point of present wisdom: an important imagination, and the way to happiness.

THOMAS TRAHERNE, (1636–1674) British clergyman, poet, mystic. *Centuries,* "Fourth Century," no. 20 (written c. 1672, first published 1908).

Magic

1 Indubitably, Magick is one of the sublest and most difficult of the sciences and arts. There is more opportunity for errors of comprehension, judgement and practice than in any other branch of physics.

ALEISTER CROWLEY, (1875–1947) British occultist. *The Confessions of Aleister Crowley,* ch. 20 (1929). Ed. (1970).

Majority, the

1 When great changes occur in history, when great principles are involved, as a rule the majority are wrong.

EUGENE VICTOR DEBS, (1855– 1926) U.S. trade unionist, Socialist leader. *Eugene V. Debs Speaks,* ed. Jean Y. Tussey (1970). Speech, Sept. 11, 1918, Cleveland, Ohio.

Defending himself against charges of sedition; found guilty, he was subsequently jailed for three years.

Malice

1 In doing good, we are generally cold, and languid, and sluggish; and of all things afraid of being too much in the right. But the works of malice and injustice are quite in another style. They are finished with a bold, masterly hand; touched as they are with the spirit of those vehement passions that call forth all our energies, whenever we oppress and persecute.

EDMUND BURKE, (1729–1797) Irish philosopher, statesman. "Speech at Bristol, Previous to the Election" (1780) published in *Works,* vol. 2 (1899).

2 There's no possibility of being witty without a little ill–nature—
The malice of a good thing is the barb that makes it stick.

RICHARD BRINSLEY SHERIDAN, (1751–1816) Anglo–Irish dramatist. Lady Sneerwell, in *The School for Scandal,* act 1, sc. 1, l. 144–5 (1777).

Management

1 Damn the great executives, the men of measured merriment, damn the men with careful smiles, damn the men that run the shops, oh, damn their measured merriment.

SINCLAIR LEWIS, (1885–1951) U.S. novelist. Martin Arrowsmith, in *Arrowsmith,* ch. 25 (1925).

Manners

1 Manners must adorn knowledge, and smooth its way through the world.

PHILIP DORMER STANHOPE, 4TH EARL CHESTERFIELD, (1694–1773) British statesman, man of letters. *The Letters of the Earl of Chesterfield to His Son*, vol. 1, no. 155, ed. Charles Strachey (1901). Letter, July 1, 1748, first published (1774).

2   He is the very pineapple of politeness!

RICHARD BRINSLEY SHERIDAN, (1751–1816) Anglo–Irish dramatist. Mrs. Malaprop, in *The Rivals*, act 3, sc. 3 (1775). Referring to Captain Absolute; the word intended in the "malapropism" is *pinnacle*.

Marriage

1   Marriage always demands the greatest understanding of the art of insincerity possible between two human beings.

VICKI BAUM, (1888–1960) Austrian–born U.S. novelist. For in the resurrection they neither marry, nor are given in marriage, but are as the angels of God in heaven.

2   Therefore shall a man leave his father and mother, and shall cleave unto his wife: and they shall be one flesh.

BIBLE: HEBREW, *Genesis*, 2:24.

3   Marriage. The state or condition of a community consisting of a master, a mistress and two slaves, making in all, two.

AMBROSE BIERCE, (1842–1914) U.S. author. *The Devil's Dictionary* (1881–1906), repr. in *Collected Works of Ambrose Bierce*, vol. 7 (1911).

4   If any man can shew any just cause, why they may not lawfully be joined together, let him now speak, or else hereafter for ever hold his peace.

BOOK OF COMMON PRAYER, THE, *Solemnization of Matrimony*, "Exhortation" (1662).

5   Those whom God hath joined together let no man put asunder.

BOOK OF COMMON PRAYER, THE, *Solemnization of Matrimony*, "Wedding" (1662). Taken from the words of Jesus in *Matthew* 19:6.

6   Reader, I married him.

CHARLOTTE BRONTË, (1816–1855) British novelist. Jane, in *Jane Eyre*, ch. 38 (1847). Opening words of chapter. The marriage was to Rochester: it was "a quiet wedding."

7   One was never married, and that's his hell; another is, and that's his plague.

ROBERT BURTON, (1577–1640) British clergyman, author. *The Anatomy of Melancholy*, pt. 1, sct. 2, memb. 4, subsct. 7 (1621).

8   It was very good of God to let Carlyle and Mrs. Carlyle marry one another and so make only two people miserable instead of four, besides being very amusing.

SAMUEL BUTLER, (1835–1902) British author. *Letters Between Samuel Butler and E.M.A. Savage 1871–1885* (1935). Letter, Nov. 21, 1884.

The quote has been erroneously ascribed to Tennyson.

9   Still I can't contradict, what so oft has been said,
"Though women are angels, yet wedlock's the devil."

GEORGE GORDON NOEL BYRON, 6TH BARON BYRON, (1788–1824) British poet. "To Eliza" (1807).

10   Love and marriage, love and marriage
Go together like a horse and carriage
Dad was told by mother
You can't have one without the other.

SAMMY CAHN, (1913–1993) U.S. song-writer. *"Love and Marriage" (song),* from the TV musical *Our Town* (1955), with music by Jimmy Van Heusen. The song was first aired by Frank Sinatra, for whom it was a million–seller.

11 Experience, though noon auctori-tee
Were in this world, were right
  ynogh to me
To speke of wo that is in mariage.

GEOFFREY CHAUCER, (1340–1400) British poet. *The Canterbury Tales,* "The Wife of Bath's Prologue," l. 1–3 (c. 1387–1400), repr. in *The Works of Geoffrey Chaucer,* ed. Alfred W. Pollard, et al. (1898).

12 Thus grief still treads upon the
  heels of pleasure:
Married in haste, we may repent at
  leisure.

WILLIAM CONGREVE, (1670–1729) British dramatist. Sharper, in *The Old Bachelor,* act 5, sc. 1 (1693). To which Setter replies, "Some by experience find those words misplaced: At leisure married, they repent in haste."

13 Barkis is willin'.

CHARLES DICKENS, (1812–1870) British novelist. *David Copperfield,* ch. 5 (1849–1850). Message of proposal carried by David Copperfield on behalf of Barkis to Clara Peggotty. "When a man says he's willin'," Barkis explains in ch. 8, "...it's as much as to say, that a man's waitin' for a answer." Peggotty becomes Mrs. Barkis.

14 Any intelligent woman who reads the marriage contract and then goes into it, deserves all the consequences.

ISADORA DUNCAN, (1878–1927) U.S. dancer. *My Life,* ch. 19 (1927). Duncan herself was married (for one year) to the Russian poet Sergei Yesenin.

15 Marriage as an institution developed from rape as a practice. Rape, originally defined as abduction, became marriage by capture. Marriage meant the taking was to extend in time, to be not only use of but possession of, or ownership.

ANDREA DWORKIN, (b. 1946) U.S. feminist critic. *Pornography,* ch. 1 (1981).

16 Matrimonial devotion
Doesn't seem to suit her notion.

SIR WILLIAM SCHWENCK GILBERT, (1836–1911) British librettist. Ko–Ko, in *The Mikado,* act 2 (1885), published in *The Savoy Operas* (1926).

17 Every time a woman makes herself laugh at her husband's often–told jokes she betrays him. The man who looks at his woman and says "What would I do without you?" is already destroyed.

GERMAINE GREER, (b. 1939) Australian feminist writer. *The Female Eunuch,* "Egotism" (1970).

18 The critical period in matrimony is breakfast–time.

A.P. (SIR ALAN PATRICK) HERBERT, (1890–1971) British author, politician. "Is Marriage Lawful?" *Uncommon Law* (1935).

19 There is, indeed, nothing that so much seduces reason from vigilance, as the thought of passing life with an amiable woman.

SAMUEL JOHNSON, (1709–1784) British author, lexicographer. Quoted in James Boswell, *Life of Dr. Johnson* (1791) (1791). Letter, Dec. 21, 1762.

20 Two by two in the ark of
the ache of it.

DENISE LEVERTOV, (b. 1923) Anglo-American poet. "The Ache of Marriage," *O Taste and See* (1964).

21 Marriage is the only actual bondage known to our law. There remain

no legal slaves, except the mistress of every house.

JOHN STUART MILL, (1806–1873) British philosopher, economist. *The Subjection of Women*, ch. 4 (1869). See Mill on wives.

22 Hail wedded Love, mysterious law,
      true source
    Of human offspring, sole propriety
    In Paradise of all things common
      else.

JOHN MILTON, (1608–1674) British poet. *Paradise Lost*, bk. 4, l.750–2 (1674). Repr. in *Paradise Lost*, ed. Scott Elledge (1993).

23 I feel
    The link of nature draw me: flesh of
      flesh,
    Bone of my bone thou art, and
      from thy state
    Mine shall never be parted, bliss or
      woe.

JOHN MILTON, (1608–1674) British poet. Adam, in *Paradise Lost*, bk. 9, l. 913–6 (1674). Repr. in *Paradise Lost*, ed. Scott Elledge (1993).

Addressing Eve, shortly before he partakes of "the fair enticing fruit."

24 We cannot do without it, and yet we disgrace and vilify the same. It may be compared to a cage, the birds without despair to get in, and those within despair to get out.

MICHEL DE MONTAIGNE, (1533–1592) French essayist. *Essays*, bk. 3, ch. 5 (1595), trans. by John Florio (1603).

25 One doesn't have to get anywhere in a marriage. It's not a public conveyance.

IRIS MURDOCH, (b. 1919) British novelist, philosopher. Martin Lynch–Gibbon, in *A Severed Head*, ch. 3 (1961).

26 Garth, marriage is punishment for shoplifting, in some countries.

MIKE MYERS, (b. 1964) Canadian comic, screenwriter. Wayne Campbell (Mike Myers), in *Wayne's World* (film) (1992).

The movie featured characters created by Mike Myers and developed into a comedy sketch with Dana Carvey on *Saturday Night Live* (TV show), hosted by David Letterman in 1989.

27 They dream in courtship, but in wedlock wake.

ALEXANDER POPE, (1688–1744) British satirical poet. "*The Wife of Bath*," l. 103 (1713).

28 The world must be peopled. When I said I would die a bachelor, I did not think I should live till I were married.

WILLIAM SHAKESPEARE, (1564–1616) British dramatist, poet. Benedick, in *Much Ado About Nothing*, act 2, sc. 3, l. 229–31 (1600). Justifying his change of heart about marriage.

29 'Tis safest in matrimony to begin with a little aversion.

RICHARD BRINSLEY SHERIDAN, (1751–1816) Anglo–Irish dramatist. Mrs. Malaprop, in *The Rivals*, act 1, sc. 2 (1775).

30 It resembles a pair of shears, so joined that they cannot be separated, often moving in opposite directions, yet always punishing anyone who comes between them.

SYDNEY SMITH, (1771–1845) British clergyman, writer. Quoted in *The Smith of Smiths*, ch. 11, Hesketh Pearson (1934).

31 The concerts you enjoy together
    Neighbors you annoy together
    Children you destroy together
    That make marriage a joy

STEPHEN SONDHEIM, (b. 1930) U.S. songwriter." The Little Things You Do Together" (song), *Company* (stage show, 1970).

33 The married state, with and without the affection suitable to it, is the

completest image of heaven and hell we are capable of receiving in this life.

RICHARD STEELE, (1672–1729) British dramatist, essayist, editor. *Spectator* (London, Sept. 9, 1712), no. 479, *The Spectator*, ed. D.F. Bond (1965).

33 Marriage is one long conversation, chequered by disputes.

ROBERT LOUIS STEVENSON, (1850–1894) Scottish novelist, essayist, poet. *Talk and Talkers*, paper 2, *Memories and Portraits* (1887). (Originally published 1882).

34 Once you are married, there is nothing for you, not even suicide, but to be good.

ROBERT LOUIS STEVENSON, (1850–1894) Scottish novelist, essayist, poet. *Virginibus Puerisque,* "Virginibus Puerisque," sct. 2 (1881). Stevenson referred to "matrimony at its lowest" as "no more than a sort of friendship recognised by the police."

35 The union of hands and hearts.

JEREMY TAYLOR, (1613–1667) British churchman, devotional writer. *Twenty–five Sermons Preached at Golden Grove*, "The Marriage Ring," (1653).

36 There is no road to wealth so easy and respectable as that of matrimony; that is, of course, provided that the aspirant declines the slow course of honest work.

ANTHONY TROLLOPE, (1815–1882) British novelist. *Doctor Thorne*, ch. 18 (1858).

37 That a marriage ends is less than ideal; but all things end under heaven, and if temporality is held to be invalidating, then nothing real succeeds.

JOHN UPDIKE, (b. 1932) U.S. novelist, critic. *Too Far To Go*, foreword (1979).

Marriage: Remarriage

1 She was a worthy womman al hir lyve:
Housbondes at chirche dore she hadde fyve,
Withouten oother compaignye in youthe,
But thereof nedeth nat to speke as nowthe.

GEOFFREY CHAUCER, (1340–1400) British poet. *The Canterbury Tales*, "General Prologue," l. 459–62 (1387–1400), repr. in *The Works of Geoffrey Chaucer*, ed. Alfred W. Pollard, et al. (1898). Referring to the Wife of Bath.

3 Better a serpent than a stepmother!

EURIPIDES, (480–406 B.C.) Greek dramatist. Alcestis, in *Alcestis*, l. 310, *Collected Plays of Euripides*, ed. and trans. by Gilbert Murray (1954).

3 The triumph of hope over experience.

SAMUEL JOHNSON, (1709–1784) British author, lexicographer. Quoted in James Boswell, *Life of Dr. Johnson*, entry, 1770 (1791). Referring to the remarriage of "a gentleman who had been very unhappy in marriage." On a different note, Johnson had stated on another occasion (Sept. 30, 1769), "By taking a second wife he pays the highest compliment to the first, by shewing that she made him so happy as a married man, that he wishes to be so a second time."

Martyrs and Martyrdom

1 Blessed are they which are persecuted for righteousness' sake: for theirs is the kingdom of heaven. Blessed are ye, when men shall revile you, and persecute you, and shall say all manner of evil against you falsely, for my sake.

BIBLE: NEW TESTAMENT, Jesus, in *Matthew*, 5:10–11. The seventh and eighth Beatitudes, from the Sermon on the Mount.

2   John Brown's body lies a–moldering in the grave,
His soul is marching on.

THOMAS BRIGHAM BISHOP, (1835–1905) U.S. songwriter. "John Brown's Body" (c. 1861). Attributed.

Other attributions of this song include Henry Howard Brownell and Charles Sprague Hall. Abolitionist John Brown was hanged Dec. 2, 1859; the dignity and sincerity which he displayed during his widely reported trial led many to regard him as a martyr.

3   It is a far, far better thing that I do, than I have ever done; it is a far, far better rest that I go to than I have ever known.

CHARLES DICKENS, (1812–1870) British novelist. *A Tale of Two Cities*, bk. 3, ch. 15 (1859). Sydney Carton's thoughts on the scaffold, the closing words of the book.

4   Men do not accept their prophets and slay them, but they love their martyrs and worship those whom they have tortured to death.

FEODOR DOSTOYEVSKY, (1821–1881) Russian novelist. Father Zossima, in *The Brothers Karamazov*, bk. 6, ch. 3, sct. H (1879–1880), trans. by David Magarshak (1958).

5   For all have not the gift of martyrdom.

JOHN DRYDEN, (1631–1700) British poet, dramatist, critic. the Hind, in" The Hind and the Panther," pt. 2, l. 59 (1687).

6   What signify a few lives lost in a century or two? The tree of liberty must be refreshed from time to time with the blood of patriots and tyrants. It is its natural manure.

THOMAS JEFFERSON, (1743–1826) U.S. president. *The Papers of Thomas Jefferson*, vol. 12, Julian P. Boyd (1955). Letter, Nov. 13, 1787.

Referring to Daniel Shays's Rebellion of poor farmers in Massachusetts; Jefferson, writing from Paris, was the only one of the American leaders not alarmed by news of the revolt.

7   If a man hasn't discovered something that he will die for, he isn't fit to live.

MARTIN LUTHER KING, JR., (1929–1968) U.S. clergyman, civil rights leader. Quoted in *The Days of Martin Luther King*, ch. 4, James Bishop (1971). Speech, June 23, 1963, Detroit, Michigan.

8   A thing is not necessarily true because a man dies for it.

OSCAR WILDE, (1854–1900) Anglo–Irish playwright, author. Erskine, in *The Portrait of Mr. W.H.*, ch. 1, *Blackwood's Edinburgh Magazine* (July 1889). Repr. in *Complete Works of Oscar Wilde*, ed. J.B. Foreman (1966).

Marxism

1   The Marxist analysis has got nothing to do with what happened in Stalin's Russia: it's like blaming Jesus Christ for the Inquisition in Spain.

TONY BENN, (b. 1925) British Labour politician. Quoted in *Observer* (London, April 27, 1980).

2   All I know is I'm not a Marxist.

KARL MARX, (1818–1883) German political theorist, social philosopher. Quoted in *Correspondence*, Marx and Engels (1934). Engels in letter Aug. 5, 1890, to Conrad Schmidt.

Engels had earlier quoted the same remark in French in a letter Nov. 2–3, 1882, to Eduard Bernstein *"Ce qu'il y a de certain, c'est que moi je ne suis pas Marxiste"* recalling Marx's words to his son–in–law, French socialist Paul Lafargue, when he rejected the French "Marxists" of the late 1870s.

3   What I did that was new was to prove: (1) that the existence of classes is only bound up with particular, historic phases in the development of production; (2) that the class struggle necessarily leads to the dictatorship of the proletariat;

(3) that this dictatorship itself only constitutes the transition to the abolition of all classes and to a classless society.

KARL MARX, (1818–1883) German political theorist, social philosopher. *Selected Works*, vol. 1 (1942). Letter, March 5, 1852.

4   Marxism is essentially a product of the bourgeois mind.

JOSEPH SCHUMPETER, (1883–1950) Austrian–American economist. Capitalism, *Socialism and Democracy*, ch. 1 (1942).

Masses, the

1   Learning will be cast into the mire, and trodden down under the hoofs of a swinish multitude.

EDMUND BURKE, (1729–1797) Irish philosopher, statesman. *Reflections on the Revolution in France* (1790), repr. in *Works*, vol. 3 (1865).

Masturbation

1   Hey, don't knock masturbation! It's sex with someone I love.

WOODY ALLEN, (b. 1935) U.S. filmmaker. Alvy Singer (Allen), in *Annie Hall* (film) (1977).

2   In masturbation there is nothing but loss. There is no reciprocity. There is merely the spending away of a certain force, and no return. The body remains, in a sense, a corpse, after the act of self–abuse. There is no change, only deadening. There is what we call dead loss. And this is not the case in any act of sexual intercourse between two people. Two people may destroy one another in sex. But they cannot just produce the null effect of masturbation.

D.H. (DAVID HERBERT) LAWRENCE, (1885–1930) British author. *Phoenix: The Posthumous Papers of D.H. Lawrence*, pt. 3, ed. E. McDonald (1936). *Pornography and Obscenity* (1930).

3   Masturbation: the primary sexual activity of mankind. In the nineteenth century, it was a disease; in the twentieth, it's a cure.

THOMAS SZASZ, (b. 1920) U.S. psychiatrist. "Sex," *The Second Sin* (1973).

Materialism

1   No man can serve two masters: for either he will hate the one, and love the other; or else he will hold to the one, and despise the other. Ye cannot serve God and mammon.

BIBLE: NEW TESTAMENT, Jesus, in *Matthew*, 6:24. From the Sermon on the Mount.

Mathematics

1   All science requires mathematics. The knowledge of mathematical things is almost innate in us.... This is the easiest of sciences, a fact which is obvious in that no one's brain rejects it; for laymen and people who are utterly illiterate know how to count and reckon.

ROGER BACON, (c. 1214–c. 1294) British philosopher, scientist. *Opus Maius*, pt. 4, ch. 1 (1267).

2   In mathematics he was greater
     Than Tycho Brahe, or Erra Pater:
     For he, by geometric scale,
     Could take the size of pots of ale;
     Resolve, by sines and tangents
          straight,
     If bread and butter wanted weight;

And wisely tell what hour o' th' day
The clock doth strike, by algebra.

SAMUEL BUTLER, (1612–1680) British poet. "Hudibras," pt. 1, cto. 1, l. 119–126 (1663). Eds. John Wilders and Hugh de Quehen (1973).

3   Mathematics may be compared to a mill of exquisite workmanship, which grinds your stuff to any degree of fineness; but, nevertheless, what you get out depends on what you put in; and as the grandest mill in the world will not extract wheat flour from peascods, so pages of formulae will not get a definite result out of loose data.

THOMAS HENRY HUXLEY, (1825–1895) British biologist. *Geological Reform*, vol. 8, *Collected Essays* (1894). Essay originally published 1869.

4   Stand firm in your refusal to remain conscious during algebra. In real life, I assure you, there is no such thing as algebra.

FRAN LEBOWITZ, (b. 1951) U.S. journalist. "Tips for Teens," *Social Studies* (1981).

5   I have hardly ever known a mathematician who was capable of reasoning.

PLATO, (c. 427–347 B.C.) Greek philosopher. *The Republic*, bk. 7, sct. 531e, trans. by Benjamin Jowett (1894).

6   Mathematics may be defined as the subject in which we never know what we are talking about, nor whether what we are saying is true.

BERTRAND RUSSELL [LORD RUSSELL, 3RD EARL], (1872–1970) British philosopher, mathematician. *Mysticism and Logic*, ch. 4 (1917). Article first published in *International Monthly*, vol. 4 (1901).

In a letter of March 1912 to Lady Ottoline Morrell, Russell wrote: "I like mathematics because it is not human and has nothing particular to do with this planet or with the whole

accidental universe—because, like Spinoza's God, it won't love us in return."

7   Mathematics, rightly viewed, possesses not only truth, but supreme beauty a beauty cold and austere, like that of sculpture, without appeal to any part of our weaker nature, without the gorgeous trappings of painting or music, yet sublimely pure, and capable of a stern perfection such as only the greatest art can show.

BERTRAND RUSSELL [LORD RUSSELL, 3RD EARL], (1872–1970) British philosopher, mathematician. *The Study of Mathematics*, essay written 1902, first published in *New Quarterly* (Nov. 1907). *Philosophical Essays* (1910), repr. in *Mysticism and Logic* (1918).

Maturity

1   Ah, but I was so much older then, I'm younger than that now.

BOB DYLAN [ROBERT ALLEN ZIMMERMAN], (b. 1941) U.S. singer, songwriter. "My Back Pages" (song), on the album *Another Side of Bob Dylan* (1964).

2   If you can keep your head when all about you Are losing theirs and blaming it on you, If you can trust yourself when all men doubt you, But make allowance for their doubting you; If you can wait and not be tired by waiting, Or being lied about, don't deal in lies, Or being hated, don't give way to hating, And yet don't look too good, nor talk too wise:... If you can talk with crowds and keep your virtue, Or walk with Kings—nor lose the common touch, If neither foes nor loving friends can hurt you, If all men count with you, but none too much; If you can fill the unforgiv-

ing minute With sixty seconds'
worth of distance run, Yours is the
Earth and everything that's in it,
And—which is more—you'll be a
Man, my son!

RUDYARD KIPLING, (1865–1936) British
writer, poet. "If–," st. 1 and 4, *Rewards and
Fairies* (1910).

3   Your lordship, though not clean
past your youth, have yet some
smack of age in you, some relish of
the saltness of time.

WILLIAM SHAKESPEARE, (1564–1616)
British dramatist, poet. Falstaff, in *Henry IV pt.
2*, act 1, sc. 2, l. 98–100 (1600). Speaking to
the Lord Chief Justice.

McCarthyism

1   McCarthyism is Americanism with
its sleeves rolled.

JOSEPH McCARTHY, (1908–1957) U.S.
Republican politician. Quoted in *Senator Joe
McCarthy*, ch. 1, Richard Rovere (1973).
Speech, 1952, Wisconsin.

Meat

1   Methinks sometimes I have no
more wit than a Christian or an
ordinary man has; but I am a great
eater of beef, and I believe that does
harm to my wit.

WILLIAM SHAKESPEARE, (1564–1616)
British dramatist, poet. Sir Andrew
Aguecheek, in *Twelfth Night*, act 1, sc. 3, l.
81–4 (1623). Reflecting a popular medical
belief.

Media, the

1   The medium is the message. This is
merely to say that the personal and
social consequences of any

medium—that is, of any extension
of ourselves—result from the new
scale that is introduced into our
affairs by each extension of ourselves, or by any new technology.

MARSHALL McLUHAN, (1911–1980)
Canadian communications theorist. *Understanding Media*, ch. 1 (1964).

2   The new electronic interdepen-
dence recreates the world in the
image of a global village.

MARSHALL McLUHAN, (1911–1980)
Canadian communications theorist. *The
Gutenberg Galaxy*, chapter gloss, p. 31, Uni-
versity of Toronto Press (1962).

Medicine

1   Just a spoonful of sugar helps the
medicine go down.

RICHARD SHERMAN, Songwriter. "A
Spoonful of Sugar" (song), in *Mary Poppins*
(film musical) (1964).

Julie Andrews played the title role (based on
the Mary Poppins books by P.L. Travers), one
of a series of "wholesome" roles which she
later attempted to repudiate by wearing the
badge, "Mary Poppins is a Junkie."

Mediocrity

1   This miserable state is borne by the
wretched souls of those who lived
without disgrace and without
praise.

DANTE ALIGHIERI, (1265–1321) Italian
poet. "Inferno," cto. 3, l. 34, *The Divine Comedy* (1321). Referring to the souls of the Futile
(See Dante on disgrace.).

Meetings

1   When shall we three meet again?
In thunder, lightning, or in rain?

When the hurly–burly's done,
When the battle's lost and won.

WILLIAM SHAKESPEARE, (1564–1616)
British dramatist, poet. First and Second
Witches, in *Macbeth*, act 1, sc. 1, l. 1–4
(1623). Opening lines of play.

Melancholy

1   All my joys to this are folly,
Naught so sweet as melancholy.

ROBERT BURTON, (1577–1640) British
clergyman, author. *The Anatomy of Melancholy*, "The Author's Abstract" (1621).

2   Farewell sadness
Good–day sadness
You are inscribed in the lines of
the ceiling.

PAUL ÉLUARD, (1895–1952) French poet.
Peine Défigurée, La Vie Immédiate (1932).
Bonjour Tristesse ("Good–day sadness") was
the title given to the first novel by Françise
Sagan, which became an international
bestseller in 1954.

3   Sweet bird, that shunn'st the noise
of folly,
Most musical, most melancholy!

JOHN MILTON, (1608–1674) British poet.
"Il Penseroso," l. 61 (written 1631, published
1645).

Memory

1   Memories are hunting horns
Whose sound dies on the wind.

GUILLAUME APOLLINAIRE,
(1880–1918) Italian–born French poet, critic.
"Alcools," *Cors de Chasse*, st. 2, 3 (1913).

2   But each day brings its petty dust
Our soon–choked souls to fill,
And we forget because we must,
And not because we will.

MATTHEW ARNOLD, (1822–1888) British
poet, critic. "Absence," st. 3 (1852).

3   I can only wait for the final amne-
sia, the one that can erase an entire
life.

LUIS BOÑUEL, (1900–1983) Spanish filmmaker. *My Last Sigh*, ch. 1 (1983).

"You have to begin to lose your memory, if
only in bits and pieces, to realize that memory
is what makes our lives," Boñuel wrote. "Life
without memory is no life at all, just as an
intelligence without the possibility of expression is not really an intelligence. Our memory
is our coherence, our reason, our feeling,
even our action. Without it, we are nothing."

4   Our memories are card indexes
consulted and then returned in disorder by authorities whom we do
not control.

CYRIL CONNOLLY, (1903–1974) British
critic. *The Unquiet Grave*, pt. 3 (1944, rev.
1951).

5   The struggle of man against power
is the struggle of memory against
forgetting.

MILAN KUNDERA, (b. 1929) Czech
author, critic. Mirek, in *The Book of Laughter
and Forgetting*, pt. 1, ch. 2 (1978, trans.
1980).

6   Oft, in the stilly night, Ere Slumber's chain has bound me, Fond
Memory brings the light Of other
days around me.

THOMAS MOORE, (1779–1852) Irish poet.
"Oft in the Stilly Night," *National Airs* (1815).
Repr. in *Moore's Poetical Works,* ed. A.D.
Godley (1910).

7   The richness of life lies in memories
we have forgotten.

CESARE PAVESE, (1908–1950) Italian
poet, novelist, translator. *The Burning Brand:
Diaries 1935–1950* (1950, trans. 1961). Journal entry, Feb. 13, 1944.

8   Mournful and never–ending
remembrance.

EDGAR ALLAN POE, (1809–1845) U.S.
poet, critic, short–story writer. *The Philosophy*

of Composition, *Graham's Magazine* (Philadelphia, April 1846). *Selected Writings,* ed. David Galloway (1967).

Explaining the symbolism of the bird in Poe's poem *The Raven.* The phrase was taken as the title of Kenneth Silverman's study of Poe (1992).

9   In memory everything seems to happen to music.

TENNESSEE WILLIAMS, (1914–1983) U.S. dramatist. Tom, in *The Glass Menagerie,* sc. 1 (1944).

10   Life is all memory except for the one present moment that goes by you so quick you hardly catch it going.

TENNESSEE WILLIAMS, (1914–1983) U.S. dramatist. Mrs. Goforth, in *The Milk Train Doesn't Stop Here Anymore,* sc. 3 (1963).

Men

1   Bloody men are like bloody buses—
You wait for about a year
And as soon as one approaches your stop
Two or three others appear.

WENDY COPE, (b. 1945) British poet. "Bloody Men," *Serious Concerns* (l992).

2   Only when manhood is dead—and it will perish when ravaged femininity no longer sustains it—only then will we know what it is to be free.

ANDREA DWORKIN, (b. 1946) U.S. feminist critic. *The Root Cause,* ch. 9, *Our Blood* (1976). Speech, Sept. 26, 1975, Massachusetts Institute of Technology, Cambridge.

Last words of book.

3   Men's men: gentle or simple, they're much of a muchness.

GEORGE ELIOT [MARY ANN (OR MARIAN) EVANS], (1819–1880) British novelist. Mrs. Girdle, in *Daniel Deronda,* bk. 4, ch. 31 (1874–1876).

4   Don't accept rides from strange men,
and remember that all men are as strange as hell.

ROBIN MORGAN, (b. 1941) U.S. feminist author, poet. *Sisterhood is Powerful,* "Letter to a Sister Underground" in Introduction (1970).

5   It's not the men in my life, but the life in my men.

MAE WEST, (1892–1980) U.S. screen actor. Tira (Mae West), in *I'm No Angel* (film), rephrasing a reporter's questions (1933).

Men and Women

1   With men he can be rational and unaffected, but when he has ladies to please, every feature works.

JANE AUSTEN, (1775–1817) British novelist. Mr. John Knightley, in *Emma,* ch. 13 (1816). Describing Mr. Elton.

2   Men get to be a mixture of the charming mannerisms of the women they have known.

F. SCOTT FITZGERALD, (1896–1940) U.S. author. *The Crack–Up,* "Notebook G," ed. Edmund Wilson (1945).

3   Men and women, women and men. It will never work.

ERICA JONG, (b. 1942) U.S. author. The narrator (Isadora Wing), in *Fear of Flying,* ch. 16 (1973).

4   I really think that American gentlemen are the best after all, because kissing your hand may make you feel very very good but a diamond and a sapphire bracelet lasts forever.

ANITA LOOS, (1893–1981) U.S. novelist, screenwriter. *Gentlemen Prefer Blondes,* "Paris is Divine" (1925). Lorelei Lee's journal entry, April 27.

5   What is most beautiful in virile men is something feminine; what is most beautiful in feminine women is something masculine.

SUSAN SONTAG, (b. 1933) U.S. essayist. *Notes on "Camp,"* note 9, *Against Interpretation* (1966). Originally published in *Partisan Review* (New Brunswick, NJ, 1964).

6   'Tis strange what a man may do, and a woman yet think him an angel.

WILLIAM MAKEPEACE THACKERAY, (1811–1863) British author. *The History of Henry Esmond,* bk. 1, ch. 7 (1852).

Men: Masculinity

1   Every modern male has, lying at the bottom of his psyche, a large, primitive being covered with hair down to his feet. Making contact with this Wild Man is the step the Eighties male or the Nineties male has yet to take. That bucketing–out process has yet to begin in our contemporary culture.

ROBERT BLY, (b. 1926) U.S. poet, author. *Iron John,* ch. 1, "Finding Iron John" (1990).

2   In this society, the norm of masculinity is phallic aggression. Male sexuality is, by definition, intensely and rigidly phallic. A man's identity is located in his conception of himself as the possessor of a phallus; a man's worth is located in his *pride* in phallic identity. The main characteristic of phallic identity is that *worth* is entirely contingent on the possession of a phallus. Since men have no other criteria for

worth, no other notion of identity, those who do not have phalluses are not recognized as fully human.

ANDREA DWORKIN, (b. 1946) U.S. feminist critic. "The Rape Atrocity and the Boy Next Door," ch. 4, *Our Blood* (1976). Speech, March 1, 1975, State University of New York, Stony Brook.

3   Someone has to stand up for wimps.

BARBARA EHRENREICH, (b. 1941) U.S. author, columnist. *The Worst Years of Our Lives,* "Wimps" (1991). First published in the *New York Times* (1985).

4   The tragedy of machismo is that a man is never quite man enough.

GERMAINE GREER, (b. 1939) Australian feminist writer. "My Mailer Problem," *The Madwoman's Underclothes* (1986). Article first published in *Esquire* (New York, Sept. 1971).

5   How beautiful maleness is, if it finds its right expression.

D.H. (DAVID HERBERT) LAWRENCE, (1885–1930) British author. *Sea and Sardinia,* ch. 3 (1923).

6   Masculinity is not something given to you, but something you gain. And you gain it by winning small battles with honor.

NORMAN MAILER, (b. 1923) U.S. author. *Cannibals and Christians,* "Petty Notes on Some Sex in America," (1966). First published in *Playboy* (1961–1962).

Men, Single

1   It is a truth universally acknowledged, that a single man in possession of a good fortune must be in want of a wife.

JANE AUSTEN, (1775–1817) British novelist. *Pride and Prejudice,* ch. 1 (1813). Opening words.

Menopause

1 The climacteric marks the end of apologizing. The chrysalis of conditioning has once for all to break and the female woman finally to emerge.

GERMAINE GREER, (b. 1939) Australian feminist writer. *The Change: Women, Ageing and the Menopause,* ch. 17 (1991).

Menstruation

1 If you think you are emancipated, you might consider the idea of tasting your menstrual blood—if it makes you sick, you've a long way to go, baby.

GERMAINE GREER, (b. 1939) Australian feminist writer. *The Female Eunuch,* "The Wicked Womb" (1970).

2 If men could menstruate ... clearly, menstruation would become an enviable, boast–worthy, masculine event: Men would brag about how long and how much.... Sanitary supplies would be federally funded and free.

GLORIA STEINEM, (b. 1934) U.S. feminist writer, editor. "If Men Could Menstruate," *Outrageous Acts and Everyday Rebellions* (1983). *Ms.* (New York, Oct. 1978).

Mental Illness

1 The experience and behaviour that gets labelled schizophrenic is a special strategy that a person invents in order to live in an unlivable situation.

R.D. (RONALD DAVID) LAING, (1927–1989) British psychiatrist. *The Politics of Experience,* ch. 5 (1967).

2 In the past, men created witches; now they create mental patients.

THOMAS SZASZ, (b. 1920) U.S. psychiatrist. *The Manufacture of Madness,* introduction (1971).

This sentence summarizes the book's theme. From ch. 1: "Institutional psychiatry is a continuation of the Inquisition. All that has really changed is the vocabulary and the social style."

Mercy

1 Blessed are the merciful: for they shall obtain mercy.

BIBLE: NEW TESTAMENT, Jesus, in *Matthew,* 5:7.The fifth of the Beatitudes, from the Sermon on the Mount.

2 Lord, have mercy on us.
[*Kyrie, eleison.*]

MISSAL, THE, *The Ordinary of the Mass.* Missal is book of prayers and rites used to celebrate the Roman Catholic mass during the year.

3 The quality of mercy is not strained.
It droppeth as the gentle rain from heaven
Upon the place beneath. It is twice blest:
It blesseth him that gives, and him that takes.
'Tis mightiest in the mightiest. It becomes
The thron'd monarch better than his crown.

WILLIAM SHAKESPEARE, (1564–1616) British dramatist, poet. Portia, in *The Merchant of Venice,* act 4, sc. 1, l. 181–86 (1600). Portia, disguised as a man, argues that Shylock should show mercy to Antonio—though shortly afterwards she herself shows little mercy in her dealings with Shylock. (*Strained* here means "forced," "compelled.").

4 A God all mercy is a God unjust.

EDWARD YOUNG, (1683–1765) British poet, playwright. "Night 4," l. 233, *The Complaint, or Night–Thoughts on Life, Death and Immortality* (1742–1746). Repr. in *Complete Works,* ed. J. Doran (1968).

Metaphysics

1 Metaphysics is the finding of bad reasons for what we believe upon instinct; but to find these reasons is no less an instinct.

F.H. (FRANCIS HERBERT) BRADLEY, (1846–1924) Welsh philosopher. *Appearance and Reality*, preface (1893).

2 He knew what's what, and that's as high
As metaphysic wit can fly.

SAMUEL BUTLER, (1612–1680) British poet. "Hudibras," pt. 1, cto. 1, l. 149–150 (1663). Eds. John Wilders and Hugh de Quehen (1973).

3 The mind, that ocean where each kind
Does straight its own resemblance find;
Yet it creates, transcending these,
Far other worlds, and other seas.

ANDREW MARVELL, (1621–1678) British metaphysical poet. "The Garden," st. 6 (written c. 1650, published 1681).

Middle Age

1 Years ago we discovered the exact point, the dead center of middle age. It occurs when you are too young to take up golf and too old to rush up to the net.

FRANKLIN PIERCE ADAMS, (1881–1960) U.S. journalist, humorist. *Nods and Becks*, p. 53 (1944).

2 Midway along the journey of our life [*Nel mezzo del cammin di nostra vita*] I woke to find myself in a dark wood, for I had wandered off from the straight path.

DANTE ALIGHIERI, (1265–1321) Italian poet. "Inferno," cto. 1, l. 1–3, *The Divine Comedy* (c. 1307–1321), trans. by Mark Musa (1971). First lines of the *Divine Comedy*.

3 Middle age is the time when a man is always thinking that in a week or two he will feel as good as ever.

DON MARQUIS, (1878–1937) U.S. humorist, journalist. Quoted in *O Rare Don Marquis*, ch. 11, E. Anthony (1962).

Middle Class, the

1 The most perfect political community must be amongst those who are in the middle rank, and those states are best instituted wherein these are a larger and more respectable part, if possible, than both the other; or, if that cannot be, at least than either of them separate, so that being thrown into the balance it may prevent either scale from preponderating.

ARISTOTLE, (384–322 B.C.) Greek philosopher. *Politics*, bk. 4, ch. 11, sct. 1295b (c. 343 B.C.), trans. by William Ellis (1912).

2 Bow, bow, ye lower middle classes! Bow, bow, ye tradesmen, bow, ye masses!

SIR WILLIAM SCHWENCK GILBERT, (1836–1911) British librettist. Chorus, in *Iolanthe*, act 1 (1885), published in *The Savoy Operas* (1926).

3 We of the sinking middle class ... may sink without further struggles into the working class where we belong, and probably when we get there it will not be so dreadful as we feared, for, after all, we have nothing to lose but our aitches.

GEORGE ORWELL, (1903–1950) British author. *The Road to Wigan Pier*, ch. 13 (1937).

4 It is to the middle–class we must look for the safety of England.

WILLIAM MAKEPEACE THACKERAY, (1811–1863) British author. *The Four Georges,* "George the Third" (1855).

Miller, Henry

1 Miller does have something highly important to tell us; his virulent sexism is beyond question an honest contribution to social and psychological understanding which we can hardly afford to ignore. But to confuse this neurotic hostility, this frank abuse, with sanity, is pitiable. To confuse it with freedom were vicious, were it not so very sad.

KATE MILLETT, (b. 1934) U.S. feminist author. *Sexual Politics,* ch. 6 (1970).

Milton, John

1 The reason Milton wrote in fetters when he wrote of Angels & God, and at liberty when of Devils & Hell, is because he was a true Poet, and of the Devil's party without knowing it.

WILLIAM BLAKE, (1757–1827) British poet, painter, engraver. *The Marriage of Heaven and Hell,* plate 6, "`The Voice of the Devil," (c. 1793), repr. in *Complete Writings,* ed. Geoffrey Keynes (1957).

2 He passed the flaming bounds of place and time:
The living throne, the sapphire–blaze,
Where angels tremble, while they gaze,
He saw; but blasted with excess of light,
Closed his eyes in endless night.

THOMAS GRAY, (1716–1771) British poet. "The Progress of Poesy," pt. 3, sct. 2, l. 4–8

(written 1754, published 1757). Repr. in *Poetical Works,* ed. J. Rogers (1953).

3 Milton, Madam, was a genius that could cut a Colossus from a rock; but he could not carve heads upon cherry–stones.

SAMUEL JOHNSON, (1709–1784) British author, lexicographer. Quoted in James Boswell, *Life of Dr. Johnson,* entry, June 13, 1784 (1791). Remark to author Hannah More when she wondered how a poet capable of writing *Paradise Lost* had written such poor sonnets.

4 Milton! thou should'st be living at this hour:
England hath need of thee.

WILLIAM WORDSWORTH, (1770–1850) British poet." London, 1802," written 1802, published in *Poems in Two Volumes* (1807). Opening lines.

Mind, the

1 The mind can make
Substance, and people planets of its own
With beings brighter than have been, and give
A breath to forms which can outlive all flesh.

GEORGE GORDON NOEL BYRON, 6TH BARON BYRON, (1788–1824) British poet. "The Dream," sct. 1 (1816).

2 The human head is bigger than the globe. It conceives itself as containing more. It can think and rethink itself and ourselves from any desired point outside the gravitational pull of the earth. It starts by writing one thing and later reads itself as something else. The human head is monstrous.

GÜNTHER GRASS, (b.1927) German author." Racing with the Utopias," *On Writing and Politics 1967–1983* (1984, trans. 1985).*Die Zeit* (June 16, 1978).

3 The mind is its own place, and in
itself
Can make a Heaven of Hell, a Hell
of Heaven.

JOHN MILTON, (1608–1674) British poet.
Satan, in *Paradise Lost*, bk. 1, l. 254–5 (1667).

4 Is there no way out of the mind?

SYLVIA PLATH, (1932–1963) U.S. poet.
"Apprehensions "(1971).

5 Not Chaos, not
The darkest pit of lowest Erebus,
Nor aught of blinder vacancy,
scooped out
By help of dreams can breed such
fear and awe
As fall upon us often when we look
Into our Minds, into the Mind of
Man.

WILLIAM WORDSWORTH, (1770–1850)
British poet. "The Excursion," preface (ed.
1814).

Minorities

1 Niggerization is the result of oppression—and it doesn't just apply to
the black people. Old people, poor
people, and students can also get
niggerized.

FLORYNCE R. KENNEDY, (b. 1916) U.S.
lawyer, civil rights activist. Quoted by Gloria
Steinem, in *Ms.* (New York, March 1973), "The
Verbal Karate of Florynce R. Kennedy, Esq."

Miracles

1 I do not think our successes can
compete with those of Lourdes.
There are so many more people who
believe in the miracles of the Blessed
Virgin than in the existence of the
unconscious.

SIGMUND FREUD, (1856–1939) Austrian
psychiatrist. *New Introductory Lectures on Psy-*

choanalysis, vol. 22, lecture 34, "Explanations,
Applications and Orientations," *Complete
Works, Standard Edition*, eds. James Strachey
and Anna Freud (1964). (Originally published
1933).

2 An act of God was defined as *"something which no reasonable man could
have expected."*

A.P. (SIR ALAN PATRICK) HERBERT,
(1890–1971) British author, politician. Mr.
David, in *Uncommon Law*, "Act of God"
(1935).

Miserliness

1 To the eyes of a miser a guinea is
more beautiful than the sun, and a
bag worn with the use of money has
more beautiful proportions than a
vine filled with grapes.

WILLIAM BLAKE, (1757–1827) British
poet, painter, engraver. *Complete Writings*, ed.
Geoffrey Keynes (1957). Letter, Aug. 23, 1799.

Misery

1 Man hands on misery to man.
It deepens like a coastal shelf.
Get out as early as you can,
And don't have any kids yourself.

PHILIP LARKIN, (1922–1986) British poet.
"This Be The Verse," st. 3, *High Windows*
(1974).

The poem's title quotes Robert Louis Stevenson, *Requiem*.

2 Misery acquaints a man with
strange bedfellows.

WILLIAM SHAKESPEARE, (1564–1616)
British dramatist, poet. Trinculo, in *The Tempest*, act 2, sc. 2, l. 39 (1623).

Misfortune

1 now and then
there is a person born

who is so unlucky
that he runs into accidents
which started out to happen
to somebody else

DON MARQUIS, (1878–1937) U.S.
humorist, journalist. *Archys life of mehitabel*,
"achy sayss" (1933).

2   I am the darkly shaded, the
bereaved, the inconsolate, the
prince of Aquitaine, with the
blasted tower.

GÉRARD DE NERVAL, (1808–1855)
French novelist, poet. *Les Chimères*, "El Des-
dichado," (1854).

T.S. Eliot quotes the original French of this
sonnet in *The Wasteland* (1922) pt. 5: "Le
Prince d'Aquitaine à la tour abolie."

3   Affliction is enamoured of thy
parts,
And thou art wedded to calamity.

WILLIAM SHAKESPEARE, (1564–
1616) British dramatist, poet. Friar
Laurence, in *Romeo and Juliet*, act 3,
sc. 3, l. 2–3 (1599). Speaking to Romeo.

4   There is always something infinitely
mean about other people's
tragedies.

OSCAR WILDE, (1854–1900) Anglo–
Irish playwright, author. Lord Henry,
in *The Picture of Dorian Gray*, ch. 4
(1891).

Missionaries

1   The harvest truly is plenteous, but
the labourers are few.

BIBLE: NEW TESTAMENT, Jesus, in
Matthew, 9:37. Jesus, on the lack of prose-
lytizers to the multitude, before sending out
his apostles endowed with healing powers.
Also in *Luke* 10:2, "The harvest truly is
great ...."

2   The world is my crucifix.
(Mundus mihi crucifixus est.)

ANONYMOUS, Quoted in *Catholic Quotations*, ed. Chapin (1957). Motto of the Carthu-
sian Order in the Middle Ages.

Mitigation

1   Friar Barnadine: Thou hast committed—
Barabas: Fornication? But that was
in another country; and besides,
the wench is dead.

CHRISTOPHER MARLOWE, (1564–1593)
British dramatist, poet. *The Jew of Malta*, act 4,
sc. 1, l. 40–42 (writen c. 1589, first published
1633).

Mobs

1   Certain lewd fellows of the baser sort.

BIBLE: NEW TESTAMENT, *Acts*,
17:5.Referring to a mob raised by the Jews at
Thessalonica, where Paul was preaching in
the synagogue.

2   I'm their leader, I've got to follow
them!

ALEXANDRE LEDRU–ROLLIN,
(1807–1864) French politician, revolutionary.
quoted in *Histoire Contemporaine*, no. 79
(1857). Among the Paris mob at the barricades,
1848.

Moderation

1   Be not righteous over much; neither
make thyself over wise; why
shouldest thou destroy thyself? Be
not over much wicked, neither be
thou foolish: why shouldest thou die
before thy time?

BIBLE: HEBREW, *Ecclesiastes*, 7:16–17.

2   My God, Mr. Chairman, at this
moment I stand astonished at my
own moderation!

ROBERT CLIVE, (1725–1774) British soldier, colonial administrator. Quoted in *Life of Robert*, "First Lord Clive," ch. 29, G.R. Glieg (1848). Speech, March 1773, to a select committee of the House of Commons.

Defending himself against charges of embezzlement; Clive was cleared of the charge but, becoming depressed and ill, committed suicide by stabbing himself in November 1774.

3   Bear in mind that you should conduct yourself in life as at a feast. Is some dish brought to you? Then put forth your hand and help yourself in seemly fashion. Does it pass you by? Then do not hold it back. Has it not yet come to you? Then do not stretch out for it at a distance, but wait till it is at your hand. And thus doing with regard to children, and wife, and authority, and wealth, you will be a worthy guest at the table of the gods. And if you even pass over things that are offered to you, and refuse to take of them, then you will not only share the banquet of the gods, but also their dominion.

EPICTETUS, (c. 55–c. 135) Greek Stoic philosopher. *Encheiridion*, no. 15, trans. by T.W.H. Rolleston (1881).

4   Tell a man whose house is on fire to give a moderate alarm; tell him to moderately rescue his wife from the hands of the ravisher; tell the mother to gradually extricate her babe from the fire into which it has fallen; but urge me not to use moderation in a case like the present.

WILLIAM LLOYD GARRISON, (1805–1879) U.S. abolitionist. *The Liberator* (Boston, Jan. 1, 1831), editorial.

Launching his newspaper, vocal and uncompromising in its support for Garrison's anti–slavery campaign.

5   God tempers the wind to the shorn lamb.

LAURENCE STERNE, (1713–1768) British author. Maria, in *A Sentimental Journey*, "Maria," (1768).

Quoting a French proverb, first recorded by Henri Estienne in 1594 (*Les Premices*, no. 47), but best known in English in this form.

Modern Times

1   This strange disease of modern life, With its sick hurry, its divided aims.

MATTHEW ARNOLD, (1822–1888) British poet, critic. "The Scholar–Gipsy", st. 21 (1853).

2   I sometimes think of what future historians will say of us. A single sentence will suffice for modern man: he fornicated and read the papers.

ALBERT CAMUS, (1913–1960) French–Algerian philosopher, author. The narrator (Jean–Baptiste Clamence), in *The Fall* (1956).

3   *Oh the times! Oh the customs![O tempora! O mores!].*

MARCUS TULLIUS CICERO, (106–43 B.C.) Roman orator, philosopher. *In Catalinam*, speech 1, ch. 1 (63 B.C.).

4   The reason for the sadness of this modern age and the men who live in it is that it looks for the truth in everything and finds it.

EDMOND LOUIS ANTOINE HUOT DE GONCOURT, (1822–1896) French writer, journalist. *The Goncourt Journals* (1956), repr. in *Pages from the Goncourt Journal*, ed. Robert Baldick (1962). Journal entry, Oct. 23, 1864.

5   The means by which we live have outdistanced the ends for which we live. Our scientific power has outrun our spiritual power. We have guided missiles and misguided men.

MARTIN LUTHER KING, JR., (1929–1968) U.S. clergyman, civil rights leader. *Strength to Love*, ch. 7 (1963).

Modernism and Postmodernism

1 Modernity is the transient, the fleeting, the contingent; it is one half of art, the other being the eternal and the immovable.

CHARLES BAUDELAIRE, (1821–1867) French poet. *The Painter of Modern Life*, sct. 4, first published in *L'Art Romantique* (1869). *Selected Writings on Art and Artists*, ed. P.E. Charvet (1972).

2 You are born modern, you do not become so.

JEAN BAUDRILLARD, (b. 1929) French semiologist. *America*, "Astral America" (1986, trans. 1988).

3 One cannot spend one's time in being modern when there are so many more important things to be.

WALLACE STEVENS, (1879–1955) U.S. poet. *Opus Posthumous*, "Adagia" (1959).

Modesty

1 No man, when he hath lighted a candle, putteth it in a secret place, neither under a bushel, but on a candlestick, that they which come in may see the light.

BIBLE: NEW TESTAMENT, Jesus, in *Luke*, 11:33.From the Sermon on the Mount.

2 He seems determined to make a trumpet sound like a tin whistle.

ANEURIN BEVAN, (1897–1960) British Labour politician. Quoted in *Aneurin Bevan*, vol. 1, ch. 14, Michael Foot (1962).

Referring to Labour politician (later prime minister) Clement Attlee. In playing second fiddle to Conservative Anthony Eden when the two were delegated to represent Britain at the U.N. conference in San Francisco, Attlee, according to Bevan, had "consistently under-

played his position and opportunities.... He brings to the fierce struggle of politics the tepid enthusiasm of a lazy summer afternoon at a cricket match."

3 He is a modest little man who has a good deal to be modest about.

WINSTON CHURCHILL, (1874–1965) British statesman, writer. Quoted in *Chicago Sunday Tribune Magazine of Books* (June 27, 1954).

Referring to Labour politician and prime minister Clement Attlee.

4 Modesty is the lowest of the virtues, and is a real confession of the deficiency it indicates. He who undervalues himself is justly undervalued by others.

WILLIAM HAZLITT, (1778–1830) British essayist. *Table Talk*, "On the Knowledge of Character" (1821–1822).

5 Be plain in dress, and sober in your diet; In short, my deary, kiss me and be quiet.

MARY WORTLEY, LADY MONTAGU, (1689–1762) British society figure, letter writer. "A Summary of Lord Lyttelton's Advice," (1716). Repr. in *Letters and Works of Lady Mary Wortley Montagu*, ed. Lord Wharncliffe (1837, rev. 1893).

Money

1 Money is better than poverty, if only for financial reasons.

WOODY ALLEN, (b. 1935) U.S. filmmaker. "The Early Essays," *Without Feathers* (1976).

2 Business, you know, may bring money, but friendship hardly ever does.

JANE AUSTEN, (1775–1817) British novelist. John Knightley, in *Emma*, ch. 34 (1816).

3 Money is like muck, not good except it be spread.

FRANCIS BACON, (1561–1626) British philosopher, statesman, essayist. *Essays*, "Of Seditions and Troubles" (1597–1625).

4   A feast is made for laughter, and wine maketh merry: but money answereth all things.

BIBLE: HEBREW, *Ecclesiastes*, 10:19.

5   The love of money is the root of all evil.

BIBLE: NEW TESTAMENT, St. Paul, in *1 Timothy*, 6:10.

6   The want of money is the root of all evil.

SAMUEL BUTLER, (1835–1902) British author. *Samuel Butler's Notebooks*, p. 310 (1951).

The aphorism, which has also been credited to Mark Twain, reappeared in Butler's novel, *Erewhon*, ch. 20 (1872).

7   Yes! ready money *is* Aladdin's lamp.

GEORGE GORDON NOEL BYRON, 6TH BARON BYRON, (1788–1824) British poet. *Don Juan*, cto. 12, st. 12 (1819–1824).

8   Cash–payment is not the sole nexus of man with man.

THOMAS CARLYLE, (1795–1881) Scottish essayist, historian. *Past and Present*, bk. 3, ch. 9 (1843)

In ch. 10, Carlyle writes, "Cash–payment never was, or could except for a few years be, the union–bond of man to man. Cash never yet paid one man fully his deserts to another; nor could it, nor can it, now or henceforth to the end of the world."

9   But when the bowels of the earth were sought,
    And men her golden entrails did espy,
    This mischief then into the world was brought,
    This framed the mint which coined our misery.

And thus began th'exordium of our woes,
The fatal dumb–show of our misery;
Here sprang the tree on which our mischief grows,
The dreary subject of world's tragedy.

MICHAEL DRAYTON, (1563–1631) British poet. "The Shepherd's Garland," Eclogue 8 (1593).

10   Money doesn't talk, it swears.

BOB DYLAN [ROBERT ALLEN ZIMMERMAN], (b. 1941) U.S. singer, songwriter. "It's Alright Ma (I'm Only Bleeding)" (song), on the album *Bringing it all Back Home* (1965).

11   Money, which represents the prose of life, and which is hardly spoken of in parlors without an apology, is, in its effects and laws, as beautiful as roses.

RALPH WALDO EMERSON, (1803–1882) U.S. essayist, poet, philosopher. *Essays*, "Nominalist and Realist," Second Series (1844).

12   Money is the sinews of love, as of war.

GEORGE FARQUHAR, (1678–1707) Irish dramatist. Roebuck, in *Love and a Bottle*, act 2, sc. 1 (1698). Repr. in *Complete Works*, ed. Charles Stonehill (1930).

13   Her voice is full of money.

F. SCOTT FITZGERALD, (1896–1940) U.S. author. Gatsby, in *The Great Gatsby*, ch. 7 (1925).

Referring to Daisy Buchanan. The narrator (Nick Carraway) added, "that was the inexhaustible charm that rose and fell in it, the jingle of it, the cymbals' song of it ...."

14   Money is a singular thing. It ranks with love as man's greatest source of joy. And with death as his greatest source of anxiety. Over all his-

tory it has oppressed nearly all people in one of two ways: either it has been abundant and very unreliable, or reliable and very scarce.

JOHN KENNETH GALBRAITH, (b. 1908) U.S. economist. *The Age of Uncertainty*, ch. 6 (1977).

15 But money, wife, is the true Fuller's Earth for reputations, there is not a spot or a stain but what it can take out.

JOHN GAY, (1685–1732) British dramatist, poet. Peachum, in *The Beggar's Opera*, act 1, sc. 9 (1728), ed. F.W. Bateson (1934).

16 The almighty dollar, that great object of universal devotion.

WASHINGTON IRVING, (1783–1859) U.S. author. *Wolfert's Roost*, "The Creole Village" (1855).

17 There are few ways in which a man can be more innocently employed than in getting money.

SAMUEL JOHNSON, (1709–1784) British author, lexicographer. Quoted in James Boswell, *Life of Dr. Johnson*, entry, March 27, 1775 (1791).

18 Money is like a sixth sense without which you cannot make a complete use of the other five.

W. SOMERSET MAUGHAM, (1874–1966) British author. Monsieur Foinet, in *Of Human Bondage*, ch. 51 (1915).

19 Money couldn't buy friends, but you got a better class of enemy.

SPIKE MILLIGAN, (b. 1918) British comedian, humorous writer. Mrs. Doonan, in *Puckoon*, ch. 6 (1963).

20 But it is pretty to see what money will do.

SAMUEL PEPYS, (1633–1703) British diarist. *The Diary of Samuel Pepys*, eds. Robert Latham and William Matthews (1977–1983). Journal entry, March 21, 1667.

21 My boy ... always try to rub up against money, for if you rub up against money long enough, some of it may rub off on you.

DAMON RUNYON, (1884–1946) U.S. author. *Feet Samuels, in* "A Very Honourable Guy," *Guys and Dolls* (1931). Originally published in *Cosmopolitan* (New York, Aug. 1929).

22 Pieces of eight! pieces of eight! pieces of eight!

ROBERT LOUIS STEVENSON, (1850–1894) Scottish novelist, essayist, poet.

Long John Silver's parrot, Cap'n Flint, in *Treasure Island*, pt 1, ch. 10 (1883)."Pieces of eight" were the old Spanish silver peso of eight reals—marked with an "8"—current in the 18th and 19th centuries.

23 O accursed hunger of gold, to what dost thou not compel human hearts!

VIRGIL [PUBLIUS VERGILIUS MARO], (70–19 B.C.) Roman poet. Aeneas, in *Aeneid*, bk. 3, l. 56–7 (19 B.C.), trans. by J.W. MacKail (1908).

Alluding to the story of Polydorus, who was killed for his gold by the treacherous King of Thrace during the Trojan War. In Dante's *Purgatory*, cto. 22, Virgil's lines are seemingly misconstrued by Statius.

Monopolies

1 Like many businessmen of genius he learned that free competition was wasteful, monopoly efficient. And so he simply set about achieving that efficient monopoly.

MARIO PUZO, (b. 1920) U.S. novelist. *The Godfather*, bk. 3, ch. 14 (1969). Referring to Don Vito Corleone.

Monroe, Marilyn

1 So we think of Marilyn who was every man's love affair with Amer-

ica. Marilyn Monroe who was blonde and beautiful and had a sweet little rinky–dink of a voice and all the cleanliness of all the clean American backyards.

NORMAN MAILER, (b. 1923) U.S. author. *Marilyn*, ch. 1 (1973).

2 My work is the only ground I've ever had to stand on. I seem to have a whole superstructure with no foundation—but I'm working on the foundation.

MARILYN MONROE, (1926–1962) U.S. screen actor. "Acting," *Marilyn Monroe In Her Own Words* (1990).

Monsters

1 Beware the Jabberrwock, my son!
The jaws that bite, the claws that catch!
Beware the Jubjub bird, and shun
The frumious Bandersnatch!

LEWIS CARROLL [CHARLES LUTWIDGE DODGSON], (1832–1898) British author, mathematician. *Jabberwocky* (poem) in *Through the Looking–Glass* "Looking–Glass House," (1872).

The Jubjub and Bandersnatch also occur in Carroll's poem, *The Hunting of the Snark* (1876).

2 Oh no, it wasn't the aviators, it was beauty that killed the beast.

JAMES CREELMAN, Screenwriter. Carl Denham (Robert Armstrong), in *King Kong* (film), last lines of the movie (1933).

3 O to be a dragon
a symbol of the power of Heaven—
of silkworm
size or immense; at times invisible.
Felicitous phenomenon!

MARIANNE MOORE, (1887–1972) U.S. poet. "O To Be a Dragon," *O To Be a Dragon* (1959).

Monuments

1 I would much rather have men ask why I have no statue than why I have one.

MARCUS PORCIUS CATO THE ELDER, (234–149 B.C.) Roman statesman. quoted in *Parallel Lives,* "Marcus Cato," ch. 19, sct. 4, Plutarch.

2 Their monument sticks like a fish-bone
in the city's throat.

ROBERT LOWELL, (1917–1977) U.S. poet. "For the Union Dead," st. 8, *For the Union Dead* (1964).

Moon

1 That's one small step for a man, one giant leap for mankind.

NEIL ARMSTRONG, (b. 1930) U.S. astronaut. Quoted in *The New York Times* (July 21, 1969)

On his first steps on the moon's surface, 10.56 pm (EDT), July 20, 1969. Armstrong's message—possibly garbled or obscured by static—was originally understood as "one small step for man, one giant leap for mankind."

2 The Eagle has landed.

NEIL ARMSTRONG, (b. 1930) U.S. astronaut. Quoted in *Washington Post* (July 21, 1969).

Radio message, spoken as the lunar module "Eagle" touched down, announcing the first landing on the moon, July 20, 1969. In 1975, Jack Higgins used the phrase as the title of his World War II thriller about a German kidnap attempt on Winston Churchill.

3 The moon is nothing
But a circumambulating aphrodisiac
Divinely subsidized to provoke the world
Into a rising birth–rate.

CHRISTOPHER FRY, (b. 1907) British playwright. Thomas Mendip, in *The Lady's Not for Burning*, act 3 (1949).

4   Treading the soil of the moon, pal-
pating its pebbles, tasting the panic
and splendor of the event, feeling in
the pit of one's stomach the separation from terra ... these form the
most romantic sensation an
explorer has ever known ... this is
the only thing I can say about the
matter. The utilitarian results do
not interest me.

VLADIMIR NABOKOV, (1899–1977)
Russian–born U.S. novelist, poet. *The New
York Times* (July 21, 1969). Referring to the
first moon–landing.

5   This is the greatest week in the history of the world since the Creation, because as a result of what
happened in this week, the world is
bigger, infinitely.

RICHARD NIXON, (1913–1992) U.S.
Republican politician, president. Quoted in
Nixon: The Triumph of a Politician, vol. 2, ch.
13, Stephen Ambrose (1989).

Remark, July 24, 1969 on *U.S.S. Hornet*,
welcoming back the crew of Apollo 11, four
days after the first moon–landing. A few days
later, Ambrose narrates, the evangelist Billy
Graham mentioned three greater days:
Christ's birth, Christ's death, and Christ's
resurrection. Nixon's scribbled response
was: "tell Billy RN referred to a *week* not a
day."

6   With how sad steps, O Moon, thou
climb'st the skies;
How silently, and with how wan a
face.

SIR PHILIP SIDNEY, (1554–1586) British
poet, diplomat, soldier. *Astrophel and Stella*,
sonnet 31 (1591).

Moralists

1   Compound for sins they are
inclined to
By damning those they have no
mind to.

SAMUEL BUTLER, (1612–1680) British
poet." Hudibras," pt. 1, cto. 1, l. 213–214
(1663). Eds. John Wilders and Hugh de Quehen (1973).

2   Dost thou think because thou art
virtuous there shall be no more
cakes and ale?

WILLIAM SHAKESPEARE, (1564–1616)
British dramatist, poet. Sir Toby Belch, in
Twelfth Night, act 2, sc. 3, l. 110–11 (1623).
Speaking to Malvolio. "Cakes and Ale" was
used by W. Somerset Maugham as the title of
a novel in 1930.

Morality

1   Food first, then morality.

BERTOLT BRECHT, (1898–1956) German
dramatist, poet. "What Keeps Mankind Alive?"
Act 2, sc. 6, *The Threepenny Opera*.

2   Ordinary morality is only for ordinary people.

ALEISTER CROWLEY, (1875–1947) British
occultist. *The Confessions of Aleister Crowley*,
ch. 22 (1929).

3   When we start deceiving ourselves
into thinking not that we want
something or need something, not
that it is a pragmatic necessity for
us to have it, but that it is a *moral
imperative* that we have it, then is
when we join the fashionable madmen, and then is when the thin
whine of hysteria is heard in the
land, and then is when we are in
bad trouble.

JOAN DIDION, (b. 1934) U.S. essayist.
Slouching Towards Bethlehem, "On Morality"
(1968).

4   About morals, I know only that
what is moral is what you feel good
after and what is immoral is what
you feel bad after.

ERNEST HEMINGWAY, (1899–1961) U.S. author. *Death in the Afternoon*, ch. 1 (1932).

5   We know no spectacle so ridiculous as the British public in one of its periodical fits of morality.

THOMAS BABINGTON MACAULAY, (1800–1859) British historian, Whig politician. *Moore's Life of Lord Byron, Critical and Historical Essays* (1843). *Edinburgh Review* (June 1831).

6   If your morals make you dreary, depend upon it they are wrong. I do not say "give them up," for they may be all you have; but conceal them like a vice, lest they should spoil the lives of better and simpler people.

ROBERT LOUIS STEVENSON, (1850–1894) Scottish novelist, essayist, poet. *Across the Plains*, "A Christmas Sermon," sct. 2 (1892).

Morning

1   Now Morn her rosy steps in th' eastern clime
Advancing, sowed the earth with orient pearl.

JOHN MILTON, (1608–1674) British poet. *Paradise Lost*, bk. 5 (1674). Repr. in *Paradise Lost*, ed. Scott Elledge (1993).

First lines.

Mortality

1   In my beginning is my end.

T.S. (THOMAS STEARNS) ELIOT, (1888–1965) Anglo–American poet, critic. "East Coker," pt. 1 (1940). *Four Quartets* (1942).

Opening lines of poem.

2   Let mortal man keep to his own Mortality, and not expect too much.

EURIPIDES, (480–406 B.C.) Greek dramatist. Herakles, in *Alcestis*, l. 799, *Collected Plays of Euripides*, ed. and trans. by Gilbert Murray (1954).

3   No young man ever thinks he shall die.

WILLIAM HAZLITT, (1778–1830) British essayist. *Table Talk*, "On the Fear of Death" (1821–1822).

4   There are no dead.

MAURICE MAETERLINCK, (1862–1949) Belgian author. the fairy Tyltyl, in *The Blue Bird*, act. 5, sc. 2 (1909).

5   'Tis time, my friend, 'tis time!
For rest the heart is aching;
Days follow days in flight, and
every day is taking
Fragments of being, while together
you and I
Make plans to live. Look, all is dust,
and we shall die.

ALEXANDER PUSHKIN, (1799–1837) Russian poet. "'Tis time, my friend," l. 1–5 (1834), trans. by C.M. Bowra (1943).

6   All men think all men mortal, but themselves.

EDWARD YOUNG, (1683–1765) British poet, playwright. "Night 1", l. 424, *The Complaint, or Night–Thoughts on Life, Death and Immortality* (1742–1746). Repr. in *Complete Works*, ed. J. Doran (1968).

Mothers

1   When a woman is twenty, a child deforms her; when she is thirty, he preserves her; and when forty, he makes her young again.

LION BLUM, (1872–1950) French Socialist statesman. *On Marriage*, ch. 6 (1907).

2   Whatever else is unsure in this stinking dunghill of a world a mother's love is not.

JAMES JOYCE, (1882–1941) Irish author. Cranly, in *A Portrait of the Artist as a Young Man*, ch. 5 (1916).

3   A Mother's hardest to forgive.
     Life is the fruit she longs to hand
        you,
     Ripe on a plate. And while you live,
     Relentlessly she understands you.

PHYLLIS MCGINLEY, (1905–1978) U.S. poet, author." The Adversary," *A Certain Age* (1960).

4   Who ran to help me when I fell,
     And would some pretty story tell,
     Or kiss the place to make it well?
     My mother.

ANN TAYLOR, (1782–1866) British writer of verse for children. "My Mother," st. 6, *Original Poems for Infant Minds* (1804).

5   Lord Illingworth: All women
     become like their mothers. That is
     their tragedy.
     Mrs. Allonby: No man does. That is
     his.

OSCAR WILDE, (1854–1900) Anglo–Irish playwright, author. *A Woman of No Importance*, act 2 (1893). This aphorism was also spoken by Algernon in *The Importance of Being Earnest*, act 1 (1895).

Motives

1   Never ascribe to an opponent
     motives meaner than your own.

J.M. (JAMES MATTHEW) BARRIE, (1860–1937) British playwright. Quoted in *Times* (London, May 4, 1922). Rectorial address, May 3, 1922, St Andrew's University, Scotland.

Mottos

1   Early to rise and early to bed makes
     a male healthy and wealthy and
     dead.

JAMES THURBER, (1894–1961) U.S. humorist, illustrator. "The Shrike and the Chipmunks," *Fables for our Time* (1940). Article first appeared in *The New Yorker* (Feb. 18, 1939).

Mountains

1   The hills are alive with the sound of
     music.

OSCAR HAMMERSTEIN II, (1895–1960) U.S. songwriter. "The Sound of Music" (song), *The Sound of Music* (stage musical, 1959; film, 1965).

2   Separate from the pleasure of your
     company, I don't much care if I
     never see another mountain in my
     life.

CHARLES LAMB, (1775–1834) British essayist, critic. *Complete Works*, vol. 3 (1882). Letter, Jan. 30, 1801, to William Wordsworth.

3   Mountains are the beginning and
     the end of all natural scenery.

JOHN RUSKIN, (1819–1900) British art critic, author. *Modern Painters*, vol. 4, pt. 5, sct. 20 (1856).

4   Rock of Ages, cleft for me,
     Let me hide myself in thee.

AUGUSTUS MONTAGUE TOPLADY, (1740–1778) British clergyman. "Rock of Ages "(hymn) (1775). First published in *The Gospel Magazine* (1775).

Legend has it that Toplady composed this most famous of hymns while sheltering in the Cheddar Gorge, Somerset, England, during a rainstorm. An alternative version relates it was written at nearby Bath on the ten of diamonds, during the interval between two rubbers of whist (hence the "Toplady Ring," with stones set in the pattern of the ten of diamonds). The typology of Christ as the "rock of ages" is referred to in a marginal note to Isaiah 26:4, in which "everlasting strength" is a translation of the literal Hebrew "rock of ages." John Wesley wrote of "Christ the Rock/Of eternal ages" in his hymn *Praise By All to Christ is Given* (1788); later, poet Robert Southey wrote in *Pilgrimage to Water-*

loo, pt. 2, st. 3: These waters are the well of life, and lo! The Rock of Ages, there, from whence they flow.

Mourning

1   Yes, thou art gone! and round me too the night
In ever–nearing circle weaves her shade.

MATTHEW ARNOLD, (1822–1888) British poet, critic. "Thyrsis," st. 14 (1866).

2   And desire shall fail: because man goeth to his long home, and the mourners go about the streets.

BIBLE: HEBREW, *Ecclesiastes, 12:5.*

3   Blessed are they that mourn: for they shall be comforted.

BIBLE: NEW TESTAMENT, Jesus, in *Matthew,* 5:4.The second of the Beatitudes, from the Sermon on the Mount.

4   I'm in mourning for my life.

ANTON CHEKHOV, (1860–1904) Russian dramatist, author. Masha, in *The Seagull,* act 1 (1896), trans. by Elisaveta Fen (1954).

Masha's first words in the play, in answer to the question, "Why do you always wear black?"

5   It is the blight man was born for,
It is Margaret you mourn for.

GERARD MANLEY HOPKINS, (1844–1889) British poet, Jesuit priest. *Spring and Fall: to a young child* (written 1880), published in *Poems* (1918). Last lines.

6   There should be weeping at a man's birth, not at his death.

CHARLES DE MONTESQUIEU, (1689–1755) French philosopher, lawyer. *Persian Letters,* no. 40 (1721), trans. by C.J. Betts (1973).

Multiculturalism

1   I hear that melting–pot stuff a lot, and all I can say is that we haven't melted.

JESSE JACKSON, (b. 1941) U.S. clergyman, civil rights leader. *Playboy* (Chicago, Nov. 1969).

2   It's just like when you've got some coffee that's too black, which means it's too strong. What do you do? You integrate it with cream, you make it weak. But if you pour too much cream in it, you won't even know you ever had coffee. It used to be hot, it becomes cool. It used to be strong, it becomes weak. It used to wake you up, now it puts you to sleep.

MALCOLM X [MALCOLM LITTLE], (1925–1965) U.S. African-American leader. "Message to the Grass Roots," published in *Malcolm X Speaks,* ch. 1 (1965). Speech, Nov. 1963, Detroit.

Murder

1   Mordre wol out; that se we day by day.

GEOFFREY CHAUCER, (1340–1400) British poet. *The Canterbury Tales,* "The Nun's Priest's Tale," l. 4242 (1387–1400), repr. in *The Works of Geoffrey Chaucer,* ed. Alfred W. Pollard, et al. (1898).

2   Every murderer is probably somebody's old friend.

AGATHA CHRISTIE, (1890–1976) British mystery writer. Hercule Poirot, in *The Mysterious Affair at Styles,* ch. 11 (1920).

3   If once a man indulges himself in murder, very soon he comes to think little of robbing; and from robbing he comes next to drinking

and Sabbath–breaking, and from that to incivility and procrastination.

THOMAS DE QUINCEY, (1785–1859) British author. "Murder Considered As One of the Fine Arts," *The Collected Writings of Thomas de Quincey*, ed. D. Masson (1889). *Blackwood's Edinburgh Magazine* (1827).

4   Every murder turns on a bright hot light, and a lot of people ... have to walk out of the shadows.

ALBERT MALTZ, U.S. screenwriter. Narrator, in *The Naked City* (film) (1948).

Mark Hellinger's last production was narrated by himself.

5   Murder most foul, as in the best it is,
But this most foul, strange, and unnatural.

WILLIAM SHAKESPEARE, (1564–1616) British dramatist, poet. Ghost, in *Hamlet*, act 1, sc. 5, l. 27–8 (1604). The ghost claims the "foul" murderer was his brother.

6   Yet who would have thought the old man to have had so much blood in him?

WILLIAM SHAKESPEARE, (1564–1616) British dramatist, poet. Lady Macbeth, in *Macbeth*, act 5, sc. 1, l. 36–8 (1623). Of the murdered Duncan.

7   I met Murder on the way—
He had a mask like Castlereagh.

PERCY BYSSHE SHELLEY, (1792–1822) British poet. *The Mask of Anarchy*, st. 2 (written 1819, published 1832).

In common with other critics of the Tory administration of the day, Shelley despised above all Robert Stewart, Viscount Castlereagh, though there is nothing to suggest that the latter had any specific role in the "Peterloo Massacre" in August 1819, when military forces fired on a Reform meeting in Manchester—an event that stirred Shelley to write "The Mask." See Byron on epitaphs.

8   Other sins only speak; murder shrieks out:

The element of water moistens the earth,
But blood flies upwards, and bedews the heavens.

JOHN WEBSTER, (1580–1625) British dramatist. Bosola, in *The Duchess of Malfi*, act 4, sc. 2, l. 260–2 (1623). Repr. in *The Complete Works of John Webster*, ed. F.L. Lucas (1927).

Museums and Galleries

1   The Louvre is like the morgue; one goes there to identify one's friends.

JEAN COCTEAU, (1889–1963) French author, filmmaker. *Le Secret Professionnel, Le Rappel à l'Ordre* (1926), repr. in *Collected Works*, vol. 9 (1950).(Originally published 1922).

Music and Musicians

1   A verbal art like poetry is reflective; it stops to think. Music is immediate, it goes on to become.

W.H. (WYSTAN HUGH) AUDEN, (1907–1973) Anglo–U.S. poet. *The Dyer's Hand*, pt. 8, "Notes on Music and Opera" (1962).

2   Great music is that which penetrates the ear with facility and leaves the memory with difficulty. Magical music never leaves the memory.

THOMAS BEECHAM, (1879–1961) British conductor. Quoted in *Sunday Times* (London, Sept. 16, 1962).

3   The English may not like music, but they absolutely love the noise it makes.

THOMAS BEECHAM, (1879–1961) British conductor. *New York Herald Tribune* (March 9, 1961).

4   It is better to make a piece of music than to perform one, better to per-

form one than to listen to one, better to listen to one than to misuse it as a means of distraction, entertainment, or acquisition of "culture."

JOHN CAGE, (1912–1992) U.S. composer. "Forerunners of Modern Music: At Random, Tiger's Eye" (New York, March 1949). *Silence* (1961).

5   Music has charms to soothe a savage breast,
To soften rocks, or bend a knotted oak.

WILLIAM CONGREVE, (1670–1729) British dramatist. Almeria, in *The Mourning Bride*, act 1, sc. 1 (1697). Opening lines of play.

6   Classic music is th' kind that we keep thinkin'll turn into a tune.

KIN HUBBARD (F. [FRANK] McKINNEY HUBBARD), (1868–1930) U.S. humorist, journalist. *Comments of Abe Martin and His Neighbors* (1923).

7   Difficult do you call it, Sir? I wish it were impossible.

SAMUEL JOHNSON, (1709–1784) British author, lexicographer. quoted in" Anecdotes by William Seward," repr. in *Johnsonian Miscellanies*, vol. 2, p. 308, ed. George Birkbeck Hill (1897). *Anecdotes of Distinguished Persons* (1797).

Referring to a violinist's playing.

8   It is the only sensual pleasure without vice.

SAMUEL JOHNSON, (1709–1784) British author, lexicographer. Quoted in "Anecdotes by William Seward,"*European Magazine* (1795). Repr. in *Johnsonian Miscellanies*, vol. 2, p. 301, ed. George Birkbeck Hill (1897).

9   'Tis the common disease of all your musicians that they know no mean, to be entreated, either to begin or end.

BEN JONSON, (c. 1572–1637) British dramatist, poet. Julia, in *The Poetaster*, act 2, sc. 2, l. 179–80 (performed 1601, published 1616). Repr. in *The Complete Plays*, vol. 2, ed. G.A. Wilkes (1981).

10   Heard melodies are sweet, but those unheard
Are sweeter.

JOHN KEATS, (1795–1821) British poet. "Ode on a Grecian Urn," st. 2, *Lamia, Isabella, The Eve of St. Agnes and Other Poems* (1820).

11   There is something suspicious about music, gentlemen. I insist that she is, by her nature, equivocal. I shall not be going too far in saying at once that she is politically suspect.

THOMAS MANN, (1875–1955) German author, critic. Herr Settembrini, in *The Magic Mountain*, ch. 4, "Politically Suspect" (1924), trans. by H.T. Lowe–Porter (1928).

12   The harp that once through Tara's halls The soul of music shed, Now hangs as mute on Tara's walls As if that soul were fled.

THOMAS MOORE, (1779–1852) Irish poet. "The Harp that Once Through Tara's Halls," st. 1, *Irish Melodies* (1807). Repr. in *Moore's Poetical Works*, ed. A.D. Godley (1910).

13   Music is your own experience, your own thoughts, your wisdom. If you don't live it, it won't come out of your horn. They teach you there's a boundary line to music. But, man, there's no boundary line to art.

CHARLIE PARKER, (1920—1955) U.S. jazz musician. Quoted in *Children of Albion: Poetry of the Underground in Britain*, "Afterwords," sct. 3, ed. Michael Horovitz (1969).

14   All art constantly aspires towards the condition of music.

WALTER PATER, (1839–1894) British essayist, critic. *Studies in the History of the Renaissance*, "The School of Giorgione" (1873).

15　If music be the food of love, play
　　　on,
　　Give me excess of it that, surfeiting,
　　The appetite may sicken and so die.

> **WILLIAM SHAKESPEARE**, (1564–1616)
> British dramatist, poet. Orsino, in *Twelfth
> Night*, act 1, sc. 1, l. 1–3 (1623).
>
> Opening lines of play. The words are recalled
> in Shakespeare's later work, *Antony and
> Cleopatra*, when Cleopatra calls out for music,
> "moody food/Of us that trade in love." Act 2,
> sc. 5, l. 1.

16　Oh, I'm a martyr to music.

> **DYLAN THOMAS,** (1914–1953) Welsh poet.
> Mrs. Organ Morgan, in *Under Milk Wood*
> (1954).

17　Hearing often–times
　　The still, sad music of humanity,
　　Nor harsh nor grating, though of
　　　ample power
　　To chasten and subdue.

> **WILLIAM WORDSWORTH,** (1770–1850)
> British poet. "Lines Composed a Few Miles
> Above Tintern Abbey," l. 90–3, *Lyrical Ballads*
> (1798).

Music: Reggae

1　Brothers and sisters rocking, a dread
　　beat pulsing fire, burning.

> **LINTON KWESI JOHNSON,** (b. 1952)
> Anglo-Jamaican poet, singer. "Dread Beat an
> Blood" (poem and song), *Dread Beat an Blood*
> (1975).
>
> The poem was later set to music and released
> on the album *Dread, Beat and Blood* (1978).

Mystery

1　Give me a mystery—just a plain and
　　simple one—a mystery which is dif-
　　fidence and silence, a slim little,
　　barefoot mystery: give me a mys-
　　tery—just one!

> **YEVGENY YEVTUSHENKO,** (b. 1933)
> Russian poet. "Mysteries," st. 10 (1960),
> trans. by Dimitri Obolensky (1965).

Mystics and Mysticism

1　The most beautiful emotion we
　　can experience is the mystical. It is
　　the power of all true art and sci-
　　ence. He to whom this emotion is a
　　stranger, who can no longer won-
　　der and stand rapt in awe, is as
　　good as dead. To know that what is
　　inpenetrable to us really exists,
　　manifesting itself as the highest
　　wisdom and the most radiant
　　beauty, which our dull faculties
　　can comprehend only in their most
　　primitive forms—this knowledge,
　　this feeling, is at the center of true
　　religiousness. In this sense, and in
　　this sense only, I belong to the rank
　　of devoutly religious men.

> **ALBERT EINSTEIN,** (1879–1955) Ger-
> man–born U.S. theoretical physicist. quoted
> in *Einstein: His Life and Times*, ch. 12, sct. 5,
> Philipp Frank (1947).

Myths

1　I therefore claim to show, not how
　　men think in myths, but how
　　myths operate in men's minds
　　without their being aware of the
　　fact.

> **CLAUDE LÉVI–STRAUSS,** (b. 1908)
> French anthropologist. "Overture," sct. 1, *The
> Raw and the Cooked* (1964).

2　Whoso pulleth out this sword of
　　this stone and anvil is rightwise
　　King born of all England.

> **THOMAS MALORY,** (c. 1430–1471)
> British author. *Le Morte d'Arthur*, bk. 1, ch. 5
> (1485).

Names

1 I have fallen in love with American names,
The sharp, gaunt names that never get fat,
The snakeskin titles of mining claims,
The plumed war–bonnet of Medicine Hat,
Tucson and Deadwood and Lost Mule Flat.

STEPHEN VINCENT BENÉT, (1898–1943) U.S. poet, author. "American Names," st. 1.*Yale Review,* vol. 17 (1927).

2 I AM THAT I AM.

BIBLE: HEBREW, *Exodus,* 3:14.

The answer that Moses should give to the children of Israel, when they ask him, referring to the God of their fathers who has sent Moses, "What is his name?"

3 It took more than one man to change my name to Shanghai Lily.

JULES FURTHMAN, (1888–1960) U.S. screenwriter. Shanghai Lily (Marlene Dietrich), in *Shanghai Express* (film) (1932).

4 To name oneself is the first act of both the poet and the revolutionary. When we take away the right to an individual name, we symbolically take away the right to be an individual. Immigration officials did this to refugees; husbands routinely do it to wives.

ERICA JONG, (b. 1942) U.S. author. *How To Save Your Own Life,* epigraph to "My posthumous life ...," (1977).

5 The name of a man is a numbing blow from which he never recovers.

MARSHALL MCLUHAN, (1911–1980) Canadian communications theorist. *Understanding Media,* ch. 2 (1964).

6 O Romeo, Romeo, wherefore art thou Romeo?
Deny thy father and refuse thy name,
Or if thou wilt not, be but sworn my love,
And I'll no longer be a Capulet.

WILLIAM SHAKESPEARE, (1564–1616) British dramatist, poet. Juliet, in *Romeo and Juliet,* act 2, sc. 1, l. 75–8 (1599).Juliet continues, "What's in a name? That which we call a rose/By any other word would smell as sweet."

Napoleon Bonaparte

1 France has more need of me than I have need of France.

NAPOLEON BONAPARTE, (1769–1821) French general, emperor. Quoted in *Dictionnaire de Citations Françaises,* vol. 2, ed. Pierre Oster (1994). Speech, Dec. 31, 1813, to Corps Législatif, Paris.

Narcissism

1 If anyone should want to know my name, I am called Leah. And I spend all my time weaving garlands of flowers with my fair hands, to please me when I stand before the mirror; my sister Rachel sits all the day long before her own, and never moves away. She loves to contemplate her lovely eyes; I love to use my hands to adorn myself: her joy is in reflection, mine in act.

DANTE ALIGHIERI, (1265–1321) Italian poet. "Purgatory," cto. 27, l. 100–8, *The Divine Comedy* (c. 1307–1321), trans. by Mark Musa (1981).

Leah and Rachel, of whom Dante dreams on the seventh stair of Purgatory before ascending to the Earthly Paradise, traditionally stood for the active and the contemplative life.

National Debt

1   On 16 September 1985, when the Commerce Department announced that the United States had become a debtor nation, the American Empire died.

GORE VIDAL, (b. 1925) U.S. novelist, critic. *Armageddon? Essays 1983–1987,* `"The Day the American Empire Ran Out of Gas," (1987).

Nationalism

1   Patriotism is a lively sense of collective responsibility. Nationalism is a silly cock crowing on its own dunghill and calling for larger spurs and brighter beaks. I fear that nationalism is one of England's many spurious gifts to the world.

RICHARD ALDINGTON, (1892–1962) British author. Purfleet, in *The Colonel's Daughter,* pt. 1, ch. 6 (1931).

2   It is humiliating to remain with our hands folded while others write history. It matters little who wins. To make a people great it is necessary to send them to battle even if you have to kick them in the pants. That is what I shall do.

BENITO MUSSOLINI, (1883–1945) Italian dictator. Recorded in *Diary 1939–1943,* Galeazzo Ciano (1946). Journal entry, April 11, 1940.

Said to Count Ciano, Mussolini's son–in–law and Minister for Foreign Affairs. Italy entered World War II on June 10, 1940.

Nations

1   Righteousness exalteth a nation: but sin is a reproach to any people.

BIBLE: HEBREW, *Proverbs,* 14:34.

2   The history of every country begins in the heart of a man or a woman.

WILLA CATHER, (1876–1947) U.S. author. *O Pioneers!* pt. 1, ch. 5 (1913).

3   History teaches us that men and nations behave wisely once they have exhausted all other alternatives.

ABBA EBAN, (b. 1915) Israeli politician, diplomat. quoted in *Times* (London, Dec. 17, 1970). Speech, Dec. 16, 1970, London.

4   If nations always moved from one set of furnished rooms to another—and always into a better set—things might be easier, but the trouble is that there is no one to prepare the new rooms. The future is worse than the ocean—there is nothing there. It will be what men and circumstances make it.

ALEXANDER HERZEN, (1812–1870) Russian journalist, political thinker. *From the Other Shore,* ch. 3 (1849).

5   The great nations have always acted like gangsters, and the small nations like prostitutes.

STANLEY KUBRICK, (b. 1928) U.S. filmmaker. *Guardian* (London, June 5, 1963).

6   Methinks I see in my mind a noble and puissant nation rousing herself like a strong man after sleep, and shaking her invincible locks. Methinks I see her as an eagle mewing her mighty youth, and kindling her undazzled eyes at the full midday beam.

JOHN MILTON, (1608–1674) British poet. *Areopagitica: a Speech for the Liberty of Unlicensed Printing to the Parliament of England* (1644).

Native Americans

1 Bury my heart at Wounded Knee.

STEPHEN VINCENT BENÉT, (1898–1943) U.S. poet, author. "American Names," st. 7. *Yale Review*, vol. 17 (1927).

Wounded Knee, a creek in South Dakota, was site of the last major battle of the Indian Wars, 1890.

2 By this you may see who are the rude and barbarous Indians: for verily there is no savage nation under the cope of Heaven, that is more absurdly barbarous than the Christian World. They that go naked and drink water and live upon roots are like Adam, or Angels in comparison of us.

THOMAS TRAHERNE, (1636–1674) British clergyman, poet, mystic. *Centuries*, "Third Century," no. 12 (written c. 1672, first published 1908).

Nature

1 Nature, to be commanded, must be obeyed.

FRANCIS BACON, (1561–1626) British philosopher, essayist, statesman. *Novum Organum*, bk. 1, aph. 129 (1620).

2 The tree which moves some to tears of joy is in the eyes of others only a green thing that stands in the way. Some see nature all ridicule and deformity ... and some scarce see nature at all. But to the eyes of the man of imagination, nature is imagination itself.

WILLIAM BLAKE, (1757–1827) British poet, painter, engraver. *The Letters of William Blake*, ed. Geoffrey Keynes (1956). Letter, Aug. 23, 1799.

3 Man masters nature not by force but by understanding. This is why science has succeeded where magic failed: because it has looked for no spell to cast over nature.

JACOB BRONOWSKI, (1908–1974) British scientist, author. "The Creative Mind," *Science and Human Values*, sct. 4 (1961). Lecture, Feb. 26, 1953, given at the Massachusetts Institute of Technology.

4 All things are artificial, for nature is the art of God.

THOMAS BROWNE, (1605–1682) British physician, author. *Religio Medici*, pt. 1, sct. 16 (1643). A related idea was expressed earlier in the *Enneads* of Plotinus (bk. 3, ch. 2, sct. 16): "The energy of nature is artificial, as when a dancer moves."

5 Glory be to God for dappled things—
For skies of couple–colour as a brinded cow;
For rose–moles all in stipple upon trout that swim.

GERARD MANLEY HOPKINS, (1844–1889) British poet, Jesuit priest. "Pied Beauty" (written 1877), published in *Poems* (1918).

6 The mountains, the forest, and the sea, render men savage; they develop the fierce, but yet do not destroy the human.

VICTOR HUGO, (1802–1885) French poet, dramatist, novelist. *Les Misérables*, pt. 1, bk. 2, ch. 6 (1862).

7 Nature abhors a vacuum.

FRANÇOIS RABELAIS, (c. 1494–1553) French monk, humanist, satirist, physician. *Gargantua and Pantagruel*, bk. 1, ch. 5 (1534), trans. by J.M. Cohen (1955).

Originally a Latin proverb, *"Natura abhorret vacuum."*

8 Nature, red in tooth and claw.

ALFRED TENNYSON, 1ST BARON TENNYSON, (1809–1892) British poet." In *Memoriam A.H.H.*", cto. 56, st. 4 (1850).

9   For I have learned
    To look on nature, not as in the
        hour
    Of thoughtless youth, but hearing
        oftentimes
    The still, sad music of humanity.

WILLIAM WORDSWORTH, (1770–1850)
British poet." Lines Composed a Few Miles
Above Tintern Abbey," l. 89–92, *Lyrical Ballads* (1798).

Navy, the

1   The Royal Navy of England hath
ever been its greatest defence and
ornament; it is its ancient and natural strength; the floating bulwark
of the island.

WILLIAM BLACKSTONE, (1723–1780)
British jurist. *Commentaries on the Laws of England*, bk. 1, ch. 13 (1765–1769).

2   Don't talk to me about naval tradition. It's nothing but rum, sodomy
and the lash.

WINSTON CHURCHILL, (1874–1965)
British statesman, writer. Quoted in *Former Naval Person*, ch. 1, Sir Peter Gretton (1968).
Remark made in 1911.

3   I must have the gentleman to haul
and draw with the mariner, and the
mariner with the gentleman.... I
would know him, that would refuse
to set his hand to a rope, but I
know there is not any such here.

FRANCIS, SIR DRAKE, (1540–1596)
British navigator. Quoted in *Drake and the Tudor Navy*, vol. 1, ch. 9, Sir Julian Corbett (1898). Speech, May 1578.

To his crew off Puerto San Julian, Argentina, shortly before entering the Magellan Straits—from which he sailed the Pacific to become the first Englishman to circumnavigate the globe.

4   No man will be a sailor who has
contrivance enough to get himself
into a jail; for being in a ship is
being in a jail, with the chance of
being drowned.... A man in a jail
has more room, better food and
commonly better company.

SAMUEL JOHNSON, (1709–1784) British
author, lexicographer. Quoted in James
Boswell, *Life of Dr. Johnson*, entry, March 16,
1759 (1791).

On another occasion, when told, "We find
people fond of being sailors," Johnson replied,
"I cannot account for that, any more than I
can account for other strange perversions of
imagination." (April 10, 1778).

5   Making the world safe for
hypocrisy.

THOMAS WOLFE, (1900–1938) U.S.
author. Luke, in *Look Homeward, Angel*, pt.
3, ch. 36 (1929).

Referring to the Norfolk naval base; see Wilson under democracy, on "making the world
safe for democracy."

Nazis

1   When Hitler attacked the Jews ... I
was not a Jew, therefore, I was not
concerned. And when Hitler
attacked the Catholics, I was not a
Catholic, and therefore, I was not
concerned. And when Hitler
attacked the unions and the industrialists, I was not a member of the
unions and I was not concerned.
Then, Hitler attacked me and the
Protestant church—and there was
nobody left to be concerned.

MARTIN NIEMLLER, (1892–1984) German Protestant pastor, theologian. Attributed
in *Congressional Record*, vol. 114, p. 31636
(Oct. 14, 1968)

The words have never been authenticated.
Though Niemller had earlier supported the
Nazi régime, he became an outspoken opponent of the Nazis and was incarcerated in
Sachsenhausen and Dachau concentration
camps 1937–1945. A submarine commander
in World War I, he volunteered (unsuccess-

fully) to serve again in the German navy in 1941, despite his opposition to Hitler—later arguing that he had a duty to "give unto Caesar what is Caesar's." In 1945, Niemller signed a "Declaration of Guilt" on behalf of the German churches for not opposing Hitler more forcefully.

Necessity

1   Must it be? It must be.
[Muss es sein? Es muss sein.]

LUDWIG VAN BEETHOVEN, (1770–1827) German composer. *String Quartet in F Major,* Opus 135, epigraph to 4th movement (1826).

The movement was entitled, *Der schwer gefasste Entschluss,* or "The Decision Taken with Difficulty." "Es muss sein" was one of Beethoven's favorite phrases. (Quoted in *The Letters of Beethoven,* vol. 3, no. 1318, ed. Emily Anderson, 1961).

2   Necessity hath no law.

OLIVER CROMWELL, (1599–1658) British Parliamentarian general, Lord Protector of England. Quoted in *Oliver Cromwell's Letters and Speeches,* Thomas Carlyle (1845). Speech, Sept. 12, 1654, to Parliament.

The proverb has a lineage extending as far back as Plutarch.

3   We do what we must, and call it by the best names.

RALPH WALDO EMERSON, (1803–1882) U.S. essayist, poet, philosopher. *The Conduct of Life,* "Considerations by the Way" (1860).

4   Freedom is the recognition of necessity.

FRIEDRICH ENGELS, (1820–1895) German social philosopher. Quoted in *The Harvest of a Quiet Eye,* Alan L. Mackay (1977).

5   The necessary has never been man's top priority. The passionate pursuit of the nonessential and the extravagant is one of the chief traits of human uniqueness. Unlike other forms of life, man's greatest exertions are made in the pursuit not of necessities but of superfluities.

ERIC HOFFER, (1902–1983) U.S. philosopher. *The New York Times* (July 21, 1969).

6   Necessity gives the law and does not itself receive it.

PUBLILIUS SYRUS, (1st century B.C.) Roman writer of mimes. *Sententiae,* no. 399.

7   Thy necessity is yet greater than mine.

SIR PHILIP SIDNEY, (1554–1586) British poet, diplomat, soldier. Quoted in *Life of Sir Philip Sidney,* ch. 12, Sir Fulke Greville (1652).

Offering his water to a dying soldier, at the battle of Zutphen, Sept. 22, 1586, where Sidney himself had received a mortal wound.

Neglect

1   A little neglect may breed mischief ... for want of a nail, the shoe was lost; for want of a shoe the horse was lost; and for want of a horse the rider was lost.

BENJAMIN FRANKLIN, (1706–1790) U.S. statesman, writer. *Poor Richard's Almanac,* preface (1758).

Negotiation

1   Better to jaw–jaw than to war–war.

WINSTON CHURCHILL, (1874–1965) British statesman, writer. Quoted in *The New York Times* (June 27, 1954). Remark, June 26 1954, White House.

The words, which were reported afterwards, are quoted with slight variations in different newspapers, and also within the same edition of the *The New York Times.*

2   Let us never negotiate out of fear, but let us never fear to negotiate.

JOHN FITZGERALD KENNEDY, (1917–1963) U.S. Democratic politician, president. inaugural address, quoted in *Kennedy*, pt. 3, ch. 9, Theodore C. Sorenson (1965). Jan. 20, 1961.

3   Only free men can negotiate. Prisoners cannot enter into contracts.

NELSON MANDELA, (b. 1918) South African political leader. Quoted in *Higher than Hope*, pt. 4, ch. 30, Fatima Meer (1988). Statement from prison, Feb. 10, 1985.

Refusing the terms offered for his release by South African President P.W. Botha. The statement was read by Zindzi Mandela, Nelson's daughter, at a UDF rally at the Jabulani Stadium, Soweto.

Neighbors

1   My apple trees will never get across
And eat the cones under his pines, I tell him.
He only says, "Good fences make good neighbors."

ROBERT FROST, (1874–1963) U.S. poet. "Mending Wall," *North of Boston* (1914).

Nerves

1   You mistake me, my dear. I have a high respect for your nerves. They are my old friends. I have heard you mention them with consideration these twenty years at least.

JANE AUSTEN, (1775–1817) British novelist. Mr. Bennet, in *Pride and Prejudice*, ch. 1 (1813).

In answer to Mrs. Bennet's accusation that her husband had "no compassion on my poor nerves."

Neuroses

1   We are all ill: but even a universal sickness implies an idea of health.

LIONEL TRILLING, (1905–1975) U.S. critic. "Art and Neurosis," *The Liberal Imagination* (1950).

Referring to neurosis. In a notebook entry for 1946, Trilling wrote: "Every neurosis is a primitive form of legal proceeding in which the accused carries on the prosecution, imposes judgment and executes the sentence: *all to the end that someone else should not perform the same process.*" (Published in *Partisan Review 50th Anniversary Edition,* ed. William Philips, 1985).

New Age, the

1   This is the dawning of the age of Aquarius.

JAMES RADO, (b. 1939) U.S. songwriter. "Aquarius" (song), from the show *Hair* (1967). Music by Galt MacDermot.

New England and the East

1   There is no pleasing New Englanders, my dear, their soil is all rocks and their hearts are bloodless absolutes.

JOHN UPDIKE, (b. 1932) U.S. author, critic. The Statesman Buchanan, in *Buchanan Dying*, act 2 (1974).

New World, the

1   I called the New World into existence, to redress the balance of the Old.

GEORGE CANNING, (1770–1827) British statesman, prime minister. *Speeches of George Canning* (1828). "Speech on the affairs of Portugal," Dec. 12, 1826.

On his policy of recognizing the independence of Spain's former colonies in the New World, thereby preventing French influence in the zone: "I resolved that if France had Spain, it should not be Spain with the Indies."

2   The pious ones of Plymouth who,

reaching the Rock, first fell upon their own knees and then upon the aborigines.

WILLIAM EVARTS, (1818–1901) U.S. statesman. Quoted by Henry Watterson in *Louisville Courier–Journal* (July 4, 1913).

Also attributed to several others, including Oliver Wendell Holmes Sr. and Bill Nye.

3 For a transitory enchanted moment man must have held his breath in the presence of this continent, compelled into an aesthetic contemplation he neither understood nor desired, face to face for the last time in history with something commensurate to his capacity for wonder.

F. SCOTT FITZGERALD, (1896–1940) U.S. author. The narrator (Nick Carraway), in *The Great Gatsby*, ch. 9 (1926).

4 Religion stands on tiptoe in our land, Ready to pass to the American strand.

GEORGE HERBERT, (1593–1633) British poet, clergyman. "The Church Militant," l. 235, *The Temple* (1633). Repr. in *The Works of George Herbert*, ed. Helen Gardner (1961).

New Year

1 Should auld acquaintance be forgot And never brought to mind?
. . . .
We'll tak a cup o'kindness yet, For auld lang syne.

ROBERT BURNS, (1759–1796) Scottish poet. "Auld Lang Syne," l. 1–2 and last two lines of chorus (1796). This traditional New Year's Eve song is one adapted by Burns from older poems and songs. "Auld Lang Syne" means "old long since" or "long ago."

New York City

1 New York is a sucked orange.

RALPH WALDO EMERSON, (1803–1882) U.S. essayist, poet, philosopher. *The Conduct of Life*, "Culture" (1860).

2 Downtown Manhattan, clear winter noon, and I've been up all night, talking,
talking, reading the Kaddish aloud,
listening to Ray Charles blues shout blind on the phonograph

ALLEN GINSBERG, (b. 1926) U.S. poet. "Kaddish," sct. 1, *Kaddish and Other Poems* (1960).

3 If ever there was an aviary over-stocked with jays it is that Yap-town–on–the–Hudson, called New York.

O. HENRY [WILLIAM SYDNEY PORTER], (1862–1910) U.S. short–story writer. "A Tempered Wind," *The Gentle Grafter* (1908).

O. Henry also referred to New York as "Baghdad–on–the–Subway" in various of his stories.

News

1 As cold waters to a thirsty soul, so is good news from a far country.

BIBLE: HEBREW, *Proverbs*, 25:25.

2 News is the first rough draft of history.

PHILIP L. GRAHAM, (1915–1963) U.S. newspaper publisher. *Attributed.*

Also ascribed to *Washington Post* editor Ben C. Bradlee; but Bradlee himself, inter-viewed in *Vanity Fair* (New York, Sept. 1991), credited it to Graham, his former boss at the *Post.*

3 News is what a chap who doesn't care much about anything wants to read. And it's only news until he's read it. After that it's dead.

EVELYN WAUGH, (1903–1966) British novelist. Corker, in *Scoop*, bk. 1, ch. 5, sct. 1 (1938).

Newspapers and Magazines

1 I read the newspapers avidly. It is my one form of continuous fiction.

ANEURIN BEVAN, (1897–1960) British Labour politician. *Times* (London, March 29, 1960).

2 Reading someone else's newspaper is like sleeping with someone else's wife. Nothing seems to be precisely in the right place, and when you find what you are looking for, it is not clear then how to respond to it.

MALCOLM BRADBURY, (b. 1932) British author. Dr. Jochum, in *Stepping Westward*, bk. 1, ch. 1 (1965).

3 Whate'er men do, or say, or think, or dream,
Our motley paper seizes for its
   theme.

JUVENAL, (c. 60–c. 130) Roman satiric poet. "Satires," no. 1, l. 85–6.

Translated thus, by Alexander Pope, this appeared as epigraph to the "Prospectus" in the first issue of Richard Steele's *Tatler* magazine, April 12, 1709. Juvenal's original, with a more inclusive list of topics (summed up as a *farrago*), referred to a "little book" or "notebook" (*libellus*), rather than a journal.

4 Newspapers always excite curiosity. No one ever lays one down without a feeling of disappointment.

CHARLES LAMB, (1775–1834) British essayist, critic. *The Last Essays of Elia*, "Detached Thoughts on Books and Reading" (1833).

5 The art of newspaper paragraphing is to stroke a platitude until it purrs like an epigram.

DON MARQUIS, (1878–1937) U.S. humorist, journalist. Quoted in *O Rare Don Marquis*, ch. 11, E. Anthony (1962).

Adlai Stevenson borrowed this idea when he quipped, "The Republicans stroke platitudes until they purr like epigrams." (Quoted in Leon Harris, *The Fine Art of Political Wit*, ch. 1, 1964).

6 A good newspaper, I suppose, is a nation talking to itself.

ARTHUR MILLER, (b. 1915) U.S. dramatist. Quoted in *Observer* (London, Nov. 26, 1961).

7 A journal produced by office–boys for office–boys.

ROBERT CECIL, MARQUIS OF SALISBURY, (1830–1903) British politician, prime minister. Quoted in *Northcliffe: an Intimate Biography*, ch. 4, H. Hamilton Fyfe (1930).

Of the London *Daily Mail*.

Newton, Sir Isaac

1 Nature and Nature's laws lay hid in night;
God said *Let Newton be!* and all was light.

ALEXANDER POPE, (1688–1744) British satirical poet. "Epitaph Intended for Sir Isaac Newton in Westminster Abbey" (1730).

British author J.C. (Sir John) Squire (1884–1958) coined the following epigram in answer to Pope's: It did not last: the Devil, howling "Ho! Let Einstein be!" Restored the status quo.

2 Where the statue stood
Of Newton with his prism, and
   silent face:
The marble index of a mind for
   ever
Voyaging through strange seas of
   thought, alone.

WILLIAM WORDSWORTH, (1770–1850) British poet. *The Prelude*, bk. 3, l. 60–3 (1850).

Referring to the statue of Newton at Trinity College, Cambridge University.

Nicknames

1 A nickname is the heaviest stone that the devil can throw at a man. It is a bugbear to the imagination, and, though we do not believe in it, it still haunts our apprehensions.

WILLIAM HAZLITT, (1778–1830) British essayist. *Sketches and Essays*, "On Nicknames" (1839).

Night

1 Night makes no difference 'twixt the Priest and Clerk;
Joan as my Lady is as good i' th' dark.

ROBERT HERRICK, (1591–1674) British poet, clergyman. "No Difference i' th' Dark," *Hesperides* (1648).

repr. in *The Poems of Robert Herrick*, ed. L.C. Martin (1956).

2 I wake and feel the fell of dark, not day.
What hours, O what black hours we have spent
This night!

GERARD MANLEY HOPKINS, (1844–1889) British poet, Jesuit priest. "I Wake and Feel the Fell of Dark," *Poems* (1918).

3 To begin at the beginning: It is spring, moonless night in the small town, starless and bible–black, the cobblestreets silent and the hunched courters'–and–rabbits' wood limping invisible down to the sloeblack, slow, black, crowblack, fishingboat–bobbing sea.

DYLAN THOMAS, (1914–1953) Welsh poet. "Under Milk Wood" (1954).

4 By night an atheist half believes a God.

EDWARD YOUNG, (1683–1765) British poet, playwright. "Night 5," l. 176, "The Complaint, or Night-Thoughts on Life, Death and Immortality" (1742–1746). Repr. in *Complete Works*, ed. J. Doran (1968).

Nixon, Richard Milhous

1 Do you realize the responsibility I carry? I'm the only person between Nixon and the White House.

JOHN FITZGERALD KENNEDY, (1917–1963) U.S. Democratic politician, president. quoted in *Kennedy*, pt. 2, ch. 7, Theodore C. Sorensen (1965).

Teasing remark to a liberal supporter during the 1960 election campaign. In the event, Nixon won 49.6 percent of the total vote, giving Kennedy the narrowest victory in a presidential election since 1888.

2 As I leave you I want you to know—just think how much you're going to be missing. You won't have Nixon to kick around any more because, gentlemen, this is my last press conference.

RICHARD NIXON, (1913–1992) U.S. Republican politician, president. *The New York Times* (Nov. 8, 1962). Press conference, Nov. 5, 1962.

Speech following his defeat in the California gubernatorial election.

Nonconformity

1 So much they scorn the crowd, that
if the throng
By chance go right, they purposely go wrong.

ALEXANDER POPE, (1688–1744) British satirical poet. "Essay on Criticism," l. 426–7 (1711).

Nonsense

1 'Twas brillig, and the slithy toves
Did gyre and gimble in the wabe:
All mimsy were the borogoves,
And the mome raths outgrabe.

**LEWIS CARROLL [CHARLES LUTWIDGE
DODGSON]**, (1832–1898) British author,
mathematician. "Jabberwocky" (poem) in
Through the Looking-Glass, "Looking-Glass
House" (1872).

This opening stanza of Carroll's nonsense poem
first appeared in a private periodical which he
wrote and illustrated in 1855, aged 23. Calling it
a "stanza of Anglo-Saxon poetry," Carroll interpreted the words and gave the literal "translation" as follows: "It was evening, and the smooth
active badgers were scratching and boring holes
in the hill-side; all unhappy were the parrots;
and the grave turtles squeaked out." (*The Anno-
tated Alice*, ed. Martin Gardner, 1960.)

2 It is a far, far better thing to have a
firm anchor in nonsense than to put
out on the troubled seas of thought.

JOHN KENNETH GALBRAITH, (b. 1908)
U.S. economist. *The Affluent Society*, ch. 11,
sct. 4 (1958).

Referring to the resistance of conventional wisdom to "the economics of affluence."

3 Ying tong iddle I po.

SPIKE MILLIGAN, (b. 1918) British comedian, humorous writer. Ned Seagoon (Harry Sec-
ombe), in *The Goon Show* (BBC radio comedy
series), broadcast (1951–1960), published in *The
Goon Show Scripts*, ed. Spike Milligan (1972).

Running gag, later set to music as "The Ying
Tong Song," released Oct. 1956.

4 Supercalifragilisticexpialidocious!

RICHARD SHERMAN, Songwriter. "Supercalifragilisticexpialidocious!" (Song), in *Mary
Poppins* (film musical) (1964).

Nonviolence

1 The only thing that's been a worse
flop than the organization of

non-violence has been the organization of violence.

JOAN BAEZ, (b. 1941) U.S. singer. "What
Would You Do?" *Daybreak* (1968).

Baez set up an Institute for Nonviolence in
California in 1965.

2 Nonviolence is the first article of
my faith. It is also the last article of
my creed.

**MOHANDAS KARAMCHAND
(MAHATMA) GANDHI,** (1869–948)
Indian political and spiritual leader. Quoted in
Young India (Mar. 23, 1922). Speech, March
18, 1922, defense trial.

Gandhi was charged with sedition after he
had organized a mass campaign of civil dis-
obedience which had degenerated into riots.
Sentenced to six years' imprisonment, he was
released after two because of ill health.

3 It is my hope that as the Negro
plunges deeper into the quest
for freedom and justice he will
plunge even deeper into the philosophy of non-violence. The Negro
all over the South must come to
the point that he can say to his
white brother: "We will match
your capacity to inflict suffering
with our capacity to endure suffering. We will meet your physical
force with soul force. We will
not hate you, but we will not obey
your evil laws. We will soon wear
you down by pure capacity to
suffer."

MARTIN LUTHER KING, JR.,
(1929–1968) U.S. clergyman, civil rights
leader. Quoted in *Dictionary of Political Quotations*, ed. Robert Stewart (1984). Letter, Oct.
28, 1957.

4 We who engage in nonviolent
direct action are not the creators of
tension. We merely bring to the
surface the hidden tension that is
already alive.

MARTIN LUTHER KING, JR.,
(1929–1968) U.S. clergyman, civil rights
leader. "Letter from Birmingham Jail," *Why
We Can't Wait* (1963). Open letter to clergymen, Apr. 16, 1963.

Noses

1 Thy nose is as the tower of Lebanon
which looketh toward Damascus.

BIBLE: HEBREW, *Song of Solomon*, 7:4.

2 A large nose is the mark of a witty,
courteous, affable, generous, and
liberal man.

SAVINIEN CYRANO DE BERGERAC,
(1619–1655) French author, playwright. A
"lunarian," in *The Other World: States and
Empires of the Moon*, ch. 8 (1656).

The "lunarian" inhabitants of the moon tell
the time by using a natural sundial composed
of their long noses, which project their shadows onto the "dial" of their teeth. The speech
was taken almost verbatim by Edmond Rostand in his 1897 dramatization of Cyrano's
life, *Cyrano de Bergerac* (act 1, sc. 4).

Nostalgia

1 The "good old times"—all times
when old are good.

**GEORGE GORDON NOEL BYRON, 6TH
BARON BYRON,** (1788–1824) British poet.
"The Age of Bronze," l. 1 (1823).

2 That is the land of lost content,
I see it shining plain,
The happy highways where I went
And cannot come again.

A.E. (ALFRED EDWARD) HOUSMAN,
(1859–1936) British poet, classical scholar. "A
Shropshire Lad," no. 40 (1896).

3 Remembrance of things past.

WILLIAM SHAKESPEARE, (1564–1616)
British dramatist, poet. *Sonnet 30* (1609).

This phrase was used by Scott Moncrieff as
the title for his translation of Proust's *A La
Recherche du Temps Perdu* (1913–1927).

4 What though the radiance which
was once so bright
Be now for ever taken from my
sight,
Though nothing can bring back the
hour
Of splendour in the grass, of glory
in the flower;
We will grieve not, rather find
Strength in what remains behind.

WILLIAM WORDSWORTH, (1770–1850)
British poet. "Intimations of Immortality," l.
178–83, *Poems in Two Volumes* (1807). The
source for the title of Elia Kazan's movie,
Splendor in the Grass, which was released in
1961, based on the original screenplay by
William Inge.

5 When you are old and gray and full
of sleep,
And nodding by the fire, take down
this book,
And slowly read, and dream of the
soft look
Your eyes had once, and of their
shadows deep.

WILLIAM BUTLER YEATS, (1865–1939)
Irish poet, playwright. "When You Are Old,"
st. 1, *The Rose* (1893).

Novelty

1 The thing that hath been, it is that
which shall be; and that which is
done is that which shall be done:
and there is no new thing under the
sun.

BIBLE: HEBREW, *Ecclesiastes*, 1:9.

2 And now for something completely
different.

MONTY PYTHON'S FLYING CIRCUS,
Catch–phrase, in *Monty Python's Flying Circus*
(TV series) (1969–1974).

Originating as a phrase spoken by John Cleese
posing as a newsreader, the words came to be
used by various characters as a link between
sketches. Monty Python episodes were written
and performed by Graham Chapman
(1941–1989); John Cleese (b. 1939); Terry
Gilliam (b. 1940); Eric Idle (b. 1943); Terry
Jones (b. 1942); and Michael Palin (b. 1943).

Nuclear Age

1 REST IN PEACE. THE MISTAKE
SHALL NOT BE REPEATED.

ANONYMOUS, Quoted in *The Harvest of a
Quiet Eye*, Alan L. Mackay (1977).

Inscription on the cenotaph at Hiroshima,
Japan.

2 For they have sown the wind, and
they shall reap the whirlwind.

BIBLE: HEBREW, *Hosea*, 8:7. A prophecy
against idolators.

3 We have grasped the mystery of the
atom and rejected the Sermon on
the Mount.... The world has
achieved brilliance without wisdom,
power without conscience. Ours is a
world of nuclear giants and ethical
infants.

OMAR BRADLEY, (1893–1981) U.S. general. *Collected Writings*, vol. 1 (1967). Speech,
Nov. 11, 1948, Armistice Day.

4 The unleashed power of the atom
has changed everything save our
modes of thinking and we thus drift
toward unparalleled catastrophe.

ALBERT EINSTEIN, (1879–1955) German–born U.S. theoretical physicist. Quoted
in *The New York Times* (May 25, 1946).
Telegram, May 24, 1946, sent to prominent
Americans.

5 There is no evil in the atom; only in
men's souls.

ADLAI STEVENSON, (1900–1965) U.S.
Democratic politician. `"The Atomic Future,"
Speeches* (1953). Speech, Sept. 18, 1952,
Hartford, Connecticut.

Nuclear War

1 I'm not saying we wouldn't get our
hair mussed, Mister President, but I
do say not more than ten to twenty
million dead depending on the
breaks.

STANLEY KUBRICK, (b. 1928) U.S. filmmaker. General "Buck" Turgidson (George C.
Scott), in *Dr. Strangelove: Or How I Learned
To Stop Worrying And Love The Bomb* (film),
weighing–up probable losses after nuclear
combat (1963).

Nudity

1 Nakedness reveals itself. Nudity is
placed on display.... The nude is
condemned to never being naked.
Nudity is a form of dress.

JOHN BERGER, (b. 1926) British author,
critic. *Ways of Seeing*, ch. 3 (1972).

2 And they were both naked, the man
and his wife, and were not ashamed.

BIBLE: HEBREW, *Genesis*, 2:25.

3 Naked came I out of my mother's
womb, and naked shall I return
thither.

BIBLE: HEBREW, Job, in *Job*, 1:21.
Almost identical words appear in *Aesop's
Fables*, No. 120 (6th century B.C.).

4 Full nakedness! All joys are due to
thee,
As souls unbodied, bodies
unclothed must be,
To taste whole joys.

JOHN DONNE, (c. 1572–1631) British
divine, metaphysical poet. "To His Mistress
Going to Bed," Elegies (composed

1590–1600, published 1669). Repr. in *Complete Poetry and Selected Prose*, ed. John Hayward (1929).

5   It's not true I had nothing on. I had the radio on.

MARILYN MONROE, (1926–1962) U.S. screen actor. *Time* (New York, 1952).

6   We shift and bedeck and bed
     rape us,
     Thou art noble and nude and
     antique.

A.C. (ALGERNON CHARLES) SWINBURNE, (1837–1909) British poet, critic. "Dolores," st. 7 (1866).

Nurses

1   No *man*, not even a doctor, ever gives any other definition of what a nurse should be than this— "devoted and obedient." This definition would do just as well for a porter. It might even do for a horse. It would not do for a policeman.

FLORENCE NIGHTINGALE, (1820–1910) British nurse. *Notes on Nursing* (1860).

Oaths

1   Lars Porsena of Clusium
     By the Nine Gods he swore
     That the great house of Tarquin
     Should suffer wrongs no more.

THOMAS BABINGTON MACAULAY, (1800–1859) British historian, Whig politician. *Horatius*, st. 1, *Lays of Ancient Rome* (1842).

Opening lines.

Obedience

1   Speak, Lord; for thy servant heareth.

BIBLE: HEBREW, Eli, in *1 Samuel*, 3:9. Advice to Samuel, on how to respond to God's call.

2   He that complies against his will
     Is of his own opinion still.

SAMUEL BUTLER, (1612–1680) British poet. "Hudibras," pt. 3, cto. 3, l. 547–548 (1678). Eds. John Wilders and Hugh de Quehen (1973).

3   The doctrine of blind obedience and unqualified submission to any human power, whether civil or ecclesiastical, is the doctrine of despotism, and ought to have no place 'mong Republicans and Christians.

ANGELINA GRIMKI, (1805–1879) U.S. abolitionist, feminist. "Appeal to the Christian Women of the South," *The Oven Birds: American Women on Womanhood 1820–1920*, ed. Gail Parker (1972). *Anti–Slavery Examiner* (Sept. 1836).

4   It is much safer to obey, than to govern.

THOMAS À KEMPIS, (c. 1380–1471) German monk, mystic. *The Imitation of Christ*, pt. 1, ch. 9 (written c. 1426, published 1486).

Obesity

1   Outside every fat man there was an even fatter man trying to close in.

KINGSLEY AMIS, (b. 1922) British novelist. *One Fat Englishman*, ch. 3 (1963).

Roger Micheldene, "a shortish fat Englishman of forty," musing over a particularly heavy lunch. For the probable inspiration of this, see Connolly on obesity.

2   Imprisoned in every fat man a thin one is wildly signalling to be let out.

CYRIL CONNOLLY, (1903–1974) British critic. *The Unquiet Grave*, pt. 2 (1944, rev. 1951).

There is a similar observation in George Orwell's *Coming Up For Air*, pt. 1, ch. 3

(1939): "I'm fat, but I'm thin inside. Has it ever struck you that there's a thin man inside every fat man, just as they say there's a statue inside every block of stone?" For a later variant, see Amis on obesity.

3 it's a sex object if you're pretty and no love or love and no sex if you're fat

NIKKI GIOVANNI, (b. 1943) U.S. poet. "Woman Poem," *Black Feeling/Black Talk/Black Judgement* (1970).

4 Let me have men about me that are fat,
Sleek–headed men and such as sleep a–nights.
Yon Cassius has a lean and hungry look.
He thinks too much. Such men are dangerous.

WILLIAM SHAKESPEARE, (1564–1616) British dramatist, poet. Caesar, in *Julius Caesar*, act 1, sc. 2, l. 193–6 (1623).

5 Thou seest I have more flesh than another man, and therefore more frailty.

WILLIAM SHAKESPEARE, (1564–1616) British dramatist, poet. Oldcastle (Falstaff), in *Henry IV pt. 1*, act 3, sc. 3, l. 167–9 (1598).

Oblivion

1 But the iniquity of oblivion blindly scattereth her poppy, and deals with the memory of men without distinction to merit of perpetuity.

THOMAS BROWNE, (1605–1682) British physician, author. *Urn Burial*, ch. 5 (1658).

2 A few more days, and this essay will follow the *Defensio Populi* to the dust and silence of the upper shelf.... For a month or two it will occupy a few minutes of chat in every drawing–room, and a few

columns in every magazine; and it will then ... be withdrawn, to make room for the forthcoming novelties.

THOMAS BABINGTON MACAULAY, (1800–1859) British historian, Whig politician. *Milton, Critical and Historical Essays* (1843). *Edinburgh Review* (Aug. 1825).

Referring to Milton's long lost *Treatise on the Doctrines of Christianity*.

Obscenity

1 The reading or non–reading a book will never keep down a single petticoat.

GEORGE GORDON NOEL BYRON, 6TH BARON BYRON, (1788–1824) British poet. *Byron's Letters and Journals*, vol. 6, ed. Leslie A Marchand (1976). Letter, Oct. 29, 1819.

Referring to Byron's poem, *Don Juan*, which women had been warned not to read.

2 My English text is chaste, and all licentious passages are left in the obscurity of a learned language.

EDWARD GIBBON, (1737–1794) British historian. *Memoirs of My Life*, ch. 8 (1796), published in "World's Classics," p .212, as *Autobiography*.

Sometimes misquoted as "decent obscurity," following the parody in *The Anti–Jacobin Review and Magazine* of the time.

3 Would you approve of your young sons, young daughters—because girls can read as well as boys—reading this book? Is it a book that you would have lying around in your own house? Is it a book that you would even wish your wife or your servants to read?

MERVYN GRIFFITH–JONES, (1909–1979) British lawyer. Quoted in *The Trial of Lady Chatterley*, ed. C.H. Rolph (1961). Opening address, Oct. 20, 1961, to jury during the prosecution of Penguin Books Ltd, London.

Griffith–Jones was senior prosecuting counsel in the case brought against Penguin for publishing an unexpurgated edition of D.H. Lawrence's *Lady Chatterley's Lover*.

Obscurity

1   The growing good of the world is partly dependent on unhistoric acts; and that things are not so ill with you and me as they might have been, is half owing to the number who lived faithfully a hidden life, and rest in unvisited tombs.

GEORGE ELIOT [MARY ANN (OR MARIAN) EVANS], (1819–1880) British novelist. *Middlemarch*, bk. 8, "Finale," (1871–1872).

Closing words.

2   The mind's passion is all for singling out.
Obscurity has another tale to tell.

ADRIENNE RICH, (b. 1929) U.S. poet. *Focus*, st. 7, "Necessities of Life" (1966).

Obsessions

1   Anger and jealousy can no more bear to lose sight of their objects than love.

GEORGE ELIOT [MARY ANN (OR MARIAN) EVANS], (1819–1880) British novelist. *The Mill on the Floss*, bk. 1, ch. 10 (1860).

2   I'm your number–one fan.

WILLIAM GOLDMAN, (b. 1931) U.S. screenwriter. Annie Wilkes (Kathy Bates), in *Misery* (film) (1990).

Obsolescence

1   You behold a range of exhausted volcanoes. Not a flame flickers on a single pallid crest.

BENJAMIN DISRAELI, (1804–1881) British statesman, author. *Selected Speeches of the Late Right Honourable the Earl of Beaconsfield*, vol. 2, "Conservative Principles," ed. T.E. Kebbes (1882). Speech, April 3, 1872, Manchester, England.

Referring to the government Treasury Bench. Edmund Burke had previously referred to old religious factions as "volcanos burnt out" (speech, May 11, 1792).

Obstinacy

1   Still bent to make some port he knows not where,
Still standing for some false impossible shore.

MATTHEW ARNOLD, (1822–1888) British poet, critic. "A Summer Night," l. 68–9 (1852).

2   Obstinacy in a bad cause is but constancy in a good.

THOMAS BROWNE, (1605–1682) British physician, author. *Religio Medici*, pt. 1, sct. 25 (1643).

3   Like all weak men he laid an exaggerated stress on not changing one's mind.

W. SOMERSET MAUGHAM, (1874–1966) British author. *Of Human Bondage*, ch. 39 (1915). Referring to the Vicar of Blackstable.

Obviousness

1   Elementary, my dear Watson!

SIR ARTHUR CONAN DOYLE, (1859–1930) British author. *Attributed*.

The words are not found in any of the Sherlock Holmes stories, though the great detective does utter "Elementary" to Watson in *The Crooked Man* (in *The Memoirs of Sherlock Holmes*, 1894). The phrase appears in the closing lines of the first Sherlock Holmes "talkie," *The Return of Sherlock Holmes* (1929), and became popularized with subsequent movie versions of the stories with Basil Rathbone in the leading part.

Offices

1 He [Robert Benchley] and I had an office so tiny that an inch smaller and it would have been adultery.

DOROTHY PARKER, (1893–1967) U.S. humorous writer. Interview in *Writers at Work*, First Series, ed. Malcolm Cowley (1958).

Benchley himself probably originated this remark, ascribed to him in *The New Yorker* Jan. 5, 1946, "One square foot less and it would be adulterous."

Old Age

1 Age appears to be best in four things—old wood best to burn, old wine to drink, old friends to trust, and old authors to read.

FRANCIS BACON, (1561–1626) British philosopher, essayist, statesman. *Apophthegms*, no. 97 (1625). Quoting Alonso of Aragon.

2 Men of age object too much, consult too long, adventure too little, repent too soon, and seldom drive business home to the full period, but content themselves with a mediocrity of success.

FRANCIS BACON, (1561–1626) British philosopher, essayist, statesman. *Essays*, "Of Youth and Age" (1597–1625).

3 To me, old age is always fifteen years older than I am.

BERNARD BARUCH, (1870–1965) U.S. financier. Quoted in *Observer* (London, Aug. 21, 1955).

4 Since it is the Other within us who is old, it is natural that the revelation of our age should come to us from outside—from others. We do not accept it willingly.

SIMONE DE BEAUVOIR, (1908–1986) French novelist, essayist. *The Coming of Age*, pt. 2, ch. 5 (1970, trans. 1972).

5 With the ancient is wisdom; and in length of days understanding.

BIBLE: HEBREW, *Job*, 12:12.

6 My days are in the yellow leaf;
The flowers and fruits of Love are gone;
The worm—the canker, and the grief
Are mine alone!

GEORGE GORDON NOEL BYRON, 6TH BARON BYRON, (1788–1824) British poet. "On This Day I Complete My Thirty–Sixth Year," written 1824, published in *Byron's Letters and Journals*, vol. 11, ed. Leslie A. Marchand (1981).

The poem was the final entry in his last journal, written in Greece; he died three months later. See also Macbeth on old age.

7 What is the worst of woes that wait on age?
What stamps the wrinkle deeper on the brow?
To view each loved one blotted from life's page,
And be alone on earth, as I am now.

GEORGE GORDON NOEL BYRON, 6TH BARON BYRON, (1788–1824) British poet. "Childe Harold's Pilgrimage," cto. 2, st. 98 (1812–1818).

8 "You are old, father William," the young man said,
"And your hair has become very white;
And yet you incessantly stand on your head
Do you think, at your age, it is right?"

LEWIS CARROLL [CHARLES LUTWIDGE DODGSON], (1832–1898) British author, mathematician. Alice, in *Alice's Adventures in Wonderland*" Advice from a Caterpillar," (1865).

A parody of Robert Southey's didactic poem, "The Old Man's Comforts and How He Gained Them" (1799), which begins: "You are old, father William," the young man cried, "The few locks which are left you are grey;

You are hale, father William, a hearty old
man; Now tell me the reason I pray."

9 Old age isn't so bad when you consider the alternative.

MAURICE CHEVALIER, (1888–1972)
French singer, actor. Quoted in *The New York
Times* (Oct. 9, 1960).

10 I never heard of an old man forgetting where he had buried his
money! Old people remember what
interests them: the dates fixed for
their lawsuits, and the names of
their debtors and creditors.

MARCUS TULLIUS CICERO, (106–43
B.C.) Roman orator, philosopher. *De Senec-
tute,* ch. 6, sct. 20 (44 B.C.).

11 Here I am, an old man in a dry
month,
Being read to by a boy, waiting for
rain.

T.S. (THOMAS STEARNS) ELIOT,
(1888–1965) Anglo–American poet, critic.
"Gerontion," *Ara Vos Prec* (1941).

Opening lines of poem.

12 We do not count a man's years
until he has nothing else to count.

RALPH WALDO EMERSON, (1803–1882)
U.S. essayist, poet, philosopher. *Society and
Solitude,* "Old Age" (1870).

13 Being an old maid is like death
by drowning, a really delightful
sensation after you cease to
struggle.

EDNA FERBER, (1887–1968) U.S. author.
Quoted in *The Algonquin Wits,* ed. Robert E.
Drennan (1968).

14 And now in age I bud again,
After so many deaths I live and
write;
I once more smell the dew and rain,
And relish versing: O my only light,
It cannot be

That I am he
On whom thy tempests fell all night.

GEORGE HERBERT, (1593–1633) British
poet, clergyman. "The Flower," st. 6, *The Temple* (1633). Repr. in *The Works of George Herbert,* ed. Helen Gardner (1961).

15 The best part of the art of living is to
know how to grow old gracefully.

ERIC HOFFER, (1902–1983) U.S. philosopher. *The Passionate State of Mind,* aph. 235
(1955).

16 Wrecked on the lee shore of age.

SARAH ORNE JEWETT, (1849–1909) U.S.
author. *The Country of the Pointed Firs and
Other Stories,* ch. 7 (1896).

17 Talking is the disease of age.

BEN JONSON, (c. 1572–1637) British dramatist, poet. *Timber, or Discoveries Made upon
Men and Matter,* para. 46, "Lingua Sapientis"
(1641), ed. Felix E. Schelling (1892).

18 Few people know how to be old.

**FRANÇOIS LA ROCHEFOUCAULD, DUC
DE,** (1613–1680) French writer, moralist. *Sentences et Maximes Morales,* no. 423 (1678).

19 O what a thing is age! Death without death's quiet.

WALTER SAVAGE LANDOR, (1775–1864)
British author, poet. "Epicurus, Leontion, and
Ternissa," *Imaginary Conversations*
(1824–1829).

20 Perhaps being old is having lighted
rooms
Inside your head, and people in
them, acting.
People you know, yet can't quite
name.

PHILIP LARKIN, (1922–1986) British poet.
"The Old Fools," st. 3, *High Windows* (1974).

21 My youth i shall never forget
but there s nothing i really regret
wotthehell wotthehell
there s a dance in the old dame yet

toujours gai toujours gai

DON MARQUIS, (1878–1937) U.S. humorist, journalist. *Archy and mehitabel,* "the song of mehitabel" (1927).

22 Growing old is no more than a bad habit which a busy man has no time to form.

ANDRÉ MAUROIS, (1885–1967) French author and critic. "The Art of Growing Old," *The Art of Living* (1940).

23 Not till the fire is dying in the grate, Look we for any kinship with the stars.
Oh, wisdom never comes when it is gold,
And the great price we paid for it full worth:
We have it only when we are half earth.
Little avails that coinage to the old!

GEORGE MEREDITH, (1828–1909) British author. *Modern Love,* Sonnet 4 (1862).

Cecil Day Lewis, Professor of Poetry at Oxford, wrote of this extract in his Introduction to the 1948 edition of the volume, that it was not originality that made it memorable, "it is a commonplace, whose force we are at last made to feel, through and through, by the inner conviction and the expressive grandeur of its utterance."

24 Nature should have been pleased to have made this age miserable, without making it also ridiculous.

MICHEL DE MONTAIGNE, (1533–1592) French essayist. *Essays,* bk. 3, ch. 5 (1595), trans. by John Florio (1603).

Montaigne was referring to the age of the "eleventh *lustre,*" or fifty–five, his own age.

25 Have you not a moist eye, a dry hand, a yellow cheek, a white beard, a decreasing leg, an increasing belly? Is not your voice broken, your wind short, your chin double, your wit single, and every part about you blasted with antiquity?

WILLIAM SHAKESPEARE, (1564–1616) British dramatist, poet. Lord Chief Justice, in *Henry IV pt. 2,* act 1, sc. 2, l. 181–5 (1600).

Listing Falstaff's "characters of age" after the latter had dared to set down his name "in the scroll of youth."

26 And now the end is near
And so I face the final curtain,
I'll state my case of which I'm certain.
I've lived a life that's full, I traveled each and ev'ry highway,
And more, much more than this. I did it my way.

FRANK SINATRA, (b. 1915) U.S. singer, actor. "My Way," written by Claude François, Jacques Revaux, and Paul Anka (1969).

The Canadian songwriter Paul Anka is generally credited with adapting this song—from a French original, "Comme D'Habitude"—for Sinatra, with whom it has become indelibly linked.

27 Old age grows cold to love.

VIRGIL [PUBLIUS VERGILIUS MARO], (70–19 B.C.) Roman poet. *Georgics,* bk. 3, l. 97 (29 B.C.), trans. by Kate Hughes (1995).

28 O Time and Change!—with hair as gray
As was my sire's that winter day,
How strange it seems, with so much gone
Of life and love, to still live on!

JOHN GREENLEAF WHITTIER, (1807–1892) U.S. poet." Snow–Bound, a Winter Idyll," l. 179–182 (1866). Repr. in *The Poetical Works of John Greenleaf Whittier,* ed. W. Garrett Horder (1911).

29 An aged man is but a paltry thing, A tattered coat upon a stick, unless Soul clap its hands and sing, and louder sing
For every tatter in its mortal dress.

WILLIAM BUTLER YEATS, (1865–1939) Irish poet, playwright. "Sailing to Byzantium," st. 2, *The Tower* (1928).

Opera

1 The opera isn't over till the fat lady sings.

ANONYMOUS.

A modern proverb along the lines of "don't count your chickens before they're hatched." This form of words has no precise origin, though both *Bartlett's Familiar Quotations* (16th ed., 1992) and *The Concise Oxford Dictionary of Proverbs* (ed. John Simpson, 1982) state that the words were first recorded in *Washington Post*, June 13, 1978, said by sports commentator Dan Cook. *Bartlett's* notes another version in *Southern Words and Sayings* (eds. Fabia Rue Smith and Charles Rayford Smith, 1976): "Church ain't out till the fat lady sings."

Opinion

1 Where an opinion is general, it is usually correct.

JANE AUSTEN, (1775–1817) British novelist. Mary Crawford, in *Mansfield Park*, ch. 11 (1814).

2 The man who never alters his opinion is like standing water, and breeds reptiles of the mind.

WILLIAM BLAKE, (1757–1827) British poet, painter, engraver. *The Marriage of Heaven and Hell*, plates 17–20, "A Memorable Fancy" (c. 1793), repr. in *Complete Writings*, ed. Geoffrey Keynes (1957).

3 The public buys its opinions as it buys its meat, or takes in its milk, on the principle that it is cheaper to do this than to keep a cow. So it is, but the milk is more likely to be watered.

SAMUEL BUTLER, (1835–1902) British author. *Notebooks*, "Sequel to Alps and Sanctuaries" (1912).

4 The only means of strengthening one's intellect is to make up one's mind about nothing—to let the mind be a thoroughfare for all thoughts. Not a select party.

JOHN KEATS, (1795–1821) British poet. *Letters of John Keats*, no. 156, ed. Frederick Page (1954). Letter, Sept. 17–27, 1819, to his brother and sister-in-law, George and Georgiana Keats.

5 A study of the history of opinion is a necessary preliminary to the emancipation of the mind.

JOHN MAYNARD KEYNES, (1883–1946) British economist. *The End of Laissez–Faire*, ch. 1 (1926).

6 Nothing can contribute more to peace of soul than the lack of any opinion whatever.

GEORG CHRISTOPH LICHTENBERG, (1742–1799) German physicist, philosopher. "Notebook E," aph. 11, *Aphorisms* (written 1765–1799), trans. by R.J. Hollingdale (1990).

7 Few opinions are always suspected, and usually opposed, without any other reason but because they are not already common.

JOHN LOCKE, (1632–1704) British philosopher. *An Enquiry Concerning Human Understanding*, dedicatory epistle (1690).

8 False opinions are like false money, struck first of all by guilty men and thereafter circulated by honest people who perpetuate the crime without knowing what they are doing.

JOSEPH DE MAISTRE, (1753–1821) French diplomat, philosopher. the Count, in *Les Soirées de Saint–Pétersbourg*, "First Dialogue," (1821), repr. in *The Works of Joseph de Maistre*, ed. Jack Lively (1965).

9 Opinions cannot survive if one has no chance to fight for them.

THOMAS MANN, (1875–1955) German author, critic. *The Magic Mountain*, ch. 6, "Of The City of God" (1924), trans. by H.T. Lowe–Porter (1928).

10 So many men, so many opinions;
    everyone his own way.

    TERENCE, (c. 190–159 B.C.) Roman drama-
    tist. *Phormio*, l. 454.

Opportunities

1 Thou strong seducer, Opportunity!

    JOHN DRYDEN, (1631–1700) British poet,
    dramatist, critic. Almahide, in *The Conquest
    of Granada*, pt. 2, act 4, sc. 3 (1670).

2 Opportunity is the great bawd.

    BENJAMIN FRANKLIN, (1706–1790) U.S.
    statesman, writer. *Poor Richard's Almanac*,
    September (1735).

3 There is a tide in the affairs of men
    Which, taken at the flood, leads on
        to fortune;
    Omitted, all the voyage of their life
    Is bound in shallows and in mis-
        eries.

    WILLIAM SHAKESPEARE, (1564–1616)
    British dramatist, poet. Brutus, in *Julius
    Caesar*, act 4, sc. 2, l. 272–5 (1623).

4 Never miss a chance to have sex or
    appear on television.

    GORE VIDAL, (b. 1925) U.S. novelist,
    critic. Attributed, *Macmillan Dictionary of
    Quotations* (1989).

Opposites

1 Without contraries is no progres-
    sion. Attraction and repulsion,
    reason and energy, love and
    hate, are necessary to human
    existence.

    WILLIAM BLAKE, (1757–1827) British
    poet, painter, engraver. *The Marriage of
    Heaven and Hell*, plate 3, "The Argument" (c.
    1793), repr. in *Complete Writings*, ed. Geof-
    frey Keynes (1957).

2 The more I see
    Pleasures about me, so much more I
        feel
    Torment within me, as from the
        hateful siege
    Of contraries; all good to me
        becomes
    Bane, and in heav'n much worse
        would be my state.

    JOHN MILTON, (1608–1674) British poet.
    Satan, in *Paradise Lost*, bk. 9, l.119–23 (1674).

3 War is peace. Freedom is slavery.
    Ignorance is strength.

    GEORGE ORWELL, (1903–1950) British
    author. *Nineteen Eighty–Four*, pt. 1, ch. 1
    (1949).

    Ingsoc party slogan.

4 Fair is foul, and foul is fair,
    Hover through the fog and filthy
        air.

    WILLIAM SHAKESPEARE, (1564–1616)
    British dramatist, poet. The three witches, in
    Macbeth, act 1, sc. 1, l. 10–11 (1623).

    End of the play's opening exchange, emphasis-
    ing the disruption of the natural order.

Opposition

1 No Government can be long secure
    without a formidable Opposition. It
    reduces their supporters to that
    tractable number which can be
    managed by the joint influences of
    fruition and hope. It offers
    vengeance to the discontented, and
    distinction to the ambitious; and
    employs the energies of aspiring
    spirits, who otherwise may prove
    traitors in a division or assassins in
    a debate.

    BENJAMIN DISRAELI, (1804–1881)
    British statesman, author. *Coningsby*, bk. 2, ch.
    1 (1844).

Oppression

1   You may write me down in history
With your bitter, twisted lies,
You may trod me in the very dirt
But still, like dust, I'll rise.

MAYA ANGELOU, (b. 1928) U.S. author.
"Still I Rise," *And Still I Rise* (1978).

2   Everybody knows there is no fineness or accuracy of suppression; if
you hold down one thing, you hold
down the adjoining.

SAUL BELLOW, (b. 1915) U.S. novelist. *The
Adventures of Augie March*, ch. 1 (1953).

3   Let my people go.

BIBLE: HEBREW, *Exodus*, 5:1.The plea of
Aaron and Moses to Pharaoh.

4   What mean ye that ye beat my
people to pieces, and grind the faces
of the poor?

BIBLE: HEBREW, Isaiah, 3:15.

5   The most potent weapon in the
hands of the oppressor is the mind
of the oppressed.

STEVE BIKO, (1946–1977) South African
political leader. Quoted in *Dictionary of Political Quotations*, ed. Robert Stewart (1984).
Address, 1971, to the Cape Town Conference
on Inter–Racial Studies.

6   In every cry of every man,
In every infant's cry of fear,
In every voice, in every ban,
The mind–forg'd manacles I hear.

WILLIAM BLAKE, (1757–1827) British
poet, painter, engraver. *Songs of Experience*,
"London" (1794), repr. in *Complete Writings*,
ed. Geoffrey Keynes (1957).

7   Where justice is denied, where
poverty is enforced, where ignorance prevails, and where any one
class is made to feel that society is
in an organized conspiracy to
oppress, rob, and degrade them, neither persons nor property will be
safe.

FREDERICK DOUGLASS, (c.1817–1895)
U.S. abolitionist. *The Frederick Douglass
Papers*, ed. John W. Blassingame (1982).
Speech, April 1886, Washington, DC.

Made on the 24th anniversary of Emancipation
in the District of Columbia.

8   You can't hold a man down without
staying down with him.

BOOKER T. WASHINGTON, (1856–1915)
U.S. educator. *Attributed.*

Optimism

1   The world is the best of all possible
worlds, and everything in it is a necessary evil.

F.H. (FRANCIS HERBERT) BRADLEY,
(1846–1924) Welsh philosopher. *Appearance
and Reality*, preface (1893). See Voltaire and
Cabell on pessimism.

2   These are not dark days: these are
great days—the greatest days our
country has ever lived.

WINSTON CHURCHILL, (1874–1965)
British statesman, writer. Vol. 6, *Winston S.
Churchill: His Complete Speeches, 1897–1963*,
ed. Robert Rhodes James (1974). Speech, Oct.
29, 1941, Harrow School, England.

3   I'm a pessimist because of intelligence, but an optimist because of
will.

ANTONIO GRAMSCI, (1891–1937) Italian
political theorist. *Gramsci: Letters from Prison*,
trans. by Raymond Rosenthal (1993). Letter,
Dec. 19, 1929.

4   Optimism is the opium of the
people.

MILAN KUNDERA, (b. 1929) Czech author,
critic. *The Joke*, pt. 3, ch. 3 (1967, trans. 1982).

The line, written by Ludvik on a postcard, was used by the Party as incriminating evidence against him, though it was only meant as "a joke."

5   an optimist is a guy
     who has never had
     much experience.

DON MARQUIS, (1878–1937) U.S. humorist, journalist. *Archy and mehitabel,* "certain maxims of archy" (1927).

6   After all, tomorrow is another day.

MARGARET MITCHELL, (1900–1949) U.S. novelist. Scarlett O'Hara, in *Gone with the Wind,* pt. 5, ch. 63 (1936).

Closing words of the book—and film.

7   Some things in life are bad
     They can really make you mad
     Other things just make you swear
       and curse
     When you're chewing on life's gris-
       tle
     Don't grumble, give a whistle
     And this'll help turn things out for
       the best ...
     And ... always look on the bright
       side of life.

MONTY PYTHON'S FLYING CIRCUS, Mr. Frisbee III (Eric Idle), in *Monty Python's Life of Brian* (film), written and conceived by John Cleese, Graham Chapman, Terry Gilliam, Eric Idle, Terry Jones and Michael Palin (1979).

First lines of a song that closes the film.

8   Oh yet we trust that somehow good
     Will be the final goal of ill!

ALFRED TENNYSON, 1ST BARON TENNYSON, (1809–1892) British poet. "In Memoriam," cto. 54, st. 1 (1850).

9   In this best of all possible worlds ...
     everything is for the best.

VOLTAIRE [FRANÇOIS MARIE AROUET], (1694–1778) French philosopher, author. *Candide,* ch. 1 (1759).

Later in ch. 6, Candide muses, "If this is the best of all possible worlds, what are the others like?"

Order

1   A place for everything and every-
     thing in its place.

ISABELLA BEETON, (1836–1865) British writer on domestic science. *Book of Household Management,* ch. 2, sct. 55 (1861).

The maxim was already in circulation, and appeared in Frederick Marryat's novel *Masterman Ready* (1842).

Orgasm

1   I finally had an orgasm and my
     doctor told me it was the wrong
     kind.

WOODY ALLEN, (b. 1935) U.S. filmmaker. Polly (Tisa Farrow), in *Manhattan* (film) (1979). Woody Allen.

repr. in *Four Films of Woody Allen* (1982).

2   I'll have what she's having.

NORA EPHRON, (b. 1941) U.S. author, journalist.

Woman diner, in *When Harry Met Sally* (film), observing Sally Albright (Meg Ryan) acting an orgasm, addressed to the waiter taking an order in a restaurant (1989).

3   But did thee feel the earth move?

ERNEST HEMINGWAY, (1899–1961) U.S. author. Robert Jordan, in *For Whom the Bell Tolls,* ch. 13 (1940).

Spoken to Maria. During their lovemaking, Jordan had "felt the earth move out and away from under them." The words do not appear in the 1943 film version.

4   The orgasm has replaced the Cross
     as the focus of longing and the
     image of fulfillment.

MALCOLM MUGGERIDGE, (1903–1990) British broadcaster. "Down with Sex," *Tread Softly for You Tread on My Jokes* (1966).

Originality

1   Long shall we seek his likeness, long
    in vain,
    And turn to all of him which may
    remain,
    Sighing that Nature formed but
    one such man,
    And broke the die—in moulding
    Sheridan!

GEORGE GORDON NOEL BYRON, 6TH BARON BYRON, (1788–1824) British poet. "Monody on the Death of Sheridan," l. 115–8 (1816).

Last lines. Compare Ariosto's *Orlando Furioso*, cto. 10, st. 84: "Nature made him, and then broke the mold." (1532).

2   When a work appears to be ahead
    of its time, it is only the time that is
    behind the work.

JEAN COCTEAU, (1889–1963) French author, filmmaker. *Le Coq et l'Arlequin, Le Rappel à l'Ordre* (1926), repr. in *Collected Works*, vol. 9 (1950). (Originally published 1918).

3   It is a matter of perfect indifference
    where a thing originated; the only
    question is: "Is it true in and for
    itself?"

GEORG HEGEL, (1770–1831) German philosopher. *The Philosophy of History*, pt. 3, sct. 3, ch. 2 (1837).

4   A thought is often original, though
    you have uttered it a hundred
    times.

OLIVER WENDELL HOLMES, SR., (1809–1894) U.S. writer, physician. *The Autocrat of the Breakfast–Table*, ch. 1 (1858).

5   Everything has been said, and
    we have come too late, now that

men have been living and thinking for seven thousand years and
more.

JEAN DE LA BRUYÈRE, (1645–1696) French writer, moralist. *Characters*, "Of Books" aph. 1 (1688).

6   In fact nothing is said that has not
    been said before.

TERENCE, (c. 190–159 B.C.) Roman dramatist. *Eunuchus*, prologue, l. 41.

Orphans

1   To lose one parent may be regarded
    as a misfortune ... to lose both
    seems like carelessness.

OSCAR WILDE, (1854–1900) Anglo–Irish playwright, author. Lady Bracknell, in *The Importance of Being Earnest*, act 1.

Other People

1   I do not want people to be very
    agreeable, as it saves me the trouble
    of liking them a great deal.

JANE AUSTEN, (1775–1817) British novelist. *Jane Austen's Letters*, ed. R.W. Chapman (1952). Letter, Dec. 24, 1798, to her sister, Cassandra.

2   And finally I twist my heart round
    again, so that the bad is on the out-
    side and the good is on the inside,
    and keep on trying to find a way of
    becoming what I would so like to
    be, and could be, if ... there weren't
    any other people living in the world.

ANNE FRANK, (1929–1945) German Jewish refugee, diarist. *The Diary of a Young Girl* (1947, trans. 1952). Journal entry, Aug. 1, 1944.

Last words of last entry. Three days later, Anne Frank was arrested and sent to a concentration camp in Germany.

3   Hell is other people.

JEAN–PAUL SARTRE, (1905–1980) French philosopher, author. Garcin, in *Huis Clos*, sc. 5 (1944).

4   It is absurd to divide people into good and bad. People are either charming or tedious.

OSCAR WILDE, (1854–1900) Anglo–Irish playwright, author. Lord Darlington, in *Lady Windermere's Fan*, act 1 (1893).

5   Each had his past shut in him like the leaves of a book known to him by heart; and his friends could only read the title, James Spalding, or Charles Budgeon, and the passengers going the opposite way could read nothing at all—save "a man with a red moustache," "a young man in grey smoking a pipe."

VIRGINIA WOOLF, (1882–1941) British novelist. *Jacob's Room*, ch. 5 (1922).

Referring to passengers on an omnibus.

Outcasts

1   His hand will be against every man, and every man's hand against him.

BIBLE: HEBREW, *Genesis*, 16:12.The prophecy spoken to Hagar, the hand–maiden of Abraham, of their unborn son Ishmael. He was banished into the desert, and is traditionally considered the father of the Arab nation.

2   He gnawed the rectitude of his life; he felt that he had been outcast from life's feast.

JAMES JOYCE, (1882–1941) Irish author. *Dubliners*, "A Painful Case" (1916). Referring to Mr. Duffy.

Outlaws

1   These, having not the law, are a law unto themselves.

BIBLE: NEW TESTAMENT, St. Paul, in *Romans*, 2:14.

2   To live outside the law, you must be honest.

BOB DYLAN [ROBERT ALLEN ZIM-MERMAN], (b. 1941) U.S. singer, songwriter. "Absolutely Sweet Marie" (song), on the album *Blonde on Blonde* (1968).

A similar observation was made in Don Siegel's 1958 film, *The Line–Up*.

Pacifism

1   The wolf also shall dwell with the lamb, and the leopard shall lie down with the kid; and the calf and the young lion and the fatling together; and a little child shall lead them.

BIBLE: HEBREW, *ISAIAH*, 11:6.

2   All that a pacifist can undertake—but it is a very great deal—is to refuse to kill, injure or otherwise cause suffering to another human creature, and untiringly to order his life by the rule of love though others may be captured by hate.

VERA BRITTAIN, (1896–1970) British author, pacifist. "What Can We Do In Wartime?" *Wartime Chronicle: Vera Brittain's Diary 1939–1945* (1989). Article published in *Forward* (Scotland, Sept. 9, 1939).

3   It is useless for the sheep to pass resolutions in favour of vegetarianism, while the wolf remains of a different opinion.

WILLIAM RALPH INGE, (1860–1954) British Dean of St. Paul's, London. *"Patriotism," Outspoken Essays,* First Series (1919). (first publ. 1915).

4   All we are saying is give peace a chance.

JOHN LENNON, (1940–1980) British songwriter, rock musician. "Give Peace a Chance" (song), on the album *Live Peace in Toronto* (1969).

The song is also credited to Paul McCartney.

5   War hath no fury like a non–combatant.

C.E. (CHARLES EDWARD) MONTAGUE, (1867–1928) British author, journalist. *Disenchantment*, ch. 16 (1922).

Pain

1   After great pain, a formal feeling comes—
The Nerves sit ceremonious, like Tombs—

EMILY DICKINSON, (1830–1886) U.S. poet. "After Great Pain, a Formal Feeling Comes" (written c. 1862, published 1929). Repr. in *The Complete Poems*, no. 341, Harvard *variorum* edition (1955).

Painters and Painting

1   It is impossible for me to envisage a picture as being other than a window, and ... my first concern is then to know what it *looks out* on.

ANDRÉ BRETON, (1896–1966) French surrealist. *Surrealism and Painting* (1928).

Palestine

1   His Majesty's Government view with favour the establishment in Palestine of a national home for the Jewish people, and will use their best endeavours to facilitate the achievement of this object, it being clearly understood that nothing shall be done which may prejudice the civil and religious rights of existing non–Jewish communities in Palestine, or the rights and political status enjoyed by Jews in any other country.

A.J. (ARTHUR JAMES) BALFOUR, (1848–1930) British Conservative politician, prime minister. "The Balfour Declaration," *The Middle East Conflict: Notes and Documents (1915–1967)*. Letter, Nov. 2, 1917.

The document, which committed British support for a Jewish national home in Palestine, made a significant departure from the wording proposed by Chaim Weizmann on behalf of the Zionist Organization, that Britain accepted "the principle of recognizing Palestine as the National Home of the Jewish people."

Paradise

1   *Et in Arcadia ego.*
[I too am in Arcadia.]

ANONYMOUS.

Tomb inscription, appearing in classical paintings by Guercino and Poussin, among others. The words probably mean that even the most ideal earthly lives are mortal. Arcadia, a mountainous region in the central Peloponnese, Greece, was the rustic abode of Pan, depicted in literature and art as a land of innocence and ease, and was the title of Sir Philip Sidney's pastoral romance (1590).

2   A damsel with a dulcimer
In a vision once I saw:
It was an Abyssinian maid.
And on her dulcimer she played,
Singing of Mount Abora.
Could I revive within me
Her symphony and song,
To such a deep delight 'twould win me,
That with music loud and long,
I would build that dome in air,
That sunny dome! those caves of ice!
And all who heard should see them there,
And all should cry, Beware! Beware!
His flashing eyes, his floating hair!
Weave a circle round him thrice,

And close your eyes with holy
dread,
For he on honey–dew hath fed,
And drunk the milk of Paradise.

SAMUEL TAYLOR COLERIDGE,
(1772–1834) British poet. "Kubla Khan," l.
37–54 (written 1797, published 1816). See
Coleridge on Asia.

3   A fool's paradise is a wise man's
hell!

THOMAS FULLER, (1608–1661) British
cleric. *The Holy State and the Profane State,*
bk. 4, ch. 20 (1642).

4   Somewhere over the rainbow
Way up high,
There's a land that I heard of
Once in a lullaby.

YIP HARBURG, (1898–1981) U.S. songwriter. "Over the Rainbow" (song), *The Wizard of Oz* (film, 1939).

Sung by Judy Garland. Author born Isidore
Hochberg, name changed to Edgar Y.
Harburg.

5   They paved paradise
And put up a parking lot.

JONI MITCHELL, (b. 1943) Canadian-born
U.S. singer, songwriter. "Big Yellow Taxi"
(song), from the album *Ladies of the Canyon*
(1970).

6   Everyone who has ever built anywhere a "new heaven" first found
the power thereto in his own hell.

FRIEDRICH NIETZSCHE, (1844–1900)
German philosopher. *The Genealogy of
Morals,* essay 3, aph. 10 (1887).

7   The land of joy, the lovely glades of
the fortunate woods and the home
of the blest.

**VIRGIL [PUBLIUS VERGILIUS
MARO],** (70–19 B.C.) Roman poet. *Aeneid,*
bk. 6, l. 638 (19 B.C.), trans. by David West
(1991).

Referring to the Elysian Fields, a stop on
Aeneas's journey to the Underworld.

Paranoia

1   A paranoiac ... like a poet, is born,
not made.

LUIS BUÑUEL, (1900–1983) Spanish filmmaker. *My Last Sigh,* ch. 18 (1983).

2   Something is happening here
But you don't know what it is
Do you, Mister Jones?

**BOB DYLAN [ROBERT ALLEN ZIM-
MERMAN],** (b. 1941) U.S. singer, songwriter. "Ballad of a Thin Man" (song), on the
album *Highway 61 Revisited* (1968).

The identity of Mr. Jones has been a source of
some perplexity: several people thought the
song was addressed to them.

Parents

1   Honor thy father and thy mother:
that thy days may be long upon the
land which the Lord thy God giveth
thee.

BIBLE: HEBREW, *Exodus,* 20:12. The
fifth commandment.

2   There are times when parenthood
seems nothing but feeding the
mouth that bites you.

PETER DE VRIES, (b. 1910) U.S. author.
The Tunnel of Love, ch. 5 (1954).

3   You don't have to deserve your
mother's love. You have to deserve
your father's. He's more particular.... The father is always a Republican towards his son, and his
mother's always a Democrat.

ROBERT FROST, (1874–1963) U.S. poet.
Interview in *Writers at Work,* Second Series,
ed. George Plimpton (1963).

4   They fuck you up, your mum and
dad.
They may not mean to, but they do.

They fill you with the faults they had
And add some extra, just for you.

PHILIP LARKIN, (1922–1986) British poet. "This Be the Verse," st. 1, *High Windows* (1974). (Written April 1971).

In a letter, June 6, 1982, published in *Selected Letters* (1992), Larkin complained of the notoriety of this poem, which "will clearly be my 'Lake Isle of Innisfree.' I fully expect to hear it recited by a thousand Girl Guides before I die."

5 I am the slave of my baptism. Parents, you have caused my misfortune, and you have caused your own.

ARTHUR RIMBAUD, (1854–1891) French poet. *Une Saison en Enfer*, "Nuit de l'Enfer" (originally published 1874). Repr. in *Collected Poems*, ed. Oliver Bernard (1962).

6 I wish either my father or my mother, or indeed both of them, as they were in duty both equally bound to it, had minded what they were about when they begot me.

LAURENCE STERNE, (1713–1768) British author. *Tristram Shandy*, bk. 1, ch. 1 (1759–1767).

Opening words of book.

7 Children begin by loving their parents. After a time they judge them. Rarely, if ever, do they forgive them.

OSCAR WILDE, (1854–1900) Anglo–Irish playwright, author. Lord Illingworth, in *A Woman of No Importance*, act 2 (1891).

Wilde had used almost the same words in *The Picture of Dorian Gray*, ch. 5 (1891).

8 A slavish bondage to parents cramps every faculty of the mind.

MARY WOLLSTONECRAFT, (1759–1797) British feminist writer. *A Vindication of the Rights of Women*, ch. 11 (1792).

Paris

1 The American arrives in Paris with a few French phrases he has culled from a conversational guide or picked up from a friend who owns a beret.

FRED ALLEN, (1894–1957) U.S. radio comic. Quoted in *Paris After Dark*, introduction, Art Buchwald (1954).

2 Good Americans, when they die, go to Paris.

THOMAS APPLETON, (1812–1884) U.S. author. Quoted in *The Autocrat of the Breakfast–Table*, ch. 6, Oliver Wendell Holmes Sr. (1858).

The saying also found its way into Oscar Wilde's *The Picture of Dorian Gray*, ch. 3 (1891) and *A Woman of No Importance*, act 1 (1893).

3 And trade is art, and art's
   philosophy,
In Paris.

ELIZABETH BARRETT BROWNING, (1806–1861) British poet. "Aurora Leigh," bk. 6, l. 96 (1857).

4 The last time I saw Paris
Her heart was warm and gay,
I heard the laughter of her heart in
   every street café.

OSCAR HAMMERSTEIN II, (1895–1960) U.S. songwriter. "The Last Time I Saw Paris" (song), *Lady Be Good* (film, 1941).

Hammerstein's last major collaboration with Jerome Kern was inspired by news of the German occupation of Paris, and won an Oscar. The movie bears no relation to the stage musical scored by Gershwin in 1924.

5 If you are lucky enough to have lived in Paris as a young man, then wherever you go for the rest of your life it stays with you, for Paris is a moveable feast.

ERNEST HEMINGWAY, (1899–1961) U.S. author. Quoted in *Papa Hemingway*, pt. 1, ch. 3, A.E. Hotchner (1966).

The words "a moveable feast" were used—on Hotchner's recommendation—as the title for Hemingway's posthumously published Paris memoirs. The above paragraph appeared as the book's epigraph.

6   As an artist, a man has no home in Europe save in Paris.

FRIEDRICH NIETZSCHE, (1844–1900) German philosopher. *Ecce Homo*, "Why I Am So Clever" sct. 5 (1888).

7   When Paris sneezes, Europe catches cold.

PRINCE METTERNICH, (1773–1859) Austrian statesman. attributed, in *A Dictionary of Historical Quotations*, eds. Alan and Veronica Palmer (1985).

Comment, 1830.

Parliament

1   Parliament is not a *congress* of ambassadors from different and hostile interests; which interests each must maintain, as an agent and advocate, against other agents and advocates; but parliament is a *deliberative* assembly of *one* nation, with *one* interest, that of the whole; where, not local purposes, not local prejudices ought to guide, but the general good, resulting from the general reason of the whole. You choose a member indeed; but when you have chosen him, he is not a member of Bristol, but he is a member of *parliament*.

EDMUND BURKE, (1729–1797) Irish philosopher, statesman. "Speech to the Electors of Bristol," *Works*, vol. 2 (1899). Speech, Nov. 3, 1774.

2   You have sat too long for any good you have been doing. Depart, I say, and let us have done with you. In the name of God, go!

OLIVER CROMWELL, (1599–1658) British Parliamentarian general, Lord Protector of England. *Memorials of the English Affairs*, Bulstrode Whitelock (1732). Speech, Apr. 20, 1653, dismissing the "rump" of the Long Parliament.

Cromwell later justified his action: "When I was there, I did not think to have done this. But perceiving the Spirit of God so strong upon me, I would not consult flesh and blood." The move was a popular one in the nation, inspiring the ditty: "Brave Oliver came to the House like a sprite, His fiery face struck the Speaker dumb; 'Begone,' said he, 'you have sat long enough, Do you think to sit here till Doomsday come?'" (quoted in G.M. Trevelyan's *History of England* (1927) bk. 4, ch. 4 Three centuries later, Cromwell's words were addressed by the Conservative politician Leo Amery in a speech of May 7, 1940, to the government of Neville Chamberlain, who stepped down in favor of Winston Churchill's wartime coalition government three days later.

3   This place is the longest running farce in the West End.

CYRIL SMITH, (b. 1928) British Liberal politician. Quoted in *Big Cyril* (autobiography), ch. 8, Cyril Smith (1977). Comment, July 1973.

Parliament, House of Commons

1   The Commons, faithful to their system, remained in a wise and masterly inactivity.

JAMES MACKINTOSH, (1765–1832) Scottish philosopher. *Vindiciae Gallicae*, ch. 1 (1791).

Parliament, House of Lords

1   A severe though not unfriendly critic of our institutions said that "the cure for admiring the House of Lords was to go and look at it."

WALTER BAGEHOT, (1826–1877) British economist, critic. *The English Constitution*, ch. 4 (1867).

2   I am dead: dead, but in the Elysian fields.

BENJAMIN DISRAELI, (1804–1881) British statesman, author. Quoted in *The Life of Benjamin Disraeli*, vol. 5, ch. 13, W. Monypenny and G. Buckle (1920).

Referring to his elevation to the House of Lords.

3   My Lord Bath, you and I are now two as insignificant men as any in England.

ROBERT WALPOLE, (1676–1745) British statesman. Quoted in *Political and Literary Anecdotes*, p. 43, William King (1819). Remark, Feb. 1742, to Pulteney, Earl of Bath.

On their elevation to the House of Lords.

Parties

1   Let us have wine and women, mirth and laughter,
Sermons and soda–water the day after.

GEORGE GORDON NOEL BYRON, 6TH BARON BYRON, (1788–1824) British poet. "Don Juan," cto. 2, st. 178 (1819–1824).

2   Like other parties of the kind, it was first silent, then talky, then argumentative, then disputatious, then unintelligible, then altogethery, then inarticulate, and then drunk. When we had reached the last step of this glorious ladder, it was difficult to get down again without stumbling.

GEORGE GORDON NOEL BYRON, 6TH BARON BYRON, (1788–1824) British poet. *Byron's Letters and Journals*, vol. 4, ed. Leslie A. Marchand (1975). Letter, Oct. 31, 1815, to poet Thomas Moore.

3   Fasten your seat belts. It's going to be a bumpy night.

JOSEPH L. MANKIEWICZ, U.S. screenwriter. Margo Channing (Bette Davis), in *All About Eve* (film), anticipating a rocky party (1950).

4   Enjoyed it! One more drink and I'd have been under the host.

DOROTHY PARKER, (1893–1967) U.S. humorous writer. Quoted in *The Algonquin Wits*, ed. Robert E. Drennan (1968).

On being asked whether she had enjoyed a party.

Partnership

1   Mr. Morgan buys his partners; I grow my own.

ANDREW CARNEGIE, (1835–1919) U.S. industrialist, philanthropist. quoted in *Life of Andrew Carnegie*, ch. 15, sct. 2, Burton J. Hendrick (1932).

Referring to the banker J.P. Morgan's habit of incorporating men who had made brilliant careers in other houses.

2   When a man's partner is killed he's supposed to do something about it. It doesn't make any difference what you thought of him. He was your partner, and you're supposed to do something about it.

DASHIELL HAMMETT, (1894–1961) U.S. crime writer. Sam Spade, in *The Maltese Falcon*, "If They Hang You" (1930).

The words are spoken thus by Humphrey Bogart in the movie *The Maltese Falcon*, scripted and directed by John Huston (1941).

Passion

1   What the public wants is the image of passion, not passion itself.

ROLAND BARTHES, (1915–1980) French semiologist. *Mythologies*, "Le monde où l'on catche" (1957).

2   For one heat, all know, doth drive out another, One passion doth expel another still.

GEORGE CHAPMAN, (c. 1559–1634) British dramatist, poet, translator. Vandome, in *Monsieur d'Olive,* act 5, sc. 1, l. 8–9 (1606). Repr. in *Plays and Poems of George Chapman: The Comedies,* ed. Thomas Marc Parrott (1914).

Proposing to distract the countess Marcellina from her melancholy.

3   There is only one passion, the passion for happiness.

DENIS DIDEROT, (1713–1784) French philosopher. *Elements of Physiology,* "Will, Freedom" (notes written 1774–1780, originally published 1875–1877). Repr. in *Selected Writings,* ed. Lester G. Crocker (1966).

4   The trouble is that no devastating or redeeming fires have ever burnt in my life.... My life began by flickering out.

IVAN GONCHAROV, (1812–1891) Russian novelist. Oblomov, in *Oblomov,* pt. 2, ch. 4 (1859), trans. by David Magarshak (1954).

5   A man who has not passed through the inferno of his passions has never overcome them.

CARL JUNG, (1875–1961) Swiss psychiatrist. *Memories, Dreams, Reflections,* ch. 9 (1962).

6   Passions spin the plot:
    We are betrayed by what is false
        within.

GEORGE MEREDITH, (1828–1909) British author. *Modern Love,* Sonnet 43 (1862).

7   As a bathtub lined with white
        porcelain,
    When the hot water gives out or
        goes tepid,
    So is the slow cooling of our chival-
        rous passion,
    O my much praised but–not–alto-
        gether–satisfactory lady.

EZRA POUND, (1885–1972) U.S. poet, critic. "The Bath Tub," *Lustra* (1916). Repr. in *Collected Shorter Poems* (1984).

The poem is thought to be addressed to Pound's fiancée Dorothy Shakespear, whom he married in April 1914.

8   Our passions are most like to floods
    and streams,
    The shallow murmur, but the deep
    are dumb.

SIR WALTER RALEIGH, (1552–1618) British author, soldier, explorer. "Sir Walter Raleigh to the Queen," st. 1 (written c. 1599, published 1655).

Passivity

1   I am a camera with its shutter open, quite passive, recording, not thinking.

CHRISTOPHER ISHERWOOD, (1904–1986) British novelist. "Berlin Diary," *Goodbye to Berlin* (1939).

Opening sentence.

Passover

1   And they shall eat the flesh in that night, roast with fire, and unleavened bread; and with bitter herbs they shall eat it. Eat not of it raw, nor sodden at all with water, but roast with fire; his head with his legs, and with the purtenance thereof. And ye shall let nothing of it remain until the morning; and that which remaineth of it until the morning ye shall burn with fire. And thus shall ye eat it; with your loins girded, your shoes on your feet, and your staff in your hand; and ye shall eat it in haste: it is the Lord's passover.

BIBLE: HEBREW, *Exodus,* 12:8–11.

2   And this day shall be unto you for a memorial; and ye shall keep it a feast to the Lord throughout your generations; ye shall keep it a feast by an ordinance for ever.

BIBLE: HEBREW, *Exodus,* 12:14.

Past, the

1   As all historians know, the past is a great darkness, and filled with echoes. Voices may reach us from it; but what they say to us is imbued with the obscurity of the matrix out of which they come; and try as we may, we cannot always decipher them precisely in the clearer light of our day.

MARGARET ATWOOD, (b. 1939) Canadian novelist, poet, critic. *The Handmaid's Tale*, "Historical Note" (1986).

2   Who controls the past controls the future: who controls the present controls the past.

GEORGE ORWELL, (1903–1950) British author. *Nineteen Eighty–Four*, pt. 1, ch. 3 (1949).

Ingsoc party slogan.

3   Those who cannot remember the past are condemned to repeat it.

GEORGE SANTAYANA, (1863–1952) U.S. philosopher, poet. *Life of Reason*, "Reason in Common Sense" ch. 12 (1905–6).

William L. Shirer made these words the epigraph for his *Rise and Fall of the Third Reich* (1959).

4   People who are always praising the past
And especially the times of faith as best
Ought to go and live in the Middle Ages
And be burnt at the stake as witches and sages.

STEVIE SMITH, (1902–1971) British poet, novelist. "The Past," *Selected Poems* (1962).

Patience

1   Behold, we count them happy which endure. Ye have heard of the patience of Job.

BIBLE: NEW TESTAMENT, *James*, 5:11.

2   With close–lipp'd Patience for our only friend,
Sad Patience, too near neighbour to Despair.

MATTHEW ARNOLD, (1822–1888) British poet, critic. *The Scholar–Gipsy*, st. 20 (1853).

3   Patience. A minor form of despair disguised as a virtue.

AMBROSE BIERCE, (1842–1914) U.S. author. *The Devil's Dictionary* (1881–1906), repr. in *Collected Works of Ambrose Bierce*, vol. 7 (1911).

4   What I say is, patience, and shuffle the cards.

MIGUEL DE CERVANTES, (1547–1616) Spanish author. Durandarte, in *Don Quixote*, pt. 2, ch. 23 (1615), trans. by P. Motteux.

5   Beware the fury of a patient man.

JOHN DRYDEN, (1631–1700) British poet, dramatist, critic. "Absalom and Achitophel," pt. 1, l. 1005 (1681).

6   Patience, that blending of moral courage with physical timidity.

THOMAS HARDY, (1840–1928) British novelist, poet. *Tess of the D'Urbervilles*, ch. 43 (1891).

7   Patience, the beggar's virtue, Shall find no harbour here.

PHILIP MASSINGER, (1583–1640) British dramatist. Sir Giles Overreach, "a cruel extortioner," in *A New Way To Pay Old Debts*, act 5, sc. 1, l. 244–6 (1632). Repr. in *The Plays and Poems of Philip Massinger*, eds. P. Edwards and C. Gibson (1976).

8   They also serve who only stand and wait.

JOHN MILTON, (1608–1674) British poet. Sonnet 19, "On His Blindness," (written c. 1652, published 1673)."Patience" is the speaker.

Sonnet also called "When I Consider How My Light is Spent" [1st line].

Patriotism

1 I realise that patriotism is not enough. I must have no hatred or bitterness towards anyone.

EDITH CAVELL, (1865–1915) British nurse. quoted in *Times* (London, Oct. 23, 1915).

Words spoken Oct. 11, 1915, in conversation with her chaplain Reverend Stirling Gahan, shortly before her execution in Brussels as a spy. In fact she was guilty of breaking the rules of war by using her status as a Red Cross nurse to help Allied prisoners escape from German–occupied territory. The words are inscribed on her monument in London.

2 "My country, right or wrong" is a thing that no patriot would think of saying except in a desperate case. It is like saying "My mother, drunk or sober."

GILBERT KEITH CHESTERTON, (1874–1936) British author. *The Defendant*, "Defence of Patriotism" (1901).

See Decatur.

3 Our country! In her intercourse with foreign nations, may she always be in the right; but our country, right or wrong.

STEPHEN DECATUR, (1779–1820) U.S. naval commander. Quoted in *Life of Stephen Decatur*, ch. 14, Alexander Slidell Mackenzie (1846).

Toast proposed at a banquet in Norfolk, Virginia, April 1816, to celebrate Decatur's victory over Algerian "Barbary pirates." The words were revived in a speech by Carl Schurz (1829–1906, German orator, later U.S. general and senator) to the U.S. Senate, Jan. 17, 1872: "Our country right or wrong. When right, to be kept right; when wrong, to be put right." See also Chesterton.

4 Never was patriot yet, but was a fool.

JOHN DRYDEN, (1631–1700) British poet, dramatist, critic. "Absalom and Achitophel," pt. 1, l. 968 (1681).

5 Patriotism is the last refuge of a scoundrel.

SAMUEL JOHNSON, (1709–1784) British author, lexicographer. Quoted in James Boswell, *Life of Dr. Johnson*, entry, April 7, 1775 (1791).

Ambrose Bierce, in his entry under *Patriotism* in his *Devil's Dictionary* (1881–1906), wrote: "In Dr. Johnson's famous dictionary patriotism is defined as the last resort of a scoundrel. With all due respect to an enlightened but inferior lexicographer I beg to submit that it is the first."

6 My fellow Americans, ask not what your country can do for you—ask what you can do for your country.

JOHN FITZGERALD KENNEDY, (1917–1963) U.S. Democratic politician, president. quoted in *Kennedy*, pt. 3, ch. 9, Theodore C. Sorenson (1965). Inaugural address, Jan. 20, 1961, Washington D.C.

Kennedy continued, "My fellow citizens of the world, ask not what America will do for you, but what together we can do for the freedom of man." He expressed the same idea earlier, in a televised campaign address of Sept. 20, 1960. Many antecedents have been cited, including Oliver Wendell Holmes Sr. in his Memorial Day Address, 1884: "It is now the moment ... to recall what our country has done for each of us, and to ask ourselves what we can do for our country in return."

7 When a nation is filled with strife, then do patriots flourish.

LAO–TZU, (6th century B.C.) Chinese philosopher. *Tao–te–ching*, bk. 1, ch. 18, trans. by T.C. Lau (1963).

8 A man who is good enough to shed his blood for his country is good enough to be given a square deal afterwards. More than that no man is entitled to, and less than that no man shall have.

THEODORE ROOSEVELT, (1858–1919) U.S. Republican (later Progressive) politician, president. *Addresses and Presidential Messages* (1904). Speech, June 4, 1903, Springfield, Illinois.

9 It was always accounted a virtue in a man to love his country. With us it is now something more than a virtue. It is a necessity. When an American says that he loves his country, he means not only that he loves the New England hills, the prairies glistening in the sun, the wide and rising plains, the great mountains, and the sea. He means that he loves an inner air, an inner light in which freedom lives and in which a man can draw the breath of self–respect.

ADLAI STEVENSON, (1900–1965) U.S. Democratic politician. "The Nature of Patriotism," *Speeches* (1953). Speech, Aug. 27, 1952, to American Legion Convention, New York City.

10 What do we mean by patriotism in the context of our times? I venture to suggest that what we mean is a sense of national responsibility ... a patriotism which is not short, frenzied outbursts of emotion, but the tranquil and steady dedication of a lifetime.

ADLAI STEVENSON, (1900–1965) U.S. Democratic politician. "The Nature of Patriotism," *Speeches* (1953). Speech, Aug. 27, 1952, to American Legion Convention, New York City.

Patronage

1 Is not a patron, my lord, one who looks with unconcern on a man struggling for life in the water, and, when he has reached ground, encumbers him with help? The notice which you have been pleased to take of my labours, had it been early, had been kind; but it has been delayed till I am indifferent, and cannot enjoy it; till I am soli-

tary, and cannot impart it; till I am known, and do not want it.

SAMUEL JOHNSON, (1709–1784) British author, lexicographer. Quoted in James Boswell, *Life of Dr. Johnson* (1791). Letter, Feb. 7, 1755, to his patron Lord Chesterfield.

In his *Dictionary of the English Language* (1755), Johnson defined *patron* as "one who countenances, supports or protects. Commonly a wretch who supports with insolence, and is paid with flattery."

2 Every time I bestow a vacant office I make a hundred discontented persons and one ingrate.

LOUIS XIV, (1638–1715) French king. Quoted in *Le Siècle de Louis XIV*, ch. 26, Voltaire (1751). Remark made following the disgrace of the Duke of Lauzun, c. 1669.

Payment

1 Alas! how deeply painful is all payment!

GEORGE GORDON NOEL BYRON, 6TH BARON BYRON, (1788–1824) British poet. *Don Juan*, cto. 10, st. 79 (1819–1824).

Peace

1 Blessed are the peacemakers: for they shall be called the children of God.

BIBLE: NEW TESTAMENT, Jesus, in *Matthew*, 5:9.The seventh of the Beatitudes, from the Sermon on the Mount.

2 They shall beat their swords into plowshares, and their spears into pruninghooks: nation shall not lift up sword against nation, neither shall they learn war any more.

BIBLE: HEBREW, *Isaiah*, 2:4.The words reappear in *Micah* 4:3, and the reverse injunction is made in *Joel* 3:10 ("Beat your plowshares into swords ...") The motto of the BBC—"Nation shall speak peace unto nation"—is thought to derive from these lines. "Study War No More" is the title of a well–known African–American spiritual.

3 What they could do with round here is a good war. What else can you expect with peace running wild all over the place? You know what the trouble with peace is? No organization.

BERTOLT BRECHT, (1898–1956) German dramatist, poet. The sergeant, in *Mother Courage and Her Children*, sc. 1 (1939), trans. by Eric Bentley (1941).

4 Lord Salisbury and myself have brought you back peace but a peace I hope with honour.

BENJAMIN DISRAELI, (1804–1881) British statesman, author. Quoted in *Times* (London, July 17, 1878).

Remark on returning from the Berlin Congress convened to resolve the European crisis (the "Eastern Question").

See John Russell's comment on peace. The words "peace with honour" were used by Neville Chamberlain in 1938. See Chamberlain's comment on World War II.

5 Peace hath her victories
No less renowned than War.

JOHN MILTON, (1608–1674) British poet. *To the Lord General Cromwell, May 1652* (1652).

6 If peace cannot be maintained with honour, it is no longer peace.

JOHN RUSSELL, 1ST EARL RUSSELL, (1792–1878) British Whig politician. quoted in *Times* (London, Sept. 21, 1853). Speech, Sept. 19, 1853, Greenock, Scotland.

On the growing crisis in the Crimea, which erupted into war the following year.

People, the

2 But we are the people of England; and we have not spoken yet.

Smile at us, pay us, pass us. But do not quite forget.

G.K. GILBERT KEITH CHESTERTON, (1874–1936) British author. "The Secret People," *Poems* (1915).

Closing lines of poem.

Perception

1 If the doors of perception were cleansed everything would appear to man as it is, infinite.

WILLIAM BLAKE, (1757–1827) British poet, painter, engraver. *The Marriage of Heaven and Hell*, plate 14, "A Memorable Fancy" (c. 1793), repr. in *Complete Writings*, ed. Geoffrey Keynes (1957).

"The Doors of Perception" was the title of Aldous Huxley's essay on his experience with mescaline (1954); the 1960s rock group The Doors also reputedly took their name from Blake's aphorism. Blake continued, "For man has closed himself up, till he sees all things thro' narrow chinks of his cavern."

2 The world is for thousands a freak show; the images flicker past and vanish; the impressions remain flat and unconnected in the soul. Thus they are easily led by the opinions of others, are content to let their impressions be shuffled and rearranged and evaluated differently.

JOHANN WOLFGANG VON GOETHE, (1749–1832) German poet, dramatist. "Third Pilgrimage to Erwin's Grave," *Aus Goethes Brieftasche* (1776).

Perfection

1 The pursuit of perfection, then, is the pursuit of sweetness and light.... He who works for sweetness and light united, works to make reason and the will of God prevail.

MATTHEW ARNOLD, (1822–1888) British poet, critic. *Culture and Anarchy*, ch. 1 (1869).

These words recall Swift's evocation of mankind's "two noblest of things, which are sweetness and light." (See culture.).

2   Faultily faultless, icily regular, splendidly null,
Dead perfection, no more.

ALFRED TENNYSON, 1ST BARON TENNYSON, (1809–1892) British poet. "Maud," pt. 1, sct. 2, *Maud, and Other Poems* (1855).

3   The intellect of man is forced to choose
Perfection of the life, or of the work,
And if it take the second must refuse
A heavenly mansion, raging in the dark.

WILLIAM BUTLER YEATS, (1865–1939) Irish poet, playwright. "The Choice," st. 1, *The Winding Stair* (1933).

Persecution

1   Saul, Saul, why persecutest thou me?

BIBLE: NEW TESTAMENT, Jesus, in *Acts,* 9:4.The words of Christ to Saul (St. Paul) on his way to Damascus.

2   They'll stone you when you're riding in your car.
They'll stone you when you're playing your guitar.
Yes, but I would not feel so all alone,
Everybody must get stoned.

BOB DYLAN [ROBERT ALLEN ZIMMERMAN], (b. 1941) U.S. singer, songwriter. "Rainy Day Women #12 & 35" (song), on the album *Blonde on Blonde* (1968).

3   Persecution produced its natural effect on them. It found them a sect; it made them a faction.

THOMAS BABINGTON MACAULAY, (1800–1859) British historian, Whig politician. *History of England,* vol. 1, ch. 1 (1849). Referring to the Puritans and Calvinists.

Perseverance

1   Put your shoulder to the wheel.

AESOP, (6th century B.C.) Greek fabulist. *Fables,* "Hercules and the Wagoner."

2   The troubles of our proud and angry dust
Are from eternity, and shall not fail.
Bear them we can, and if we can we must.
Shoulder the sky, my lad, and drink your ale.

A.E. (ALFRED EDWARD) HOUSMAN, (1859–1936) British poet, classical scholar. *Last Poems,* no. 9 (1922).

3   Neither evil tongues,
Rash judgements, nor the sneers of selfish men,
Nor greetings where no kindness is, nor all
The dreary intercourse of daily life,
Shall e'er prevail against us.

WILLIAM WORDSWORTH, (1770–1850) British poet. "Lines Composed a Few Miles Above Tintern Abbey," l. 129–33, *Lyrical Ballads* (1798).

Personality

1   Two souls, alas! reside within my breast.

JOHANN WOLFGANG VON GOETHE, (1749–1832) German poet, dramatist. Faust, in *Faust,* pt. 1, ch. 2, "Before The City Gate," l. 1112 (1808), trans. by Bayard Taylor (1870–1871).

2   Personality is the supreme realization of the innate idiosyncrasy of a living being. It is an act of high courage flung in the face of life, the absolute affirmation of all that constitutes the individual, the most successful adaptation to

the universal conditions of existence coupled with the greatest
possible freedom for self–determi-
nation.

CARL JUNG, (1875–1961) Swiss psychiatrist.
The Development of Personality (1934), repr.
in *Collected Works*, vol. 17, ed. William
McGuire (1954).

Persuasion

1 There is a holy mistaken zeal in politics, as well as in religion. By per-
suading others, we convince ourselves.

JUNIUS (PSEUDONYM OF WRITER
NEVER I, *The Letters of Junius*, letter 35
(1772). *Public Advertiser* (London, December
19, 1769).

Pessimism

1 The optimist proclaims that we
live in the best of all possible
worlds; and the pessimist fears this
is true.

JAMES BRANCH CABELL, (1879–1958)
U.S. novelist, essayist. *The Silver Stallion*, bk.
4, ch. 26 (1926).

See Bradley and Voltaire on optimism.

2 It is wisdom in prosperity, when all
is as thou wouldst have it, to fear
and suspect the worst.

DESIDERIUS ERASMUS, (c.1466–1536)
Dutch humanist. *Proverbs or Adages of Erasmus*, fol. 32 (1545).

3 If we see light at the end of the
tunnel,
It's the light of the oncoming train.

ROBERT LOWELL, (1917–1977) U.S. poet."
Since 1939," *Day by Day* (1977).

Philosophy and
Philosophers

1 A little philosophy inclineth man's
mind to atheism, but depth in philosophy bringeth men's minds
about to religion.

FRANCIS BACON, (1561–1626) British
philosopher, essayist, statesman. *Essays*, "Of
Atheism" (1597–1625).

2 We are much beholden to Machiavel and others, that write what
men do, and not what they ought
to do.

FRANCIS BACON, (1561–1626) British
philosopher, essayist, statesman. *The
Advancement of Learning*, bk. 2, ch. 21, sct. 9
(1605).

3 Philosophy, like medicine, has
plenty of drugs, few good remedies,
and hardly any specific cures.

SÉBASTIEN–ROCH NICOLAS DE
CHAMFORT, (1741–1794) French writer,
wit. *Maxims and Considerations*, vol. 1, no.
17 (1796), trans. by E. Powys Mathers (1926).

4 For hym was levere have at his
beddes heed,
Twenty bookes, clad in blak or
reed,
Of Aristotle and his philosophie,
Than robes riche, or fithele, or gay
sautrie:
But al be that he was a
philosophre,
Yet hadde he but litel gold in cofre.

GEOFFREY CHAUCER, (1340–1400)
British poet. *The Canterbury Tales*, "General
Prologue," l. 293–8 (1387–1400), repr. in *The
Works of Geoffrey Chaucer*, ed. Alfred W.
Pollard, et al. (1898).

Referring to the Clerk of Oxenford; the last
couplet alludes to the "philosophy" of
alchemy.

5   There is nothing so absurd but some philosopher has said it.

MARCUS TULLIUS CICERO, (106–43 BC) Roman orator, philosopher. *De Divinatione,* bk. 2, sct. 58 (45 B.C.).

6   And new Philosophy calls all in doubt,
The element of fire is quite put out;
The Sun is lost, and th'earth, and no mans wit
Can well direct him where to look for it.

JOHN DONNE, (c. 1572–1631) British divine, metaphysical poet. "An Anatomy of the World: First Anniversary," l. 205–8 (1611). Repr. in *Complete Poetry and Selected Prose,* ed. John Hayward (1929).

7   Do not all charms fly
At the mere touch of cold philosophy?
There was an awful rainbow once in heaven:
We know her woof, her texture; she is given
In the dull catalogue of common things.
Philosophy will clip an angel's wings,
Conquer all mysteries by rule and line,
Empty the haunted air, and gnomed mine
Unweave a rainbow.

JOHN KEATS, (1795–1821) British poet. *Lamia,* pt. 2, l. 229–37, *Lamia, Isabella, The Eve of St. Agnes and Other Poems* (1820).

8   Philosophy always requires something more, requires the eternal, the true, in contrast to which even the fullest existence as such is but a happy moment.

SOREN KIERKEGAARD, (1813–1855) Danish philosopher. *The Concept of Irony,* introduction to pt. 1 (1841, trans. 1966).

9   The philosophers have only *interpreted* the world in various ways; the point, however, is to *change* it.

KARL MARX, (1818–1883) German political theorist, social philosopher. *Theses on Feuerbach,* no. 11 (written 1845, published 1888). Repr. in *Selected Works,* vol. 1 (1942).

The observation also appeared in Marx, *The German Ideology* (1846) and was inscribed as the epitaph on his tomb in Highgate Cemetery, London.

10   How charming is divine philosophy!
Not harsh and crabb'd, as dull fools suppose,
But musical as is Apollo's lute,
And a perpetual feast of nectared sweets,
Where no crude surfeit reigns.

JOHN MILTON, (1608–1674) British poet. Second brother, in "Comus," l. 476–80 (1637).

11   Bishop Berkeley destroyed this world in one volume octavo; and nothing remained, after his time, but mind; which experienced a similar fate from the hand of Hume in 1737.

SYDNEY SMITH, (1771–1845) British writer, clergyman. *Sketches of Moral Philosophy,* introduction (1850).

12   The philosopher proves that the philosopher exists. The poet merely enjoys existence.

WALLACE STEVENS, (1879–1955) U.S. poet. "The Figure of the Youth as Virile Poet," lecture, Aug. 1943, *The Necessary Angel* (1951). (Originally published 1944).

13   Philosophy is a battle against the bewitchment of our intelligence by means of language.

LUDWIG WITTGENSTEIN, (1889–1951) Austrian philosopher. *Philosophical Investigations,* pt. 1, sct. 109 (1953).

In the book, Wittgenstein argued that most philosophical problems arose from the systematic misuse of language, and could be solved by a new critical method of linguistic analysis.

Photography

1 It is not at all monstrous in me to say ... that I would rather have such a memorial of one I dearly loved, than the noblest artist's work ever produced.

ELIZABETH BARRETT BROWNING, (1806–1861) British poet. *Elizabeth Barrett to Miss Mitford* (1954). Letter, Dec. 7, 1843, to author Mary Russell Mitford.

"It is not merely the likeness which is precious," Barrett wrote, " ... but the association and the sense of nearness involved in the thing ... the fact of the very shadow of the *person* lying there fixed forever! It is the very sanctification of portraits."

2 The photographer both loots and preserves, denounces and consecrates.

SUSAN SONTAG, (b. 1933) U.S. essayist. *On Photography*, "Melancholy Objects" (1977).

3 Most modern reproducers of life, even including the camera, really repudiate it. We gulp down evil, choke at good.

WALLACE STEVENS, (1879–1955) U.S. poet. *Opus Posthumous*, "Adagia" (1959).

Physics

1 To see a world in a grain of sand
And a heaven in a wild flower,
Hold infinity in the palm of your
  hand
And eternity in an hour.

WILLIAM BLAKE, (1757–1827) British poet, painter, engraver. "Auguries of Inno-

cence," l. 1–4, *Poems from the Pickering Manuscript* (c. 1803), repr. in *Complete Writings*, ed. Geoffrey Keynes (1957).

2 $E=mc^2$

ALBERT EINSTEIN, (1879–1955) German–born U.S. theoretical physicist. "Does the Inertia of a Body Depend upon Its Energy Content?" *Annalen der Physik*, no. 17 (Sept. 1905). Repr. in *The Principle of Relativity*, eds. Einstein, H.A. Lorentz, et al (1923).

Einstein's Special Theory of Relativity contained the formula, "If a body gives off the energy E in the form of radiation its mass diminishes by E/C≤" (represented by the equation $E=mc^2$). The equation does not appear in this form in Einstein's original paper, which at first met with indifferent or negative reactions. Roland Barthes later wrote: "Through the mythology of Einstein, the world blissfully regained the image of knowledge reduced to a formula" (*Mythologies*, "The Brain of Einstein" 1957).

3 *Three quarks for Muster Mark!*

JAMES JOYCE, (1882–1941) Irish author. *Finnegans Wake*, pt. 2 (1939).

This seabirds' chorus provided the name for the hypothetical particle postulated by physicists Murray Gell–Mann and George Zweig in 1963.

Piety

1 Bernard always had a few prayers in the hall and some whiskey afterwards as he was rather pious.

DAISY ASHFORD, (1881–1972) British writer. *The Young Visiters*, ch.3, "The First Evening," (published 1919).

Written when the author was aged nine.

2 But I gae mad at their grimaces,
Their sighin', cantin', grace–proud
  faces,
Their three–mile prayers, an'
  half–mile graces.

ROBERT BURNS, (1759–1796) Scottish poet. "To the Rev. John M'Math," (written 1785, published 1808). Repr. in *Poetical*

Works, vol. 2, ed. William Scott Douglas (1891).

Referring to members of the Scottish kirk.

lop–shell was the symbol worn by pilgrims. Raleigh was reprieved, though imprisoned for the next 12 years, and finally condemned and beheaded in 1616.

Pilgrimages

1 There's no discouragement
Shall make him once relent
His first avowed intent
  To be a pilgrim.

JOHN BUNYAN, (1628–1688) British Baptist preacher, author. Valiant–for–Truth, in *The Pilgrim's Progress*, pt. 2 (1684).

2 Whan Zephirus eek with his swete breeth,
Inspired hath in every holt and heeth
The tendre croppes, and the yonge sonne
Hath in the Ram his halfe cours yronne,
And smale foweles maken melodye,
That slepen al the nyght with open eye,
(So priketh hem Nature in hir corages);
Thanne longen folk to goon on pilgrimages.

GEOFFREY CHAUCER, (1340–1400) British poet. *The Canterbury Tales*, "General Prologue" l. 5–12 (1387–1400), repr. in *The Works of Geoffrey Chaucer*, ed. Alfred W. Pollard, et al. (1898).

3 Give me my scallop–shell of quiet,
My staff of faith to walk upon,
My scrip of joy, immortal diet,
My bottle of salvation,
My gown of glory, hope's true gage,
And thus I'll take my pilgrimage.

SIR WALTER RALEIGH, (1552–1618) British author, soldier, explorer. "The Passionate Man's Pilgrimage," *The Poems of Sir Walter Raleigh*, ed. Agnes M. Latham (1951).

Poem written while waiting execution on charges of treason against James I. The scal-

Pirates

1 Fifteen men on the dead man's chest—
Yo–ho–ho, and a bottle of rum!
Drink and the devil had done for the rest—
Yo–ho–ho, and a bottle of rum!

ROBERT LOUIS STEVENSON, (1850–1894) Scottish novelist, essayist, poet. The captain, in *Treasure Island*, pt. 1, ch. 1 (1883).

Pity

1 Poor man. Poor mankind.

WILLIAM FAULKNER, (1897–1962) U.S. novelist. Hightower, in *Light in August*, ch. 4 (1932).

Referring to Joe Christmas, suspected of murder and liable to be lynched.

2 If a madman were to come into this room with a stick in his hand, no doubt we should pity the state of his mind; but our primary consideration would be to take care of ourselves. We should knock him down first, and pity him afterwards.

SAMUEL JOHNSON, (1709–1784) British author, lexicographer. Quoted in James Boswell, *Life of Dr. Johnson*, entry, April 3, 1776 (1791).

3 Pity is the feeling which arrests the mind in the presence of whatsoever is grave and constant in human sufferings and unites it with the human sufferer. Terror is the feeling which arrests the mind in the presence of whatsoever is grave and

constant in human sufferings and unites it with the secret cause.

JAMES JOYCE, (1882–1941) Irish author. Stephen Dedalus, in *A Portrait of the Artist as a Young Man*, ch. 5 (1916).

Outlining his aesthetic theory.

4 Pity is for the living, envy is for the dead.

MARK TWAIN, (1835–1910) U.S. author. *Following the Equator*, ch. 19, "Pudd'nhead Wilson's New Calendar" (1897).

Places

1 Last night I dreamt I went to Manderley again.

DAPHNE DU MAURIER, (1907–1989) British novelist. *Rebecca*, ch. 1 (1938). Opening words.

2 Bugger Bognor.

GEORGE V, (1865–1936) British monarch, King of Great Britain and Ireland.

Attributed deathbed remark, on being assured by a courtier that he would soon be in Bognor. It has also been suggested that the king's exclamation was made in 1929, in response to a suggestion that the town should be named Bognor Regis, in commemoration of his convalescence there after a serious illness.

3 The accent of one's birthplace remains in the mind and in the heart as in one's speech.

FRANÇOIS LA ROCHEFOUCAULD, DUC DE, (1613–1680) French writer, moralist. *Sentences et Maximes Morales*, no. 342 (1678).

Plagiarism

1 They lard their lean books with the fat of others' works.

ROBERT BURTON, (1577–1640) British clergyman, author. *The Anatomy of Melancholy*, "Democritus to the Reader" (1621).

2 He invades authors like a monarch; and what would be theft in other poets is only victory in him.

JOHN DRYDEN, (1631–1700) British poet, dramatist, critic. Neander, in *Essay of Dramatic Poesy* (1668).

Referring to dramatist Ben Jonson.

3 If you steal from one author, it's plagiarism; if you steal from many, it's research.

WILSON MIZNER, (1876–1933) U.S. dramatist, wit. Quoted in *The Legendary Mizners*, ch. 4, Alva Johnson (1953).

4 Whatever is well said by another, is mine.

SENECA, (c. 5–65) Roman writer, philosopher, statesman. *Epistulae ad Lucilium*, epistle 16, sct. 7.

5 Immature artists imitate. Mature artists steal.

LIONEL TRILLING, (1905–1975) U.S. critic. *Esquire* (New York, Sept. 1962).

6 I made my song a coat
Covered with embroideries
Out of old mythologies
From heel to throat;
But the fools caught it,
Wore it in the world's eyes
As though they'd wrought it.
Song, let them take it
For there's more enterprise
In walking naked.

WILLIAM BUTLER YEATS, (1865–1939) Irish poet, playwright. "A Coat," *Responsibilities* (1914).

Planning

1 The best laid schemes o' mice and men
Gang aft agley;
An' lea'e us nought but grief an' pain,

For promis'd joy!

ROBERT BURNS, (1759–1796) Scottish poet. *"To a Mouse,"* st. 7 (1786). Repr. in *Poetical Works,* vol. 1, ed. William Scott Douglas (1891).

2   *Long run* is a misleading guide to current affairs. In the *long run* we are all dead.

JOHN MAYNARD KEYNES, (1883–1946) British economist. *A Tract on Monetary Reform,* ch. 3 (1923).

Pleasures

1   One half of the world cannot understand the pleasures of the other.

JANE AUSTEN, (1775–1817) British novelist. Emma, in *Emma,* ch. 9 (1816).

2   Stolen waters are sweet, and bread eaten in secret is pleasant.

BIBLE: HEBREW, *Proverbs,* 9:17.Speech of "a foolish woman" to "him that wanteth understanding."

3   Most men pursue pleasure with such breathless haste that they hurry past it.

SOREN KIERKEGAARD, (1813–1855) Danish philosopher. *Either/Or,* vol. 1, "Diapsalmata" (1843, trans. 1987).

4   Let us roll all our strength, and all
Our sweetness, up into one ball:
And tear our pleasures with rough
  strife,
Thorough the iron gates of life.
Thus, though we cannot make our
  sun
Stand still, yet we will make him
  run.

ANDREW MARVELL, (1621–1678) British metaphysical poet. "To His Coy Mistress," l. 41–6 (written c. 1650, published 1681).

5   The truth is, I do indulge myself a little the more in pleasure, knowing

that this is the proper age of my life to do it; and, out of my observation that most men that do thrive in the world do forget to take pleasure during the time that they are getting their estate, but reserve that till they have got one, and then it is too late for them to enjoy it.

SAMUEL PEPYS, (1633–1703) British diarist. *The Diary of Samuel Pepys,* eds. Robert Latham and William Matthews (1977–83). Journal entry, March 10, 1666.

Written aged 33.

6   All the things I really like to do are either immoral, illegal, or fattening.

ALEXANDER WOOLLCOTT, (1887–1943) U.S. columnist, critic. Quoted in *The Algonquin Wits,* ed. Robert E. Drennan (1968).

Poe, Edgar Allan

1   There comes Poe, with his raven,
  like Barnaby Rudge,
Three–fifths of him genius, and
  two–fifths sheer fudge.
Who talks like a book of iambs and
  pentameters,
In a way to make people of common sense damn metres,
Who has written some things quite
  the best of their kind,
But the heart somehow seems all
  squeezed out by the mind.

JAMES RUSSELL LOWELL, (1819–1891) U.S. poet, editor. "Poe and Longfellow," l. 1216, *A Fable for Critics* (1848).

Poetry and Poets

1   Earth, receive an honoured guest:
William Yeats is laid to rest.
Let the Irish vessel lie
Emptied of its poetry.

W.H. (WYSTAN HUGH) AUDEN,
(1907–1973) Anglo–U.S. poet. "In Memory of
W.B. Yeats," *Another Time* (1940).

2 It is a sad fact about our culture
that a poet can earn much more
money writing or talking about his
art than he can by practicing it.

W.H. (WYSTAN HUGH) AUDEN,
(1907–1973) Anglo–American poet. *The
Dyer's Hand*, foreword (1962).

Opening words.

3 You will be a poet because you will
always be humiliated.

W.H. (WYSTAN HUGH) AUDEN,
(1907–1973) Anglo–U.S. poet. Quoted in
Journals 1939–1983, Stephen Spender (1985).
Journal entry, April 11, 1979.

Auden's remark was recalled by Spender,
reminiscing on his first meeting with Auden at
Oxford.

4 The poet is like the prince of the
clouds
Who haunts the tempest and laughs
at the archer;
Exiled on the ground in the midst
of jeers,
His giant's wings prevent him from
walking.

CHARLES BAUDELAIRE, (1821–1867)
French poet. "L'Albatros," st. 4, *Les Fleurs du
Mal* (1857).

5 At last came Malherbe, the first in
France
To give to verse a smooth cadence.

NICOLAS BOILEAU–DESPRÉAUX,
(1636–1711) French poet, critic. *L'Art Politique*, cto. 1, l. 131–132 (1674).

François Malherbe (1555–1628) exercised a
profound influence on French verse, initiating
a reaction against the florid Baroque poetry of
his day in favor of a clear, neo–classical style.

6 Every individual ought to know at
least one poet from cover to cover:

if not as a guide through the world,
then as a yardstick for the language.

JOSEPH BRODSKY, (b. 1940)
Russian–born U.S. poet, critic. "To Please a
Shadow," sct. 5, *Less Than One: Selected
Essays* (1986). (Essay written 1983).

Brodsky recommended W.H. Auden as qualified on both counts.

7 Shakespeare was of us, Milton was
for us,
Burns, Shelley, were with us—they
watch from their graves!

ROBERT BROWNING, (1812–1889) British
poet. "The Lost Leader," st. 1, *Dramatic
Romances and Lyrics* (1845).

8 What's this, Aurora Leigh,
You write so of the poets and not
laugh?
Those virtuous liars, dreamers after
dark,
Exaggerators of the sun and moon,
And soothsayers in a tea–cup? I
write so
Of the only truth–tellers, now left
to God,
The only speakers of essential truth,
Opposed to relative, comparative,
And temporal truths;...
The only teachers who instruct
mankind,
From just a shadow on a
charnel–wall.

ELIZABETH BARRETT BROWNING,
(1806–1861) British poet. "Aurora Leigh,"
bk.1, l. 853–64 (1857).

9 I by no means rank poetry high in
the scale of intelligence—this may
look like affectation but it is my real
opinion. It is the lava of the imagination whose eruption prevents an
earthquake.

**GEORGE GORDON NOEL BYRON, 6TH
BARON BYRON,** (1788–1824) British poet.
Byron's Letters and Journals, vol. 3, ed. Leslie

Marchand (1974). Letter, Nov. 29, 1813, to
Annabella Milbanke (later Lady Byron).

10   Little do such men know the toil,
       the pains,
     The daily, nightly racking of the
       brains,
     To range the thoughts, the matter to
       digest,
     To cull fit phrases, and reject the
       rest.

CHARLES CHURCHILL, (1731–1764)
British clergyman, poet. *Gotham*, bk. 2, l. 11
(1764).

11   The worst tragedy for a poet is to be
     admired through being misunder-
     stood.

JEAN COCTEAU, (1889–1963) French
author, filmmaker. *Le Coq et l'Arlequin, Le
Rappel à l'Ordre* (1926), repr. in *Collected
Works*, vol. 9 (1950). (Originally published
1918).

12   I wish our clever young poets would
     remember my homely definitions of
     prose and poetry; that is, prose =
     words in their best order;—poetry =
     the *best* words in the best order.

SAMUEL TAYLOR COLERIDGE,
(1772–1834) British poet, critic. *Table Talk,*
"12 July 1827," *Specimens of the Table Talk of
Samuel Taylor Coleridge*, ed. Henry Nelson
Coleridge (1835). Repr. in *Collected Works*,
vol. 14, ed. Kathleen Coburn (1990).

13   No man was ever yet a great poet,
     without being at the same time a
     profound philosopher.

SAMUEL TAYLOR COLERIDGE,
(1772–1834) British poet, critic. *Biographia
Literaria*, ch. 15 (1817).

14   That willing suspension of disbelief
     for the moment, which constitutes
     poetic faith.

SAMUEL TAYLOR COLERIDGE,
(1772–1834) British poet, critic. *Biographia
Literaria*, ch. 14 (1817).

15   Then Pope, as harmony itself exact,
     In verse well disciplined, complete,
       compact,
     Gave virtue and morality a grace,
     That, quite eclipsing pleasure's
       painted face,
     Levied a tax of wonder and
       applause,
     Even on the fools that trampled on
       their laws.
     But he (his musical finesse was such,
     So nice his ear, so delicate his
       touch)
     Made poetry a mere mechanic art;
     And every warbler has his tune by
       heart.

WILLIAM COWPER, (1731–1800) British
poet. *Table Talk*, l. 646–55 (1782). Repr. in
Poetical Works, ed. H.S. Milford (1934).

16   It is the logic of our times,
     No subject for immortal verse—
     That we who lived by honest
       dreams
     Defend the bad against the worse.

CECIL DAY LEWIS, (1904–1972) British
poet. "Where Are the War Poets?" *Word Over
All* (1943).

17   This is my letter to the World
     That never wrote to Me—
     The simple News that Nature
       told—
     With tender Majesty.

EMILY DICKINSON, (1830–1886) U.S.
poet. "This is My Letter to the World," st. 1
(written c. 1862, published 1890). Repr. in
The Complete Poems, no. 441, Harvard *variorum* edition (1955).

18   I am two fools, I know,
     For loving, and for saying so
     In whining poetry.

JOHN DONNE, (c. 1572–1631) British
divine, metaphysical poet. "The Triple Fool,"
Songs and Sonnets (1633). Repr. in *Complete
Poetry and Selected Prose*, ed. John Hayward
(1929).

19 For that fine madness still he did
    retain
    Which rightly should possess a
    poet's brain.

MICHAEL DRAYTON, (1563–1631) British
poet. "To Henry Reynolds," *Of Poets and
Poesy*, l. 109 (1627).

Referring to Christopher Marlowe.

20 'Tis sufficient to say, according to the
    proverb, that here is God's plenty.

JOHN DRYDEN, (1631–1700) British poet,
dramatist, critic. *Fables Ancient and Modern*,
preface (1700).

Referring to Geoffrey Chaucer.

21 Immature poets imitate; mature
    poets steal.

T.S. (THOMAS STEARNS) ELIOT,
(1888–1965) Anglo–American poet, critic. *The
Sacred Wood*, "Philip Massinger" (1920).

22 Poetry is not a turning loose of
    emotion, but an escape from emo-
    tion; it is not the expression of per-
    sonality, but an escape from person-
    ality. But, of course, only those who
    have personality and emotions
    know what it means to want to
    escape from these things.

T.S. (THOMAS STEARNS) ELIOT,
(1888–1965) Anglo–American poet, critic.
"Tradition and the Individual Talent," sct. 1,
Selected Prose of T.S. Eliot, ed. Frank Kermode
(1975). First published in *Egoist* (London, Sept.
and Dec. 1919).

23 Poetry is a mere drug, Sir.

GEORGE FARQUHAR, (1678–1707) Irish
dramatist. Pamphlet, in *Love and a Bottle*, act
3, sc. 2 (1698). Repr. in *Complete Works*, ed.
Charles Stonehill (1930).

24 Constantly risking absurdity and
    death whenever he performs above
    the heads of his audience the poet
    like an acrobat climbs on rime to a
    high wire of his own making.

LAWRENCE FERLINGHETTI, (b. 1919)
U.S. poet, publisher. "A Coney Island of the
Mind," sct. 15 (1958).

25 A poem ... begins as a lump in the
    throat, a sense of wrong, a home-
    sickness, a lovesickness.... It finds
    the thought and the thought finds
    the words.

ROBERT FROST, (1874–1963) U.S. poet.
*The Letters of Robert Frost to Louis Unter-
meyer* (1963).

Letter, Jan. 1, 1916, to poet and anthologist
Louis Untermeyer.

26 No wonder poets sometimes have
    to *seem*
    So much more business–like than
    business men.
    Their wares are so much harder to
    get rid of.

ROBERT FROST, (1874–1963) U.S. poet.
"New Hampshire," *New Hampshire* (1923).

27 Poetry is a way of taking life by the
    throat.

ROBERT FROST, (1874–1963) U.S. poet.
Quoted in Elizabeth S. Sergeant, *Robert Frost:
the Trial by Existence*, ch. 18 (1960).

28 Writing free verse is like playing
    tennis with the net down.

ROBERT FROST, (1874–1963) U.S. poet.
Address, May 17, 1935, Milton Academy,
Massachusetts.

29 Poetry is the language in which
    man explores his own amaze-
    ment ...says heaven and earth in
    one word ... speaks of himself
    and his predicament as though for
    the first time. It has the virtue of
    being able to say twice as much as
    prose in half the time, and the
    drawback, if you do not give it
    your full attention, of seeming
    to say half as much in twice the
    time.

CHRISTOPHER FRY, (b. 1907) British playwright. *Time* (New York, April 3, 1950).

30 What thoughts I have of you
tonight, Walt Whitman, for I walked
down the sidestreets under the trees
with a headache self–conscious looking at the full moon.
  In my hungry fatigue, and shopping for images, I went into the
neon fruit supermarket, dreaming
of your enumerations!

ALLEN GINSBERG, (b. 1926) U.S. poet. "A Supermarket in California," *Howl and Other Poems* (1956).

Opening lines.

31 If there's no money in poetry,
neither is there poetry in money.

ROBERT GRAVES, (1895–1985) British poet, novelist. "Mammon," *Mammon and the Black Goddess* (1965). Speech, Dec. 6, 1963, London School of Economics.

32 Nine–tenths of English poetic
literature is the result either of vulgar careerism or of a poet trying to
keep his hand in. Most poets are
dead by their late twenties.

ROBERT GRAVES, (1895–1985) British poet, novelist. Quoted in *Observer* (London, Nov. 11, 1962).

33 He indeed cloys with sweetness; he
obscures with splendour; he fatigues
with gaiety. We are stifled on beds of
roses.

WILLIAM HAZLITT, (1778–1830) British essayist. *The Spirit of the Age*, "T. Moore Leigh Hunt," (1825). Referring to the poet Thomas Moore.

34 Poetry is the universal language
which the heart holds with nature
and itself. He who has a contempt
for poetry, cannot have much respect
for himself, or for anything else.

WILLIAM HAZLITT, (1778–1830) British essayist. *Lectures on the English Poets*, "On Poetry in General" (1818).

35 Hearken unto a Verser, who may
chance
Rhyme thee to good, and make a
bait of pleasure.
A verse may find him, who a sermon flies,
And turn delight into a sacrifice.

GEORGE HERBERT, (1593–1633) British poet, clergyman. "The Church Porch," st. 1, *The Temple* (1633). Repr. in *The Works of George Herbert*, ed. Helen Gardner (1961).

36 Who says that fictions only and
false hair
Become a verse? Is there in truth no
beauty?
Is all good structure in a winding
stair?
May no lines pass, except they do
their duty
Not to a true, but painted chair?

GEORGE HERBERT, (1593–1633) British poet, clergyman. "Jordan (I)", st. 1, *The Temple* (1633). Repr. in *The Works of George Herbert*, ed. Helen Gardner (1961).

The Winding Stair was the title of a volume of verse by W.B. Yeats (1933).

37 Experience has taught me, when I
am shaving of a morning, to keep
watch over my thoughts, because, if
a line of poetry strays into my
memory, my skin bristles so that
the razor ceases to act.

A.E. (ALFRED EDWARD) HOUSMAN, (1859–1936) British poet. "The Name and Nature of Poetry." Lecture, May 9, 1933, at Senate House, Cambridge, England.

"The seat of this sensation," Housman explained, "is the pit of the stomach."

38 Donne, for not keeping of accent,
deserved hanging ... Shakespeare

wanted art ... Sharpham, Day,
Dekker, were all rogues.

BEN JONSON, (c. 1572–1637) British
dramatist, poet. *Conversations with William
Drummond of Hawthornden* (written 1619,
published 1711). Repr. in *Ben Jonson's Conversations with William Drummond of
Hawthornden*, ed. R.F. Patterson (1923).

39 Poetry should surprise by a fine
excess and not by singularity—it
should strike the reader as a wording of his own highest thoughts,
and appear almost a remembrance.

JOHN KEATS, (1795–1821) British poet.
Letters of John Keats, no. 51, ed. Frederick
Page (1954). Letter, Feb. 27, 1818.

40 We hate poetry that has a palpable
design upon us—and if we do not
agree, seems to put its hand in its
breeches pocket. Poetry should be
great and unobtrusive, a thing
which enters into one's soul, and
does not startle it or amaze it with
itself, but with its subject.

JOHN KEATS, (1795–1821) British poet.
Letters of John Keats, no. 44, ed. Frederick
Page (1954). Letter, Feb. 3, 1818.

41 When power leads man towards
arrogance, poetry reminds him
of his limitations. When power
narrows the area of man's concern,
poetry reminds him of the richness and diversity of existence.
When power corrupts, poetry
cleanses.

JOHN FITZGERALD KENNEDY,
(1917–1963) U.S. Democratic politician, president. quoted in *The New York Times* (Oct.
27, 1963). Address, at dedication of Robert
Frost Library, Amherst College, Oct. 26, 1963.

Last major public address. Previously, in a
speech to the annual meeting of the Harvard
Alumni Association, Cambridge, Massachusetts, June 14, 1956, Kennedy said, "If more
politicians knew poetry, and more poets knew
politics, I am convinced the world would be a
little better place to live."

42 Prose on certain occasions can bear
a great deal of poetry; on the other
hand, poetry sinks and swoons
under a moderate weight of prose.

WALTER SAVAGE LANDOR, (1775–1864)
British author. *Imaginary Conversations,*
"Archdeacon Hare and Walter Landor," *The
Last Fruit of an Old Tree* (1853).

43 As civilization advances, poetry
almost necessarily declines.

THOMAS BABINGTON MACAULAY,
(1800–1859) British historian, Whig politician.
"Milton, Critical and Historical Essays" (1843).
Originally published in *Edinburgh Review*
(Aug. 1825).

Macaulay went on to explain: "In proportion as
men know more and think more, they look less
at individuals and more at classes. They therefore make better theories and worse poems."

44 Perhaps no person can be a poet, or
can even enjoy poetry, without a
certain unsoundness of mind.

THOMAS BABINGTON MACAULAY,
(1800–1859) British historian, Whig politician.
"Milton, Critical and Historical Essays" (1843).
Originally published in *Edinburgh Review*
(Aug. 1825).

45 Poetry is what Milton saw when he
went blind.

DON MARQUIS, (1878–1937) U.S.
humorist, journalist. Quoted in *O Rare Don
Marquis*, ch. 11, E. Anthony (1962).

46 Writing a book of poetry is like dropping a rose petal down the Grand
Canyon and waiting for the echo.

DON MARQUIS, (1878–1937) U.S.
humorist, journalist. Quoted in *O Rare Don
Marquis*, ch. 6, E. Anthony (1962).

This aphorism was published alone, in Don
Marquis's "Sun Dial" column, instead of a long
piece on the futility of writing poetry, abandoned on the grounds that it was too much of a
plaint.

47 My verse
    has brought me

no roubles to spare:
no craftsmen have made
mahogany chairs for my house.

VLADIMIR MAYAKOVSKY, (1893–1930)
Russian poet, dramatist. "*At the top of my
voice*—First Prelude to a Poem of the Five Year
Plan," (1929–1930), trans. by George Reavey.

This was Mayakovsky's last completed poem
before his suicide.

48   Most people ignore most poetry
because
most poetry ignores most people.

ADRIAN MITCHELL, (b. 1932) British
poet, author. *Poems*, epigraph (1964).

49   Poetry, that is to say the poetic, is a
primal necessity.

MARIANNE MOORE, (1887–1972) U.S.
poet. "Comment," *Complete Prose* (1987).First
published in *Dial*, no. 81 (New York, Aug.
1926).

50   The high–water mark, so to
speak, of Socialist literature is W.H.
Auden, a sort of gutless Kipling.

GEORGE ORWELL, (1903–1950) British
author. *The Road to Wigan Pier*, ch. 11 (1937).

51   Cibber! write all thy verses upon
glasses,
The only way to save 'em from our
arses.

ALEXANDER POPE, (1688–1744) British
satirical poet. "Epigrams Occasioned by Cibber's Verses in Praise of Nash," no. 2, *Minor
Poems*, eds. Norman Ault and John Butt (1954).

Referring to Colley Cibber, dramatist and poet.
Cibber (1671–1757) was Poet Laureate for 27
years from 1730, and is generally considered
one of the worst poets to hold the office,
admitting himself that he was given the post
principally for being a good Whig.

52   Sir, I admit your general rule,
That every poet is a fool,
But you yourself may serve to show
it,

That every fool is not a poet.

ALEXANDER POPE, (1688–1744) British
satirical poet. "Epigram from the French"
(1732).

53   Now, again, poetry
violent, arcane, common,
hewn of the commonest living substance
into archway, portal, frame
I grasp for you, your bloodstained
splinters, your
ancient and stubborn poise
—as the earth trembles—
burning out from the grain

ADRIENNE RICH, (b. 1929) U.S. poet.
"The Fact of a Doorframe," st. 3, *The Fact of a
Doorframe* (1974).

54   I invented the colors of the vowels!—*A* black, *E* white, *I* red, *O*
blue, *U* green—I made rules for the
form and movement of each con-
sonant, and, and with instinctive
rhythms, I flattered myself that I
had created a poetic language
accessible, some day, to all the
senses.

ARTHUR RIMBAUD, (1854–1891) French
poet. *Une Saison en Enfer*, "Délires II:
Alchimie du Verbe" (1874). Repr. in *Collected
Poems*, ed. Oliver Bernard (1962).

Rimbaud had already expressed the notion of
the vowels possessing particular colors in the
poem "Voyelles" 1871.

55   Not marble nor the gilded
monuments
Of princes shall outlive this powerful rhyme.

WILLIAM SHAKESPEARE, (1564–1616)
British dramatist, poet. "Sonnet 55" (1609).

Opening lines.

56   Poetry is the record of the best and
happiest moments of the happiest
and best minds.

PERCY BYSSHE SHELLEY, (1792–1822) British poet. *A Defence of Poetry* (written 1821, published 1840).

57 Poets are the hierophants of an unapprehended inspiration; the mirrors of the gigantic shadows which futurity casts upon the present; the words which express what they understand not; the trumpets which sing to battle and feel not what they inspire; the influence which is moved not, but moves. Poets are the unacknowledged legislators of the world.

PERCY BYSSHE SHELLEY, (1792–1822) British poet. *A Defence of Poetry* (written 1821, published 1840).

Last words. In his *History of Rasselas* (1759) ch. 10, Dr. Samuel Johnson similarly wrote that the poet "must write as the interpreter of nature, and the legislator of mankind, and consider himself as presiding over the thoughts and manners of future generations." In our own century, W.H. Auden wrote—in *The Dyer's Hand*—"'The unacknowledged legislators of the world' describes the secret police, not the poets."

58 Poetry ... is ... a speaking picture, with this end: to teach and delight.

SIR PHILIP SIDNEY, (1554–1586) British poet, diplomat, soldier. "An Apology for Poetry" (written 1579–1580, published 1595), ed. J. Churton Collins (1907).

59 Poetry is the supreme fiction, madame.
Take the moral law and make a nave of it
And from the nave build haunted heaven.

WALLACE STEVENS, (1879–1955) U.S. poet. "A High-Toned Old Christian Woman," *Harmonium* (1923).

60 What poet would not grieve to see His brother write as well as he? But rather than they should excel,

He'd wish his rivals all in Hell.

JONATHAN SWIFT, (1667–1745) Anglo–Irish satirist. "Verses on the Death of Dr Swift," l. 31–4 (1731). Repr. in *The Poems of Jonathan Swift*, ed. H. Williams (1958).

61 A poet can survive everything but a misprint.

OSCAR WILDE, (1854–1900) Anglo–Irish playwright, author. "The Children of the Poets," *Pall Mall Gazette* (London, Oct. 14, 1886). Quoted in *The Fireworks of Oscar Wilde*, ed. Owen Dudley Edwards (1989).

62 All good poetry is the spontaneous overflow of powerful feelings: it takes its origin from emotion recollected in tranquillity.

WILLIAM WORDSWORTH, (1770–1850) British poet. *Lyrical Ballads*, preface, 2nd edition (1801).

This sentiment, which is a central tenet in Wordsworth's criticism, has parallels in Schiller, *Ueber Bürgers Gedichte*, as well as Coleridge's *Notebooks*, in which he speaks of "recalling passion in tranquillity."

63 We poets in our youth begin in gladness;
But thereof comes in the end despondency and madness.

WILLIAM WORDSWORTH, (1770–1850) British poet. "Resolution and Independence," st. 7, *Poems in Two Volumes* (1807).

64 Irish poets, learn your trade, Sing whatever is well made, Scorn the sort now growing up All out of shape from toe to top.

WILLIAM BUTLER YEATS, (1865–1939) Irish poet and playwright. "Under Ben Bulben," sct. 5, *Last Poems* (1939).

Written five months before Yeats's death.

65 We make out of the quarrel with others, rhetoric, but of the quarrel with ourselves, poetry.

WILLIAM BUTLER YEATS, (1865–1939) Irish poet, playwright. "Anima Hominis," sct. 5, *Essays* (1924).

Police

1 When constabulary duty's to be
 done,
 A policeman's lot is not a happy
 one.

SIR WILLIAM SCHWENCK GILBERT, (1836–1911) British librettist. The police chorus, in *The Pirates of Penzance*, act 2 (1879), published in *The Savoy Operas* (1926).

2 Every society gets the kind of criminal it deserves. What is equally true is that every community gets the kind of law enforcement it insists on.

ROBERT KENNEDY, (1925–1968) U.S. attorney general, Democratic politician. *The Pursuit of Justice*, pt. 3, "Eradicating Free Enterprise in Organized Crime" (1964).

3 As far as I can see, the Polis as Polis, in this city, is Null an' Void!

SEAN O'CASEY, (1884–1964) Irish dramatist. Mrs. Madigan, in *Juno and the Paycock*, act 3 (1924). Referring to Dublin during the Irish Civil War in 1922.

4 Evenin' all.

JACK WARNER, (1895–1981) British actor. George Dixon (Jack Warner), in *Dixon of Dock Green* (TV series), created by Ted Willis (1955–1976).

Dixon started life in the film *The Blue Lamp* (1949). Though shot dead, he was resurrected by the BBC 6 years later, each episode ending with Dixon's familiar salute and "evenin' all."

Policy

1 The right honourable gentleman caught the Whigs bathing, and walked away with their clothes. He

has left them in the full enjoyment of their liberal positions, and he is himself a strict conservative of their garments.

BENJAMIN DISRAELI, (1804–1881) British statesman, author. Quoted in *The Fine Art of Political Wit*, ch. 4, Leon Harris (1964). Speech, Feb. 28, 1845.

Referring to the embracing of Whig policy on free trade by prime minister and fellow Tory, Robert Peel.

2 The longest suicide note in history.

GERALD KAUFMAN, (b. 1930) British Labour politician. Quoted in *The Time of My Life*, ch. 23, Denis Healey (1989).

Referring to the Labour Party's *New Hope For Britain* manifesto for the 1983 general election, which Labour lost: "the scale of our defeat was devastating," Healey wrote.

3 Where's the beef?

WALTER MONDALE, (b. 1928) U.S. Democratic politician, vice president. *Advertising and political slogan*. Campaign slogan for 1984 Democratic presidential nomination.

Originally used to advertise Wendy's Hamburgers, the words were taken up by Mondale's campaign team after a televised debate in which the candidate told rival Gary Hart, "When I hear your new ideas, I'm reminded of that ad, *Where's the beef?*" (March 11, 1984).

Political Correctness

1 It seems our fate to be incorrect ... and in our incorrectness stand.

ALICE WALKER, (b. 1944) U.S. author, critic. "From an Interview," *In Search of Our Mothers' Gardens* (1983). Originally published in *Interviews with Black Writers*, ed. John O'Brien (1973).

Political Parties

1 When great questions end, little parties begin.

WALTER BAGEHOT, (1826–1877) British economist, critic. *The English Constitution*, ch. 9 (1867).

2   No amount of cajolery, and no attempts at ethical or social seduction, can eradicate from my heart a deep burning hatred for the Tory Party.... So far as I am concerned they are lower than vermin.

ANEURIN BEVAN, (1897–1960) British Labour politician. Quoted in *Times* (London, July 5, 1948). Speech, July 4, 1948, Manchester.

Referring to the social policies of the Conservative Party, which "condemned millions of first–class people to semi–starvation." Bevan's words, which formed part of his speech to inaugurate the National Health Service, provoked widespread criticism by the press and embarrassment within his own party.

3   Party leads to vicious, corrupt and unprofitable legislation, for the sole purpose of defeating party.

JAMES FENIMORE COOPER, (1789–1851) U.S. novelist. *The American Democrat*, "On Party" (1838).

4   A Conservative government is an organised hypocrisy.

BENJAMIN DISRAELI, (1804–1881) British statesman, author. *Selected Speeches of the Late Right Honourable the Earl of Beaconsfield*, vol. 1, "Agricultural Distress," ed. T.E. Kebbes (1882). Speech, March 17, 1845, addressing Prime Minister Sir Robert Peel in the House of Commons, London.

Closing words of speech, on the abandonment of Peel's Protectionist policies on which his government had been elected.

5   A sect or a party is an elegant incognito, devised to save a man from the vexation of thinking.

RALPH WALDO EMERSON, (1803–1882) U.S. essayist, poet, philosopher. *Journals* (1909–1914). Journal entry, June 20, 1831.

6   A party of order or stability, and a party of progress or reform, are

both necessary elements of a healthy state of political life.

JOHN STUART MILL, (1806–1873) British philosopher, economist. *On Liberty*, ch. 2 (1859).

7   I find myself ... hoping a total end of all the unhappy divisions of mankind by party–spirit, which at best is but the madness of many for the gain of a few.

ALEXANDER POPE, (1688–1744) British satirical poet. *The Correspondence of Alexander Pope*, vol. 1, ed. George Sherburn (1956). Letter, Aug. 27, 1714.

Pope's words are also noted in their more quoted form in Swift's *Miscellanies*, "Thoughts on Various Subjects" (1727): "Party is the madness of many for the gain of a few."

8   You are pitiful isolated individuals; you are bankrupts; your role is played out. Go where you belong from now on—into the dustbin of history!

LEON TROTSKY, (1879–1940) Russian revolutionary. *History of the Russian Revolution*, vol. 3, ch. 10 (1933). Addressed to the Mensheviks, who participated in Kerensky's provisional government in 1917, overthrown by the Bolsheviks.

Politics

1   I agree with you that in politics, the middle way is none at all.

JOHN ADAMS, (1735–1826) U.S. statesman, president. *The Papers of John Adams*, vol. 4, Third Series, ed. R.J. Taylor (1979). Letter, March 23, 1776.

2   Man is naturally a political animal.

ARISTOTLE, (384–322 B.C.) Greek philosopher. *Politics*, bk. 1, ch. 2, sct. 1253a (c. 343 B.C.), trans. by William Ellis (1912).

3   Politics is the art of the possible.

OTTO VON BISMARCK, (1815–1898) Prussian statesman. Quoted in *Complete*

Works, vol. 7 (1924). Remark, Aug. 11, 1867.

Almost equally famous is Bismarck's dictum, "Politics is not an exact science" (speech, Dec 18, 1863, to Prussian legislature).

4   Politics are usually the executive expression of human immaturity.

VERA BRITTAIN, (1896–1970) British author, pacifist. *The Rebel Passion*, ch. 1 (1964).

5   Magnanimity in politics is not seldom the truest wisdom; and a great empire and little minds go ill together.

EDMUND BURKE, (1729–1797) Irish philosopher, statesman. *Speech on Conciliation with America: The Thirteen Resolutions, Works*, vol. 2 (1899). Speech, March 22, 1775, House of Commons, London.

6   In politics, what begins in fear usually ends in folly.

SAMUEL TAYLOR COLERIDGE, (1772–1834) British poet, critic. *Table Talk*, "5 Oct 1830," *Specimens of the Table Talk of Samuel Taylor Coleridge*, ed. Henry Nelson Coleridge (1835). Repr. in *Collected Works*, vol. 14, ed. Kathleen Coburn (1990).

7   Politics is not the art of the possible. It consists in choosing between the disastrous and the unpalatable.

JOHN KENNETH GALBRAITH, (b. 1908) U.S. economist. *Ambassador's Journal* (1969). Letter, March 2, 1962, to President Kennedy.

Written while Galbraith was serving as U.S. ambassador in India. See Bismarck on politics.

8   Whenever a man has cast a longing eye on [political offices], a rottenness begins in his conduct.

THOMAS JEFFERSON, (1743–1826) U.S. president. *The Writings of Thomas Jefferson*, vol. 7, ed. Paul L. Ford (1896). Letter, May 21, 1799.

9   Politics begin where the masses are, not where there are thousands, but where there are millions, that is where serious politics begin.

VLADIMIR ILYICH LENIN, (1870–1924) Russian revolutionary leader. (1920), published in *Selected Works*, vol. 7 (1937). Report to Seventh Congress of the Russian Communist Party, March 7, 1918.

10   Politics is war without bloodshed while war is politics with bloodshed.

MAO ZEDONG, (1893–1976) Chinese founder of the People's Republic of China. "On Protracted War," *Selected Works*, vol. 2 (1965). Lecture, May 1938.

11   In our time, political speech and writing are largely the defence of the indefensible.

GEORGE ORWELL, (1903–1950) British author. *Shooting an Elephant*, "Politics and the English Language" (1950). (Originally published 1946).

12   A radical is a man with both feet firmly planted in the air. A conservative is a man with two perfectly good legs, who, however, has never learned to walk forward. A reactionary is a somnambulist walking backwards. A liberal is a man who uses his legs and his hands at the behest ... of his head.

FRANKLIN DELANO ROOSEVELT, (1882–1945) U.S. Democratic politician, president. *Public Papers and Addresses of Franklin D. Roosevelt*, vol. 8 (1941). Radio broadcast, Oct. 26, 1939.

Politics and Politicians

1   The trouble with this country is that there are too many politicians who believe, with a conviction based on experience, that you can fool all of the people all of the time.

FRANKIN PIERCE ADAMS, (1881–1960) U.S. journalist, humorist. *Nods and Becks*, p. 74 (1944).

James Thurber had earlier written, "You can fool too many of the people too much of the time" in *The New Yorker*, April 29, 1939 (Repr. in *Fables for our Time*, "The Owl Who Was God," 1940). See Abraham Lincoln's comment on deception.

2   A political leader must keep looking over his shoulder all the time to see if the boys are still there. If they aren't still there, he's no longer a political leader.

BERNARD BARUCH, (1870–1965) U.S. financier. Quoted in obituary, *The New York Times* (June 21, 1965).

3   The Prime Minister has an absolute genius for putting flamboyant labels on empty luggage.

ANEURIN BEVAN, (1897–1960) British Labour politician. Quoted in *Aneurin Bevan*, vol. 2, ch. 16, Michael Foot (1973). Queen's Speech debate, House of Commons, Nov. 3, 1959.

Referring to Harold Macmillan.

4   Your representative owes you, not his industry only, but his judgement; and he betrays instead of serving you if he sacrifices it to your opinion.

EDMUND BURKE, (1729–1797) Irish philosopher, statesman. *Speech to the Electors of Bristol, Works*, vol. 2 (1899). Speech, Nov. 3, 1774.

5   a politician is an arse upon which everyone has sat except a man.

E.E. (EDWARD ESTLIN) CUMMINGS, (1894–1962) U.S. poet. "A politician," *1 x 1* (1944).

6   A sophistical rhetorician, inebriated with the exuberance of his own verbosity, and gifted with an egotistical imagination that can at all times command an interminable and inconsistent series of arguments to malign an opponent and to glorify himself.

BENJAMIN DISRAELI, (1804–1881) British statesman, author. Quoted in *Times* (London, July 29, 1878). Speech, July 27, 1878, Knightsbridge, London.

Referring to Prime Minister Gladstone. On another occasion, Disraeli said of Gladstone, "He has not a single redeeming defect."

7   Resolved to ruin or to rule the state.

JOHN DRYDEN, (1631–1700) British poet, dramatist, critic. *Absalom and Achitophel*, pt. 1, l. 174 (1681).

Referring to Achitophel, who in the poem represents the statesman Anthony Ashley Cooper, Earl of Shaftesbury, "In friendship false, implacable in hate."

8   It is not necessary that every time he rises he should give his famous imitation of a semi–house–trained polecat.

MICHAEL FOOT, (b. 1913) British Labour politician, prime minister. *Hansard*, col. 668. Speech, March 2, 1978, House of Commons.

Referring to Conservative politician Norman Tebbit.

9   Politicians are the same all over: they promise to build a bridge even where there is no river.

NIKITA KHRUSHCHEV, (1894–1971) Soviet premier. Quoted in *New York Herald–Tribune* (Aug. 22, 1963).

Khrushchev is earlier reported to have uttered these words at a press conference, Oct. 1960, Glen Cove, New York.

10   Did you ever
notice that when
a politician
does get an idea
he usually
gets it all wrong.

DON MARQUIS, (1878–1937) U.S. humorist, journalist. *Archys life of mehitabel*, ch. 11 (1933).

11 We assume that politicians are without honor. We read their statements
trying to crack the code. The scan-
dals of their politics: not so much
that men in high places lie, only that
they do so with such indifference, so
endlessly, still expecting to be
believed. We are accustomed to the
contempt inherent in the political lie.

ADRIENNE RICH, (b. 1929) U.S. poet.
"Women and Honor: Some Notes on Lying"
(originally published 1977). Repr. in *On Lies,
Secrets, and Silence* (1980).

Paper read at Hartwick College, New York,
June 1975.

12 We all know that Prime Ministers
are wedded to the truth, but like
other wedded couples they sometimes live apart.

[**H.H. (HECTOR HUGH) MUNRO**]
SAKI, (1870–1916) Scottish author. Lady Caroline, in *The Unbearable Bassington*, ch. 13
(1912).

13 Faith, there hath been many great
men that have flattered the people
who ne'er loved them.

WILLIAM SHAKESPEARE, (1564–1616)
British dramatist, poet. Second Officer, in *Cori-
olanus*, act 2, sc. 2, l. 7–8 (1623).

14 Get thee glass eyes,
And, like a scurvy politician, seem
To see the things thou dost not.

WILLIAM SHAKESPEARE, (1564–1616)
British dramatist, poet. Lear, in *King Lear*, act 4,
sc. 5, l. 166–8 (1623).

15 A politician is a statesman who
approaches every question with
an open mouth.

ADLAI STEVENSON, (1900–1965) U.S.
Democratic politician. Quoted in *The Fine Art
of Political Wit*, ch. 10, Leon Harris (1964).

16 He aspired to power instead of influence, and as a result forfeited both.

**A.J.P. (ALAN JOHN PERCIVALE) TAY-
LOR,** (1906–1990) British historian. *English
History, 1914–1945*, ch. 1 (1965).

Referring to press magnate Lord Northcliffe,
who made the London *Times* and other newspapers mouthpieces for his political ambitions.

17 Only he has the calling for politics
who is sure that he will not crumble
when the world from his point of
view is too stupid or base for what
he wants to offer. Only he who in
the face of all this can say "In spite
of all!" has the calling for politics.

MAX WEBER, (1864–1920) German sociologist. "Politics as a Vocation," *Essays in Soci-
ology*, eds. H.H. Gerth and C. Wright Mills
(1946). (Essay originally published 1919).

Polls

1 A straw vote only shows which way
the hot air blows.

**O. HENRY [WILLIAM SYDNEY
PORTER],** (1862–1910) U.S. short–story
writer. *Rolling Stones*, "A Ruler of Men"
(1913).

Pope, the

1 The Papacy is no other than the
ghost of the deceased Roman
Empire, sitting crowned upon the
grave thereof.

THOMAS HOBBES, (1588–1679) British
philosopher. *Leviathan*, pt. 4, ch. 47 (1651).

Popular Culture

1 Popular art is normally decried as
vulgar by the cultivated people of
its time; then it loses favor with its
original audience as a new generation grows up; then it begins to

merge into the softer lighting of "quaint," and cultivated people become interested in it, and finally it begins to take on the archaic dignity of the primitive.

NORTHROP FRYE, (b. 1912) Canadian literary critic.. "Mythical Phase: Symbol as Archetype,"' *Anatomy of Criticism* (1957).

2   Two things only the people
       anxiously desire,
     Bread and circuses.

JUVENAL, (c. 60–c. 130) Roman satiric poet. *Satires*, no. 10, l. 80–1.

Popular Music

1   Extraordinary how potent cheap
     music is.

NOËL COWARD, (1899–1973) British actor, playwright, composer. Amanda, in *Private Lives*, act 1 (1930), published in *Play Parade* (1931).

In the 1930 recording of the play, the words (spoken by Gertrude Lawrence) were "Strange how potent cheap music is."

Popularity

1   Popularity? It's glory's small
     change.

VICTOR HUGO, (1802–1885) French poet, dramatist, novelist. Don Salluste, in *Ruy Blas*, act 3, sc. 5 (1838).

2   He's liked, but he's not well liked.

ARTHUR MILLER, (b. 1915) U.S. dramatist. Biff, in *Death of a Salesman*, act 1 (1949).

Referring to Bernard, his schoolmate.

Population

1   Population, when unchecked,
     increases in a geometrical ratio.
     Subsistence increases only in an

arithmetical ratio. A slight acquaintance with numbers will show the immensity of the first power in comparison of the second.

THOMAS ROBERT MALTHUS, (1766–1834) British economist, sociologist. *An Essay on the Principle of Population*, ch. 1 (1798).

Pornography

1   What I wanted to get at is the value
     difference between pornographic
     playing–cards when you're a kid,
     and pornographic playing–cards
     when you're older. It's that when
     you're a kid you use the cards as a
     substitute for a real experience, and
     when you're older you use real expe-
     rience as a substitute for the fantasy.

EDWARD ALBEE, (b. 1928) U.S. playwright. Jerry, in *The Zoo Story* (1959).

2   Pornography is the attempt to insult
     sex, to do dirt on it.

D.H. (DAVID HERBERT) LAWRENCE, (1885–1930) British author. *Phoenix: The Posthumous Papers of D.H. Lawrence*, pt. 3, ed. E. McDonald (1936). *Pornography and Obscenity* (1930).

Lawrence admitted, however, that the definition of pornography varied according to the individual: "What is pornography to one man is the laughter of genius to another."

3   What pornography is really about,
     ultimately, isn't sex but death.

SUSAN SONTAG, (b. 1933) U.S. essayist. "The Pornographic Imagination," sct. 4, *Styles of Radical Will* (1969). Originally published in *Partisan Review* (New Brunswick, NJ, Spring 1967).

Portents

1   The Pharisees also with the Sad-
     ducees came, and tempting desired

him that he would shew them a sign from heaven. He answered and said unto them, When it is evening, ye say, It will be fair weather: for the sky is red. And in the morning, It will be foul weather today: for the sky is red and lowring. O ye hypocrites, ye can discern the face of the sky; but can ye not discern the signs of the times?

BIBLE: NEW TESTAMENT, Jesus, in *Matthew*, 16:1–3.

2   The Ides of March have come.

GAIUS CAESAR [GAIUS JULIUS CAESAR], (100–44 B.C.) Roman general and emperor. Quoted in *Parallel Lives*, "Caesar," sct. 63, Plutarch.

Reputedly spoken by Caesar on his way to the forum on March 15, 44 B.C., the day of his assassination, recalling the warning of a soothsayer.

3   I saw ten thousand talkers whose tongues were all broken,
I saw guns and sharp swords in the hands of young children,
And it's a hard, it's a hard, it's a hard, it's a hard,
It's a hard rain's a–gonna fall.

BOB DYLAN [ROBERT ALLEN ZIMMERMAN], (b. 1941) U.S. singer, songwriter. "A Hard Rain's A–Gonna Fall" (song), on the album *The Freewheelin' Bob Dylan* (1963).

Portraits

1   Mr. Lely, I desire you would use all your skill to paint my picture truly like me, and not flatter me at all; but remark all these roughnesses, pimples, warts, and everything as you see me, otherwise I will never pay a farthing for it.

OLIVER CROMWELL, (1599–1658) British Parliamentarian general, Lord Protector of

England. Quoted in *Anecdotes of Painting in England*, vol. 3, ch. 1, Horace Walpole (1763).

Remark to painter Sir Peter Lely, c. 1657, usually quoted "warts and all."

2   There are only two styles of portrait painting; the serious and the smirk.

CHARLES DICKENS, (1812–1870) British novelist. Miss La Creevy, in *Nicholas Nickleby*, ch. 10 (1838–1839).

3   She is older than the rocks among which she sits; like the vampire, she has been dead many times, and learned the secrets of the grave.

WALTER PATER, (1839–1894) British essayist, critic. *Studies in the History of the Renaissance*, "Leonardo da Vinci" (1873).

Referring to the Mona Lisa.

Possibility

1   I dwell in Possibility—
A fairer House than Prose—
More numerous of Windows—
Superior—for Doors—

EMILY DICKINSON, (1830–1886) U.S. poet. "I Dwell in Possibility" (written c. 1862, published 1929). Repr. in *The Complete Poems*, no. 657, Harvard *variorum* edition (1955).

Posterity

1   "We are always doing," says he, "something for posterity, but I would fain see posterity do something for us."

JOSEPH ADDISON, (1672–1719) British essayist. *Spectator* (London, Aug. 20, 1714), no. 583, *The Spectator*, ed. D.F. Bond (1965).

In the style of an old fellow of a college, articulating the feelings of "most people."

2 After being Turned Down by numerous Publishers, he had decided to write for Posterity.

GEORGE ADE, (1866–1944) U.S. humorist, playwright. "The Fable of the Bohemian who had Hard Luck," *Fables in Slang* (1899).

Of the "main Bohemian."

3 To be remembered after we are dead, is but poor recompense for being treated with contempt while we are living.

WILLIAM HAZLITT, (1778–1830) British essayist. *Characteristics: In the Manner of Rochefoucault's Maxims,* no. 429 (1823), repr. in *The Complete Works of William Hazlitt,* vol. 9, ed. P.P. Howe (1932).

4 Your descendants shall gather your fruits.

VIRGIL [PUBLIUS VERGILIUS MARO], (70–19 B.C.) Roman poet. *Eclogues,* no. 9, l. 50 (37 B.C.).

Potential

1 One's prime is elusive. You little girls, when you grow up, must be on the alert to recognize your prime at whatever time of your life it may occur. You must then live it to the full.

MURIEL SPARK, (b. 1918) British novelist. Miss Brodie, in *The Prime of Miss Jean Brodie,* ch. 1 (1961).

Pound, Ezra

1 He was a village explainer, excellent if you were a village, but if you were not, not.

GERTRUDE STEIN, (1874–1946) U.S. author. *The Autobiography of Alice B. Toklas,* ch. 7 (1933).

When asked later what she meant by calling Pound (whom she "liked ... but did not find

amusing") "a village explainer," Stein told Thornton Wilder, "Ezra Pound still lives in a village and his world is a kind of village and people keep explaining things when they live in a village.... I have come not to mind if certain people live in villages and some of my friends still appear to live in villages and a village can be cozy as well as intuitive but must one really keep perpetually explaining and elucidating?" (Quoted in Frederic Prokosch *Voices: A Memoir,* "The Evil Corner," 1983).

Poverty and the Poor

1 Poverty is an anomaly to rich people. It is very difficult to make out why people who want dinner do not ring the bell.

WALTER BAGEHOT, (1826–1877) British economist, critic. *The Waverley Novels,* vol. 2, *Literary Studies* (1878). (Article originally published 1858).

2 Blessed are the poor in spirit: for theirs is the kingdom of heaven.

BIBLE: NEW TESTAMENT, Jesus, in *Matthew,* 5:3.The first of the Beatitudes, from the Sermon on the Mount.

3 Almost every desire a poor man has is a punishable offence.

LOUIS–FERDINAND CÉLINE, (1894–1961) French author. The narrator (Ferdinand Bardamu), in *Journey to the End of the Night* (1932, trans. 1934).

4 There is no scandal like rags, nor any crime so shameful as poverty.

GEORGE FARQUHAR, (1678–1707) Irish dramatist. Archer, a "gentleman of broken fortunes," in *The Beaux' Stratagem,* act 1, sc. 1 (1707). Repr. in *Complete Works,* ed. Charles Stonehill (1930).

5 I used to think I was poor. Then they told me I wasn't poor, I was needy. Then they told me it was self–defeating to think of myself as needy, I was deprived. Then they told me deprived was a bad image, I was underprivileged. Then they told me underprivileged was overused, I was disadvantaged. I still don't have a dime. But I sure have a great vocabulary.

JULES FEIFFER, (b. 1929) U.S. cartoonist. Quoted in *Political Dictionary*, "Disadvantaged," William Safire (1968, rev. 1978). Cartoon, 1965.

6 Let not ambition mock their useful toil,
Their homely joys, and destiny obscure;
Nor grandeur hear with a disdainful smile,
The short and simple annals of the poor.

THOMAS GRAY, (1716–1771) British poet. "Elegy Written in a Country Churchyard," st. 8 (1751). Repr. in *Poetical Works*, ed. J. Rogers (1953).

7 Too poor for a bribe, and too proud to importune,
He had not the method of making a fortune.

THOMAS GRAY, (1716–1771) British poet. "Sketch of his Own Character "(written 1761), published in *Poetical Works*, ed. J. Rogers (1953).

8 That the poor are invisible is one of the most important things about them. They are not simply neglected and forgotten as in the old rhetoric of reform; what is much worse, they are not seen.

MICHAEL HARRINGTON, (1928–1989) U.S. social scientist, author. *The Other America*, ch. 1, sct. 1 (1962).

9 Oh, God! that bread should be so dear,
And flesh and blood so cheap!

THOMAS HOOD, (1799–1845) British poet. "The Song of the Shirt," st. 5 (1843). Repr. in *Complete Poetical Works*, ed. Walter Jerrold (1906).

10 It's no disgrace t' be poor, but it might as well be.

KIN HUBBARD (F. [FRANK] McKINNEY HUBBARD), (1868–1930) U.S. humorist, journalist. *Abe Martin's Sayings and Sketches* (1915). *Short Furrows* (1911).

11 Resolve not to be poor: whatever you have, spend less. Poverty is a great enemy to human happiness; it certainly destroys liberty, and it makes some virtues impracticable, and others extremely difficult.

SAMUEL JOHNSON, (1709–1784) British author, lexicographer. Quoted in James Boswell, *Life of Dr. Johnson* (1791). Letter, Dec. 7, 1782, to Boswell.

12 This mournful truth is ev'rywhere confessed,
Slow rises worth by poverty depressed.

SAMUEL JOHNSON, (1709–1784) British author, lexicographer. "London," l. 176–7 (1738). Repr. in *Works of Samuel Johnson*, Yale Edition, vol. 6, eds. E.L. McAdam, Jr. and G. Milne (1964).

13 Here we all live in a state of ambitious poverty.

JUVENAL, (c. 60–c. 130) Roman satiric poet. *Satires*, no. 3, l.182.

14 If a free society cannot help the many who are poor, it cannot save the few who are rich.

JOHN FITZGERALD KENNEDY, (1917–1963) U.S. Democratic politician, president. "Inaugural address," *Public Papers of the Presidents of the United States: John F. Kennedy, 1961*. Jan. 20, 1961, Washington D.C.

15 The forgotten man at the bottom of the economic pyramid.

FRANKLIN DELANO ROOSEVELT, (1882–1945) U.S. Democratic politician, president. *Public Papers and Addresses of Franklin D. Roosevelt*, vol. 1 (1938). Radio broadcast, April 7, 1932.

16 Poverty keeps together more homes than it breaks up.

[H.H. (Hector Hugh) Munro]
Saki, (1870–1916) Scottish author. *The Baroness*, in "Esmé" *The Chronicles of Clovis* (1911).

17 Oh, I realize it's a penny here and a penny there, but look at me: I've worked myself up from nothing to a state of extreme poverty.

Arthur Sheekman, U.S. screenwriter. Groucho Marx as himself, in *Monkey Business* (film) (1931). Norman McLeod.

18 How to live well on nothing a year.

William Makepeace Thackeray, (1811–1863) British author. *Vanity Fair*, ch. 36 (title of chapter) (1848).

Power

1 Power tends to corrupt, and absolute power corrupts absolutely. Great men are almost always bad man.

John Emerich Edward Dalberg, 1st Baron Acton, (1834–1902) British historian. *The Life and Letters of Mandell Creighton*, vol. 1, ch. 13, ed. Louise Creighton (1904). Letter, April 3, 1887, to Bishop Mandell Creighton.

William Pitt the Elder had made a similar observation, in a speech to the House of Lords, Jan. 9, 1770: "Unlimited power is apt to corrupt the minds of those who possess it." In the present century, the economist J.W. Galbraith wrote, "In the United States, though power corrupts, the expectation of power paralyzes." ("The United States," published in *New York* Nov. 15, 1971, repr. in *A View from the Stands*, 1986).

2 Power tires only those who do not have it.

Giulio Andreotti, (b. 1919) Italian Christian Democrat politician, prime minister. Quoted in *Independent on Sunday* (London, April 5, 1992).

Reply when asked how he had survived so long in power.

3 It is a strange desire, to seek power, and to lose liberty; or to seek power over others, and to lose power over a man's self.

Francis Bacon, (1561–1626) British philosopher, essayist, statesman. *Essays*, "Of Great Place" (1597–1625).

4 The purpose of getting power is to be able to give it away.

Aneurin Bevan, (1897–1960) British Labour politician. Quoted in *Aneurin Bevan*, vol. 1, ch. 1, Michael Foot (1962).

5 I am monarch of all I survey,
My right there is none to dispute.

William Cowper, (1731–1800) British poet. "Verses Supposed to be Written by Alexander Selkirk," l. 1–2 (1782). Repr. in *Poetical Works*, ed. H.S. Milford (1934).

6 Power is given only to those who dare to lower themselves and pick it up. Only one thing matters, one thing; to be able to dare!

Feodor Dostoyevsky, (1821–1881) Russian novelist. Raskolnikov, in *Crime and Punishment*, pt. 5, ch. 4 (published 1866), trans. by David McDuff (1991).

Raskolnikov explains to Sonya his motives for committing murder: "I wanted to *make the dare*, and so I killed someone."

7 The love of liberty is the love of others; the love of power is the love of ourselves.

William Hazlitt, (1778–1830) British essayist. *Political Essays*, "The Times Newspaper" (1819).

8 Political power grows out of the barrel of a gun.

Mao Zedong, (1893–1976) Chinese founder of the People's Republic of China. "Problems of War and Strategy,'" *Selected Works*, vol. 2 (1965). Speech, Nov. 6, 1938.

9 By the power elite, we refer to those political, economic, and military

circles which as an intricate set of overlapping cliques share decisions having at least national conse-quences. In so far as national events are decided, the power elite are those who decide them.

C. Wright Mills, (1916–1962) U.S. sociologist. *The Power Elite*, ch. 1, "The Higher Circles" (1956).

10   Power, like a desolating pestilence,
     Pollutes whate'er it touches.

Percy Bysshe Shelley, (1792–1822) British poet. "Queen Mab," pt. 3, l. 176–7 (1813).

11   Power can be taken, but not given. The process of the taking is empowerment in itself.

Gloria Steinem, (b. 1934) U.S. feminist writer, editor. "Far From the Opposite Shore," *Outrageous Acts and Everyday Rebellions* (1983). *Ms.* (New York, July 1978 and July/Aug. 1982).

12   The good old rule
     Sufficeth them, the simple plan,
     That they should take, who have
        the power,
     And they should keep who can.

William Wordsworth, (1770–1850) British poet. "Rob Roy's Grave," st. 9, *Poems in Two Volumes* (1807).

Pragmatism

1   Mahomet made the people believe that he would call a hill to him, and from the top of it offer up his prayers for the observers of the Law. The people assembled; Mahomet called the hill to come to him again and again; and when the hill stood still, he was never a whit abashed, but said, *If the hill will not come to Mahomet, Mahomet will go to the hill.*

Francis Bacon, (1561–1626) British philosopher, essayist, statesman. *Essays*, "Of Boldness" (1597–1625).

Referring to a tradition relating to Muham-mad. "So," Bacon explained, "these men, when they have promised great matters, and failed most shamefully (yet if they have the perfection of boldness), they will but slight it over, and make a turn, and no more ado." This is the first appearance of the proverb in English.

Praise

1   Let us now praise famous men, and our fathers that begat us.

Apocrypha, *Apocrypha, Ecclesiasticus* 44:1.

2   The advantage of doing one's praising for oneself is that one can lay it on so thick and exactly in the right places.

Samuel Butler, (1835–1902) British author. *The Way of All Flesh*, ch. 34 (1903).

3   Usually we praise only to be praised.

François La Rochefoucauld, Duc De, (1613–1680) French writer, moralist. *Sentences et Maximes Morales*, no. 146 (1678).

4   Fondly we think we honour merit then,
     When we but praise ourselves in other men.

Alexander Pope, (1688–1744) British satirical poet. "An Essay on Criticism," l. 454–5 (1711).

5   Among the smaller duties of life I hardly know any one more impor-tant than that of not praising where praise is not due.

Sydney Smith, (1771–1845) British cler-gyman, writer. *Sketches of Moral Philosophy*, lecture 9 (1850).

Prayers

1   After this manner therefore pray ye:
Our Father which art in heaven,
Hallowed be thy name. Thy kingdom come. Thy will be done in
earth, as it is in heaven. Give us this
day our daily bread. And forgive us
our debts, as we forgive our debtors.
And lead us not into temptation, but
deliver us from evil: For thine is the
kingdom, and the power, and the
glory, for ever. Amen.

BIBLE: NEW TESTAMENT, Jesus, in
Matthew, 6:9–13.The Lord's Prayer. In *Luke*
11:4, the words are "forgive us our sins; for
we also forgive everyone that is indebted to
us." The Book of Common Prayer gives the
most common usage, "forgive us our tres-
passes, as we forgive them that trespass
against us."

2   The wish to pray is a prayer in itself
... God can ask no more than that of
us.

GEORGES BERNANOS, (1888–1948)
French novelist, political writer. *The Diary of a
Country Priest,* ch. 4 (1936).

3   I throw myself down in my chamber, and I call in, and invite God,
and his Angels thither, and when
they are there, I neglect God and his
Angels, for the noise of a fly, for the
rattling of a coach, for the whining
of a door.

JOHN DONNE, (c. 1572–1631) British
divine, metaphysical poet. *Eighty Sermons,* no.
80, sct. 3 (preached Dec. 12, 1626, published
1640). Repr. in *Complete Poetry and Selected
Prose,* ed. John Hayward (1929).

4   And some to Meccah turn to pray,
and I toward thy bed, Yasmin.

JAMES ELROY FLECKER, (1884–1915)
British poet. Hassan, in *Hassan,* act 1, sc. 2
(1922).

5   There are thoughts which are
prayers. There are moments when,
whatever the posture of the body,
the soul is on its knees.

VICTOR HUGO, (1802–1885) French poet,
dramatist, novelist. Marius, in *Les Misérables,*
pt. 4, bk. 5, ch. 4 (1862).

6   A single thankful thought towards
heaven is the most perfect of all
prayers.

GOTTHOLD EPHRAIM LESSING,
(1729–1881) German dramatist, critic.
Fröulein, in *Minna von Barnhelm,* act 2, sc. 7
(1767).

7   Our Father which art in heaven
Stay there
And we will stay on earth
Which is sometimes so pretty.

JACQUES PRÉVERT, (1900–1977) French
poet. "Pater Noster," *Paroles* (1946;
rev.1949), trans. by Lawrence Ferlinghetti
(1958). Opening lines.

8   Lord, make me an instrument of
Your peace!
Where there is hatred let me sow
love;
Where there is injury, pardon;
Where there is doubt, faith;
Where there is despair, hope;
Where there is darkness, light;
Where there is sadness, joy.

SAINT FRANCIS, (c.1182–1226) Italian
friar, founder of the Franciscan Order. *"Prayer
of St Francis" (attributed).*

This prayer for harmony was famously paraphrased by Mrs. Thatcher on the steps of 10
Downing Street, 4 May 1979, after her first
election victory: "Where there is discord, may
we bring harmony. Where there is error may
we bring truth. Where there is doubt may we
bring faith. Where there is despair may we
bring hope" (quoted in Hugo Young's biography *One of Us,* ch. 9, 1989).

Preaching

1   I preached as never sure to preach
again,

And as a dying man to dying men.

RICHARD BAXTER, (1615–1691) British nonconformist cleric. "Love Breathing Thanks and Praise," *Poetical Fragments* (1681).

2   Truth from his lips prevailed with
    double sway,
    And fools, who came to scoff,
    remained to pray.

OLIVER GOLDSMITH, (1728–1774) Anglo–Irish author, poet, playwright. "The Deserted Village," l. 179–180 (1770).

Referring to the village preacher.

3   A woman preaching is like a dog's
    walking on his hinder legs. It is not
    done well; but you are surprised to
    find it done at all.

SAMUEL JOHNSON, (1709–1784) British author, lexicographer. Quoted in James Boswell, *Life of Dr. Johnson*, entry, July 31, 1763 (1791).

4   But, good my brother,
    Do not, as some ungracious pastors
    do,
    Show me the steep and thorny way
    to heaven
    Whilst like a puffed and reckless
    libertine
    Himself the primrose path of dal-
    liance treads
    And recks not his own rede.

WILLIAM SHAKESPEARE, (1564–1616) British dramatist, poet. Ophelia, in *Hamlet*, act 1, sc. 3, l. 46–51 (1604).

In response to the lengthy advice given by her brother Polonius before his departure for France; the last line means "heeds not his own advice." Shakespeare also conveyed the idea of a flower–strewn path to hell in *Hamlet* act 2, sc. 3, l. 18, "the primrose way to th'ever-lasting bonfire."

Precedent

1   The glory of each generation is to
    make its own precedents.

BELVA LOCKWOOD, (1830–1917) U.S. lawyer, feminist. Quoted in *Lady for the Defense*, pt. 3, ch. 13, Mary Virginia Fox (1975).

Lockwood was arguing in favor of admitting women to practice in the U.S. Supreme Court, for which there was no precedent. In 1879 she became the first woman to practice there.

2   A precedent embalms a principle.

WILLIAM SCOTT, BARON STOWELL, (1745–1836) British lawyer. "Quoted by Benjamin Disraeli," *Hansard,* col. 1066. Speech, Feb. 22, 1848, House of Commons.

The axiom is often erroneously ascribed to Disraeli. William Scott also known as Lord Stowell.

Precociousness

1   So wise so young, they say, do never
    live long.

WILLIAM SHAKESPEARE, (1564–1616) British dramatist, poet. Gloucester (later Richard III), in *Richard III*, act 3, sc. 1, l. 79 (1597).

Referring to of Prince Edward, who is dead by act 4, sc. 3.

Predicaments

1   Here's another nice mess you've got-
    ten me into.

STAN LAUREL, (1890–1965) British–born U.S. comedian. *The Laurel–Hardy Murder Case* (film) (1930).

This is the earliest use of this famous catch-phrase featured in various Laurel and Hardy films, always uttered by Oliver Hardy to Laurel, though Laurel is credited with most of the script-work, and directed many of the films. The words are generally misquoted as "another fine mess," which was the title of a Laurel and Hardy short released in 1930, but they were only ever used in this form in *The Wedding Night* (1938 or 1943).

Prediction

1   Beware the ides of March.

WILLIAM SHAKESPEARE, (1564–1616) British dramatist, poet. Soothsayer, in *Julius Caesar*, act 1, sc. 2, l. 19 (1623).

This warning of danger is repeated twice to Caesar and rejected ("He is a dreamer. Let us leave him. Pass!"). According to the Julian calendar the ides were the 15th day in March, May, July and October.

Pregnancy and Childbirth

1 If men could get pregnant, abortion would be a sacrament.

FLORYNCE R. KENNEDY, (b. 1916) U.S. lawyer, civil rights activist. "The Verbal Karate of Florynce R. Kennedy, Esq," quoted by Gloria Steinem, in *Ms.* (New York, March 1973).

Prejudice

1 Prejudice. A vagrant opinion without visible means of support.

AMBROSE BIERCE, (1842–1914) U.S. author. *The Devil's Dictionary* (1881–1906), repr. in *Collected Works of Ambrose Bierce,* vol. 7 (1911).

2 A little grit in the eye destroyeth the sight of the very heavens, and a little malice or envy a world of joys. One wry principle in the mind is of infinite consequence.

THOMAS TRAHERNE, (1636–1674) British clergyman, poet, mystic. *Centuries,* "Fourth Century," no. 17 (written c. 1672, first published 1908).

Present, the

1 We were wise indeed, could we discern truly the signs of our own time; and by knowledge of its wants and advantages, wisely adjust our own position in it. Let us, instead of gazing idly into the obscure distance, look calmly around us, for a little, on the perplexed scene where we stand.

Perhaps, on a more serious inspection, something of its perplexity will disappear, some of its distinctive characters and deeper tendencies more clearly reveal themselves; whereby our own relations to it, our own true aims and endeavours in it, may also become clearer.

THOMAS CARLYLE, (1795–1881) Scottish essayist, historian. "Signs of the Times," first published in *Edinburgh Review,* no. 98 (1829). *Critical and Miscellaneous Essays* (1839–1857).

2 Time past and time future
What might have been and what
    has been
Point to one end, which is always
    present.

T.S. (THOMAS STEARNS) ELIOT, (1888–1965) Anglo–American poet, critic. "Burnt Norton," pt. 1 (1936). *Four Quartets* (1942).

3 The present is an age of talkers, and not of doers; and the reason is, that the world is growing old. We are so far advanced in the Arts and Sciences, that we live in retrospect, and dote on past achievement.

WILLIAM HAZLITT, (1778–1830) British essayist. *The Spirit of the Age,* "Coleridge" (1825).

4 Will lovely, lively, virginal today
Shatter for us with a wing's
    drunken blow
This hard, forgotten lake haunted
    in snow
By the sheer ice of flocks not flown
    away!

STÉPHANE MALLARMÉ, (1842–1898) French symbolist poet. *Plusieurs Sonnets,* no. 2, st. 1, *Mallarmé: The Poems,* trans. by and ed. Keith Bosley (1977). *Poésies* (1887).

5 I balanced all, brought all to mind,
The years to come seemed waste of
    breath,

A waste of breath the years behind
In balance with this life, this death.

WILLIAM BUTLER YEATS, (1865–1939)
Irish poet, playwright. "An Irish Airman Fore-
sees His Death, "*The Wild Swans at Coole*
(1919).

Last lines.

Presidency, U.S.

1   But even the President of the United
States
Sometimes must have
To stand naked.

**BOB DYLAN [ROBERT ALLEN ZIM-
MERMAN],** (b. 1941) U.S. singer, songwriter.
"It's Alright Ma (I'm Only Bleeding)" (song), on
the album *Bringing it all Back Home* (1965).

2   Jerry Ford is so dumb he can't fart
and chew gum at the same time.

LYNDON BAINES JOHNSON, (1908–1973)
U.S. Democratic politician, president. Quoted
in *A Ford, Not a Lincoln*, ch. 1, Richard Reeves
(1975).

Reeves alleges that Johnson's remark was
"cleaned up" by "the late President's aides and
history."

3   All this will not be finished in the
first 100 days. Nor will it be finished
in the first 1,000 days, nor in the life
of this Administration,
nor even perhaps in our lifetime on
this planet. But let us begin.

JOHN FITZGERALD KENNEDY,
(1917–1963) U.S. Democratic politician, president. "Inaugural address," *Public Papers of the
Presidents of the United States: John F. Kennedy,
1961.* Jan. 20, 1961, Washington D.C..

Kennedy's administration lasted a little over
1,000 days, described in Arthur M.
Schlesinger's *A Thousand Days* (1965).
Schlesinger was appointed Kennedy's
special assistant in 1961.

4   When the President does it, that
means that it is not illegal.

RICHARD NIXON, (1913–1992) U.S.
Republican politician, president. Quoted in *I
Gave Them a Sword*, ch. 8, David Frost
(1978). TV interview with David Frost, May
20, 1977.

5   In America any boy may become
President, and I suppose it's just
one of the risks he takes!

ADLAI STEVENSON, (1900–1965) U.S.
Democratic politician. *Major Campaign
Speeches of Adlai E. Stevenson: 1952* (1953).
Speech, Sept. 26, 1952, Indianapolis, Ind.

6   To be President of the United
States, sir, is to act as advocate for a
blind, venomous, and ungrateful
client; still, one must make the best
of the case, for the purposes of
Providence.

JOHN UPDIKE, (b. 1932) U.S. author,
critic. President James Polk, in *Buchanan
Dying*, act 2 (1974).

7   In America the President reigns for
four years, and Journalism governs
for ever and ever.

OSCAR WILDE, (1854–1900) Anglo–Irish
playwright, author. "The Soul of Man Under
Socialism" (1895) *Fortnightly Review* (London, Feb. 1891). Repr. in *Complete Works of
Oscar Wilde*, ed. J.B. Foreman (1966).

President and First Lady of
the United States

1   She would rather light a candle
than curse the darkness, and her
glow has warmed the world.

ADLAI STEVENSON, (1900–1965) U.S.
Democratic politician. Quoted in *The New
York Times* (Nov. 8, 1962).

Comment on learning of Eleanor Roosevelt's
death. Stevenson was quoting the motto of the
Christopher Society, "It is better to light one
candle than curse the darkness." According to
Brewer's Quotations, ed. Nigel Rees (1994),
this in turn is a Chinese proverb.

President and the Vice President

1 The Republican Vice Presidential Candidate ... asks you to place him a heartbeat from the Presidency.

ADLAI STEVENSON, (1900–1965) U.S. Democratic politician. *"The Hiss Case," Speeches* (1953). Speech, Oct. 23, 1952, Cleveland, Ohio.

Referring to Richard Milhous Nixon, who became Vice President in 1952 (reelected 1956).

Press, the

1 The price of justice is eternal publicity.

ARNOLD BENNETT, (1867–1931) British novelist. *Things That Have Interested Me,* "Secret Trials," Second Series (1923).

2 The liberty of the Press is the *Palladium* of all the civil, political and religious rights of an Englishman.

JUNIUS (PSEUDONYM OF WRITER NEVER I, "Dedication to the English Nation," *The Letters of Junius* (1772).

3 Power without responsibility—the prerogative of the harlot throughout the ages.

RUDYARD KIPLING, (1865–1936) British author, poet. Quoted in *The Kipling Journal* (Dec. 1971).

The quotation is often ascribed to British prime minister Stanley Baldwin, Kipling's cousin. Baldwin used the words in a speech, Mar. 17, 1931, attacking press barons Lord Beaverbrook and Lord Rothermere, whose newspapers he called "engines of propaganda."

4 The men with the muck–rakes are often indispensable to the well–being of society; but only if they know when to stop raking the muck.

THEODORE ROOSEVELT, (1858–1919) U.S. Republican (later Progressive) politician, president. *The Penguin Book of Twentieth Century Speeches,* ed. Brian MacArthur (1992). Speech, April 14, 1906, Washington, D.C..

The "Man with the Muck–rake" is a character in John Bunyan's *Pilgrim's Progress.*

5 In old days men had the rack. Now they have the Press.

OSCAR WILDE, (1854–1900) Anglo–Irish playwright, author. "The Soul of Man Under Socialism " (1895) *Fortnightly Review* (London, Feb. 1891). Repr. in *Complete Works of Oscar Wilde,* ed. J.B. Foreman (1966).

Pride

1 He that toucheth pitch shall be defiled therewith; and he that hath fellowship with a proud man shall be like unto him.

APOCRYPHA, *Ecclesiasticus,* 13:1.

2 I cannot dig; to beg I am ashamed.

BIBLE: NEW TESTAMENT, *Luke,* 16:3.The unjust steward in the Parable of the Unjust Steward.

3 Pride goeth before destruction, andan haughty spirit before a fall.

BIBLE: HEBREW, *Proverbs,* 16:18.

4 My family pride is something inconceivable. I can't help it. I was born sneering.

SIR WILLIAM SCHWENCK GILBERT, (1836–1911) British librettist. Pooh-Bah, in *The Mikado,* act 1 (1885), published in *The Savoy Operas* (1926).

Primitive Life

1 No arts; no letters; no society; and which is worst of all, continual fear, and danger of violent death; and the life of man, solitary, poor, nasty, brutish, and short.

THOMAS HOBBES, (1588–1679) British philosopher. *Leviathan*, pt. 1, ch. 13 (1651).

Describing the state "wherein men live without other security, than what their own strength and their own invention shall furnish them."

Principles

1 Amid the pressure of great events, a general principle gives no help.

GEORG HEGEL, (1770–1831) German philosopher. *The Philosophy of History*, "Introduction," sct. 2 (1837).

2 When a fellow says, it hain't the money but the principle o' the thing, it's th' money.

KIN HUBBARD (F. [FRANK] McKINNEY HUBBARD), (1868–1930) U.S. humorist, journalist. *Hoss Sense and Nonsense* (1926).

Priorities

1 The three most important things a man has are, briefly, his private parts, his money, and his religious opinions.

SAMUEL BUTLER, (1835–1902) British author. *Samuel Butler's Notebooks*, "Untraced Notes" (1951).

2 The least pain in our little finger gives us more concern and uneasiness than the destruction of millions of our fellow–beings.

WILLIAM HAZLITT, (1778–1830) British essayist. *American Literature Dr. Channing*, first published in *Edinburgh Review* (Oct. 1829). *Complete Works*, vol. 16, ed. P.P. Howe (1932).

Prison

1 If you want to know who your friends are, get yourself a jail sentence.

CHARLES BUKOWSKI, (1920–1994) U.S. author, poet. *Notes From a Dirty Old Man* (1969).

2 Go to jail. Go directly to jail. Do not pass go. Do not collect $200.

CHARLES BRACE DARROW, (1889–1967) U.S. inventor. Instruction in the game, *Monopoly* (1933).

Monopoly was devised by Darrow in 1931.

3 We are all conceived in close prison; in our mothers' wombs, we are close prisoners all; when we are born, we are born but to the liberty of the house; prisoners still, though within larger walls; and then all our life is but a going out to the place of execution, to death.

JOHN DONNE, (c. 1572–1631) British divine, metaphysical poet. *Eighty Sermons*, no. 27 (published 1640). Repr. in *Complete Poetry and Selected Prose*, ed. John Hayward (1929).

4 I see my light come shining
From the west unto the east
Any day now, any day now,
I shall be released.

BOB DYLAN [ROBERT ALLEN ZIMMERMAN], (b. 1941) U.S. singer, songwriter. "I Shall Be Released" (song), recorded 1967, on the album *The Basement Tapes* (1975).

5 Stone walls do not a prison make
Nor iron bars a cage; Minds innocent and quiet take That for an hermitage.

RICHARD LOVELACE, (1618–1658) British poet. "To Althea, from Prison," st. 4 (1649). Repr. in *Poems*, ed. C.H. Wilkinson (1930).

6 I know not whether Laws be right
Or whether Laws be wrong;
All that we know who live in gaol
Is that the wall is strong;
And that each day is like a year,
A year whose days are long.

OSCAR WILDE, (1854–1900) Anglo–Irish playwright, author. "The Ballad of Reading Gaol," pt. 5, st. 1 (1898). Repr. in *Complete Works of Oscar Wilde*, ed. J.B. Foreman (1966).

Privacy

1 There is no private life which has not been determined by a wider public life.

GEORGE ELIOT [MARY ANN (OR MARIAN) EVANS], (1819–1880) British novelist, editor. Felix Holt, *The Radical*, ch. 3 (1866).

Privilege

1 I perceive that God is no respecter of persons.

BIBLE: NEW TESTAMENT, *Acts*, 10:34. Said by Peter at Caesarea; similar wording is found in *Romans* 2:11: "There is no respect of persons with God."

2 What men prize most is a privilege, even if it be that of chief mourner at a funeral.

JAMES RUSSELL LOWELL, (1819–1891) U.S. poet, editor. *Democracy, Democracy and Other Addresses* (1887). Address, Oct. 6, 1884, Birmingham, England.

3 I was born with a plastic spoon in my mouth.

PETE TOWNSHEND, (b. 1945) British rock musician. "Substitute" (song), on the album *My Generation* (1965).

Problems

1 I thought a lot about our nation and what I should do as president. And Sunday night before last, I made a speech about two problems of our country—energy and malaise.

JIMMY CARTER, (b. 1924) U.S. Democratic politician, president. *Public Papers of the Presidents of the United States: Jimmy Carter, 1979*. Remarks at town meeting, July 31, 1979, Bardstown, Kentucky.

The speech referred to by Carter, broadcast July 15 from the White House, did not include the word *malaise*.

2 I'm no good at being noble, but it doesn't take much to see that the problems of three little people don't amount to a hill of beans in this crazy world. Someday you'll understand that.

JULIUS J. EPSTEIN, U.S. screenwriter. Rick Blaine (Humphrey Bogart), in *Casablanca* (film), spoken in the final scenes of the film to Ilsa Lund (Ingrid Bergman), departing from Casablanca with her husband (1942).

Procrastination

1 procrastination is the
art of keeping
up with yesterday

DON MARQUIS, (1878–1937) U.S. humorist, journalist. *Archy and mehitabel*, "certain maxims of archy" (1927).

2 Procrastination is the thief of time.

EDWARD YOUNG, (1683–1765) British poet, playwright. "Night 1," l. 393, *The Complaint, or Night–Thoughts on Life, Death and Immortality* (1742–1746). Repr. in *Complete Works*, ed. J. Doran (1968).

Procreation

1 I could be content that we might procreate like trees, without conjunction, or that there were any way to perpetuate the world without this trivial and vulgar way of coition.

THOMAS BROWNE, (1605–1682) British physician, author. *Religio Medici*, pt. 2, sct. 9 (1643).

2 A hen is only an egg's way of making another egg.

SAMUEL BUTLER, (1835–1902) British author. *Life and Habit*, ch. 8 (1877).

3 Get thee to a nunnery. Why wouldst thou be a breeder of sinners?

WILLIAM SHAKESPEARE, (1564–1616) British dramatist, poet. Hamlet, in *Hamlet,* act 3, sc. 1, l. 123–4 (1604).

Speaking to Ophelia. Hamlet's reasoned thus: "I could accuse me of such things that it were better my mother had not borne me.... What should such fellows as I do crawling between heaven and earth? We are arrant knaves, all."

4 "Pray my dear," quoth my mother, "have you not forgot to wind up the clock?"—"Good G—!" cried my father, making an exclamation, but taking care to moderate his voice at the same time,—"Did ever woman, since the creation of the world, interrupt a man with such a silly question?"

LAURENCE STERNE, (1713–1768) British author. *Tristram Shandy*, bk. 1, ch. 1 (1759–1767).

Events occurring at the conception of Tristram Shandy, on account of which, according to his father, "My Tristram's misfortunes began nine months before ever he came into the world."

Professions

1 I'm a lumberjack
And I'm OK,
I sleep all night
And I work all day.

MONTY PYTHON'S FLYING CIRCUS, *Monty Python's Flying Circus* (TV series), episode 9, "The Lumberjack Song" (1969–1974) published in *Monty Python's Big Red Book* (1971). Broadcast Dec. 1969.

Monty Python episodes were written and performed by Graham Chapman (1941–1989);

John Cleese (b. 1939); Terry Gilliam (b. 1940); Eric Idle (b. 1943); Terry Jones (b. 1942); and Michael Palin (b. 1943).

Profit

1 To whose gain?
[Cui bono]

MARCUS TULLIUS CICERO, (106–43 B.C.) Roman orator, philosopher. *Pro Milone*, ch. 12, sct. 32 (44–43 B.C.).

Quoting the tribune L. Cassius Longinus, when urging the voters how to decide; the phrase is often misapplied as meaning "what's the good?"

2 Civilization and profits go hand in hand.

CALVIN COOLIDGE, (1872–1933) U.S. Republican politician, president. quoted in *The New York Times* (Nov. 28, 1920). Speech, Nov. 27, 1920, New York City.

Progress

1 Progress, man's distinctive mark alone,
Not God's, and not the beasts': God is, they are,
Man partly is and wholly hopes to be.

ROBERT BROWNING, (1812–1889) British poet. "A Death in the Desert," l. 586–8, *Dramatis Personae* (1864).

2 The United States has to move very fast to even stand still.

JOHN FITZGERALD KENNEDY, (1917–1963) U.S. Democratic politician, president. Quoted in *Observer* (London, July 21, 1963).

3 Today, the notion of progress in a single line without goal or limit seems perhaps the most parochial notion of a very parochial century.

LEWIS MUMFORD, (1895–1990) U.S. social philosopher. *Technics and Civilization*, ch. 8, sct. 12 (1934).

Promiscuity

1   You were born with your legs apart.
    They'll send you to the grave in a
    Y–shaped coffin.

    JOE ORTON, (1933–1967) British play-
    wright. Dr. Prentice, in *What the Butler Saw,*
    act 1 (1969).

    Speaking to Mrs. Prentice.

2   That woman speaks eighteen lan-
    guages and can't say No in any of
    them.

    DOROTHY PARKER, (1893–1967) U.S.
    humorous writer. Quoted in *While Rome
    Burns,* "Our Mrs. Parker," Alexander Woollcott
    (1934).

    Referring to a departing guest.

3   Chaste to her husband, frank to all
      beside,
    A teeming mistress, but a barren
      bride.

    ALEXANDER POPE, (1688–1744) British
    satirical poet. "Epistle to a Lady," l. 71–2
    (1735).

4   If you can't be with the one you
      love,
    Love the one you're with.

    STEPHEN STILLS, (b. 1945) U.S. rock
    musician. "Love the One You're With," refrain,
    Stephen Stills (album, 1970).

    The lyrics recall the 1947 song by Yip Har-
    burg, "When I'm Not Near the Girl I Love":
    "When I'm not near the girl I love, I love the
    girl I'm near." (Music by Burton Lane).

Promised Land

1   And I am come down to deliver
    them out of the hand of the Egyp-
    tians, and to bring them up out of
    that land unto a good land and a
    large, unto a land flowing with milk
    and honey; unto the place of the
    Canaanites, and the Hittites, and the
    Amorites, and the Perizzites, and
    the Hivites, and the Jebusites.

    BIBLE: HEBREW, *Exodus,* 3:8.

Promises

1   It is not the oath that makes us
    believe the man, but the man the
    oath.

    AESCHYLUS, (525–456 B.C.) Greek drama-
    tist. *Fragments,* no. 385, trans. by M.H. Mor-
    gan.

2   The rule is, jam tomorrow and jam
    yesterday—but never jam today.

    **LEWIS CARROLL [CHARLES
    LUTWIDGE DODGSON],** (1832–1898)
    British author, mathematician. The White
    Queen, in *Through the Looking–Glass,* "Wool
    and Water" (1872).

3   What a woman says to her avid
      lover
    Should be written in wind and run-
      ning water.

    **CATULLUS [GAIUS VALERIUS CAT-
    ULLUS],** (87–54 B.C.) Roman lyric poet.
    "Carmina," no. 70, l. 3–4.

4   'Twas but my tongue, 'twas not my
    soul that swore.

    EURIPIDES, (480–406 B.C.) Greek drama-
    tist. Hippolytus, in *Hippolytus,* l. 612, *Col-
    lected Plays of Euripides,* ed. and trans. by
    Gilbert Murray (1954).

5   The woods are lovely, dark and
      deep.
    But I have promises to keep,
    And miles to go before I sleep,
    And miles to go before I sleep.

    ROBERT FROST, (1874–1963) U.S. poet.
    "Stopping by Woods on a Snowy Evening,'
    New Hampshire (1923).

    These words were found on a scrap of paper
    on the desk of Indian prime minister Jawahar-
    lal Nehru when he died—presumed to be the
    last words he saw. John F. Kennedy regularly

used the lines to wind up speeches during his presidential campaign.

Promotion

1   Fain would I climb, yet fear I to fall.

SIR WALTER RALEIGH, (1552–1618) British author, soldier, explorer. Quoted in *History of the Worthies of England,* "Devonshire," Thomas Fuller (1662).

Line scratched with a diamond ring on a window–pane, to which Queen Elizabeth replied, using the same method, "If thy heart fail thee, climb not at all."

2   When I give a man an office, I watch him carefully to see whether he is swelling or growing.

WOODROW WILSON, (1856–1924) U.S. Democratic politician, president.

Speech, May 15, 1916, National Press Club, Washington D.C..

Propaganda

1   Words that are saturated with lies or atrocity, do not easily resume life.

GEORGE STEINER, (b. 1929) French–born U.S. critic, novelist. "K," *Language and Silence* (1967). (Essay originally published 1963.)

Property

1   Thieves respect property. They merely wish the property to become their property that they may more perfectly respect it.

GILBERT KEITH CHESTERTON, (1874–1936) British author. Policeman, in *The Man Who Was Thursday,* ch. 4 (1908).

2   Property has its duties as well as its rights.

THOMAS DRUMMOND, (1797–1840) Scottish statesman, engineer. *Life and Letters,* R. Barry O'Brien (1889). Letter, May 22, 1838.

Disraeli also used these words in his novel *Sybil,* bk. 1, ch. 11 (1845).

3   Government has no other end but the preservation of Property.

JOHN LOCKE, (1632–1704) British philosopher. *Second Treatise on Civil Government,* ch. 6 (written 1681, publ. 1690).

4   What is yours is mine, and whatever is mine is yours.

PLAUTUS, (254–184 B.C.) Roman playwright. Lysiteles, in *Trinummus,* act 2, sc. 2, l. 48, trans. by E.F. Watling (1964).

Prophecy

1   Among all forms of mistake, prophecy is the most gratuitous.

GEORGE ELIOT [MARY ANN (OR MARIAN) EVANS], (1819–1880) British novelist. *Middlemarch,* bk. 1, ch. 10 (1872).

Prophets

1   A prophet is not without honour, save in his own country, and in his own house.

BIBLE: NEW TESTAMENT, Jesus, in *Matthew,* 13:57.

2   Beware of false prophets, which come to you in sheep's clothing, but inwardly they are ravening wolves.

BIBLE: NEW TESTAMENT, Jesus, in *Matthew,* 7:15.From the Sermon on the Mount.

Prostitution and Prostitutes

1   But most thro' midnight streets I hear
How the youthful harlot's curse
Blasts the new born infant's tear,

And blights with plagues the marriage hearse.

WILLIAM BLAKE, (1757–1827) British
poet, painter, engraver. *Songs of Experience,*
"London," (1794), repr. in *Complete Writings,*
ed. Geoffrey Keynes (1957).

Protest

1   We shall overcome, we shall
overcome,
We shall overcome some day.
Oh, deep in my heart I do believe
We shall overcome some day.

ANONYMOUS.

According to *Bartlett's Familiar Quotations*
(16th ed., 1992) and *Oxford Dictionary of
Quotations* (4th ed., 1992), this 19th–century
song was adapted as a Baptist hymn by C.
Albert Tindley in 1901, and revived in the
1940s by black tobacco workers in Charleston,
S.C. The 1960s civil rights movement trans-
formed it into an anthem.

2   Can't Pay? Won't Pay!
[Non si paga, non si paga.]

DARIO FO, (b. 1926) Italian dramatist. *Can't
Pay? Won't Pay!* (Play) (1974, trans. 1978).

Adopted as slogan by anti–Poll–Tax protesters
in Britain, 1990s. The play's title was originally
translated as *We Can't Pay? We Won't Pay!*

3   Let us be realistic and demand the
impossible.
*[Soyons réalistes, demandons l'impos-
sible.]*

GRAFFITO, *Paris '68,* ch. 2, Marc Rohan
(1988).

4   One–fifth of the people are against
everything all the time.

ROBERT KENNEDY, (1925–1968) U.S.
attorney general, Democratic politician.
Quoted in *Philadelphia Inquirer* (May 7, 1964).
Speech, May, 6 1964, University of Pennsylvania.

5   I submit that an individual who
breaks a law that conscience tells

him is unjust, and willingly accepts
the penalty by staying in jail in
order to arouse the conscience of
the community over its injustice, is
in reality expressing the very highest respect for law.

MARTIN LUTHER KING, JR.,
(1929–1968) U.S. clergyman, civil rights
leader. "Letter from Birmingham Jail," *Why
We Can't Wait* (1963). Open letter to clergymen, Apr. 16, 1963.

6   Unfortunately, I am involved in a
freedom ride protesting the loss of
the minority rights belonging to
the few remaining earthbound
stars. All we demanded was our
right to twinkle.

MARILYN MONROE, (1926–1962) U.S.
screen actor. *Marilyn: Something's Got to
Give* (TV program, Channel 4), broadcast
(Aug. 2, 1992).

Telegram, June 13, 1962, to Mr. and Mrs.
Robert Kennedy, turning down a party invita-
tion.

7   I pondered all these things, and
how men fight and lose the battle,
and the thing that they fought for
comes about in spite of their
defeat, and when it comes turns
out not to be what they meant, and
other men have to fight for what
they meant under another name.

WILLIAM MORRIS, (1834–1896) British
artist, writer, printer. *A Dream of John Ball,*
ch. 4 (1888).

Protestantism

1   All Protestantism, even the most
cold and passive, is a sort of dissent. But the religion most preva-
lent in our northern colonies is a
refinement on the principle of
resistance; it is the dissidence of
dissent, and the Protestantism of
the Protestant religion.

EDMUND BURKE, (1729–1797) Irish philosopher, statesman. "Second Speech on Conciliation with America: The Thirteen Resolutions," *Works*, vol. 2 (1899). Speech, March 22, 1775, House of Commons, London.

2   The Church of England is the Tory Party at prayer.

BENJAMIN DISRAELI, (1804–1881) British statesman, author. *Attributed.*

Disraeli's biographer, the historian Robert Blake, has not been able to confirm that Disraeli ever wrote or spoke these words.

3   This is what the Church is said to want, not party men, but sensible, temperate, sober, well–judging persons, to guide it through the channel of no–meaning, between the Scylla and Charybdis of Aye and No.

CARDINAL JOHN HENRY NEWMAN, (1801–1890) British churchman, theologian. "History of My Religious Opinions from 1839–1841," *Apologia Pro Vita Sua* (1864).

Provincialism

1   The dead level of provincial existence.

GEORGE ELIOT [MARY ANN (OR MARIAN) EVANS], (1819–1880) British novelist. Philip, in *The Mill on the Floss*, bk. 5, ch. 3 (1860).

2   There are few who would not rather be taken in adultery than in provincialism.

ALDOUS HUXLEY, (1894–1963) British author. Mr. Boldero, in *Antic Hay*, ch. 10 (1923).

3   When you're growing up in a small town
You know you'll grow down in a small town
There is only one good use for a small town

You hate it and you know you'll have to leave.

LOU REED, (b. 1944) U.S. rock musician. "Small Town" (song), from the album *Songs for Drella* (1990).

Provocation

1   Go ahead. Make my day.

JOSEPH STINSON, Screenwriter. Harry Callahan (Clint Eastwood), in *Sudden Impact* (film) (1983).

Psychiatry

1   If the nineteenth century was the age of the editorial chair, ours is the century of the psychiatrist's couch.

MARSHALL MCLUHAN, (1911–1980) Canadian communications theorist. *Understanding Media*, introduction (1964).

2   Canst thou not minister to a mind diseased,
Pluck from the memory a rooted sorrow,
Raze out the written troubles of the brain,
And with some sweet oblivious antidote
Cleanse the fraught bosom of that perilous stuff
Which weighs upon the heart?

WILLIAM SHAKESPEARE, (1564–1616) British dramatist, poet. Macbeth, in *Macbeth*, act 5, sc. 3, l. 42–7 (1623). Speaking to the Doctor of Physic.

Psychoanalysis

1   Where *id* was, there *ego* shall be.

SIGMUND FREUD, (1856–1939) Austrian psychiatrist. *New Introductory Lectures on Psychoanalysis*, vol. 22, lecture 31, "The Dissection of the Psychical Personality," *Com-*

plete Works, Standard Edition, eds. James Strachey and Anna Freud (1964). (Originally published 1933.)

The intention of psychoanalysis, Freud explained, is "to strengthen the ego, to make it more independent of the super–ego, to widen its field of perception and enlarge its organization, so that it can appropriate fresh portions of the id.... It is a work of culture," he added in the closing words of the lecture, "not unlike the draining of the Zuider Zee."

2   Freud is the father of psychoanalysis. It had no mother.

GERMAINE GREER, (b. 1939) Australian feminist writer. *The Female Eunuch*, "The Psychological Sell' ' (1970).

Psychology

1   To understand the true quality of people, you must look into their minds, and examine their pursuits and aversions.

MARCUS AURELIUS, (121–180) Roman emperor, philosopher. *Meditations*, bk. 4, sct. 38, trans. by Jeremy Collier.

2   There is no psychology; there is only biography and autobiography.

THOMAS SZASZ, (b. 1920) U.S. psychiatrist. "Psychology," *The Second Sin* (1973).

Public life

1   Private faces in public places
Are wiser and nicer
Than public faces in private places.

W.H. (WYSTAN HUGH) AUDEN, (1907–1973) Anglo–American poet. *Orators*, epigraph (1932). Repr. in *Collected Shorter Poems 1927–1957* (1966) "Shorts."

2   You're not an M.P., you're a gastronomic pimp.

ANEURIN BEVAN, (1897–1960) British Labour politician. Quoted in *Aneurin Bevan*, vol. 2, ch. 6, Michael Foot (1973).

Said to a colleague who complained of attending too many public dinners.

3   How dreary—to be—Somebody!
How public—like a frog—
To tell one's name—the livelong June—
To an admiring Bog!

EMILY DICKINSON, (1830–1886) U.S. poet. "I'm Nobody! Who Are You?" (Written c. 1861, published 1891). Repr. in *The Complete Poems*, no. 288, Harvard *variorum* edition (1955).

4   We are persons of quality, I assure you, and women of fashion, and come to see and to be seen.

BEN JONSON, (c. 1572–1637) British dramatist, poet. Mirth, in *The Staple of News*, "Induction," l. 8–10 (1626). Repr. in *The Complete Plays*, vol. 2, ed. G.A. Wilkes (1981).

See Ovid on fashion.

Public Office

1   Prudent dullness marked him for a mayor.

CHARLES CHURCHILL, (1731–1764) British clergyman, poet. "The Rosciad," l. 596 (1761).

Public Opinion

1   It is a besetting vice of democracies to substitute public opinion for law. This is the usual form in which masses of men exhibit their tyranny.

JAMES FENIMORE COOPER, (1789–1851) U.S. novelist. *The American Democrat*, "On the Disadvantages of Democracy" (1838).

2   It is the folly of too many to mistake the echo of a London

coffee–house for the voice of the kingdom.

JONATHAN SWIFT, (1667–1745) Anglo–Irish satirist. *The Conduct of the Allies* (1711). Repr. in *Jonathan Swift: A Critical Edition of the Major Works*, eds. Angus Ross and David Woolley (1984).

Public, the

1   There is not a more mean, stupid, dastardly, pitiful, selfish, spiteful, envious, ungrateful animal than the Public. It is the greatest of cowards, for it is afraid of itself.

WILLIAM HAZLITT, (1778–1830) British essayist. *Table Talk*, "On Living to One's Self" (1821–1822).

2   The public seldom forgive twice.

JOHANN KASPAR LAVATER, (1741–1801) Swiss divine, poet. *Aphorisms on Man*, no. 595 (1788).

Publicity

1   All publicity is good, except an obituary notice.

BRENDAN BEHAN, (1923–1964) Irish playwright. Quoted in *Sunday Express* (London, Jan. 5, 1964).

2   To have news value is to have a tin can tied to one's tail.

T.E. (THOMAS EDWARD) LAWRENCE, (1888–1935) British soldier, scholar. *The Letters of T.E. Lawrence*, ed. Malcolm Brown (1988). Letter, April 1, 1935.

Publishers and Publishing

1   Some said, John, print it; others said, Not so:
Some said, It might do good; others said, No.

JOHN BUNYAN, (1628–1688) British Baptist preacher, author. *The Pilgrim's Progress*, pt. 1, "Author's Apology" (1678).

2   Now Barabbas was a publisher.

THOMAS CAMPBELL, (1777–1844) Scottish poet. Quoted in *A Publisher and his Friends*, vol. 1, ch. 14, Samuel Smiles (1891).

Parodying the gospel of John 18: 40. The joke is also ascribed to Lord Byron.

Punctuality

1   Punctuality is the politeness of kings.

LOUIS XVIII, (1755–1824) French king. attributed, in *Souvenirs de Jean Lafitte*, bk. 1, ch. 3 (1844). Remark c. 1814.

2   I've been on a calendar, but never on time.

MARILYN MONROE, (1926–1962) U.S. screen actor. *Look* (New York, Jan. 16, 1962).

3   Punctuality is the virtue of the bored.

EVELYN WAUGH, (1903–1966) British novelist. *The Diaries of Evelyn Waugh*, ed. Michael Davie (1976). Journal entry, March 26, 1962.

Punishment

1   "Medusa, come, we'll turn him into stone," they shouted all together glaring down, "how wrong we were to let off Theseus lightly!"

DANTE ALIGHIERI, (1265–1321) Italian poet. "Inferno," cto. 9, l. 52–4, *The Divine Comedy* (c. 1307–1321), trans. by Mark Musa (1971).

Dante is threatened by the three Furies at the gates of Dis, the Infernal City. Theseus, king of Athens, had tried and failed to carry off Persephone, queen of the classical underworld; he was rescued by Hercules.

2   Distrust everyone in whom the impulse to punish is powerful!

FRIEDRICH NIETZSCHE, (1844–1900) German philosopher. *Thus Spoke Zarathustra*, pt. 2, ch. 29 (1883–1891).

3 And where th'offence is, let the great axe fall.

WILLIAM SHAKESPEARE, (1564–1616) British dramatist, poet. Claudius, in *Hamlet*, act 4, sc. 5, l. 216 (1604).

Punishment, Corporal

1 Love is a boy, by poets styled,
Then spare the rod and spoil the
child.

SAMUEL BUTLER, (1612–1680) British poet. "Hudibras," pt. 2, cto. 1, l. 843 (1664). Eds. John Wilders and Hugh de Quehen (1973).

2 I'm all for bringing back the birch,
but only between consenting adults.

GORE VIDAL, (b. 1925) U.S. novelist, critic. Quoted in *Sunday Times Magazine* (London, Sept. 16, 1973). TV interview with David Frost.

Punk

1 I am an Anti–Christ
I am an anarchist
Don't know what I want but I know
where to get it
I wanna destroy passers–by
Because I wanna be anarchy!

SEX PISTOLS, THE, "Anarchy in the U.K." (song) (1976), on the album *Never Mind the Bollocks* (1977).

Puns

1 For my own part I think no innocent species of wit or pleasantry
should be suppressed: and that a
good pun may be admitted among
the smaller excellencies of lively
conversation.

JAMES BOSWELL, (1740–1795) Scottish lawyer, biographer. *Life of Dr Johnson*, entry for June 19, 1784 (1791).

2 A man who could make so vile a
pun would not scruple to pick a
pocket.

JOHN DENNIS, (1657–1734) British playwright, critic. *The Gentleman's Magazine*, vol. 51, editorial note (1781).

3 A pun is not bound by the laws
which limit nicer wit. It is a pistol
let off at the ear; not a feather to
tickle the intellect.

CHARLES LAMB, (1775–1834) British essayist, critic. *Last Essays of Elia*, "Popular Fallacies: That the Worst Puns are the Best" (1833).

Puritans

1 A puritan is a person who pours
righteous indignation into the
wrong things.

G.K. GILBERT KEITH CHESTERTON, (1874–1936) British author. *The New York Times* (Nov. 21, 1930).

2 To the Puritan, all things are
impure, as somebody says.

D.H. (DAVID HERBERT) LAWRENCE, (1885–1930) British author. *Etruscan Places*, 'Cerveteri' (written 1927, published 1932).

Lawrence was probably thinking of St. Paul's words in the New Testament: "Unto the pure all things are pure." (*Titus* 1:15).

3 The Puritan hated bearbaiting, not
because it gave pain to the bear, but
because it gave pleasure to the spectators.

THOMAS BABINGTON MACAULAY, (1800—1859) British historian, Whig politician. *History of England*, vol. 1, ch. 2 (1849).

Purity

1   Blessed are the pure in heart: for they shall see God.

BIBLE: NEW TESTAMENT, Jesus, in Matthew, 5:8.The sixth of the Beatitudes, from the Sermon on the Mount.

2   Stand by thyself, come not near to me; for I am holier than thou.

BIBLE: HEBREW, Isaiah, 65:5.God, upbraiding hypocrisy among the Jews.

3   Unto the pure all things are pure: but unto them that are defiled and unbelieving is nothing pure; but even their mind and conscience is defiled.

BIBLE: NEW TESTAMENT, St. Paul, in Titus, 1:15.See Lawrence on Puritans.

4   I'm as pure as the driven slush.

TALLULAH BANKHEAD, (1903–1968) U.S. screen actor. Quoted in Saturday Evening Post (April 12, 1947). Quoted by Maurice Zolotow.

5   What stronger breastplate than a heart untainted?
Thrice is he armed that hath his quarrel just;
And he but naked, though locked up in steel,
Whose conscience with injustice is corrupted.

WILLIAM SHAKESPEARE, (1564–1616) British dramatist, poet. King Henry, in King Henry VI pt. 2, act 3, sc. 2, l. 232–5 (1600).

6   My strength is as the strength of ten,
Because my heart is pure.

ALFRED TENNYSON, 1ST BARON TENNYSON, (1809–1892) British poet. "Sir Galahad," st. 1 (1842).

7   Purity is the power to contemplate defilement.

SIMONE WEIL, (1909–1943) French philosopher, mystic. Gravity and Grace, ``Attention and Will'' (1947, trans. 1952).

Quarrels

1   Let's contend no more, Love
Strive nor weep:
All be as before, Love,
—Only sleep!

ROBERT BROWNING, (1812–1889) British poet. "A Woman's Last Word," st. 1, Men and Women, vol. 1 (1855).

2   The falling out of faithful friends, renewing is of love.

RICHARD EDWARDS, (c.1523–1566) British poet. "Amantium Irae," The Paradise of Dainty Devices (1576).

This last line of each of the poem's stanzas is an echo of an older line, from which the poem's Latin title is taken: see Terence.

3   Though a quarrel in the streets is a thing to be hated, the energies displayed in it are fine; the commonest man shows a grace in his quarrel.

JOHN KEATS, (1795–1821) British poet. Letters of John Keats, no. 123, ed. Frederick Page (1954).

Letter, written Feb. 14–May 3, 1819, to his brother and sister-in-law, George and Georgiana Keats.

4   Love-quarrels oft in pleasing concord end.

JOHN MILTON, (1608–1674) British poet. Samson, in "Samson Agonistes," l. 1008 (1671). Repr. in Milton's Poetical Works, ed. Douglas Bush (1966).

5   I find my wiffe hath something in her gizzard, that only waits an opportunity of being provoked to bring up; but I will not, for my content-sake, give it.

SAMUEL PEPYS, (1633–1703) British diarist. The Diary of Samuel Pepys, eds.

Robert Latham and William Matthews (1977-1983). Journal entry, June 17, 1668.

6　A plague o' both your houses. They have made worms' meat of me.

WILLIAM SHAKESPEARE, (1564–1616) British dramatist, poet. Mercutio, in *Romeo and Juliet*, act 3, sc. 1, l. 106-7 (1599).

This is the third time Mercutio utters this oath within the space of fifteen lines, when he is struck under Romeo's arm when the latter intervened to pry apart the duelling Mercutio and Tybalt.

7　The course of true love never did run smooth.

WILLIAM SHAKESPEARE, (1564–1616) British dramatist, poet. Lysander, in *A Midsummer Night's Dream*, act 1, sc. 1, l. 134 (1600).

8　Lovers' quarrels are the renewal of love.

TERENCE, (c. 190–159 B.C.) Roman dramatist. Chremes, in *Andria*, act 3, sc. 3, l. 555.

Quixote de la Mancha, Don

1　Nor has his death the world deceiv'd
Less than his wondrous life sur-priz'd;
For if he like a madman liv'd
At least he like a wise one dy'd.

MIGUEL DE CERVANTES, (1547–1616) Spanish author. *Don Quixote*, pt. 2, bk. 4, ch. 74 (1615), trans. by P. Motteux.

Don Quixote's epitaph.

2　The Knight of the Doleful Countenance.

MIGUEL DE CERVANTES, (1547–1616) Spanish author. *Don Quixote*, pt. 1, ch. 19 and *passim* (1605).

Sancho Panza's appellation referring to Don Quixote.

Quotations

1　One must be a wise reader to quote wisely and well.

A. BRONSON ALCOTT [AMOS BRONSON ALCOTT], (1799–1888) U.S. educator, social reformer. "Quotation," bk. 1, *Table Talk* (1877).

2　Quotations in my work are like wayside robbers who leap out armed and relieve the stroller of his conviction.

WALTER BENJAMIN, (1892–1940) German critic, philosopher. *One-Way Street*, "Hardware" (1928), repr. in *One-Way Street and Other Writings* (1978).

3　Ah, yes, I wrote the "Purple Cow"—
I'm sorry, now, I wrote it!
But I can tell you, anyhow,
I'll kill you if you quote it.

GELETT BURGESS, (1866–1951) U.S. humorist, illustrator. *Cinq Ans Après*, *The Burgess Nonsense Book* (1914).

4　It is a good thing for an uneducated man to read books of quotations.... The quotations, when engraved upon the memory, give you good thoughts. They also make you anxious to read the authors and look for more.

WINSTON CHURCHILL, (1874–1965) British statesman, writer. *My Early Life*, ch. 9 (1930).

5　I hate quotations. Tell me what you know.

RALPH WALDO EMERSON, (1803–1882) U.S. essayist, poet, philosopher. *Journals* (1909-1914). Journal entry, May 1849.

6　Next to the originator of a good sentence is the first quoter of it. Many will read the book before one thinks of quoting a passage. As

soon as he has done this, that line
will be quoted east and west.

RALPH WALDO EMERSON, (1803–1882)
U.S. essayist, poet, philosopher. *Journals*, vol.
16, eds. Ronald Bosco and Glen Johnson
(1982). Journal entry, 1867.

The passage later appeared in *Letters and Social
Aims*, "Quotation and Originality" (1876), in
which Emerson commented, "By necessity, by
proclivity, and by delight, we all quote."

7 Classical quotation is the *parole* of
literary men all over the world.

SAMUEL JOHNSON, (1709–1784) British
author, lexicographer. Quoted in James
Boswell, *Life of Dr. Johnson*, entry, May 8,
1781 (1791).

8 Every quotation contributes something to the stability or enlargement
of the language.

SAMUEL JOHNSON, (1709–1784) British
author, lexicographer. *Dictionary of the English
Langauge*, preface (1755).

9 Fidelity to the subject's thought and
to his characteristic way of expressing himself is the *sine qua non* of
journalistic quotation.

JANET MALCOLM, (b. 1934) U.S. author.
The Journalist and the Murderer, "Afterword"
(1990).

Malcolm was at the center of a legal dispute in
which she was accused of fabricating quotations. In her book, Malcolm argued that accurate quotation is impossible: "When we talk
with somebody, we are not aware of the language we are speaking. Our ear takes it in as
English, and only if we see it transcribed verbatim do we realize that it is a kind of foreign
tongue."

10 A book that furnishes no quotations
is, *me judice*, no book—it is a play-
thing.

THOMAS LOVE PEACOCK, (1785–1866)
British author. Dr. Folliot, in *Crotchet Castle*,
ch. 9 (1831).

11 To be occasionally quoted is the
only fame I care for.

ALEXANDER SMITH, (1830–1867) Scottish
poet. *Dreamthorp*, "Men of Letters" (1863).

12 Some, for renown, on scraps of
learning dote,
And think they grow immortal as
they quote.

EDWARD YOUNG, (1683–1765) British
poet, playwright. "Love of Fame: The Universal Passion," satire 1, l. 89-90 (1725-1728).
Repr.In *Complete Works*, ed. J. Doran (1968).

Race

1 It is a great shock at the age of five
or six to find that in a world of Gary
Coopers you are the Indian.

JAMES BALDWIN, (1924–1987) U.S.
author. *The New York Times Magazine* (Mar.
7, 1965). Speech, Feb. 17, 1965, Cambridge
Union, Cambridge University, England.

2 The true worth of a race must be
measured by the character of its
womanhood.

MARY McLEOD BETHUNE, (1875–1955)
U.S. educator. "A Century of Progress of Negro
Women," *Black Women in White America*,
ed. Gerda Lerner (1972). Address, June 3,
1933, to Chicago Women's Federation.

3 I am black, but comely, O ye daughters of Jerusalem, as the tents of
Kedar, as the curtains of Solomon.

BIBLE: HEBREW, *Song of Solomon*,
1:5.The Latin words—*nigra sum, sed her-
mosa*—appear as an inscription on icons of
the Black Madonna in some Mediterranean
countries.

4 The problem of the twentieth
century is the problem of the color-
line—the relation of the darker to
the lighter races of men in Asia and
Africa, in America and the islands of
the sea. It was a phase of this problem that caused the Civil War.

**W.E.B. (WILLIAM EDWARD
BURGHARDT) DU BOIS,** (1868–1963)

U.S. civil rights leader, author. *The Souls of Black Folk*, ch. 2 (1903).

Du Bois discussed the problem of "the color-line" on a number of occasions, incorporating the concept in a speech at the first Pan-African Conference, January 1900, in London.

5   No one has been barred on account of his race from fighting or dying for America—there are no "white" or "colored" signs on the foxholes or graveyards of battle.

JOHN FITZGERALD KENNEDY, (1917–1963) U.S. Democratic politician, president. Quoted in *The New York Times* (June 20, 1963). Message to Congress, June 19, 1963.

Referring to the proposed civil rights bill.

6   I have no purpose to introduce political and social equality between the white and black races. There is a physical difference between the two, which, in my judgment, will probably for ever forbid their living together upon the footing of perfect equality; and inasmuch as it becomes a necessity that there must be a difference, I ... am in favour of the race to which I belong having the superior position.

ABRAHAM LINCOLN, (1809–1865) U.S. president. *Collected Works of Abraham Lincoln*, vol. 2, ed. Roy P. Basler (1953). speech, Aug. 21, 1858, Ottawa, Illinois.

One of the debates with Stephen A. Douglas for election to the Senate.

7   In this country American means white. Everybody else has to hyphenate.

TONI MORRISON, (b. 1931) U.S. novelist, editor. *Guardian* (London, Jan. 29, 1992).

Racism

1   Racism is an *ism* to which everyone in the world today is exposed; for or against, we must take sides. And the history of the future will differ according to the decision which we make.

RUTH BENEDICT, (1887–1948) U.S. anthropologist. *Race: Science and Politics*, ch. 1 (1940).

2   Race prejudice is not only a shadow over the colored—it is a shadow over all of us, and the shadow is darkest over those who feel it least and allow its evil effects to go on.

PEARL S. BUCK, (1892–1973) U.S. author. *What America Means to Me*, ch. 1 (1943).

3   Southern trees bear a strange fruit
Blood on the leaf and blood at the
    root
Black bodies swingin' in the south
    ern breeze
Strange fruit hangin' in the poplar
    trees.

BILLIE HOLIDAY [ELEANOR FAGAN], (1915–1959) U.S. blues singer. "Strange Fruit" (song) (1939).

Anti-lynching poem written by Lewis Allen, set to music by Danny Mendlson and pianist Sonny White.

4   If you're born in America with a black skin, you're born in prison, and the masses of black people in America today are beginning to regard our plight or predicament in this society as one of a prison inmate.

MALCOLM X [MALCOLM LITTLE], (1925–1965) U.S. African-American leader. *Malcolm X: The Man and His Times*, pt. 3, "Malcolm X Talks with Kenneth B. Clark," ed. John Henrik Clarke (1969). Interview June 1963.

5   Until the philosophy which holds one race superior and another inferior is finally and permanently discredited and abandoned, everywhere is war ... and until there are no

longer first-class and second-class citizens of any nation, until the color of a man's skin is of no more significance than the color of his eyes, me seh war. And until the basic human rights are equally guaranteed to all without regard to race, there is war. And until that day, the dream of lasting peace, world citizenship, rule of international morality, will remain but a fleeting illusion to be pursued, but never attained ... now everywhere is war.

BOB MARLEY, (1945–1981) Jamaican reggae musician. "War" (song), from the album *Rastaman Vibration* (1976).

The words of the song are based on a speech given to the United Nations by the Ethiopian emperor Haile Selassie in 1968.

Radicalism

1   What we're saying today is that you're either part of the solution or you're part of the problem.

ELDRIDGE CLEAVER, (b. 1935) U.S. African–American leader, writer. *Eldridge Cleaver, Post Prison Writings and Speeches*, ed. R. Scheer (1969). Speech, 1968, San Francisco.

Radicals

1   I never dared be radical when young
For fear it would make me conservative when old.

ROBERT FROST, (1874–1963) U.S. poet. "Precaution," *A Further Range* (1936).

2   Radical Chic, after all, is only radical in Style; in its heart it is part of Society and its traditions—Politics, like Rock, Pop, and Camp, has its uses.

TOM WOLFE, (b. 1931) U.S. author, journalist. "Radical Chic and Mau-Mauing the Flak-Catchers "(1970). Essay originally published in *New York* (June 8, 1970).

Rain

1   Nature, like man, sometimes weeps from gladness.

BENJAMIN DISRAELI, (1804–1881) British statesman, author. *Coningsby*, bk. 7, ch. 5 (1844).

2   The rain in Spain stays mainly in the plain.

ALAN JAY LERNER, (1918–1986) U.S. songwriter. "The Rain in Spain" (song), *My Fair Lady* (show, 1956; film, 1964). Henry Higgins's phonetic exercise for Eliza Doolittle.

Rank

1   Must! Is *must* a word to be addressed to princes? Little man, little man! thy father, if he had been alive, durst not have used that word.

ELIZABETH I, (1533–1603) British Queen of England. Quoted in *A Short History of the English People*, ch. 7, J.R. Green (1874).

Attributed remonstrance to Sir Robert Cecil, who had urged her to go to bed in her last illness, March 1603; both Robert and his father William Cecil (Lord Burghley) were secretaries of state to Elizabeth.

2   When every one is somebodee, Then no one's anybody!

SIR WILLIAM SCHWENCK GILBERT, (1836–1911) British librettist. The Gondoliers, in *The Gondoliers*, act 2 (1889), published in *The Savoy Operas* (1926).

Rape

1   Rape is no excess, no aberration, no accident, no mistake—it embodies sexuality as the culture defines it.

As long as these definitions remain intact—that is, as long as men are defined as sexual aggressors and women are defined as passive receptors lacking integrity—men who are exemplars of the norm will rape women.

ANDREA DWORKIN, (b. 1946) U.S. feminist critic. "The Rape Atrocity and the Boy Next Door," *Our Blood,* ch. 4 (1976). Speech, March 1, 1975, State University of New York, Stony Brook.

Reactionaries

1 He is a man walking backwards with his face to the future.

ANEURIN BEVAN, (1897–1960) British Labour politician. Quoted in *The Fine Art of Political Wit,* ch. 9, Leon Harris (1964).

Referring to Conservative politician Sir Walter Elliot.

2 The march of the human mind is slow.

EDMUND BURKE, (1729–1797) Irish philosopher, statesman. "Second Speech on Conciliation with America: The Thirteen Resolutions," *Works,* vol. 2 (1899). Speech, March 22, 1775, House of Commons, London.

3 All the reputedly powerful reactionaries are merely paper tigers. The reason is that they are divorced from the people. Look! Was not Hitler a paper tiger? Was Hitler not overthrown?... U.S. imperialism has not yet been overthrown and it has the atomic bomb. I believe it also will be overthrown. It, too, is a paper tiger.

MAO ZEDONG, (1893–1976) Chinese founder of the People's Republic of China. *Quotations from Chairman Mao Tse-Tung,* ch. 6, speech, Nov. 18, 1957, to the International Congress of Communist and Workers' Parties, Moscow.

Mao's first recorded reference to "paper tigers" was in 1946, in "Talk with the American Correspondent Anne Louise Strong," Aug. 1946, published in *Selected Works,* vol. 4 (1961).

Reading

1 Read not to contradict and confute; nor to believe and take for granted; nor to find talk and discourse; but to weigh and consider.

FRANCIS BACON, (1561–1626) British philosopher, essayist, statesman. *Essays,* "Of Studies" (1597-1625).

2 Hypocrite reader—my fellow—my brother!
 (Hypocrite lecteurmon semblablemon frère!)

CHARLES BAUDELAIRE, (1821–1867) French poet. *Les Fleurs du Mal,* Preface "Au Lecteur," (1857). The line is quoted by T.S. Eliot in "The Wasteland," l. 76 (1922).

3 Read, mark, learn, and inwardly digest.

BOOK OF COMMON PRAYER, THE, *The Second Sunday in Advent,* "The Collect" (1662). Referring to the Scriptures.

4 Until you understand a writer's ignorance, presume yourself ignorant of his understanding.

SAMUEL TAYLOR COLERIDGE, (1772–1834) British poet, critic. *Biographia Literaria,* ch. 12 (1817).

5 Never read any book that is not a year old.

RALPH WALDO EMERSON, (1803–1882) U.S. essayist, poet, philosopher. *Society and Solitude,* "Books" (1870).

One of Emerson's three "practical rules" for reading.

6 There is then creative reading as well as creative writing. When the mind is braced by labor and invention, the page of whatever book we

read becomes luminous with manifold allusion. Every sentence is doubly significant, and the sense of our author is as broad as the world.

RALPH WALDO EMERSON, (1803–1882) U.S. essayist, poet, philosopher. *The American Scholar, Nature, Addresses and Lectures* (1849). Lecture, Aug. 31, 1837, delivered before the Phi Beta Kappa Society, Harvard University.

7 No tears in the writer, no tears in the reader.

ROBERT FROST, (1874–1963) U.S. poet. "The Figure a Poem Makes," *Collected Poems* (1939).

8 A man ought to read just as his inclination leads him; for what he reads as a task will do him little good.

SAMUEL JOHNSON, (1709–1784) British author, lexicographer. Quoted in James Boswell, *Life of Dr. Johnson*, entry, July 14, 1763 (1791).

Johnson continued, however, by prescribing that "A young man should read five hours in a day, and so may acquire a great deal of knowledge."

9 What is written without effort is in general read without pleasure.

SAMUEL JOHNSON, (1709–1784) British author, lexicographer. Quoted in *Anecdotes by William Seward, Johnsonian Miscellanies*, vol. 2, ed. George Birkbeck Hill (1897).

10 Everywhere I have sought rest and not found it, except sitting in a corner by myself with a little book.

THOMAS À KEMPIS, (c. 1380–1471) German monk, mystic. Attributed in *The Imitation of Christ*, preface (1617 edition).

The words are inscribed on the picture of Thomas Kempis at Zwoll, Holland, where he is buried.

11 Much reading has brought upon us a learned barbarism.

GEORG CHRISTOPH LICHTENBERG, (1742–1799) German physicist, philosopher. "Notebook F," aph. 144, *Aphorisms* (written 1765-99), trans. by R.J. Hollingdale (1990).

12 Tonstant Weader fwowed up.

DOROTHY PARKER, (1893–1967) U.S. humorous writer. *The New Yorker* (Oct. 20, 1928), repr. in *The Collected Dorothy Parker*, pt. 2 (1973).

Closing words of review of *The House at Pooh Corner*, in Parker's "Constant Reader" column.

13 With one day's reading a man may have the key in his hands.

EZRA POUND, (1885–1972) U.S. poet, critic. "Canto 74," *Pisan Cantos* (1948).

In contrast, Pound had once confided to William Carlos Williams that, "It is not necessary to read everything in a book in order to speak intelligently of it," adding, "Don't tell everybody I said so." (Quoted in Williams' *Kora in Hell* (1920) p.13).

14 Be sure that you go to the author to get at *his* meaning, not to find yours.

JOHN RUSKIN, (1819–1900) British art critic, author. *"Of Kings' Treasuries,"* lecture 1, *Sesame and Lilies* (1865). Repr. in *The Works of John Ruskin*, vol. 28, eds. E.T. Cook and Alexander Weddesburn (1905).

15 People say that life is the thing, but I prefer reading.

LOGAN PEARSALL SMITH, (1865–1946) U.S. essayist, aphorist. *Afterthoughts*, "Myself" (1931).

16 Digressions, incontestably, are the sunshine;—they are the life, the soul of reading!—take them out of this book, for instance,—you might as well take the book along with them;—one cold external winter would reign in every page of it; restore them to the writer;—he steps forth like a bridegroom,—

bids All-hail; brings in variety, and forbids the appetite to fail.

LAURENCE STERNE, (1713–1768) British author. *Tristram Shandy*, bk. 1, ch. 22 (1759-1767).

Reagan, Ronald

1   I'm proud to be his partner. We've had triumphs, we've made mistakes, we've had sex.

GEORGE BUSH, (b. 1924) U.S. Republican politician, president. Quoted by Alexander Cockburn in *New Statesman* (London, May 27, 1988), repr. in *Corruptions of Empire* (1988). Speech, May 6, 1988, College of Southern Idaho.

Bush's gaffe occurred in a speech extolling the Reagan/Bush administration. He corrected himself: "Setbacks, we've had setbacks.... I feel like the javelin competitor who won the toss and elected to receive."

2   A triumph of the embalmer's art.

GORE VIDAL, (b. 1925) U.S. novelist, critic. Quoted in *Observer* (London, April 26, 1981).

Referring to Reagan. In the same newspaper, Feb. 7, 1982, Vidal was quoted: "As the age of television progresses the Reagans will be the rule, not the exception. To be perfect for television is all a President has to be these days."

Reality and Realism

1   The very definition of the real becomes: *that of which it is possible to give an equivalent reproduction....* The real is not only what can be reproduced, but *that which is always already reproduced*. The hyperreal.

JEAN BAUDRILLARD, (b. 1929) French semiologist. *Simulations*, pt. 2, "The Hyperrealism of Simulation" (1983).

Baudrillard goes on to say, "Reality no longer has the time to take on the appearance of real-ity. It no longer even surpasses fiction: it captures every dream even before it takes on the appearance of a dream."

2   Human kind
Cannot bear very much reality.

T.S. (THOMAS STEARNS) ELIOT, (1888–1965) Anglo-American poet, critic. "Burnt Norton," pt. 1 (1936). *Four Quartets* (1942).

The words also appear in Eliot's "Murder in the Cathedral," pt. 2, spoken by Thomas.

Reason

1   Everything that is beautiful and noble is the product of reason and calculation.

CHARLES BAUDELAIRE, (1821–1867) French poet. "The Painter of Modern Life," sct. 11, published in *L'Art Romantique* (1869). *Selected Writings*, ed. P.E. Charvet (1972).

2   It was not reason that besieged Troy; it was not reason that sent forth the Saracen from the desert to conquer the world; that inspired the crusades; that instituted the monastic orders; it was not reason that produced the Jesuits; above all, it was not reason that created the French Revolution. Man is only great when he acts from the passions; never irresistible but when he appeals to the imagination.

BENJAMIN DISRAELI, (1804–1881) British statesman, author. Sidonia, in *Coningsby*, bk. 4, ch. 13 (1844).

3   I'll not listen to reason.... Reason always means what someone else has got to say.

ELIZABETH GASKELL, (1810–1865) British novelist. Miss Matty's maid, Martha, in *Cranford*, ch. 14 (1853).

4   To him who looks upon the world rationally, the world in its turn pre-

sents a rational aspect. The relation is mutual.

GEORG HEGEL, (1770–1831) German philosopher. *The Philosophy of History*, "Introduction," sct. 3 (1837).

5   Irrationally held truths may be more harmful than reasoned errors.

THOMAS HENRY HUXLEY, (1825–1895) British biologist. "The Coming of Age of The Origin of Species," *Science and Culture* (1881).

6   What is a man
If his chief good and market of his time
Be but to sleep and feed?—a beast, no more.
Sure, he that made us with such large discourse,
Looking before and after, gave us not
That capability and god-like reason
To fust in us unused.

WILLIAM SHAKESPEARE, (1564–1616) British dramatist, poet. Hamlet, in *Hamlet*, act 4, sc. 4, l. 27-30 (1604).

This passage is absent from the 1623 Folio edition.

Rebellion

1   Rebellion to tyrants is obedience to God.

JOHN BRADSHAW, (1602–1659) British lawyer, regicide. *Motto.*

Inscription at Bradshaw's final burial place near Martha Bay, Jamaica. Bradshaw, the President of the Parliamentary Commission which tried and sentenced King Charles I, was originally buried in Westminster Abbey, but his remains, along with those of Cromwell and Ireton, were dug up in 1660, and hanged at Tyburn, London, where rebels and common criminals were executed. Both Benjamin Franklin and Thomas Jefferson were attributed with sayings similar to Bradshaw's epitaph, and the words appeared on Jefferson's seal.

2   What is a rebel? A man who says no.

ALBERT CAMUS, (1913–1960) French-Algerian philosopher, author. *The Rebel*, ch. 1 (1951, trans. 1953).

Opening sentence.

3   A civilization which leaves so large a number of its participants unsatisfied and drives them into revolt neither has nor deserves the prospect of a lasting existence.

SIGMUND FREUD, (1856–1939) Austrian psychiatrist. *The Future of an Illusion*, vol. 6, ch. 2, *Complete Works, Standard Edition*, eds. James Strachey and Anna Freud (1961). (Originally published 1927).

4   I struck the board, and cried, "No more.
I will abroad."
What? Shall I ever sigh and pine?
My lines and life are free; free as the road,
Loose as the wind, as large as store.
Shall I be still in suit?

GEORGE HERBERT, (1593–1633) British poet, clergyman. "The Collar," *The Temple* (1633). Repr. in *The Works of George Herbert*, ed. Helen Gardner (1961).

Herbert's poem describes the anguished decision which directed him toward the "collar" (the Church)—see Herbert on vocation.

5   I hold it that a little rebellion, now and then, is a good thing, and as necessary in the political world as storms in the physical.... It is a medicine necessary for the sound health of government.

THOMAS JEFFERSON, (1743–1826) U.S. president. *The Papers of Thomas Jefferson*, vol. 11, Julian P. Boyd (1955). Letter, Jan. 30, 1787, to statesman (later president) James Madison.

Speaking of Daniel Shays's Rebellion of poor farmers in Massachusetts; Jefferson, writing from Paris, was the only one of the American leaders not alarmed by news of the revolt.

Recession

1 Can anybody remember when the times were not hard, and money not scarce?

RALPH WALDO EMERSON, (1803–1882) U.S. essayist, poet, philosopher. *Society and Solitude,* "Works and Days" (1870).

Recklessness

1 Fools rush in where angels fear to tread.

ALEXANDER POPE, (1688–1744) British satirical poet. "An Essay on Criticism," l. 625 (1711).

2 Live fast, die young and have a good-looking corpse.

DANIEL TARADASH, U.S. screenwriter. Nick Romano (John Derek), in *Knock On Any Door* (film) (1949). Nicholas Ray.

Reckoning

1 Be not deceived; God is not mocked: for whatsoever a man soweth, that shall he also reap.

BIBLE: NEW TESTAMENT, St. Paul, in *Galatians,* 6:7.

Reclusiveness

1 To fly from, need not be to hate, mankind:
   All are not fit with them to stir and toil,
   Nor is it discontent to keep the mind
   Deep in its fountain, lest it overboil.

GEORGE GORDON NOEL BYRON, 6TH BARON BYRON, (1788–1824) British poet. "Childe Harold's Pilgrimage" cto. 3, st. 69 (1812-1818).

2 In this world without quiet corners, there can be no easy escapes from history, from hullabaloo, from terrible, unquiet fuss.

SALMAN RUSHDIE, (b. 1947) Indian–born British author. "Outside the Whale," *Imaginary Homelands* (1991). (Essay originally published 1984).

Reconciliation

1 Now is the winter of our discontent
   Made glorious by this son of York;
   And all the clouds that loured upon
   our house
   In the deep bosom of the ocean
   buried.

WILLIAM SHAKESPEARE, (1564–1616) British dramatist, poet. Richard, in *Richard III,* act 1, sc. 1, l. 1-4 (1597).

The play opens with Richard's soliloquy about his brother, now installed on the throne as Edward IV.

Recreation

1 One way of getting an idea of our fellow-countrymen's miseries is to go and look at their pleasures.

GEORGE ELIOT [MARY ANN (OR MARIAN) EVANS], (1819–1880) British novelist. *Felix Holt, the Radical,* ch. 28 (1866).

2 If I had no duties, and no reference to futurity, I would spend my life in driving briskly in a post-chaise with a pretty woman.

SAMUEL JOHNSON, (1709–1784) British author, lexicographer. quoted in James Boswell, *Life of Dr. Johnson,* entry, Sept. 19, 1777 (1791).

Reform

1 You begin saving the world by saving one man at a time; all else

is grandiose romanticism or politics.

CHARLES BUKOWSKI, (1920–1994) U.S. author, poet. "Too Sensitive," *Tales of Ordinary Madness* (1967).

2 Every reform, however necessary, will by weak minds be carried to an excess, which will itself need reforming.

SAMUEL TAYLOR COLERIDGE, (1772–1834) British poet, critic. *Biographia Literaria*, ch. 1 (1817).

3 Why, Sir, most schemes of political improvement are very laughable things.

SAMUEL JOHNSON, (1709–1784) British author, lexicographer. quoted in James Boswell, *Life of Dr. Johnson*, entry, Oct. 20, 1769 (1791).

4 Turn where we may, within, around, the voice of great events is proclaiming to us, Reform, that you may preserve!

THOMAS BABINGTON MACAULAY, (1800–1859) British historian, Whig politician. *Complete Writings of Lord Macaulay*, vol. 17 (1900). Speech to House of Commons, March 2, 1831.

The First Reform Bill debate.

5 Of all follies there is none greater than wanting to make the world a better place.

MOLIÈRE [JEAN BAPTISTE POQUELIN], (1622–1673) French dramatist. Philinte, in *Le Misanthrope*, act 1, sc. 1 (1666).

6 Nothing so needs reforming as other people's habits.

MARK TWAIN, (1835–1910) U.S. author. *Pudd'nhead Wilson*, ch. 15, "Pudd'nhead Wilson's Calendar" (1894).

7 The inevitability of gradualness cannot fail to be appreciated.

SIDNEY WEBB (LORD PASSFIELD, OR BARON PASS, (1859–1947) British socialist. *The Labour Party on the Threshold* (pamphlet) (1923). Speech, June 26, 1923, Labour Party Conference, London.

Referring to the program of the Labour Party, then in opposition.

Regret

1 O plunge your hands in water,
   Plunge them in up to the wrist;
   Stare, stare in the basin
   And wonder what you've missed.

W.H. (WYSTAN HUGH) AUDEN, (1907–1973) Anglo-American poet. "As I Walked Out One Evening," *Another Time* (1940).

Refrain by "all the clocks in the city."

2 There is no greater sorrow than to recall a happy time in the midst of wretchedness.

DANTE ALIGHIERI, (1265–1321) Italian poet. "Inferno," cto. 5, l. 121-3, *The Divine Comedy* (1321). Spoken by Francesca da Rimini. This thought appears in Boethius's *Consolation of Philosophy*, bk. 2 (6th century).

3 Footfalls echo in the memory
   Down the passage which we did not take
   Towards the door we never opened
   Into the rose-garden.

T.S. (THOMAS STEARNS) ELIOT, (1888–1965) Anglo-American poet, critic. "Burnt Norton," pt. 1 (1936). *Four Quartets* (1942).

4 *(Non! Rien de rien.... Non, je ne regrette rien! Ni le bien qu'on m'a fait, Ni le mal. Tout ça m'est bien égal!)* No, I regret nothing.... Neither the good nor the bad, It's all the same for me.

EDITH PIAF, (1918–1963) French singer. "Non, Je ne Regrette Rien" (song), written by Charles Dumont and Michael Vaucaire (1961).

5   For of all sad words of tongue or pen,
    The saddest are these: "It might have
    been!"

    JOHN GREENLEAF WHITTIER,
    (1807–1892) U.S. poet. "Maud Muller," l. 105-6
    (1856). Repr. in *The Poetical Works of John
    Greenleaf Whittier*, ed. W. Garrett Horder
    (1911).

Reincarnation

1   If there is a transmigration of souls
    then I am not yet on the bottom
    rung. My life is a hesitation before
    birth.

    FRANZ KAFKA, (1883–1924) Czech novel-
    ist, short-story writer. *The Diaries of Franz
    Kafka: 1910-1923*, ed. Max Brod (1948). Jour-
    nal entry, Jan. 24, 1922.

Relationships

1   Me Tarzan, you Jane.

    EDGAR RICE BURROUGHS, (1875–1950)
    Johnny Weissmuller (Tarzan), in *Tarzan the Ape
    Man* (film) (1932).

    In Burroughs' book *Tarzan of the Apes* (1914),
    Tarzan's words are: "I am Tarzan of the Apes. I
    want you. I am yours. You are mine." (Ch. 18.)

Relativity

1   God keep me from the divinity of
    Yes and No ... the Yea Nay Creeping
    Jesus, from supposing Up and Down
    to be the same thing as all experi-
    mentalists must suppose.

    WILLIAM BLAKE, (1757–1827) British poet,
    painter, engraver. *The Letters of William Blake*,
    ed. Geoffrey Keynes (1956). Letter, April 12,
    1827.

2   By an application of the theory of
    relativity to the taste of readers,
    today in Germany I am called a Ger-
    man man of science, and in England
    I am represented as a Swiss Jew. If I

come to be regarded as a *bête noire*
the descriptions will be reversed,
and I shall become a Swiss Jew for
the Germans and a German man of
science for the English!

ALBERT EINSTEIN, (1879–1955) German-born U.S. theoretical physicist. *Times*
(London, Nov. 28, 1919).

Einstein used variations of this idea on different occasions.

Religion

1   Of all possible sexual perversions,
    religion is the only one to haveever
    been scientifically systematized.

    LOUIS ARAGON, (1897–1982) French
    poet. *Treatise on Style*, pt. 1, "The Pen" (1928).

2   The true meaning of religion is
    thus, not simply *morality*, but
    morality touched by *emotion*.

    MATTHEW ARNOLD, (1822–1888)
    British poet, critic. *Literature and Dogma*,
    ch. 1, sct. 2 (1873).

3   Pure religion and undefiled before
    God and the Father is this, to visit
    the fatherless and widows in their
    affliction, and to keep himself
    unspotted from the world.

    BIBLE: NEW TESTAMENT *James*, 1:27.

4   Religion! what treasure untold
    Resides in that heavenly word!

    WILLIAM COWPER, (1731–1800) British
    poet. "Verses Supposed to be Written by
    Alexander Selkirk", l. 25-6 (1782). Repr. in
    Poetical Works, ed. H.S. Milford (1934).

5   Science without religion is lame,
    religion without science is blind.

    ALBERT EINSTEIN, (1879–1955) Ger-
    man-born U.S. theoretical physicist. *Out of
    My Later Years*, ch. 8, pt. 1 (1950, rev. 1970).

    Einstein used the words in a scientific paper
    in 1940.

6 Religion
Has made an honest woman of the
   supernatural,
And we won't have it kicking over
   the traces again.

CHRISTOPHER FRY, (b. 1907) British
playwright. Tappercoom, in *The Lady's Not
for Burning*, act 2 (1949).

7 For it is with the mysteries of our
religion, as with wholesome pills
for the sick, which swallowed
whole, have the virtue to cure; but
chewed, are for the most part cast
up again without effect.

THOMAS HOBBES, (1588–1679) British
philosopher. *Leviathan*, pt. 3, ch. 32 (1651).

8 I count religion but a childish toy,
And hold there is no sin but ignorance.

CHRISTOPHER MARLOWE, (1564–1593)
British dramatist, poet. Machiavel, in *The Jew
of Malta*, "Prologue," (writen c. 1589, first
published 1633).

The second line sometimes appears, "no sin
but innocence."

9 The idea of the sacred is quite simply one of the most conservative
notions in any culture, because it
seeks to turn other ideas—uncertainty, progress, change—into
crimes.

SALMAN RUSHDIE, (b. 1947) Indian–born
British author. "Is Nothing Sacred?" (1990).
Herbert Read Memorial Lecture, Feb. 6, 1990,
ICA, London.

10 We have just enough religion to
make us *hate*, but not enough to
make us *love* one another.

JONATHAN SWIFT, (1667–1745) Anglo-
Irish satirist. "Various Thoughts Moral and
Diverting," *Miscellanies in Prose and Verse*
(1711). Repr. in *Jonathan Swift: A Critical Edi-
tion of the Major Works*, eds. Angus Ross and
David Woolley (1984).

Reminiscences

1 I wept as I remembered how often
   you and I
Had tired the sun with talking and
   sent him down the sky.

CALLIMACHUS, (c.305–240 B.C.) Alexan-
drian poet, grammarian. *Heraclitus*, trans. by
William Johnson Cory (1858).

Addressing the poet Heraclitus of Halicarnas-
sus, on the news of his death.

2 One man's remorse is another
man's reminiscence.

OGDEN NASH, (1902–1971) U.S. poet. 'A
Clean Conscience Never Relaxes,' *I'm a
Stranger Here Myself* (1938).

Repentance

1 Though your sins be as scarlet, they
shall be as white as snow; though
they be red like crimson, they shall
be as wool.

BIBLE: HEBREW, *Isaiah*, 1:18.

2 For while my former flames remain
within,
Repentance is but want of power to
   sin.

JOHN DRYDEN, (1631–1700) British poet,
dramatist, critic. Arcite, in *Palamon and Arcite*,
bk. 3, l. 812-3 (1700).

Repression

1 If they take you in the morning, they
will be coming for us that night.

JAMES BALDWIN, (1924–1987) U.S. author.
"Open Letter to my Sister, Angela Davis." *New
York Review of Books* (Jan. 7, 1971).

2 In the groves of their academy, at
the end of every vista, you see nothing but the gallows.

EDMUND BURKE, (1729–1797) Irish philosopher, statesman. *Reflections on the Revolution in France* (1790), repr. in *Works*, vol. 3 (1865).

Referring to the aftermath of the French Revolution.

3   We can never be sure that the opinion we are endeavouring to stifle is a false opinion; and even if we were sure, stifling it would be an evil still.

JOHN STUART MILL, (1806–1873) British philosopher, economist. *On Liberty*, ch. 2 (1859).

Reproach

1   You silly twisted boy!

SPIKE MILLIGAN, (b. 1918) British comedian, humorous writer. Lance Brigadier Grytpype-Thynne (Peter Sellers), in *The Goon Show* (BBC radio comedy series), broadcast (1951-1960). Published in *The Goon Show Scripts*, ed. Spike Milligan (1972).

Running gag.

Republicanism

1   The republican is the only form of government which is not eternally at open or secret war with the rights of mankind.

THOMAS JEFFERSON, (1743–1826) U.S. president. *The Papers of Thomas Jefferson*, vol. 16, Julian P. Boyd (1963). Letter, March 11, 1790.

Reputations

1   For my name and memory I leave it to men's charitable speeches, and to foreign nations, and the next ages.

FRANCIS BACON, (1561–1626) British philosopher, essayist, statesman. *Works of Francis Bacon*, vol. 3 (ed. 1765). Last will, Dec. 19, 1625.

Appointed Lord Chancellor in 1618, Bacon was removed from office three years later for accepting a bribe from a litigant. Alexander Pope summed up his character thus: "If parts allure thee, think how Bacon shined, The wisest, brightest, meanest of mankind." (*Essay on Man*, epistle 4, l. 281-2.)

2   A good name is better than precious ointment.

BIBLE: HEBREW, *Ecclesiastes*, 7:1.

3   A good reputation is more valuable than money.

PUBLILIUS SYRUS, (1st century B.C.) Roman writer of mimes. *Sententiae*, no. 108.

4   Reputation, reputation, reputation! O, I ha' lost my reputation, I ha' lost the immortal part of myself, and what remains is bestial!

WILLIAM SHAKESPEARE, (1564–1616) British dramatist, poet. Cassio, in *Othello*, act 2, sc. 3, l. 256-8 (1623).

Research

1   To write it, it took three months; to conceive it—three minutes; to collect the data in it—all my life.

F. SCOTT FITZGERALD, (1896–1940) U.S. author. "The Author's Apology," published in *The Letters of F. Scott Fitzgerald*, ed. Andrew Turnbull (1963). Letter to the Booksellers' Convention, April 1920.

Referring to his novel *This Side of Paradise*.

2   Knowledge is of two kinds. We know a subject ourselves, or we know where we can find information upon it.

SAMUEL JOHNSON, (1709–1784) British author, lexicographer. Quoted in James

Boswell, *Life of Dr. Johnson*, entry, April 18, 1775 (1791).

3 If politics is the art of the possible, research is surely the art of the soluble. Both are immensely practical-minded affairs.

PETER B. MEDAWAR, (1915–1987) British immunologist. "The Act of Creation," first published in *New Statesman* (London, June 19, 1964). *The Art of the Soluble* (1967).

Resentment

1 I was angry with my friend:
I told my wrath, my wrath did end.
I was angry with my foe:
I told it not, my wrath did grow.

WILLIAM BLAKE, (1757–1827) British poet, painter, engraver. *Songs of Experience,* "A Poison Tree," st. 1 (1794), repr. in *Complete Writings*, ed. Geoffrey Keynes (1957).

2 In ceremonies of the horsemen,
Even the pawn must hold a grudge.

BOB DYLAN [ROBERT ALLEN ZIM-MERMAN], (b. 1941) U.S. singer, songwriter. "Love Minus Zero/No Limit" (song), on the album *Bringing it all Back Home* (1965).

Reserve

1 There is safety in reserve, but no attraction. One cannot love a reserved person.

JANE AUSTEN, (1775–1817) British novelist. Frank Churchill, in *Emma*, ch. 24 (1816).

Emma replies, "Not till the reserve ceases towards one's self; and then the attraction may be the greater."

Resignation

1 We'd like to fight but we fear defeat,

We'd like to work but we're feeling too weak,
We'd like to be sick but we'd get the sack,
We'd like to behave, we'd like to believe,
We'd like to love, but we've lost the knack.

CECIL DAY LEWIS, (1904–1972) British poet. "The Magnetic Mountain," sct. 33 (1933). Repr. in *Collected Poems 1929-1936* (1948).

2 I can imagine no more comfortable frame of mind for the conduct of life than a humorous resignation.

W. SOMERSET MAUGHAM, (1874–1966) British author. *A Writer's Notebook*, entry, 1902 (1949).

Resistance

1 Be strong, and quit yourselves like men, O ye Philistines, that ye be not servants unto the Hebrews, as they have been to you; quit yourselves like men, and fight.

BIBLE: HEBREW, *1 Samuel*, 4:9.

2 We shall fight on the beaches, we shall fight on the landing grounds, we shall fight in the fields and in the streets, we shall fight in the hills; we shall never surrender.

WINSTON CHURCHILL, (1874–1965) British statesman, writer. Vol. 6, *Winston S. Churchill: His Complete Speeches, 1897-1963,* ed. Robert Rhodes James (1974). Speech, June 4, 1940, House of Commons, London.

After the retreat from Dunkirk, France.

3 *No pasarón!* (They shall not pass!)

DOLORES IBARRURI (*LA PASIONARIA*), (1895–1989) Spanish Communist leader. Quoted in *The Spanish Civil War*, bk. 2, ch. 16, Hugh Thomas (1961, rev.

1965). Radio broadcast, July 18, 1936, from Paris.

Calling on the women of Spain to defend the Republic. The expression, like "It is better to die on your feet than to live on your knees" (said in the same broadcast; see Ibarurri on revolutionaries), became a slogan in the ensuing civil war. Previous attributions for this rallying cry include Marshal Pétain (1856-1951) during World War I: *Ils ne passeront pas.*

4   Fight the power that be. Fight the power.

K. SHOCKLEE, E. SADLER, C. RIDEN-HOUR, "Fight the Power," on Public Enemy's album, *Fear of a Black Planet,* and theme song in *Do The Right Thing* (film), directed and co-produced by Spike Lee (1989).

Resolve

1   Moral of the Work. In war: resolution. In defeat: defiance. In victory: magnanimity. In peace: goodwill.

WINSTON CHURCHILL, (1874–1965) British statesman, writer. *The Second World War,* epigraph (1948-1954).

Churchill first used the words with reference to World War I..

2   I am in earnest—I will not equivocate—I will not excuse—I will not retreat a single inch—and I will be heard!

WILLIAM LLOYD GARRISON, (1805–1879) U.S. abolitionist. *Liberator* (Boston, Jan. 1, 1831).

Salutatory address of Garrison's anti-slavery newspaper, which was edited by him for the next 34 years in the face of savage opposition.

3   What reinforcement we may gain from hope;
    If not, what resolution from despair.

JOHN MILTON, (1608–1674) British poet. Satan, in *Paradise Lost,* bk. 1, l. 190-1 (1667).

Results

1   Wherefore by their fruits ye shall know them.

BIBLE: NEW TESTAMENT Jesus, in *Matthew,* 7:20.From the Sermon on the Mount.

Retirement

1   Lord Tyrawley and I have been dead these two years, but we don't choose to have it known.

PHILIP DORMER STANHOPE, 4TH EARL CHESTERFIELD, (1694–1773) British statesman, man of letters. Quoted by Dr. Samuel Johnson in James Boswell, *Life of Dr. Johnson,* April 3, 1773 (1791).

2   Learn to live well, or fairly make your will;
    You've played, and loved, and eat, and drunk your fill:
    Walk sober off; before a sprightlier age
    Comes tittering on, and shoves you from the stage:
    Leave such to trifle with more grace and ease,
    Whom Folly pleases, and whose follies please.

ALEXANDER POPE, (1688–1744) British satirical poet. *Imitations of Horace,* bk. 2, epistle 2, l. 322-7 (1737).

Last lines of bk. 2, epistle 2.

Revenge

1   Revenge is a kind of wild justice, which the more a man's nature runs to, the more ought law to weed it out.

FRANCIS BACON, (1561–1626) British philosopher, essayist, statesman. *Essays,* "Of Revenge" (1597–1625)."A man that studieth revenge," Bacon added later in the essay, "keeps his own wounds green."

2 And if any mischief follow, then thou shalt give life for life, eye for eye, tooth for tooth, hand for hand, foot for foot, burning for burning, wound for wound, stripe for stripe.

BIBLE: HEBREW, *Exodus,* 21:23-25.

3 Dearly beloved, avenge not yourselves, but rather give place unto wrath: for it is written, Vengeance is mine; I will repay, saith the Lord. Therefore if thine enemy hunger, feed him; if he thirst, give him drink: for in so doing thou shalt heap coals of fire on his head. Be not overcome of evil, but overcome evil with good.

BIBLE: NEW TESTAMENT St. Paul, in *Romans,* 12:19-21.Paul is referring to *Deuteronomy* 32:35: "To me belongeth vengeance, and recompence."

4 And, re-assembling our afflicted powers,
Consult how we may henceforth most offend.

JOHN MILTON, (1608–1674) British poet. Satan, in *Paradise Lost,* bk.1, l. 186-7 (1667).

Revolution

1 All modern revolutions have ended in a reinforcement of the power of the state.

ALBERT CAMUS, (1913–1960) French-Algerian philosopher, author. *The Rebel* (1951, trans. 1953).

2 You can never have a revolution in order to establish a democracy. You must have a democracy in order to have a revolution.

GILBERT KEITH CHESTERTON, (1874–1936) British author. *Tremendous Trifles,* "The Wind and The Trees" (1909).

3 All successful revolutions are the kicking in of a rotten door. The violence of revolutions is the violence of men who charge into a vacuum.

JOHN KENNETH GALBRAITH, (b. 1908) U.S. economist. *The Age of Uncertainty,* ch. 3 (1977).

4 The surest guide to the correctness of the path that women take is *joy in the struggle.* Revolution is the festival of the oppressed.

GERMAINE GREER, (b. 1939) Australian feminist writer. *The Female Eunuch,* " Revolution" (1970).

5 The brutalities of progress are called revolutions. When they are over we realize this: that the human race has been roughly handled, but that it has advanced.

VICTOR HUGO, (1802–1885) French poet, dramatist, novelist. The old revolutionary, in *Les Misérables,* pt. 1, bk. 1, ch. 10 (1862).

6 Those who make peaceful revolution impossible will make violent revolution inevitable.

JOHN FITZGERALD KENNEDY, (1917–1963) U.S. Democratic politician, president. *Public Papers of the Presidents of the United States: John F. Kennedy, 1962.* Speech, March 13, 1962, the White House.

Addressing the diplomatic corps of the Latin American republics.

7 Without revolutionary theory there can be no revolutionary movement.

VLADIMIR ILYICH LENIN, (1870–1924) Russian revolutionary leader. *What Is To Be Done?* (1902).

8 A revolution is not a dinner party, or writing an essay, or painting a

picture, or doing embroidery; it cannot be so refined, so leisurely and gentle, so temperate, kind, courteous, restrained and magnanimous. A revolution is an insurrection, an act of violence by which one class overthrows another.

MAO ZEDONG, (1893–1976) Chinese founder of the People's Republic of China. *Selected Works,* vol. 1 (1954).

Report, March 1927.

9　Let the ruling classes tremble at a communist revolution. The proletarians have nothing to lose but their chains. They have a world to win. Workingmen of all countries, unite!

KARL MARX, (1818–1883) German political theorist, social philosopher. *The Communist Manifesto,* sct. 4 (1848). Repr. in *Karl Marx: Selected Works,* vol. 1 (1942).

These closing words are commonly rendered, "Workers of the world unite, you have nothing to lose but your chains!"

10　When the people contend for their liberty they seldom get anything by their victory but new masters.

GEORGE SAVILE, LORD HALIFAX, (1633–1695) British statesman, author. "Of Prerogative, Power and Liberty," *Political, Moral and Miscellaneous Thoughts and Reflections* (1750). Repr. in *Works,* ed. Walter Raleigh (1912).

11　Revolutions are always verbose.

LEON TROTSKY, (1879–1940) Russian revolutionary. *The History of the Russian Revolution,* vol. 2, ch. 12 (1933).

Revolution: American

1　Our cause is just. Our union is perfect.

JOHN DICKINSON, (1732–1808) U.S. statesman, essayist. *Declaration on the Causes*

and Necessity of Taking Up Arms (pamphlet) (1775). Quoted in C.J. Stillé, *The Life and Times of John Dickinson,* ch. 5 (1891).

2　Freedom of religion, freedom of the press, and freedom of person under the protection of *habeas corpus,* and trial by juries impartially selected. These principles form the bright constellation which has gone before us, and guided our steps through an age of revolution and reformation.

THOMAS JEFFERSON, (1743–1826) U.S. president. "First Inaugural Address', vol. 3, *The Writings of Thomas Jefferson,* ed. Andrew A. Lipscomb (1904). Speech, March 4, 1801.

3　Fourscore and seven years ago, our fathers brought forth on this continent a new nation, conceived in liberty, and dedicated to the proposition that all men are created equal.

ABRAHAM LINCOLN, (1809–1865) U.S. president. "Gettysburg Address", repr. in *Collected Works of Abraham Lincoln,* vol. 7, ed. Roy P. Basler (1953). speech, Nov. 19, 1863.

Revolution: French

1　It was the best of times, it was the worst of times, it was the age of wisdom, it was the age of foolishness, it was the epoch of belief, it was the epoch of incredulity, it was the season of Light, it was the season of Darkness, it was the spring of hope, it was the winter of despair, we had everything before us, we had nothing before us, we were all going direct to Heaven, we were all going direct the other way—in short, the period was so far like the present period, that some of its noisiest authorities insisted on its being received, for good or for evil, in the superlative degree of comparison only.

CHARLES DICKENS, (1812–1870) British novelist. *A Tale of Two Cities*, bk. 1, ch. 1 (1859).

Opening lines.

2 How much the greatest event it is that ever happened in the world! and how much the best!

CHARLES JAMES FOX, (1749–1806) British Whig politician. Quoted in *The Life and Times of C.J. Fox*, vol. 2, Lord John Russell (1859). Letter, July 30, 1789.

Referring to the fall of the Bastille. Fox's support for the French Revolution led to the rupture of his cherished friendship with Edmund Burke.

3 Bliss was it in that dawn to be alive, But to be young was very heaven!

WILLIAM WORDSWORTH, (1770–1850) British poet. *The Prelude*, bk. 11, l. 108–9 (1850).

These lines are from an earlier composition, *The French Revolution as it Appeared to Enthusiasts* (written 1804, published 1809), incorporated by Wordsworth in *The Prelude*.

Revolutionaries

1 I must study politics and war that my sons may have liberty to study mathematics and philosophy.

JOHN ADAMS, (1735–1826) U.S. statesman, president. *The Adams Family Correspondence*, vol. 3, ed. L.H. Butterfield (1973). Letter, May 1780, to his wife Abigail Adams.

2 History will absolve me.
[La historia me absolver.]

FIDEL CASTRO, (b. 1926) Cuban revolutionary, premier. *La Historia Me Absolver* (pamphlet) (1953).

Castro used the words during his trial in 1953, referring to his unsuccessful assault on the

Moncada barracks. Though sentenced to fifteen years' imprisonment, he was released under an amnesty within a year and returned from exile in 1958 to oust the Batista régime and assume power.

3 It is better to die on your feet than to live on your knees!

DOLORES IBARRURI (LA PASIONARIA), (1895–1989) Spanish Communist leader. Quoted in *The Spanish Civil War*, bk. 2, ch. 16, Hugh Thomas (1961, rev. 1965). Radio broadcast, Sept. 3, 1936, from Paris.

Calling on the women of Spain to defend the Republic. In her autobiography (1966), Ibarruri stated that she had first used the words in an earlier broadcast in Spain, July 18. The expression, which became a slogan in the ensuing civil war, has an earlier attribution, to Mexican revolutionary Emiliano Zapata (c. 1877–1919).

4 People who talk about revolution and class struggle without referring explicitly to everyday life, without understanding what is subversive about love and what is positive in the refusal of constraints, such people have a corpse in their mouth.

RAOUL VANEIGEM, (b. 1934) Belgian situationist philosopher. *The Revolution of Everyday Life*, ch. 1, sct. 4 (1967, trans. 1983).

The last words were graffitied onto walls in Paris during the 1968 revolt.

Rewards

1 Thou preparest a table before me in the presence of mine enemies; thou anointest my head with oil; my cup runneth over.

BIBLE: HEBREW, *Psalms*, 23:5.

Rich, the

1 He that maketh haste to be rich shall not be innocent.

BIBLE: HEBREW, *Proverbs*, 28:20.

2   It is easier for a camel to go through the eye of a needle, than for a rich man to enter into the kingdom of God.

BIBLE: NEW TESTAMENT, Jesus, in *Matthew*, 19:24.

3   The day is not far distant when the man who dies leaving behind him millions of available wealth, which was free for him to administer during life, will pass away "unwept, unhonored, and unsung," no matter to what uses he leave the dross which he cannot take with him. Of such as these the public verdict will then be: "The man who dies thus rich dies disgraced." Such, in my opinion, is the true gospel concerning wealth, obedience to which is destined some day to solve the problem of the rich and the poor.

ANDREW CARNEGIE, (1835–1919) U.S. industrialist, philanthropist. "The Gospel of Wealth," quoted in *Life of Andrew Carnegie*, vol. 1, ch. 17, Burton J. Hendrick (1932). First published in *North American Review*, Cedar Falls, Iowa (June 1889).

4   Poor little rich girl,
You're a bewitched girl,
Better beware!

NOËL COWARD, (1899–1973) British playwright, actor, composer. "Poor Little Rich Girl" (song), *On With the Dance* (musical revue, 1925), published in *Collected Sketches and Lyrics* (1931).

5   Let me tell you about the very rich. They are different from you and me. They possess and enjoy early, and it does something to them, makes them soft where we are hard, and cynical where we are trustful, in a way that, unless you were born rich, it is very difficult to understand. They think, deep in their hearts, that they are better than we are because we had to discover the compensations and refuges of life for ourselves. Even when they enter deep into our world or sink below us, they still think that they are better than we are. They are different.

F. SCOTT FITZGERALD, (1896–1940) U.S. author. *All the Sad Young Men*, "The Rich Boy" (1926). The first sentence also occurs in Fitzgerald's notebooks (*The Crack-Up*, "Notebook E," 1945) and was taken up by Hemingway in his story "The Snows of Kilimanjaro" (1936). See Hemingway on the rich.

6   The rich were dull and they drank too much or they played too much backgammon. They were dull and they were repetitious. He remembered poor Julian and his romantic awe of them and how he had started a story once that began, "The very rich are different from you and me." And how someone had said to Julian, "Yes, they have more money."

ERNEST HEMINGWAY, (1899–1961) U.S. author. "The Snows of Kilimanjaro', *The Fifth Column and the First Forty-Nine Stories* (1938). First published in *Esquire* (New York, Aug. 1936).

In its original publication, "Julian" was named as F. Scott Fitzgerald.

7   For just as poets love their own works, and fathers their own children, in the same way those who have created a fortune value their money, not merely for its uses, like other persons, but because it is their own production. This makes them moreover disagreeable companions, because they will praise nothing but riches.

PLATO, (c. 427–347 B.C.) Greek philosopher. Socrates, in *The Republic*, bk. 1 sct. 330.

8   O, what a world of vile ill-favoured
     faults,
     Looks handsome in three hundred
     pounds a year!

WILLIAM SHAKESPEARE, (1564–1616)
British dramatist, poet. Anne, in *The Merry
Wives of Windsor*, act 3, sc. 4, l. 31-2
(1602).

9   If Heaven had looked upon riches to
     be a valuable thing, it would not
     have given them to such a
     scoundrel.

JONATHAN SWIFT, (1667–1745) Anglo-
Irish satirist. *The Correspondence of Jonathan
Swift*, vol. 2, ed. H. Williams (1963). letter,
Aug. 12, 1720.

Ridicule

1   It is commonly said, and more par-
     ticularly by Lord Shaftesbury, that
     ridicule is the best test of truth; for
     that it will not stick where it is not
     just. I deny it. A truth learned in a
     certain light, and attacked in certain
     words, by men of wit and humour,
     may, and often doth, become ridicu-
     lous, at least so far, that the truth is
     only remembered and repeated for
     the sake of the ridicule.

**PHILIP DORMER STANHOPE, 4TH
EARL CHESTERFIELD,** (1694–1773) British
statesman, man of letters. *The Letters of the Earl
of Chesterfield to His Son*, vol. 2, no. 270, ed.
Charles Strachey (1901). Letter, Feb. 6, 1752,
first published (1774).

Lord Shaftesbury wrote: "How comes it to pass,
then, that we appear such cowards in reasoning, and are so afraid to stand the test of
ridicule?" (*A Letter Concerning Enthusiasm*, sct.
2, 1708).

2   I believe they talked of me, for they
     laughed consumedly.

GEORGE FARQUHAR, (1678–1707) Irish
dramatist. Scrub, in *The Beaux' Stratagem*, act
3, sc. 1 (1707). Repr. in *Complete Works*, ed.
Charles Stonehill (1930).

Rights

1   Glittering generalities! They are
     blazing ubiquities!

RALPH WALDO EMERSON, (1803–1882)
U.S. essayist, poet, philosopher. *Attributed.*

Remark made referring to the criticism by
Rufus Choate of the Declaration of Independence in a letter to the Maine Whig Central
Committee, August 9, 1856: "Its constitution
the glittering and sounding generalities of natural right which make up the Declaration of
Independence." Published in *The Works of
Rufus Choate with a Memoir of his Life*, vol.
1, ed. S.G. Brown (1862).

Rivers

1   Flow gently, sweet Afton, among
     thy green braes,
     Flow gently, sweet river, the theme
     of my lays;
     My Mary's asleep by thy murmur-
     ing stream,
     Flow gently, sweet Afton, disturb
     not her dream.

ROBERT BURNS, (1759–1796) Scottish
poet. "Afton Water," st. 6, *Johnson's Musical
Museum*, vol. 4 (1792). *Poetical Works*, vol.
1, ed. William Scott Douglas (1891).

Closing lines.

2   I do not know much about gods;
     but I think that the river
     Is a strong brown god—sullen,
     untamed and intractable.

T.S. (THOMAS STEARNS) ELIOT,
(1888–1965) Anglo-American poet, critic.
"The Dry Salvages," pt. 1 (1941). *Four Quartets* (1942).

Opening lines of poem.

3   Ol' man river, dat ol' man river,
     He must know sumpin', but don't
     say nothin'
     He just keeps rollin',
     He keeps on rollin' along.

OSCAR HAMMERSTEIN II, (1895–1960) U.S. songwriter. "Ol' Man River " (song), *Show Boat* (stage musical, 1927).

4   By shallow rivers, to whose falls
Melodious birds sing madrigals.

CHRISTOPHER MARLOWE, (1564–1593) British dramatist, poet. "The Passionate Shepherd to his Love" (c. 1589).

These lines also appear in Shakespeare's *The Merry Wives of Windsor*, sung by Evans in act 3, sc. 1.

Roads

1   The road to the City of Emeralds is
paved with yellow brick.

L. FRANK BAUM, (1856–1919) U.S. author. *The Wonderful Wizard of Oz*, ch. 2 (1900).

The words do not appear thus in the film (1939), which features the song, "Follow the Yellow Brick Road."

2   The rolling English drunkard made
    the rolling English road.
A reeling road, a rolling road, that
    rambles round the shire.

GILBERT KEITH CHESTERTON, (1874–1936) British author. "The Rolling English Road," *The Flying Inn*, ch. 21 (1914).

Robots

1   Let's start with the three fundamental Rules of Robotics.... We have: one, a robot may not injure a human being, or, through inaction, allow a human being to come to harm. Two, a robot must obey the orders given it by human beings except where such orders would conflict with the First Law. And three, a robot must protect its own existence as long as such protection does not conflict with the First or Second Laws.

ISAAC ASIMOV, (1920–1992) Russian-born - U.S. author. Powell, in "Runaround," story first published in *Astounding Science Fiction* (March 1942). *I, Robot* (1950).

These three laws have been generally adopted by writers on robots, according to Asimov, who called the formulation his most important contribution to science fiction, and also claimed that this passage contains the first recorded use of the term, "Robotics" (see "My Robots" in *Robot Visions*, 1993).

2   The danger of the past was that men
became slaves. The danger of the
future is that men may become
robots. True enough, robots do not
rebel. But given man's nature, robots
cannot live and remain sane, they
become "Golems," they will destroy
their world and themselves because
they cannot stand any longer the
boredom of a meaningless life.

ERICH FROMM, (1900–1980) U.S. psychologist. *The Sane Society*, ch. 9 (1955).

Recalling a remark of Adlai Stevenson in a speech at Columbia University in 1954: "We are not in danger of becoming slaves any more, but of becoming robots."

Rock 'n' Roll

1   Roll over, Beethoven,
And tell Tchaikovsky the news.

CHUCK BERRY, (b. 1926) U.S. rock musician. "Roll Over, Beethoven" (song) (1956).

2   Sex and drugs and rock and roll.

IAN DURY, (b. 1942) British rock musician. "Sex and Drugs and Rock and Roll" *(song)*, on the album *New Boots and Panties!!* (1977).

3   I know it's only rock 'n' roll but I
like it.

MICK JAGGER, (b. 1943) British rock musician. "It's Only Rock 'n' Roll" *(song)*, on the album *It's Only Rock 'n' Roll* (1974).

4   It's one for the money,
Two for the show,

Three to get ready,
Now go, cat, go!
But don't you step on my Blue
Suede Shoes.
You can do anything but lay off my
Blue Suede Shoes.

CARL PERKINS, (b. 1932) U.S. rock musician. "Blue Suede Shoes" (song) (1956). A million-seller, the song topped both country and rhythm 'n' blues charts, and reached no. 2 in the pop charts.

Rome

1   Everyone soon or late comes round by Rome.

ROBERT BROWNING, (1812–1889) British poet. *The Ring and the Book*, bk. 5, l. 296 (1868-1869).

Royalty

1   A *family* on the throne is an interesting idea.... It brings down the pride of sovereignty to the level of petty life.

WALTER BAGEHOT, (1826–1877) British economist, critic. *The English Constitution*, ch. 3 (1867).

All the same, Bagehot warned, the British monarchy's "mystery is its life. We must not let in daylight upon magic."

2   The Sovereign has, under a constitutional monarchy such as ours, three rights—the right to be consulted, the right to encourage, the right to warn. And a king of great sense and sagacity would want no others.

WALTER BAGEHOT, (1826–1877) British economist, critic. *The English Constitution*, ch. 3 (1867).

Bagehot construed the formula, "I do not oppose, it is my duty not to oppose; but observe that I warn," as a notional statement by a British constitutional sovereign.

3   Put not your trust in princes.

BIBLE: HEBREW, *Psalms,* 146:3.

4   Curtsey while you're thinking what to say. It saves time.

LEWIS CARROLL [CHARLES LUTWIDGE DODGSON], (1832–1898) British author, mathematician. The Red Queen, in *Through the Looking-Glass,* "The Garden of Live Flowers" (1872).

5   The royal refugee our breed restores
With foreign courtiers and with
foreign whores,
And carefully repeopled us again,
Throughout his lazy, long, lascivious reign.

DANIEL DEFOE, (1660–1731) British author, poet, journalist. "The True-Born Englishman," pt. 1, l. 233-236 (1701). Repr. in *Works*, ed. Keltie (1869).

Referring to Charles II.

6   Everyone likes flattery; and when you come to Royalty you should lay it on with a trowel.

BENJAMIN DISRAELI, (1804–1881) British statesman, author. Quoted in *Collections and Recollections*, ch. 23, G.W.E. Russell (1898)

Remark to critic and poet Matthew Arnold, c. 1880.

7   I have found it impossible to carry the heavy burden of responsibility and to discharge my duties as King as I would wish to do without the help and support of the woman I love.... I now quit altogether public affairs, and I lay down my burden.

EDWARD VIII, KING, (1894–1972) British King of Great Britain and Northern Ireland. Abdication speech, in *Times* (London, Dec. 12, 1936). Radio broadcast, Dec. 11, 1936.

Edward VIII renounced the throne in order to marry Wallis Simpson, an American whose second marriage had ended in divorce three weeks earlier. Winston Churchill is said to have had a hand in composing Edward's abdication speech. The wedding of Edward and "Mrs. Simpson" took place in June 1937, and the couple spent the rest of their lives as the Duke and Duchess of Windsor, living mostly in Paris and ostracized by the British royal family.

8   I am your anointed Queen. I will never be by violence constrained to do anything. I thank God I am endued with such qualities that if I were turned out of the Realm in my petticoat I were able to live in any place in Christome.

ELIZABETH I, (1533–1603) British Queen of England. Quoted in *Elizabeth I and her Parliaments 1559-1581*, pt. 3, ch. 1, J.E. Neale (1953). Speech, Nov. 5, 1566, to Deputation of Lords and Commons.

9   I declare before you all that my whole life, whether it be long or short, shall be devoted to your service and the service of our great Imperial family to which we all belong.

ELIZABETH II, (b. 1926) British monarch, Queen of Great Britain and Northern Ireland. Quoted in the *Times* (London, April 22, 1947). Speech to the Commonwealth, April 21, 1947, Cape Town, South Africa.

10   I'm glad we've been bombed. It makes me feel I can look the East End in the face.

ELIZABETH, QUEEN MOTHER, (b. 1900) British wife of King George VI of Great Britain and Northern Ireland. Quoted in *King George VI*, pt. 3, ch. 6, John Wheeler-Bennett (1958). September 1940.

Said to a policeman after the bombing of Buckingham Palace by German planes. The East End—predominantly working-class—bore the brunt of the bombing during the blitz on London in World War II. When it was suggested that the royal family be evacuated, the Queen is reported to have said, "The children will not leave unless I do. I shall not leave unless their father does, and the King will not leave the country in any circumstances whatever."

11   The state of monarchy is the supremest thing upon earth: for kings are not only God's Lieutenants upon earth, and sit upon God's throne, but even by God himself they are called gods.

JAMES I OF ENGLAND, JAMES VI OF SCOTLAND, (1566–1625) British King of England and Scotland. Quoted in *England Under the Stuarts*, ch. 4, G.M. Trevelyan (1904, rev. 1925). Address, March 21, 1609, to Parliament, London.

12   In a few years there will be only five kings in the world—the King of England and the four kings in a pack of cards.

KING FAROUK, (1920–1965) Egyptian king. Quoted in *Life* (New York, April 10, 1950).

Remark to the agriculturalist Lord Boyd-Orr.

13   What are kings, when regiment is gone,
But perfect shadows in a sunshine day?

CHRISTOPHER MARLOWE, (1564–1593) British dramatist, poet. Edward, in *Edward II*, act 5, sc. 1, l. 26-7 (1593).

14   Uneasy lies the head that wears a crown.

WILLIAM SHAKESPEARE, (1564–1616) British dramatist, poet. King Henry, in *Henry IV pt. 2*, act 3, sc. 1, l. 31 (1600).

The phrase may originally have derived from Erasmus' *Institutio Principis* (1516), though it had become proverbial by Shakespeare's time.

Russia and the Russians

1   O Russia! O my wife! Our long and narrow
    Road lies clear though distressed.
    Our road with an old Tatar free-
    dom's arrow
    Has deeply pierced our breast.

ALEXANDER BLOK, (1880–1921) Russian poet. "On the Field of Kulikovo," st. 2 (1908), trans. by Vladimir Markov and Merril Sparks (1966).

Recalling the Russian victory over the Tatars in 1380.

2   I cannot forecast to you the action of Russia. It is a riddle wrapped in a mystery inside an enigma.

WINSTON CHURCHILL, (1874–1965) British statesman, writer. Vol. 6, *Winston S. Churchill: His Complete Speeches, 1897-1963*, ed. Robert Rhodes James (1974). Radio broadcast, Oct. 1, 1939.

Churchill added: "But perhaps there is a key ...Russian national interest."

3   From being a patriotic myth, the Russian people have become an awful reality.

LEON TROTSKY, (1879–1940) Russian revolutionary. *The History of the Russian Revolution*, vol. 3, ch. 7 (1933).

On the chaotic aftermath of the October Revolution, 1917.

Russian Revolution

1   And before, with banner red,
Through the blizzard snow unseen,
All unharmed by hail of lead,
With a step like snow so light,
Showered in myriad pearls of snow.
Crowned in wreath of roses white,
Christ leads onward as they go.

ALEXANDER BLOK, (1880–1921) Russian poet. "The Twelve," sct. 12 (1918), trans. by Gerard Shelley (1942).

Last lines of poem, referring to twelve guards during the October Revolution.

2   Ten days that shook the world.

JOHN REED, (1887–1920) U.S. journalist, author. *Ten Days That Shook the World* (1919).

Reed's pioneering work of reportage was an eye-witness account of the October Revolu-

tion as it unfolded in St. Petersburg. His experiences made him a fervent apologist for the Bolsheviks, and, after helping to found the Communist Labor Party in the United States, he returned to the Soviet Union to work in the bureau of propaganda. He was buried in the Kremlin.

Sacrifices

1   He is brought as a lamb to the slaughter, and as a sheep before her shearers is dumb, so he openeth not his mouth.

BIBLE: HEBREW, *Isaiah*, 53:7.Foretelling Christ's passion.

2   The stern hand of fate has scourged us to an elevation where we can see the great everlasting things which matter for a nation the great peaks we had forgotten, of Honour, Duty, Patriotism, and, clad in glittering white, the great pinnacle of Sacrifice pointing like a rugged finger to Heaven.

DAVID LLOYD GEORGE, (1863–1945) British Liberal politician, Prime Minister. quoted in *Times* (London, Sept. 20, 1914). Speech, Sept. 19, 1914, Queen's Hall, London.

3   The whole earth, perpetually steeped in blood, is nothing but an immense altar on which every living thing must be sacrificed without end, without restraint, without respite until the consummation of the world, the extinction of evil, the death of death.

JOSEPH DE MAISTRE, (1753–1821) French diplomat, philosopher. the senator, in *Les Soirées de Saint-Pétersbourg*, "Seventh Dialogue," (1821), repr. in *The Works of Joseph de Maistre*, ed. Jack Lively (1965).

4   The darkness of a day elapsed, of a day nourished with our sad blood.

PABLO NERUDA, (1904–1973) Chilean poet. *There Is No Forgetting: Sonata, Residencia en la Tierra (1925-1935)* (1935).

7 Too long a sacrifice
Can make a stone of the heart.
O when may it suffice?

WILLIAM BUTLER YEATS, (1865–1939) Irish poet, playwright. "Easter 1916," st. 4, *Michael Robartes and the Dancer* (1920).

Saints

1 I have fought a good fight, I have finished my course, I have kept the faith.

BIBLE: NEW TESTAMENT St. Paul, in *2 Timothy*, 4:7.

2 Precious in the sight of the Lord is the death of his saints.

BIBLE: HEBREW, *Psalms*, 116:15

In the Book of Common Prayer, the lines are rendered: "Right dear in the sight of the Lord is the death of his saints." (Psalm 116:13.)

3 Saint. A dead sinner revised and edited.

AMBROSE BIERCE, (1842–1914) U.S. author. *The Devil's Dictionary* (1881-1906), repr. in *Collected Works of Ambrose Bierce*, vol. 7 (1911).

4 What after all
Is a halo? It's only one more thing to keep clean.

CHRISTOPHER FRY, (b. 1907) British playwright. Thomas, in *The Lady's Not for Burning*, act 1 (1949).

5 If I am not, may God put me there; and if I am, may God so keep me.

JOAN OF ARC, (c.1412–1431) French patriot, martyr. Quoted in *The Trial of Jeanne d'Arc*, ed. W.P. Barrett (1931).

On being asked whether she knew she was in God's grace.

Sales and Marketing

1 Nobody dast blame this man.... For a salesman, there is no rock bottom to the life. He don't put a bolt to a nut, he don't tell you the law or give you medicine. He's a man way out there in the blue, riding on a smile and a shoeshine. And when they start not smiling back—that's an earthquake. And then you get yourself a couple of spots on your hat, and you're finished. Nobody dast blame this man. A salesman is got to dream, boy. It comes with   the territory.

ARTHUR MILLER, (b. 1915) U.S. dramatist. Charley, in *Death of a Salesman*, "Requiem" (1949).

Salvation

1 It is the final proof of God's omnipotence that he need not exist in order to save us.

PETER DE VRIES, (b. 1910) U.S. author. The Reverend Andrew Mackerel, in *The Mackerel Plaza*, ch. 1 (1958).

"This aphorism," De Vries added, "seemed to his hearers so much better than anything Voltaire had said on the subject that he was given an immediate hike in pay and invited out to more dinners than he could possibly eat."

2 To the question, What shall we do to be saved in this World? there is no answer but this, Look to your Moat.

GEORGE SAVILE, LORD HALIFAX, (1633–1695) British statesman, author. *A Rough Draft of a New Model at Sea* (1694). Repr. in *Works*, ed. Walter Raleigh (1912).

Sarcasm

1 What I claim is to live to the full the contradiction of my time, which

may well make sarcasm the condition of truth.

ROLAND BARTHES, (1915–1980) French semiologist. *Mythologies*, preface (1957).

2   Sarcasm I now see to be, in general, the language of the Devil; for which reason I have long since as good as renounced it.

THOMAS CARLYLE, (1795–1881) Scottish essayist, historian. *Sartor Resartus*, bk. 2, ch. 4 (1833-1834).

Satire

1   I'll publish, right or wrong:
    Fools are my theme, let satire be
       my song.

GEORGE GORDON NOEL BYRON, 6TH BARON BYRON, (1788–1824) British poet. "English Bards and Scotch Reviewers," l. 5-6 (1809).

2   It is difficult not to write satire.

JUVENAL, (c. 60–c. 130) Roman satiric poet. *Satires*, no. 1, l. 30.

3   Satire is a sort of glass, wherein beholders do generally discover everybody's face but their own; which is the chief reason for that kind of reception it meets in the world, and that so very few are offended with it.

JONATHAN SWIFT, (1667–1745) Anglo-Irish satirist. *The Battle of the Books*, preface (written 1697, published 1704). Repr. in *Jonathan Swift: A Critical Edition of the Major Works*, eds. Angus Ross and David Woolley (1984).

Scandal

1   An event has happened, upon which it is difficult to speak, and impossible to be silent.

EDMUND BURKE, (1729–1797) Irish philosopher, statesman. *Speeches ... in the Trial of Warren Hastings*, vol. 2, ed. E.A. Bond (1859). Speech, May 5, 1789, Westminster Hall, London.

Referring to the impeachment of Warren Hastings on charges of corruption.

2   In the case of scandal, as in that of robbery, the receiver is always thought as bad as the thief.

PHILIP DORMER STANHOPE, 4TH EARL CHESTERFIELD, (1694–1773) British statesman, man of letters. *The Letters of the Earl of Chesterfield to His Son*, vol. 1, no. 166, ed. Charles Strachey (1901). Letter, Oct. 19, 1748, first published (1774).

3   It is the public scandal that offends; to sin in secret is no sin at all.

MOLIÈRE [JEAN BAPTISTE POQUELIN], (1622–1673) French dramatist. *Tartuffe*, in *Le Tartuffe*, act 4, sc. 5 (written 1664, performed 1669).

Scholars and Scholarship

1   Of making many books there is no end; and much study is a weariness of the flesh.

BIBLE: HEBREW, *Ecclesiastes*, 12:12.

2   And let a scholar all earth's volumes carry,
    He will be but a walking dictionary:
    A mere articulate clock.

GEORGE CHAPMAN, (1559–1634) British dramatist, poet, translator. "The Tears of Peace," l. 530-2 (1609).

3   The clever men at Oxford
    Know all that there is to be knowed.
    But they none of them know one
       half as much
    As intelligent Mr. Toad!

KENNETH GRAHAME, (1859–1932) British essayist, writer of children's books. *The Wind in the Willows*, ch. 10 (1908).

4 The world's great men have not commonly been great scholars, nor its great scholars great men.

OLIVER WENDELL HOLMES, SR., (1809–1894) U.S. writer, physician. *The Autocrat of the Breakfast-Table,* ch. 6 (1858).

5 I have purchased knowledge at the expense of all the common comforts of life: I have missed the endearing elegance of female friendship, and the happy commerce of domestic tenderness.

SAMUEL JOHNSON, (1709–1784) British author, lexicographer. The astronomer, in *The History of Rasselas,* ch. 46 (1759)

Explaining his plight, the astronomer adds, "I am not able to instruct you. I can only tell that I have chosen wrong. I have passed my time in study without experience; in the attainment of sciences which can, for the most part, be but remotely useful to mankind."

6 There mark what ills the scholar's life assail,
Toil, envy, want, the patron, and the gaol.

SAMUEL JOHNSON, (1709–1784) British author, lexicographer. *The Vanity of Human Wishes,* l. 159-60 (1749). Repr. in *Works of Samuel Johnson,* Yale Edition, vol. 6, eds. E.L. McAdam, Jr. and G. Milne (1964).

In his *Life of Dr. Johnson* (1791), Boswell noted that the second line of Johnson's couplet had read, "Toil, envy, want, the *garret,* and the gaol," but had changed it "after experiencing the uneasiness which Lord Chesterfield's fallacious patronage made him feel." For further views of Chesterfield and patrons in general, see Johnson on patronage.

7 He was a rake among scholars, and a scholar among rakes.

THOMAS BABINGTON MACAULAY, (1800–1859) British historian, Whig politician. "Aikin's Life and Writings of Addison," repr. in *Critical and Historical Essays,* vol. 3 (1860). *Edinburgh Review* (July 1843).

Referring to essayist and dramatist Sir Richard Steele.

8 Beholding the bright countenance of truth in the quiet and still air of delightful studies.

JOHN MILTON, (1608–1674) British poet. *The Reason of Church Government,* introduction to bk. 2 (1642).

School

1 No trace of slavery ought to mix with the studies of the freeborn man.... No study, pursued under compulsion, remains rooted in the memory.

PLATO, (c. 427–347 B.C.) Greek philosopher. Socrates, in *The Republic,* bk. 7, sct. 536e.

School: Private

1 What we must look for here is, 1st, religious and moral principles; 2ndly, gentlemanly conduct; 3rdly, intellectual ability.

THOMAS ARNOLD, (1795–1842) British educator, scholar. Quoted in *The Life and Correspondence of Thomas Arnold, DD,* vol. 1, ch. 3, ed. Arthur Penrhyn Stanley (1845). Address to Rugby School.

2 Minerva House ... was "a finishing establishment for young ladies," where some twenty girls of the ages from thirteen to nineteen inclusive, acquired a smattering of everything and a knowledge of nothing.

CHARLES DICKENS, (1812–1870) British novelist. *Sketches by Boz,* "Tales," ch. 3, "Sentiment" (1833–1835).

3 Probably the battle of Waterloo *was* won on the playing-fields of Eton, but the opening battles of all subsequent wars have been lost there.

GEORGE ORWELL, (1903–1950) British author. *The Lion and the Unicorn,* pt. 1, "England Your England" (1941).

Science

1   Science knows only one commandment—contribute to science.

BERTOLT BRECHT, (1898–1956) German dramatist, poet. Andrea, in *The Life of Galileo*, sc. 14 (1939), trans. by Howard Brenton (1980).

2   That is the essence of science: ask an impertinent question, and you are on the way to a pertinent answer.

JACOB BRONOWSKI, (1908–1974) British scientist, author. *The Ascent of Man*, ch. 4 (1973).

3   Science has a simple faith, which transcends utility. Nearly all men of science, all men of learning for that matter, and men of simple ways too, have it in some form and in some degree. It is the faith that it is the privilege of man to learn to understand, and that this is his mission. If we abandon that mission under stress we shall abandon it forever, for stress will not cease. Knowledge for the sake of understanding, not merely to prevail, that is the essence of our being. None can define its limits, or set its ultimate boundaries.

VANNEVAR BUSH, (1890–1974) U.S. electrical engineer, physicist. "The Search for Understanding," *Science Is Not Enough* (1967).

Vannevar Bush was a zealous believer in the "missionary" function of science: during World War II, he led the U.S. Office of Scientific Research and Development, directing such programs as the development of the first atomic bomb.

4   "Faith" is a fine invention
When Gentlemen can *see*—
But *Microscopes* are prudent
In an Emergency.

EMILY DICKINSON, (1830–1886) U.S. poet. "Faith Is a Fine Invention" (written c. 1860, published 1891). Repr. in *The Complete Poems*, no. 185, Harvard *variorum* edition (1955).

5   Do you see this egg? With this you can topple every theological theory, every church or temple in the world.

DENIS DIDEROT, (1713–1784) French philosopher. *D'Alembert's Dream*, "Conversation between d'Alembert and Diderot," (written 1769, published 1830). Repr. in *Selected Writings*, ed. Lester G. Crocker (1966).

6   The whole of science is nothing more than a refinement of everyday thinking.

ALBERT EINSTEIN, (1879–1955) German-born U.S. theoretical physicist. *Out of My Later Years*, ch. 12 (1950, rev. 1970).

7   The great tragedy of science—the slaying of a beautiful theory by an ugly fact.

THOMAS HENRY HUXLEY, (1825–1895) British biologist. "Biogenesis and Abiogenesis," vol. 8, *Collected Essays* (1894). Presidential address, 1870, to the British Association for the Advancement of Science.

8   In everything that relates to *science*, I am a whole Encyclopaedia behind the rest of the world.

CHARLES LAMB, (1775–1834) British essayist, critic. *The Essays of Elia*, "The Old and the New Schoolmaster" (1820-1823).

9   Science is all metaphor.

TIMOTHY LEARY, (b. 1920) U.S. psychologist. *Contemporary Authors*, vol. 107 (1983). Interview, Sept. 24, 1980.

10   From man or angel the great Architect
Did wisely to conceal, and not divulge

His secrets to be scanned by them
who ought
Rather admire; or if they list to try
Conjecture, he his fabric of the
heav'ns
Hath left to their disputes, perhaps
to move
His laughter at their quaint
opinions wide
Hereafter, when they come to
model heav'n
And calculate the stars, how they
will wield
The mighty frame, how build,
unbuild, contrive
To save appearances, how gird the
sphere
With centric and eccentric scrib-
bled o'er,
Cycle and epicycle, orb in orb.

JOHN MILTON, (1608–1674) British poet.
the angel Raphael, in *Paradise Lost*, bk. 8, l.
72-84 (1667).

11 One science only will one genius
fit;
So vast is art, so narrow human
wit.

ALEXANDER POPE, (1688–1744) British
satirical poet. "An Essay on Criticism," l. 60-1
(1711).

12 Science is a cemetery of dead
ideas.

MIGUEL DE UNAMUNO, (1864–1936)
Spanish philosophical writer. *The Tragic
Sense of Life*, ch. 5 (1913, trans. 1921).

Science and Society

1 *Vanity of science.* Knowledge of
physical science will not console
me for ignorance of morality in
time of affliction, but knowledge of
morality will always console me for
ignorance of physical science.

BLAISE PASCAL, (1623–1662) French
scientist and philosopher. *Pensées*, no. 23,
ed. Krailsheimer; no. 67, ed. Brunschvicg
(1670).

Science Fiction

1 Everything is becoming science
fiction. From the margins of an
almost invisible literature has
sprung the intact reality of the
20th century.

J.G. (JAMES GRAHAM) BALLARD,
(b. 1930) British author. "Fictions of Every
Kind," *Re/Search* (San Francisco) no. 8/9
(1984). Originally published in *Books and
Bookmen* (London, Feb. 1971).

Ballard continued: "Even the worst science
fiction is better ... than the best conventional fiction. The future is a better key to
the present than the past."

2 May the Force be with you!

GEORGE W. LUCAS, (b. 1944) U.S.
film director, producer. Ben "Obi-wan"
Kenobi (Alec Guinness), in *Star Wars* (film)
(1977).

Scientists

1 When I find myself in the company of scientists, I feel like a
shabby curate who has strayed by
mistake into a drawing room full
of dukes.

W.H. (WYSTAN HUGH) AUDEN,
(1907–1973) Anglo-U.S. poet. *The Dyer's
Hand*, pt. 2, "The Poet & the City" (1962).

2 It is a good morning exercise for a
research scientist to discard a pet
hypothesis every day before
breakfast. It keeps him young.

KONRAD LORENZ, (1903–1989) Austrian ethologist. *On Aggression*, ch. 2
(1963, trans. 1966).

Scotland and the Scots

1   There are few more impressive
sights in the world than a Scotsman
on the make.

J.M. (JAMES MATTHEW) BARRIE,
(1860–1937) British playwright. David Wylie,
in *What Every Woman Knows*, act 2 (performed 1908, published 1918).

2   My heart's in the Highlands, my
heart is not here;
My heart's in the Highlands a-chas-
ing the deer;
Chasing the wild deer, and following the roe:
My heart's in the Highlands, wherever I go.

ROBERT BURNS, (1759–1796) Scottish
poet. "My Heart's in the Highlands," st. 4,
Johnson's Musical Museum, vol. 3 (1790).
Poetical Works, vol. 1, ed. William Scott Douglas (1891).

The lines are based on a traditional air.

3   A land of meanness, sophistry and
mist.
Each breeze from foggy mount and
marshy plain
Dilutes with drivel every drizzly
brain.

**GEORGE GORDON NOEL BYRON, 6TH
BARON BYRON,** (1788–1824) British poet.
"The Curse of Minerva," l. 138-40 (1812).

4   Much ... may be made of a Scotchman, if he be *caught* young.

SAMUEL JOHNSON, (1709–1784) British
author, lexicographer. Quoted in James
Boswell, *Life of Dr. Johnson*, entry, spring
1772 (1791).

5   Norway, too, has noble prospects;
and Lapland is remarkable for
prodigious noble wild prospects.
But, Sir, let me tell you, the noblest
prospect which a Scotchman ever
sees is the high road that leads him
to England!

SAMUEL JOHNSON, (1709–1784) British
author, lexicographer. Quoted in James
Boswell, *Life of Dr. Johnson*, entry, July 6,
1763 (1791).

6   It requires a surgical operation
to get a joke well into a Scotch
understanding. The only idea of
wit, or rather that inferior variety
of the electric talent which prevails
occasionally in the North, and
which, under the name of "Wut,"
is so infinitely distressing to people
of good taste, is laughing immod-
erately at stated intervals.

SYDNEY SMITH, (1771–1845) British clergyman, writer. Quoted in *Memoir*, vol. 1, ch.
2, Lady Holland (1855).

7   That garret of the earth—that
knuckle-end of England—that
land of Calvin, oat-cakes, and sul-
phur.

SYDNEY SMITH, (1771–1845) British clergyman, writer. Quoted in *Memoir*, vol. 1, ch.
2, Lady Holland (1855).

8   Mourn, hapless Caledonia, mourn
Thy banished peace, thy laurels
torn.

TOBIAS SMOLLETT, (1721–1771) Scottish
novelist, surgeon. *The Tears of Scotland*
(1746). Repr. in *The Works of Tobias Smollett*,
ed. George Saintsbury (1895).

Sculpture

1   The marble not yet carved can hold
the form Of every thought the
greatest artist has.

MICHELANGELO BUONARROTI,
(1475–1564) Italian sculptor, painter, poet.
"Sonnet 15," *The Sonnets of Michelangelo*,
trans. by Elizabeth Jennings (1961).

Sea

1 Hitherto shalt thou come, but no further: and here shall thy proud waves be stayed.

BIBLE: HEBREW, *Job*, 38:11.God speaking to Job, of how he "shut up the sea with doors." See Parnell on nationalism.

2 They that go down to the sea in ships, that do business in great waters, these see the works of the Lord and his wonders in the deep.

BIBLE: HEBREW, *Psalms*, 107:23-4.

3 Water, water, everywhere, And all the boards did shrink; Water, water, everywhere Nor any drop to drink.

SAMUEL TAYLOR COLERIDGE, (1772–1834) British poet. *The Rime of the Ancient Mariner*, pt. 2, st. 9 (1798). "And the Albatross begins to be avenged."

4 The sea has never been friendly to man. At most it has been the accomplice of human restlessness.

JOSEPH CONRAD, (1857–1924) Polish-born British novelist. *The Mirror of the Sea*, ch. 35 (1906).

"The sea—this truth must be confessed—has no generosity. No display of manly qualities—courage, hardihood, endurance, faithfulness—has ever been known to touch its irresponsible consciousness of power." (Ch. 36).

5 for whatever we lose (like a you or a me) it's always ourselves we find in the sea

E.E. (EDWARD ESTLIN) CUMMINGS, (1894–1962) U.S. poet. "Maggie and milly and molly and may."

6 The snotgreen sea. The scro-tumtightening sea.

JAMES JOYCE, (1882–1941) Irish author. Buck Mulligan, in *Ulysses*, ch. 1 of 1984 edition (1922).

7 Beneath the azure current floweth; Above, the golden sunlight glows. Rebellious, the storm it wooeth, As if the storms could give repose.

MIKHAIL LERMONTOV, (1814–1841) Russian poet. "A Sail," st. 3 (written 1832, published 1841), trans. by C.M. Bowra (1943).

8 There is nothing so desperately monotonous as the sea, and I no longer wonder at the cruelty of pirates.

JAMES RUSSELL LOWELL, (1819–1891) U.S. poet, editor. "At Sea," *Fireside Travels* (1864).

9 I must down to the seas again for the call of the running tide Is a wild call and a clear call that may not be denied.

JOHN MASEFIELD, (1874–1967) British poet, playwright. "Sea Fever," st. 2, *Salt-Water Ballads* (1902).

The line appears as "I must go down to the seas again ... " in some collections, and in John Ireland's musical setting of the poem; though apparently not in Masefield's drafts, nor in the first published version.

10 I will go back to the great sweet mother, Mother and lover of men, the sea. I will go down to her, I and no other, Close with her, kiss her and mix her with me.

A.C. (ALGERNON CHARLES) SWIN-BURNE, (1837–1909) British poet, critic. "The Triumph of Time," st. 33 (1866).

Seasons

1 To everything there is a season, and a time to every purpose under the heaven: a time to be born and a time to die; a time to plant, and a time to pluck up that which is planted; a time to kill, and a time to

heal; a time to break down, and a time to build up; a time to weep, and a time to laugh; a time to mourn and a time to dance; a time to cast away stones, and a time to gather stones together; a time to embrace, and a time to refrain from embracing; a time to get, and a time to lose; a time to keep, and a time to cast away; a time to rend, and a time to sew; a time to keep silence, and a time to speak; a time to love, and a time to hate; a time of war, and a time of peace.

BIBLE: HEBREW, *Ecclesiastes*, 3:1-8.The lines were set to music by Pete Seeger and recorded by the Byrds in 1966 (*Turn! Turn! Turn!*).

Second Coming

1   Now I know
    That twenty centuries of stony sleep
    Were vexed to nightmare by a rock-
        ing cradle,
    And what rough beast, its hour
        come round at last,
    Slouches towards Bethlehem to be
        born?

WILLIAM BUTLER YEATS, (1865–1939) Irish poet, playwright. "The Second Coming, st. 2," *Michael Robartes and the Dancer* (1921).

Secrets

1   Every thing secret degenerates, even the administration of justice; nothing is safe that does not show how it can bear discussion and publicity.

JOHN EMERICH EDWARD DALBERG, 1ST BARON ACTON, (1834–1902) British historian. *Lord Acton and his Circle*, letter 74, ed. Abbot Gasquet (1906). Letter, Jan. 23, 1861.

2   We dance round in a ring and
        suppose,
    But the Secret sits in the middle and
        knows.

ROBERT FROST, (1874–1963) U.S. poet. "The Secret Sits," *The Witness Tree* (1942).

3   Something nasty in the woodshed.

STELLA GIBBONS, (1902–1989) British author. *Cold Comfort Farm*, ch. 8 and passim (1932).

Recurring motif of some unspecific secret and shameful act, witnessed in the past, and used in the novel as an ironic symbol of corrupting knowledge.

4   The secret thoughts of a man run over all things, holy, profane, clean, obscene, grave, and light, without shame or blame.

THOMAS HOBBES, (1588–1679) British philosopher. *Leviathan*, pt. 1, ch. 8 (1651).

5   No one can keep a secret better than a child.

VICTOR HUGO, (1802–1885) French poet, dramatist, novelist. *Les Misérables*, pt. 2, bk. 8, ch. 8 (1862).

6   But he that hides a dark soul and
        foul thoughts
    Benighted walks under the mid-day
        sun;
    Himself is his own dungeon.

JOHN MILTON, (1608–1674) British poet. Second brother, in "Comus," l. 383-5 (1637).

Sects

1   Fanatics have their dreams, where-
        with they weave
    A paradise for a sect.

JOHN KEATS, (1795–1821) British poet. *The Fall of Hyperion*, cto. 1 (written 1819).

Opening lines.

Seduction

1 Licence my roving hands, and let
 them go
Before, behind, between, above,
 below.
O my America, my new found land,
My kingdom, safeliest when with
 one man manned.

JOHN DONNE, (c. 1572–1631) British divine, metaphysical poet. "To His Mistress Going to Bed," *Elegies* (1633). Repr. in *Complete Poetry and Selected Prose*, ed. John Hayward (1929).

2 Seduction is often difficult to distinguish from rape. In seduction, the rapist often bothers to buy a bottle of wine.

ANDREA DWORKIN, (b. 1946) U.S. feminist critic. "Sexual Economics: The Terrible Truth," *Letters from a War-Zone* (1987). Speech, 1976.

3 Can love be controlled by advice?
Will Cupid our mothers obey?
Though my heart were as frozen as
 ice,
At his flame 'twould have melted
 away.
When he kissed me so closely he
 pressed,
'Twas so sweet that I must have
 complied:
So I thought it both safest and best
To marry, for fear you should chide.

JOHN GAY, (1685–1732) British dramatist, poet. Polly, in *The Beggar's Opera*, act 1, sc. 8, air 8 (1728), ed. F.W. Bateson (1934).

4 When lovely woman stoops to folly,
And finds too late that men betray,
What charm can soothe her melancholy,
What art can wash her guilt away?

OLIVER GOLDSMITH, (1728–1774) Anglo-Irish author, poet, playwright. Song sung

by Olivia, in *The Vicar of Wakefield*, ch. 24 (written 1761-1762, published 1766).

5 Had we but world enough, and
 time,
This coyness, lady, were no crime.

ANDREW MARVELL, (1621–1678) British metaphysical poet. "To His Coy Mistress," l. 1-2 (written c. 1650, published 1681).

6 Let this great maxim be my virtue's
guide—In part she is to blame that
has been tried: He comes too near
that comes to be denied.

MARY WORTLEY, LADY MONTAGU, (1689–1762) British society figure, letter writer. "The Lady's Resolve," *The Plain Dealer* (London, April 27, 1724). Repr. in *Letters and Works of Lady Mary Wortley Montagu,* ed. Lord Wharncliffe (1837, rev. 1893).

7 Why don't you come up sometime
'n see me ? I'm home every evening
... come on up, I'll tell your fortune.

HARVEY THEW, Screenwriter. Lady Lou (Mae West), in *She Done Him Wrong* (film) (1933).

8 Mrs. Robinson, you're trying to
seduce me. Aren't you?

CALDER WILLINGHAM, Screenwriter. Ben Braddock (Dustin Hoffman), in *The Graduate* (film) (1967).

Self

1 We are all serving a life-sentence in
the dungeon of self.

CYRIL CONNOLLY, (1903–1974) British critic. *The Unquiet Grave*, pt. 2 (1944, rev. 1951).

2 The *self* is hateful.

BLAISE PASCAL, (1623–1662) French scientist, philosopher. *Pensées*, no. 597, ed. Krailsheimer; no. 455, ed. Brunschvicg (1670, trans. 1688), rev. A.J. Krailsheimer (1966).

Self-Confidence

1   I wish I was as cocksure of anything as Tom Macaulay is of everything.

WILLIAM LAMB MELBOURNE, 2ND VISCOUNT, (1779–1848) British statesman, prime minister. Quoted in *Lord Melbourne's Papers*, preface (1889).

Comment reported by Melbourne's nephew Earl Cowper.

Self-Control

1   He who doesn't lose his wits over certain things has no wits to lose.

GOTTHOLD EPHRAIM LESSING, (1729–1881) German dramatist, critic. Orsina, in *Emilia Galotti*, act 4, sc. 7 (1772).

The words are repeated by Odoardo in act 5, sc. 5.

2   He that would govern others, first should be The master of himself.

PHILIP MASSINGER, (1583–1640) British dramatist. Timoleon, in *The Bondman*, act 1, sc. 3 (1624). Repr. in *The Plays and Poems of Philip Massinger,* eds. P. Edwards and C. Gibson (1976).

3   When angry, count four; when very angry, swear.

MARK TWAIN, (1835–1910) U.S. author. *Pudd'nhead Wilson*, ch. 10, "Pudd'nhead Wilson's Calendar" (1894).

Self-Deception

1   A man is his own easiest dupe, for what he wishes to be true he generally believes to be true.

DEMOSTHENES, (c. 384–322 B.C.) Greek orator. *Third Olynthiac*, sct. 19 (349 B.C.).

2   We lie loudest when we lie to ourselves.

ERIC HOFFER, (1902–1983) U.S. philosopher. *The Passionate State of Mind*, aph. 70 (1955).

3   The surest way to be deceived is to consider oneself cleverer than others.

FRANÇOIS LA ROCHEFOUCAULD, DUC DE, (1613–1680) French writer, moralist. *Sentences et Maximes Morales*, no. 127 (1678).

Self-Destructiveness

1   But I do nothing upon myself, and yet am mine own executioner.

JOHN DONNE, (c. 1572–1631) British divine, metaphysical poet. *Devotions upon Emergent Occasions*, meditation 12 (1624). Repr. in *Complete Poetry and Selected Prose*, ed. John Hayward (1929).

Self-Expression

1   I will tell you what I will do and what I will not do. I will not serve that in which I no longer believe, whether it call itself my home, my fatherland, or my church: and I will try to express myself in some mode of life or art as freely as I can and as wholly as I can, using for my defence the only arms I allow myself to use—silence, exile and cunning.

JAMES JOYCE, (1882–1941) Irish author. Stephen Dedalus, in *A Portrait of the Artist as a Young Man*, ch. 5 (1916).

Self-Image

1   O wad some pow'r the giftie gie us
To see oursels as others see us!
It wad frae monie a blunder free us,
    And foolish notion.

ROBERT BURNS, (1759–1796) Scottish poet. "To a Louse," st. 8 (1786). Repr. in *Poetical Works*, vol. 1, ed. William Scott Douglas (1891).

2   You've no idea what a poor opinion I have of myself—and how little I deserve it.

SIR WILLIAM SCHWENCK GILBERT, (1836–1911) British librettist. Sir Ruthven Murgatroyd (disguised as Robin Oakapple), in *Ruddigore*, act 1 (1887), published in *The Savoy Operas* (1926).

3   It is no use to blame the looking glass if your face is awry.

NIKOLAI VASILYEVICH GOGOL, (1809–1852) Russian author, dramatist. *The Inspector-General*, epigraph (1936).

4   It is terrible to destroy a person's picture of himself in the interests of truth or some other abstraction.

DORIS LESSING, (b. 1919) British novelist. *The Grass is Singing*, ch. 2 (1950).

5   The attempt to force human beings to despise themselves ... is what I call hell.

ANDRÉ MALRAUX, (1901–1976) French man of letters, statesman. *Anti-Memoirs*, "The Human Condition," sct. 2 (1967), trans. by Terence Kilmartin (1968).

Referring to the concentration camps in Nazi Germany.

6   No one can make you feel inferior without your consent.

ELEANOR ROOSEVELT, (1884–1962) U.S. columnist, lecturer, wife of Franklin Roosevelt. Quoted in *Catholic Digest* (St. Paul, Minnesota, Oct. 1960).

Warning to wives of future presidents.

Self-Improvement

1   Whoever will cultivate their own mind will find full employment.

Every virtue does not only require great care in the planting, but as much daily solicitude in cherishing as exotic fruits and flowers; the vices and passions (which I am afraid are the natural product of the soil) demand perpetual weeding. Add to this the search after knowledge ... and the longest life is too short.

MARY WORTLEY, LADY MONTAGU, (1689–1762) British society figure, letter writer. *Selected Letters*, ed. Robert Halsband (1970). Letter, March 6, 1753, to her daughter Lady Bute.

Self-Interest

1   That smooth-faced gentleman,
       tickling commodity;
    Commodity, the bias of the world.

WILLIAM SHAKESPEARE, (1564–1616) British dramatist, poet. The bastard, in *King John*, act 2, sc. 1, l. 574-75 (1623).

2   It is not from the benevolence of the butcher, the brewer, or the baker, that we expect our dinner, but from their regard to their own interest. We address ourselves, not to their humanity but to their self-love, and never talk to them of our necessities but of their advantages.

ADAM SMITH, (1723–1790) Scottish economist. *The Wealth of Nations*, vol. 1, bk. 1, ch. 2 (1776).

Self-Knowledge

1   Ful wys is he that kan hymselven knowe!

GEOFFREY CHAUCER, (1340–1400) British poet. *The Canterbury Tales*, "The Monk's Tale," l. 3329 (1387-1400), repr. in *The Works of Geoffrey Chaucer*, ed. Alfred W. Pollard, et al. (1898).

2 Know thyself.
(Gnothi seauton)

DELPHIC ORACLE, *Inscription on the Oracle of Apollo at Delphi, Greece,* 6th century B.C..

The words are traditionally ascribed to the "Seven Sages" or "Seven Wise Men" of ancient Greece, and specifically to Solon of Athens (c. 640-c. 558 B.C.).

3 She imagines herself clean as a fish, evasive, solitary, dumb. Her prayer: to make peace with her own monstrous nature.

ELAINE FEINSTEIN, (b. 1930) British author, poet. "Patience," *Some Unease and Angels* (1977).

4 He knows the universe and does not know himself.

JEAN DE LA FONTAINE, (1621–1695) French poet, fabulist. *"Démocrite et les Abdéritains,"* bk. 8, fable 26, *Fables* (1678-1679).

5 He who knows others is clever; He who knows himself has discernment.

LAO-TZU, (6th century B.C.) Chinese philosopher. *Tao-te-ching,* bk. 1, ch. 33, trans. by T.C. Lau (1963).

Self-Pity

1 The dupe of friendship, and the fool of love; have I not reason to hate and to despise myself? Indeed I do; and chiefly for not having hated and despised the world enough.

WILLIAM HAZLITT, (1778–1830) British essayist. *The Plain Speaker,* "On the Pleasure of Hating" (1826).

2 I never saw a wild thing
Sorry for itself.
A small bird will drop frozen dead
From a bough

Without ever having felt sorry for itself.

D.H. (DAVID HERBERT) LAWRENCE, (1885–1930) British author. "Self-Pity," *Pansies* (1929).

Self-Promotion

1 I am the greatest.

MUHAMMAD ALI, (b. 1942) U.S. boxer. *Slogan.*

Used from c. 1962.

2 To establish oneself in the world, one does all one can to seem established there already.

FRANÇOIS LA ROCHEFOUCAULD, DUC DE, (1613–1680) French writer, moralist. *Sentences et Maximes Morales,* no. 56 (1678).

Self-Sacrifice

1 Greater love hath no man than this, that a man lay down his life for his friends.

BIBLE: NEW TESTAMENT Jesus, in *John,* 15:13.

In *Ulysses,* James Joyce wrote, "Greater love than this ... no man hath that a man lay down his wife for his friend."

2 I gave my life for freedom—this I know:
For those who bade me fight had told me so.

W.N. (WILLIAM NORMAN) EWER, (1885–1976) British journalist. *"Five Souls,"* *Five Souls and Other Verses* (1917).

Self-Sufficiency

1 And seeing the snail, which everywhere doth roam,

Carrying his own house still, still is
at home,
Follow (for he is easy paced) this
snail,
Be thine own palace, or the world's
thy gaol.

JOHN DONNE, (c. 1572–1631) British
divine, metaphysical poet. "Verse Letter to Sir
Henry Wotton" (1633). Repr. in *Complete
Poetry and Selected Prose*, ed. John Hayward
(1929).

2 He travels the fastest who travels
alone.

RUDYARD KIPLING, (1865–1936) British
author, poet. "The Winners," refrain, *The Story
of the Gadsbys* (1890).

3 Know how to live within yourself:
there is in your soul a whole world
of mysterious and enchanted
thoughts; they will be drowned by
the noise without; daylight will
drive them away: listen to their
singing and be silent.

FYODOR TYUTCHEV, (1803–1873) Russian poet. "Silentium," st. 3 (1836), trans. by
Dimitri Obolensky (1965).

4 We must cultivate our own garden.... When man was put in the
garden of Eden he was put there so
that he should work, which proves
that man was not born to rest.

**VOLTAIRE [FRANÇOIS MARIE
AROUET],** (1694–1778) French philosopher,
author. *Candide*, ch. 30 (1759).

Candide and Pangloss, exchanging the fruits of
their experience. This passage is held to encap-
sulate Voltaire's philosophy of common sense
as against the complacency of "optimism."

Sensuality

1 So must pure lovers' souls descend
T'affections, and to faculties,
Which sense may reach and appre-
hend,

Else a great Prince in prison lies.

JOHN DONNE, (c. 1572–1631) British
divine, metaphysical poet. "The Ecstasy,'
Songs and Sonnets (1633). Repr. in *Complete
Poetry and Selected Prose*, ed. John Hayward
(1929).

2 Age cannot wither her, nor custom
stale
Her infinite variety. Other women
cloy
The appetites they feed, but she
makes hungry
Where most she satisfies.

WILLIAM SHAKESPEARE, (1564–1616)
British dramatist, poet. Enobarbus, in *Antony
and Cleopatra*, act 2, sc. 2, l. 241-4 (1623).

Referring to Cleopatra.

Sentimentality

1 It is as healthy to enjoy sentiment as
to enjoy jam.

GILBERT KEITH CHESTERTON,
(1874–1936) British author. *Generally Speaking*, "On Sentiment" (1928).

2 Sentimentality is the emotional
promiscuity of those who have no
sentiment.

NORMAN MAILER, (b. 1923) U.S. author.
Cannibals and Christians, "My Hope for
America," (1966).

Review of book by Lyndon B. Johnson.

3 Sentimentality is only sentiment that rubs you up the wrong
way.

W. SOMERSET MAUGHAM,
(1874–1966) British author. *A Writer's Notebook*, entry, 1941 (1949).

Servants

1 Well done, thou good and faithful
servant.

BIBLE: NEW TESTAMENT Jesus, in *Matthew*, 25:21.

Here and in 25:23, said to the two "profitable servants" in the parable of the talents.

2 A servant with this clause
Makes drudgery divine:
Who sweeps a room as for Thy laws
Makes that and th' action fine.

GEORGE HERBERT, (1593–1633) British poet, clergyman. "The Elixir," st. 5, *The Temple* (1633). Repr. in *The Works of George Herbert*, ed. Helen Gardner (1961).

3 Though I've belted you and flayed you,
By the livin' Gawd that made you,
You're a better man than I am,
Gunga Din!

RUDYARD KIPLING, (1865–1936) British writer, poet. "Gunga Din," *Barrack-Room Ballads* (1892).

Last lines.

4 Few men have been admired of their familiars.

MICHEL DE MONTAIGNE, (1533–1592) French essayist. *Essays*, bk. 3, ch. 2 (1595), trans. by John Florio (1603).

Madame de Corneul (1605–1694) is attributed with the saying, "No man is a hero to his valet."

Servility

1 Whenever he met a great man he grovelled before him, and my-lorded him as only a free-born Briton can do.

WILLIAM MAKEPEACE THACKERAY, (1811–1863) British author. *Vanity Fair*, ch. 13 (1848).

Referring to Mr. Osborne.

Sex

1 The Englishman can get along with sex quite perfectly so long as he can pretend that it isn't sex but something else.

JAMES AGATE, (1866–1944) British drama critic. "Ego 1," *The Selective Ego*, ed. Tim Beaumont (1976).

Journal entry, Oct. 14, 1932.

2 That was the most fun I've ever had without laughing.

WOODY ALLEN, (b. 1935) U.S. filmmaker. Alvy Singer (Woody Allen), in *Annie Hall* (film) (1977).

Repr. in *Four Films of Woody Allen* (1982).

3 Embraces are cominglings from the head even to the feet,
And not a pompous high priest entering by a secret place.

WILLIAM BLAKE, (1757–1827) British poet, painter, engraver. *Jerusalem*, ch. 3, plate 69, l. 43-4 (c. 1820), repr. in *Complete Writings*, ed. Geoffrey Keynes (1957).

4 Sex. In America an obsession. In other parts of the world a fact.

MARLENE DIETRICH, (1904–1992) German-born U.S. film actress. "Sex," *Marlene Dietrich's ABC* (1962).

5 No woman needs intercourse; few women escape it.

ANDREA DWORKIN, (b. 1946) U.S. feminist critic. *Right-Wing Women*, ch. 3 (1978).

6 The zipless fuck is absolutely pure. It is free of ulterior motives. There is no power game. The man is not "taking" and the woman is not "giving." No one is attempting to cuckold a husband or humiliate a wife. No one is trying to prove anything or get anything out of anyone. The zipless fuck is the purest thing there is. And it is rarer than the unicorn. And I have never had one.

ERICA JONG, (b. 1942) U.S. author. *Fear of Flying*, ch. 1 (1973).

Jong explained, "Zipless ... because the incident has all the swift compression of a dream and is seemingly free of all remorse and guilt."

7   Sexual intercourse began
    In nineteen sixty-three
    (Which was rather late for me)—
    Between the end of the *Chatterley*
      ban
    And the Beatles' first LP.

PHILIP LARKIN, (1922–1986) British poet. "Annus Mirabilis," st. 1, *High Windows* (1974). (Written June 16, 1967.)

8   Continental people have sex lives; the English have hot-water bottles.

GEORGE MIKES, (1912–1987) Hungarian-born British humorist. *How To Be An Alien,* ch. 1, sct. 6 (1946).

Thirty years later, Mikes referred to this notorious pronouncement: "Things *have* progressed. Not on the continent, where people still have sex lives; but they have progressed here because the English now have electric blankets. It's a pity that electricity so often fails in this country." (*How To Be Decadent,* 1977.)

9   Skill makes love unending.

OVID (PUBLIUS OVIDIUS NASO), (43 B.C.–A.D.17) Roman poet. *Ars Amatoria,* bk. 3, l. 42.

10 Everything you always wanted to know about sex, but were afraid to ask.

DAVID REUBEN, (b. 1933) U.S. psychiatrist. *Everything You Always Wanted to Know About Sex, But Were Afraid to Ask* (book title) (1969).

Reuben's manual became America's number-one nonfiction bestseller. Woody Allen's satirical movie of the same name was released in 1972. In the screenplay, Allen asked: "Is sex dirty? Only if it is done right."

11 Sex is like money; only too much is enough.

JOHN UPDIKE, (b. 1932) U.S. author, critic. Piet Hanema, in *Couples,* ch. 5 (1968).

12 All this fuss about sleeping together. For physical pleasure I'd sooner go to my dentist any day.

EVELYN WAUGH, (1903–1966) British novelist. Nina Blount, in *Vile Bodies,* ch. 6 (1930).

Spoken to her fiancé Adam Fenwick-Symes.

Sexism

1   Sexism is the foundation on which all tyranny is built. Every social form of hierarchy and abuse is modeled on male-over-female domination.

ANDREA DWORKIN, (b. 1946) U.S. feminist critic. "Redefining Nonviolence," ch. 6, *Our Blood* (1976). Speech, April 5, 1975, Boston College.

2   Any woman who chooses to behave like a full human being should be warned that the armies of the status quo will treat her as something of a dirty joke. That's their natural and first weapon. She will *need* her sisterhood.

GLORIA STEINEM, (b. 1934) U.S. feminist writer, editor." Sisterhood," *Outrageous Acts and Everyday Rebellions* (1983). *Ms.* (New York, Spring 1972).

Sexual Harassment

1   Will you take your hands off me? What are you playing, osteopath?

CHARLES LEDERER, Screenwriter. Hildy Johnson (Rosalind Russell), in *His Girl Friday* (film) (1940).

Sexuality

1   There is no such thing as a homosexual or a heterosexual person.

There are only homo- or heterosexual acts. Most people are a mixture of impulses if not practises.

GORE VIDAL, (b. 1925) U.S. novelist, critic. *Armageddon? Essays 1983-1987*, "Tennessee Williams: Someone to Laugh at the Squares With," sct. 1 (1987).

2   I believe that it's better to be looked over than it is to be overlooked.

MAE WEST, (1892–1980) U.S. screen actor. *On Sex, Health and ESP*, "Last Word," (1975).

Mae West first said these words in the 1934 film *Belle of the Nineties*, scripted by her.

Shakespeare, William

1   If we wish to know the force of human genius, we should read Shakespeare. If we wish to see the insignificance of human learning, we may study his commentators.

WILLIAM HAZLITT, (1778–1830) British essayist. *Table Talk*, "On the Ignorance of the Learned" (1821-1822). First published in *Edinburgh Magazine* (July 1818).

2   A quibble is to Shakespeare what luminous vapours are to the traveller: he follows it at all adventures; it is sure to lead him out of his way and sure to engulf him in the mire.

SAMUEL JOHNSON, (1709–1784) British author, lexicographer. *Plays of William Shakespeare*, preface (1765).

3   He was not of an age, but for all time!

BEN JONSON, (1573–1637) British dramatist, poet. "To the Memory of My Beloved, the Author, Master William Shakespeare," l. 43, originally published in Folio ed. of Shakespeare's plays (1623). Repr. in *The Complete Poems*, ed. George Parfitt (1975).

4   The players have often mentioned it as an honour to Shakespeare, that

in his writing, whatsoever he penned, he never blotted out [a] line. My answer hath been, "Would he had blotted a thousand."

BEN JONSON, (c. 1572–1637) British dramatist, poet. *Timber, or Discoveries Made upon Men and Matter*, "De Shakespeare Nostrati," (1641), ed. Felix E. Schelling (1892).Nonetheless, Jonson wrote, "I loved the man and do honour his memory, on this side idolatry, as much as any."

Shame

1   A blot in thy scutcheon to all futurity.

MIGUEL DE CERVANTES, (1547–1616) Spanish author. Merlin's nymph, in *Don Quixote*, pt. 2, ch. 35 (1615), trans. by P. Motteux.

The nymph attempts to shame Sancho for his quailing at the prospect of receiving three thousand three hundred lashes.

Shaw, Bernard

1   As a teacher, as a propagandist, Shaw is no good at all, even in his own generation. But as a personality, he is immortal.

MAX BEERBOHM, (1872–1956) British essayist, caricaturist. *Around Theatres*, "A Cursory Conspectus of G.B.S." (1924) (Written 1901.)

Closing words of essay. Shaw was Beerbohm's predecessor as dramatic critic on the London weekly, *Saturday Review*.

2   A good man fallen among Fabians.

VLADIMIR ILYICH LENIN, (1870–1924) Russian revolutionary leader. Quoted in *Six Weeks in Russia in 1919*, "Notes of a Conversation with Lenin," Arthur Ransome (1919).

Remark to Arthur Ransome.

3   A buzz of recognition came from the front rows of the pit, together with a craning of necks on the part

of those in less favoured seats. It heralded the arrival of Sherard Blaw, the dramatist who had discovered himself, and who had given so ungrudgingly of his discovery to the world.

[H.H. (HECTOR HUGH) MUNRO] SAKI, (1870–1916) Scottish author. *The Unbearable Bassington*, ch. 13 (1912).

Lady Caroline, in the audience, commented: "They say the poor man is haunted by the fear that he will die during a general election, and that his obituary notices will be seriously curtailed by the space taken up by the election results. The curse of our party system, from his point of view, is that it takes up so much room in the press."

4   An excellent man; he has no enemies; and none of his friends like him.

OSCAR WILDE, (1854–1900) Anglo-Irish playwright, author. Quoted by Shaw in *Bernard Shaw: Collected Letters*, vol. 1 (1965). Letter, Sept. 25, 1896, to actress Ellen Terry.

Shaw provided the most quoted version of this in *Sixteen Self Sketches*, ch. 17 (1949): "He hasn't an enemy in the world, and none of his friends like him."

Shelley, Percy Bysshe

1   The man Shelley, in very truth, is not entirely sane, and Shelley's poetry is not entirely sane either. The Shelley of actual life is a vision of beauty and radiance, indeed, but availing nothing, effecting nothing. And in poetry, no less than in life, he is *a beautiful and ineffectual* angel, beating in the void his luminous wings in vain."

MATTHEW ARNOLD, (1822–1888) British poet, critic. *Essays in Criticism*, "Shelley," Second Series (1888). Review first published (1886).

Closing words of review. The quotation referred to is to be found in another essay by

Arnold, "Byron" also collected in this volume. Arnold was appalled at what he considered the depravity of Shelley's personal life: "What a set! what a world!... One feels sickened for ever of the subject of irregular relations."

Ships and Boats

1   There is *nothing*—absolutely nothing—half so much worth doing as simply messing about in boats.

KENNETH GRAHAME, (1859–1932) British essayist, writer of children's books. Rat, in *The Wind in the Willows*, ch. 1 (1908).

Rat continued, "In or out of 'em, it doesn't matter. Nothing seems really to matter, that's the charm of it. Whether you get away, or whether you don't; whether you arrive at your destination or whether you reach somewhere else, or whether you never get anywhere at all, you're always busy, and you never do anything in particular; and when you've done it there's always something else to do."

Show Business

1   There's no business like show business.

IRVING BERLIN, (1888–1989) U.S. songwriter. "There's No Business Like Show Business" (song), *Annie Get Your Gun* (Broadway show 1946, film 1949).

Sung by Ethel Merman in the Broadway hit *Annie Get Your Gun*, and by Betty Hutton in the movie version, the song supplied the title to a 1954 movie starring Marilyn Monroe.

2   All my shows are great. Some of them are bad. But they are all great.

LORD GRADE, (b. 1906) British film and TV entrepreneur. Quoted in *Observer* (London, Sept. 14, 1975).

Shyness

1   And indeed there will be time To wonder, "Do I dare?" and,

"Do I dare?"
Time to turn back and descend the
  stair,
With a bald spot in the middle of
  my hair....
  Do I dare
  Disturb the universe?

T.S. (THOMAS STEARNS) ELIOT,
(1888–1965) Anglo-American poet, critic.
"The Love Song of J. Alfred Prufrock," *Prufrock
and Other Observations* (1917).

Signs of the Times

1 You don't need a weatherman
  To know which way the wind blows.

**BOB DYLAN [ROBERT ALLEN
ZIMMERMAN],** (b. 1941) U.S. singer, songwriter. "Subterranean Homesick Blues" (song),
on the album *Bringing it all Back Home* (1965).

Silence

1 And when he had opened the seventh seal, there was silence in heaven
  about the space of half an hour.

BIBLE: NEW TESTAMENT St. John the
Divine, in *Revelation*, 8:1.

2 Even a fool, when he holdeth his
  peace, is counted wise: and he that
  shutteth his lips is esteemed a man
  of understanding.

BIBLE: HEBREW, *Proverbs*, 17:28.

3 These be
  Three silent things:
  The falling snow ... the hour
  Before the dawn ... the mouth of
    one
  Just dead.

ADELAIDE CRAPSEY, (1878–1914) U.S.
poet. "Cinquain: Triad."

The "cinquain" was a poetic form, originated
by Crapsey, comprising five unrhyming lines
of, respectively, 2, 4, 6, 8 and 2 syllables.

4 That man's silence is wonderful to
  listen to.

THOMAS HARDY, (1840–1928) British
novelist, poet. Spinks, in *Under the Green-
wood Tree*, pt. 2, ch. 5 (1872). Some editions
have the variation: "That man's dumbness is
wonderful to listen to."

5 And silence, like a poultice, comes
  To heal the blows of sound.

OLIVER WENDELL HOLMES, SR.,
(1809–1894) U.S. writer, physician. "The
Music-Grinders," st. 10, *The Poetical Works
of Oliver Wendell Holmes*, ed. Eleanor M.
Tilton (1895, rev. 1975).

6 The words of the prophets
  Are written on the subway walls
  And tenement halls
  And whispered in the sounds of
    silence.

PAUL SIMON, (b. 1941) U.S. singer, songwriter. "The Sound of Silence" (song) (1965),
on the album *Sounds of Silence* (1966).

7 Whereof one cannot speak, thereof
  one must be silent.

LUDWIG WITTGENSTEIN, (1889–1951)
Austrian philosopher. *Tractatus Logico-Philo-
sophicus*, sct. 7 (1922).

Wittgenstein had elaborated in the book's
Preface: "What can be said at all can be said
clearly, and what we cannot talk about we
must pass over in silence." Karl Popper, in
his *Conjectures and Refutations* (1963)
reported Franz Urbach's rejoinder to this:
"But it is only here that speaking becomes
worthwhile."

Simplicity

1 A taste for simplicity cannot
  endure for long.

EUGÈNE DELACROIX, (1798–1863)
French artist. *The Journal of Eugène
Delacroix*, journal entry, 1847, trans. by
Walter Pach (1937).

2 Far from the madding crowd's
  ignoble strife,

Their sober wishes never learned to
stray;
Along the cool sequestered vale of
life
They kept the noiseless tenor of
their way.

THOMAS GRAY, (1716–1771) British poet.
"Elegy Written in a Country Churchyard," st.
19 (1751). Repr. in *Poetical Works*, ed. J.
Rogers (1953).

Referring to the village dead. Thomas Hardy
took the title of his 1874 novel, *Far from the
Madding Crowd*, from this stanza—"madding"
here has the sense "becoming mad, acting
madly, frenzied" (O.E.D.), rather than "mad-
dening."

3   Give me a look, give me a face,
That makes simplicity a grace;
Robes loosely flowing, hair as free:
Such sweet neglect more taketh me,
Than all the adulteries of art;
They strike mine eyes, but not my
heart.

BEN JONSON, (c. 1572–1637) British
dramatist, poet. Song sung by Boy, in *Epicene,
or The Silent Woman*, act 1, sc. 1 (performed
1609, published 1616). Repr. in *The Complete Plays*, ed. G.A. Wilkes (1981).

Sin

1   True Civilization does not lie in gas,
nor in steam, nor in turn-tables. It
lies in the reduction of the traces of
original sin.

CHARLES BAUDELAIRE, (1821–1867)
French poet. "My Heart Laid Bare,' *Intimate
Journals*, sct. 59 (1887), trans. by Christopher
Isherwood (1930), rev. Don Bachardy (1989).

2   He that is without sin among you,
let him first cast a stone at her.

BIBLE: NEW TESTAMENT Jesus, in
John, 8:7.

Said to the scribes and Pharisees who had
presented Jesus with a woman caught in
adultery, to be stoned according to the law
of Moses.

3   One leak will sink a ship: and one
sin will destroy a sinner.

JOHN BUNYAN, (1628–1688) British Baptist preacher, author. The Interpreter, in *The
Pilgrim's Progress*, pt. 2 (1684).

4   A private sin is not so prejudicial in
this world, as a public indecency.

MIGUEL DE CERVANTES, (1547–1616)
Spanish author. Don Quixote, in *Don
Quixote*, pt. 2, ch. 22 (1615), trans. by P. Mot-
teux.

5   Lord, with what care hast Thou
begirt us round!
Parents first season us; then schoolmasters
Deliver us to laws; they send us
bound
To rules of reason, holy messen-
gers,
Pulpits and Sundays, sorrow dog-
ging sin,
Afflictions sorted, anguish of all
sizes,
Fine nets and stratagems to catch us
in,
Bibles laid open, millions of sur-
prises,
Blessings beforehand, ties of grate-
fulness,
The sound of glory ringing in our
ears:
Without, our shame; within, our
consciences;
Angels and grace, eternal hopes and
fears.
Yet all these fences and their whole
array
One cunning bosom-sin blows
quite away.

GEORGE HERBERT, (1593–1633) British
clergyman, poet. "Sin," *George Herbert:
Poetry and Prose*, ed. W.H. Auden (1973).

6   Sin has always been an ugly word,
but it has been made so in a new
sense over the last half-century. It

has been made not only ugly but passé. People are no longer sinful, they are only immature or under-privileged or frightened or, more particularly, sick.

PHYLLIS MCGINLEY, (1905–1978) U.S. poet, author. "In Defense of Sin," *The Province of the Heart* (1959).

7 Few love to hear the sins they love to act.

WILLIAM SHAKESPEARE, (1564–1616) British dramatist, poet. Pericles, in *Pericles*, sc. 1, l. 135 (1609).

8 Nothing makes one so vain as being told that one is a sinner.

OSCAR WILDE, (1854–1900) Anglo-Irish playwright, author. Lord Henry, in *The Picture of Dorian Gray*, ch. 8 (1891).

Sincerity

1 A wit should no more be sincere, than a woman constant; one argues a decay of parts, as t'other of beauty.

WILLIAM CONGREVE, (1670–1729) British dramatist. Witwoud, in *The Way of the World*, act 1, sc. 1 (1700).

2 A little sincerity is a dangerous thing, and a great deal of it is absolutely fatal.

OSCAR WILDE, (1854–1900) Anglo-Irish playwright, author. Gilbert, in "The Critic as Artist," pt. 2, *Intentions* (1891). Repr. in *Complete Works of Oscar Wilde*, ed. J.B. Foreman (1966).

Skepticism

1 Truth, Sir, is a cow which will yield such people no more milk, and so they are gone to milk the bull.

SAMUEL JOHNSON, (1709–1784) British author, lexicographer. Quoted in James

Boswell, *Life of Dr. Johnson*, entry, July 21, 1763 (1791).

Referring to the philosopher David Hume, "and other sceptical innovators."

2 With a grain of salt.

PLINY THE ELDER, (23–79) Roman scholar. *Natural History*, bk. 23, sct. 8.

Pliny himself, in his writings, appeared to make no distinction between the true and the wildly fantastic.

3 Scepticism is the chastity of the intellect, and it is shameful to sur-render it too soon or to the first comer; there is nobility in preserv-ing it coolly and proudly through a long youth, until at last, in the ripeness of instinct and discretion, it can be safely exchanged for fidelity and happiness..

GEORGE SANTAYANA, (1863–1952) U.S. philosopher, poet. *Skepticism and Animal Faith*, ch. 9 (1923).

4 The skeptic does not mean him who doubts, but him who investi-gates or researches, as opposed to him who asserts and thinks that he has found.

MIGUEL DE UNAMUNO, (1864–1936) Spanish philosophical writer. "My Religion," *Essays and Soliloquies* (1924).

Sky

1 To see the Summer Sky
Is Poetry, though never in a Book it lie—
True Poems flee—

EMILY DICKINSON, (1830–1886) U.S. poet. "To See the Summer Sky" (written c. 1879, published 1945). Repr. in *The Complete Poems*, no. 1472, Harvard *variorum* edition (1955).

2 The sky is the daily bread of the eyes.

RALPH WALDO EMERSON, (1803–1882) U.S. essayist, poet, philosopher. *Journals* (1909-1914). Journal entry, May 25, 1843.

3   I never saw a man who looked
     With such a wistful eye
     Upon that little tent of blue
     Which prisoners call the sky.

OSCAR WILDE, (1854–1900) Anglo-Irish playwright, author. *The Ballad of Reading Gaol*, pt. 1, st. 3 (1898). Repr. in *Complete Works of Oscar Wilde*, ed. J.B. Foreman (1966).

Slander

1   Our disputants put me in mind of the scuttlefish that, when he is unable to extricate himself, blackens the water about him till he becomes invisible.

JOSEPH ADDISON, (1672–1719) British essayist. *Spectator* (London, Sept. 5, 1712), no. 476, *The Spectator*, ed. D.F. Bond (1965).

2   And there was that wholesale libel on a Yale prom. If all the girls attending it were laid end to end, Mrs. Parker said, she wouldn't be at all surprised.

DOROTHY PARKER, (1893–1967) U.S. humorous writer. Quoted in *While Rome Burns*, "Our Mrs. Parker," Alexander Woollcott (1934).

3   Slander-mongers and those who listen to slander, if I had my way, would all be strung up, the talkers by the tongue, the listeners by the ears.

PLAUTUS, (254–184 B.C.) Roman playwright. Callipho, in *Pseudolus*, act 1, sc. 5, l. 427-30.

4   I have been thinking that I would make a proposition to my Republican friends. That if they will stop telling lies about Democrats, we will stop telling the truth about them.

ADLAI STEVENSON, (1900–1965) U.S. Democratic politician. Quoted in *Adlai Stevenson of Illinois*, ch. 8, John Bartlow Martin (1976). Campaign speech, Sept. 10. 1952, Fresno, California.

The remark has been attributed first to Republican Chauncey Depew (senator 1899-1911) though with the party-names reversed.

5   The slanders poured down like Niagara. If you take into consideration the setting—the war and the revolution—and the character of the accused—revolutionary leaders of millions who were conducting their party to the sovereign power—you can say without exaggeration that July 1917 was the month of the most gigantic slander in world history.

LEON TROTSKY, (1879–1940) Russian revolutionary. *The History of the Russian Revolution*, vol. 2, ch. 4 (1933).

Slang and Jargon

1   All slang is metaphor, and all metaphor is poetry.

G.K. GILBERT KEITH CHESTERTON, (1874–1936) British author. *The Defendant*, "A Defence of Slang" (1901).

2   Dialect words—those terrible marks of the beast to the truly genteel.

THOMAS HARDY, (1840–1928) British novelist, poet. *The Mayor of Casterbridge*, ch. 20 (1886).

3   Slang is a language that rolls up its sleeves, spits on its hands and goes to work.

CARL SANDBURG, (1878–1967) U.S. poet. *The New York Times* (Feb. 13, 1959).

Slavery

1 It cannot in the opinion of His Majesty's Government be classified as slavery in the extreme acceptance of the word without some risk of terminological inexactitude.

WINSTON CHURCHILL, (1874–1965) British statesman, writer. *Hansard*, col. 555. speech, Feb. 22, 1906, House of Commons.

Referring to the position of indentured Chinese laborers working in the Rand mines in the Transvaal, South Africa; made soon after assuming office of Under-Secretary for the Colonies. Of Churchill's last phrase, former colonial secretary Joseph Chamberlain commented: "Eleven syllables, many of them of Latin or Greek derivation, when one good English word, a Saxon word of a single syllable, would do!"

2 Either be wholly slaves or wholly free.

JOHN DRYDEN, (1631–1700) British poet, dramatist, critic. "The Hind and the Panther," pt. 2, l. 285 (1687).

3 There're two people in the world that are not likeable: a master and a slave.

NIKKI GIOVANNI, (b. 1943) U.S. poet. *A Dialogue* (1973). conversation in London, Nov. 4, 1971, with James Baldwin.

4 In giving freedom to the slave, we assure freedom to the free—honorable alike in what we give and what we preserve. We shall nobly save, or meanly lose, the last, best hope of earth.

ABRAHAM LINCOLN, (1809–1865) U.S. president. "Second Annual Message to Congress,"*Collected Works of Abraham Lincoln,* vol. 5, ed. Roy P. Basler (1953). Speech, Dec. 1, 1862.

5 My paramount object in this struggle is to save the Union, and is not either to save or to destroy slavery.

If I could save the Union without freeing any slave, I would do it; and if I could save it by freeing all the slaves, I would do it; and if I could save it by freeing some and leaving others alone, I would also do that.

ABRAHAM LINCOLN, (1809–1865) U.S. president. *Collected Works of Abraham Lincoln*, vol. 5, ed. Roy P. Basler (1953). Letter, Aug. 11, 1862 to newspaper editor Horace Greeley.

However, Lincoln added, "I have here stated my purpose according to my views of official duty and I intend no modification of my oft-expressed personal wish that all men everywhere could be free."

Sleep

1 We term sleep a death ... by which we may be literally said to die daily; *in fine,* so like death, I dare not trust it without my prayers.

THOMAS BROWNE, (1605–1682) British physician, author. *Religio Medici*, pt. 2, sct. 12 (1643).

2 Now blessings light on him that first invented this same sleep: it covers a man all over, thoughts and all, like a cloak; 'tis meat for the hungry, drink for the thirsty, heat for the cold, and cold for the hot. 'Tis the current coin that purchases all the pleasures of the world cheap; and the balance that sets the king and the shepherd, the fool and the wise-man even. There is only one thing ... that I dislike in sleep; 'tis that it resembles death; there's very little difference between a man in his first sleep, and a man in his last sleep.

MIGUEL DE CERVANTES, (1547–1616) Spanish author. Sancho Panza, in *Don Quixote*, pt. 2, ch. 68 (1615), trans. by P. Motteux.

3   Oh Sleep! it is a gentle thing,
     Beloved from pole to pole!
     To Mary Queen the praise be given!
     She sent the gentle sleep from
       Heaven,
     That slid into my soul.

SAMUEL TAYLOR COLERIDGE,
(1772–1834) British poet, critic. "The Rime of
the Ancient Mariner," pt. 5, st. 1 (1798).

4   We are not hypocrites in our sleep.

WILLIAM HAZLITT, (1778–1830) British
essayist. *The Plain Speaker,* "On Dreams" (1826).

5   Methought I heard a voice cry,
     "sleep no more,
     Macbeth does murder sleep"—the
       innocent sleep,
     Sleep that knits up the ravelled
       sleave of care,
     The death of each day's life, sore
       labour's bath,
     Balm of hurt minds, great nature's
       second course,
     Chief nourisher in life's feast.

WILLIAM SHAKESPEARE, (1564–1616)
British dramatist, poet. Macbeth, in *Macbeth,*
act 2, sc. 2, l. 33-38 (1623).

To Lady Macbeth, following the murder of the
sleeping Duncan.

6   Come Sleep! Oh Sleep, the certain
       knot of peace,
     The baiting-place of wit, the balm of
       woe,
     The poor man's wealth, the pris-
       oner's release,
     Th'indifferent judge between the
       high and low.

SIR PHILIP SIDNEY, (1554–1586) British
poet, diplomat, soldier. *Astrophel and Stella,*
sonnet 39 (1591).

Slums

1   I've been in many of them and to
     some extent I would have to say this:

If you've seen one city slum you've
seen them all.

SPIRO T. AGNEW, (b. 1918) U.S. Republi-
can politician, vice president. *Detroit Free
Press* (Oct. 19, 1968). Speech, Oct. 18, 1968,
Detroit.

Smells

1   They haven't got no noses
     The fallen sons of Eve;
     Even the smell of roses
     Is not what they supposes;
     But more than mind discloses
     And more than men believe.

GILBERT KEITH CHESTERTON,
(1874–1936) British author. "The Song of
Quoodle," *The Flying Inn,* ch. 15 (1914).

Smiling

1   What's the use of worrying?
     It never was worth while,
     So, pack up your troubles in your
       old kit-bag,
     And smile, smile, smile.

GEORGE ASAF, (1880–1951) British songwriter. "Pack up your Troubles" (song) (1915).

2   She gave me a smile I could feel in
     my hip pocket.

RAYMOND CHANDLER, (1888–1959)
U.S. author. Philip Marlowe, in *Farewell, My
Lovely,* ch. 18 (1940).

Referring to Helen Grayle.

Smoking and Smokers

1   Tobacco, divine, rare, superexcel-
     lent tobacco, which goes far beyond
     all the panaceas, potable gold, and
     philosophers' stones, a sovereign
     remedy to all diseases ... but as it is
     commonly abused by most men,
     which take it as tinkers do ale, 'tis a

plague, a mischief, a violent purger of goods, lands, health; hellish, devilish and damned tobacco, the ruin and overthrow of body and soul.

Robert Burton, (1577–1640) British clergyman, author. *The Anatomy of Melancholy,* pt. 2, sct. 4, memb. 2, subsct. 1 (1621).

2 Sublime tobacco! which from east to west
Cheers the tar's labour or the Turkman's rest.

George Gordon Noel Byron, 6th Baron Byron, (1788–1824) British poet. "The Island," cto. 2, st. 19 (1823).

3 Pernicious weed! whose scent the fair annoys,
Unfriendly to society's chief joys.

William Cowper, (1731–1800) British poet. "Conversation," l. 251-2 (1782). Repr. in *Poetical Works,* ed. H.S. Milford (1934).

4 The pipe, with solemn interposing puff,
Makes half a sentence at a time enough;
The dozing sages drop the drowsy strain,
Then pause, and puff—and speak, and pause again.

William Cowper, (1731–1800) British poet. "Conversation," l. 245-8 (1782). Repr. in *Poetical Works,* ed. H.S. Milford (1934).

5 Anybody got a match?

Jules Furthman, (1888–1960) U.S. screenwriter. Marie Browning (Lauren Bacall), in *To Have And To Have Not* (film) (1944).

Lauren Bacall's screen-debut line.

6 A custom loathsome to the eye, hateful to the nose, harmful to the brain, dangerous to the lungs, and in the black, stinking fume thereof nearest resembling the horrible Stygian smoke of the pit that is bottomless.

James i Of England, James vi Of Scotland, (1566–1625) British King. *A Counterblast to Tobacco* (1604).

Written shortly after Sir Walter Raleigh introduced tobacco to England from the New World.

7 A million surplus Maggies are willing to bear the yoke;
And a woman is only a woman, but a good cigar is a Smoke.

Rudyard Kipling, (1865–1936) British writer, poet. "The Betrothed," *Departmental Ditties* (1886).

8 There's nothing quite like tobacco: it's the passion of decent folk, and whoever lives without tobacco doesn't deserve to live.

Molière [Jean Baptiste Poquelin], (1622–1673) French dramatist. Sganarelle, in *Dom Juan,* act 1, sc. 1 (1665).

9 Cigarette me, big boy.

Robert Presnell, Screenwriter. Ginger Rogers, in *Young Man of Manhattan* (film) (1930).

In her first screen part.

10 A cigarette is the perfect type of a perfect pleasure. It is exquisite, and it leaves one unsatisfied. What more can one want?

Oscar Wilde, (1854–1900) Anglo-Irish playwright, author. Lord Henry, in *The Picture of Dorian Gray,* ch. 6 (1891).

Smuggling

1 Five and twenty ponies
Trotting through the dark—
Brandy for the Parson, 'Baccy for the Clerk;
Laces for a lady, letters for a spy,
And watch the wall, my darling, while the Gentlemen go by!

Rudyard Kipling, (1865–1936) British writer, poet. "A Smuggler's Song," *Puck of Pook's Hill* (1906).

Smugness

1   Of all the horrid, hideous notes of
    woe,
    Sadder than owl-songs or the mid-
    night blast,
    Is that portentous phrase, "I told
    you so,"
    Uttered by friends, those prophets
    of the past.

**GEORGE GORDON NOEL BYRON, 6TH
BARON BYRON,** (1788–1824) British poet.
Don Juan, cto. 14, st. 50 (1819-1824).

2   And then, in the fulness of joy and
    hope,
    Seemed washing his hands with
    invisible soap
    In imperceptible water.

THOMAS HOOD, (1799–1845) British poet.
Miss Kilmansegg and her Precious Leg, "Her
Christening," st. 10 (1841 1843). Repr. in
Complete Poetical Works, ed. Walter Jerrold
(1906).

Referring to Sir Jacob Kilmansegg, at his
daughter's christening.

Snobbery

1   It is impossible, in our condition of
    Society, not to be sometimes a
    Snob.

WILLIAM MAKEPEACE THACKERAY,
(1811–1863) British author. *The Book of
Snobs*, ch. 3 (1848).

Snow

1   Yes, the newspapers were right:
    snow was general all over Ireland. It
    was falling on every part of the dark
    central plain, on the treeless hills,
    falling softly upon the Bog of Allen
    and, farther westward, softly falling
    into the dark mutinous Shannon
    waves. It was falling, too, upon
every part of the lonely churchyard
on the hill where Michael Furey lay
buried. It lay thickly drifted on the
crooked crosses and headstones, on
the spears of the little gate, on the
barren thorns. His soul swooned
slowly as he heard the snow falling
faintly through the universe and
faintly falling, like the descent of
their last end, upon all the living
and the dead.

JAMES JOYCE, (1882–1941) Irish author.
Dubliners, "The Dead" (1916).

Closing passage of the story.

2   Snow, snow over the whole land
    across all boundaries.
    The candle burned on the table,
    the candle burned.

BORIS PASTERNAK, (1890–1960) Russian
poet, novelist, translator. "Winter Night," st. 1,
Doctor Zhivago: the Poems (1958), trans. by
Richard McKane (1985).

Snubs

1   Mrs. Montagu has dropped me.
    Now, Sir, there are people whom
    one should like very well to drop,
    but would not wish to be dropped
    by.

SAMUEL JOHNSON, (1709–1784) British
author, lexicographer. Quoted in James
Boswell, *Life of Dr. Johnson*, entry, March
1781 (1791).

Referring to Lady Mary Wortley Montagu.

Social Sciences

1   Thou shalt not sit
    With statisticians nor commit
    A social science.

W.H. (WYSTAN HUGH) AUDEN,
(1907–1973) Anglo-American poet. "Under
Which Lyre," st. 27 (1946). Repr. in *Selected
Poems*, ed. Edward Mendelson (1979).

2   The true science and study of man,
     is man himself.
     (La vraye science et le vray étude de
     l'homme, c'est l'homme.)

     PIERRE CHARRON, (1541–1603) French
     philosopher. *Of Wisdom*, bk. 1, preface (1601).

Socialism

1   I pass the test that says a man who
     isn't a socialist at 20 has no heart,
     and a man who is a socialist at 40
     has no head.

     WILLIAM CASEY, (1913–1987) U.S. intel-
     ligence chief, director of the CIA. Quoted in
     Washington Post obituary (May 7, 1987).

     The saying referred to by Casey has been
     attributed to French socialist politician and
     premier Aristide Briand.

2   Socialism with a human face.

     ALEXANDER DUBCEK, (1921–1992)
     Czechoslovakian politician.*Attributed.*

     Dubcek's words ("in the service of the people
     we followed a policy so that socialism would
     not lose its human face") became a watch-
     word of the "Prague Spring" of 1968, which
     led to his replacement as first secretary of the
     party by Husak, and the withdrawal of his
     party membership in 1970.

3   Socialism can only arrive by bicycle.

     JOSÉ ANTONIO VIERA GALLO, (b.
     1943) Chilean politician in Allende's govern-
     ment. Quoted in *Energy and Equity*, foreword,
     Ivan Illich (1974).

4   As with the Christian religion, the
     worst advertisement for Socialism
     is its adherents.

     GEORGE ORWELL, (1903–1950) British
     author. *The Road to Wigan Pier*, ch. 11 (1937).

Socializing

1   In the dime stores and bus stations,
     People talk of situations,

Read books, repeat quotations,
Draw conclusions on the wall.

BOB DYLAN [ROBERT ALLEN
ZIMMERMAN], (b. 1941) U.S. singer,
songwriter. "Love Minus Zero/No Limit"
(song), on the album *Bringing it all Back
Home* (1965).

Society

1   Society is indeed a contract....
     It is a partnership in all science; a
     partnership in all art; a partnership
     in every virtue, and in all perfec-
     tion. As the ends of such a partner-
     ship cannot be obtained in many
     generations, it becomes a partner-
     ship not only between those
     who are living, but between
     those who are living, those who
     are dead, and those who are to be
     born.

     EDMUND BURKE, (1729–1797) Irish
     philosopher, statesman. *Reflections on the
     Revolution in France* (1790), repr. in *Works*,
     vol. 3 (1865).

2   Never speak disrespectfully of
     Society, Algernon. Only people
     who can't get into it do that.

     OSCAR WILDE, (1854–1900) Anglo-Irish
     playwright, author. Lady Bracknell, in *The
     Importance of Being Earnest*, act 4 (1895).

Solidarity

1   You'll never walk alone.

     OSCAR HAMMERSTEIN II, (1895–1960)
     U.S. songwriter. "You'll Never Walk Alone"
     (song), *Carousel* (stage musical, 1945; film,
     1956).

     The song, recorded at various times by Judy
     Garland, Frank Sinatra and Gerry and the
     Pacemakers, has since become a perennial
     anthem among crowds at British football
     matches, particularly associated with Liver-
     pool.

Solitude

1 Whosoever is delighted in solitude is either a wild beast or a god.

ARISTOTLE, (384–322 B.C.) Greek philosopher. *Politics*, bk. 1, ch. 2, sct. 1253a, trans. by Francis Bacon, *Essays*, "Of Friendship" (1597-1625).

2 In solitude, where we are *least* alone.

GEORGE GORDON NOEL BYRON, 6TH BARON BYRON, (1788–1824) British poet. "Childe Harold's Pilgrimage," cto. 3, st. 90 (1812-1818).

3 I want to be alone ... I just want to be alone.

WILLIAM A. DRAKE, Screenwriter. Grusinskaya (Greta Garbo), in *Grand Hotel* (film) (1932).

The phrase was associated with Garbo although she claims never to have said it word for word: "I only said I want to be *let* alone." In the movie *The Single Standard*, she spoke the line: "I am walking alone because I want to be alone."

4 By all means use sometimes to be alone.
Salute thyself: see what thy soul doth wear.
Dare to look in thy chest; for 'tis thine own:
And tumble up and down what thou find'st there.
Who cannot rest till he good fellows find,
He breaks up house, turns out of doors his mind.

GEORGE HERBERT, (1593–1633) British clergyman, poet. "The Church Porch," st. 25, *The Temple* (1633).

5 If you are idle, be not solitary; if you are solitary, be not idle.

SAMUEL JOHNSON, (1709–1784) British author, lexicographer. Quoted in James Boswell, *Life of Dr. Johnson* (1791). letter, Oct. 27, 1779, to Boswell.

6 Solitude is un-American.

ERICA JONG, (b. 1942) U.S. author. *Fear of Flying*, ch. 1 (1973).

7 A solitude is the audience-chamber of God.

WALTER SAVAGE LANDOR, (1775–1864) British author. "Lord Brooke and Sir Philip Sidney," *Imaginary Conversations* (1824-1829).

8 But 'twas beyond a mortal's share
To wander solitary there:
Two Paradises 'twere in one,
To live in Paradise alone.

ANDREW MARVELL, (1621–1678) British metaphysical poet. "The Garden," st. 8 (written c. 1650, published 1681).

9 In solitude
What happiness? Who can enjoy alone
Or all enjoying, what contentment find?

JOHN MILTON, (1608–1674) British poet. Adam, in *Paradise Lost*, bk. 8, l. 364-6 (1667).

God responds to Adam thus: "What call'st thou solitude? Is not the earth With various living creatures, and the air Replenished, and all these at thy command To come and play before thee?" (L. 369-72) The plea is finally granted by the creation of Eve.

Solutions

1 Sure the disease and kill the patient.

FRANCIS BACON, (1561–1626) British philosopher, essayist, statesman. *Essays*, "Of Friendship" (1597-1625).

2 And if thy right eye offend thee, pluck it out, and cast it from thee: for it is profitable for thee that one of thy members should perish, and not that thy whole body should be cast into hell. And if thy right hand offend thee, cut it off, and cast it from thee: for it is profitable for

thee that one of thy members should perish, and not that thy whole body should be cast into hell.

BIBLE: NEW TESTAMENT Jesus, in *Matthew*, 5:29-30. From the Sermon on the Mount.

3 The best way out is always through.

ROBERT FROST, (1874–1963) U.S. poet. *A Servant to Servants, North of Boston* (1914).

Songs

1 That's the wise thrush; he sings
each song twice over,
Lest you should think he never
could recapture
The first fine careless rapture!

ROBERT BROWNING, (1812–1889) British poet. "Home Thoughts, From Abroad," st. 2, *Dramatic Romances and Lyrics* (1845).

2 Wait a minute, wait a minute, you ain't heard nothing yet. Wait a minute I tell you. You ain't heard nothing yet. Do you want to hear "Toot, Toot, Tootsie?"

ALFREAD A. COHEN, U.S. Jakie Rabinowitz (Al Jolson), in *The Jazz Singer* (film) (1927).

Al Jolson's first spoken words in one of the first ever talking pictures, guaranteeing its place in cinema history.

3 Swans sing before they die—'twere
no bad thing
Should certain persons die before
they sing.

SAMUEL TAYLOR COLERIDGE, (1772–1834) British poet, critic. "Epigram on a Bad Singer," *Poetical Works*, ed. James Dyke Campbell (1893).

4 A song is anything that can walk by itself.

BOB DYLAN [ROBERT ALLEN ZIMMERMAN], (b. 1941) U.S. singer, song-

writer. *Bringing It All Back Home* (album), sleeve notes (1965).

5 Play it Sam. Play "As Time Goes By."

JULIUS J. EPSTEIN, Screenwriter. Ilsa Lund (Ingrid Bergman), in *Casablanca* (film), Ilsa Lund (Ingrid Bergman) making a request to Sam (Dooley Wilson) the piano player. (1942).

Later in the film, Rick Blaine (Humphrey Bogart) repeats the request: "You played it for her, you can play it for me. If she can stand it, I can. Play it!" (Usually misquoted "Play it again Sam"—the title of Woody Allen's 1972 movie). For the song, see Hupfeld on love.

6 Odds life! must one swear to the truth of a song?

MATTHEW PRIOR, (1664–1721) British poet, diplomat. "A Better Answer, Poems" (1718). Repr. in *The Literary Works of Matthew Prior*, eds. H.B. Wright and M.K. Spears (1959).

7 I would rather be remembered by a song than by a victory.

ALEXANDER SMITH, (1830–1867) Scottish poet. *Dreamthorp*, "Men of Letters" (1863).

Sons

1 This is my beloved Son, in whom I am well pleased.

BIBLE: NEW TESTAMENT *Matthew*, 3:17. A "voice from heaven," following the baptism of Jesus by John the Baptist.

2 If a man has been his mother's undisputed darling he retains throughout life the triumphant feeling, the confidence in success, which not seldom brings actual success along with it.

SIGMUND FREUD, (1856–1939) Austrian psychiatrist. *A Childhood Recollection from Dichtung und Wahrheit*, vol. 17, *Complete Works, Standard Edition*, eds. James Strachey and Anna Freud (1955). (Originally published 1917).

Sorrow

1   Sorrow is better than laughter: for by the sadness of the countenance the heart is made better. The heart of the wise is in the house of mourning: but the heart of fools is in the house of mirth.

Bible: Hebrew, *Ecclesiastes,* 7:3-4.

2   To fight aloud is very brave—
But *gallanter,* I know
Who charge within the bosom
The Cavalry of Woe—

Emily Dickinson, (1830–1886) U.S. poet. "To Fight Aloud Is Very Brave" (written c. 1859, published 1890). Repr. in *The Complete Poems,* no. 126, Harvard *variorum* edition (1955).

3   Sorrow, the great idealizer.

James Russell Lowell, (1819–1891) U.S. poet, editor. *Among My Books,* "Spenser," Second Series (1876).

4   Sorrow is tranquility remembered in emotion.

Dorothy Parker, (1893–1967) U.S. humorous writer. *Here Lies,* "Sentiment" (1939).

For the original, see Wordsworth on poetry.

5   But, truly, I have wept too much! The dawns are heartbreaking. Every moon is atrocious and every sun bitter.

Arthur Rimbaud, (1854–1891) French poet. "Le Bateau Ivre" (written 1871). Repr. in *Collected Poems,* ed. Oliver Bernard (1962).

6   When sorrows come they come not single spies,
But in battalions.

William Shakespeare, (1564–1616) British dramatist, poet. Claudius, in *Hamlet,* act 4, sc. 5, l. 76-7 (1604).

7   O Sorrow, wilt Thou live with me
No casual mistress, but a wife.

Alfred Tennyson, 1st Baron Tennyson, (1809–1892) British poet. "In Memoriam A.H.H.," cto. 59, st. 1 (1850).

Soul

1   Ah! from the soul itself must issue forth
A light, a glory, a fair luminous cloud
Enveloping the Earth.

Samuel Taylor Coleridge, (1772–1834) British poet, critic. "Dejection: An Ode," st. 4, *Morning Post* (Oct. 4, 1802). *Sibylline Leaves* (1817), repr. in *Poetical Works,* ed. James Dyke Campbell (1893).

2   The Soul unto itself
Is an imperial friend—
Or the most agonizing Spy—
An Enemy—could send—

Emily Dickinson, (1830–1886) U.S. poet. "The Soul Unto Itself" (written c. 1862, published 1891). Repr. in *The Complete Poems,* no. 683, Harvard *variorum* edition (1955).

3   You are a little soul carrying around a corpse.

Epictetus, (c. 55–c. 135) Greek stoic philosopher. *Fragments,* vol. 2, no. 26, *Epictetus: The Discourses, The Manual and Fragments,* ed. and trans. by W. Oldfather (1928).

4   In a real dark night of the soul it is always three o'clock in the morning, day after day.

F. Scott Fitzgerald, (1896–1940) U.S. author. "Handle With Care," first published in *Esquire* (New York, March 1936). *The Crack-Up,* ed. Edmund Wilson (1945).

The article constituted the second part of Fitzgerald's *Crack-Up* series. "The Dark Night of the Soul" is the title of a poem and commentary by the 16th-century Spanish mystic San Juan de la Cruz (St. John of the Cross).

5   Every soul is a melody which needs renewing.

STÉPHANE MALLARMÉ, (1842–1898) French symbolist poet. *Variations on a Subject,* "Verse Crisis," *Complete Works* (1945). *La Revue Blanche* (Paris, Sept. 1895).

6   On the pavement
of my trampled soul
the soles of madmen
stamp the prints of rude, crude
    words.

VLADIMIR MAYAKOVSKY, (1893–1930) Russian poet, dramatist. "1," no. 1 (1913). Repr. in *Listen!: Early Poems 1913-1918,* trans. by Maria Enzenberger (1987).

7   Ah, what a dusty answer gets the
    soul
When hot for certainties in this our
life!

GEORGE MEREDITH, (1828–1909) British author. *Modern Love,* Sonnet 50 (1862).

8   The soul can split the sky in two,
And let the face of God shine
    through.

EDNA ST. VINCENT MILLAY, (1892–1950) U.S. poet. "Renascence," st. 8, *Renascence and Other Poems* (1917).

South (American)

1   Southerners can never resist a losing cause.

MARGARET MITCHELL, (1900–1949) U.S. novelist. Rhett Butler, in *Gone with the Wind,* vol. 2, pt. 4, ch. 34 (1936).

2   Being a Georgia author is a rather specious dignity, on the same order as, for the pig, being a Talmadge ham.

FLANNERY O'CONNOR, (1925–1964) U.S. author. "The Regional Writer," *Mystery and Manners,* eds. Sally and Robert Fitzgerald (1972). *Esprit* (University of Scranton, Pennsylvania, Winter 1963).

South Africa

1   Together, hand in hand, with that stick of matches, with our necklace, we shall liberate this country.

WINNIE MANDELA, (b. 1934) South African political leader. Quoted in *Guardian* (London, April 15, 1986). Speech in black townships.

Soviet Union

1   It was a time when only the dead smiled, happy in their peace.

. . . .

Stars of Death stood over us,
and innocent Russia squirmed
under the bloody boots,
under the wheels of black Marias.

ANNA AKHMATOVA, (1889–1966) Russian poet. "Requiem," introduction, trans. by Richard McKane (1985).

Though Akhmatova's long poem about the Stalinist purges—during which time her only son was arrested—was written mainly 1935-1940, it was not published until 1963 in West Germany, and not in its entirety in the Soviet Union until 1987.

2   Those who wait for that must wait until a shrimp learns to whistle.

NIKITA KHRUSHCHEV, (1894–1971) Soviet premier. Quoted in *The New York Times* (Sept. 18, 1955). Speech, Sept. 17, 1955, Moscow.

Referring to the possibility of the Soviet Union rejecting communism.

Space

1 Space is the stature of God.

JOSEPH JOUBERT, (1754–1824) French essayist, moralist. *Pensées,* ch. 12 (1842), trans. by and ed. H.P. Collins (1928).

2 Oh! I have slipped the surly bonds of earth, And danced the skies on laughter-silvered wings;... And while with silent lifting mind I've trod The high, untrespassed sanctity of space, Put out my hand and touched the face of God.

JOHN GILLESPIE MAGEE, (1922–1941) U.S. pilot with Royal Canadian Air Force. "High Flight," (written 1941), publ. in *More Poems from the Forces,* ed. K. Rhys (1943).

First and concluding lines of the sonnet quoted by President Ronald Reagan following the Challenger space shuttle disaster in 1986. Magee died while on a bombing mission over Germany.

4 Space—the final frontier. These are the voyages of the starship *Enterprise.* Its five-year mission: to explore strange new worlds, to seek out new life and new civilizations, to boldly go where no man has gone before.

GENE RODDENBERRY, (1921–1991) U.S. writer. *Star Trek* (television series), preamble (1966-1969).

The words include what is probably the most famous split infinitive ever recorded.

Speech

1 The stroke of the whip maketh marks in the flesh: but the stroke of the tongue breaketh the bones. Many have fallen by the edge of the sword: but not so many as have fallen by the tongue.

APOCRYPHA, *Ecclesiasticus,* 28:17-8.

2 Let your speech be always with grace, seasoned with salt, that ye may know how ye ought to answer every man.

BIBLE: NEW TESTAMENT St. Paul, in *Colossians,* 4:6.

3 Soun is noght but air ybroken,
And every speche that is spoken,
Loud or privee, foul or fair,
In his substaunce is but air;
For as flaumbe is but lighted
    smoke,
Right so soun is air ybroke.

GEOFFREY CHAUCER, (1340–1400) British poet. The eagle, in "The House of Fame," bk. 2, l. 257-62 (1374-1385), repr. in *The Works of Geoffrey Chaucer,* ed. Alfred W. Pollard, et al. (1898).

4 When you have nothing to say, say nothing.

C.C. (CHARLES CALEB) COLTON, (1780–1832) British author, clergyman. *Lacon,* vol. 1, no. 183 (1820).

5 True and false are attributes of speech not of things. And where speech is not, there is neither truth nor falsehood. Error there may be, as when we expect that which shall not be; or suspect what has not been: but in neither case can a man be charged with untruth.

THOMAS HOBBES, (1588–1679) British philosopher. *Leviathan,* pt. 1, ch. 4 (1651).

6 Good Heavens! For more than forty years I have been speaking prose without knowing it.

MOLIÈRE [JEAN BAPTISTE POQUELIN], (1622–1673) French dramatist. M. Jourdain, in *Le Bourgois Gentilhomme,* act 2, sc. 4 (1671).

7 Speech is the mirror of the soul.

PUBLILIUS SYRUS, (1st century B.C.) Roman writer of mimes. *Sententiae,* no. 1073.

8   Taffeta phrases, silken phrases
        precise,
     Three-piled hyperbole, spruce
        affectation,
     Figures pedantical—these summer
        flies
     Have blown me full of maggot
        ostentation.
     I do forswear them.

WILLIAM SHAKESPEARE, (1564–1616)
British dramatist, poet. Biron, in *Love's
Labour's Lost*, act 5, sc. 2, l. 407-11 (1598).

Biron vows to abandon his verbosity in his
attempts to woo the ladies.

Speeches and Speechmaking

1   Let thy speech be short, compre-
     hending much in few words.

APOCRYPHA, *Ecclesiasticus*, 32:8.

2   I do not object to people looking
     at their watches when I am speak-
     ing. But I strongly object when they
     start shaking them to make certain
     they are still going.

WILLIAM NORMAN BIRKETT,
(1883–1962) British lawyer, politician.
Quoted in *Observer* (London, Oct. 30, 1960).

3   And adepts in the speaking trade
     Keep a cough by them ready made.

CHARLES CHURCHILL, (1731–1764)
British clergyman, poet. "The Ghost," bk. 2, l.
545-6 (1763).

4   He is one of those orators of whom
     it was well said, "Before they get up,
     they do not know what they are
     going to say; when they are speak-
     ing, they do not know what they are
     saying; and when they have sat
     down, they do not know what they
     have said."

WINSTON CHURCHILL, (1874–1965)
British statesman, writer. *Hansard*, col.
1893. speech, Dec. 20, 1912, House of
Commons.

Referring to naval commander Lord Charles
Beresford.

5   My husband and I ...

ELIZABETH II, (b. 1926) British monarch,
Queen of Great Britain and Northern Ireland.
Christmas Message, 1953, New Zealand.

This form of words used by the Queen to ini-
tiate a speech quickly became a regular feature of her delivery, though the alternative
"Prince Philip and I ..." appeared in the 1960s
when it was apparent that the familiar formula was becoming a joke.

6   The world will little note nor long
     remember what we say here.

ABRAHAM LINCOLN, (1809–1865)
U.S. president. "Gettysburg Address,"
Collected Works of Abraham Lincoln, vol. 7,
ed. Roy P. Basler (1953). Speech, Nov. 19,
1863.

Lincoln's *Gettysburg Address*—taking him
only about three minutes to deliver—is perhaps the most quoted speech of all time.

7   The object of oratory alone is not
     truth, but persuasion.

THOMAS BABINGTON MACAULAY,
(1800–1859) British historian, Whig politician. "Essay on Athenian Orators," *Knight's
Quarterly Magazine* (Aug. 1824). *The Works
of Lord Macaulay*, vol. 11 (1898).

8   So having said, a while he stood,
        expecting
     Their universal shout and high
        applause
     To fill his ear; when contrary, he
        hears,
     On all sides, from innumerable
        tongues
     A dismal universal hiss, the sound
     Of public scorn.

JOHN MILTON, (1608–1674) British poet.
Paradise Lost, bk. 10, l. 504-9 (1667).

9   He's a wonderful talker, who has the art of telling you nothing in a great harangue.

MOLIÉRE [JEAN BAPTISTE POQUELIN], (1622–1673) French dramatist. Céliméne, in *Le Misanthrope*, act 2, sc. 5 (1666).

Referring to Damon.

10   Speak the speech ... trippingly on the tongue; but if you mouth it ... I had as lief the town crier had spoke my lines. Nor do not saw the air too much with your hand, thus, but use all gently; for in the very torrent, tempest, and as I may say the whirl-wind of your passion, you must acquire and beget a temperance that may give it smoothness.

WILLIAM SHAKESPEARE, (1564–1616)British dramatist, poet. Hamlet, in *Hamlet*, act3, sc. 2, l. 1-8 (1604).

Instructing the players how to deliver the speech he has written for insertion in the play to be performed before Claudius and Gertrude.

11   Sure if I reprehend anything in this world, it is the use of my oracular tongue, and a nice derangement of epitaphs.

RICHARD BRINSLEY SHERIDAN, (1751–1816) Anglo-Irish dramatist. Mrs. Malaprop, in *The Rivals*, act 3, sc. 3 (1775).

A "correct" version of this "malapropism" might be: "If I apprehend anything in this world, it is the use of my vernacular tongue, and a nice arrangement of epithets."

Speed

1   And bid the devil take the hin'most.

SAMUEL BUTLER, (1612–1680) British poet. "Hudibras," pt. 1, cto. 2, l. 633 (1663). eds. John Wilders and Hugh de Quehen (1973).

2   A new beauty has been added to the splendor of the world—the beauty of speed.

TOMMASO MARINETTI, (1876–1944) Italian playwright. "Foundation and Manifesto of Futurism," *Figaro* (Paris, Feb. 20, 1909). Repr. in *Marinetti: Selected Writings,* ed. by R.W. Flint (1971).

3   I'll put a girdle round about the earth
In forty minutes.

WILLIAM SHAKESPEARE, (1564–1616) British dramatist, poet. Robin Goodfellow (Puck), in *A Midsummer Night's Dream*, act 2, sc. 1, l. 175-76 (1600).

Boasting of how short a time it will take him to fetch the love charm wanted by Oberon.

Spirit

1   Man doth not live by bread only, but by every word that proceedeth out of the mouth of the Lord doth man live.

BIBLE: HEBREW, *Deuteronomy*, 8:3. Jesus recalls these words in *Matthew* 4:4.

2   There's nought, no doubt, so much the spirit calms
As rum and true religion.

GEORGE GORDON NOEL BYRON, 6TH BARON BYRON, (1788–1824) British poet. *Don Juan*, cto. 2, st. 34 (1819-1824).

Spontaneity

1   Improvisation is too good to leave to chance.

PAUL SIMON, (b. 1941) U.S. singer, songwriter. *International Herald Tribune* (Paris, Oct. 12, 1990).

Sports

1   Then ye returned to your trinkets; then ye contented your souls
With the flannelled fools at the

wicket or the muddied oafs at the goals.

RUDYARD KIPLING, (1865–1936) British writer, poet. "The Islanders," *The Five Nations* (1903).

2   Serious sport has nothing to do with fair play. It is bound up with hatred, jealousy, boastfulness, and disregard of all the rules.

GEORGE ORWELL, (1903–1950) British author. *Shooting an Elephant,* "I Write As I Please" (1950).

Spring

1   O months of blossoming, months of transfigurations,
May without cloud and June stabbed to the heart,
I shall not ever forget the lilacs or the roses
Nor those the spring has kept folded away apart.

LOUIS ARAGON, (1897–1982) French poet. "Les Lilas et les Roses" (trans. by Louis MacNeice), *Le Créve-Coeur* (1940).

2   April is the cruellest month, breeding
Lilacs out of the dead land, mixing
Memory and desire, stirring
Dull roots with spring rain.

T.S. (THOMAS STEARNS) ELIOT, (1888–1965) Anglo-American poet, critic. *The Waste Land,* pt. 1, "The Burial of the Dead" (1922). Opening lines of poem.

3   June is bustin' out all over.

OSCAR HAMMERSTEIN II, (1895–1960) U.S. songwriter. "June is Bustin' Out All Over" (song), *Carousel* (stage musical, 1945; film, 1956).

4   Sweet spring, full of sweet days and roses,
A box where sweets compacted lie;

My music shows ye have your closes,
And all must die.

GEORGE HERBERT, (1593–1633) British poet, clergyman. "Virtue," st. 3, *The Temple* (1633). Repr. in *The Works of George Herbert,* ed. Helen Gardner (1961).

5   Nothing is so beautiful as spring—
When weeds, in wheels, shoot long and lovely and lush;
Thrush's eggs look little low heavens, and thrush
Through the echoing timber does so rinse and wring
The ear, it strikes like lightning to hear him sing.

GERARD MANLEY HOPKINS, (1844–1889) British poet, Jesuit priest. "Spring," st. 1 (written 1877), published in *Poems* (1918).

6   For like as herbs and trees bringen forth fruit and flourish in May, in likewise every lusty heart that is in any manner a lover, springeth and flourisheth in lusty deeds.

THOMAS MALORY, (c. 1430–1471) British author. *Le Morte d'Arthur,* bk. 18, ch. 25 (1485).

7   Now the bright morning star, day's harbinger,
Comes dancing from the east, and leads with her
The flow'ry May, who from her green lap throws
The yellow cowslip and the pale primrose.
Hail, bounteous May, that dost inspire
Mirth and youth and warm desire!
Woods and groves are of thy dressing,
Hill and dale doth boast thy blessing.

JOHN MILTON, (1608–1674) British poet. "Song: On May Morning" (c. 1630). Repr. in

Milton's Poetical Works, ed. Douglas Bush (1966).

8   Poor, dear, silly Spring, preparing her annual surprise!

WALLACE STEVENS, (1879–1955) U.S. poet. *Souvenirs and Prophecies: the Young Wallace Stevens*, ch. 8, ed. Holly Stevens (1977). Journal entry, March 4, 1906.

9   For winter's rains and ruins are
         over,
      And all the seasons of snows and
         sins;
      The days dividing lover and lover,
      The light that loses, the night that
         wins;
      And time remembered is grief for-
         gotten,
      And frosts are slain and flowers
         begotten,
      And in green underwood and
         cover
      Blossom by blossom the spring
         begins.

A.C. (ALGERNON CHARLES) SWIN-BURNE, (1837–1909) British poet, critic. "Atalanta in Calydon," chorus, st. 4 (1865).

Stalin, Josef

1   It was the supreme expression of the mediocrity of the apparatus that Stalin himself rose to his position.

LEON TROTSKY, (1879–1940) Russian revolutionary. *My Life*, ch. 40 (1930).

In his last book, *Stalin* (published 1947), drafted while in exile in Mexico, Trotsky wrote: "Our paths diverged so long ago and so far, and in my eyes he is so much the instrument of historical forces that are alien and hostile to me, that my feelings towards him differ little from those I have towards Hitler or the Mikado. The personal element burned out long ago." Trotsky was assassinated on Stalin's orders before the book could be finished.

Stardom

1   There is not a more unhappy being than a superannuated idol.

JOSEPH ADDISON, (1672–1719) British essayist. *Spectator* (London, May 24, 1711), no. 73, *The Spectator*, ed. D.F. Bond (1965).

2   No memory of having starred
      Atones for later disregard,
      Or keeps the end from being hard.

ROBERT FROST, (1874–1963) U.S. poet. "Provide, Provide," st. 6, *A Further Range* (1936).

3   I *am* big. It's the pictures that got small.

BILLY WILDER, (b. 1906) U.S. film director. Norma Desmond (Gloria Swanson), in *Sunset Boulevard* (film), in response to the remark by Joe Gillis (William Holden), in one of their opening scenes together: "You're Norma Desmond! You used to be in silent pictures. Used to be big." (1950).

Staring

1   What is this life if, full of care,
      We have no time to stand and stare?

WILLIAM HENRY DAVIES, (1871–1940) British poet. *Leisure, Songs of Joy* (1911).

Stars

1   And we came out to see once more the stars.

DANTE ALIGHIERI, (1265–1321) Italian poet. "Inferno," cto. 34, l. 139, *The Divine Comedy* (c. 1307-1321), trans. by Mark Musa (1971).

Final line of the "Inferno"—each of the books of the *Divine Comedy* closes with a reference to the stars.

2   Twinkle, twinkle, little star,
      How I wonder what you are!

Up above the world so high,
Like a diamond in the sky!

ANN TAYLOR, (1782–1866) British writer of verse for children. *The Star,* st. 1, *Rhymes for the Nursery* (1806).

In Lewis Carroll's *Alice in Wonderland,* the Mad Hatter sings: "Twinkle, twinkle, little bat! How I wonder what you're at! Up above the world you fly, Like a tea-tray in the sky." The burlesque may refer to a professor of mathematics at Oxford known as "The Bat," probably from his tendency when lecturing to soar above the heads of his listeners.

Stars, the

1   The stars move still, time runs, the
clock will strike,
    The devil will come, and Faustus
must be damned.
    O I'll leap up to my God: who pulls
me down?
    See, see, where Christ's blood
streams in the firmament.
    One drop would save my soul, half
a drop, ah my Christ.

CHRISTOPHER MARLOWE, (1564–1593) British dramatist, poet. Faustus, in *The Tragical History of Dr. Faustus,* act 5, sc. 1 (1604).

State, the

1   The state is not "abolished," it
withers away.

FRIEDRICH ENGELS, (1820–1895) German social philosopher. *Anti-Düring,* pt. 3, ch. 2 (1878).

2   As high as mind stands above
nature, so high does the state stand
above physical life. Man must
therefore venerate the state as a secular deity.... The march of God in
the world, that is what the State is.

GEORG HEGEL, (1770–1831) German philosopher. *The Philosophy of Right,* "The State," addition 164 (1821, trans. 1942).

3   The obligation of subjects to the
sovereign is understood to last as
long, and no longer, than the
power lasteth by which he is able
to protect them.

THOMAS HOBBES, (1588–1679) British philosopher. *Leviathan,* pt. 2, ch. 21 (1651).

4   While the State exists there can be
no freedom; when there is freedom there will be no State.

VLADIMIR ILYICH LENIN, (1870–1924) Russian revolutionary leader. *The State and Revolution,* ch. 5, sct. 4 (1919).

5   In a free society the state does
not administer the affairs of
men. It administers justice among
men who conduct their own
affairs.

WALTER LIPPMANN, (1889–1974) U.S. journalist. *The Good Society,* ch. 12 (1937).

6   The worth of a State, in the long
run, is the worth of the individuals composing it ... a State
which dwarfs its men, in order
that they may be more docile
instruments in its hands even
for beneficial purposes—will
find that with small men no
great thing can really be accomplished.

JOHN STUART MILL, (1806–1873) British philosopher, economist. *On Liberty,* ch. 5 (1859).

Statesmanship

1   A constitutional statesman is in
general a man of common opinions and uncommon abilities.

WALTER BAGEHOT, (1826–1877) British economist, critic. "The Character of Sir Robert Peel," *Biographical Studies* (1881).

2   In statesmanship get the formalities right, never mind about the moralities.

> **MARK TWAIN,** (1835–1910) U.S. author. *Following the Equator,* ch. 65, "Pudd'nhead Wilson's New Calendar" (1897).

Statistics

1   There are three kinds of lies: lies, damned lies and statistics.

> **BENJAMIN DISRAELI,** (1804–1881) British statesman, author. Quoted by Mark Twain in his *Autobiography,* ch. 29, Mark Twain (1924), rev. Charles Neider (1959).
>
> The words have never been found among Disraeli's works; alternative attributions include the radical journalist and politician Henry Labouchére (1831-1912).

2   He uses statistics as a drunken man uses lamp-posts—for support rather than illumination.

> **ANDREW LANG,** (1844–1912) Scottish author. Quoted in *The Harvest of a Quiet Eye,* Alan L. Mackay (1977).

Status Quo

1   The powers that be are ordained of God.

> **BIBLE:** New Testament. St. Paul, in *Romans,* 13:1.

Stock Market

1   On Wall Street he and a few others—how many?—three hundred, four hundred, five hundred?—had become precisely that ... Masters of the Universe.

> **TOM WOLFE,** (b. 1931) U.S. author, journalist. *The Bonfire of the Vanities,* ch. 1 (1979).

Stories and Storytelling

1   Listen, little Elia: draw your chair up close to the edge of the precipice and I'll tell you a story.

> **F. SCOTT FITZGERALD,** (1896–1940) U.S. author. *The Crack-Up,* "Notebook N," ed. Edmund Wilson (1945).

2   Are you sitting comfortably? Then we'll begin.

> **JULIA LANG,** (b. 1921) British broadcaster. *Listen with Mother,* BBC radio program (1950-1982).
>
> Introductory words to daily children's stories.

3   There yet remains but one
    concluding tale,
And then this chronicle of mine is
    ended—
Fulfilled, the duty God ordained to
    me,
A sinner. Not without purpose did
    the Lord
Put me to witness much for many
    years
And educate me in the love of books.
One day some indefatigable monk
Will find my conscientious,
    unsigned work;
Like me, he will light up his ikon-
    lamp
And, shaking from the scroll the age-
    old dust,
He will transcribe these tales in all
    their truth.

> **ALEXANDER PUSHKIN,** (1799–1837) Russian poet. Father Pimen, in *Boris Godunov,* prologue, sct. 5, l. 18-28 (1825), trans. by Philip L. Barbour (1953).

Strangers

1   If a man be gracious and courteous to strangers, it shows he is a citizen

of the world, and that his heart is no island cut off from others lands, but a continent that joins to them.

FRANCIS BACON, (1561–1626) British philosopher, essayist, statesman. *Essays*, "Of Goodness, and Goodness of Nature" (1597-1625).

2 Be not forgetful to entertain strangers: for thereby some have entertained angels unawares.

BIBLE: NEW TESTAMENT, St. Paul, in *Hebrews*, 13:2. This recalls the story of Lot's hospitality at Sodom, in *Genesis* 19.

3 Some enchanted evening,
You may see a stranger,
You may see a stranger,
Across a crowded room.

OSCAR HAMMERSTEIN II, (1895–1960) U.S. songwriter. "Some Enchanted Evening" (song), *South Pacific* (stage musical, 1949; film, 1958).

4 I do desire we may be better strangers.

WILLIAM SHAKESPEARE, (1564–1616) British dramatist, poet. Orlando, in *As You Like It*, act 3, sc. 2, l. 253 (1623).

Speaking to Jaques.

5 I have always depended on the kindness of strangers.

TENNESSEE WILLIAMS, (1914–1983) U.S. dramatist. Blanche DuBois, in *A Streetcar Named Desire*, sc. 11 (1947).

Blanche's final words in the play.

Students

1 Study to be quiet, and to do your own business.

BIBLE: NEW TESTAMENT, St. Paul, in *1 Thessalonians*, 4:11.

2 Generally young men are regarded as radicals. This is a popular mis-

conception. The most conservative persons I ever met are college undergraduates. The radicals are the men past middle life.

WOODROW WILSON, (1856–1924) U.S. Democratic politician, president. *The Papers of Woodrow Wilson*, vol. 16, ed. Arthur S. Link (1974). Speech, Nov. 19, 1905, New York City.

Stupidity

1 You're not too smart, are you? I like that in a man.

LAWRENCE KASDAN, Screenwriter, director. Matty Walker (Kathleen Turner), in *Body Heat* (film) (1981).

2 There is no sin except stupidity.

OSCAR WILDE, (1854–1900) Anglo-Irish playwright, author. Gilbert, in *The Critic as Artist*, pt. 2, *Intentions* (1891). Repr. in *Complete Works of Oscar Wilde*, ed. J.B. Foreman (1966).

Style

1 Behold, Esau my brother is a hairy man, and I am a smooth man.

BIBLE: HEBREW, Jacob, in *Genesis*, 27:11.To his mother Rebekah, explaining how the blind Isaac might discover the ploy of his pretending to be Esau. "Esau was a cunning hunter, a man of the field; and Jacob was a plain man, dwelling in tents." (25:27).

2 Well, less is more, Lucrezia.

ROBERT BROWNING, (1812–1889) British poet. "Andrea del Sarto," l. 78, *Men and Women*, vol. 2 (1855).

"Less is more" is said to have been one of the favorite maxims of architect Mies Van der Rohe.

3 Style is the man himself.
[Le style c'est l'homme même.]

LECLERC, GEORGE-LOUIS BUFFON, COMTE DE, (1707–1788) French naturalist. *Discours sur le Style* (1753). Inaugural address, Aug. 25, 1753, Académie Française, Paris.

4 Style is the dress of thoughts; and let them be ever so just, if your style is homely, coarse, and vulgar, they will appear to as much disadvantage, and be as ill received, as your person, though ever so well-proportioned, would if dressed in rags, dirt, and tatters.

PHILIP DORMER STANHOPE, 4TH EARL CHESTERFIELD, (1694–1773) British statesman, man of letters. *The Letters of the Earl of Chesterfield to His Son*, vol. 1, no. 203, ed. Charles Strachey (1901). Letter, Nov. 24, 1749, first published (1774).

5 Happy Rome, born in my consulship!

MARCUS TULLIUS CICERO, (106–43 B.C.) Roman orator, philosopher. Quoted in *Satires*, bk. 10, l. 122, Juvenal.

Satirized by Juvenal as an example of Cicero's lack of poetic style (*O fortunatam natam me consule Romam!*).

6 'Tisn't beauty, so to speak, nor good talk necessarily. It's just IT. Some women'll stay in a man's memory if they once walked down a street.

RUDYARD KIPLING, (1865–1936) British author, poet. Pyecroft, in "Mrs. Bathurst," *Traffics and Discoveries* (1904).

Referring to Mrs. Bathurst.

7 Our own epoch is determining, day by day, its own style. Our eyes, unhappily, are unable yet to discern it.

LE CORBUSIER [CHARLE ÉDOUARD JEANNE], (1887–1965) Swiss-born French architect. *Toward a New Architecture*, ch. 1, "Eyes Which Do Not See" (1923, trans. 1946).

8 Style [is] the hallmark of a temperament stamped on the material in hand.

ANDRÉ MAUROIS, (1885–1967) French author and critic. *The Art of Writing*, "The Writer's Craft" sct. 2 (1960).

9 Camp is a vision of the world in terms of style—but a particular kind of style. It is the love of the exaggerated, the "off," of things-being-what-they-are-not.

SUSAN SONTAG, (b. 1933) U.S. essayist. *Notes on "Camp,"* note 8, *Against Interpretation* (1966). Originally published in *Partisan Review* (New Brunswick, NJ, 1964).

10 Style is not something applied. It is something that permeates. It is of the nature of that in which it is found, whether the poem, the manner of a god, the bearing of a man. It is not a dress.

WALLACE STEVENS, (1879–1955) U.S. poet. *Opus Posthumous*, "Two or Three Ideas" (1959). (Originally published 1951.)

11 *Feather-footed through the plashy fen passes the questing vole.*

EVELYN WAUGH, (1903–1966) British novelist. Mr. Salter, in *Scoop*, bk. 1, ch. 1, sct. 4 (1938).

Example of "good style."

12 His style is chaos illumined by flashes of lightning. As a writer he has mastered everything except language.

OSCAR WILDE, (1854–1900) Anglo-Irish playwright, author. Vivian, in "The Decay of Lying, "*Intentions* (1891). Repr. in *Complete Works of Oscar Wilde*, ed. J.B. Foreman (1966).

Referring to novelist and poet George Meredith. On the subject of Meredith and Robert Browning, Wilde wrote: "Meredith's a prose Browning, and so is Browning. He uses poetry as a medium for writing in prose." (*The Critic as Artist*, pt. 1, 1891).

Subjection

1 It does not matter what the whip is; it is none the less a whip, because you have cut thongs for it out of your own souls.

JOHN RUSKIN, (1819–1900) British art critic, author. "Crown of Wild Olives," lecture 3, sct. 119 (1865), repr. in *The Works of John Ruskin*, vol. 18, eds. E.T. Cook and Alexander Weddesburn (1905). Address, 1865, Royal Military Academy.

Subjugation

1   Ask for this great deliverer now, and find him
    Eyeless in Gaza at the mill with slaves,
    Himself in bonds under Philistian yoke.

JOHN MILTON, (1608–1674) British poet. "Samson Agonistes," l. 40-2 (1671). Aldous Huxley called his novel of ideas *Eyeless in Gaza* (1936).

Suburbs

1   Come, friendly bombs, and fall on Slough!
    It isn't fit for humans now,
    There isn't grass to graze a cow.
    Swarm over, Death!

JOHN BETJEMAN, (1906–1984) British poet. "Slough," st. 1, *Continental Dew* (1937).

Betjeman was renowned for his antipathy toward modern architecture and town planning.

2   The women there do all they ought;
    The men observe the Rules of Thought.
    They love the Good; they worship Truth;
    They laugh uproariously in youth;
    (And when they get to feeling old,
    They up and shoot themselves, I'm told) ...

RUPERT BROOKE, (1887–1915) British poet. "The Old Vicarage," *Grantchester, 1914 and Other Poems* (1915).

Of the people of Grantchester, outside Cambridge, England.

3   And the wind shall say "Here were decent godless people;
    Their only monument the asphalt road
    And a thousand lost golf balls."

T.S. (THOMAS STEARNS) ELIOT, (1888–1965) Anglo-American poet, critic. "The Rock," pt. 1 (1934).

Success

1   'Tis not in mortals to command success,
    But we'll do more, Sempronius, we'll deserve it.

JOSEPH ADDISON, (1672–1719) British essayist. Portius, in *Cato*, act 1, sc. 2 (1713). Repr. in *Works of Addison*, ed. R. Hurd (1883).

"Curse on the stripling!" Responds Sempronius, father of Portius, "... ambitiously sententious."

2   One's religion is whatever he is most interested in, and yours is Success.

J.M. (JAMES MATTHEW) BARRIE, (1860–1937) British playwright. Kate, in *The Twelve-Pound Look* (performed 1910, published 1921).

3   Success is counted sweetest
    By those who ne'er succeed.
    To comprehend a nectar
    Requires sorest need.

EMILY DICKINSON, (1830–1886) U.S. poet. "Success Is Counted Sweetest," st. 1 (written c. 1859, published 1878). Repr. in *The Complete Poems*, no. 67, Harvard *variorum* edition (1955).

4   If A is a success in life, then A equals x plus y plus z. Work is x; y is play; and z is keeping your mouth shut.

ALBERT EINSTEIN, (1879–1955) German-born U.S. theoretical physicist. quoted in *Observer* (London, Jan. 15, 1950).

5   The moral flabbiness born of the exclusive worship of the bitch-goddess SUCCESS. That—with the squalid cash interpretation put on the word success—is our national disease.

WILLIAM JAMES, (1843–1916) U.S. psychologist, philosopher. *The Letters of William James*, vol. 2 (1920). Letter, Sept. 11, 1906, to H.G. Wells.

6   The common idea that success spoils people by making them vain, egotistic, and self-complacent is erroneous; on the contrary, it makes them, for the most part, humble, tolerant, and kind. Failure makes people cruel and bitter.

W. SOMERSET MAUGHAM, (1874–1966) British author. *The Summing Up*, ch. 48 (1938).

7   A hit, a very palpable hit.

WILLIAM SHAKESPEARE, (1564–1616) British dramatist, poet. Osric, in *Hamlet*, act 5, sc. 2, l. 232 (1604).

Judging that Hamlet has struck Laertes, his opponent in a duel.

8   It is not enough to succeed. Others must fail.

GORE VIDAL, (b. 1925) U.S. novelist, critic. Quoted in *Antipanegyric for Tom Driberg* (requiem mass), Dec. 8, 1976, Reverend Gerard Irvine.

Other sources give "It is not enough to be seen to succeed—others must be seen to fail."

Suffering

1   Mankind are more disposed to suffer, while evils are sufferable, than to right themselves by abolishing the forms to which they are accustomed.

THOMAS JEFFERSON, (1743–1826) U.S. president. "The Declaration of Independence," *The Papers of Thomas Jefferson*, vol. 1, Julian P. Boyd (1950).

Adopted by the Second Continental Congress, July 4, 1776.

2   It is not true that suffering ennobles the character; happiness does that sometimes, but suffering, for the most part, makes men petty and vindictive.

W. SOMERSET MAUGHAM, (1874–1966) British author. *The Moon and Sixpence*, ch. 17 (1919).

Nearly twenty years later, Maugham used almost identical words to describe the suffering he witnessed as a medical student, in *The Summing Up*, ch. 19 (1938).

3   No pain, no palm; no thorns, no throne; no gall, no glory; no cross, no crown.

WILLIAM PENN, (1644–1718) British religious leader, founder of Pennsylvania. *No Cross, No Crown* (pamphlet) (1669).

Suicide

1   It is not worth the bother of killing yourself, since you always kill yourself *too late*.

E.M. (EMIL MIHAI) CIORAN, (1911–1995) Romanian-born French philosopher. *The Trouble with Being Born*, ch. 2 (1973).

2   Whensoever any affliction assails me, me thinks I have the keyes of my prison in mine owne hand, and no remedy presents it selfe so soone to my heart, as mine own sword. Often meditation of this hath wonne me to a charitable interpretation of their action, who dy so: and provoked me a little to watch and exagitate their reasons, which pronounce so peremptory judgements upon them.

John Donne, (c. 1572–1631) British divine, metaphysical poet. "Biathanatos," preface (written c. 1608, published 1646). Repr. in *Complete Poetry and Selected Prose*, ed. John Hayward (1929).

3   However great a man's fear of life, suicide remains the courageous act, the clear-headed act of a mathematician. The suicide has judged by the laws of chance—so many odds against one that to live will be more miserable than to die. His sense of mathematics is greater than his sense of survival.

Graham Greene, (1904–1991) British novelist. Dr. Magiot, in *The Comedians*, bk. 3, pt. 1, ch. 1, sct. 1 (1966).

4   Death has a thousand doors to let out life, I shall find one.... From a loath'd life, I'll not an hour outlive.

Philip Massinger, (1583–1640) British dramatist. Almera (daughter of the Viceroy of Sicily), in *A Very Woman*, act 5, sc. 4 (1655). Repr. in *The Plays and Poems of Philip Massinger,* eds. P. Edwards and C. Gibson (1976).

This image of death was a common one, used by Massinger and John Fletcher in *The Custom of the Country,* John Webster in *The Duchess of Malfi,* and much earlier by Seneca in *Phoenissae* (1st century A.D.).

5   It is always consoling to think of suicide: in that way one gets through many a bad night.

Friedrich Nietzsche, (1844–1900) German philosopher. *Beyond Good and Evil,* ch. 4, aph. 157 (1886).

"When one *does away with* oneself one does the most estimable thing possible: one thereby almost deserves to live." (*Twilight of the Idols,* "Expeditions of an Untimely Man," aph. 36, 1889).

6   Razors pain you;
Rivers are damp;
Acids stain you;
And drugs cause cramp.
Guns aren't lawful;

Nooses give;
Gas smells awful;
You might as well live.

Dorothy Parker, (1893–1967) U.S. humorous writer. "Résumé." *Enough Rope* (1926).

7   No one ever lacks a good reason for suicide.

Cesare Pavese, (1908–1950) Italian poet, novelist, translator. *The Burning Brand: Diaries 1935-1950* (1950, trans. 1961). Journal entry, March 23, 1938.

Suicide was a continuing theme in Pavese's diaries; he took his own life on Aug. 27, 1950, shortly after being awarded the Strega Prize for literature.

8   The woman is perfected.
Her dead
Body wears the smile of accomplishment.

Sylvia Plath, (1932–1963) U.S. poet. "Edge," *Ariel* (1965).

Opening lines of Sylvia Plath's last poem, written a week before her suicide.

9   But suicides have a special language.
Like carpenters they want to know *which tools.*
They never ask *why build.*

Anne Sexton, (1928–1974) U.S. poet. "Wanting to Die," st. 3, *Live or Die* (1966).

Sexton committed suicide in October 1974, after several failed attempts.

10   For who would bare the whips and scorns of time,
Th'oppressor's wrong, the proud man's contumely,
The pangs of disprized love, the law's delay,
The insolence of office, and the spurns
That patient merit of th'unworthy takes,

When he himself might his quietus
make
With a bare bodkin?

WILLIAM SHAKESPEARE, (1564–1616)
British dramatist, poet. Hamlet, in *Hamlet*,
act 3, sc. 1, l. 72-78 (1604).

Part of Hamlet's meditative soliloquy on the
question of "To be, or not to be."

11   Oh, no no no, it was too cold
always
(Still the dead one lay moaning)
I was much too far out all my life
And not waving but drowning.

STEVIE SMITH, (1902–1971) British poet,
novelist. *Not Waving But Drowning*, "Not
Waving But Drowning" (1957).

Summer

1   Sumer is icumen in,
Lhude sing cuccu!
Groweth sed, and bloweth med,
And springth the wude nu—
Sing cuccu!

ANONYMOUS, *Cuckoo Song* (c. 1250).

This hymn is still sung annually at Reading
Abbey, England. Ezra Pound's *Ancient
Music* was a pastiche of this (originally
dropped from the 1916 edition of *Lustra*
when it was considered offensive, later rein-
stated): Winter is icummen in, Lhude sing
Goddamm, Raineth drop and staineth slop,
And how the wind doth ramm! Sing:
Goddamm.

2   Summer has set in with its usual
severity.

SAMUEL TAYLOR COLERIDGE,
(1772–1834) British poet, critic. Quoted in
Letters of Charles Lamb, vol. 2, ed. Alfed
Ainger (1888). Letter, May 9, 1826, by essayist Charles Lamb.

3   Summertime and the living is easy,
Fish are jumping, and the cotton is
high.

IRA GERSHWIN, (1896–1983) U.S. "Summertime" (song), *Porgy and Bess* (show, 1935).

The song was a hit for Billie Holiday in 1936.
Music by George Gershwin.

4   Shall I compare thee to a summer's
day?
Thou art more lovely and more
temperate.
Rough winds do shake the darling
buds of May,
And summer's lease hath all too
short a date.

WILLIAM SHAKESPEARE, (1564–1616)
British dramatist, poet. "Sonnet 18" (1609).

5   Summer set lip to earth's bosom
bare
And left the flushed print in a
poppy there.

FRANCIS THOMPSON, (1859–1907)
British poet. "The Poppy," *Poems* (1913).

Sun

1   Busy old fool, unruly Sun,
Why dost thou thus,
Through windows and through
curtains call on us?
Must to thy motions lovers' seasons
run?

JOHN DONNE, (c. 1572–1631) British
divine, metaphysical poet. "The Sun Rising,"
Songs and Sonnets (1633). Repr. in *Complete
Poetry and Selected Prose*, ed. John Hayward
(1929).

2   The day of the sun is like the day
of a king. It is a promenade in
the morning, a sitting on the
throne at noon, a pageant in the
evening.

WALLACE STEVENS, (1879–1955) U.S.
poet. *Souvenirs and Prophecies: the Young
Wallace Stevens*, ch. 6, ed. Holly Stevens
(1966). Journal entry, April 20, 1920.

Sunday and the Sabbath

1 Remember the sabbath day, to keep it holy. Six days shalt thou labour, and do all thy work: but the seventh day is the sabbath of the Lord thy God: in it thou shalt not do any work, thou, nor thy son, nor thy daughter, thy manservant, nor thy maidservant, nor thy cattle, nor thy stranger that is within thy gates: for in six days the Lord made heaven and earth, the sea, and all that in them is, and rested the seventh day: wherefore the Lord blessed the sabbath day, and hallowed it.

BIBLE: HEBREW, *Exodus*, 20:8-11.The fourth commandment.

2 Some keep the Sabbath going to Church—
I keep it, staying at Home—
With a Bobolink for a Chorister—
And an Orchard, for a Dome—

EMILY DICKINSON, (1830–1886) U.S. poet. "Some Keep the Sabbath Going to Church," st. 1 (written c. 1860, published 1864). Repr. in *The Complete Poems*, no. 324, Harvard *variorum* edition (1955).

3 Why do I do this every Sunday? Even the book reviews seem to be the same as last week's. Different books—same reviews.

JOHN OSBORNE, (1929–1994) British playwright. Jimmy Porter, in *Look Back in Anger*, act 1 (1956).

Opening words of play.

4 Anybody can observe the Sabbath, but making it holy surely takes the rest of the week.

ALICE WALKER, (b. 1944) U.S. author, critic. "To the Editors of *Ms.* Magazine," *In Search of Our Mothers' Gardens* (1983).

Sundays

1 It was a Sunday afternoon, wet and cheerless; and a duller spectacle this earth of ours has not to show than a rainy Sunday in London.

THOMAS DE QUINCEY, (1785–1859) British author. *Confessions of an English Opium-Eater*, pt. 2, "The Pleasures of Opium," (1822).

Recalling the day in 1804 when he first took opium.

Superstition

1 Superstition is the religion of feeble minds.

EDMUND BURKE, (1729–1797) Irish philosopher, statesman. *Reflections on the Revolution in France* (1790), repr. in *Works*, vol. 3 (1865).

Surprises

1 Nobody expects the Spanish Inquisition.

MONTY PYTHON'S FLYING CIRCUS, Michael Palin, in *Monty Python's Flying Circus* (BBC TV comedy series), 2nd series, episode 2, written and conceived by John Cleese, Graham Chapman, Terry Gilliam, Eric Idle, Terry Jones and Michael Palin (1969-1974), published in *Monty Python's Flying Circus: Just the Words*, ed. Roger Wilmut, vol. 1, ch. 15 (1989). First broadcast Sept. 22, 1970.

Surrealism

1 To be a surrealist ... means barring from your mind all remembrance of what you have seen, and being always on the lookout for what has never been.

RENÉ MAGRITTE, (1898–1967) Belgian surrealist painter. Quoted in Uwe M. Scheede's essay, "Sightless Vision," published in *Max*

Ernst, ed. Werner Spies (1991). *Time* (New York, April 21, 1947).

Surveillance

1   BIG BROTHER IS WATCHING YOU.

GEORGE ORWELL, (1903–1950) British author. *Nineteen Eighty-Four,* pt. 1, ch. 1 (1949).

Caption to Ingsoc poster—"... one of those pictures which are so contrived that the eyes follow you about when you move."

Survival

1   And therfore, at the kynges court, my brother,
    Ech man for hymself, ther is noon oother.

GEOFFREY CHAUCER, (1340–1400) British poet. *The Canterbury Tales,* Arcite, in "The Knight's Tale," l. 1181-2 (c. 1387-1400), repr. in *The Works of Geoffrey Chaucer,* ed. Alfred W. Pollard, et al. (1898).

2   These fragments I have shored against my ruins.

T.S. (THOMAS STEARNS) ELIOT, (1888–1965) Anglo-American poet, critic. *The Waste Land,* pt. 5: "What the Thunder Said" (1922).

3   I tell the tale that I heard told. Mithridates, he died old.

A.E. (ALFRED EDWARD) HOUSMAN, (1859–1936) British poet. "A Shropshire Lad", no. 62 (1896). Repr. in *The Collected Poems of A.E. Housman* (1939).

Mithridates the Great (c. 135-63 B.C.) made himself immune to poison by the continuous taking of antidotes. When captured by the Romans he was unable to poison himself, so he ordered a Gallic mercenary to kill him.

4   The chess-board is the world; the pieces are the phenomena of the universe; the rules of the game are what we call the laws of Nature. The player on the other side is hidden from us. We know that his play is always fair, just, and patient. But also we know, to our cost, that he never overlooks a mistake, or makes the smallest allowance for ignorance.

THOMAS HENRY HUXLEY, (1825–1895) British biologist. "A Liberal Education," *Lay Sermons, Addresses, and Reviews* (1870). (Essay originally published 1868).

5   From birth to 18 a girl needs good parents. From 18 to 35, she needs good looks. From 35 to 55, good personality. From 55 on, she needs good cash. I'm saving my money.

SOPHIE TUCKER [SOPHIE KALISH ABUZA], (1884–1966) Russian-born - U.S. singer. Quoted in *Sophie,* "When They Get Too Wild For Everyone Else," Michael Freedland (1978). Remark from 1953.

Sophie Tucker called herself "The Last of the Red-Hot Mamas" after her most famous song.

Suspicion

1   There is nothing makes a man suspect much, more than to know little.

FRANCIS BACON, (1561–1626) British philosopher, essayist, statesman. *Essays,* "Of Suspicion" (1597-1625).

2   What loneliness is more lonely than distrust?

GEORGE ELIOT [MARY ANN (OR MARIAN) EVANS], (1819–1880) British novelist. *Middlemarch,* bk. 5, ch. 44 (1872).

3   A new disease? I know not, new or old,
    But it may well be called poor mortals' plague:
    For, like a pestilence, it doth infect
    The houses of the brain ...

Till not a thought, or motion, in
  the mind,
Be free from the black poison of
  suspect.

BEN JONSON, (c. 1572–1637) British
dramatist, poet. Kitely, in *Every Man in His
Humour*, act 2, sc. 3, l. 55-67 (performed
1598, published 1616). Repr. in *The Complete Plays*, vol. 1, ed. G.A. Wilkes, 1981).

4   We have to distrust each other. It is
our only defence against betrayal.

TENNESSEE WILLIAMS, (1914–1983)
U.S. dramatist. Marguerite Gautier, in *Camino
Real*, Block 10 (1953).

Swearing

1   Grant me some wild expressions,
Heavens, or I shall burst.

GEORGE FARQUHAR, (1678–1707) Irish
dramatist. Lady Lurewell, in *The Constant
Couple*, act 5, sc. 3 (1699). Repr. in *Complete
Works*, ed. Charles Stonehill (1930).

2   Ethelberta breathed a sort of exclamation, not right out, but stealthily,
like a parson's damn.

THOMAS HARDY, (1840–1928) British
novelist, poet. *The Hand of Ethelberta*, ch. 26
(1876).

3   Swear me, Kate, like a lady as thou
art,
A good mouth-filling oath.

WILLIAM SHAKESPEARE, (1564–1616)
British dramatist, poet. Hotspur, in *Henry IV
pt. 1*, act 3, sc. 1, l. 249-50 (1598).

Speaking to his wife (Lady Percy).

Switzerland and the Swiss

1   Switzerland is a small, steep country, much more up and down than
sideways, and is all stuck over with

large brown hotels built on the
cuckoo clock style of architecture.

ERNEST HEMINGWAY, (1899–1961) U.S.
author. Quoted in *Toronto Star Weekly*
(March 4, 1922).

2   I look upon Switzerland as an inferior sort of Scotland.

SYDNEY SMITH, (1771–1845) British clergyman, writer. Quoted in *Memoir*, vol. 2,
Lady Holland (1855). Letter to Lord Holland,
1815.

Sympathy

1   I can sympathise with people's
pains, but not with their pleasures.
There is something curiously boring about somebody else's happiness.

ALDOUS HUXLEY, (1894–1963) British
author. "Cynthia," *Limbo* (1920).

Taboo

1   We find many things to which the
prohibition of them constitutes the
only temptation.

WILLIAM HAZLITT, (1778–1830) British
essayist. *Characteristics: In the Manner of
Rochefoucault's Maxims*, no. 140 (1823),
repr. in *The Complete Works Of William
Hazlitt*, vol. 9, ed. P.P. Howe (1932).

Tact

1   A soft answer turneth away wrath:
but grievous words stir up anger.

BIBLE: HEBREW, *Proverbs*, 15:1.

2   Tact in audacity consists in knowing how far we may go too far.

JEAN COCTEAU, (1889–1963) French
author, filmmaker. *Le Coq et l'Arlequin, Le*

Rappel à l'Ordre (1926), repr. in Collected Works, vol. 9 (1950). (Originally published 1918).

3 Tact is after all a kind of mind-reading.

SARAH ORNE JEWETT, (1849–1909) U.S. author. The Country of the Pointed Firs and Other Stories, ch. 10 (1896).

4 Give thy thoughts no tongue,
Nor any unproportioned thought
   his act.
Be thou familiar but by no means
   vulgar.

WILLIAM SHAKESPEARE, (1564–1616) British dramatist, poet. Polonius, in Hamlet, act 1, sc. 3, l. 59-61 (1604).

Advice to his son Laertes, departing for France ("unproportioned" means "inappropriate").

Talent

1 It takes little talent to see clearly what lies under one's nose, a good deal of it to know in which direction to point that organ.

W.H. (WYSTAN HUGH) AUDEN, (1907–1973) Anglo-American poet. The Dyer's Hand, pt. 1, "Writing" (1962).

2 Whom the gods wish to destroy they first call promising.

CYRIL CONNOLLY, (1903–1974) British critic. Enemies of Promise, pt. 2, ch. 13 (1938).

3 If a man can write a better book, preach a better sermon, or make a better mouse-trap, than his neighbor, though he build his house in the woods, the world will make a beaten path to his door.

RALPH WALDO EMERSON, (1803–1882) U.S. essayist, poet, philosopher. Attributed.

Ascribed to Emerson by Sarah Yule in the anthology Borrowings (1889), later said by her

to originate in a lecture given by Emerson in 1871. A similar passage appears in Emerson's Journals (1909-1914), which provided material for many of his lectures and writings. The remark's authorship was also claimed by Elbert Hubbard in A Thousand and One Epigrams (1911). In The Worst Years of Our Lives, "The Cult of Busyness" (1991), Barbara Ehrenreich wrote: "Anyone who has invented a better mousetrap, or the contemporary equivalent, can expect to be harassed by strangers demanding that you read their unpublished manuscripts or undergo the humiliation of public speaking, usually on remote Midwestern campuses."

4 I think this is the most extra-ordinary collection of talent, of human knowledge, that has ever been gathered together at the White House—with the possible exception of when Thomas Jefferson dined alone.

JOHN FITZGERALD KENNEDY, (1917–1963) U.S. Democratic politician, president. Public Papers of the Presidents of the United States: John F. Kennedy, 1962. Remark, April 29, 1962, Washington D.C..

At a dinner for Nobel Prize winners.

5 If a man has a talent and cannot use it, he has failed. If he has a talent and uses only half of it, he has partly failed. If he has a talent and learns somehow to use the whole of it, he has gloriously succeeded, and won a satisfaction and a triumph few men ever know.

THOMAS WOLFE, (1900–1938) U.S. author. The Web and the Rock, ch. 29 (1939).

Taste

1 What is exhilarating in bad taste is the aristocratic pleasure of giving offense.

CHARLES BAUDELAIRE, (1821–1867) French poet. Squibs, Intimate Journals, sct. 18 (1887), trans. by Christopher Isherwood (1930), rev. Don Bachardy (1989).

2   To achieve harmony in bad taste is the height of elegance.

JEAN GENET, (1910–1986) French playwright, novelist. *The Thief's Journal* (1949).

3   I love everything that's old: old friends, old times, old manners, old books, old wines; and, I believe, Dorothy, you'll own I have been pretty fond of an old wife.

OLIVER GOLDSMITH, (1728–1774) Anglo-Irish author, poet, playwright. Hardcastle, in *She Stoops to Conquer*, act 1, sc. 1 (1773).

4   Between good sense and good taste there lies the difference between a cause and its effect.

JEAN DE LA BRUYÈRE, (1645–1696) French writer, moralist. *Characters,* "Of Opinions," aph. 56 (1688).

5   I wish you all manner of prosperity, with a little more taste.

ALAIN-RENÉ LE SAGE, (1668–1747) French playwright, novelist. The Archbishop of Grenada, in *The Adventures of Gil Blas*, bk. 7, ch. 4 (1715-1735).

Dismissing Gil Blas, who had incurred the Archbishop's disfavor by criticizing one of his sermons.

6   People who like this sort of thing will find this the sort of thing they like.

ABRAHAM LINCOLN, (1809–1865) U.S. president. Quoted in *Collections and Recollections*, ch. 30, G.W.E. Russell (1898).

Referring to "an unreadably sentimental book." According to Gross' *Lincoln's Own Stories*, Lincoln's remark was to Robert Dale Owen, a spiritualist who had insisted on reading to Lincoln a long manuscript on spiritualism.

7   The arbiter of taste.

TACITUS, (c. 55–c. 120) Roman historian. *Annals,* bk. 15, ch. 18.

Referring to the satirist Petronius, often given the name Arbiter.

8   Either that wallpaper goes, or I do.

OSCAR WILDE, (1854–1900) Anglo-Irish playwright, author. *Attributed.*

Last words as he lay dying in a drab Paris hotel room, recorded in variant forms in R.H. Sherard, *Life of Oscar Wilde* (1906) and Richard Ellmann, *Oscar Wilde* (1988).

Taxes

1   To tax and to please, no more than to love and to be wise, is not given to men.

EDMUND BURKE, (1729–1797) Irish philosopher, statesman. "First Speech on Conciliation with America: American Taxation," *Works*, vol. 2 (1899). Speech, April 19, 1774, House of Commons, London.

2   Read my lips: no new taxes.

GEORGE BUSH, (b. 1924) U.S. Republican politician, president. Acceptance speech, *The New York Times* (August 19, 1988). August 18, 1988, New Orleans.

The expression has been in general usage since at least the 1970s. Bush eventually raised taxes.

3   We don't pay taxes. Only the little people pay taxes.

LEONA HELMSLEY, (b. 1920) U.S. businesswoman. Quoted in *The New York Times* (July 12, 1989).

Reported by Helmsley's former housekeeper during her trial for tax evasion; in March 1992 Leona Helmsley was sentenced to four years' imprisonment.

Tea

1   Thank God for tea! What would the world do without tea? How did it exist?

SYDNEY SMITH, (1771–1845) British clergyman, writer. *Memoir,* vol. 1, ch. 11, Lady Holland (1855).

Teachers

1 The true teacher defends his pupils against his own personal influence. He inspires self-distrust. He guides their eyes from himself to the spirit that quickens him. He will have no disciple.

A. BRONSON ALCOTT [AMOS BRONSON ALCOTT], (1799–1888) U.S. educator, social reformer. "The Teacher," *Orphic Sayings* (1840). *The Dial* (July 1840).

2 My object will be, if possible, to form Christian men, for Christian boys I can scarcely hope to make.

THOMAS ARNOLD, (1795–1842) British educator, scholar. *The Life and Correspondence of Thomas Arnold, DD*, vol. 1, ch. 2, ed. Arthur Penrhyn Stanley (1845). Letter, March 2, 1828.

Written on appointment as headmaster of Rugby School.

3 A schoolmaster should have an atmosphere of awe, and walk wonderingly, as if he was amazed at being himself.

WALTER BAGEHOT, (1826–1877) British economist, critic. *Hartley Coleridge*, vol. 1, *Literary Studies* (1878). (Article originally published 1852).

4 Teaching is not a lost art, but the regard for it is a lost tradition.

JACQUES BARZUN, (b. 1907) U.S. scholar. *Newsweek* (New York, Dec. 5, 1955).

5 Once more I would adopt the graver style—
A teacher should be sparing of his smile.

WILLIAM COWPER, (1731–1800) British poet. "Charity", l. 489-90 (1782). Repr. in *Poetical Works*, ed. H.S. Milford (1934).

6 We loved the doctrine for the teacher's sake.

DANIEL DEFOE, (1660–1731) British author, poet, journalist. "The Character of the Late Dr. S. Annesly," (1697), repr. in *Works*, ed. Keltie (1869).

7 We love the precepts for the teacher's sake.

GEORGE FARQUHAR, (1678–1707) Irish dramatist. Sir Harry Wildair, in *The Constant Couple*, act 5, sc. 3 (1699). Repr. in *Complete Works*, ed. Charles Stonehill (1930).

8 Well had the boding tremblers learned to trace
The day's disasters in his morning face.

OLIVER GOLDSMITH, (1728–1774) Anglo-Irish author, poet, playwright. *The Deserted Village*, l. 199-200 (1770).

Referring to the village schoolmaster.

9 George—don't do that.

JOYCE GRENFELL, (1910–1979) British actress, writer. Catch phrase (various sketches), GeorgeDon't Do That (1977).

10 Give me a girl at an impressionable age, and she is mine for life!

MURIEL SPARK, (b. 1918) British novelist. Miss Brodie, in *The Prime of Miss Jean Brodie*, ch. 1 (1961).

11 A teacher should have maximal authority, and minimal power.

THOMAS SZASZ, (b. 1920) U.S. psychiatrist. "Education," *The Second Sin* (1973).

Teachers and Teaching

1 Teaching is not a lost art, but the regard for it is a lost tradition.

JACQUES BARZUN, (b. 1907) U.S. scholar. *Newsweek* (New York, Dec. 5, 1955).

Technology

1 Technology ... the knack of so arranging the world that we don't have to experience it.

MAX FRISCH, (1911–1991) Swiss author, architect. Hanna, in *Homo Faber*, "Second Stop" (1957, trans. 1959).

Teeth

1 I hope all your teeth have cavities, and don't forget; abscess makes the heart grow fonder.

MORRIE RYSKIND, Screenwriter. Hammer (Groucho Marx), in *The Cocoanuts* (film) (1929). Robert Florey and Joseph Santley.

Telephones

1 Well, if I called the wrong number, why did you answer the phone?

JAMES THURBER, (1894–1961) U.S. humorist, illustrator. Cartoon caption, in *The New Yorker* (June 5, 1937).

Temper

1 There is a great deal of unmapped country within us which would have to be taken into account in an explanation of our gusts and storms.

GEORGE ELIOT [MARY ANN (OR MARIAN) EVANS], (1819–1880) British novelist. *Daniel Deronda*, bk. 3, ch. 24 (1876).

2 We boil at different degrees.

RALPH WALDO EMERSON, (1803–1882) U.S. essayist, poet, philosopher. *Society and Solitude*, "Eloquence" (1870).

3 A tart temper never mellows with age, and a sharp tongue is the only edged tool that grows keener with constant use.

WASHINGTON IRVING, (1783–1859) U.S. author. *The Sketch Book of Geoffrey Crayon, Gent.* "Rip Van Winkle" (1819-1820).

Temptation

1 Get thee behind me, Satan: thou art an offence unto me: for thou savourest not the things that be of God, but those that be of men.

BIBLE: NEW TESTAMENT Jesus, in *Matthew*, 16:23. Said to Peter, who had suggested that Jesus not go into Jerusalem to meet his fate.

2 Watch and pray, that ye enter not into temptation: the spirit indeed is willing, but the flesh is weak.

BIBLE: NEW TESTAMENT Jesus, in *Matthew*, 26:41.

3 "I am," she sang, "the sweet Siren, I am, whose song beguiles the sailors in mid-sea, enticing them, inviting them to joy! My singing made Ulysses turn away from his desired course; who dwells with me seldom departs, I satisfy so well."

DANTE ALIGHIERI, (1265–1321) Italian poet. "Purgatory," cto. 19, l. 19-24, *The Divine Comedy* (c. 1307-1321), trans. by Mark Musa (1981).

Sung by the Siren to Dante, in his dream on the fourth cornice of Purgatory.

4 There are several good protections against temptations but the surest is cowardice.

MARK TWAIN, (1835–1910) U.S. author. *Following the Equator*, ch. 36, "Pudd'nhead Wilson's New Calendar" (1897).

The epigram also appears as an entry, 1898, in Twain *Notebook*, ch. 31, ed. Albert Bigelow Paine (1935).

5 I can resist everything except temptation.

OSCAR WILDE, (1854–1900) Anglo-Irish playwright, author. Lord Darlington, in *Lady Windermere's Fan*, act 1 (1893).

This was a favorite theme of Wilde's. In *An Ideal Husband*, act 2 (performed 1895, published 1899), Sir Robert Chiltern says to Lord

Goring, "Do you really think, Arthur, that it is weakness that yields to temptation? I tell you that there are terrible temptations that it requires strength, strength and courage, to yield to." Again, in *The Picture of Dorian Gray*, ch. 2 (1891), Wilde wrote: "The only way to get rid of a temptation is to yield to it."

Tenderness

1 If you wish —
   ... I'll be irreproachably tender;
   not a man, but—a cloud in
      trousers!

   VLADIMIR MAYAKOVSKY, (1893–1930) Russian poet, dramatist. "The Cloud in Trousers" (1915), trans. by Samuel Charteris.

Tennis

1 Miss J. Hunter Dunn, Miss J.
      Hunter Dunn,
   Furnish'd and burnish'd by Alder-
      shot sun,
   What strenuous singles we played
      after tea,
   We in the tournament—you
      against me!

   JOHN BETJEMAN, (1906–1984) British poet. "A Subaltern's Love-song", st. 1, *New Bats in Old Belfries* (1945).

Terrorism

1 The man who throws a bomb is an
   artist, because he prefers a great
   moment to everything.

   GILBERT KEITH CHESTERTON, (1874–1936) British author. Gregory, in *The Man Who Was Thursday*, ch. 1 (1908).

Terrorists

1 The terrorist and the policeman
   both come from the same basket.

Revolution, legality—counter-moves in the same game; forms of idleness at bottom identical.

JOSEPH CONRAD, (1857–1924) Polish-born British novelist. *The Secret Agent*, ch. 4 (1907).

Texas

1 Texas is a state of mind. Texas is an obsession. Above all, Texas is a nation in every sense of the word. And there's an opening convey of generalities. A Texan outside of Texas is a foreigner.

   JOHN STEINBECK, (1902–1968) U.S. author. *Travels With Charley: In Search of America*, pt. 4 (1962).

Theater

1 "*Theater of cruelty*" means a theater difficult and cruel for myself first of all. And, on the level of performance, it is not the cruelty we can exercise upon each other by hacking at each other's bodies, carving up our personal anatomies, or, like Assyrian emperors, sending parcels of human ears, noses, or neatly detached nostrils through the mail, but the much more terrible and necessary cruelty which things can exercise against us. We are not free. And the sky can still fall on our heads. And the theater has been created to teach us that first of all.

   ANTONIN ARTAUD, (1896–1948) French theater producer, actor, theorist. *The Theater and Its Double*, ch. 1 (1938, trans. 1958).

2 All tragedies are finished by a death,
   All comedies are ended by a marriage.

   GEORGE GORDON NOEL BYRON, 6TH BARON BYRON, (1788–1824) British poet. *Don Juan*, cto. 3, st. 9 (1819-1824).

3 The drama's laws, the drama's
   patrons give,
   For we that live to please, must
      please to live.

SAMUEL JOHNSON, (1709–1784) British
author, lexicographer. "Prologue at the Opening of the Theatre in Drury Lane," l. 53-4
(1747). Repr. in *Works of Samuel Johnson,* Yale
Edition, vol. 6, eds. E.L. McAdam, Jr. and G.
Milne (1964).

4 Come, leave the loathed stage,
   And the more loathsome age,
   Where pride and impudence, in fac-
      tion knit,
   Usurp the chair of wit:
   Indicting and arraigning every day
   Something they call a play.
   Let their fastidious, vain
   Commission of the brain
   Run on and rage, sweat, censure, and
      condemn:
   They were not made for thee, less
      thou for them.

BEN JONSON, (c. 1572–1637) British dramatist, poet. "Ode To Himself," st. 1 (1632). Repr.
in *The Complete Poems,* ed. George Parfitt
(1975).

Written on the poor reception to Jonson's late
comedy, *The New Inn.*

5 We respond to a drama to that
   extent to which it corresponds to our
   dreamlife.

DAVID MAMET, (b. 1947) U.S. playwright.
Writing in Restaurants, "A National Dream-Life"
(1986).

6 *House Beautiful* is the play lousy.

DOROTHY PARKER, (1893–1967) U.S.
humorous writer. Quoted in *While Rome Burns,*
"Our Mrs. Parker," Alexander Woollcott (1934).
The New Yorker (1933).

Review of *House Beautiful* by Channing Pollock.

7 Exit, pursued by a bear.

WILLIAM SHAKESPEARE, (1564–1616)
British dramatist, poet. Stage direction, in *The
Winter's Tale,* act 3, sc. 3, l. 57 (1623).

This most famous of all stage directions, referring to the sudden exit of Antigonus, has led
some critics to ask whether the bear was real,
introduced as a theatrical coup. Most stage
directions in Shakespeare's plays were addi-
tions by later editors.

8 The play's the thing
   Wherein I'll catch the conscience of
      the King.

WILLIAM SHAKESPEARE, (1564–1616)
British dramatist, poet. Hamlet, in *Hamlet,* act
2, sc. 2, l. 605-6 (1604).

Referring to the performance of a play depict-
ing his father's murder, as described by the
ghost, and the guilty reaction of King
Claudius.

Theory

1 In order to shake a hypothesis, it is
   sometimes not necessary to do anything more than push it as far as it
   will go.

DENIS DIDEROT, (1713–1784) French
philosopher. *On the Interpretation of Nature,*
no. 50 (1753). Repr. in *Selected Writings,* ed.
Lester G. Crocker (1966).

2 It is a capital mistake to theorize
   before one has data.

SIR ARTHUR CONAN DOYLE,
(1859–1930) British author. Sherlock Holmes,
in *The Adventures of Sherlock Holmes,* "Scandal in Bohemia" (1892).

In *A Study in Scarlet,* ch. 3, Holmes reiterated,
"It is a capital mistake to theorize before you
have all the evidence. It biases the judgement."

Thieves and Thievery

1 Thou shalt not steal.

BIBLE: HEBREW, *Exodus,* 20:15. The
eighth commandment.

2 The thief. Once committed beyond
   a certain point he should not worry

himself too much about not being a thief any more. Thieving is God's message to him. Let him try and be a good thief.

SAMUEL BUTLER, (1835–1902) British author. *Samuel Butler's Notebooks*, p. 113 (1951).

3 My father named me Autolycus, who being, as I am, littered under Mercury, was likewise a snapper-up of unconsidered trifles.

WILLIAM SHAKESPEARE, (1564–1616) British dramatist, poet. Autolycus, in *The Winter's Tale*, act 4, sc. 3, l. 24-6 (1623).

In mythology, Autolycus was the son of Mercury (god of thieves); here, Autolycus was born when the planet Mercury was in the ascendant.

Things

1 For we brought nothing into this world, and it is certain we can carry nothing out.

BIBLE: NEW TESTAMENT, St. Paul, in *1 Timothy*, 6:7. The words also appear in the Book of Common Prayer, "Burial of the Dead."

Things, Trivial

1 My own idear is that these things are as piffle before the wind.

DAISY ASHFORD, (1881–1972) British writer. The Earl of Clincham, in *The Young Visiters*, ch. 5, "The Chrystal Palace," (published 1919).

Written when the author was aged nine.

Thinking and Thought

1 True thoughts are those alone which do not understand themselves.

THEODOR W. ADORNO, (1903–1969) German philosopher, sociologist, music critic. *Minima Moralia*, pt. 3, sct. 122, "Monograms" (1951), trans. by G.F.N. Jephcott (1978).

2 One thought fills immensity.

WILLIAM BLAKE, (1757–1827) British poet, painter, engraver. *The Marriage of Heaven and Hell*, plate 8, "Proverbs of Hell," (c. 1793), repr. in *Complete Writings*, ed. Geoffrey Keynes (1957).

3 I think, therefore I am.
[Cogito, ergo sum.]

RENÉ DESCARTES, (1596–1650) French philosopher, mathematician. *Le Discours de la Méthode*, pt. 4 (1637).

4 Thought would destroy their paradise.

THOMAS GRAY, (1716–1771) British poet. "Ode on a Distant Prospect of Eton College," l. 98 (written 1742, published 1747). Repr. In *Poetical Works*, ed. J. Rogers (1953).

5 Thought is the work of the intellect, reverie is its self-indulgence. To substitute day-dreaming for thought is to confuse a poison with a source of nourishment.

VICTOR HUGO, (1802–1885) French poet, dramatist, novelist. *Les Misérables*, pt. 4, bk. 2, ch. 1 (1862).

6 Two things fill the mind with ever new and increasing wonder and awe, the more often and the more seriously reflection concentrates upon them: the starry heaven above me and the moral law within me.

IMMANUEL KANT, (1724–1804) German philosopher. *Critique of Pure Reason*, conclusion (1788).

7 He had a wonderful talent for packing thought close, and rendering it portable.

THOMAS BABINGTON MACAULAY, (1800–1859) British historian, Whig politician.

"I ord Bacon," *Edinburgh Review* (July 1837). *Critical and Historical Essays* (1843).

Referring to Francis Bacon.

8 Man
   You beheld the saddest and dreari-
      est of all the flowers of the earth
   And as with other flowers you gave
      it a name
   You called it Thought.

JACQUES PRÉVERT, (1900–1977) French poet. "Flowers and Wreaths," *Paroles* (1946), trans. by Lawrence Ferlinghetti (1958).

Opening lines of poem.

9 Thought is an infection. In the case
   of certain thoughts, it becomes an
   epidemic.

WALLACE STEVENS, (1879–1955) U.S. poet. *Opus Posthumous*, "Adagia" (1959).

10 They use thought only to justify
   their injustices, and speech only to
   disguise their thoughts.

VOLTAIRE [FRANÇOIS MARIE AROUET], (1694–1778) French philoso-pher, author. Le Chapon, in *Dialogues*, "Le Chapon et la Poularde," (1765).

Describing the ways of men; the words echo a 1676 sermon by Robert South (1634-1716), an English theologian and preacher.

Time

1 By Time and Age full many things
   are taught.

AESCHYLUS, (525–456 B.C.) Greek drama-tist. Prometheus, in *Prometheus Bound*, l. 981, trans. by Gilbert Murray.

2 Time, the avenger! unto thee I lift
   My hands, and eyes, and heart, and
      crave of thee a gift.

GEORGE GORDON NOEL BYRON, 6TH BARON BYRON, (1788–1824) British poet. "Childe Harold's Pilgrimage," cto. 4, st. 130 (1812-1818).

3 I recommend to you to take care of
   the minutes; for hours will take
   care of themselves.

PHILIP DORMER STANHOPE, 4TH EARL CHESTERFIELD, (1694–1773) British statesman, man of letters. *The Letters of the Earl of Chesterfield to His Son*, vol. 1, no. 131, ed. Charles Strachey (1901). Letter, Nov. 6, 1747, first published (1774).

4 O, for an engine, to keep back all
      clocks,
   Or make the sun forget his motion!

BEN JONSON, (c. 1572–1637) British dramatist, poet. Lady Frampul, in *The New Inn*, act 4, sc. 3 (1629). Repr. in *The Complete Plays*, ed. G.A. Wilkes (1981-1982).

5 We must use time as a tool, not as
   a couch.

JOHN FITZGERALD KENNEDY, (1917–1963) U.S. Democratic politician, president. Quoted in *Observer* (London, Dec. 10, 1961).

6 Time has no divisions to mark
   its passage, there is never a thunderstorm or blare of trumpets to
   announce the beginning of a
   new month or year. Even when a
   new century begins it is only we
   mortals who ring bells and fire off
   pistols.

THOMAS MANN, (1875–1955) German author, critic. *The Magic Mountain*, ch. 5, "Whims of Mercurius" (1924), trans. by H.T. Lowe-Porter (1928).

7 The clock, not the steam-engine, is
   the key-machine of the modern
   industrial age.

LEWIS MUMFORD, (1895–1990) U.S. social philosopher. *Technics and Civilization*, ch. 1, sct. 2 (1934).

8   Time the devourer of all things.

OVID (PUBLIUS OVIDIUS NASO), (43
B.C.–A.D.17) Roman poet. *Metamorphoses,*
bk. 15, l. 234.

9   Even such is Time, which takes in
     trust
     Our youth, our joys, and all we
     have,
     And pays us but with age and dust,
     Who in the dark and silent grave
     When we have wandered all our
     ways
     Shuts up the story of our days.
     And from which earth, and grave,
     and dust,
     The Lord shall raise me up I trust.

SIR WALTER RALEIGH, (1552–1618)
British author, soldier, explorer. "Even Such is
Time," *The Poems of Sir Walter Raleigh,* ed.
Agnes M. Latham (1951).

Written the night before his death, this version
of the last stanza of one of Raleigh's earlier
poems was found in the flyleaf of his Bible in
the Abbey Gatehouse at Westminster.

10   And thus the whirligig of time
     brings in his revenges.

WILLIAM SHAKESPEARE, (1564–1616)
British dramatist, poet. Feste, in *Twelfth Night,*
act 5, sc. 1, l. 372-3 (1623).

11   And time, that takes survey of all
     the world,
     Must have a stop.

WILLIAM SHAKESPEARE, (1564–1616)
British dramatist, poet. Hotspur, in *Henry IV,*
pt. 1, act 5, sc. 4, l. 81-2 (1598).

Hotspur's dying words to Prince Harry, who
has mortally wounded him in battle.

12   O, call back yesterday, bid time
     return.

WILLIAM SHAKESPEARE, (1564–1616)
British dramatist, poet. Salisbury, in *Richard II,*
act 3, sc. 2, l. 65 (1597).

13   Time is the only critic without
     ambition.

JOHN STEINBECK, (1902–1968) U.S. author.
Writers at Work, "On Critics," Fourth Series, ed.
George Plimpton (1977).

14   Time turns the old days to derision,
     Our loves into corpses or wives;
     And marriage and death and division
     Make barren our lives.

A.C. (ALGERNON CHARLES) SWIN-
BURNE, (1837–1909) British poet, critic.
"Dolores" st. 20 (1866).

15   Time is flying, never to return.

VIRGIL [PUBLIUS VERGILIUS MARO],
(70–19 B.C.) Roman poet. *Georgics,* bk. 3, l.
284 (29 B.C.). The Latin, *fugit irreparabile tempus,* is usually quoted *tempus fugit.*

16   Time, like an ever-rolling stream,
     Bears all its sons away;
     They fly forgotten, as a dream
     Dies at the opening day.

ISAAC WATTS, (1674–1748) British hymn-
writer. "Psalm 90," st. 5, *The Psalms of David
Imitated* (1719).

17   For time is the longest distance
     between two places.

TENNESSEE WILLIAMS, (1914–1983) U.S.
dramatist. Tom, in *The Glass Menagerie,* sc. 7
(1944).

18   The years like great black oxen
     tread the world,
     And God the herdsman treads them
     on behind,
     And I am broken by their passing feet.

WILLIAM BUTLER YEATS, (1865–1939)
Irish poet, playwright. "The Countess Cathleen,"
act 4 (1891).

Last lines.

Toasts and Salutations

1   Here's looking at you, kid.

JULIUS J. EPSTEIN, Screenwriter. Rick
Blaine (Humphrey Bogart), in *Casablanca* (film),
spoken to Ilsa Lund (Ingrid Bergman) (1942).

2   Here's to the maiden of bashful
    fifteen;
    Here's to the widow of fifty;
    Here's to the flaunting extravagant
    queen;
    And here's to the housewife that's
    thrifty.
    Let the toast pass,—
    Drink to the lass,
    I'll warrant she'll prove an excuse for
    the glass.

    RICHARD BRINSLEY SHERIDAN,
    (1751–1816) Anglo-Irish dramatist. Chorus, in
    The School for Scandal, act 3, sc. 3, l. 40-6
    (1777).

3   May you live all the days of your life.

    JONATHAN SWIFT, (1667–1745) Anglo-
    Irish satirist. The Colonel, in *Polite Conversa-
    tion*, dialogue 2 (1738), repr. in *The Prose
    Works of Jonathan Swift*, vol. 4, ed. Herbert
    Davis (1957).

Tolerance

1   For ye suffer fools gladly, seeing ye
    yourselves are wise.

    BIBLE: NEW TESTAMENT St. Paul, in *2
    Corinthians*, 11:19.

Tools

1   Man is a tool-using animal.... With-
    out tools he is nothing, with tools he
    is all.

    THOMAS CARLYLE, (1795–1881) Scottish
    essayist, historian. *Sartor Resartus*, bk. 1, ch. 5
    (1833-1834).

    Benjamin Franklin is also cited as defining man
    as a *tool-making* animal, in Boswell's *Life of
    Johnson*, entry, April 7, 1778.

Totalitarianism

1   Since it is difficult to join them
    together, it is safer to be feared than

to be loved when one of the two
must be lacking.

NICCOLÒ MACHIAVELLI, (1469–1527)
Italian political philosopher, statesman. *The
Prince*, ch. 17 (written 1513-1514, published
1532), trans. by George Bull (1961).

Touch

1   Touch me not.

    BIBLE: NEW TESTAMENT, Jesus, in
    John, 20:17. Spoken to Mary Magdalene,
    after Jesus has risen from the dead and
    made himself known to her. The words are
    best known in the Latin form in which they
    appear in the Vulgate: *Noli me tangere.*

2   O why do you walk through the
    fields in gloves,
    Missing so much and so much?
    O fat white woman whom nobody
    loves,
    Why do you walk through the
    fields in gloves,
    When the grass is soft as the breast
    of doves
    And shivering sweet to the touch?

    FRANCES CORNFORD, (1886–1960)
    British poet. "To a Fat Lady Seen from a
    Train," *Poems* (1910).

Tourists and Tourism

1   The time to enjoy a European tour
    is about three weeks after you
    unpack.

    GEORGE ADE, (1866–1944) U.S. humorist,
    playwright. "The Hungry Man from the Bird
    Center," *Forty Modern Fables* (1901).

2   Worth seeing? Yes; but not worth
    going to see.

    SAMUEL JOHNSON, (1709–1784) British
    author, lexicographer. Quoted in James
    Boswell, *Life of Dr. Johnson*, entry, Oct. 12,
    1779 (1791).

    To Boswell's question, "Is not the Giant's
    Causeway worth seeing?"

3 Does this boat go to Europe, France?

ANITA LOOS, (1893–1981) U.S. novelist, screenwriter. Marilyn Monroe, in the film *Gentlemen Prefer Blondes* (1953) directed by Howard Hawkes, screenplay by Charles Lederer, based on the original novel by Anita Loos (1925).

Town and Country

1 God the first garden made, and the first city Cain.

ABRAHAM COWLEY, (1618–1667) British essayist, poet. "The Garden," *Essays in Verse and Prose* (1668).

2 The country in the town.
[Rus in urbe.]

MARCUS VALERIUS MARTIAL, (c. 40–104) Spanish-born Roman poet, epigrammatist. *Epigrams,* bk. 12, no. 57.

Trade

1 In matter of commerce the fault of the Dutch
Is offering too little and asking too much.
The French are with equal advantage content,
So we clap on Dutch bottoms just twenty per cent.

GEORGE CANNING, (1770–1827) British statesman, prime minister. "Canning's Rhyming 'Dispatch'" to Sir Charles Bagot, Sir Harry Poland (1905). Coded letter, Jan. 31, 1826, to the English ambassador at the Hague, Holland.

2 Protection is not a principle, but an expedient.

BENJAMIN DISRAELI, (1804–1881) British statesman, author. *Selected Speeches of the Late Right Honourable the Earl of Beaconsfield,* vol. 1, "Agricultural Distress," ed. T.E. Kebbes (1882). Speech to House of Commons, March 17, 1845.

Disraeli said exactly the opposite in a speech two years earlier, April 25, 1843.

3 The greatest meliorator of the world is selfish, huckstering Trade.

RALPH WALDO EMERSON, (1803–1882) U.S. essayist, poet, philosopher. *Society and Solitude,* "Works and Days" (1870).

4 No nation was ever ruined by trade.

BENJAMIN FRANKLIN, (1706–1790) U.S. statesman, writer. *Thoughts on Commercial Subjects.*

5 Merchants have no country. The mere spot they stand on does not constitute so strong an attachment as that from which they draw their gains.

THOMAS JEFFERSON, (1743–1826) U.S. president. *The Writings of Thomas Jefferson,* vol. 9, ed. Paul L. Ford (1898). Letter, March 17, 1814.

Trade Unions

1 People of the same trade seldom meet together, even for merriment and diversion, but the conversation ends in a conspiracy against the public, or in some contrivance to raise prices.

ADAM SMITH, (1723–1790) Scottish economist. *The Wealth of Nations,* vol. 1, bk. 1, ch. 10 (1776).

Tradition

1 People will not look forward to posterity, who never look backward to their ancestors.

EDMUND BURKE, (1729–1797) Irish philosopher, statesman. *Reflections on the Revolution in France* (1790), repr. in *Works,* vol. 3 (1865).

2 It cannot be inherited, and if you want it you must obtain it by great labour.

T.S. (THOMAS STEARNS) ELIOT,
(1888–1965) Anglo-American poet, critic. "Tradition and the Individual Talent," sct. 1, *Selected Prose of T.S. Eliot*, ed. Frank Kermode (1975). First published in *Egoist* (London, Sept. and Dec. 1919).

Tragedy

1   Ours is essentially a tragic age, so we refuse to take it tragically.

D.H. (DAVID HERBERT) LAWRENCE,
(1885–1930) British author. *Lady Chatterley's Lover*, ch. 1 (written 1928, published 1959).

Opening words.

2   It's not the tragedies that kill us, it's the messes.

DOROTHY PARKER, (1893–1967) U.S. humorous writer. Interview in *Writers at Work*, First Series, ed. Malcolm Cowley (1958).

Training

1   Reading maketh a full man; conference a ready man; and writing an exact man.

FRANCIS BACON, (1561–1626) British philosopher, essayist, statesman. *Essays*, "Of Studies" (1597-1625).

2   Training is everything. The peach was once a bitter almond; cauliflower is nothing but cabbage with a college education.

MARK TWAIN, (1835–1910) U.S. author. *Pudd'nhead Wilson*, ch. 5, "Pudd'nhead Wilson's Calendar" (1894).

Trains

1   This is the Night Mail crossing the Border,
Bringing the cheque and the postal order,
Letters for the rich, letters for the poor,
The shop at the corner, the girl next door.

W.H. (WYSTAN HUGH) AUDEN,
(1907–1973) Anglo-American poet. "Night Mail," sct. 1 (1936). Repr. in *Collected Shorter Poems 1927-1957* (1966).

Opening lines; poem written as commentary for a Post Office film.

2   The only way of catching a train I have ever discovered is to miss the train before.

GILBERT KEITH CHESTERTON,
(1874–1936) British author. *Tremendous Trifles*, "The Prehistoric Railway Station" (1909).

3   Pardon me boy,
Is that the Chattanooga Choo-choo?
Track twenty nine,
Boy you can give me a shine.

MACK GORDON, (1904–1959) U.S. songwriter. "Chattanooga Choo-choo" (song) (1941).

4   ... frseeeeeeeefronnnng train somewhere whistling the strength those engines have in them like big giants and the water rolling all over and out of them all sides like the end of Loves old sweeeetsonnnng the poor men that have to be out all the night from their wives and families in those roasting engines ...

JAMES JOYCE, (1882–1941) Irish author. Molly Bloom, in *Ulysses*, ch. 18 of 1984 edition (1922).

Molly Bloom's soliloquy.

Tranquility

1   There is no such thing as inner peace. There is only nervousness or death. Any attempt to prove other-

wise constitutes unacceptable behavior.

FRAN LEBOWITZ, (b. 1951) U.S. journalist. "Manners," *Metropolitan Life* (1978).

Transience

1 How soon passeth the glory of this world.

[O quam cito transit gloria mundi.]

THOMAS À KEMPIS, (c. 1380–1471) German monk, mystic. *The Imitation of Christ*, pt. 1, ch. 3 (written c. 1426, published 1486). The words *Sic transit gloria mundi* are used at the coronation of popes, and may be of earlier origin than this citation.

Translation

1 Such is our pride, our folly, or our fate,
That few but such as cannot write, translate.

JOHN, SIR DENHAM, (1615–1669) British poet. "To Sir Richard Fanshaw upon his translation of *Pastor Fido*," l. 1-2 (1648), repr. in *The Works of Sir John Denham*, ed. T.H. Banks (1928).

The poem continues: "Nor ought a genius less than his that writ Attempt translation." (l. 9-10).

2 God employs several translators; some pieces are translated by age, some by sickness, some by war, some by justice.

JOHN DONNE, (c. 1572–1631) British divine, metaphysical poet. *Devotions Upon Emergent Occasions*, meditation 17 (1624), repr. in *Complete Poetry and Selected Prose*, ed. John Hayward (1929).

3 Poetry is what is lost in translation.

ROBERT FROST, (1874–1963) U.S. poet. Quoted in *Robert Frost: a Backward Look*, ch. 1, Louis Untermeyer (1964).

Samuel Taylor Coleridge wrote, in *Biographia Literaria* (1817), ch. 22: "In poetry, in which

every line, every phrase, may pass the ordeal of deliberation and deliberate choice, it is possible, and barely possible, to attain that *ultimatum* which I have ventured to propose as the infallible test of a blameless style; namely: its *untranslatableness* in words of the same language without injury to the meaning."

4 It were as wise to cast a violet into a crucible that you might discover the formal principle of its colour and odour, as seek to transfuse from one language into another the creations of a poet. The plant must spring again from its seed, or it will bear no flower—and this is the burthen of the curse of Babel.

PERCY BYSSHE SHELLEY, (1792–1822) British poet. *A Defence of Poetry* (written 1821, published 1840).

5 Humour is the first of the gifts to perish in a foreign tongue.

VIRGINIA WOOLF, (1882–1941) British novelist. *The Common Reader*, "On Not Knowing Greek," First Series (1925).

Transport

1 What is this that roareth thus?
Can it be a Motor Bus?
Yes, the smell and hideous hum
Indicat Motorem Bum ...
Domine, defende nos Contra hos Motores Bos!

ALFRED GODLEY, (1856–1925) British scholar. "The Motor Bus," *Reliquae*, vol. 1 (1926). Letter, Jan. 10, 1914.

Traveling and Travelers

1 In America there are two classes of travel—first class and with children.

ROBERT BENCHLEY, (1889–1945) U.S. humorous writer. Quoted in *The Algonquin Wits*, ed. Robert E. Drennan (1968).

2 Never weather-beaten sail more
willing bent to shore.

THOMAS CAMPION, (1567–1620) British
poet, musician. "Never Weather-beaten Sail,"
Two Books of Airs, "Divine and Moral Songs"
(c. 1613). Repr. in *Works of Thomas Campion*, ed. W.R. Davis (1967).

3 When you set out for Ithaca
ask that your way be long.

CONSTANTINE CAVAFY, (1863–1933)
Greek poet. "Ithaca," (1911), repr. in *Col-
lected Poems*, eds. George Savidis, trans. by
Edmund Keeley and Philip Sherrard (1975).

4 The whole object of travel is not to
set foot on foreign land; it is at last
to set foot on one's own country as
a foreign land.

GILBERT KEITH CHESTERTON,
(1874–1936) British author. *Tremendous Trifles*, "The Riddle of the Ivy" (1909).

5 Journeys, like artists, are born and
not made. A thousand differing
circumstances contribute to them,
few of them willed or determined
by the will—whatever we may
think.

LAWRENCE DURRELL, (1914–1991)
British author. *Bitter Lemons*, "Towards an
Eastern Landfall" (1957).

Opening words.

6 The soul of a journey is liberty, perfect liberty, to think, feel, do just as
one pleases.

WILLIAM HAZLITT, (1778–1830) British
essayist. *Table Talk*, "On Going a Journey"
(1821-1822).

7 As the Spanish proverb says, "He
who would bring home the wealth
of the Indies, must carry the wealth
of the Indies with him." So it is in
travelling; a man must carry knowledge with him, if he would bring
home knowledge.

SAMUEL JOHNSON, (1709–1784) British
author, lexicographer. Quoted in James
Boswell, *Life of Dr. Johnson*, entry, April 17,
1778 (1791).

8 Much have I travelled in the realms
of gold,
And many goodly states and king-
doms seen.

JOHN KEATS, (1795–1821) British poet.
"On First Looking into Chapman's Homer,"
Opening lines, *Poems* (1817).

9 Without stirring abroad, One can
know the whole world; Without
looking out of the window One can
see the way of heaven. The further
one goes The less one knows.

LAO-TZU, (6th century B.C.) Chinese
philosopher. *Tao-te-ching*, bk. 2, ch. 47, trans.
by T.C. Lau (1963).

10 For my part, I travel not to go
anywhere, but to go. I travel for
travel's sake. The great affair is to
move; to feel the needs and hitches
of our life more nearly; to come
down off this feather-bed of civilisation, and find the globe granite
underfoot and strewn with cutting
flints.

ROBERT LOUIS STEVENSON,
(1850–1894) Scottish novelist, essayist, poet.
Travels with a Donkey, "Cheylard and Luc"
(1879).

11 To travel hopefully is a better thing
than to arrive.

ROBERT LOUIS STEVENSON,
(1850–1894) Scottish novelist, essayist, poet.
Virginibus Puerisque, "El Dorado" (1881).

12 I travelled among unknown men,
In lands beyond the sea;
Nor, England! did I know till then
What love I bore to thee.

WILLIAM WORDSWORTH, (1770–1850)
British poet. "I Travelled Among Unknown

Men" (written 1801, published in *Poems in Two Volumes*, 1807).

Trees

1   O leave this barren spot to me!
     Spare, woodman, spare the
       beechen tree.

     THOMAS CAMPBELL, (1777–1844) Scottish poet. "The Beech-Tree's Petition," st. 1 (1800). Repr. in *Complete Poetical Works*, ed. J.L. Robertson (1907).

2   I like trees because they seem more
     resigned to the way they have to
     live than other things do.

     WILLA CATHER, (1876–1947) U.S. author. Marie, in *O Pioneers!* pt. 2, ch. 8 (1913).

3   One could do worse than be a
     swinger of birches.

     ROBERT FROST, (1874–1963) U.S. poet. "Birches," *Mountain Interval* (1916).

4   Tree at my window, window tree,
     My sash is lowered when night
       comes on;
     But let there never be curtain
       drawn
     Between you and me.

     ROBERT FROST, (1874–1963) U.S. poet. "Tree at My Window," st. 1, *West-Running Brook* (1928).

5   My aspens dear, whose airy cages
       quelled,
     Quelled or quenched in leaves the
       leaping sun,
     All felled, felled, are all felled;
     Of a fresh and following folded
       rank
     Not spared, not one
     That dandled a sandalled
     Shadow that swam or sank
     On meadow and river and wind-
       wandering weed-winding bank.

     GERARD MANLEY HOPKINS, (1844–1889) British poet, Jesuit priest. "Binsey Poplars," st. 1 (written 1879), published in *Poems* (1918).

6   Ten or twelve, only ten or twelve
     Strokes of havoc únselne
     The sweet especial scene,
     Rural scene, a rural scene,
     Sweet especial rural scene.

     GERARD MANLEY HOPKINS, (1844–1889) British poet, Jesuit priest. "Binsey Poplars," felled 1879 (written 1879), published in *Poems* (1918).

7   Loveliest of trees, the cherry now
     Is hung with bloom along the
       bough,
     And stands about the woodland ride
     Wearing white for Eastertide.

     A.E. (ALFRED EDWARD) HOUSMAN, (1859–1936) British poet. "A Shropshire Lad," no. 2 (1896). Repr. in *The Collected Poems of A.E. Housman* (1939).

8   I think that I shall never see
     A poem lovely as a tree.

     JOYCE KILMER, (1886–1918) U.S. poet. "Trees," *Trees and Other Poems* (1914). *Poetry* (Chicago, Aug. 1913.)

     Ogden Nash wrote a riposte: "I think that I shall never see A billboard lovely as a tree. Perhaps unless the billboards fall, I'll never see a tree at all." (*Song of the Open Road* in *Happy Days*, 1933).

9   The green trees when I saw them
     first through one of the gates trans-
     ported and ravished me, their
     sweetness and unusual beauty made
     my heart to leap, and almost mad
     with ecstasy, they were such strange
     and wonderful things.

     THOMAS TRAHERNE, (1636–1674) British clergyman, poet, mystic. *Centuries of Meditations*, "Third Century," no. 3 (written c. 1672, first published 1908).

10   One impulse from a vernal wood
     May teach you more of man,

Of moral evil and of good,
Than all the sages can.

WILLIAM WORDSWORTH, (1770–1850)
British poet. "The Tables Turned," st. 6, *Lyrical Ballads* (1798).

Trickery

1   There is death in the pot.

BIBLE: HEBREW, *2 Kings,* 4:40. Referring to poisonous herbs in a meal prepared for the sons of the prophets, which Elisha made harmless.

2   There's a snake lurking in the grass.

VIRGIL [PUBLIUS VERGILIUS MARO], (70–19 B.C.) Roman poet. "Eclogues," no. 3, l. 93 (37 B.C.).

Trouble

1   Death and taxes and childbirth! There's never any convenient time for any of them!

MARGARET MITCHELL, (1900–1949) U.S. novelist. Scarlett O'Hara, in *Gone with the Wind,* vol. 2, pt. 4, ch. 38 (1936).

Trust

1   Candid and generous and just,
Boys care but little whom they
   trust,
An error soon corrected—
For who but learns in riper years,
That man, when smoothest he
   appears,
Is most to be suspected?

WILLIAM COWPER, (1731–1800) British poet. "Friendship," l. 19-24 (written 1781, published 1800). Repr. in *Poetical Works,* ed. H.S. Milford (1934).

2   Thrust ivrybody, but cut th' ca-ards.

FINLEY PETER DUNNE, (1867–1936) U.S. journalist, humorist. *Dooley's Philosophy,* "Casual Observations" (1900).

3   It is more shameful to distrust one's friends than to be deceived by them.

FRANÇOIS LA ROCHEFOUCAULD, DUC DE, (1613–1680) French writer, satirist. *Sentences et Maximes Morales,* no. 84 (1678).

Truth

1   Too much *Truth*
Is uncouth.

FRANKIN PIERCE ADAMS, (1881–1960) U.S. journalist, humorist. "From the New England Primer," *Nods and Becks* (1944).

2   Great is Truth, and mighty above all things.

APOCRYPHA, *1 Esdras,* 4:41.

Acclamation following the speech of the bodyguard of King Darius, who proclaimed the power of truth, "the strength, kingdom, power, and majesty of all ages."

3   The first wrote, Wine is the strongest. The second wrote, The king is strongest. The third wrote, Women are strongest: but above all things Truth beareth away the victory.

APOCRYPHA, *1 Esdras,* 3:10-12.

Referring to "three young men" of the bodyguard of Darius, king of the Persians, competing for his favor.

4   For though we love both the truth and our friends, piety requires us to honor the truth first.

ARISTOTLE, (384–322 B.C.) Greek philosopher. *Nicomachean Ethics,* bk. 1, ch. 6, trans. by Terence Irwin (1985).

Often quoted (from the Latin) "Plato is dear to me, but dearer still is truth." Aristotle, who spent 20 years at Plato's Academy as pupil and teacher, referred to his philosophical colleagues at the Academy as "friends."

5 The true story is vicious
and multiple and untrue
after all. Why do you
need it? Don't ever
ask for the true story.

MARGARET ATWOOD, (b. 1939) Canadian novelist, poet, critic. "True Stories," *True Stories* (1981).

6 It is a pleasure to stand upon the shore, and to see ships tossed upon the sea: a pleasure to stand in the window of a castle, and to see a battle and the adventures thereof below: but no pleasure is comparable to standing upon the vantage ground of truth ... and to see the errors, and wanderings, and mists, and tempests, in the vale below.

FRANCIS BACON, (1561–1626) British philosopher, essayist, statesman. *Essays*, "Of Truth" (1597-1625).

7 What is truth? said jesting Pilate; and would not stay for an answer.

FRANCIS BACON, (1561–1626) British philosopher, essayist, statesman. *Essays*, "Of Truth" (1597-1625).

Opening words of essay, alluding to Bible, St. John 18:38.

8 A truth that's told with bad intent
Beats all the lies you can invent.

WILLIAM BLAKE, (1757–1827) British poet, painter, engraver. "Auguries of Innocence," l. 53-4, *Poems from the Pickering Manuscript* (c. 1803), repr. in *Complete Writings*, ed. Geoffrey Keynes (1957).

9 A man may be in as just possession of truth as of a city, and yet be forced to surrender.

THOMAS BROWNE, (1605–1682) British physician, author. *Religio Medici*, pt. 1, sct. 6 (1643).

10 Truth that peeps
Over the glasses' edge when dinner's done.

ROBERT BROWNING, (1812–1889) British poet. "Bishop Blougram's Apology," l. 17-8, *Men and Women*, vol. 1 (1855).

11 It was as true as taxes is. And nothing's truer than them.

CHARLES DICKENS, (1812–1870) British novelist. Mr. Barkis, in *David Copperfield*, ch. 21 (1849-1850).

This remark echoes Benjamin Franklin's famous gloomy observation on the inevitability of taxes (Franklin on certainty).

12 I can be expected to look for truth but not to find it.

DENIS DIDEROT, (1713–1784) French philosopher. *Philosophic Thoughts*, no. 29 (1746). Repr. in *Philosophical Works*, ed. Paul Verniére (1964).

13 When you have eliminated the impossible, whatever remains, *however improbable*, must be the truth.

ARTHUR CONAN, SIR DOYLE, (1859–1930) British author. Sherlock Holmes, in *The Sign of Four*, ch. 6 (1889).

14 Perhaps the mission of those who love mankind is to make people laugh at the truth, *to make truth laugh*, because the only truth lies in learning to free ourselves from insane passion for the truth.

UMBERTO ECO, (b. 1932) Italian semiologist, novelist. Brother William, in *The Name of the Rose*, "Seventh Day: Night (2)" (1980, trans. 1983).

15 The truth has never been of any real value to any human being—it is a symbol for mathematicians and philosophers to pursue. In human relations kindness and lies are worth a thousand truths.

GRAHAM GREENE, (1904–1991) British novelist. Scobie, in *Heart of the Matter*, bk. 1, pt. 1, ch. 2, sct. 4 (1948).

16 Such truth, as opposeth no man's profit, nor pleasure, is to all men welcome.

THOMAS HOBBES, (1588–1679) British philosopher. *Leviathan*, "A Review and Conclusion" (1651).

17 It is the customary fate of new truths, to begin as heresies, and to end as superstitions.

THOMAS HENRY HUXLEY, (1825–1895) British biologist. "The Coming of Age of The Origin of Species," *Science and Culture* (1881).

18 The true way leads along a tightrope not stretched aloft but just above the ground. It seems designed more to trip one than to be walked along.

FRANZ KAFKA, (1883–1924) Czech novelist, short-story writer. *The Collected Aphorisms*, vol. 1, no. 1, *Shorter Works*, ed. and trans. by Malcolm Pasley (1973). (Written Oct. 1917-Feb. 1918.)

19 I maintain that Truth is a pathless land, and you cannot approach it by any path whatsoever, by any religion, by any sect.

JIDDU KRISHNAMURTI, (1895–1986) Indian mystic. Quoted in *Krishnamurti*, ch. 2, Lilly Heber (1931). Speech, Aug. 3, 1929, Holland.

20 There are no new truths, but only truths that have not been recognized by those who have perceived them without noticing. A truth is something that everybody can be shown to know and to have known, as people say, all along.

MARY MCCARTHY, (1912–1989) U.S. author, critic. "The Vita Activa," first published in *The New Yorker* (Oct. 18, 1958). *On the Contrary* (1961).

21 Truth ... never comes into the world but like a Bastard, to the ignominy of him that brought her forth.

JOHN MILTON, (1608–1674) British poet. *The Doctrine and Discipline of Divorce*, introduction (1643).

22 Let us begin by committing ourselves to the truth—to see it like it is, and tell it like it is—to find the truth, to speak the truth, and to live the truth.

RICHARD NIXON, (1913–1992) U.S. Republican politician, president. *Acceptance speech for the Republican presidential nomination*. Speech, Aug. 9, 1968, Miami.

23 Truth is the most valuable thing we have. Let us economize it.

MARK TWAIN, (1835–1910) U.S. author. *Following the Equator*, ch. 7, "Pudd'nhead Wilson's New Calendar" (1897).

Twentieth Century

1 What a long strange trip it's been.

ROBERT HUNTER, U.S. rock lyricist. "Truckin'," on the Grateful Dead album *American Beauty* (1971). This best-known line from the lyrics of the Grateful Dead ("WALSTIB" to dedicated fans) has been used as title for a large number of books and articles evoking the 60s.

2 The horror of the Twentieth Century was the size of each new event, and the paucity of its reverberation.

NORMAN MAILER, (b. 1923) U.S. author. *A Fire on the Moon*, pt. 1, ch. 1 (1970).

Twentieth Century: the 1920s

1 Though the Jazz Age continued it became less and less an affair of youth. The sequel was like a children's party taken over by the elders.

F. Scott Fitzgerald, (1896–1940) U.S. author. "Echoes of the Jazz Age," article in *Scribner's* (New York, Nov. 1931). *The Crack-Up*, ed. Edmund Wilson (1945).

Twentieth Century: the 1930s

1   I pledge you, I pledge myself, to a new deal for the American people.

Franklin Delano Roosevelt, (1882–1945) U.S. Democratic politician, president. *Public Papers and Addresses of Franklin D. Roosevelt*, vol. 1 (1938). Acceptance speech, July 2, 1932, Chicago.

At the height of the economic crisis, Roosevelt's "New Deal" became the slogan of his successful campaign for the presidency.

Twentieth Century: the 1950s

1   These are the tranquilized *Fifties*, and I am forty. Ought I to regret my seedtime?

Robert Lowell, (1917–1977) U.S. poet. "Memories of West Street and Lepke," *Life Studies* (1959).

2   We live in an era of revolution— the revolution of rising expectations.

Adlai Stevenson, (1900–1965) U.S. Democratic politician. *Look* (New York, Sept. 22, 1953), *The Papers of Adlai E. Stevenson*, vol. 5 (1974).

Twentieth Century: the 1960s

1   The line it is drawn
The curse it is cast
The slow one now
Will later be fast
As the present now
Will later be past
The order is
Rapidly fadin.'
And the first one now
Will later be last
For the times they are a-changin.'

Bob Dylan [Robert Allen Zimmerman], (b. 1941) U.S. singer, songwriter." The Times They Are A-Changin'" (song), on the album *The Times They Are A-Changin'* (1964).

2   The Great Society is a place where every child can find knowledge to enrich his mind and to enlarge his talents.... It is a place where the city of man serves not only the needs of the body and the demands of commerce but the desire for beauty and the hunger for community.... It is a place where men are more concerned with the quality of their goals than the quantity of their goods.

Lyndon Baines Johnson, (1908–1973) U.S. Democratic politician, president. *Public Papers of the Presidents of the United States, Lyndon B. Johnson: 1963-64.* Speech, May 22, 1964, Ann Arbor, Michigan.

According to Hugh Sidey, in *A Very Personal Presidency* (1968), the slogan, "Great Society," had been current for several years, but was adopted for Johnson by Richard N. Goodwin, Secretary General of the International Peace Corps Secretariat and occasional speechwriter. It became a keynote of Johnson's presidency, stressed by him in his acceptance speech at the Democratic Party National Convention, August 1964.

3   We stand today on the edge of a new frontier—the frontier of the 1960s, a frontier of unknown opportunities and perils, a frontier of unfulfilled hopes and threats.... The new frontier of which I speak is not a set of promises—it is a set of challenges.

JOHN FITZGERALD KENNEDY, (1917–1963) U.S. Democratic politician, president. *Acceptance speech*, July 15, 1960, at the Democratic Convention, Los Angeles.

Theodore C. Sorensen claimed credit for drafting this speech, in his biography *Kennedy*, ch. 6 (1965).

4 My advice to people today is as follows: If you take the game of life seriously, if you take your nervous system seriously, if you take your sense organs seriously, if you take the energy process seriously, you must turn on, tune in, and drop out.

TIMOTHY LEARY, (b. 1920) U.S. psychologist. *The Politics of Ecstasy*, ch. 21 (1968). Lecture, 1966.

Twentieth Century: the 1970s

1 We are now in the Me Decade— seeing the upward roll of ... the third great religious wave in American history.

TOM WOLFE, (b. 1931) U.S. author, journalist. "The Me Decade and the Third Great Awakening," *Mauve Gloves and Madmen* (1976).

Tycoons

1 The rights and interests of the laboring man will be protected and cared for, not by the labor agitators, but by the Christian men to whom God in His infinite wisdom has given control of the property interests of the country.

GEORGE BAER, (1842–1914) U.S. railroad magnate. Open letter to the Press, Oct. 1902, during the Pennsylvania miners' strike.

Tyranny

1 In every tyrant's heart there springs in the end
This poison, that he cannot trust a friend.

AESCHYLUS, (525–456 BC) Greek dramatist. Prometheus, in *Prometheus Bound, The Complete Plays of Aeschylus*, trans. by Gilbert Murray (1951).

2 Kings will be tyrants from policy, when subjects are rebels from principle.

EDMUND BURKE, (1729–1797) Irish philosopher, statesman. *Reflections on the Revolution in France* (1790), repr. in *Works*, vol. 3 (1865).

3 I have sworn upon the altar of God eternal hostility against every form of tyranny over the mind of man.

THOMAS JEFFERSON, (1743–1826) U.S. president. *The Writings of Thomas Jefferson*, vol. 10, ed. Andrew A. Lipscomb (1904). letter, Sept. 23, 1800.

4 No government power can be abused long. Mankind will not bear it.... There is a remedy in human nature against tyranny, that will keep us safe under every form of government.

SAMUEL JOHNSON, (1709–1784) British author, lexicographer. Quoted in James Boswell, *Life of Dr. Johnson*, entry, March 31, 1772 (1791).

5 Truth forever on the scaffold, Wrong forever on the throne.

JAMES RUSSELL LOWELL, (1819–1891) U.S. poet, editor. *The Present Crisis*, st. 8 (1844). Repr. in *Poetical Works of James Russell Lowell* (1978).

6 Like Cato, give his little Senate laws,

And sit attentive to his own
applause.

ALEXANDER POPE, (1688–1744) British
satirical poet. "Epistle to Dr. Arbuthnot," l.
209-10 (1735).

A portrait of essayist Joseph Addison.

7   I met a traveller from an antique
     land
     Who said: Two vast and trunkless
     legs of stone
     Stand in the desert. Near them, on
     the sand,
     Half sunk, a shattered visage lies,
     whose frown,
     And wrinkled lip, and sneer of cold
     command,
     Tell that its sculptor well those pas-
     sions read
     Which yet survive, stamped on
     these lifeless things,
     The hand that mocked them, and
     the heart that fed:
     And on the pedestal these words
     appear:
     "My name is Ozymandias, king of
     kings:
     Look on my works, ye Mighty, and
     despair!"

PERCY BYSSHE SHELLEY, (1792–1822)
British poet. "Ozymandias," l. 1-11 (1819).
Written in December 1817, probably in
competition with Horace Smith (whose
sonnet is extant, but does not name
Ozymandias).

Ugliness

1   Against the beautiful and the clever
     and the successful, one can wage a
     pitiless war, but not against the
     unattractive: then the millstone
     weighs on the breast.

GRAHAM GREENE, (1904–1991) British
novelist. *The Heart of the Matter,* bk. 1, pt. 1,
ch. 2, sct. 2 (1948).

Uncertainty

1   The grand Perhaps! We look on
     helplessly,
     There the old misgivings, crooked
     questions are.

ROBERT BROWNING, (1812–1889) British
poet. "Bishop Blougram's Apology," l. 189-90,
Men and Women, vol. 1 (1855).

Understanding

1   You and I ought not to die before
     we have explained ourselves to
     each other.

JOHN ADAMS, (1735–1826) U.S. statesman,
president. *The Adams-Jefferson Letters,* vol. 2,
ed. L.J. Cappon (1959). Letter, July 15, 1813,
to Thomas Jefferson.

2   Come hither, and I shall light a can-
     dle of understanding in thine heart,
     which shall not be put out.

APOCRYPHA, *2 Esdras,* 14:25.

3   The world only goes round by mis-
     understanding.

CHARLES BAUDELAIRE, (1821–1867)
French poet. "My Heart Laid Bare," *Intimate
Journals,* sct. 99 (1887), trans. by Christopher
Isherwood (1930), rev. Don Bachardy (1989).

4   Perhaps I am doomed to retrace my
     steps under the illusion that I am
     exploring, doomed to try and learn
     what I should simply recognize,
     learning a mere fraction of what I
     have forgotten.

ANDRÉ BRETON, (1896–1966) French surrealist. *Nadja* (1928).

5   Sir, I have found you an argument;
     but I am not obliged to find you an
     understanding.

SAMUEL JOHNSON, (1709–1784) British
author, lexicographer. Quoted in James

Boswell, *I ife of Dr. Johnson*, entry, June 19, 1784 (1791).

6 Shallow understanding from people of good will is more frustrating than absolute misunderstanding from people of ill will.

MARTIN LUTHER KING, JR., (1929–1968) U.S. clergyman, civil rights leader. "Letter from Birmingham Jail, *"Why We Can't Wait* (1963). Open letter to clergymen, Apr. 16, 1963.

7 Society needs to condemn a little more and understand a little less.

JOHN MAJOR, (b. 1943) British Conservative politician, prime minister. Interview in *Mail on Sunday* (London, Feb. 21, 1993).

Unemployment

1 Gizza job, go on, gizzit!

ALAN BLEASDALE, (b. 1946) British dramatist. Yosser Hughes, in *The Boys from the Blackstuff* (TV series) (1983).

Catchphrase, usually quoted "gissa job!"

2 When we're unemployed, we're called lazy; when the whites are unemployed it's called a depression.

JESSE JACKSON, (b. 1941) U.S. clergyman, civil rights leader. Interview in *The Americans*, "When Whites Are Unemployed, It's Called a Depression," David Frost (1970).

Unhappiness

1 Nothing is funnier than unhappiness, I grant you that.... Yes, yes, it's the most comical thing in the world.

SAMUEL BECKETT, (1906–1989) Irish dramatist, novelist. Nell, in *Endgame* (1957, trans. 1958).

2 Let no one till his death

Be called unhappy. Measure not the work
Until the day's out and the labour done.

ELIZABETH BARRETT BROWNING, (1806–1861) British poet. "Aurora Leigh," bk. 5, l. 76-8 (1857).

See Solon on happiness.

3 Man's unhappiness, as I construe, comes of his greatness; it is because there is an Infinite in him, which with all his cunning he cannot quite bury under the Finite.

THOMAS CARLYLE, (1795–1881) Scottish essayist, historian. Teufelsdröckh, in *Sartor Resartus*, bk. 2, ch. 9 (1833-1834).

4 Unhappiness is best defined as the difference between our talents and our expectations.

EDWARD DE BONO, (b. 1933) British psychologist. Quoted in *Observer* (London, June 12, 1977).

5 He felt the loyalty we feel to unhappiness—the sense that that is where we really belong.

GRAHAM GREENE, (1904–1991) British novelist. *The Heart of the Matter*, bk. 2, pt. 2, ch. 1, sct. 1 (1948).

Referring to Harris.

6 Men who are unhappy, like men who sleep badly, are always proud of the fact.

BERTRAND RUSSELL [LORD RUSSELL, 3RD EARL], (1872–1970) British philosopher, mathematician. *The Conquest of Happiness*, ch. 1 (1930).

Uniforms

1 O, Nelly Gray! O, Nelly Gray!
Is this your love so warm?
The love that loves a scarlet coat
Should be more uniform!

THOMAS HOOD, (1799–1845) British poet. "Faithless Nelly Gray" (1826). Repr. in *Complete Poetical Works*, ed. Walter Jerrold (1906).

Unions

1 The most conservative man in the world is the British Trade Unionist when you want to change him.

ERNEST BEVIN, (1881–1951) British politician. *Report of Proceedings of the Trades Union Congress*, p. 298 (1927). Speech, Sept. 8, 1927, to Trades Union Congress, Edinburgh.

United States

1 God bless the U.S.A, so large, So friendly, and so rich.

W.H. (WYSTAN HUGH) AUDEN, (1907–1973) Anglo-U.S. poet. "On the Circuit," *Collected Poems* (1976).

2 America, thou half-brother of the world;
With something good and bad of every land.

PHILIP BAILEY, (1816–1902) British poet. "Festus," st. 10 (1839, rev. 1889).

3 From the mountains to the prairies, To the oceans white with foam, God bless America, My home sweet home!

IRVING BERLIN, (1888–1989) U.S. songwriter. "God Bless America" (song) (written 1917, published 1939).

This unofficial national anthem, originally written for the Broadway show, *Yip Yip Yaphank* (1918), is said to have provoked Woody Guthrie to compose "This Land Is Your Land" (see Guthrie on the land).

4 Young man, there is America, which at this day serves for little more than to amuse you with stories of savage men and uncouth manners.

EDMUND BURKE, (1729–1797) Irish philosopher, statesman. "Second Speech on Conciliation with America: The Thirteen Resolutions," *Works*, vol. 2 (1899). Speech, March 22, 1775, House of Commons, London.

5 America is the only nation in history which miraculously has gone directly from barbarism to degeneration without the usual interval of civilization.

GEORGES CLEMENCEAU, (1841–1929) French statesman. Attributed in *Saturday Review of Literature* (New York, Dec. 1, 1945).

6 "next to of course god america i
love you land of the pilgrims" and
so forth oh
say can you see by the dawn's early
my
country 'tis of centuries come and
go
and are no more what of it we
should worry
in every language even deafand-
dumb
thy sons acclaim your glorious name
by gorry
by jing by gee by gosh by gum

E.E. (EDWARD ESTLIN) CUMMINGS, (1894–1962) U.S. poet. "Next to of course god america i," *is 5* (1926).

7 Yes, America is gigantic, but a gigantic mistake.

SIGMUND FREUD, (1856–1939) Austrian psychiatrist. Quoted in *Memories of a Psychoanalyst*, ch. 9, Ernest Jones (1959).

"America is the most grandiose experiment the world has seen," Freud said on another occasion, "but, I am afraid, it is not going to be a success." (Ronald W. Clark, *Freud: the Man and his Cause*, pt. 3, ch. 12, 1980).

8 America I'm putting my queer shoulder to the wheel.

ALLEN GINSBERG, (b. 1926) U.S. poet. "America," *Howl and Other Poems* (1956).

Last line.

9   We have the men—the skill—the wealth—and above all, the will.... We must be the great arsenal of democracy.

FRANKLIN DELANO ROOSEVELT, (1882–1945) U.S. Democratic politician, president. "Fireside Chat," *The Penguin Book of Twentieth Century Speeches,* ed. Brian MacArthur (1992). Speech, Dec. 29, 1940, Washington, D.C..

10   I like to be in America!
     OK by me in America!
     Ev'rything free in America
     For a small fee in America!

STEPHEN SONDHEIM, (b. 1930) U.S. songwriter. "America" (song), *West Side Story* (stage show, 1957; film, 1961).

11   America is a vast conspiracy to make you happy.

JOHN UPDIKE, (b. 1932) U.S. author, critic. *Problems,* "How to Love America and Leave it at the Same Time" (1980).

12   Everywhere, spread all over in characters of living light, blazing on all its ample folds, as they float over the sea and over the land, and in every wind under the whole heavens, that other sentiment, dear to every true American heart,—Liberty *and* Union, now and for ever; one and inseparable!

DANIEL WEBSTER, (1782–1852) U.S. lawyer, statesman. "Second speech on Foote's Resolution," vol. 6, *The Writings and Speeches of Daniel Webster* (1903). Speech, Jan. 26, 1830, U.S. Senate.

13   The youth of America is their oldest tradition. It has been going on now for three hundred years.

OSCAR WILDE, (1854–1900) Anglo-Irish playwright, author. Lord Illingworth, in *A Woman of No Importance,* act 1 (1893).

14   Sometimes people call me an idealist. Well, that is the way I know I am an American.... America is the only idealistic nation in the world.

WOODROW WILSON, (1856–1924) U.S. Democratic politician, president. *The Messages and Papers of Woodrow Wilson,* vol. 2, ed. Albert Shaw (1924).

Speech, Sept. 8, 1919, Sioux Falls, North Dakota.

United States, People of

1   Our society distributes itself into Barbarians, Philistines and Populace; and America is just ourselves with the Barbarians quite left out, and the Populace nearly.

MATTHEW ARNOLD, (1822–1888) British poet, critic. *Culture and Anarchy,* preface (1859).

Arnold held that literature was of paramount importance for the education of the "Philistines."

2   A people who are still, as it were, but in the gristle, and not yet hardened into the bone of manhood.

EDMUND BURKE, (1729–1797) Irish philosopher, statesman. "Second Speech on Conciliation with America: The Thirteen Resolutions," *Works,* vol. 2 (1899). Speech, March 22, 1775, House of Commons, London.

3   There is nothing the matter with Americans except their ideals. The real American is all right; it is the ideal American who is all wrong.

GILBERT KEITH CHESTERTON, (1874–1936) British author. *The New York Times* (Feb. 1, 1931).

4   I'm a Yankee Doodle Dandy,
    A Yankee Doodle do or die;
    A real live nephew of my Uncle Sam's,
    Born on the fourth of July.

GEORGE M. COHAN, (1878–1942) U.S. songwriter, performer. "Yankee Doodle Dandy" (song), *Little Johnny Jones* (show, 1904).

Cohan claimed his own birthday was July 4, though skeptics have suggested his birthday was actually July 3. Oliver Stone's movie *Born on the Fourth of July* (1989) depicted the life of Ron Kovic, himself born on July 4th.

5   In America the geography is sublime, but the men are not; the inventions are excellent, but the inventors one is sometimes ashamed of.

RALPH WALDO EMERSON, (1803–1882) U.S. essayist, poet, philosopher. *The Conduct of Life,* "Considerations by the Way" (1860).

6   There are no second acts in American lives.

F. SCOTT FITZGERALD, (1896–1940) U.S. author. *The Last Tycoon,* "Hollywood, ETC.," ed. Edmund Wilson (1941).

7   I am not a Virginian, but an American.

PATRICK HENRY, (1736–1799) U.S. statesman. Quoted in *Diary and Biography of John Adams,* vol. 2, ed. L.H. Butterfield (1961). Speech, Sept./Oct. 1774, First Continental Congress, Philadelphia.

8   I am willing to love all mankind, *except an American.*

SAMUEL JOHNSON, (1709–1784) British author, lexicographer. Quoted in James Boswell, *Life of Dr. Johnson,* entry, April 15, 1778 (1791).

"Sir, they are a race of convicts," Johnson stated in 1769, "and ought to be thankful for anything we allow them short of hanging." (Quoted in Boswell, *Life of Dr. Johnson,* March 21, 1775.)

9   Sitting at the table doesn't make you a diner, unless you eat some of what's on that plate. Being here in America doesn't make you an American. Being born here in America doesn't make you an American.

MALCOLM X [MALCOLM LITTLE], (1925–1965) U.S. African-American leader.

Malcolm X Speaks, ch. 3 (1965). "The Ballot or the Bullet" speech, April 3, 1964, Cleveland, Ohio.

10   The whole life of an American is passed like a game of chance, a revolutionary crisis, or a battle.

ALEXIS DE TOCQUEVILLE, (1805–1859) French social philosopher. *Democracy in America,* vol. 1, ch. 18 (1835).

11   That impersonal insensitive friendliness which takes the place of ceremony in that land of waifs and strays.

EVELYN WAUGH, (1903–1966) British novelist. *The Loved One* (1948).

Of Aimée Thanatogenos, an American.

12   I was born an American; I will live an American; I shall die an American.

DANIEL WEBSTER, (1782–1852) U.S. lawyer, statesman. "Speech on the Compromise Bill," vol. 10, *The Writings and Speeches of Daniel Webster* (1903). Speech, July 17, 1850, U.S. Senate.

13   The pure products of America go crazy—mountain folk from Kentucky or the ribbed north end of Jersey with its isolate lakes and valleys, its deaf-mutes, thieves.

WILLIAM CARLOS WILLIAMS, (1883–1963) U.S. poet. "To Elsie," *Spring and All* (1923).

Unity

1   Then join hand in hand, brave
    Americans all!
   By uniting we stand, by dividing we
    fall!

JOHN DICKINSON, (1732–1808) U.S. statesman, essayist. "The Liberty Song" (1768) quoted in *The Writings of John Dickinson,* vol. 1 (1895). *Boston Gazette* (July 18, 1768).

United we stand, divided we fall! was a motto of the American revolutionaries. The slogan also appeared in "Flag of Our Union," by journalist and poet George Pope Morris: "'United we stand, divided we fall!'—It made and preserves a nation!" (*Poemss* (1853.)

2   From many, one.
     [E pluribus unus.]

VIRGIL [PUBLIUS VERGILIUS MARO], (70–19 B.C.) Roman poet. "Moretum," l. 104, trans. by Kate Hughes (1995).

The words "E pluribus unum" were inscribed on the face of the Great Seal of the United States of America, June 20, 1782.

Universe, the

1   I don't pretend to understand the Universe—it's a great deal bigger than I am.

THOMAS CARLYLE, (1795–1881) Scottish essayist, historian. Quoted by poet and diarist William Allingham in *A Diary*, ch. 10, Dec. 28, 1868, eds. H. Allingham and D. Radford (1907).

2   They cannot scare me with their
         empty spaces
     Between stars—on stars where no
         human race is.
     I have it in me so much nearer home
     To scare myself with my own desert
         places.

ROBERT FROST, (1874–1963) U.S. poet. "Desert Places," *A Further Range* (1936).

3   I accept the universe.

MARGARET FULLER, (1810–1850) U.S. writer and lecturer. Quoted in *The Varieties Of Religious Experience*, Lecture 2, "Circumscription of the Topic," William James (1902).

Said to have been a favorite utterance by Fuller, to which Thomas Carlyle, who met Fuller on her European voyage in 1846, is reported to have responded, "Gad! She'd better!"

4   My own suspicion is that the Universe is not only queerer than we suppose, but queerer than we can suppose.

J.B.S. (JOHN BURDON SANDERSON) HALDANE, (1892–1964) British scientist. *Possible Worlds*, "Possible Worlds" (1927).

Universities and Colleges

1   Home of lost causes, and forsaken beliefs, and unpopular names, and impossible loyalties!

MATTHEW ARNOLD, (1822–1888) British poet, critic. *Essays in Criticism*, preface, First Series (1865).

Referring to Oxford University; see Arnold's comment on "cities."

2   I was a modest, good-humoured boy. It is Oxford that has made me insufferable.

MAX BEERBOHM, (1872–1956) British essayist, caricaturist. *More*, "Going Back to School," (1899).

Referring to Oxford University.

3   'Tis well enough for a servant to be bred at an University. But the education is a little too pedantic for a gentleman.

WILLIAM CONGREVE, (1670–1729) British dramatist. Tattle, in *Love for Love*, act 5, sc. 1 (1695).

4   A University should be a place of light, of liberty, and of learning.

BENJAMIN DISRAELI, (1804–1881) British statesman, author. *Selected Speeches of the Late Right Honourable the Earl of Beaconsfield*, vol. 2, "Irish University Education Bill," ed. T.E. Kebbes (1882). Speech to House of Commons, March 11, 1873.

5   Ye distant spires, ye antique towers,
     That crown the wat'ry glade.

THOMAS GRAY, (1716–1771) British poet. "Ode on a Distant Prospect of Eton

College," st. 1 (written 1742, published 1747). Repr. in *Poetical Works* ed. J. Rogers (1953).

Opening lines.

6   Towery city and branchy between
     towers;
    Cuckoo-echoing, bell-swarm.:d,
     lark-charm'd, rook-racked, river-
     rounded.

GERARD MANLEY HOPKINS,
(1844–1889) British poet, Jesuit priest. "Duns Scotus's Oxford," st. 1 (written 1879), published in *Poems* (1918).

7   I am told that today rather more than 60 per cent of the men who go to university go on a Government grant. This is a new class that has entered upon the scene. It is the white-collar proletariat.... They do not go to university to acquire culture but to get a job, and when they have got one, scamp it. They have no manners and are woefully unable to deal with any social predicament. Their idea of a celebration is to go to a public house and drink six beers. They are mean, malicious and envious.... They are scum.

W. SOMERSET MAUGHAM,
(1874–1966) British author. *Sunday Times* (London, Dec. 25, 1955).

Referring to the generation of "Angry Young Men" as portrayed in Kingsley Amis's 1954 novel *Lucky Jim*. These people, Amis continued, "will in due course leave the university. Some will doubtless sink back, perhaps with relief, into the modest social class from which they emerged; some will take to drink, some to crime and go to prison.... A few will go into Parliament, become Cabinet Ministers and rule the country. I look upon myself as fortunate that I shall not live to see it."

Unknown, the

1   Whither goest thou?

BIBLE: NEW TESTAMENT, Peter, in *John*, 13:36. The words, which are repeated in *John* 16:5, are best known in the Latin form in which they appear in the Vulgate: *Quo vadis?* Jesus replies, "Whither I go, thou canst not follow me now; but thou shalt follow me afterwards."

2   There are more things in heaven
     and earth, Horatio,
    Than are dreamt of in our philoso-
     phy.

WILLIAM SHAKESPEARE, (1564–1616) British dramatist, poet. Hamlet, in *Hamlet*, act 1, sc. 5, l. 168-9 (1604).

In response to Horatio's exclamation "O day and night, but this is wondrous strange!"— which followed Hamlet's initial encounter with the ghost.

Upbringing

1   Tew bring up a child in the wa he
    should go—travel that wa yourself.

JOSH BILLINGS [HENRY WHEELER SHAW], (1818–1885) U.S. humorist. *Josh Billings, His Sayings*, ch. 78 (1865).

Recalling Proverbs 22:6: see Hebrew Bible on Education.

2   Every luxury was lavished on you—
    atheism, breast-feeding, circumci-
    sion.

JOE ORTON, (1933–1967) British playwright. Hal, in *Loot*, act 1 (1967).

Upper Class, the

1   The stately Homes of England,
    How beautiful they stand,
    To prove the upper classes
    Have still the upper hand.

NOËL COWARD, (1899–1973) British playwright, actor, composer. "The Stately Homes of England" (song), refrain, *Operette* (musical, 1938).

See Crisp on homosexuality.

Utopias

1 Imagine that it is you yourself who are erecting the edifice of human destiny with the aim of making men happy in the end, of giving them peace and contentment at last, but that to do that it is absolutely necessary, and indeed quite inevitable, to torture to death only one tiny creature, the little girl who beat her breast with her little fist, and to found the edifice on her unavenged tears—would you consent to be the architect on those conditions?

FEODOR DOSTOYEVSKY, (1821–1881) Russian novelist. Ivan Karamazov, in *The Brothers Karamazov*, bk. 5, ch. 4 (published 1879-1880), trans. by David Magarshak (1958).

2 The great universal family of men is a utopia worthy of the most mediocre logic.

ISIDORE DUCASSE, COMTE DE LAUTRÉAMONT, (1846–1870) French author, poet. "Maldoror," bk. 1, ch. 9 (1870, trans. 1978).

Vacations

1 Oh, why can't we break away from all this, just you and I, and lodge with my fleas in the hills?... I mean flee to my lodge in the hills.

ARTHUR SHEEKMAN, Screenwriter. *Monkey Business* (film) (1931).

Vanity

1 To say that a man is vain means merely that he is pleased with the effect he produces on other people. A conceited man is satisfied

with the effect he produces on himself.

MAX BEERBOHM, (1872–1956) British essayist, caricaturist. *And Even Now*, "Quia Imperfectum" (1920).

2 Vanity of vanities, saith the Preacher, vanity of vanities; all is vanity.

BIBLE: HEBREW, *Ecclesiastes*, 1:2 *passim.*

3 He is a self-made man who worships his creator.

JOHN BRIGHT, (1811–1889) British radical politician. *Attributed.*

Referring to Benjamin Disraeli.

4 What time he can spare from the adornment of his person he devotes to the neglect of his duties.

WILLIAM HEPWORTH THOMPSON, (1810–1886) British academic, Master of Trinity College, Cambridge. Quoted in *With Dearest Love to All*, ch. 7, M.R. Bobbit (1960).

Referring to a colleague at Cambridge.

5 Cure yourself of the affliction of caring how you appear to others. Concern yourself only with how you appear before God, concern yourself only with the idea that God may have of you.

MIGUEL DE UNAMUNO, (1864–1936) Spanish philosophical writer. *The Life of Don Quixote and Sancho*, "The Sepulcher of Don Quixote" (1905).

Vegetarianism

1 Most vegetarians I ever see looked enough like their food to be classed as cannibals.

FINLEY PETER DUNNE, (1867–1936) U.S. journalist, humorist. *Dooley's Philosophy*, "Casual Observations" (1900).

Venice

1 Venice is like eating an entire box of chocolate liqueurs at one go.

TRUMAN CAPOTE, (1924–1984) U.S. author. Quoted in *Observer* (London, Nov. 26, 1961).

Vices

1 Vice ... is a creature of such heejous mien ... that th' more ye see it th' betther ye like it.

FINLEY PETER DUNNE, (1867–1936) U.S. journalist, humorist. *Dooley's Opinions*, "The Crusade Against Vice" (1901).

2 It's true Heaven forbids some pleasures, but a compromise can usually be found.

MOLIÈRE [JEAN BAPTISTE POQUELIN], (1622–1673) French dramatist. Tartuffe, in *Le Tartuffe*, act 4, sc. 5 (written 1664, performed 1669).

Victims

1 Don't agonize. Organize.

FLORYNCE R. KENNEDY, (b. 1916) U.S. lawyer, civil rights activist. "The Verbal Karate of Florynce R. Kennedy, Esq." Quoted by Gloria Steinem, in *Ms.* (New York, March 1973).

2 I am a man more sinned against than sinning.

WILLIAM SHAKESPEARE, (1564–1616) British dramatist, poet. Lear, in *King Lear*, act 3, sc. 2, l. 59-60 (1623).

Victoria, Queen

1 No it is better not. She would only ask me to take a message to Albert.

BENJAMIN DISRAELI, (1804–1881) British statesman, author. Quoted in *Disraeli*, ch. 32, Robert Blake (1966).

Remark on hearing that Victoria would like to see him during his last illness. W.H. Auden quotes Disraeli's remark slightly differently: "What's the use? She would only want me to take a message to dear Albert." (*A Certain World*, "Words, Last," 1970.)

Victory

1 The problems of victory are more agreeable than the problems of defeat, but they are no less difficult.

WINSTON CHURCHILL, (1874–1965) British statesman, writer. *Hansard*, col. 28. Speech, Nov. 11, 1942, House of Commons.

2 Even victors are by victories undone.

JOHN DRYDEN, (1631–1700) British poet, dramatist, critic. "Epistle to John Driden of Chesterton," l. 164 (1700).

Vietnam

1 Nothing else in the world smells like that.... I love the smell of napalm in the morning.... It smells like victory.

FRANCIS FORD COPPOLA, (b. 1939) U.S. filmmaker. Colonel Kilgore (Robert Duvall), in *Apocalypse Now* (film) (1979).

2 You have a row of dominoes set up; you knock over the first one, and what will happen to the last one is that it will go over very quickly.

DWIGHT D. EISENHOWER, (1890–1969) U.S. general, Republican politician, president. *Public Papers of the Presidents of the United States* (1960). Address, April 7, 1954, to press conference.

Referring to the situation in south-east Asia after the defeat of the French by the Viet-Minh.

3 We are not about to send American boys 9 or 10,000 miles away from home to do what Asian boys ought to be doing for themselves.

LYNDON BAINES JOHNSON, (1908–1973) U.S. Democratic politician, president. *Public Papers of the Presidents of the United States, Lyndon B. Johnson: 1963-64.* speech, Oct. 21, 1964, Akron University, Ohio.

4   Television brought the brutality of war into the comfort of the living room. Vietnam was lost in the living rooms of America—not on the battlefields of Vietnam.

MARSHALL MCLUHAN, (1911–1980) Canadian communications theorist. Quoted in *Montreal Gazette* (May 16, 1975).

5   Let us understand: North Vietnam cannot defeat or humiliate the United States. Only Americans can do that.

RICHARD NIXON, (1913–1992) U.S. Republican politician, president. Quoted in *Nixon: The Triumph of a Politician*, ch. 14, Stephen Ambrose (1989). Television broadcast, Nov. 3, 1969.

In his *Memoirs*, Nixon commented: "Very few speeches actually influence the course of history. The November 3 speech was one of them." On the subject of Vietnam, he later wrote: "No event in American history is more misunderstood than the Vietnam War. It was misreported then, and it is misremembered now."("No More Vietnams" in *The New York Times* (March 28, 1985).)

Villains and Villainy

1   Oh, the shark has pretty teeth, dear
And he shows them pearly white
Just a jackknife has Macheath, dear
And he keeps it out of sight.

BERTOLT BRECHT, (1898–1956) German dramatist and poet. "The Ballad of Mack the Knife," in *The Threepenny Opera*, prologue (1928, trans. 1933).

Vindication

1   Though I sit down now, the time will come when you will hear me.

BENJAMIN DISRAELI, (1804–1881) British statesman, author. *Selected Speeches of the Late Right Honourable the Earl of Beaconsfield*, vol. 2, "Irish Election Petitions," ed. T.E. Kebbes (1882). Maiden speech in House of Commons, Dec. 7, 1837.

Closing words. T.E. Kebbes, editor of Disraeli's published speeches, commented on Disraeli's performance: "That in some way or another the speaker, before he had done, succeeded in making himself ridiculous is a fact too well attested to be doubted."

Violence

1   The only thing that's been a worse flop than the organization of nonviolence has been the organization of violence.

JOAN BAEZ, (b. 1941) U.S. singer. "What Would You Do If?" *Daybreak* (1968).

Baez set up an Institute for Nonviolence in California in 1965.

2   In violence we forget who we are.

MARY MCCARTHY, (1912–1989) U.S. author, critic. "Characters in Fiction," *On the Contrary*, pt. 3 (1961).

Virgil

1   Honor to the greatest poet.

DANTE ALIGHIERI, (1265–1321) Italian poet. "Inferno," cto. 4, l. 80, *The Divine Comedy* (1321).

Said of Virgil.

Virginity

1   If love the virgin's heart invade,
How, like a moth, the simple maid
Still plays about the flame!

JOHN GAY, (1685–1732) British dramatist, poet. Mrs. Peachum, in *The Beggar's Opera*, act 1, sc. 4, air 4 (1728), ed. F.W. Bateson (1934).

2   Gather ye rose-buds while ye may,
Old Time is still a-flying:
And this same flower that smiles
   to-day,
To-morrow will be dying.

> ROBERT HERRICK, (1591–1674) British poet, clergyman. "To the Virgins, to Make Much of Time," st. 1, *Hesperides* (1648). Repr. in *The Poems of Robert Herrick*, ed. L.C. Martin (1956).

3   I always thought of losing my virginity as a career move.

> MADONNA, (b. 1959) U.S. singer, actor. Quoted in *Madonna Unauthorized*, epilogue, Christopher Andersen (1991).

Virtue

1   Strait is the gate, and narrow is the way, which leadeth unto life, and few there be that find it.

> BIBLE: NEW TESTAMENT, Jesus, in *Matthew*, 7:14.From the Sermon on the Mount.

2   Every one suspects himself of at least one of the cardinal virtues.

> F. SCOTT FITZGERALD, (1896–1940) U.S. author. The narrator (Nick Carraway), in *The Great Gatsby*, ch. 3 (1925).

3   Assume a virtue if you have it not.

> WILLIAM SHAKESPEARE, (1564–1616) British dramatist, poet. Hamlet, in *Hamlet*, act 3, sc. 4, l. 151 (1604).
>
> Speaking to his mother Gertrude.

4   Men's evil manners live in brass, their virtues
We write in water.

> WILLIAM SHAKESPEARE, (1564–1616) British dramatist, poet. Griffith, in *King Henry VIII*, act 4, sc. 2, l. 45-6 (1623).

5   Be virtuous and you will be eccentric.

> MARK TWAIN, (1835–1910) U.S. author. "Mental Photographs," motto (1869), repr. in *Complete Humourous Sketches and Tales*, ed. Charles Neider (1961).

Virtue and Vice

1   There are in every man, always, two simultaneous allegiances, one to God, the other to Satan. Invocation of God, or Spirituality, is a desire to climb higher; that of Satan, or animality, is delight in descent.

> CHARLES BAUDELAIRE, (1821–1867) French poet. "My Heart Laid Bare," *Intimate Journals*, sct. 19 (1887), trans. by Christopher Isherwood (1930), rev. Don Bachardy (1989).

2   If he does really think that there is no distinction between virtue and vice, why, Sir, when he leaves our houses let us count our spoons.

> SAMUEL JOHNSON, (1709–1784) British author, lexicographer. Quoted in James Boswell, *Life of Dr. Johnson*, entry, July 14, 1763 (1791).

Vision

1   The things which are seen are temporal; but the things which are not seen are eternal.

> BIBLE: NEW TESTAMENT, St. Paul, in *2 Corinthians*, 4:18.

2   Where there is no vision, the people perish.

> BIBLE: HEBREW, *Proverbs*, 29:18.President John F. Kennedy quoted this passage on the eve of his assassination in Dallas, Texas; recorded in Theodore C. Sorenson's biography, *Kennedy*, Epilogue (1965).

3   A man that looks on glass,
On it may stay his eye;
Or if he pleaseth, through it pass,
And then the heaven espy.

GEORGE HERBERT, (1593–1633) British poet, clergyman. "The Elixir, "The Temple (1633). Repr. in *The Works of George Herbert*, ed. Helen Gardner (1961).

4   It is only with the heart that one can see rightly; what is essential is invisible to the eye.

ANTOINE DE SAINT-EXUPÉRY, (1900–1944) French aviator, author. *The Little Prince*, ch. 21 (1943).

Visionaries

1   How beautiful upon the mountains are the feet of him that bringeth good tidings, that publisheth peace.

BIBLE: HEBREW, *Isaiah*, 52:7.

2   "What," it will be questioned, "When the sun rises, do you not see a round disc of fire somewhat like a guinea?" O no, no, I see an innumerable company of the heavenly host crying
"Holy, Holy, Holy is the Lord God Almighty."

WILLIAM BLAKE, (1757–1827) British poet, painter, engraver. "A Vision of the Last Judgement" (1810), repr. in *Complete Writings*, ed. Geoffrey Keynes (1957).

3   It doesn't matter with me now. Because I've been to the mountaintop. And I don't mind. Like anybody, I would like to live a long life. Longevity has its place. But I'm not concerned about that now. I just want to do God's will. And He's allowed me to go up to the mountain. And I've looked over, and I've seen the promised land.... Mine eyes have seen the glory of the coming of the Lord.

MARTIN LUTHER KING, JR., (1929–1968) U.S. clergyman, civil rights leader. "I See the Promised Land," *A Testa-*

ment of Hope: Essential Writings, ed. James Melvin Washington (1986). Speech, Apr. 3, 1968, Memphis, Tennessee.

The speech was made the day before Martin Luther King's assassination; the epitaph on his tomb, in South View Cemetery, Atlanta, Georgia, reads: ree at last, Free at last,Thank God Almighty, I'm free at last (a reference to the spiritual with which King often closed his speeches).

Vitality

1   Who would have thought my shrivelled heart
Could have recovered greenness?

GEORGE HERBERT, (1593–1633) British poet, clergyman. "The Flower," st. 2, *The Temple* (1633). Repr. in *The Works of George Herbert*, ed. Helen Gardner (1961).

Vocation

1   But as I raved and grew more fierce and wild
At every word,
Methought I heard one calling, "Child;"
And I replied, "My Lord."

GEORGE HERBERT, (1593–1633) British poet, clergyman. "The Collar," *The Temple* (1633). Repr. in *The Works of George Herbert*, ed. Helen Gardner (1961).

Voting

1   I never vote for anyone. I always vote against.

W.C. FIELDS, (1879–1946) U.S. screen actor. Quoted in *Halliwell's Filmgoer's Companion* (1984).

2   The freeman, casting with unpurchased hand
The vote that shakes the turrets of the land.

OLIVER WENDELL HOLMES, SR.,
(1809–1894) U.S. writer, physician. "Poetry:
a Metrical Essay," l. 83-4 (1836). Repr. in *The
Poetical Works of Oliver Wendell Holmes*,
ed. Eleanor M. Tilton (1895, rev. 1975).

3   The ballot is stronger than the
     bullet.

ABRAHAM LINCOLN, (1809–1865) U.S.
president. *The Writings of Abraham Lincoln*,
ed. Arthur Brooks Lapsley (1905). Speech,
May 29, 1856, Bloomington, Illinois.

This speech to the first Republican State Convention of Illinois was reconstructed 40 years
after; more reliable sources exist for a variant—but later—form of this famous line: "To
give victory to the right, not bloody bullets,
but peaceful ballots only, are necessary."
(Speech, May 18, 1858, published in *Collected Works of Abraham Lincoln*, vol. 2, ed.
Roy P. Basler, 1953.)

Waiting

1   Estragon: Charming spot. Inspiring
     prospects. Let's go.
     Vladimir: We can't.
     Estragon: Why not?
     Vladimir: We're waiting for
       Godot.

SAMUEL BECKETT, (1906–1989) Irish
dramatist, novelist. *Waiting for Godot*, act 1
(1952, trans. 1954).

2   What are we waiting for, gathered
     in the market-place?
     The barbarians are to arrive today.

CONSTANTINE CAVAFY, (1863–1933)
Greek poet. "Waiting for the Barbarians,"
(1904). Repr. in *Collected Poems*, ed. George
Savidis, trans. by Edmund Keeley and Philip
Sherrard (1975).

Wales and the Welsh

1   Lovely the woods, waters,
       meadows, combes, vales,
     All the air things wear that build
       this world of Wales.

GERARD MANLEY HOPKINS,
(1844–1889) British poet, Jesuit priest. "In the
Valley of the Elwy," st. 2, *Poems* (1918).

2   An old and haughty nation proud in
     arms.

JOHN MILTON, (1608–1674) British poet.
Attendant Spirit, in "Comus," l. 33 (1637).
Repr. in *Milton's Poetical Works*, ed. Douglas
Bush (1966).

Referring to the tract of Wales and the Welsh
borders ruled by the Earl of Bridgewater, in
whose castle at Ludlow, Milton's masque was
first performed in 1634.

3   The land of my fathers. My fathers
     can have it.

DYLAN THOMAS, (1914–1953) Welsh poet.
Adam (London, Dec. 1953).

"Land of my Fathers" is the Welsh national
anthem.

4   We can trace almost all the disasters
     of English history to the influence of
     Wales.

EVELYN WAUGH, (1903–1966) British novelist. *Decline and Fall*, pt. 1, ch. 8 (1928).

Referring to the influence of a colleague, Dr.
Fagan.

War

1   Saul hath slain his thousands, and
     David his ten thousands.

BIBLE: NEW TESTAMENT, *1 Samuel*,
18:7. Said by the women of Israel after
David killed Goliath; and overheard by Saul,
who then determined to kill David.

2   War is like love, it always finds a way.

BERTOLT BRECHT, (1898–1956) German
dramatist, poet. The Chaplain, in *Mother
Courage and Her Children*, sc. 6 (1939), trans.
by Eric Bentley (1941).

3   The Angel of Death has been abroad
     throughout the land, you may
     almost hear the beating of his wings.

JOHN BRIGHT, (1811–1889) British politician. *Hansard,* col. 1761. Speech, Feb. 23, 1855, to House of Commons.

Appealing for an armistice in the Crimean War.

4   "Let there be light!" said God, and there was light!
"Let there be blood!" says man, and there's a sea!

GEORGE GORDON NOEL BYRON, 6TH BARON BYRON, (1788–1824) British poet. *Don Juan,* cto. 7, st. 41.

In cto. 9, st. 4 of the poem, Byron wrote, "War's a brain-spattering, windpipe-slitting art."

5   How horrible, fantastic, incredible it is that we should be digging trenches and trying on gas masks here because of a quarrel in a faraway country between people of whom we know nothing.

NEVILLE CHAMBERLAIN, (1869–1940) British politician, prime minister. Quoted in *Times* (London, Sept. 28, 1938). Radio broadcast, Sept. 27, 1938.

On Germany's annexation of the Sudetenland, Czechoslovakia.

6   Laws are silent in times of war.

MARCUS TULLIUS CICERO, (106–43 B.C.) Roman orator, philosopher. *Pro Milone,* ch. 4, sct. 11 (44-43 B.C.).

7   The sinews of war, a limitless supply of money.

MARCUS TULLIUS CICERO, (106–43 B.C.) Roman orator, philosopher. *Philippics,* oration 5, sct. 5 (44-43 B.C.).

8   War is regarded as nothing but the continuation of state policy with other means.

KARL VON CLAUSEWITZ, (1780–1831) Prussian soldier, strategist. *On War,* author's note (1833), trans. by O.J. Matthijs Jolles (1943).

The notion is expressed in variant forms in different parts of the book.

9   It is easier to make war than to make peace.

GEORGES CLEMENCEAU, (1841–1929) French statesman. *Discours de Paix* (1938). Speech, July 20, 1919, Verdun, France.

10   My home policy: I wage war; my foreign policy: I wage war. All the time I wage war.

GEORGES CLEMENCEAU, (1841–1929) French statesman. *Discours de Guerre* (1968). Speech, July 20, 1919, Chamber of Deputies.

11   All this stuff you heard about America not wanting to fight, wanting to stay out of the war, is a lot of horse dung. Americans, traditionally, love to fight. All real Americans love the sting of battle.... Americans play to win all the time. I wouldn't give a hoot in hell for a man who lost and laughed. That's why Americans have never lost—and will never lose—a war, because the very thought of losing is hateful to Americans.

FRANCIS FORD COPPOLA, (b. 1939) U.S. filmmaker. General George S. Patton Jr. (George C. Scott), in *Patton* (film).

Opening speech in which General Patton addresses the audience as though they were his troops. (1970).

12   War is the trade of Kings.

JOHN DRYDEN, (1631–1700) British poet, dramatist, critic. Arthur, in *King Arthur,* act 2, sc. 2 (1691).

13   Either war is obsolete or men are.

R. BUCKMINSTER FULLER, (1895–1983) U.S. architect, engineer. *The Bew Yorker* (Jan. 8, 1966).

14   I was always embarrassed by the words sacred, glorious and sacrifice and the expression in vain. We had heard them, sometimes standing in the rain almost out of earshot, so that only the shouted words came through, and had read them, on proclamations that were slapped up by billposters over other proclamations, now for a long time, and I had seen nothing sacred, and the things that were glorious had no glory and the sacrifices were like the stockyards at Chicago if nothing was done with the meat except to bury it.

ERNEST HEMINGWAY, (1899–1961) U.S. author. Frederic Henry, in *A Farewell to Arms,* ch. 27 (1929).

15 Force, and fraud, are in war the two cardinal virtues.

THOMAS HOBBES, (1588–1679) British philosopher. *Leviathan,* pt. 1, ch. 13 (1651).

16 Here dead lie we because we did
   not choose
To live and shame the land from
   which we sprung.
Life, to be sure, is nothing much to
   lose;
But young men think it is, and we
   were young.

A.E. (ALFRED EDWARD) HOUSMAN, (1859–1936) British poet, classical scholar. *More Poems,* no. 36 (1936).

17 If any question why we died,
Tell them, because our fathers lied.

RUDYARD KIPLING, (1865–1936) British author, poet. "Common Form," *The Years Between* (1919).

18 The most persistent sound which reverberates through man's history is the beating of war drums.

ARTHUR KOESTLER, (1905–1983) Hungarian-born British author. *Janus: A Summing Up,* "Prologue: The New Calendar," sct. 1 (1978).

19 It is well that war is so terrible: we would grow too fond of it!

ROBERT E. LEE, (1807–1870) U.S. Confederate general. *Attributed, Dictionary of War Quotations,* ed. Justin Wintle (1989). remark, Dec. 13, 1862, at the Battle of Fredericksburg.

Comment to James Longstreet, on seeing a Federal charge repulsed.

20 For the man who should loose me
   is dead,
Fighting with the Duke in Flanders,
In a pattern called a war.
Christ! What are patterns for?

AMY LOWELL, (1874–1925) U.S. poet. "Patterns," *Men, Women and Ghosts* (1916).

21 War is thus divine in itself, since it is a law of the world. War is divine through its consequences of a supernatural nature which are as much general as particular.... War is divine in the mysterious glory that surrounds it and in the no less inexplicable attraction that draws us to it.... War is divine by the manner in which it breaks out.

JOSEPH DE MAISTRE, (1753–1821) French diplomat, philosopher. the senator, in *Les Soirés de Saint-Pétersbourg,* "Seventh Dialogue," (1821) rep. in *The Works of Joseph de Maistre,* ed. Jack Lively (1965).

22 Accurst be he that first invented war.

CHRISTOPHER MARLOWE, (1564–1593) British dramatist, poet. Mycetes, King of Persia, in *Tamburlaine the Great,* pt. 1, act 2, sc. 4 (1590).

23 War alone brings up to their highest tension all human energies and imposes the stamp of nobility upon the peoples who have the courage to make it.

BENITO MUSSOLINI, (1883–1945) Italian dictator. "The Political and Social Doctrine of Fascism," publ. in *Enciclopedia Italiana* (1932).

24 The quickest way of ending a war is to lose it.

GEORGE ORWELL, (1903–1950) British author. *Shooting an Elephant,* "Second Thoughts on James Burnham" (1950). First published in *Polemic* (May 1946).

25 Wars are made to make debt.

EZRA POUND, (1885–1972) U.S. poet, critic. Interview in *Writers at Work,* Second Series, ed. George Plimpton (1963).

26 War is a contagion.

FRANKLIN DELANO ROOSEVELT, (1882–1945) U.S. Democratic politician, president. Quoted in *The Wit and Wisdom of Franklin D. Roosevelt,* "War," ed. Maxwell Meyersohn (1950). Speech, Oct. 5, 1937, Chicago.

27 Sometime they'll give a war and nobody will come.

CARL SANDBURG, (1878–1967) U.S. poet. "The People," *Yes* (1936).

The words were popularized during the antiwar protests of the 1960s, and were echoed in the 1970 movie *Suppose They Gave a War and Nobody Came?* starring Brian Keith and Tony Curtis. Allen Ginsberg also recalls the line in his 1972 poem, "Graffiti": "What if someone gave a war & Nobody came? Life would ring the bells of Ecstasy and Forever be Itself again."

28 And Caesar's spirit, ranging for revenge,
With Ate by his side come hot from hell,
Shall in these confines with a monarch's voice
Cry "havoc!" and let slip the dogs of war,
That this foul deed shall smell above the earth
With carrion men, groaning for burial.

WILLIAM SHAKESPEARE, (1564–1616) British dramatist, poet. Antony, in *Julius Caesar,* act 3, sc. 1, l. 273-8 (1623).

Prophesying the turmoil following on Caesar's assassination. Ate was, according to Hesiod, the daughter of Strife, cast out of Olympus by Zeus.

29 We go to gain a little patch of ground
That hath in it no profit but the name.

WILLIAM SHAKESPEARE, (1564–1616) British dramatist, poet. Captain, in *Hamlet,* act 4, sc. 4, l. 18 (1604).

The passage in which the Captain's speech occurs is absent from the 1623 Folio edition.

30 War is the statesman's game, the priest's delight,
The lawyer's jest, the hired assassin's trade.

PERCY BYSSHE SHELLEY, (1792–1822) British poet. "Queen Mab," pt. 4, l. 168-9 (1812).

31 War ...
What is it good for?
Absolutely nothing.

EDWIN STARR, U.S. soul singer. "War" (song), written by Norman Whitfield and Barrett Strong (1970).

32 I see wars, horrible wars, and the Tiber foaming with much blood.

VIRGIL [PUBLIUS VERGILIUS MARO], (70–19 B.C.) Roman poet. the Sibyl of Cumae, in *Aeneid,* bk. 6, l. 86 (29 B.C.).

Spoken to Aeneas, in his quest to find his father.

33 What a country calls its vital economic interests are not the things which enable its citizens to live, but the things which enable it to make war. Petrol is more likely than wheat to be a cause of international conflict.

SIMONE WEIL, (1909–1943) French philosopher, mystic. "The Power of Words," first published in *Nouveaux Cahiers* (April 1 and 15, 1937). *Selected Essays,* ed. Richard Rees (1962).

34 As long as war is regarded as wicked, it will always have its fasci-

nation. When it is looked upon as vulgar, it will cease to be popular.

OSCAR WILDE, (1854–1900) Anglo-Irish playwright, author. Gilbert, in *The Critic as Artist*, pt. 2, *Intentions* (1891), repr. in *Complete Works of Oscar Wilde*, ed. J.B. Foreman (1966).

35 Once lead this people into war and they will forget there ever was such a thing as tolerance.

WOODROW WILSON, (1856–1924) U.S. Democrat, president. Quoted in *Mr. Wilson's War*, pt. 3, ch. 12, John Dos Passos (1917).See Wilson's comment on "World War I."

36 I think it better that in times like these
A poet's mouth be silent, for in truth
We have no gift to set a statesman right.

WILLIAM BUTLER YEATS, (1865–1939) Irish poet, playwright. "On Being Asked for a War Poem," l. 1-3, *The Wild Swans at Coole* (1919).

War and Peace

1 We make war that we may live in peace.

ARISTOTLE, (384–322 B.C.) Greek philosopher. *Nicomachean Ethics*, bk. 10, ch. 7, sct. 1177b.

2 There never was a good war or a bad peace.

BENJAMIN FRANKLIN, (1706–1790) U.S. statesman, writer. *Complete Works*, vol. 8, ed. John Bigelow (1887-1888). Letter, July 27, 1783, to the botanist Sir Joseph Banks.

Franklin used the same words in a letter of Sept. 11, 1783, to New England revolutionary Josiah Quincy.

3 My argument is that War makes rattling good history; but Peace is poor reading.

THOMAS HARDY, (1840–1928) British novelist, poet. "Spirit Sinister," in *The Dynasts*, pt. 1, act 2, sc. 5 (1904).

War Crimes

1 I do not know a method of drawing up an indictment against a whole people.

EDMUND BURKE, (1729–1797) Irish philosopher, statesman. "Second Speech on Conciliation with America: The Thirteen Resolutions," *Works*, vol. 2 (1899). Speech, March 22, 1775, House of Commons, London.

Warhol, Andy

1 If you want to know all about Andy Warhol, just look at the surface: of my paintings and films and me, and there I am. There's nothing behind it.

ANDY WARHOL, (c. 1928–1987) U.S. pop artist. "Warhol in his own Words," article first published in Los Angeles *Free Press* (March 17, 1967). *Andy Warhol: A Retrospective* (1986).

Washington, D.C.

1 Washington is a city of Southern efficiency and Northern charm.

JOHN FITZGERALD KENNEDY, (1917–1963) U.S. Democratic politician, president. Quoted in *Portrait of a President*, William Manchester (1962).

Remark, Nov. 1961.

Water

1 The thirsty earth soaks up the rain, And drinks, and gapes for drink again.

The plants suck in the earth, and are
With constant drinking fresh and fair.

ABRAHAM COWLEY, (1618–1667) British essayist, poet. "Drinking, "*Anacreon* (1656).

Watergate Affair

1   Our long national nightmare is over. Our Constitution works; our great Republic is a government of laws and not of men. Here the people rule.

GERALD FORD, (b. 1913) U.S. Republican politician, president. *Public Papers of the Presidents* (1974). Speech, Aug. 9, 1974.

On succeeding Richard Nixon as president.

2   There can be no whitewash at the White House.

RICHARD NIXON, (1913–1992) U.S. Republican politician, president. *The New York Times* (May 1, 1973). Television address on Watergate, April 30, 1973.

In July 1972 agents of Nixon's reelection committee were arrested in Democratic Party headquarters after an attempt to tap telephones there.

Weakness

1   The weak have one weapon: the errors of those who think they are strong.

GEORGES BIDAULT, (1899–1983) French resistance leader, statesman. Quoted in "Sayings of the Week," *Observer* (London, July 15, 1962).

2   I see and approve better things, but follow worse.

OVID (PUBLIUS OVIDIUS NASO), (43 B.C.–A.D.17) Roman poet. *Metamorphoses,* bk. 7, l. 20.

See Bible: New Testament on fallibility.

3   Union of the weakest develops strength
Not wisdom. Can all men, together, avenge
One of the leaves that have fallen in autumn?
But the wise man avenges by building his city in snow.

WALLACE STEVENS, (1879–1955) U.S. poet. "Like Decorations in a Nigger Cemetery," sct. 50, *Ideas of Order* (1936).

Wealth and the Wealthy

1   Lay not up for yourselves treasures upon earth, where moth and rust doth corrupt, and where thieves break through and steal: but lay up for yourselves treasures in heaven, where neither moth nor rust doth corrupt, and where thieves do not break through nor steal: for where your treasure is, there will your heart be also.

BIBLE: NEW TESTAMENT, Jesus, in *Matthew*, 6:19-21.

2   Wealth, howsoever got, in England makes
Lords of mechanics, gentlemen of rakes;
Antiquity and birth are needless here;
'Tis impudence and money makes a peer.

DANIEL DEFOE, (1660–1731) British author, poet, journalist. "The True-Born Englishman," pt. 1, l. 360-363 (1701). Repr. in *Works*, ed. Keltie (1869).

3   Wealth is not without its advantages and the case to the contrary, although it has often been made, has never proved widely persuasive.

JOHN KENNETH GALBRAITH, (b. 1908) U.S. economist. *The Affluent Society*, ch. 1, sct. 1 (1958).

4   Ill fares the land, to hast'ning ills a
     prey,
     Where wealth accumulates, and
     men decay.

     OLIVER GOLDSMITH, (1728–1774)
     Anglo-Irish author, poet, playwright. "The
     Deserted Village," l. 51-2 (1770).

5   Let none admire
     That riches grow in hell; that soil
     may best
     Deserve the precious bane.

     JOHN MILTON, (1608–1674) British poet.
     Paradise Lost, bk. 1, l. 690-3 (1667).

6   But Satan now is wiser than of yore,
     And tempts by making rich, not
     making poor.

     ALEXANDER POPE, (1688–1744) British
     satirical poet. "Epistle to Lord Bathurst," l.
     351-2 (1733).

7   What difference does it make how
     much you have? What you do not
     have amounts to much more.

     SENECA, (c. 5–65) Roman writer, philoso-
     pher, statesman. Attributed in Noctes Atticae,
     bk. 12, ch. 2, sct. 13, Aulus Gellius (second
     century A.D.).

8   I've been rich and I've been poor.
     Believe me, honey, rich is better.

     SOPHIE TUCKER [SOPHIE KALISH
     ABRA], (1884–1966) Russian-born U.S.
     singer. "Some of These Days" (1945).

Weather

1   He maketh his sun to rise on the
     evil and on the good, and sendeth
     rain on the just and on the unjust.

     BIBLE: NEW TESTAMENT, Jesus, in
     Matthew, 5:45.

2   Heat, ma'am! It was so dreadful
     here that I found there was nothing
     left for it but to take off my flesh
     and sit in my bones.

     SYDNEY SMITH, (1771–1845) British cler-
     gyman, writer. Quoted in Memoir, vol. 1, ch.
     9, Lady Holland (1855).

3   Everybody talks about the weather,
     but nobody does anything about it.

     MARK TWAIN, (1835–1910) U.S. author.
     Attributed in Hartford Courant (Connecticut,
     Aug. 27, 1897), editorial.

     Quoted by Charles D. Warner, though his
     actual words were, "A well-known U.S. writer
     once said that while everyone talked about
     the weather, nobody seemed to do anything
     about it." The remark is generally ascribed to
     Twain, with whom Warner collaborated on
     the novel, The Gilded Age (1873).

Webster, Daniel

1   Daniel Webster struck me much
     like a steam-engine in trousers.

     SYDNEY SMITH, (1771–1845) British cler-
     gyman, writer. Quoted in Memoir, vol. 1, ch.
     9, Lady Holland (1855).

     Thomas Carlyle described Webster thus:
     "A terrible, beetle-browed, mastiff-mouthed,
     yellow-skinned, broad-bottomed, grim-taci-
     turn individual; with a pair of dull-cruel-
     looking black eyes, and as much Parliamen-
     tary intellect and silent-rage in him ... as I
     have ever seen in any man." (Letter, June 24,
     1824, in New Letters of Thomas Carlyle,
     1904.)

Weddings

1   A princely marriage is the brilliant
     edition of a universal fact, and, as
     such, it rivets mankind.

     WALTER BAGEHOT, (1826–1877) British
     economist, critic. The English Constitution,
     ch. 3 (1867).

2   Dearly beloved, we are gathered
     together here in the sight of God,
     and in the face of this congregation,

to join together this Man and this Woman in holy Matrimony.

BOOK OF COMMON PRAYER, THE, *Solemnization of Matrimony,* "Exhortation" (1662).

3 With this Ring I thee wed, with my body I thee worship, and with all my worldly goods I thee endow.

BOOK OF COMMON PRAYER, THE, *Solemnization of Matrimony,* "Wedding" (1662).

4 Happy, happy, happy pair!
None but the brave
None but the brave
None but the brave deserves the fair.

JOHN DRYDEN, (1631–1700) British poet, dramatist, critic. "Alexander's Feast, " l. 12-15 (1697).

Referring to Alexander and Dais at the "Royal Feast for Persia won."

5 I'm getting married in the morning,
Ding! dong! the bells are gonna chime.
Pull out the stopper;
Let's have a whopper;
But get me to the church on time!

ALAN JAY LERNER, (1918–1986) U.S. songwriter. "Get Me to the Church on Time" (song), *My Fair Lady* (show, 1956; film, 1964).

6 Strange, to see what delight we married people have to see these poor fools decoyed into our condition, every man and wife gazing and smiling at them.

SAMUEL PEPYS, (1633–1703) British diarist. *The Diary of Samuel Pepys,* eds. Robert Latham and William Matthews (1977-83). Journal entry, Dec. 25, 1665.

7 We will have rings, and things, and fine array;
And kiss me, Kate. We will be married o' Sunday.

WILLIAM SHAKESPEARE, (1564–1616) British dramatist, poet. Petruccio, in *The Taming of the Shrew,* act 2, sc. 1, l. 319-20 (1623)."Kiss Me Kate" was the title of a musical by Cole Porter.

Welfare

1 And having looked to government for bread, on the very first scarcity they will turn and bite the hand that fed them. To avoid that evil, government will redouble the causes of it; and then it will become inveterate and incurable.

EDMUND BURKE, (1729–1797) Irish philosopher, statesman. *Thoughts and Details on Scarcity* (Nov. 1790), repr. in *Works,* vol. 5.

Cautioning against the "attempt to feed the people out of the hands of the magistrates."

2 A decent provision for the poor is the true test of civilization.

SAMUEL JOHNSON, (1709–1784) British author, lexicographer. Quoted in James Boswell, *Life of Dr. Johnson,* entry, 1770 (1791).

As quoted by the Rev. Dr. Maxwell.

West, the (U.S.)

1 Reporter: "Mr. Gandhi, what do you think of Western civilization?"
Gandhi: "I think it would be a very good idea."

MOHANDAS KARAMCHAND (MAHATMA) GANDHI, (1869–1948) Indian political and spiritual leader. *Attributed.*

There is no evidence of this exchange having occurred in fact, though E.F. Schumacher mentions seeing a film of Gandhi disembarking at Southampton, England, in 1930, in which Gandhi is asked his opinion on *modern civilization,* and gives the answer as above. (*Good Work,* ch. 2, 1979).

Whites

1 Every time I embrace a black woman I'm embracing slavery, and when I put my arms around a white woman, well, I'm hugging freedom. The white man forbade me to have the white woman on pain of death.... I will not be free until the day I can have a white woman in my bed.

ELDRIDGE CLEAVER, (b. 1935) U.S. African–American leader, writer. Lazarus, in *Soul on Ice*, "Allegory of the Black Eunuchs" (1968).

2 The so called white races are really pinko-grey.

E.M. (EDWARD MORGAN) FORSTER, (1879–1970) British novelist, essayist. Mr. Fielding, in *A Passage to India*, pt. 1, ch. 7 (1924).

This aside caused scandal at Fielding's Anglo-Indian club.

3 At the ground of all these noble races, the beast of prey, the splendid, *blond beast*, lustfully roving in search of spoils and victory, cannot be mistaken.

FRIEDRICH NIETZSCHE, (1844–1900) German philosopher. *The Genealogy of Morals*, essay 1, aph. 11 (1887, trans. 1899).

4 The truth is that Mozart, Pascal, Boolean algebra, Shakespeare, parliamentary government, baroque churches, Newton, the emancipation of women, Kant, Marx, and Balanchine ballets don't redeem what this particular civilization has wrought upon the world. The white race *is* the cancer of human history.

SUSAN SONTAG, (b. 1933) U.S. essayist. "What's Happening in America" (*1966*), *Styles of Radical Will* (1969). *Partisan Review* (New Brunswick, NJ, Spring 1967).

Wickedness

1 There is no peace, saith the Lord, unto the wicked.

BIBLE: HEBREW, *Isaiah*, 48:22.Repeated in *Isaiah* 57:21.

2 Wicked is not much worse than indiscreet.

JOHN DONNE, (c. 1572–1631) British divine, metaphysical poet. "An Anatomy of the World: First Anniversary" (1611). Repr. in *Complete Poetry and Selected Prose*, ed. John Hayward (1929).

Widows

1 Give unto them beauty for ashes, the oil of joy for mourning.

BIBLE: HEBREW, *Isaiah*, 61:3.

2 Take example by your father, my boy, and be very careful o' widders all your life, specially if they've kept a public house, Sammy.

CHARLES DICKENS, (1812–1870) British novelist. Mr. Weller, in *The Pickwick Papers*, ch. 20 (1836-1837).

3 The comfortable estate of widowhood is the only hope that keeps up a wife's spirits.

JOHN GAY, (1685–1732) British dramatist, poet. Peachum, in *The Beggar's Opera*, act 1, sc. 10 (1728), ed. F.W. Bateson (1934).

4 Methought I saw my late espous'd saint
Brought to me like Alcestis from the grave.

JOHN MILTON, (1608–1674) British poet. "Methought I saw my late espous'd saint," "Sonnet 23 (1658). Repr. in *Milton's Poetical Works*, ed. Douglas Bush (1966).

Opening lines.

5 Widow. The word consumes
   itself ...

SYLVIA PLATH, (1932–1963) U.S. poet.
"Widow" (1971). *Crossing the Water.*

Wilde, Oscar

1 He rose, and he put down *The Yellow Book.*
   He staggered—and, terrible-eyed,
   He brushed past the palms on the
   staircase
   And was helped to a hansom outside.

JOHN BETJEMAN, (1906–1984) British
poet. "The Arrest of Oscar Wilde at the Cado-
gan Hotel," st. 9, *Continual Dew* (1937).

Closing lines.

2 If, with the literate, I am
   Impelled to try an epigram,
   I never seek to take the credit;
   We all assume that Oscar said it.

DOROTHY PARKER, (1893–1967) U.S.
humorous writer. "A Pig's-Eye View of Literature," *Sunset Gun* (1928).

Wilderness

1 What would the world be, once
   bereft
   Of wet and wildness? Let them be
   left,
   O let them be left, wildness and wet;
   Long live the weeds and the wilderness yet.

GERARD MANLEY HOPKINS,
(1844–1889) British poet, Jesuit priest. "Inver-
snaid," st. 4 (written 1881), published in
Poems (1918).

2 I love all waste
   And solitary places; where we taste
   The pleasure of believing what we see

Is boundless, as we wish our souls
   to be.

PERCY BYSSHE SHELLEY, (1792–1822)
British poet. "Julian and Maddalo, "l. 14-17
(1818).

Wind

1 The answer, my friend, is blowin' in
   the wind,
   The answer is blowin' in the wind.

**BOB DYLAN [ROBERT ALLEN ZIM-
MERMAN],** (b. 1941) U.S. singer, songwriter. "Blowin' in the Wind, "chorus, on the
album *The Freewheelin' Bob Dylan* (1962).

On the sleeve notes to the record, Dylan
wrote: "The first way to answer the questions
in the song is by asking them. But lots of people have to first find the wind."

2 Who has seen the wind?
      Neither you nor I:
   But when the trees bow down their
      heads,
   The wind is passing by.

CHRISTINA ROSSETTI, (1830–1894)
British poet, lyricist. "Who has seen the
wind?" st. 2 (written 1869), published in *Sing-
Song* (1872).

3 O wild West Wind, thou breath of
      Autumn's being,
   Thou, from whose unseen presence
      the leaves dead
   Are driven, like ghosts from an
      enchanter fleeing,
   Yellow, and black, and pale, and
      hectic red,
   Pestilence-stricken multitudes.

PERCY BYSSHE SHELLEY, (1792–1822)
British poet. "Ode to the West Wind," l. 1-5
(1819).

Opening lines.

4 Willows whiten, aspens quiver,
   Little breezes dusk and shiver.

ALFRED TENNYSON, 1ST BARON TENNYSON, (1809–1892) British poet. "The Lady of Shalott," pt. 1, st. 2 (1832, rev. 1842).

Wine

1 Drink no longer water, but use a little wine for thy stomach's sake and thine often infirmities.

BIBLE: NEW TESTAMENT, St. Paul, in *1 Timothy*, 5:23.

2 The Grape that can with Logic absolute The Two-and-Seventy jarring Sects confute.

OMAR KHAYYAM, (11–12th century) Persian astronomer, poet. *The Rubaiyat of Omar Khayyam*, st. 43, trans. by Edward FitzGerald, first edition (1859).

3 It's a naive domestic Burgundy without any breeding, but I think you'll be amused by its presumption.

JAMES THURBER, (1894–1961) U.S. humorist, illustrator. Cartoon caption, in *The New Yorker* (March 27, 1937).

Winning

1 We will get everything out of her that you can squeeze out of a lemon and a bit more.... I will squeeze her until you can hear the pips squeak.

SIR ERIC GEDDES, (1875–1937) British Conservative politician. Quoted in *A Dictionary of Political Quotations*, ed. Robert Stewart (1984). Speech, Dec. 9, 1918, the Guildhall, Cambridge, England.

On German war reparations following World War I. Geddes repeated the speech the following night, adding, "My only doubt is not whether we can squeeze hard enough, but whether there is enough juice."

Winter

1 The English winter—ending in July,
To recommence in August.

GEORGE GORDON NOEL BYRON, 6TH BARON BYRON, (1788–1824) British poet. *Don Juan*, cto. 13, st. 42 (1819-1824).

2 There's a certain Slant of light,
Winter Afternoons—
That oppresses, like the Heft
Of Cathedral Tunes—

EMILY DICKINSON, (1830–1886) U.S. poet. "There's a Certain Slant of Light," st. 1 (written c. 1861, published 1890). Repr. in *The Complete Poems*, no. 258, Harvard *variorum* edition (1955).

The word "heft" was altered to "weight" in the first edition of Dickinson's verse, edited in 1890 by Thomas Wentworth Higginson and Mabel Loomis Todd.

3 Winter is icummen in,
Lhude sing Goddamm,
Raineth drop and staineth slop,
And how the wind doth ramm!
Sing: Goddamm.

EZRA POUND, (1885–1972) U.S. poet, critic. "Ancient Music, " *Lustra* (1917).

Pound's pastiche of the medieval song (see Anonymous, summer) was originally dropped from the 1916 edition of *Lustra* as being offensive, though it was later reinstated.

4 O, Wind,
If Winter comes, can Spring be far behind?

PERCY BYSSHE SHELLEY, (1792–1822) British poet. "Ode to the West Wind," l. 69-70 (1819).

Wisdom

1 The fear of the Lord is the beginning of wisdom.

BIBLE: HEBREW, *Psalms*, 111:10.

2   Wisdom hath builded her house,
     she hath hewn out her seven pillars.

     BIBLE: HEBREW, *Proverbs*, 9:1.

3   Wisdom is the principal thing;
     therefore get wisdom: and with all
     thy getting get understanding.

     BIBLE: HEBREW, *Proverbs*, 4:7.

4   Wisdom we know is the knowledge
     of good and evil not the strength to
     choose between the two.

     JOHN CHEEVER, (1912–1982) U.S. author.
     John Cheever: The Journals, "The Late Forties
     and the Fifties," ed. Robert Gottlieb (1991).
     Journal entry, 1956.

5   The art of being wise is the art of
     knowing what to overlook.

     WILLIAM JAMES, (1842–1910) U.S. psy-
     chologist, philosopher. *Principles of Psychol-
     ogy*, vol. 2, ch. 22 (1890).

6   Knowledge comes, but wisdom
     lingers, and he bears a laden
       breast,
     Full of sad experience, moving
       towards the stillness of his rest.

     ALFRED TENNYSON, 1ST BARON TEN-
     NYSON, (1809–1892) British poet. "Locksley
     Hall," l. 141 (1842).

Wit

1   Wit is the salt of conversation, not
     the food.

     WILLIAM HAZLITT, (1778–1830) British
     essayist. *Lectures on the English Comic Writ-
     ers*, "On Wit and Humour" (1819).

2   True wit is nature to advantage
       dressed,
     What oft was thought, but ne'er so
       well expressed.

ALEXANDER POPE, (1688–1744) British
satirical poet. "An Essay on Criticism," l. 297-
8 (1711).

3   Brevity is the soul of wit,
     And tediousness the limbs and out-
       ward flourishes.

     WILLIAM SHAKESPEARE, (1564–1616)
     British dramatist, poet. Polonius, in *Hamlet*,
     act 2, sc. 2, l. 91-2 (1604).

     Said in the middle of a lengthy and rhetorical
     speech.

4   He's winding up the watch of his
     wit. By and by it will strike.

     WILLIAM SHAKESPEARE, (1564–1616)
     British dramatist, poet. Sebastian, in *The
     Tempest*, act 2, sc. 1, l. 13-4 (1623).

     Referring to Gonzalo's attempts to cheer up
     Alonso.

Witches

1   Double, double, toil and trouble
     Fire burn, and cauldron bubble.

     WILLIAM SHAKESPEARE, (1564–1616)
     British dramatist, poet. The three witches, in
     Macbeth, act 4, sc. 1, l. 10-11 (1623).

Wives

1   Wives are young men's mistresses,
     companions for middle age, and
     old men's nurses.

     FRANCIS BACON, (1561–1626) British
     philosopher, essayist, statesman. *Essays*, "Of
     Marriage and Single Life" (1597-1625).

2   Whoso findeth a wife findeth a
     good thing, and obtaineth favour of
     the Lord.

     BIBLE: HEBREW, *Proverbs*, 18:22.

3   Wilt thou have this Woman to thy
     wedded wife, to live together after
     God's ordinance in the holy estate

of Matrimony? Wilt thou love her, comfort her, honour, and keep her in sickness and in health; and, forsaking all other, keep thee only unto her, so long as ye both shall live?

BOOK OF COMMON PRAYER, THE, *Solemnization of Matrimony,* "Betrothal" (1662).

In general practise, the man promises only "to love and to cherish" his wife and uses the words "I plight thee my troth."

4 Caesar's wife must be above suspicion.

GAIUS CAESAR [GAIUS JULIUS CAESAR], (100–44 B.C.) Roman general, emperor. Quoted in *Parallel Lives,* "Caesar," sct. 10, Plutarch.

Pompeia, Caesar's wife, involved in an accusation against P. Clodius, was divorced by Caesar solely on these grounds.

5 The true index of a man's character is the health of his wife.

CYRIL CONNOLLY, (1903–1974) British critic. *The Unquiet Grave,* pt. 2 (1944, rev. 1951).

6 Accidents will occur in the best-regulated families; and in families not regulated by that pervading influence which sanctifies while it enhances ... in short, by the influence of Woman, in the lofty character of Wife, they may be expected with confidence, and must be borne with philos-ophy.

CHARLES DICKENS, (1812–1870) British novelist. Mr. Micawber, in *David Copperfield,* ch. 28 (1850).

7 He knows little, who will tell his wife all he knows.

THOMAS FULLER, (1608–1661) British cleric. *The Holy State and the Profane State,* bk. 1, "The Good Husband" (1642).

8 I ... chose my wife as she did her wedding-gown, not for a fine glossy surface, but such qualities as would wear well.

OLIVER GOLDSMITH, (1728–1774) Anglo-Irish author, poet, playwright. The narrator (Dr. Charles Primrose), in *The Vicar of Wakefield,* ch. 1 (1766).

9 No slave is a slave to the same lengths, and in so full a sense of the word, as a wife is.

JOHN STUART MILL, (1806–1873) British philosopher, economist. *The Subjection of Women,* ch. 2 (1869).

See Mill on marriage.

10 To suckle fools, and chronicle small beer.

WILLIAM SHAKESPEARE, (1564–1616) British dramatist, poet. Iago, in *Othello,* act 2, sc. 1, l. 163 (1623).

Describing the role of "a deserving woman." Desdemona calls this a "most lame and impotent conclusion."

11 Trusty, dusky, vivid, true,
With eyes of gold and bramble-
dew,
Steel-true and blade-straight
The great artificer
Made my mate.

ROBERT LOUIS STEVENSON, (1850–1894) Scottish novelist, essayist, poet. "My Wife," *Songs of Travel* (1896).

The lines "Steel-true, blade-straight" are inscribed on the gravestone of Arthur Conan Doyle, Hampshire, England.

Women

1 Men themselves have wondered
What they see in me.
They try so much
But they can't touch
My inner mystery.
When I try to show them,
They say they still can't see.
I say,

It's in the arch of my back,
The sun of my smile,
The ride of my breasts,
The grace of my style.
I'm a woman
Phenomenally.
Phenomenal woman,
That's me.

MAYA ANGELOU, (b. 1928) U.S. author. "Phenomenal Woman, "*And Still I Rise* (1978).

2 A homely face and no figure have aided many women heavenward.

MINNA ANTRIM, (1861–?) U.S. epigrammist. *Naked Truth and Veiled Allusions*, p. 16 (1901).

3 A woman, especially, if she have the misfortune of knowing anything, should conceal it as well as she can.

JANE AUSTEN, (1775–1817) British novelist. *Northanger Abbey*, ch. 14 (1818).

4 One is not born, but rather becomes, a woman.

SIMONE DE BEAUVOIR, (1908–1986) French novelist, essayist. *The Second Sex*, bk. 2, pt. 4, ch. 1 (1953).

5 All I ask, is the privilege for my masculine part, the poet in me.... If I must not, because of my sex, have this freedom ... I lay down my quill and you shall hear no more of me.

APHRA BEHN, (1640–1689) British playwright, poet. "The Lucky Chance," preface (1686). Repr. in *The Works of Aphra Behn*, vol. 2, ed. M. Summers (1915).

6 In sorrow thou shalt bring forth children; and thy desire shall be to thy husband, and he shall rule over thee.

BIBLE: HEBREW, *Genesis*, 3:16. God's judgment on Eve.

7 Who can find a virtuous woman? for her price is far above rubies.

BIBLE: HEBREW, *Proverbs*, 31:10.

8 Women have no wilderness in them,
They are provident instead,
Content in the tight hot cell of their hearts
To eat dusty bread.

LOUISE BOGAN, (1897–1970) U.S. poet, critic. "Women," st. 1, *Body of this Death* (1923).

9 I am obnoxious to each carping tongue
Who says my hand a needle better fits,
A poet's pen, all scorn, I should thus wrong;
For such despite they cast on female wits:
If what I do prove well, it won't advance,
They'll say it's stolen, or else it was by chance.

ANNE BRADSTREET, (c. 1612–1672) U.S. poet. "The Prologue," (1650). Repr. in *Several Poems Compiled with Great Variety of Wit and Learning* (1678).

10 Women are supposed to be very calm generally: but women feel just as men feel; they need exercise for their faculties, and a field for their efforts as much as their brothers do; they suffer from too rigid a restraint, too absolute a stagnation, precisely as men would suffer; and it is narrow-minded in their more privileged fellow creatures to say that they ought to confine themselves to making puddings and knitting stockings, to playing on the piano and embroidering bags. It is thoughtless to condemn them, or laugh at them, if they seek to do more or learn more than custom has pronounced necessary for their sex.

CHARLOTTE BRONTË, (1816–1855) British novelist. *Jane Eyre*, ch. 12 (1847).

11 Good women always think it is their fault when someone else is being offensive. Bad women never take the blame for anything.

ANITA BROOKNER, (b. 1938) British author. Mr. Neville, in *Hotel du Lac*, ch. 7 (1984).

12 Eve is a twofold mystery.

ELIZABETH BARRETT BROWNING, (1806–1861) British poet. "The Poet's Vow," pt. 1, st. 1, *The Seraphim and Other Poems* (1838).

Opening words.

13 And what is better than wisdom? Womman. And what is bettre than a good womman? Nothyng.

GEOFFREY CHAUCER, (1340–1400) British poet. *The Canterbury Tales*, Prudence, in "The Tale of Melibee," l 1107 (c. 1387 1400), repr. in *The Works of Geoffrey Chaucer*, ed. Alfred W. Pollard, etc. (1898).

14 Certain women should be struck regularly like gongs.

NOËL COWARD, (1899–1973) British actor, playwright, composer. Elyot, in *Private Lives*, act 3 (1930), published in *Play Parade* (1931).

15 Look for the woman!
[Cherchez la femme!]

ALEXANDRE DUMAS, (1802–1870) French dramatist. *The Mohicans of Paris*, vol. 3, ch. 10 (1854-1855).

The phrase, which is used to imply that a mystery will be understood when the involvement of a woman can be shown, has also been attributed to revolutionary and statesman Joseph Fouché (1763-1829).

16 I know that I have the body of a weak and feeble woman, but I have the heart and stomach of a king, and of a king of England too.

ELIZABETH I, (1533–1603) British Queen of England. Quoted in *The Tudors*, ch. 7, Christo-pher Morris (1955). Speech, Aug. 8, 1588, at Tilbury, England.

Address to troops on the approach of the Spanish Armada.

17 The great question that has never been answered, and which I have not yet been able to answer, despite my thirty years of research into the feminine soul, is "What does a woman want?" *[Was will das Weib?]*

SIGMUND FREUD, (1856–1939) Austrian psychiatrist. Quoted in *Sigmund Freud: Life and Work*, vol. 2, pt. 3, ch. 16, Ernest Jones (1955).

Quoted from a letter to Marie Bonaparte. Freud's views on women are summed up in Peter Gay, *Freud: A Life of Our Time*, pt. 10 (1988). On the subject of women's psyche, Oscar Wilde wrote, "The strength of women comes from the fact that psychology cannot explain us. Men can be analysed, women ... merely adored." (Mrs. Chieveley, in *The Ideal Husband*, act 1, 1895).

18 The Woman-Soul leadeth us Upward and on!

JOHANN WOLFGANG VON GOETHE, (1749–1832) German poet, dramatist. Chorus Mysticus, in *Faust*, pt. 2, act 5, sc. 7 (1832), trans. by Bayard Taylor (1870-1871).

Last words of play.

19 Women are reputed never to be disgusted. The sad fact is that they often are, but not with men; following the lead of men, they are most often disgusted with themselves.

GERMAINE GREER, (b. 1939) Australian feminist writer. *The Female Eunuch*, "Loathing and Disgust" (1970).

20 A woman's whole life is a history of the affections. The heart is her world: it is there her ambition strives for empire; it is there her avarice seeks for hidden treasures. She sends forth her sympathies on adventure; she embarks her whole soul on the traffic of affection; and if shipwrecked, her case is hopeless—for it is a bankruptcy of the heart.

WASHINGTON IRVING, (1783–1859) U.S. author. *The Sketch Book of Geoffrey Crayon, Gent.* "The Broken Heart" (1819-1820).

21 The opinion I have of the generality of women—who appear to me as children to whom I would rather give a sugar plum than my time, forms a barrier against matrimony which I rejoice in.

JOHN KEATS, (1795–1821) British poet. *Letters of John Keats,* no. 94, ed. Frederick Page (1954). Letter, Oct. 14-31, 1818, to his brother and sister-in-law, George and Georgiana Keats.

Two years later (Aug. 1820) Keats wrote, "I am certain that I have said nothing in a spirit to displease any woman I would care to please; but still there is a tendency to class women in my books with roses and sweetmeats."

22 The monstrous regiment of women.

JOHN KNOX, (1505–1572) Scottish Presbyterian leader. *The First Blast of the Trumpet Against the Monstrous Regiment of Women,* pamphlet (1558).

In his pamphlet, Knox wrote, "Nature doth paint them further to be weak, frail, impatient, feeble and foolish; and experience hath declared them to be unconstant, variable, cruel, and lacking the spirit of counsel."

23 Being a woman is of special interest only to aspiring male transsexuals. To actual women it is merely a good excuse not to play football.

FRAN LEBOWITZ, (b. 1951) U.S. journalist. "Letters," *Metropolitan Life* (1978).

24 If woman is inconstant, good, I am faithful to

ebb and flow, I fall
in season and now
is a time of ripening.

DENISE LEVERTOV, (b. 1923) Anglo–American poet. "Stepping Westward," *The Sorrow Dance* (1967).

25 But if God had wanted us to think just with our wombs, why did He give us a brain?

CLARE BOOTHE LUCE, (1903–1987) U.S. playwright, diplomat. Nora, in *Slam the Door Softly* (1970).

26 Aren't women prudes if they don't and prostitutes if they do?

KATE MILLETT, (b. 1934) U.S. feminist author. In *The Quotable Woman,* ed. Elaine Partnow (1982). Speech, March 22, 1975, Women's Writers' Conference, Los Angeles.

27 We are educated in the grossest ignorance, and no art omitted to stifle our natural reason; if some few get above their nurses' instructions, our knowledge must rest concealed and be as useless to the world as gold in the mine.

MARY WORTLEY, LADY MONTAGU, (1689–1762) British society figure, letter writer. *Selected Letters,* ed. Robert Halsband (1970). Letter, Oct. 10, 1753, to her daughter Lady Bute.

28 Woman is the nigger of the world.

YOKO ONO, (b. 1933) U.S. artist. Quoted in *The Lennon Tapes* (1981). Interview in *Nova* (New York, 1968).

The words—used by John Lennon as a song title on the album *Some Time in New York City* (1972)—recall those of Zora Neale Hurston: "De nigger woman is de mule uh de world so fur as Ah can see." (*Their Eyes Were Watching God,* ch. 2, 1937.)

29 Every woman adores a Fascist,
The boot in the face, the brute
Brute heart of a brute like you.

SYLVIA PLATH, (1932–1963) U.S. poet. "Daddy," st. 10, *Ariel* (1965). *Encounter* (London, Oct. 1963).

30 Most women have no characters at all.

ALEXANDER POPE, (1688–1744) British satirical poet. "Epistle to a Lady," l. 2 (1735).

Towards the end of the poem, (l. 269-70), Pope writes "And yet, believe me, good as well as ill, Woman's at best a contradiction still."

31 For my part I distrust *all* generalizations about women, favourable and unfavourable, masculine and feminine, ancient and modern; all alike, I should say, result from paucity of experience.

BERTRAND RUSSELL [LORD RUSSELL, 3RD EARL], (1872–1970) British philosopher, mathematician. *Unpopular Essays*, "An Outline of Intellectual Rubbish" (1950).

32 Let me not think on't; frailty, thy name is woman.

WILLIAM SHAKESPEARE, (1564–1616) British dramatist, poet. Hamlet, in *Hamlet*, act 1, sc. 2, l. 146 (1604).

In Hamlet's first soliloquy he voices his unhappiness at the haste with which his mother had remarried when she had seemed so devoted to his father and had mourned him "Like Niobe, all tears."

33 Paradoxically, the most constructive thing women can do ... is to write, for in the *act* of writing we deny our muteness and begin to eliminate some of the difficulties that have been put upon us.

DALE SPENDER, (b. 1943) Australian feminist, author. *Man Made Language*, ch. 7 (1980).

34 The New Women! I could barely recognise them as being of the same sex as myself, their buttocks arrogant in tight jeans, openly inviting, breasts falling free and shameless and feeling no apparent obligation to smile, look pleasant or keep their voices low. And how they live! Just look at them to know how! If a man doesn't bring them to orgasm, they look for another who does. If by mistake they fall pregnant, they abort by vacuum aspiration. If they don't like the food, they push the plate away. If the job doesn't suit them, they hand in their notice. They are satiated by everything, hungry for nothing. They are what I wanted to be; they are what I worked for them to be: and now I see them, I hate them.

FAY WELDON, (b. 1933) British novelist. The narrator (Praxis Duveen), in *Praxis*, ch. 2 (1978).

35 Alas! a woman that attempts the pen,
Such a presumptuous creature is esteemed,
The fault can by no virtue be redeemed.
They tell us we mistake our sex and way;
Good breeding, fashion, dancing, dressing, play,
Are the accomplishments we should desire;
To write, or read, or think, or to enquire,
Would cloud our beauty, and exhaust our time,
And interrupt the conquests of our prime,
Whilst the dull manage of a servile house
Is held by some our utmost art and use.

ANNE FINCH, LADY WINCHILSEA, (1660–1720) British poet. "The Introduction," l. 10-20 (1713). Repr. in *Poems*, ed. M. Reynolds (1903).

Women and Men

1   Women are only children of a larger growth.... A man of sense only trifles with them, plays with them, humours and flatters them, as he does with a sprightly and forward child; but he neither consults them about, nor trusts them with, serious matters.

PHILIP DORMER STANHOPE, 4TH EARL CHESTERFIELD, (1694–1773) British statesman, man of letters. *The Letters of the Earl of Chesterfield to His Son*, vol. 1, no. 161, ed. Charles Strachey (1901). Letter, Sept. 5, 1748, first published (1774).

John Dryden wrote "Men are but children of a larger growth" in *All For Love*, act 4, sc. 1 (1678).

2   I should like to know what is the proper function of women, if it is not to make reasons for husbands to stay at home, and still stronger reasons for bachelors to go out.

GEORGE ELIOT [MARY ANN (OR MARIAN) EVANS], (1819–1880) British novelist. Stephen Guest, in *The Mill on the Floss*, bk. 6, ch. 6 (1860).

3   I must have women—there is nothing unbends the mind like them.

JOHN GAY, (1685–1732) British dramatist, poet. Macheath, in *The Beggar's Opera*, act 2, sc. 3 (1728), ed. F.W. Bateson (1934).

4   Women have very little idea of how much men hate them.

GERMAINE GREER, (b. 1939) Australian feminist writer. *The Female Eunuch*, "Loathing and Disgust" (1970).

5   For the female of the species is more deadly than the male.

RUDYARD KIPLING, (1865–1936) British writer, poet. "The Female of the Species," *Rudyard Kipling's Verse* (1919).

6   I expect that Woman will be the last thing civilised by Man.

GEORGE MEREDITH, (1828–1909) British author. *The Ordeal of Richard Feverel*, ch. 1 (1859).

An aphorism from the "The Pilgrim's Scrip."

7   I yielded, and unlocked her all my heart,
Who with a grain of manhood well resolved
Might easily have shook off all her snares;
But foul effeminacy held me yoked
Her bondslave.

JOHN MILTON, (1608–1674) British poet. Samson, in "Samson Agonistes," l. 407-11 (1671). Repr. in *Milton's Poetical Works*, ed. Douglas Bush (1966).

Referring to Délila (Delilah).

8   A woman without a man is like a fish without a bicycle.

GLORIA STEINEM, (b. 1934) U.S. feminist writer. *Attributed*.

Although the quote is generally attributed to Steinem, there is evidence that the words were current as a graffito in the 1970s, in the form, "A woman needs a man like a fish needs a bicycle."

9   Some of us are becoming the men we wanted to marry.

GLORIA STEINEM, (b. 1934) U.S. feminist writer, editor. Speech, Sept. 1981, Yale University, New Haven, Connecticut.

Steinem's words reappeared in an article in *Ms* (New York, July/Aug. 1982).

10   Women have served all these centuries as looking-glasses possessing the magic and delicious power of reflecting the figure of man at twice its natural size.

VIRGINIA WOOLF, (1882–1941) British novelist. *A Room Of One's Own*, ch. 2 (1929).

Women and Politics

1   Women—one half the human race at least—care fifty times more for a marriage than a ministry.

WALTER BAGEHOT, (1826–1877) British economist, critic. *The English Constitution*, ch. 3 (1867).

2   There is no hope even that woman, with her right to vote, will ever purify politics.

EMMA GOLDMAN, (1869–1940) U.S. anarchist. *Anarchism and Other Essays*, "The Tragedy of Women's Emancipation" (1910).

Women and the Arts

1   I'm a writer first & a woman after.

KATHERINE MANSFIELD, (1888–1923) New Zealand-born British author. *Collected Letters*, eds. Vincent O'Sullivan and Margaret Scott (1984). Letter, Dec. 3, 1920, to her husband John Middleton Murry.

2   As artists they're rot, but as providers they're oil wells; they gush. Norris said she never wrote a story unless it was fun to do. I understand Ferber whistles at her typewriter. And there was that poor sucker Flaubert rolling around on his floor for three days looking for the right word.

DOROTHY PARKER, (1893–1967) U.S. humorous writer. Interview in *Writers at Work*, First Series, ed. Malcolm Cowley (1958).

3   The composition of a tragedy requires *testicles*.

VOLTAIRE [FRANÇOIS MARIE AROUET], (1694–1778) French philosopher, author. Quoted in *Byron's Letters and Journals*, vol. 5, ed. Leslie A. Marchand (1976). Letter, April 2, 1817, to publisher John Murray.

In answer to the question "why no woman has ever written a tolerable tragedy," attributed by Byron.

4   A woman must have money and a room of her own if she is to write fiction.

VIRGINIA WOOLF, (1882–1941) British novelist. *A Room Of One's Own*, ch. 1 (1929).

Women: Single

1   Then be not coy, but use your time;
And while ye may, go marry:
For having lost but once your
    prime,
You may for ever tarry.

ROBERT HERRICK, (1591–1674) British poet, clergyman. "To the Virgins, to Make Much of Time, "st. 4, *Hesperides* (1648). Repr. in *The Poems of Robert Herrick*, ed. L.C. Martin (1956).

Wonder

1   There be three things which are too wonderful for me, yea, four which I know not: the way of an eagle in the air; the way of a serpent upon a rock; the way of a ship in the midst of the sea; and the way of a man with a maid.

BIBLE: HEBREW, *Proverbs*, 30:18-19. From the oracle of Agur, son of Jakeh.

2   Curiouser and curiouser!

LEWIS CARROLL [CHARLES LUTWIDGE DODGSON], (1832–1898) British author, mathematician. Alice, in *Alice's Adventures in Wonderland*, "The Pool of Tears" (1865).

On eating the cake marked "Eat Me," and growing taller.

3 Astonish me.
[...*tonne-moi.*]

SERGEI DIAGHILEV, (1872–1929) Russian ballet impresario. Quoted in *Journals of Jean Cocteau,* ch. 1, ed. Wallace Fowlie (1956).

Said to Jean Cocteau, Paris 1912, who had complained to Diaghilev that he was not getting enough artistic notice.

4 O wonder!
How many goodly creatures are
there here!
How beauteous mankind is! O
brave new world
That has such people in't!

WILLIAM SHAKESPEARE, (1564–1616) British dramatist, poet. Miranda, in *The Tempest,* act 5, sc. 1, l. 184-7 (1623).

Prospero replies: "'Tis new to thee." *Brave New World* became the title of Aldous Huxley's dystopian novel of 1932.

5 O what venerable and reverend creatures did the aged seem! Immortal Cherubims! And young men glittering and sparkling Angels, and maids strange seraphic pieces of life and beauty! Boys and girls tumbling in the street, and playing, were moving jewels. I knew not that they were born or should die; but all things abided eternally as they were in their proper places.

THOMAS TRAHERNE, (1636–1674) British clergyman, poet, mystic. *Centuries of Meditations,* "Third Century," no. 3 (written c. 1672, first published 1908).

Words

1 "When *I* use a word," Humpty Dumpty said in rather a scornful tone, "it means just what I choose it to mean neither more nor less."

LEWIS CARROLL [CHARLES LUTWIDGE DODGSON], (1832–1898) British author, mathematician. *Through the Looking-Glass,* "Humpty Dumpty" (1872).

"'The question is,' said Alice, 'whether you *can* make words mean so many different things.' 'The question is,' said Humpty Dumpty, 'which is to be master that's all.'"

2 A word is dead
When it is said,
Some say.
I say it just
Begins to live
That day.

EMILY DICKINSON, (1830–1886) U.S. poet. "A Word Is Dead" (written c. 1872, published 1894). Repr. in *The Complete Poems,* no. 1212, Harvard *variorum* edition (1955).

3 All our words from loose using
have lost their edge.

ERNEST HEMINGWAY, (1899–1961) U.S. author. *Death in the Afternoon,* ch. 7 (1932).

4 Poor Faulkner. Does he really think big emotions come from big words? He thinks I don't know the ten-dollar words. I know them all right. But there are older and simpler and better words, and those are the ones I use.

ERNEST HEMINGWAY, (1899–1961) U.S. author.

Quoted in *Papa Hemingway,* pt. 1, ch. 4, A.E. Hotchner (1966). Hemingway's comment was made after being informed (by Hotchner) that William Faulkner considered Hemingway "had no courage" and "had never been known to use a word that might send the reader to the dictionary." Hemingway also described Faulkner as "Old Corndrinking Mellifluous." (Quoted in Carlos Baker, *Ernest Hemingway, A Life Story,* 1969, rev. 1973.)

5 Words are wise men's counters, they do but reckon by them: but they are the money of fools.

THOMAS HOBBES, (1588–1679) British philosopher. *Leviathan,* pt. 1, ch. 4 (1651).

6 The word is the Verb, and the Verb is God.

> VICTOR HUGO, (1802–1885) French poet, dramatist, novelist. *Les Contemplations*, "Suite," pt. 1, ch. 8 (1856).

7 I am not yet so lost in lexicography as to forget that words are the daughters of earth, and that things are the sons of heaven. Language is only the instrument of science, and words are but the signs of ideas: I wish, however, that the instrument might be less apt to decay, and that signs might be permanent, like the things which they denote.

> SAMUEL JOHNSON, (1709–1784) British author, lexicographer. *Dictionary of the English Language*, preface (1755).
>
> Johnson was paraphrasing a line from Samuel Madden's poem, *Boulter's Monument* (1745), which Johnson had revised for publication: "Words are men's daughters, but God's sons are things."

8 I fear those big words which make us so unhappy.

> JAMES JOYCE, (1882–1941) Irish author. Stephen Dedalus, in *Ulysses*, ch. 2 of 1984 edition (1922).

9 Words ought to be a little wild for they are the assault of thoughts on the unthinking.

> JOHN MAYNARD KEYNES, (1883–1946) British economist. *New Statesman and Nation* (London, July 15, 1933).

10 Words are, of course, the most powerful drug used by mankind.

> RUDYARD KIPLING, (1865–1936) British author, poet. Quoted in *Times* (London, Feb. 15, 1923), speech, Feb. 14, 1923.

11 Truthful words are not beautiful; beautiful words are not truthful. Good words are not persuasive; persuasive words are not good.

> LAO-TZU, (6th century B.C.) Chinese philosopher. *Tao-te-ching*, bk. 2, ch. 81, trans. by T.C. Lau (1963).

12 In a society in which equality is a fact, not merely a word, words of racial or sexual assault and humiliation will be nonsense syllables.

> CATHARINE A. MACKINNON, U.S. lawyer. *Only Words*, ch. 3 (1993).

13 One of our defects as a nation is a tendency to use what have been called "weasel words." When a weasel sucks eggs the meat is sucked out of the egg. If you use a "weasel word" after another there is nothing left of the other.

> THEODORE ROOSEVELT, (1858–1919) U.S. Republican (later Progressive) politician, president. *Works*, vol. 24 (1926). Speech, May 31, 1916, St. Louis, Missouri.
>
> Referring to Woodrow Wilson's proposal for "universal voluntary military training."

14 For words, like Nature, half reveal
And half conceal the soul within.

> ALFRED TENNYSON, 1ST BARON TENNYSON, (1809–1892) British poet. "In Memoriam A.H.H.," cto. 5, st. 1 (1850).

Wordsworth, William

1 We that had loved him so, followed
him, honoured him,
Lived in his mild and magnificent
eye,
Learned his great language, caught
his clear accents,
Made him our pattern to live and
to die!
Shakespeare was of us, Milton was
for us,
Burns, Shelley, were with us—they
watch from their
graves!

He alone breaks from the van and
the freemen,
—He alone sinks to the rear and the
slaves!

ROBERT BROWNING, (1812–1889) British
poet. "The Lost Leader," st. 1, *Dramatic
Romances and Lyrics* (1845).

2 For the sake of a few fine imaginative or domestic passages, are we to
be bullied into a certain philosophy
engendered in the whims of an
egotist?

JOHN KEATS, (1705–1821) British poet. *Letters of John Keats*, no. 44, ed. Frederick Page
(1954). Letter, Feb. 3, 1818.

3 Wordsworth went to the Lakes, but
he was never a lake poet. He found
in stones the sermons he had already
hidden there.

OSCAR WILDE, (1854–1900) Anglo-Irish
playwright, author. Vivian, in "The Decay of
Lying," *Intentions* (1891). Repr. in *Complete
Works of Oscar Wilde*, ed. J.B. Foreman
(1966).

The words recall Shakespeare, *As You Like It*,
act 2, sc. 1, l. 15-17: "And this our life,
exempt from public haunt, Finds tongues in
trees, books in the running brooks, Sermons in
stones, and good in everything."

Work

1 Whatsoever thy hand findeth to do,
do it with thy might; for there is no
work, nor device, nor knowledge,
nor wisdom, in the grave, whither
thou goest.

BIBLE: HEBREW, *Ecclesiastes*, 9:10.

2 I do most of my work sitting down.
That's where I shine.

ROBERT BENCHLEY, (1889–1945) U.S.
humorous writer. Quoted in *The Algonquin
Wits*, ed. Robert E. Drennan (1968).

In the same book, Benchley is quoted,
"Anyone can do any amount of work, provided it isn't the work he is supposed to be
doing."

3 Nowher so bisy a man as he ther
nas,
And yet he semed bisier than he
was.

GEOFFREY CHAUCER, (1340–1400)
British poet. *The Canterbury Tales*, "General
Prologue," l. 323-4 (c. 1387-1400), repr. in
The Works of Geoffrey Chaucer, ed. Alfred W.
Pollard, et al. (1898).

Referring to the Sergeant of Law.

4 Nice work if you can get it,
And you can get it if you try.

IRA GERSHWIN, (1896–1983) U.S. lyricist.
"Nice Work If You Can Get It" (song), *Damsel
in Distress* (film, 1937).

Music by George Gershwin.

5 Work—work—work,
In the dull December light,
And work—work—work,
When the weather is warm and
bright—
While underneath the eaves
The brooding swallows cling
As if to show me their sunny backs
And twit me with the spring.

THOMAS HOOD, (1799–1845) British poet.
"The Song of the Shirt," st. 8 (1843). Repr. in
Complete Poetical Works, ed. Walter Jerrold
(1906).

6 I like work; it fascinates me. I can
sit and look at it for hours. I love to
keep it by me; the idea of getting rid
of it nearly breaks my heart.

JEROME K. JEROME, (1859–1927) British
author. *Three Men in a Boat*, ch. 15 (1889).

7 I am gradually approaching the
period in my life when work comes
first.... No longer diverted by other

emotions, I work the way a cow grazes.

KÄTHE KOLLWITZ, (1867–1945) German artist. *Diaries and Letters*, ed. Hans Kollwitz (1955). Journal entry, April 1910.

In an entry Jan. 1, 1912, Kollwitz wrote: "For the last third of life there remains only work. It alone is always stimulating, rejuvenating, exciting and satisfying."

8   All work and no play makes Jack a dull boy.

STANLEY KUBRICK, (b. 1928) U.S. film-maker. Jack Torrance (Jack Nicholson), in *The Shining* (film) (1980).

The words typed by Nicholson cover the pages of the manuscript he is supposed to be working on. The proverb has been in common usage since at least the 17th century, when it was recorded in Howell's *English Proverbs* (1659). In Samuel Smiles's celebrated *Self-Help*, ch. 11, there appears the warning: "'All work and no play makes Jack a dull boy.' But all play and no work makes him something greatly worse."

9   Why should I let the toad *work*
    Squat on my life?
    Can't I use my wit as a pitchfork
    And drive the brute off?

PHILIP LARKIN, (1922–1986) British poet. "Toads," st. 1, *The Less Deceived* (1955).

10 No man is born into the world,
    whose work
    Is not born with him; there is
    always work,
    And tools to work withal, for those
    who will:
    And bless'd are the horny hands of
    toil!

JAMES RUSSELL LOWELL, (1819–1891) U.S. poet, editor. "A Glance Behind the Curtains" (1844). Repr. in *Poetical Works of James Russell Lowell* (1978).

11 To work—to work! It is such infinite delight to know that we still have the best things to do.

KATHERINE MANSFIELD, (1888–1923) New Zealand-born British author. *Collected Letters*, vol. 1, eds. Vincent O'Sullivan and Margaret Scott (1984). Letter, Dec. 7, 1916, to Bertrand Russell.

12 In communist society, where nobody has one exclusive sphere of activity but each can become accomplished in any branch he wishes, society regulates the general production and thus makes it possible for me to do one thing today and another tomorrow, to hunt in the morning, fish in the afternoon, rear cattle in the evening, criticize after dinner, just as I have a mind, without ever becoming hunter, fisherman, shepherd or critic.

KARL MARX, (1818–1883) German political theorist, social philosopher. *The German Ideology*, sct. 1 (1846), repr. in Karl Marx and Friedrich Engels: *Collected Works*, vol. 5 (1976).

This thesis represented Marx's attempt later abandoned to reconcile his conflicting doctrines of the abolition of the division of labor, and the necessity of highly developed forms of production.

13 The reward of labour is *life*. Is that not enough?

WILLIAM MORRIS, (1834–1896) British artist, writer, printer. Hammond, in *News From Nowhere*, ch. 15 (1891).

14 Perpetual devotion to what a man calls his business, is only to be sustained by perpetual neglect of many other things.

ROBERT LOUIS STEVENSON, (1850–1894) Scottish novelist, essayist, poet. *Virginibus Puerisque*, "An Apology for Idlers" (1881).

15 All aglow is the work.

VIRGIL [PUBLIUS VERGILIUS MARO], (70–19 B.C.) Roman poet. *Georgics*, bk. 4, l. 169 (29 B.C.), trans. by H. Rushton Fairclough (1967).

Virgil compares bees to Vulcan's workmen, the Cyclopes.

16 Work is the curse of the drinking classes.

OSCAR WILDE, (1854–1900) Anglo-Irish playwright, author. Quoted in *Life of Oscar Wilde*, ch. 12, Hesketh Pearson (1946).

17 The fascination of what's difficult
Has dried the sap out of my veins,
   and rent
Spontaneous joy and natural content
Out of my heart.

WILLIAM BUTLER YEATS, (1865–1939) Irish poet, playwright. "The Fascination of What's Difficult," *The Green Helmet and Other Poems* (1910).

Working Class, the

1 The working-class ... is now issuing from its hiding-place to assert an Englishman's heaven-born privilege of doing as he likes, and is beginning to perplex us by marching where it likes, meeting where it likes, bawling what it likes, breaking what it likes.

MATTHEW ARNOLD, (1822–1888) British poet, critic. *Culture and Anarchy*, ch. 3 (1869).

2 The history of all countries shows that the working class exclusively by its own effort is able to develop only trade-union consciousness.

VLADIMIR ILYICH LENIN, (1870–1924) Russian revolutionary leader. *What Is To Be Done?* ch. 2, sct. A (1902).

The pamphlet's title was originally the title of N.G. Chernyshevsky's novel of 1863, which expounded the author's ideas of true revolutionary practise, and was later regarded as a classic in the Soviet Union.

3 Really, if the lower orders don't set us a good example, what on earth is the use of them? They seem, as a class, to have absolutely no sense of moral responsibility.

OSCAR WILDE, (1854–1900) Anglo-Irish playwright, author. Algernon, in *The Importance of Being Earnest*, act 1 (1895).

World War I

1 Their bodies are buried in peace; but their name liveth for evermore.

APOCRYPHA, *Ecclesiasticus*, 44:14.

The line "their name liveth for evermore" was chosen by Rudyard Kipling on behalf of the Imperial War Graves Commission as an epitaph to be used in Commonwealth War Cemeteries. Kipling had himself lost a son in the fighting.

2 Now, God be thanked Who has matched us with His hour,
And caught our youth, and wakened us from sleeping,
With hand made sure, clear eye, and sharpened power,
To turn, as swimmers into cleanness leaping.

RUPERT BROOKE, (1887–1915) British poet. "Peace," *1914 and Other Poems* (1915). *New Numbers*, no. 4 (1914).

3 Keep the home fires burning,
While your hearts are yearning,
Though your lads are far away
They dream of home.
There's a silver lining
Through the dark cloud shining;
Turn the dark cloud inside out,
Till the boys come home.

LENA GUILBERT FORD, (1870–1916) U.S. poet. "Till the Boys Come Home!" (Song) (1914).

4 The lamps are going out all over Europe; we shall not see them lit again in our lifetime.

SIR EDWARD GREY, (1862–1933) British statesman. *Twenty-Five Years*, vol. 2, ch. 18 (1925). Remark, Aug. 3, 1914 (eve of Britain's declaration of war against Germany), London.

5 What God abandoned, these
   defended,
   And saved the sum of things for pay.

A.E. (ALFRED EDWARD) HOUSMAN,
(1859–1936) British poet. "Epitaph on an Army
of Mercenaries," no. 37, *Last Poems* (1922).
Repr. in *The Collected Poems of A.E. Housman*
(1939).

6 Oh what a lovely war!

JOAN LITTLEWOOD, (b. 1914) British stage
director. "Song and title of stage show" (stage
show, 1963; film, 1969).

7 I hope we may say that thus, this
   fateful morning, came to an end all
   wars.

DAVID LLOYD GEORGE, (1863–1945)
British Liberal politician, prime minister.
Hansard, col. 2463. Speech, Nov. 11, 1918,
House of Commons, London.

On the day that the armistice was signed
between the allied powers and Germany. *The
war that will end war* had already been used as
the title of a novel by H.G. Wells (1914).

8 There died a myriad,
   And of the best, among them,
   For an old bitch gone in the teeth,
   For a botched civilization.

EZRA POUND, (1885–1972) U.S. poet,
critic. *Hugh Selwyn Mauberley,* "E.P. Ode
Pour l'Election de Son Sépulchre," pt. 5 (1920).

9 As a lover of truth, the national propaganda of all the belligerent
   nations sickened me. As a
   lover of civilization, the return to
     barbarism appalled me.

**BERTRAND RUSSELL [LORD RUSSELL,
3RD EARL],** (1872–1970) British philosopher, mathematician. *The Autobiography of
Bertrand Russell,* vol. 2, ch. 1 (1968).

Referring to World War I.

10 All of you young people who served
    in the war. You are a lost genera-
    tion.... You have no respect for any-
    thing. You drink yourselves to
    death.

GERTRUDE STEIN, (1874–1946) U.S.
author. Quoted in *A Moveable Feast,* ch. 3,
Ernest Hemingway (1964).

Remark to Hemingway, used by him as the
epigraph in *The Sun Also Rises* (1926).

World War II

1 Gracious Lord, oh bomb the
   Germans.
   Spare their women for Thy Sake,
   And if that is not too easy
   We will pardon Thy Mistake.
   But gracious Lord, whate'er shall
     be,
   Don't let anyone bomb me.

JOHN BETJEMAN, (1906–1984) British
poet. "In Westminster Abbey," st. 2, *Old
Lights for New Chancels* (1940).

2 Springtime for Hitler and
   Germany,
   Winter for France and Poland.

MEL BROOKS, (b. 1926) U.S. filmmaker,
screen actor. Max Bialystok (Zero Mostel), in
The Producers (film) (1968).

3 This morning the British Ambassador in Berlin handed the German
   Government a final Note stating
   that, unless we heard from them by
   11 o'clock that they were prepared
   at once to withdraw their troops
   from Poland, a state of war would
   exist between us. I have to tell you
   now that no such undertaking has
   been received, and that conse-
   quently this country is at war with
   Germany.

NEVILLE CHAMBERLAIN, (1869–1940)
British politician, prime minister. *The Penguin
Book of Twentieth Century Speeches,* ed.
Brian MacArthur (1992). BBC Radio broad-
cast, Sept. 3, 1939, on the declaration of war.

4 Let us therefore brace ourselves to
   our duties, and so bear ourselves
   that if the British Empire and its

Commonwealth last for a thousand years, men will still say, "This was their finest hour."

SIR WINSTON CHURCHILL, (1874–1965) British statesman, writer. Vol. 6, *Winston S. Churchill: His Complete Speeches, 1897-1963,* ed. Robert Rhodes James (1974). Speech, June 18, 1940, House of Commons, London.

Announcing the fall of France, and the start of the "Battle of Britain." Two days later, a week after the Germans had entered Paris, France concluded an armistice with Germany.

5 France has lost a battle. But France has not lost the war!

CHARLES DE GAULLE, (1890–1970) French general, president. *Speeches of General de Gaulle* (1941). Speech, broadcast June 18, 1940, from London.

De Gaulle's famous words were not part of the official typescript for this speech, and not issued in written form until the following month.

6 And while I am talking to you mothers and fathers, I give you one more assurance. I have said this before, but I shall say it again and again and again: Your boys are not going to be sent into any foreign wars.

FRANKLIN DELANO ROOSEVELT, (1882–1945) U.S. Democratic politician, president. *Public Papers and Addresses of Franklin D. Roosevelt,* vol. 9 (1941). Speech, Oct. 30, 1940, Boston.

Roosevelt made the speech while campaigning for his third term as president. He declared war against Japan just over a year later, the day following Japan's attack on Pearl Harbor, Dec. 7, 1941—denounced by Roosevelt as "a date which will live on in infamy."

World, the

1 The world is gradually becoming a place
Where I do not care to be any more.

JOHN BERRYMAN, (1914–1972) U.S. poet. *His Toy, His Dream, His Rest,* no. 149 (1968).

Berryman ended his life by jumping off a bridge over the Mississippi River.

2 What is this world? what asketh men to have?
Now with his love, now in his colde grave
Allone, withouten any compaignye.

GEOFFREY CHAUCER, (1340–1400) British poet. *The Canterbury Tales,* Arcite, in "The Knight's Tale," l. 2777-9 (c. 1387-1400), repr. in *The Works of Geoffrey Chaucer,* ed. Alfred W. Pollard, et al. (1898).

3 That cold accretion called the world, which, so terrible in the mass, is so unformidable, even pitiable, in its units.

THOMAS HARDY, (1840–1928) British novelist, poet. *Tess of the D'Urbervilles,* ch. 13 (1891).

4 The world is a fine place and worth fighting for.

ERNEST HEMINGWAY, (1899–1961) U.S. author. Robert Jordan, in *For Whom the Bell Tolls,* ch. 43 (1940).

5 Call the world if you please "the vale of soul-making." Then you will find out the use of the world.

JOHN KEATS, (1795–1821) British poet. *Letters of John Keats,* no. 123, ed. Frederick Page (1954). Letter, written Feb. 14-May 3, 1819, to his brother and sister-in-law, George and Georgiana Keats.

6 This whole world is wild at heart and weird on top.

DAVID LYNCH, (b. 1947) U.S. filmmaker. Lula (Laura Dern), in *Wild at Heart* (film) (1990).

7 But you think ... that it is time for me to have done with the world, and so I would if I could get into a better before I was called into the best, and not die here in a rage, like a poisoned rat in a hole.

JONATHAN SWIFT, (1667–1745) Anglo-Irish satirist. *The Correspondence of Jonathan Swift*, vol. 3. Letter, March 21, 1729, to statesman and author Viscount Bolingbroke.

Worldliness

1   I have been in love, and in debt, and in drink,
    This many and many a year.

ALEXANDER BROME, (1620–1666) British poet. "The Mad Lover," *Songs and Other Poems*, 2nd ed. (1664).

Opening lines.

2   He, in his developed manhood, stood,
    A little sunburnt by the glare of life.

ELIZABETH BARRETT BROWNING, (1806–1861) British poet. "Aurora Leigh," bk. 4, l. 1139-40 (1857).

Referring to Aurora's cousin, Romney Leigh.

Worship

1   Thou shalt not make unto thee any graven image, or any likeness of any thing that is in heaven above, or that is in the earth beneath, or that is in the water under the earth.

BIBLE: HEBREW, *Exodus*, 20:4. The second commandment.

2   Walking, and leaping, and praising God.

BIBLE: NEW TESTAMENT, *Acts*, 3:8. Referring to the miraculous recovery of a lame man, through the intervention of Peter.

3   Worship is transcendent wonder.

THOMAS CARLYLE, (1795–1881) Scottish essayist, historian. *On Heroes and Hero-Worship*, lecture 1, "The Hero as Divinity" (1841).

4   Man, so long as he remains free, has no more constant and agonizing

anxiety than find as quickly as possible someone to worship.

FEODOR DOSTOYEVSKY, (1821–1881) Russian novelist. Ivan Karamazov, in *The Brothers Karamazov*, bk. 5, ch. 5 (published 1879-1880), trans. by David Magarshak (1958).

Reporting the words of the Grand Inquisitor.

Worth

1   If a thing is worth doing, it is worth doing badly.

GILBERT KEITH CHESTERTON, (1874–1936) British author. *What's Wrong With the World*, pt. 4, ch. 14 (1910).

2   What is a weed? A plant whose virtues have not yet been discovered.

RALPH WALDO EMERSON, (1803–1882) U.S. essayist, poet, philosopher. *Fortune of the Republic* (1878).

3   The real price of everything, what everything really costs to the man who wants to acquire it, is the toil and trouble of acquiring it.

ADAM SMITH, (1723–1790) Scottish economist. *The Wealth of Nations*, vol. 1, bk. 1, ch. 5 (1776).

Writers and Writing

1   Everyone thinks writers must know more about the inside of the human head, but that is wrong. They know less, that's why they write. Trying to find out what everyone else takes for granted.

MARGARET ATWOOD, (b. 1939) Canadian novelist, poet, critic. *Dancing Girls*, "Lives of the Poets" (1977).

2   No poet or novelist wishes he were the only one who ever lived, but most of them wish they were the

only one alive, and quite a number fondly believe their wish has been granted.

W.H. (WYSTAN HUGH) AUDEN, (1907–1973) Anglo-American poet. *The Dyer's Hand*, pt. 1, "Writing" (1962).

3   It took me fifteen years to discover that I had no talent for writing, but I couldn't give it up because by that time I was too famous.

ROBERT BENCHLEY, (1889–1945) U.S. humorous writer. Quoted in *Robert Benchley*, ch. 1, Nathaniel Benchley (1955).

4   Essential characteristic of the really great novelist: a Christ-like, all-embracing compassion.

ARNOLD BENNETT, (1867–1931) British novelist. *The Journals of Arnold Bennett*, ed. Frank Swinnerton (1932). Entry, Oct. 25, 1897.

5   No one who cannot limit himself has ever been able to write.

NICOLAS BOILEAU-DESPRÉAUX, (1636–1711) French poet, critic. "L'Art Politique," cto. 1, l. 63 (1674).

6   The aim, if reached or not, makes great the life:
Try to be Shakespeare, leave the rest to fate!

ROBERT BROWNING, (1812–1889) British poet. "Bishop Blougram's Apology," l. 491-2, *Men and Women*, vol. 1 (1855).

7   Without, or with, offence to friends or foes,
I sketch your world exactly as it goes.

GEORGE GORDON NOEL BYRON, 6TH BARON BYRON, (1788–1824) British poet. *Don Juan*, cto. 8, st. 89 (1819-1824).

8   Who often, but without success, have prayed
For apt Alliteration's artful aid.

CHARLES CHURCHILL, (1731–1764) British clergyman, poet. "The Prophecy of Famine," l. 85-6 (1763).

9   I shall christen this style the Mandarin, since it is beloved by literary pundits, by those who would make the written word as unlike as possible to the spoken one. It is the style of all those writers whose tendency is to make their language convey more than they mean or more than they feel, it is the style of most artists and all humbugs.

CYRIL CONNOLLY, (1903–1974) British critic. *Enemies of Promise*, ch. 2 (1938).

Referring to a style of English prose popularized by authors such as Addison—"responsible for many of the evils from which English prose has since suffered. He made prose artful and whimsical, he made it sonorous when sonority was not needed, affected when it did not require affectation."

10   The more books we read, the clearer it becomes that the true function of a writer is to produce a masterpiece and that no other task is of any consequence.

CYRIL CONNOLLY, (1903–1974) British critic. *The Unquiet Grave*, pt. 1 (1944, rev. 1951).

11   Writers are always selling somebody out.

JOAN DIDION, (b. 1934) U.S. essayist. *Slouching Towards Bethlehem*, preface (1968).

12   An author who speaks about his own books is almost as bad as a mother who talks about her own children.

BENJAMIN DISRAELI, (1804–1881) British statesman, author. quoted in *Times* (London, Nov. 20, 1873). Speech, Nov. 19, 1873, Glasgow.

At a banquet given by the city of Glasgow to Disraeli, on his inauguration as Lord Rector of Glasgow University.

13 Each venture
Is a new beginning, a raid on the
    inarticulate
With shabby equipment always
    deteriorating
In the general mess of imprecision
    of feeling.

T.S. (THOMAS STEARNS) ELIOT,
(1888–1965) Anglo-American poet, critic.
"East Coker," pt. 5 (1940). *Four Quartets*
(1942).

14 Writing, madam, 's a mechanic
part of wit! A gentleman should
never go beyond a song or a *billet*.

GEORGE ETHEREGE, (1635–1691) British
dramatist, diplomat. Sir Fopling, in *The Man
of Mode*, act 4, sc. 1 (1676).

15 I encountered the mama of dada
again ... and as usual withdrew
worsted.

CLIFTON FADIMAN, (b. 1904) U.S.
essayist. *Party of One*, p. 90 (1955).

Referring to Gertrude Stein.

16 All good writing is *swimming under
water* and holding your breath.

F. SCOTT FITZGERALD, (1896–1940)
U.S. author. *The Crack-Up*, ed. Edmund Wil-
son (1945). Letter (undated) to his daughter
Frances Scott Fitzgerald.

17 My idea is always to reach my
generation. The wise writer ...
writes for the youth of his own
generation, the critics of the next,
and the schoolmasters of ever
afterward.

F. SCOTT FITZGERALD, (1896–1940)
U.S. author. "Self-interview," published in
New York Tribune (May 7, 1920). Repr. in
Matthew J. Bruccoli's biography, *Some Sort of
Epic Grandeur*, ch. 16 (1981).

The interview was later used by Fitzgerald in
The Author's Apology, a letter to the American Booksellers Convention, May 1920.

18 Often I think writing is a sheer paring away of oneself leaving always
something thinner, barer, more
meager.

F. SCOTT FITZGERALD, (1896–1940)
U.S. author. *The Letters of F. Scott Fitzgerald*,
ed. Andrew Turnbull (1963). Letter, April 27,
1940, to his daughter Frances Scott Fitzgerald.

19 Any fool may write a most valuable
book by chance, if he will only tell
us what he heard and saw, with
veracity.

THOMAS GRAY, (1716–1771) British poet.
Correspondence of Thomas Gray, vol. 3, ed.
H.W. Starr (1971). Letter, Feb. 25, 1768, to
Horace Walpole.

20 A serious writer is not to be con-
founded with a solemn writer. A
serious writer may be a hawk or a
buzzard or even a popinjay, but a
solemn writer is always a bloody
owl.

ERNEST HEMINGWAY, (1899–1961) U.S.
author. *Death in the Afternoon*, ch. 16 (1932).

21 The most essential gift for a good
writer is a built-in, shock-proof,
shit detector. This is the writer's
radar and all great writers have
had it.

ERNEST HEMINGWAY, (1899–1961) U.S.
author. Interview in *Writers at Work*, Second
Series, ed. George Plimpton (1963). First published in *Paris Review* (Flushing, NY, spring
1958).

22 In all pointed sentences, some
degree of accuracy must be sacrificed to conciseness.

SAMUEL JOHNSON, (1709–1784) British
author, lexicographer. "On the Bravery of the
English Common Soldier," *The British Magazine* (Jan. 1760). Repr. in *Works of Samuel
Johnson, LL.D.*, vol. 10, ed. Sir John Hawkins
(1787) and *Works of Samuel Johnson*,
Yale Edition, vol. 10.

23 The greatest part of a writer's time is spent in reading, in order to write; a man will turn over half a library to make one book.

SAMUEL JOHNSON, (1709–1784) British author, lexicographer. Quoted in James Boswell, *Life of Dr. Johnson*, entry, April 6, 1775 (1791).

24 One man is as good as another until he has written a book.

BENJAMIN JOWETT, (1817–1893) British scholar, essayist. Quoted in *The Life and Letters of Benjamin Jowett*, vol. 1, ch. 8, eds. Evelyn Abbott and Lewis Campbell (1897).

25 Making a book is a craft, like making a clock; it needs more than native wit to be an author.

JEAN DE LA BRUYÈRE, (1645–1696) French writer, moralist. *Characters*, "Of Books," aph. 3 (1688).

26 I always write a good first line, but I have trouble in writing the others.

MOLIÈRE [JEAN BAPTISTE POQUELIN], (1622–1673) French dramatist. Mascarille, in *Les Précieuses Ridicules*, sc. 11, l. 122 (1659).

27 A writer is unfair to himself when he is unable to be hard on himself.

MARIANNE MOORE, (1887–1972) U.S. poet. Interview in *Writers at Work*, Second Series, ed. George Plimpton (1963).

28 The last thing one discovers in composing a work is what to put first.

BLAISE PASCAL, (1623–1662) French scientist, philosopher. *Pensées*, no. 976, ed. Krailsheimer; no. 19, ed. Brunschvicg (1670, trans. 1688), rev. A.J. Krailsheimer (1966).

29 True ease in writing comes from art, not chance,
As those move easiest who have learned to dance.

'Tis not enough no harshness gives offence,
The sound must seem an echo to the sense.

ALEXANDER POPE, (1688–1744) British satirical poet. "An Essay on Criticism," l. 362-5 (1711).

30 Why did I write? what sin to me unknown
Dipt me in ink, my parents', or my own?

ALEXANDER POPE, (1688–1744) British satirical poet. "Epistle to Dr. Arbuthnot," l. 125-6 (1735).

31 Thus, with child to speak, and helpless in my throes,
Biting my truant pen, beating myself for spite:
Fool! said my muse to me, look in thy heart, and write.

SIR PHILIP SIDNEY, (1554–1586) British poet, diplomat, soldier. "Astrophel and Stella," sonnet 1 (1591).

32 Writing, when properly managed (as you may be sure I think mine is) is but a different name for conversation.

LAURENCE STERNE, (1713–1768) British author. *Tristram Shandy*, bk. 2, ch. 11 (1759-1767).

33 O Grub Street! how do I bemoan thee,
Whose graceless children scorn to own thee!
... Yet *thou* hast greater cause to be Ashamed of them, than they of thee.

JONATHAN SWIFT, (1667–1745) Anglo-Irish satirist. "On Poetry: A Rhapsody," l. 357-64 (1733), repr. in *The Poems of Jonathan Swift*, ed. H. Williams (1958).

Dr Johnson, in his *Dictionary* of 1755, defined *Grub Street*: "Originally the name of a street in

Moorfields in London, much inhabited by writers of small histories, dictionaries, and temporary poems, whence any mean production is called *grubstreet*."

34   Three hours a day will produce as much as a man ought to write.

ANTHONY TROLLOPE, (1815–1882) British novelist. *Autobiography*, ch. 15 (1883).

35   It is dangerous to leave written that which is badly written. A chance word, upon paper, may destroy the world. Watch carefully and erase, while the power is still yours, I say to myself, for all that is put down, once it escapes, may rot its way into a thousand minds, the corn become a black smut, and all libraries, of necessity, be burned to the ground as a consequence. Only one answer: write carelessly so that nothing that is not green will survive.

WILLIAM CARLOS WILLIAMS, (1883–1963) U.S. poet. *Paterson*, bk. 3, "The Library," sct. 3 (1949, rev. 1963).

36   We are nauseated by the sight of trivial personalities decomposing in the eternity of print.

VIRGINIA WOOLF, (1882–1941) British novelist. *The Common Reader*, "The Modern Essay," First Series (1925).Referring to inferior essayists.

Youth

1   It is good for a man that he bear the yoke in his youth.

BIBLE: HEBREW, *Lamentations of Jeremiah*, 3:27.

2   Rejoice, O young man, in thy youth; and let thy heart cheer thee in the days of thy youth, and walk in the ways of thine heart, and in the sight of thine eyes: but know thou, that for all these things God will bring thee into judgment.

BIBLE: HEBREW, *Ecclesiastes*, 11:9.

3   O yonge fresshe folkes, he or she,
In which that love up-groweth with your age,
Repeyreth hoom fro worldly vanitee,
And of your herte up-casteth the visage
To thilke God that after his image
Yow made, and thynketh al nis but a faire
This world, that passeth sone as floures faire.

GEOFFREY CHAUCER, (1340–1400) British poet. *Troilus and Criseyde*, bk. 5, l. 1835-41 (c. 1385), repr. in *The Works of Geoffrey Chaucer*, ed. Alfred W. Pollard, etc. (1898).

4   I remember my youth and the feeling that will never come back any more—the feeling that I could last for ever, outlast the sea, the earth, and all men; the deceitful feeling that lures us on to joys, to perils, to love, to vain effort—to death; the triumphant conviction of strength, the heat of life in the handful of dust, the glow in the heart that with every year grows dim, grows cold, grows small, and expires—and expires, too soon, too soon—before life itself.

JOSEPH CONRAD, (1857–1924) Polish-born British novelist. Marlow, in *Youth* (1902).

5   We live in an age when to be young and to be indifferent can be no longer synonymous. We must prepare for the coming hour. The claims of the Future are represented by suffering millions; and the

Youth of a Nation are the trustees of Posterity.

BENJAMIN DISRAELI, (1804–1881) British statesman, author. *Sybil*, bk. 6, ch. 13 (1845).

Closing words of novel.

6 He wears the rose
Of youth upon him, from which the world should note
Something particular.

WILLIAM SHAKESPEARE, (1564–1616) British dramatist, poet. Mark Antony, in *Antony and Cleopatra*, act 3, sc. 13, l. 19-21 (1623).

Referring to Octavius Caesar.

7 All appeared new, and strange at first, inexpressibly rare and delightful and beautiful. I was a little stranger, which at my entrance into the world was saluted and surrounded with innumerable joys. My knowledge was divine. I knew by intuition those things which since my Apostasy, I collected again by the highest reason.

THOMAS TRAHERNE, (1636–1674) British clergyman, poet, mystic. *Centuries of Meditations*, "Third Century," no. 2 (written c. 1672, first published 1908).

Youth and Age

1 What Youth deemed crystal, Age finds out was dew.

ROBERT BROWNING, (1812–1889) British poet. "Jochanan Hakkadosh," st. 101, *Jocoseria* (1883).

2 If ye live enough befure thirty ye won't care to live at all afther fifty.

FINLEY PETER DUNNE, (1867–1936) U.S. journalist, humorist. *Dooley's Opinions*, "Casual Observations," (1901).

3 Crabbed age and youth cannot live together:
Youth is full of pleasance, age is full of care;
Youth like summer morn, age like winter weather;
Youth like summer brave, age like winter bare.

WILLIAM SHAKESPEARE, (1564–1616) British dramatist, poet. "The Passionate Pilgrim, Poem" 12 (1599).

Shakespeare's authorship of *The Passionate Pilgrim* has never been proved.

4 The denunciation of the young is a necessary part of the hygiene of older people, and greatly assists the circulation of their blood.

LOGAN PEARSALL SMITH, (1865–1946) U.S. essayist, aphorist. *All Trivia*, "Last Words (1933).

Zoos

1 A Robin Redbreast in a cage
Puts all Heaven in a Rage.

WILLIAM BLAKE, (1757–1827) British poet, painter, engraver. "Auguries of Innocence," l. 5-6, *Poems from the Pickering Manuscript* (c. 1803), repr. in *Complete Writings*, ed. Geoffrey Keynes (1957).

Index of Sources

Index of Key Words

Adult
To be a. ADULTHOOD/ADULT DEVELOPMENT, 3

Adultery
A. ADULTERY, 6; a. LUST, 2; committed a. ADULTERY, 3;
rather be taken in a. PROVINCIALISM, 2; shalt not
commit a. ADULTERY, 2

Advantage
them as take a. GETTING AHEAD, 3

Adventure
a. ADVENTURES AND ADVENTURERS, 1; awfully big a.
DEATH AND DYING, 5

Adventures
large spiritual a. CANADA AND THE CANADIANS, 1

Adversary
Treating your a. ENEMIES, 4

Adversity
A. ADVERSITY, 4; learn to endure a. ADVERSITY, 12;
Sweet are the uses of a. ADVERSITY, 11

Advertisement
Promise is. . . soul of an a. ADVERTISING, 2

Affection
a. HYPOCRISY, 2; Set your a. AFFECTION, 1

Affections
holiness of the heart's a. CERTAINTY, 4

Affliction
A. MISFORTUNE, 3

Afraid
not that I'm a. DEATH AND DYING, 2

Africa
new out of A. AFRICA AND AFRICANS, 4

Afternoon
At five in the a. AFTERNOON, 1; What'll we do with
ourselves this a. ENNUI, 1

Against
His hand will be a. OUTCASTS, 1

Age
A. OLD AGE, 1; A. SENSUALITY, 2; A. YOUTH AND AGE, 1;
At twenty years of a. AGE AND AGING, 5; dead center of
middle a. MIDDLE AGE, 1; Give me a girl at an impressionable a. TEACHERS, 10; in a. OLD AGE, 14; Judges
don't a. JUDGES, 1; lady of a certain a. AGE, 2; lee shore
of a. OLD AGE, 16; Men of a. OLD AGE, 2; Middle a.
MIDDLE AGE, 3; No woman should. . . be accurate
about her a. AGE, 7; Old a. OLD AGE, 9; revelation of
our a. OLD AGE, 4; what a thing is a. OLD AGE, 19

Aged
a. OLD AGE, 29

Agrees
person who a. AGREEMENT, 1

Aid
what's it all in a. CONFORMITY, 3

Ailments
a. COMPATIBILITY, 3

Air
Soun is noght but a. SPEECH, 3; Wild a. AIR, 1

Albatross
A. CURSES, 1

Albert
take a message to A. VICTORIA, QUEEN, 1

Alcohol
A. ALCOHOL, 3; A. ALCOHOL, 7

Alcoholism
Lying is like a. LIES AND LYING, 15

Ale
fed purely upon a. ALCOHOL, 8

Algebra
no such thing as a. MATHEMATICS, 4

Alive
Bliss was it in that dawn to be a. REVOLUTION:
FRENCH, 3; wish they were the only one a. WRITERS
AND WRITING, 2

All
one for a. FELLOWSHIP, 3

Allegiances
two simultaneous a. Satan VIRTUE AND VICE, 1

Alliance
A. ALLIANCES, 1; a. FRIENDS AND FRIENDSHIP, 16

Alliances
steer clear of permanent a. ALLIANCES, 4

Alliteration
A. WRITERS AND WRITING, 8

Alms
doest thine a. CHARITY, 2

Alone
A. LONELINESS, 2; fastest who travels a. SELF−SUFFI-
CIENCY, 2; I want to be a. SOLITUDE, 3; use sometimes
to be a. SOLITUDE, 4; we can survive a. ISOLATION, 1;
You'll never walk a. SOLIDARITY, 1

Along
If you want to get a. GETTING AHEAD, 5

Alpha
A. GOD, 3

Ambition
A. AMBITION, 10; A. AMBITION, 3; Vaulting a. AMBI-
TION, 9

Ambitions
All a. AMBITION, 4

Ambitious
as he was a. AMBITION, 8

Amen
A. END OF THE WORLD, 1

America
A. UNITED STATES, 7; A. UNITED STATES, 11; Being here
in A. UNITED STATES: PEOPLE OF, 9; Everybody in A.
COMPLACENCY, 2; everything in common with A. ENG-
LISH LANGUAGE, 1; God bless A. UNITED STATES, 3; In
A. TRAVELING AND TRAVELERS, 1; In A. UNITED
STATES: PEOPLE OF, 5; keep A. AMERICAN DREAM, 1;
like to be in A. UNITED STATES, 10; pure products of A.
UNITED STATES: PEOPLE OF, 13

American
A. CONFORMITY, 1; adult A. AFRICAN AMERICANS, 1;
blacks upon A. AFRICAN AMERICANS, 5; faults of A.
LANGUAGE, 2; I was born an A. UNITED STATES: PEO-

a. GOD, 23; Never trust the a. CRITICISM AND THE ARTS, 4

Artistic
A. ARTISTS, 2; a. ARTISTS, 3

Artists
A. ART AND SOCIETY, 1; As a. WOMEN: AND THE ARTS, 2

Ashes
beauty for a. WIDOWS, 1

Asia
A. ASIA, 5

Ask
A. FULFILLMENT, 1

Aspens
a. TREES, 4

Aspiration
our finest a. IDEALISM, 6

Assassination
A. ASSASSINATION, 1; A. ASSASSINATION, 4

Assault
words of racial or sexual a. WORDS, 12

Assent
A. DISSENT, 3

Astonish
A. WONDER, 3

Asylums
comfortably padded lunatic a. ARISTOCRACY, 12

Atheism
God never wrought miracle to convince a. ATHEISM, 1; owlet A. ATHEISM, 3

Atheist
embittered a. ATHEISM, 4

Atom
no evil in the a. NUCLEAR AGE, 5; unleashed power of the a. NUCLEAR AGE, 4

Attack
A. ATTACK, 2

Attacked
rather be a. CRITICISM AND THE ARTS, 2

Attention
a. FAILURE, 8

Attorney
he is an a. LAWYERS, 2

Aunt William
A. GIVE AND TAKE, 2

Auschwitz
day's work at A. CULTURE, 6

Author
a. WRITERS AND WRITING, 12; native wit to be an a. WRITERS AND WRITING, 25

Authority
A. AUTHORITY, 1

Authors
damn those a. CRITICS, 3; invades a. PLAGIARISM, 2; praise of ancient a. BOOKS: CLASSICS, 1

Autobiography
a. AUTOBIOGRAPHY, 1

Autolycus
My father named me A. THIEVES AND THIEVERY, 3

Autumn
A. AUTUMN, 1; harmony/In a. AUTUMN, 4

Avarice
A. ECONOMY, THE, 2; A. GREED, 5; I must take up with a. GREED, 4

Awake
We are a. DREAMS AND DREAMING, 8

Azure
Beneath the a. SEA, 7

Babes
Out of the mouth of b. BABIES, 1

Babies
milk into b. BABIES, 2; who hates dogs and b. ECCENTRICITY, 1

Baby
When the first b. FAIRIES, 2

Babylon
a modern B. LONDON, 2; By the rivers of B. EXILE, 1

Backwards
walking b. REACTIONARIES, 1

Bad taste
harmony in b. TASTE, 2

Bad
When b. ALLIANCES, 2

Baggage
b. CRITICISM, 2

Baldness
b. BALDNESS, 1; far side of b. BALDNESS, 2

Ballet
can never be a b. DANCE, 6

Ban
recommend they b. CENSORSHIP, 2

Bananas
they have no b. CONTRADICTION, 4

Bane
all good to me becomes/B. OPPOSITES, 2

Bank
compared with founding a b. BANKING AND CURRENCY, 1; cry all the way to the b. CRITICISM AND THE ARTS, 5

Bankers
Bats have no b. ANIMALS, 1

Baptism
slave of my b. PARENTS, 5

Barabbas
crowd will always save B. CROWDS, 1

Barb
no more steely b. INFINITY, 1

Barbarians
without the b. BARBARISM, 1

Barbarism
from b. UNITED STATES, 5; return to b. WORLD WAR I, 9

Barge
b. CLEOPATRA, 3

Barricks
single men in b. ARMY, 11
Baseball
better learn b. BASEBALL, 1
Bastard
all my eggs in one b. ABORTION, 1
Bastards
at first princes' b. ARISTOCRACY, 2
Bathe
B. HYGIENE, 1
Bathtub
As a b. PASSION, 7
Bathurst
Dear B. HATE, 4
Battles
jewel and the mother of b. GULF WAR, THE, 1; winning small b. MEN: MASCULINITY, 6
Be
To b. DILEMMAS, 1
Beak
Take thy b. DESTINY, 4
Beam
B. DEPARTURE, 4
Beamish
b. DANGER, 1
Beast
beauty that killed the b. MONSTERS, 2
Beat
b. OPPRESSION, 4
Beautiful
better to be b. BEAUTY, 11; How b. VISIONARIES, 1; indisputably b. FLATTERY, 1
Beauty
B. BEAUTY, 1; B. BEAUTY, 10; B. BEAUTY, 3; b. BEAUTY, 5; b. CRITICISM AND THE ARTS, 3; I have loved the principle of b. KEATS, JOHN, 3; sat B. BEAUTY, 8; world's b. BEAUTY, 6
Bed
And so to b. BED, 3; long black passage up to b. BED, 4; lying awake in b. BED, 2; My mind is not a b. INDECISION, 1
Bedlam
general B. MADNESS, 11
Bee–hive
not good for the b. ENVIRONMENT, 2
Bee
doth the little busy b. INSECTS, 3
Beef
great eater of b. MEAT, 1; Where's the b. POLICY, 3
Beep
B. COMMUNICATION, 3
Beer
Life isn't all b. LEISURE, 3; They who drink b. ALCOHOL, 13
Beg
to b. PRIDE, 2

Beginning
Each venture/Is a new b. WRITERS AND WRITING, 13; end of the b. ENDURANCE, 2; In the b. CREATION, THE, 3; In my b. MORTALITY, 1
Behold
B. JESUS CHRIST, 1
Belial
wander forth the sons Of B. ALCOHOL AND DRUNKENNESS, 17
Belief
founded on a blind b. BELIEF, 5
Believe
I b. CREEDS, 2
Belif
abdication of B. BELIEF, 4
Belly
Better b. ALCOHOL, 24; does not mind his b. FOOD AND EATING, 8
Beloved
My b. LOVERS, 1
Benediction
Perpetual b. ANNIVERSARIES, 2
Benevolence
not from the b. SELF–INTEREST, 2
Berkeley
Bishop B. PHILOSOPHY AND PHILOSOPHERS, 11
Berliner
Ich bin ein B. GERMANY AND THE GERMANS, 2
Best–dressed
gentleman to be the b. DRESS, 10
Best–seller
b. BOOKS: BESTSELLERS, 1
Best
b. EXCELLENCE, 3; everything is for the b. OPTIMISM, 9; It was the b. REVOLUTION: FRENCH, 1
Betray
All things b. BETRAYAL, 4; guts to b. CAUSES, 3
Betrayal
defence against b. SUSPICION, 4
Beware
B. PREDICTION, 1
Bewitched
B. CONFUSION, 1
Bible
English B. BIBLE, 6; read the B. BIBLE, 3; We have used the B. constable's handbook BIBLE, 5
Bills
inflammation of his weekly b. BILLS, 1; not paying one's b. BILLS, 2; She Paid the B. EPITAPHS, 9
Binds
He who b. JOY, 1
Biographies
geniuses have the shortest b. BIOGRAPHY, 4
Biography
B. BIOGRAPHY, 1; B. BIOGRAPHY, 6; difficult. . . to write b. BIOGRAPHY, 8; Judas who writes the b. DISCIPLES, 3;

Celebrity
C. FAME, 9; C. FAME, 2

Cell
Life is. . . a solitary c. ISOLATION, 3

Censure
C. FAME, 8

Centre
My c. ATTACK, 1

Ceremony
thou idol c. CEREMONY, 1

Certain
nothing. . . c. CERTAINTY, 3

Certainties
if a man will begin with c. CERTAINTY, 1

Chains
nothing to lose but their c. REVOLUTION, 9

Chair
draw your c. STORIES AND STORYTELLING, 1

Chamber
throw myself down in my c. PRAYER, 3

Chance
write a most valuable book by c. WRITERS AND WRITING, 19

Change
c. CHANGE, 2; more things c. CHANGE, 3; necessary for everything to c. CHANGE, 4; not necessary to c. CHANGE, 1; O Time and C. OLD AGE, 28; ringing grooves of c. CHANGE, 6

Changing
exaggerated stress on not c. OBSTINACY, 3

Chapter
one c. DEATH, 20

Character
index of a man's c. WIVES, 5

Characters
c. FICTION, 4

Charity
C. CHARITY, 4; organized c. CHARITY, 3

Charm
What is c. CHARM, 3

Charming
c. CHARM, 2

Charms
Do not all c. PHILOSOPHY AND PHILOSOPHERS, 7

Chaste
C. PROMISCUITY, 3; My English text is c. OBSCENITY, 2; What. . . does a c. CHASTITY, 1

Chastity
c. CHASTITY, 2

Chattanooga
C. TRAINS, 3

Cheerful
c. GIFTS AND GIVING, 2

Cheese
c. FOOD AND EATING, 7; different kinds of c. FRANCE AND THE FRENCH, 5

Chequer–board
C. DESTINY, 3

Cherubic
Soft–C. LADIES, 1

Chess–board
c. SURVIVAL, 4

Chickens
Do not count your c. ANTICIPATION, 1

Child
anything. . . to change in the c. CHILDREN, 13; Become a C. CHRISTMAS, 2; c. ADULTHOOD/ADULT DEVELOPMENT, 4; c. CHILDREN, 12; c. CHILDREN, 20; c. CHILDREN, 7; healthy c. CHILDREN, 18; Monday's c. CHILDREN, 1; Tew bring up a c. UPBRINGING, 1; Train up a c. EDUCATION, 1; When I was a c. ADULTHOOD/ADULT DEVELOPMENT, 1

Childhood
c. CHILDHOOD, 1; C. CHILDHOOD, 4; c. CHILDHOOD, 5; one moment in c. CHILDHOOD, 2; Where c. CHILDHOOD, 6

Children
better reasons for having c. BIRTH CONTROL, 4; C. CHILDREN, 2; C. PARENTS, 7; How inimitably graceful c. DANCE, 5; Suffer the little c. CHILDREN, 5; violations committed by c. CHILDREN, 6; we do not like c. CHILDREN, 11; We shelter c. FRIENDS AND FRIENDSHIP, 25

Chime
set a c. LIFE, 24

Chivalry
age of c. CHIVALRY, 1; age of c. CHIVALRY, 2

Chocolate
entire box of c. VENICE, 1

Choose
strength to c. WISDOM, 4

Christ
C. ADVERSITY, 9; C. EVANGELISM, 1; C. ITALY AND THE ITALIANS, 6; Why did you kill C. JESUS CHRIST, 5

Christian
in what peace a C. DEATH AND DYING, 1; persuadest me to be a C. CONVERSION, 1; to form C. TEACHERS, 2

Christianity
loving C. CHRISTIANITY AND THE CHRISTIANS, 5

Christians
Whatever makes men good C. CITIZENSHIP, 5

Christmas
dreaming of a white C. CHRISTMAS, 1

Church clock
Stands the C. HERITAGE, 1, 2

Church
Some keep the Sabbath going to C. SUNDAY AND THE SABBATH, 2

Cibber
C. POETRY AND POETS, 51

Cigarette
C. SMOKING AND SMOKERS, 9; C. SMOKING AND SMOKERS, 10

NISM, 1

Communists
theory of the C. COMMUNISM, 7

Company
C. COMPANY, 6; crowd is not c. LOVE, 2; give me your bill of c. DINNER PARTIES, 4; My idea of good c. COMPANY, 1; Tell me thy c. COMPANY, 4

Complainers
loudest c. COMPLAINT, 2

Complaints
When c. COMPLAINT, 4

Complies
c. OBEDIENCE, 2

Compliment
c. COMPLIMENTS, 1

Compositions
Read your own c. EDITING, 3

Compromise
c. COMPROMISE, 1

Conceited
c. VANITY, 1

Conceivable
every c. BIRTH CONTROL, 3

Conceived
There is a man child c. DESPAIR, 1

Conception
c. DOUBTS, 2

Concepts
up the stairs of his c. AMBITION, 11

Confession
no refuge from c. CONFESSION, 3

Confinement
solitary c. ISOLATION, 4

Conformity
C. CONFORMITY, 2

Congress
American criminal class except C. CONGRESS (U.S.), 1

Conquered
I will be c. DEATH AND DYING, 28

Conquest
c. EMPIRES, 2

Conscience
C. CONSCIENCE, 8; C. CONSCIENCE, 2; c. DELIBERATION, 3; clear c. CONSCIENCE, 5; man's c. CONSCIENCE, 4; Non–Conformist C. CONSCIENCE, 1

Conservatism
What is c. CONSERVATIVES, 3

Conservative
C. CONSERVATIVES, 1; makes a man more c. CONSERVATIVES, 2; man's the true C. CONSERVATIVES, 4; most c. UNIONS, 1

Consistent
only completely c. CONSISTENCY, 1

Conspiracy
organized c. OPPRESSION, 7

Constitution
Like the British C. INCONSISTENCY, 2; proposed C.

Constitution (U.S.), 1

Constitutional
c. ROYALTY, 2

Constructive
most c. WOMEN, 33

Consul
C. DIPLOMACY, 1

Consumer
C. CONSUMER SOCIETY, 2

Consumption
Conspicuous c. CONSUMER SOCIETY, 3

Contemporaries
life of. . . his c. CONTEMPORARIES, 1

Contend
Let's c. QUARRELS, 1

Content
I have learned. . . to be c. CONTENTMENT, 1; That is the land of lost c. NOSTALGIA, 2

Contentment
peace and c. UTOPIAS, 1

Continent
man must have held his breath in the presence. NEW WORLD, THE, 3; On the C. ENGLAND AND THE ENGLISH, 16

Contraception
oral c. BIRTH CONTROL, 1

Contract
verbal c. CONTRACTS, 1

Contradiction
violent c. CONTRADICTION, 1

Contraries
Without c. OPPOSITES, 1

Controversy
ceases to be a subject of c. CONTROVERSY, 1

Conventionality
C. IRREVERENCE, 1

Conversation
different name for c. WRITERS AND WRITING, 32; no such thing as c. CONVERSATION, 5; stick on c. CONVERSATION, 3

Conversing
With thee c. CONVERSATION, 4

Converted
You have not c. ARGUMENT, 5

Cookery
Kissing don't last: c. COOKERY, 3

Coopers
in a world of Gary C. RACE, 1

Copperfield
David C. AUTOBIOGRAPHY, 2

Corn
al this new c. KNOWLEDGE, 8; c. COUNTRYSIDE, 3; c. COUNTRYSIDE, 6; two ears of c. FARMERS AND FARMING, 4

Corporation
C. BUSINESS AND COMMERCE, 2

may f. DECEPTION, 1
Foolish
f. CONTRADICTION, 2
Fools
F. RECKLESSNESS, 1; Let us be thankful for the f. FOOLS
AND FOLLIES, 8; suffer f. TOLERANCE, 1; To suckle f.
WIVES, 10; two f. POETRY AND POETS, 18; what f. FOOLS
AND FOLLIES, 6
Footfalls
F. REGRET, 3
Foppery
excellent f. ASTROLOGY, 2
Force
May the F. SCIENCE FICTION, 2; use of f. FORCE, 2;
Where f. FORCE, 4
Ford
I am a F. FORD, GERALD R., 1
Foreign policy
F. FOREIGN POLICY, 6
Foreign
perish in a f. TRANSLATION, 5
Forever
would you live f. ARMY, 7
Forget
Lest we forget<ND>lest we f. DEAD, THE, 6
Forgets
busy hand f. DIARIES, 1
Forgetting
memory against f. MEMORY, 5
Forgive
f. BORES, 4; stupid neither f. FORGIVENESS, 6
Forgot
Should auld acquaintance be f. NEW YEAR, 1
Forgotten
f. DEFEAT, 1; f. LOVE: ENDED, 11; If you would not be f.
IMMORTALITY, 4
Fornicated
f. MODERN TIMES, 2
Fortunes
of f. ADVERSITY, 6
Forty–five
At f. AGE: THE FORTIES, 1
Forty
F. AGE AND AGING, 1; fool at f. AGE: THE FORTIES, 3;
Life begins at f. AGE: THE FORTIES, 2
Foxes
With f. CUNNING, 3
Foxholes
f. RACE, 5
Fragments
These f. SURVIVAL, 2
Frailty
f. WOMEN, 32
France
F. FRANCE AND THE FRENCH, 2; F. NAPOLEON BONA-
PARTE, 1; They order. . . this matter better in F.
FRANCE AND THE FRENCH, 7

Franklin
body/Of/Benjamin F. EPITAPHS, 4
Freak
world is for thousands a f. PERCEPTION, 2
Free
Man is born f. FREEDOM, 15; men naturally were born
f. LIBERTY, 5; no people ought to be f. DECOLONIZA-
TION, 1; thyng as any spirit f. LOVE, 12
Freedom
caged bird/sings of f. FREEDOM, 1; F. FREEDOM, 8; F.
FREEDOM, 9; f. FREEDOM, 2; F. FREEDOM, 13; f. FREE-
DOM, 17; F. FREEDOM, 3; F. FREEDOM, 7; F. NECESSITY,
4; F. REVOLUTION: AMERICAN, 2; None can love f. FREEDOM, 12;
SELF—SACRIFICE, 2; None can love f. FREEDOM, 12;
progress. . . of f. FREEDOM, 5
Freedoms
four essential human f. FREEDOM, 14
Freemen
He alone breaks from the van and the f.
WORDSWORTH, WILLIAM, 1; nation of f. DESTRUCTIVE-
NESS, 2
Frenchmen
Fifty million F. FRANCE AND THE FRENCH, 1
Frend
good f. EPITAPHS, 8
Freud
trouble with F. FREUD, SIGMUND, 2
Friday
My name's F. DETECTIVES, 3
Friend
A f. FRIENDS AND FRIENDSHIP, 11; f. FRIENDS AND
FRIENDSHIP, 12; Forsake not an old f. FRIENDS AND
FRIENDSHIP, 1; mistress. . . only after that a f. FRIEND-
SHIP AND LOVE, 2; no man is useless while he has a f.
FRIENDS AND FRIENDSHIP, 22; Whenever a f. FRIENDS
AND FRIENDSHIP, 24
Friendless
F. FRIENDLESSNESS, 1
Friendliness
impersonal insensitive f. UNITED STATES: PEOPLE OF, 11
Friends
f. FRIENDS AND FRIENDSHIP, 21; falling out of faithful
f. QUARRELS, 2; shameful to distrust one's f. TRUST, 3;
we want f. FRIENDS AND FRIENDSHIP, 14
Friendship
beginning of a beautiful f. FRIENDS AND FRIENDSHIP,
13; dupe of f. SELF—PITY, 1; F. FRIENDSHIP AND LOVE, 1;
F. FRIENDSHIP AND LOVE, 3; full joys of f. FRIENDS
AND FRIENDSHIP, 7; holy passion of f. FRIENDS AND
FRIENDSHIP, 23; keep his f. FRIENDS AND FRIENDSHIP,
17; Thy f. FRIENDS AND FRIENDSHIP, 5; wing of f. COM-
PANY, 5
Friendships
man's f. FRIENDS AND FRIENDSHIP, 6
Frigate
no F. BOOKS, 7

Glory

G. NATURE, 5; I go to g. LAST WORDS, 1; passeth the g. TRANSIENCE, 1; paths of g. GLORY, 3

Gloves

walk through the field in g. TOUCH, 2

God–like

Man. . . with his g. HUMANKIND, 8

God

every man with him was G. EXTREMISM, 1; G. CHILDREN, 14; G. CHRISTIANITY AND THE CHRISTIANS, 1; G. CONTENTMENT, 2; G. CREATION, THE, 7; G. GOD, 7; G. GOD, 9; G. GOD, 10; G. GOD, 12; G. GOD, 19; G. GOD, 20; G. GOD, 25; G. GOD, 6; G. HEAVEN, 3; G. MERCY, 4; Had I but served my G. LOYALTY, 5; honest G. GOD, 16; If G. GOD, 26; it's like kissing G. DRUGS, 2; Just are the ways of G. GOD, 21; may G. SAINTS, 5; My G. ABANDONMENT, 1; The world is charged with the grandeur of G. GOD, 14; they shall see G. PURITY, 1; Those who marry G. CHURCH, THE, 8; When G. CREATION, THE, 6; when g. CREATION, THE, 5; whom G. MARRIAGE, 5; "G. ABSENCE, 6

Goddamm

Lhude sing G. WINTER, 3

Goddess

concerning this great g. ART, 1

Gods

By the Nine G. OATHS, 1; civilization is destroyed. . . when its g. GODS AND GODDESSES, 5; convenient that there be g. GODS AND GODDESSES, 7; do not know much about g. RIVERS, 2; g. GODS AND GODDESSES, 8; man who would argue with the g. HEROES AND HEROINES, 22; no other g. GODS AND GODDESSES, 3; there are innumerable g. GODS AND GODDESSES, 4; When men make g. GODS AND GODDESSES, 6; Whom the g. TALENT, 2; Ye shall be as g. HUMANKIND, 4

Gold

O accursed hunger of g. MONEY, 23

Golden

repeat that on the G. JOKES AND JOKERS, 3

Good

Be g. GOODNESS, 2; g. NOSTALGIA, 1; g. OPTIMISM, 8; in me. . . dwelleth no g. FALLIBILITY, 1; really g. IDEALISM, 3; The g. FICTION, 7

Goodness

vulgar standard of g. GOODNESS, 3

Gorgonised

G. BRITISH, THE, 5

Gossip

G. GOSSIP, 6

Govern

He that would g. SELF–CONTROL, 2; No man is good enough to g. DEMOCRACY, 9

Government

Every country has the g. GOVERNMENT, 13; family is the basic cell of g. FAMILIES, 7; feeble g. GOVERNMENT, 5; For forms of G. GOVERNMENT, 15; Freedom of men under g. GOVERNMENT, 11; g. GOVERNMENT, 1; Good g. GOVERNMENT, 7; meddling g. GOVERNMENT, 12; people's g. GOVERNMENT, 17

Governments

G. GOVERNMENT, 16

Grace

G. COURAGE, 3; nor summer beauty hath such g. AUTUMN, 2

Gracefully

how to grow old g. OLD AGE AND AGING, 15

Grammar

G. GRAMMAR, SPELLING AND PUNCTUATION, 5

Grand

horror about everything g. GREATNESS, 11

Grape

G. WINE, 2

Grass

g. ESCAPE, 1

Gratitude

g. GRATITUDE, 1

Grave

lies a–moldering in the g. MARTYRS AND MARTYRDOM, 2

Graveyards

no bone to pick with g. GRAVES, 1

Gravy

for a person who disliked g. COMPATIBILITY, 2

Great

disbelief in g. GREATNESS, 6; g. GREATNESS, 10; G. GREATNESS, 15; g. GREATNESS, 3; g. POLITICS AND POLITICIANS, 13; I am not a g. FITZGERALD, F. SCOTT, 1; Some are born g. GREATNESS, 13; To be g. GREATNESS, 8

Greater

Thy necessity is yet g. NECESSITY, 7

Greatest

I am the g. SELF–PROMOTION, 1

Greatness

G. GREATNESS, 12; highest point of all my g. GLORY, 6; nature of all g. GREATNESS, 2

Greece

isles of G. GREECE AND THE GREEKS, 2

Greed

g. GREED, 2; not enough for everyone's g. GREED, 3

Greeks

you are G. ANCESTRY, 1

Green

g. GARDENS AND GARDENING, 3

Grey

little g. INTELLIGENCE, 1

Grief

G. GRIEF, 9; g. GRIEF, 10; Nothing becomes so offensive so quickly as g. GRIEF, 8; silent manliness of g. GRIEF, 5; such a capacity for genuine g. KENNEDY FAMILY, 1

Grimaces

gae mad at their g. PIETY, 2

THE, 2; keep your h. MATURITY, 2; Son of man hath
not where to lay his h. HOMELESS, THE, 1

Health
universal sickness implies an idea of h. NEUROSES, 1

Healthy
kind of h. COUNTRYSIDE, 5

Hear
h. GOSSIP, 2; time will come when you will h. VINDI-
CATION, 1

Heard
I will be h. RESOLVE, 2; you ain't h. SONGS, 2

Heart
h. ABSENCE, 3; his h. STRANGERS, 1; How else but
through a broken h. HEARTBREAK, 2; I twist my h.
OTHER PEOPLE, 2; my shrivelled h. VITALITY, 1; Open
my h. ITALY AND THE ITALIANS, 2; strings in the
human h. HEART, 1; that have a h. BLAME, 1

Heartbeat
h. PRESIDENT AND THE VICE PRESIDENT, 1

Hearts
live in h. DEATH, 13

Heav'n
built in h. ARCHITECTURE, 7

Heaven
distant from h. HEAVEN, 4; Heaven I'm in H. DANCE, 1;
in the day when h. ARMY, 8; silence in h. SILENCE, 1;
steep and thorny way to h. PREACHING, 4; voice from
h. HEAVEN, 2; what's a h. IDEALISM, 2

Hebraism
H. CLASSICISM AND ANTIQUITY, 1

Heels
upon the h. MARRIAGE, 12

Heifer
plowed with my h. CUNNING, 1

Heir
weeping of an h. INHERITANCE, 6

Heiresses
All h. INHERITANCE, 2

Helen
H. BEAUTY, 7

Helicon
watered our houses in H. INSPIRATION, 2

Hell
Better to reign in H. DEVIL, THE, 5; first found the
power. . . in his own h. PARADISE, 6; gates of H. HELL,
8; H. HELL, 4; H. HELL, 6; H. OTHER PEOPLE, 3; hot
from h. WAR, 28; I believe that I am in h. HELL, 7;
safest road to H. HELL, 5; starless air of H. HELL, 1

Hellespont
straight H. BREASTS, 2

Hello
H. GREETINGS, 3

Help
h. GODS, THE, 1; Who ran to h. MOTHERS, 4

Henry
Poor H. JAMES, HENRY, 3

Hero
Every h. HEROES AND HEROINES, 9; h. COWARDICE, 2;
h. HEROES AND HEROINES, 5; Show me a h. HEROES
AND HEROINES, 10

Heroes
have no h. HEROES AND HEROINES, 7; land. . . in need
of h. HEROES AND HEROINES, 1; make Britain a fit
country for h. HEROES AND HEROINES, 20; world
doesn't make any h. HEROES AND HEROINES, 12

Heroic
greatest obstacle to being h. HEROES AND HEROINES,
13

Heroism
opportunities for h. HEROES AND HEROINES, 25

Hew
When we h. or delve ECOLOGY, 1

Hierarchy
h. BUSINESS AND COMMERCE, 10

Highlands
heart's in the H. SCOTLAND AND THE SCOTS, 2

Hilarity
h. JOKES AND JOKERS, 2

Hill
we flung us on the windy h. JOY, 2

Hills
flee to my lodge in the h. VACATIONS, 1

Hired
they h. DEBT, 1

Historical
world–h. HISTORY, 13

Histories
H. HISTORY, 1; true h. HISTORY, 6

History
arms folded while others write h. NATIONALISM, 2;
greatest week in the h. Creation MOON, 5; h. COLD
WAR, THE, 4; h. CULTURE, 1; h. HISTORY, 9; H. HISTORY,
11; h. HISTORY, 16; H. HISTORY, 3; h. HISTORY, 5; h.
NATIONS, 2; longest suicide note in h. POLICY, 2;
nation without a h. HISTORY, 2; never learned anything from h. HISTORY, 12; people without h. HISTORY,
10; principal office of h. HISTORY, 15; writing h. CINE-
MA, 7

Hit
h. SUCCESS, 7

Hitler
If H. HITLER, ADOLF, 2; When H. NAZIS, 1

Hives
fill our h. CULTURE, 7

Hoard
sage does not h. GENEROSITY, 2

Hobby–Horse
man rides his H. ECCENTRICITY, 2

Holier
h. PURITY, 2

Hollywood
H. HOLLYWOOD, CALIFORNIA, 3; invited to H. HOLLY-
WOOD AND WRITERS, 2; phony tinsel of H. HOLLY-

WOOD, CALIFORNIA, 4

Holy Ghost
pencil of the H. BIBLE, 2

Home
H. HOUSES AND HOMES, 4; Keep the h. WORLD WAR I,
3; Should we have stayed at h. FOREIGN COUNTRIES, 2

Homely
h. WOMEN, 2

Homos
stately h. HOMOSEXUALITY, 1

Homosexual
no such thing as a h. SEXUALITY, 1

Homosexuality
preoccupied with his latent h. HOMOSEXUALITY, 4

Honest
few h. HONESTY, 1; H. HONESTY, 3

Honey
Pedigree of H. ARISTOCRACY, 5

Honor
cross of the Legion of H. AWARDS, 1; H. PARENTS, 1;
louder he talked of his h. HONOR, 1

Honour
H. BUSINESS AND COMMERCE, 7; h. HYPOCRISY, 8;
Loved I not h. HONOR, 2; peace cannot be maintained
with h. PEACE, 6

Hook
God. . . left the receiver off the h. END OF THE WORLD,
5

HOPE
ABANDON EVERY H. HELL, 2; H. HOPE, 2; nursing
the unconquerable h. HOPE, 1; reinforcement we may
gain from h. RESOLVE, 3; triumph of h. MARRIAGE:
REMARRIAGE, 3; what is H. HOPE, 3

Horny
h. WORK, 10

Horrible
h. LIFE, 3

Horror
h. HORROR, 1; Where there is no imagination there is
no h. HORROR, 2

Horse
behold a pale h. DEATH, 6; My kingdom for a h. HORS-
ES, 3; never look at another h. DOCTORS, 5

Horses
frighten the h. ENTHUSIASM, 1

Hostage
H. HOSTAGES, 1

Houndes
they been lyk to h. HABIT, 1

Hour
I also had my h. ANIMALS, 5; This was their finest h.
WORLD WAR II, 4

House
admiring the H. PARLIAMENT: HOUSE OF LORDS, 1; h.
HOUSES AND HOMES, 6; young and inexperienced h.
HOUSES AND HOMES, 5

Houses
H. HOUSES AND HOMES, 1; Have nothing in your h.
HOUSES AND HOMES, 7; plague o' both your h. QUAR-
RELS, 6; spaces between the h. CITIES AND CITY LIFE, 6

Hugging
I'm h. WHITES, 1

Human nature
great deal of h. HUMAN NATURE, 1

Human
h. AIDS, 1

Humanity
H. HUMANKIND, 6

Humble</heyword> We are so very [æumble] HUMILI-
TY, 2

Humiliated
you will always be h. POETRY AND POETS, 3

Humility
H. GENERALS, 3

Humor
H. HUMOR, 6; h. HUMOR, 3

Hunchback
h. HOBOS, 1

Hundred</keyword> first [100] days PRESIDENCY: U.S.,
3

Hunger
I offer only h. HEROES AND HEROINES, 11

Hungry
h. HUNGER, 4

Hunter
h. BURIAL, 2

Hunting
passion for h. HUNTING, 2

Hurry
Whoever is in a h. HASTE, 3

Husband
accept me as a h. HUSBANDS, 4; desire shall be to thy
h. WOMEN, 6; good h. HUSBANDS, 6; laugh at her h.
MARRIAGE, 17; little in drink. . . your faithful h. HUS-
BANDS, 8; My h. SPEECHES AND SPEECHMAKING, 5

Husbands
H. HUSBANDS, 2

Hymself
Ech man for h. SURVIVAL, 1

Hypocrisy
H. HYPOCRISY, 5; H. HYPOCRISY, 6; Making the world
safe for h. NAVY, THE, 5; man nor angel can discern H.
HYPOCRISY, 7; organised h. POLITICAL PARTIES, 4

Hypocrite
h. HYPOCRISY, 5; H. READING, 2

Hypocrites
not h. SLEEP, 4

Hypothesis
In order to shake a h. THEORY, 1

I
I. IDENTITY, 1; I. NAMES, 2

Iced
three parts i. AGE: THE THIRTIES, 1

IT
  It's just I. STYLE, 6
Italia
  I. ITALY AND THE ITALIANS, 4
Italy
  Creator made I. ITALY AND THE ITALIANS, 9; I. ITALY AND THE ITALIANS, 7; man who has not been in I. ITALY AND THE ITALIANS, 5
Ithaca
  When you set out for I. TRAVELING AND TRAVELERS, 3
Jabberrwock
  Beware the J. MONSTERS, 1
Jail
  get yourself a j. PRISON, 1; Go to j. PRISON, 2
Jam
  never j. PROMISES, 2
James
  less journalistic talent than J. JAMES, HENRY, 1; Mr. Henry J. JAMES, HENRY, 4
Jaw–jaw
  Better to j. NEGOTIATION, 1
Jazz
  J. TWENTIETH CENTURY: THE 1920S, 1
Jealous
  j. GOD, 2
Jealousy
  J. JEALOUSY, 2; J. JEALOUSY, 3; Nor j. JEALOUSY, 4
Jefferson
  when Thomas J. TALENT, 4
Jest
  Life is a j. COMEDY AND COMEDIANS, 3
Jests
  He j. JOKES AND JOKERS, 6; indebted to his memory for his j. FANTASY, 4
Jesus
  J. CIVILIZATION, 6; J. GRIEF, 1; more popular than J. CHRISTIANITY AND THE CHRISTIANS, 7; Yea Nay Creeping J. RELATIVITY, 1
Jew
  Christian was the theorizing J. JUDAISM AND JEWISH PEOPLE, 4; I determine who is a J. JUDAISM AND JEWISH PEOPLE, 3; what one J. JUDAISM AND JEWISH PEOPLE, 2
Jewelry
  Don't. . . wear artistic j. JEWELRY, 1; just rattle your j. APPLAUSE, 3
Jewish
  J. JUDAISM AND JEWISH PEOPLE, 4; national home for the J. PALESTINE, 1
Jiu–jitsu
  moral j. ACCEPTANCE, 2
Job
  Gizza j. UNEMPLOYMENT, 1
Johnson
  Dr. J. JOHNSON, DR. SAMUEL, 2
Joined
  name will be j. IMMORTALITY, 6

Joke
  dirty j. JOKES AND JOKERS, 4; life has been one great big j. JOKES AND JOKERS, 1
Jokes
  difference of tastes in j. HUMOR, 4; every ten j. JOKES AND JOKERS, 7; my little j. GOD, 11
Jolt
  sudden violent j. ALCOHOL, 4
Jostling
  no man lives without j. INJURY, 2
Journalism
  j. JOURNALISM AND JOURNALISTS, 1; J. PRESIDENCY: U.S., 7
Journalist
  Every j. JOURNALISM AND JOURNALISTS, 5
Journey
  j. MIDDLE AGE, 2; soul of a j. TRAVELING AND TRAVELERS, 6
Journeys
  J. TRAVELING AND TRAVELERS, 5
Joy
  full value of a j. JOY, 3; land of j. PARADISE, 7
Joys
  j. MELANCHOLY, 1
Judge
  J. JUDGMENT, 1; say that you are my j. JUDGMENT, 4; The cold neutrality of an impartial j. JUDGES, 3
Judges
  What harsh j. FATHER–SON RELATIONSHIPS, 2
Judgment
  fear more to deliver j. HERESY, 1
June
  J. SPRING, 3
Junk
  J. DRUGS, 3
Just
  cause is j. REVOLUTION: AMERICAN, 1; j. JUSTICE, 9
Justice
  J. JUSTICE, 6; Let j. JUSTICE, 5; love of j. JUSTICE, 7; price of j. PRESS, THE, 1; temper so/J. JUSTICE, 8; This even–handed j. JUSTICE, 10; where mystery begins j. JUSTICE, 3; you have ravished j. INJUSTICE, 2
Kansas
  not in K. FOREIGN COUNTRIES, 6
Kant
  read K. COMPANY, 7
Kennedy
  man who accompanied Jacqueline K. FIRST LADIES OF THE UNITED STATES, 1
Kew
  Highness' dog at K. CLASS, 3
Keyes
  k. SUICIDE, 2
Kick
  Against a spike/K. ADVERSITY, 1; k. ADVERSITY, 2
Kidnapped
  Being born is like being k. BIRTH, 4

1; M. MUSIC AND MUSICIANS, 5; M. MUSIC AND MUSI-
CIANS, 13; m. MUSIC AND MUSICIANS, 15; Magical m.
MUSIC AND MUSICIANS, 2; something suspicious about
m. MUSIC AND MUSICIANS, 11

Musicians
common disease of all your m. MUSIC AND MUSI-
CIANS, 9

Must
Is m. RANK, 1; It m. NECESSITY, 1

Mutability
Nought may endure but M. CHANGE, 5

My–lorded
m. SERVILITY, 1

Mysterious
moves in a m. GOD, 8

Mystery
Give me a m. MYSTERY, 1

Mystical
most beautiful emotion. . . is the m. MYSTICS AND
MYSTICISM, 1

Mythology
species of m. FICTION, 5

Myths
m. MYTHS, 1

Naked
N. NUDITY, 3; they were both n. NUDITY, 2

Nakedness
Full n. NUDITY, 4

Name
For my n. REPUTATIONS, 1; good n. REPUTATIONS, 2;
left a n. FAME, 1; n. NAMES, 4; n. NAMES, 5; n. WORLD
WAR I, 1; rather make my n. ANCESTRY, 5; Whose N.
KEATS, JOHN, 2

Names
call it by the best n. NECESSITY, 3; fallen in love with
American n. NAMES, 1

Napalm
smell of n. VIETNAM, 1

Narcotics
Two great European n. CHRISTIANITY AND THE
CHRISTIANS, 8

Nasty
Something n. SECRETS, 3

Nation
a new n. REVOLUTION: AMERICAN, 3; n. IMMIGRATION
AND IMMIGRANTS, 2; n. NEWSPAPERS AND MAGAZINES,
6; noble and puissant n. NATIONS, 6; old and haughty
n. WALES AND THE WELSH, 2; real favors from n.
INTERNATIONAL RELATIONS, 2; what our N. BRITISH,
THE, 1

Nationalism
N. NATIONALISM, 1

Nations
Other n. FORCE, 5; Two n. INEQUALITY, 6

Natural selection
N. EVOLUTION, 2

Natural
n. INSTINCT, 1; prevents our being n. AFFECTATION, 1

Nature
Man masters n. NATURE, 3; N. AMBITION, 6; N.
NATURE, 1; N. NATURE, 8

Naught
It is n. BARGAINING, 1

Navy
See the N. ARMY, 10; The Royal N. NAVY, THE, 1

Near
n. DEPRESSION, 2

Necessarily
It ain't n. BIBLE, 4

Necessary
n. NECESSITY, 5

Necessities
There are only n. NATURE, 7

Necessity
N. BARGAINING, 2; N. NECESSITY, 2

Neck
stick my n. CAUSES, 2

Need
You get what you n. EFFORT, 2

Neglect
n. NEGLECT, 1

Negotiate
never n. NEGOTIATION, 2; Only free men can n. NEGO-
TIATION, 3

Negro
oppression that affects the N. AFRICA AND AFRICANS,
1

Neighborhood
narrowed to a n. FELLOWSHIP, 4

Nelly
poor N. LAST WORDS, 3

Nerve
You got a lotta n. FRIENDS AND FRIENDSHIP, 10

Nerves
high respect for your n. NERVES, 1

Nets
Fine n. SIN, 5

Neurotic
expression of a n. ACTORS AND ACTING, 3

New Jersey
strange beings who landed in N. ALIENS, 1

New Englanders
no pleasing N. NEW ENGLAND AND THE EAST, 1

New World
called the N. NEW WORLD, THE, 1

New York
N. NEW YORK CITY, 1

New deal
n. TWENTIETH CENTURY: THE 1930S, 1

New
all who told it added something n. GOSSIP, 7; All
appeared n. YOUTH, 7; find something n. ADVENTURES
AND ADVENTURERS, 4; n. INNOVATION, 2; no n. NOVEL-

Richness
r. MEMORY, 7
Ridicule
that r. RIDICULE, 1
Right
<i>the r. COURAGE, 8; Always do r. GOOD DEEDS, 4;
defend to the death your r. FREEDOM OF SPEECH, 6
Righteousness
R. NATIONS, 1
Rights
abstract r. FEMINISM, 8; Stand up for your r. CIVIL
RIGHTS, 2
Ripeness
R. DEATH AND DYING, 45
Ripped
from his mother's womb/Untimely r. CHILDBIRTH, 2
Rises
No man r. GETTING AHEAD, 1
River
Ol' man r. RIVERS, 3; On a tree by a r. BIRDS, 3
Road
rolling English r. ROADS, 2
Roads
Two r. CHOICE, 1
Robbers
like wayside r. QUOTATIONS, 2
Robin
R. ZOOS, 1, 2
Robinson
Mrs. R. SEDUCTION, 8
Robotics
fundamental Rules of R. ROBOTS, 1
Robots
men may become r. ROBOTS, 2
Rock 'n' roll
it's only r. ROCK 'N' ROLL, 3
Rock
R. MOUNTAINS, 4; upon this r. CHURCH, THE, 3
Rocket
life like a r. LIFE, 26
Rome
Everyone. . . comes round by R. ROME, 1; Happy R.
STYLE, 5
Romeo
wherefore art thou R. NAMES, 6
Ronald
Lord R. EXASPERATION, 1
Root
eaten on the insane r. ILLUSION, 3
Rose–buds
Gather ye r. VIRGINITY, 2
Rose
dropping a r. POETRY AND POETS, 46; He r. WILDE,
OSCAR, 1; how strangely /the r. FLOWERS, 2; O R. COR-
RUPTION, 1; One perfect r. GIFTS AND GIVING, 4; R.
FLOWERS, 8; r. YOUTH, 6

Roses
stifled on beds of r. POETRY AND POETS, 33
Royalty
R. GOVERNMENT, 3
Ruin
Resolved to r. POLITICS AND POLITICIANS, 7
Ruined
No nation was ever r. TRADE, 4
Rule
Here the people r. WATERGATE AFFAIR, 1
Rulers
Of the best r. GOVERNMENT, 10
Rum
r. NAVY, THE, 2; r. SPIRIT, 2
Rumour
distillation of r. HISTORY, 8
Run
He can r. BOXING, 2
Running
all the r. HASTE, 1
Rural
Sweet especial r. TREES, 6
Russia
I cannot forecast. . . the action of R. RUSSIA AND THE
RUSSIANS, 2; O R. RUSSIA AND RUSSIANS, 1
Russian
R. RUSSIA AND THE RUSSIANS, 3
Rye
catcher in the r. DREAMS AND DREAMING, 11
Sabbath
Anybody can observe the S. SUNDAY AND THE SAB-
BATH, 4; Remember the s. SUNDAY AND THE SABBATH,
1
Sacred
idea of the s. RELIGION, 9; not much is really s. CON-
SUMER SOCIETY, 1
Sacrifice
Too long a s. SACRIFICES, 5
Sad
How s. LOVE, 10
Sadness
Farewell s. MELANCHOLY, 2
Safer
s. FREEDOM, 6
Said
Everything has been s. ORIGINALITY, 5; has not been s.
ORIGINALITY, 6; Whatever is well s. PLAGIARISM, 4
Sail
Never weather–beaten s. TRAVELING AND TRAVELERS,
2
Sailor
No man will be a s. NAVY, THE, 4
Saint
no sinner like a young s. CHILDREN, 3; S. SAINTS, 3
Saints
death of his s. SAINTS, 2

Star

Without troubling of a s. COSMOS, 4

Stardust

We are s. HIPPIES, 1

Stare

time to stand and s. STARING, 1

Starless

S. NIGHT, 3

Starred

No memory of having s. STARDOM, 2

Stars

see once more the s. STARS, 1; Wandering s. DAMNA-
TION, 1; we have the s. DREAMS AND DREAMING, 10;
You s. ASTROLOGY, 1

State

free society the s. STATE, THE, 5; main foundations of
every s. ARMS, 3; s. STATE, THE, 1; there will be no S.
STATE, THE, 4; venerate the s. STATE, THE, 2; worth of a
S. STATE, THE, 6

Stately

S. UPPER CLASS, THE, 1

Statesman

constitutional s. STATESMANSHIP, 1

Statesmanship

In s. STATESMANSHIP, 2

Statisticians

shalt not sit/With s. SOCIAL SCIENCES, 1

Statistics

he uses s. STATISTICS, 2

Statue

ask why I have no s. MONUMENTS, 1

Stay

S. GUESTS, 3

Steal

Thou shalt not s. THIEVES AND THIEVERY, 1

Stealth

do a good action by s. GOOD DEEDS, 3

Steam–engine

S. WEBSTER, DANIEL, 1

Step

one small s. MOON, 1

Stepmother

serpent than a s. MARRIAGE: REMARRIAGE, 2

Stepping–stones

Men may rise on s. EXPERIENCE, 5

Still

be wholly s. INERTIA, 2

Stirrup

I sprang to the s. DEPARTURE, 1

Stomach

army marches on its s. ARMY, 1

Stone

first cast a s. SIN, 2; to s. CRYING, 2

Stoned

Everybody must get s. PERSECUTION, 2

Stories

eight million s. CITIES AND CITY LIFE, 7

Strange

Don't accept rides from s. MEN, 4

Stranger

S. FOREIGN COUNTRIES, 1

Strangers

kindness of s. STRANGERS, 5; we may be better s.
STRANGERS, 4

Straw

S. POLLS, 1

Street

On Wall S. Universe STOCK MARKET, 1

Strength

My s. PURITY, 6

Strenuous

doctrine of the s. EFFORT, 3

Strife

nation is filled with s. PATRIOTISM, 7

Struck

women should be s. WOMEN, 14

Study

S. SCHOOL, 1; S. STUDENTS, 1

Stumbling

Negro's great s. LIBERALS, 5

Stygian

S. SMOKING AND SMOKERS, 6

Style

adopt the graver s. TEACHERS, 5; S. STYLE, 8; S. STYLE,
10; S. STYLE, 12; S. STYLE, 3; S. STYLE, 4

Sublime

S. ABSURDITY, 2

Sublimity

S. EXCELLENCE, 2

Subtlest

S. MAGIC, 1

Succeed

not enough to s. SUCCESS, 8

Success

'Tis not in mortals to command s. SUCCESS, 1; his lack
of s. FAILURE, 5; If A is a s. SUCCESS, 4; no s. FAILURE,
2; One's religion is. . . S. SUCCESS, 2; s. SUCCESS, 6; S.
SUCCESS, 3

Sucker

Never give a s. CREDULITY, 2; s. CREDULITY, 1

Suez

Ship me somewhere east of S. EXPATRIATES, 1

Suffer

Mankind are more disposed to s. SUFFERING, 1

Suffering

S. SUFFERING, 2

Sugar

spoonful of s. MEDICINE, 1

Suicide

consoling to think of s. SUICIDE, 5; lacks a good reason for s. SUICIDE, 7; s. SUICIDE, 3

Suicides

S. SUICIDE, 9